Philanthropy and
Cultural Imperialism

Edited by
Robert F. Arnove

Philanthropy and Cultural Imperialism
The Foundations at Home and Abroad

Indiana University Press *Bloomington*

First Midland Book Edition 1982

Manufactured in the United States of America

Library of Congress Cataloging in Publication Data
Main entry under title:
Philanthropy and cultural imperialism.
Reprint. Originally published: Boston: G.K. Hall & Co., © 1980
Includes index.
1. Endowments—United States—History—Addresses, essays, lectures. I. Arnove, Robert F.
HV16.P44   361.7′63   82-48055   AACR2
ISBN 978-0-253-20303-8 pbk
1   2   3   4   5   86   85   84   83   82

Contents

The major foundations function as public rather than private institutions. Inevitably they have become one of the major institutional forces of the modern state. In particular, their influence is of increasing importance in the determination of educational policy, the goals of research in all fields, and the direction of thinking in international affairs.

Wolfgang Friedmann, *Law in a Changing Society*
(Harmondsworth, England: Penguin Books, 1972
2nd edition), p. 318.

Robert F. Arnove

Introduction

Philanthropy and Cultural Imperialism is intended as a source book on the origins, workings, and consequences of modern general-purpose founda- tions. The text encompasses the activities of foundations—principally Carnegie, Rockefeller, and Ford—in the production of culture and the formation of public policy. Particular attention is given to the policies of the big foundations in the fields of education and social science research.

The authors write from the perspectives of history, sociology, compar- ative education, and educational policy studies. Their chapters are based on original research undertaken, in most cases, for doctoral dissertations. While the contributors do not share a uniform ideological framework, they do have in common a structural point of view—they examine foundations with regard to their functioning in society. They analyze the implications of foundations' organizational characteristics, modus oper- andi, and substantive decisions for social control or social change.

A distinguishing feature of *Philanthropy and Cultural Imperialism* is its systematic, critical analysis of the sociopolitical consequences of these powerful institutions. A central thesis is that foundations like Carnegie, Rockefeller, and Ford have a corrosive influence on a democratic society; they represent relatively unregulated and unaccountable concentrations of power and wealth which buy talent, promote causes, and, in effect, establish an agenda of what merits society's attention. They serve as "cooling-out" agencies, delaying and preventing more radical, structural change. They help maintain an economic and political order, international in scope, which benefits the ruling-class interests of philanthropists and philanthropoids[1]—a system which, as the various chapters document, has worked against the interests of minorities, the working class, and Third World peoples. Ross notes that

> . . .philanthropy has always been the reflection of a class society because it has depended on a division between rich givers and poor recipients. . . . The wealthy have not only given because

they have more but because, by alleviating distress, they have
secured their own positions against those who might displace
them and thus have avoided revolt.[2]

With the exception of Lindeman's pioneering study of *Wealth and
Culture* (1936),[3] no other book, to my knowledge, has systematically
focused on the involvement of philanthropic foundations in the fields of
education and research, and the implications of these interventions for
cultural domination at home and abroad.[4] Cultural imperialism has been
selected as an organizing theme of this book. Despite the imprecise and
rhetorical nature of the term, cultural imperialism captures the scope and
impact of foundation involvement in public education, professional training, and research activities, both nationally and internationally. In part, it
denotes the ethnocentrism of an elite group from a particular class and
cultural background,[5] who arrogate the right to determine public policies
in critical areas of culture not only for U.S. society but other societies as
well. The term, furthermore, denotes "the use of political and economic
power to exalt and spread the values and habits of a foreign culture at the
expense of a native culture" (*The Harper Dictionary of Modern Thought*),[6]
and "the deliberate and calculated process of forcing a cultural minority
to adopt the culture of the dominant group in a society" (*Dictionary of
Social Science*).[7] And cultural imperialism comprehends the contribution
of educational programs to the functioning of an international class-
system intimately related to situations of classical colonialism (nation to
nation domination), internal colonialism (the economic, political, cultural, and legal subjugation of groups within a nation), and neocolonialism (the continuing economic and cultural dependency of politically
independent countries on the metropolitan centers of North America and
Europe).[8]

Closely related to cultural imperialism and the arguments of this book
is the concept of cultural or ideological hegemony. The concept, first
articulated by Marx and Engels,[9] was subsequently elaborated by the
Italian cultural Marxist Antonio Gramsci. As summarized by Apple,

> . . . for Gramsci symbolic and cultural control—hegemony—is
> as critical as overt political and economic interest and manipula-
> tion in enhancing the power of dominant groups; thus, the
> ideological structures and meanings that organize our everyday
> lives in schools and elsewhere become prime elements in any
> explanation of how an unequal society maintains itself.[10]

The cultural hegemony exercised by dominant groups in a society defines,
in the words of Thompson, "the limits of what is possible" and "inhibits
the growth of alternative horizons and expectations."[11]

For Gramsci, intellectuals and schools were crucial to the development of consensus in society, to the rationalization and legitimation of a given social order. Cultural hegemony mitigated the necessity for the State to use its coercive apparatus to control groups which might otherwise be disaffected.[12] This concept serves as a useful tool for examining the centrality, for foundations, of educational investments. Education—and higher education, in particular—has been the primary target of foundation funding activities.

Lindeman believed that "nearly all donors appeared to have education in mind when they made their bequests."[13] His survey of foundation disbursements for the period 1921–1930 indicated that education accounted for 43 percent of all expenditures, followed by health with 32 percent.[14] Within education, Lindeman estimated that 61 percent of the grants were expended on higher education.[15] Fifty years later, education still is the number one priority of foundations, accounting for approximately 30 percent of expenditures, the highest percentage in any single area.[16] Similarly, an analysis of the investment patterns of nine major donors (Carnegie, Danforth, Ford, Grant, Kellogg, Lilly, Mott, Rockefeller, and Russell Sage) reveals that approximately eight times more was spent on higher education than on precollegiate education.[17] And within higher education, the lion's share of expenditures during the first half of this century went to graduate-level academic and professional programs at private colleges and universities.[18] Closely aligned with institution-building grants in higher education are foundation competency-building fellowship and scholarship awards to individuals.[19] Ford Foundation president McGeorge Bundy, in his 1968 annual review, touched upon the significance of education and expertise:

> The oldest and strongest of the ties that connect this foundation to other parts of society are those that bind us to the world of education. We depend on learned men for advice and special study on nearly every subject we take up. More deeply still, we have supposed, from our very beginning, that the health and strength of American education was in and of itself an area of central importance to the national well-being.[20]

Foundation involvement in the areas of education and research is often used to justify the existence of organized philanthropy. According to F. Emerson Andrews, widely considered to be the most articulate spokesperson on foundations, "the funds of foundations are largely the venture capital of philanthropy, best invested in activities requiring risk and foresight that are not likely to be supported either by government or private individuals. The usual purpose is not relief or even cure; it is prevention, research, and discovery. . . ."[21]

Large-scale, organized philanthropy, as embodied in the notion of "scientific giving" and in the institution of foundations, is a uniquely American phenomenon. Whitaker, in *The Philanthropoids,* estimates that 95 percent of the major foundations in the world with assets of over $10 million are situated in the United States.[22] For Kiger, "American foundations are the result of a capitalistic system which, contrary to its European counterpart, allowed neither church nor state a monopoly on philanthropic activity."[23] As a "flowering of the American capitalistic system,"[24] American foundations are characterized by unprecedented scope and freedom of action. Throughout the twentieth century they have financed welfare and planning activities that in many European, Commonwealth— and certainly in all socialist—countries are the responsibility of the State.[25]

The emergence of American philanthropic foundations represented a confluence of economic, political, and social forces at the beginning of the twentieth century. These included the following: the amassing of great industrial fortunes; the industrial processes and social relations of production that led to both great wealth in the hands of a few and to poverty and discontent on the part of many; the social reformism of the period that proposed the application of rational social planning and scientific expertise to the amelioration of social ills; and the recognition on the part of the federal government, corporate management, and the conservative wing of the labor movement that they must work together to address common problems or face the prospects of radical social change. With regard to this last point, Karl and Katz observe that

> Many of those involved understood perfectly well that the new cooperative structures might provide an alterntive to socialism and the welfare state, both of which seemed inevitable in contemporary Europe, in which the American private sector could retain its dominant position in the formulation of public policy. In this effort, it is not too hard to see, the role of the philanthropic foundation might well prove central to the ambitions of the private sector.[26]

By the 1920s, the general-purpose foundation had emerged and crystallized with many of the features it exhibits today as "a nongovernment, nonprofit organization having a principal fund of its own, managed by its own trustees or directors, and established to maintain or aid. . .activities serving the common welfare."[27] Foundations had succeeded in winning unprecedented autonomy not only because they were aligned with powerful interests and commanded vast resources, but because the doctrine of independent institutions efficiently administering surplus wealth in the public interest accorded with the American belief in pluralism and a thriving private sector.[28] The foundations represented a vehicle for proposing and implementing programs of social remediation at a time when the federal government was greatly limited by law or by what the public was willing to support.[29] And foundation policies accorded with, and reinforced, the growing American belief in education, research, and science as the surest path to progress.

From their beginnings, the activities of the giant philanthropic foundations were concerned not only with promoting stability and orderly change in the emergent national society, but with extending the "benefits" of Western science, technology, and value systems abroad. Ford, Rockefeller, and Carnegie have been key investors in the growth and development of higher education institutions, think tanks, and research centers around the world. Indeed, the Ford Foundation has been described as the "the world's largest investor in new ideas."[30] They have been the principal architects of international networks of scholars and agencies involved in the production and dissemination of knowledge—networks which connect talented individuals and their institutional bases to one another as well as to the benefactors. Through these institutions and networks, they have been in a unique position to influence cultural and social policies on an international scale.

It is testimony to the power and impact of these giant foundations that many of their priorities, policies, and practices have been assumed by the public sector. This has been a main objective of philanthropic endeavor, that their pilot projects and initial "seed" investments be incorporated into public policy. Millett, a former foundation executive, offers this evidence.

> The National Institutes of Health were modeled from the medical and health-related research activities of general purpose foundations. The National Science Foundation not only utilizes the techniques of the private foundation but also enjoys the very same designation. . . . The Corporation for Public Broadcasting is the product of one private foundation study and employs the procedures of another foundation. More recently, the Education Amendments of 1972 provided for the creation of the National Institute of Education and the National Fund for the Improvement of Postsecondary Education.[31]

Internationally, Yarmolinsky believes, "If it is a fair test of the success of new private initiatives whether they are later incorporated into public policy, then foundation initiatives in development assistance get high marks."[32] One example cited by Yarmolinsky is the 1970 Presidential Task Force on International Development, which observed that "the United States should seek to operate these programs (Technical Assistance) more as a private foundation would," and recommended that "an increasing proportion of the work should be carried out largely through private channels."[33]

In international as in national affairs the role of foundations like Ford and Rockefeller has been that of catalyst and broker of ideas and programs, which better-endowed national and international agencies then assume the responsibility for funding. As a case in point, the International Division of the Ford Foundation stated in 1972 that "leaders in the international development assistance field, notably including John Hannah, head of AID, and Paul Gerin-Lajoie, head of the Canadian International Development Agency, along with Robert McNamara and David Hopper [head of the International Development Research Centre of Canada] have urged the foundation to play a larger role in helping the aid community assess the need for development aid, evaluate progress, and establish further work for others as well as ourselves."[34] And as the International Division further notes, "as other funding agencies improve in quantity and quality, the Foundation has the opportunity (and is steadily urged) to work on the problems of highest sensitivity, of largest policy content, and of potentially greatest leverage."[35]

Despite the disclaimers of the big foundations that the federal government spends 150 times more than all private foundations (which account for less than 10 percent of all charitable giving), and 1,500 times more than the Ford Foundation,[36] their assets are nevertheless substantial. Mavity and Ylivasker (former program head of Public Affairs for the Ford Foundation) note: "With millions and sometimes billions of private dollars both available and at stake, the Carnegies, Rockefellers, Fords— even more so, the paid philanthropoids who followed in their name—were able to fix on patterns of social need and charitable opportunity that were regional, national, and international in scope. . . ."[37] Whitaker estimates that, in the early 1970s, foundations owned nearly 1 percent of the wealth of the United States—three times the proportion they possessed before the Second World War.[38] The late U.S. Representative Wright Patman, who investigated the financial activities of foundations, wrote in the *Progressive* in 1967: "During the four years 1961 through 1964, they took in $4.6 billion. . .nearly thirty percent higher than the combined net operating earnings—$3.6 billion after taxes—of the fifty largest banks in the United States. . .they had capital gains of $1.3 billion." "Here," as he noted, "is a huge amount of income."[39] And despite the decrease in foundation assets due to stock market declines in the mid-1970s, the big foundations, like Ford, continue to command enormous resources. Ford, with assets of $2.3 billion in 1978,[40] was the premier foundation.[41] The Rockefeller Foundation, with assets of $740 million in 1978, was the fifth largest; and Carnegie, with over $284 million in late 1977, the eleventh.[42] Historically, these three foundations have occupied the apex of a pyramid consisting of some 22,000 foundations in the United States—a pyramid in which the top forty-one foundations accounted in 1978 for 40.4 percent of all assets of the principal 3,000 active grant-making foundations.[43] As Schrag has remarked, "it is by now impossible to conceive of contemporary enterprise in education, research and international development without thinking of Carnegie, Rockefeller and Ford."[44] The chapters in this book detail the activities of these foundations and a handful of others (such as Russell Sage) in the construction of ideology, the training of leadership, and the formation of public policy.

Content

This edited collection is designed to be used both in its entirety and in part, according to the information sought. As a guide to the reader, the content of each chapter is summarized below.

HISTORICAL AND SOCIAL ORIGINS

Chapter 1 by Howe describes the origins and issues surrounding the emergency of "scientific philanthropy" in the period 1900–1920. The chapter focuses on the activities and professed motivations of the wealthiest and most visible of the new millionaires—Andrew Carnegie and John D. Rockefeller—and on the factors influencing their decision to systematize and institutionalize charitable giving. The philanthropic activities of these industrial giants led to widespread concern over the concentration of corporate wealth and power in unregulated institutions closely involved in the shaping of educational and cultural policies. The chapter gives substantial attention to the congressionally authorized Walsh Commission of 1915, which served as a forum for debating the role of the general-purpose foundation in American society. As Howe notes, not for another forty years would foundations be subjected to such critical examination and public scrutiny. The foundations survived the congressional challenge by obtaining unrestrictive state, rather than national, charters. The institutional autonomy they secured and the funding policies they pursued, in response to public outcry over their more blatant forms of self-serving grant-making, have continued relatively intact to the present day.

THE CONSTRUCTION AND DISSEMINATION OF IDEOLOGIES

This section consists of the introductory overview by Slaughter and Silva, followed by the two case studies of Marks and Brown. As Slaughter and

Silva point out, philanthropic foundations in the Progressive Period were created and controlled by satisfied resource holders. Philanthropists intervened in the era's vibrant marketplace of ideas, using their vast resources to further those groups who produced and disseminated world views supportive of the status quo, and using the weapons at their disposal to contain and discredit alternative, especially socialistic, ideologies.

The authors select for case study the funding patterns of the Russell Sage Foundation, the Carnegie Institute of Washington, and the Rockefeller Foundation. Russell Sage is analyzed with regard to its pioneering role in organizing the field of social work according to a model of professionally directed reform which was nonthreatening to existing power arrangements. The Carnegie Institute is studied with regard to its support for university-based academics who would address social issues of concern to the owners and managers of capital. As in the case of the Russell Sage Foundation and social work, the role of Carnegie was to mobilize and efficiently organize talent on a national scale. New knowledge, then as now, was considered a valuable resource to be mined in the interest of policy formation. A new breed of entrepreneur was also formed in the process: the "university managers," individuals who were able to traverse freely among the academic, business, and foundation worlds, mounting projects and administering the research activities of intellectual workers.[45] The Rockefeller Foundation is examined with regard to the operating procedures it developed in response to the Walsh Commission investigation of its involvement in labor-management strife in the coal fields of Colorado. The foundation, accused of public relations activities on behalf of the Colorado Lead and Fuel Company (which was 40 percent owned by the Rockefeller family), moved to separate its activities from that of the family, and to separate grant-making from project management.[46] Moreover, the foundation moved to gain respectability—to project an aura of disinterested detachment—by channeling its resources through intermediary agencies such as the American Council of Learned Societies and subsequently the Social Science Research Council. As later chapters detail, these mechanisms and modes of grant-making are very much characteristic of the big foundations to this day.

Marks, in his chapter on "individual differences," provides an example of the manufacture of ideology. As he observes, the concept of "individual differences" has served the purpose of bridging the gap between the American dream of upward mobility open to all and the grim realities of the workplace. The concept legitimates class differences and unequal distribution of rewards on the basis of "innate ability," as measured by scientific instruments, commonly known as "IQ" tests. The Carnegie and Rockefeller philanthropies provided the funding and helped disseminate the work of leading proponents of intelligence tests, such as Edward L.

Thorndike, during the first half of this century. Their resources were put to work in the "social construction" of a set of explanatory concepts which justified different futures for differently endowed individuals. A principal educational ramification of these concepts was a differentiated curriculum which consigned working-class and minority children, especially blacks (see Chapters 5 and 6) to dead-end academic tracks, preparing them for menial work at the bottom of the economic hierarchy. At the same time, the differential curriculum prepared a select few, the children of dominant groups in the society, for higher education and the apex of the economic pyramid. (Those who were talented were considered to be both more virtuous and deserving of the most prestigious, influential, and lucrative positions in the society.) The social implications of these notions of individual differences were eugenics policies involving forced sterilization of those deemed incompetent (as well as degenerate) and immigrant laws designed to prevent the entry of undesirable stock into the American gene pool.

Brown, in his chapter on Rockefeller programs in pre-1949 China, provides a case study of not only the export of Western medicine but of an infrastructure the Rockefellers and their advisors believed necessary to China's development along Western lines. The Peking Union Medical College represented a vehicle through which China would assimilate "the best that is known to Western civilization not only in medical science but in mental development and spiritual culture."[47]

Medical and health programs also were a gateway for U.S. access to raw materials and to markets for its manufactured products. Such programs worked better than machine guns, and possibly missionaries, in winning admission to a country, for what could be more neutral and less objectionable than health? Unfortunately, the consequences of pursuing medical training, according to Western notions of professionalism, meant the suppression of alternative and more traditional forms of health care. The minuscule number of medical doctors trained by the Rockefeller programs served the elites, while the majority were abandoned. But, as Brown reminds us, the role of these doctors was not exclusively, primarily, to meet the health needs of the country; they were trained as an elite stratum to carry out cultural and technological transformations in Chinese society. For the benefactors and apostles of the faith, the physicians were "Chinese leaders who will do the things we have so long done for China" and "who will do the things we wish to see done."[48]

The medical education programs of the Rockefeller philanthropies highlight several contradictions. There is the contradiction between the international health programs of Rockefeller, designed to improve the health of a work force—thereby increasing productivity and profits—and the medical training programs that emphasize a curative approach for an elite rather than a preventive approach for the many. And there was the contradiction between the professed humanitarianism of the philanthropists and the exploitative policies and deleterious consequences of such interventions in other societies. Herein lies the roots and dynamics of cultural imperialism, for, as Brown observes:

> Their humanitarianism was shaped by their ethnocentrism, their class interests, and their support for the imperialist objectives of their own country. By the time their humanitarianism was expressed in programs, it was so intertwined with the interests of American capitalism as to be indistinguishable.

EDUCATION OF AFRO-AMERICANS AND AFRICANS

Health and minority education programs are frequently pointed to as examples of the noblest undertakings of philanthropy. If we are to hold foundations accountable to their statements of goals and achievements, then, their past record in the field of education of American blacks is dismal. For well over fifty years, the record of northern philanthropies— starting with the Peabody Education Fund (considered by F. Emerson Andrews to be the first of the modern foundations),[49] Slater, Phelps-Stokes, and the giants in the field (Rockefeller, through the General Education Board, and Carnegie)—was one of promoting "segregated betterment"[50] and Jim Crowism. Northern philanthropies were to assist efforts of southern leaders in maintaining a system of de jure segregation and denial of power. Blacks were to remain on the bottom, serving the interests of a coalition of northern and southern industrialists who set out to reconstruct a new South in the post–Civil War period. The model that was developed for the education of blacks in the United States was considered to be so successful and relevant that it was embraced by British colonial offices and missionary societies working in Africa in the period between the two world wars. Chapters 5 and 6 by Anderson and Berman document the development of these educational policies and their export to other colonial areas of the world.

Anderson contrasts the differences between missionary and industrial philanthropists in their approaches to the education of blacks in the post–Civil War period. According to Anderson, missionary leaders supported a classical-liberal education for black Americans as a means to achieve racial equality in civil and political life. While the missionaries by no means proposed radical change, they did assume that the newly emancipated blacks were capable of becoming what they chose, limited only by their own ability and effort. By contrast, industrial philanthropists were less concerned with equal rights. They viewed black education as a vehicle to provide them with a disciplined, semiskilled, and cheap labor force which would guarantee political stability and economic efficiency. The education system envisioned by northern philanthropists and philanthropoids was one that taught blacks "the discipline of manual labor and the boundaries of the 'natural environment.' " Very much in accordance with the notions of individual differences propagated by foundation-backed psychologists and educational testers, schooling for the Afro-American was to "adapt" him to his limited capacities and inferior station in life. For the most talented of the blacks, there would be a few select colleges to train a conservative elite in a limited number of fields, principally education. Thus a dual education system was developed for blacks that operated within an overall racially segregated system. But, as Anderson points out, a number of black educators and students were able to use these institutions to their own advantage and thereby partially subvert the intentions of the donors.

Edward Berman, in Chapter 6, discusses the activities of the Phelps-Stokes Fund in exporting the U.S. model of "adaptation" and industrial education for blacks to British Africa in the period between 1910 and 1945. The assumptions both U.S. and British colonialists shared were (1) that neither the African nor the American Negro would be self-governing in the foreseeable future and (2) that a narrowly defined vocational education could be used to train American Negroes and Africans to become productive, docile, and permanent underclasses in their respective societies.

Berman finds little sentimentality and scant evidence of humanitarianism in the pronouncements and policies of northern philanthropists and British colonial officers. Moreover, contrary to Anderson's belief in the more humanitarian goals of missionary philanthropists in the United States, Berman believes that missionaries on both sides of the Atlantic were very much involved in promoting educational policies which would ensure a system of enduring segregation and inferiority. The involvement of American philanthropy in advising South Africa in the development of its apartheid policies is also documented. What is made evident in the Berman chapter is not only the emergence of a national but an international network of corporate interests, philanthropists, and policymakers who increasingly coordinate activities to their advantage.

Assumptions concerning the permanent exclusion of Africans from decision-making roles in their societies, and the continuance of the British Empire as a framework within which compatible U.S. interests could work, were shattered by World War II. With the demise of classical colonialism and the creation of independent states governed by Africans, American philanthropies, as Berman describes in Chapter 7, pursued new policies in education which would link the emergent indigenous leadership to U.S. values, modus operandi, and institutions. These policies were designed to ensure that U.S. vested economic and strategic interests were not threatened. Chapter 7 details the activities of the big three foundations (Ford, Carnegie, and Rockefeller) that led to

> 1) the creation of lead universities located in countries [Nigeria, Zaire, Ethiopia, Tanzania, Kenya] considered of geo-strategic and/or economic importance to the United States; 2) an emphasis within these institutions on social science research and related manpower planning programs; 3) programs to train public administrators; 4) teacher training and curriculum development projects; and 5) training programs which brought African nationals to select universities in the United States for advanced training and returned them home to assume positions of leadership.

The overriding concern, according to Berman, was to train elite cadres who would work within a pro-Western, procapitalistic framework to promote evolutionary change.

THE SOCIAL SCIENCES AND SOCIAL CONTROL

Foundations, in their concern with orderly growth at home and abroad, have placed particular emphasis on the development of research competencies of social scientists. As previous chapters (1 through 3) have noted, philanthropic foundations look to social and behavioral scientists to provide policymakers with knowledge and insights to help undergird and guide planning on a national scale. In the United States, researchers have been looked to as a source of understanding—even, possibly, of solutions—to pressing economic, political, and social issues. Overseas, researchers have represented a valuable source of insight into change processes and a means of comprehending institutions and value systems different from ours.

Fisher documents (in his case study of the Rockefeller philanthropies in England, before and after World War II) how the direction in which the social sciences developed in Britain tended both to serve and to perpetuate the ideological perspective of American philanthropy. This perspective was, according to a key Rockefeller spokesman, that the social sciences become more scientific so that they would help solve more efficiently the "real," "practical" problems facing society.[51] Extensive support was given to those individuals and institutions which pursued useful lines of inquiry. For example, "functionalist" anthropology was supported because of its supposed value to the British colonial administration in providing detailed knowledge of the workings of indigenous societies and those structures which contributed to group stability and continuity. Fisher concludes that the Rockefeller philanthropies, in the period between the two world wars, determined that the social sciences in Britain should help preserve that society's economic structure and its overseas empire.

Seybold, in Chapter 9, examines what he terms "the revolution in American political science" in the years 1948–1961. During this period, the traditional substantive concerns of the field (with issues of ends of the State and the nature of the good polity) were replaced by a new behavioral approach and a different set of substantive issues. The chapter focuses on the role of the Ford Foundation in engineering this dramatic shift; and the implications of this new approach for social control are raised:

> The fundamental restructuring of the social sciences was not
> simply a product of Ford's benevolence. It was rather a product
> of their effort to elicit the social sciences in the struggle to
> provide social stability. It was essential that a problem-solving
> orientation be promoted in the behavioral sciences.

Both the Fisher and Seybold chapters provide extensive documentation on the means by which foundations structure a scholarly field. These include the funding of leading individuals and institutions; the identification, recruitment, and training of promising young scholars; the capturing of key journals in a field as well as the leadership of professional associations; and the use of prestigious intermediary agencies, such as the Social Science Research Council and the American Council of Learned Societies. An important point made by Seybold is that foundations do not simply respond to dominant trends in a field, nor do they merely reflect the views of preeminent sholars. Foundations first determine the direction a field should take; then, they solicit requests from individuals who are likely to share their interests. In come cases, they may even approach researchers and proffer support before a proposal has been submitted to them.

Once the initial funding or "seeding" period is over (usually a period of 10 to 20 years), foundation-supported institutions and mechanisms are so entrenched as to be self-perpetuating. The research agenda is set. Foundations may recede into the background, but the seminal influence they exerted is very much manifest in the issues which are examined, the research paradigms and methods that are used, and the center-stage individuals who determine the nature and direction of the field's endeavors.

Arnove, in Chapter 10, points out that by the late 1960s it was becoming increasingly evident that the research paradigms the foundations had so heavily invested in were incapable of explaining events in the Third

World—or at home. The context of research had so changed that it was no longer possible or desirable for United States and European academics to conduct research overseas. New regional and international networks of interaction and influence had to be constructed and a new set of competencies had to be fostered in individuals. These competencies combined rigorous quantitative methodologies with the theoretical insights and analytic frameworks of neo-Marxist and conflight paradigms.[52] Emphasis was placed on identifying, supporting, and connecting such Third World researchers to one another, as well as to research centers and scholars in the metropolitan centers of North America and Europe. As to who benefits from these arrangements, Arnove speculates that it is primarily the metropolitan centers. Third World countries not only are producing and exporting valuable raw materials but they are also generating data which provide metropolitan policymakers with more accurate assessments of social forces at work overseas.

ELITIST AND TECHNOCRATIC EDUCATION

The international context of big power rivalries was a key factor in the domestic education policies of the big foundations in the post–World War II period. Chapters 11 through 13 analyze the types of programs funded by Ford and Carnegie in response to the Cold War. The social-engineering approach to controlled change, described in the preceding chapters on social science research, is very much evident in foundation programs in public education.

In the parallel chapters 11 and 12, Buss and Weischadle[53] analyze the educational funding policies and modus operandi of the Ford Foundation and Carnegie Corporation during the past twenty-five years. Both chapters point out the priority given by Ford and Carnegie to the quest for excellence. Brain power was deemed to be an important component of national strength. This quest resulted in the bulk of domestic educational funding being allocated to programs to identify and support talented youth and to develop curricula which would teach the structure of disciplines at the earliest possible age. Emphasis was placed on individual as well as national testing and assessment. Faced with a teacher shortage, the foundations also turned to educational technologies, notably television, to multiply the impact of high-quality instructors. At the same time, new teacher training programs were funded that emphasized greater preparation in academic subject matter. As an integral part of these reforms, state teachers colleges were to be gradually replaced by prestigious universities as the locus of teacher education. Concomitantly, the then existing educational establishment—consisting of teacher educators, officials in state educational bureaucracies and teacher associations—was to be replaced by a national elite of like-minded university superstars, like Conant of Harvard, who moved with aplomb among academia, government, and the foundation world.

The two chapters (11 and 12) examine the various modes of influence exerted by the foundations to capture a national policymaking role in primary and secondary education. The levers used are very similar to those described in previous chapters. In addition, Weischadle discusses, in his study of Carnegie, a new dimension—the "Washington connection"—to foundation influence on policy formation. As he points out, no matter which political party was in power in the decades of the 1950s and 1960s, there was heavy reliance on Carnegie advisors as well as appointment of Carnegie-affiliated individuals to national-level positions in the capital. Special attention is given to the period 1963–1965, when three men with close ties to Carnegie—John Gardner, Harold Howe II, and Francis Keppel—occupied the positions of Secretary of the Department of Health, Education, and Welfare, Assistant Secretary for Education, and U.S. Commissioner of Education.[54] In these posts they promoted policies which very much reflected Carnegie priorities and provided funding to projects and intermediary agencies (such as the Educational Testing Service and the Education Development Center) which had been favored recipients of Ford and Carnegie grants. The Office of Education, in its grant-making activities and style of operation, assumed the characteristics of a general-purpose foundation.

Both chapters also point out the belated response of the Carnegie and Ford Foundations to the problems of racial segregation and inequality in American education. It was only after significant outbursts of racial violence occurred in the late 1960s that they moved to give priority to these issues. And when they did, foundation priorities tended to be linked to the more traditional approaches of identifying and supporting talented minority youth to continue higher education studies. Buss analyzes the implications of recent Ford Foundation support for legal and financial approaches to remedying racial inequality in the schools, and whether or not they are likely to have a significant impact on improving racial integration and mobility opportunities for disadvantaged sectors of the society.

Criticism of foundation practices, as the two authors indicate, is strongly resisted by foundation managers and staff. Weischadle discusses the "pathological professionalism" of the foundation world—the suspicion and distrust of those outside their tightly knit group of responsible experts—as well as the expectation foundation officials have that the research and evaluation activities they support will reach the correct conclusions; and Buss reviews the promotional techniques used by foundations to advance their so-called "experimental" projects as well as the ridicule they direct at those who oppose them.

The strategies, policies, and mechanisms of the power elite are further elaborated by Darknell, in Chapter 13, on the Carnegie influence on higher education. Using the analytical framework of G. William Domhoff, Darknell analyzes the workings of the Carnegie Commission (1967–1971) and its successor, the Carnegie Council on Higher Education (1972–1979), as examples of agencies through which dominant groups in American society are able to achieve consensus and map out strategies of social action. Using case studies of the California Master Plan for Higher Education[55] and the development of a Doctorate of Arts Degree for instructors in two-year colleges, Darknell sets out to show that Carnegie has fostered a system of classification and channeling in higher education which parallels the system of class- and race-biased testing and tracking in the lower levels of the American education system. Policies aimed at containing and directing the flow of students in higher education, according to Darknell, have helped provide, in the short run, a trained and ideologically prepared work force in sufficient numbers to meet corporate needs; in the long run, they have maintained the organization and stability of higher education by controlling supply and demand for its services.

As is the case in previous chapters, Darknell traces the steps by which foundations are able to shape the framework of public debate on important issues:

> The Carnegie policy group monitors developments in higher education and publicly defines what issues merit national attention. It then funds investigations into problems arising out of such issues. The resulting conclusions, arrived at by reliable scholars at leading elite universities are published, often under Carnegie sponsorship. The results are then directed toward key people in higher education and concerned members of the lay public, reaching the latter via the press and serious opinion journals and magazines. Finally, study results and new policy proposals dealing with the problems earlier identified are directed toward government decision-makers who now find a mobilized constituency supporting Carnegie proposals in the apparent absence of anything else.

FRONTIER RESEARCH ON FOUNDATIONS

Similarly, working with the framework of Domhoff, Colwell, in Chapter 15, sets out to document the linkages between foundations and key policy-formation groups (such as the Council on Foreign Relations, the Committee for Economic Development, the Brookings Institution, and the Overseas Development Council). This research represents a significant contribution to the empirical verification of trustee overlaps as well as mutual membership of trustees in elite social clubs, such as the Century Association. The study focuses on a select sample of twenty out of the 400 foundations with assets over $10 million in 1974, and on thirty-one policy organizations funded by these foundations.

Three sets of linkages are studied: foundation to foundation; foundation to organization; organization to organization. The extensive data which Colwell painstakingly marshals do indeed indicate substantial overlaps at all three levels. These overlapping board memberships, as the author notes, provide a nexus for communication and interactions which may influence grants as well as the perspectives and projects of the policy formation groups.

Colwell's conclusions cast doubt on the assertion frequently made by philanthropoids that nonprofit organizations and foundations—the so-called "third sector"—provide an independent, countervailing force to big business and government, that they serve as a channel of access for citizens/consumers which is more open and participatory. The author ends with a call for more research to illuminate the processes of decision-making in public policy matters.

Conclusions

Philanthropic foundations, since their origins at the turn of the century, have played the role of unofficial planning agencies for both a national American society and an increasingly interconnected world-system with the United States at its center. The power of foundations like Carnegie, Rockefeller, and Ford has long resided in their providing necessary seed money for professional advancement and institutional growth, for innovation and research in unchartered and perhaps risky areas where other sources of funding are unavailable. Through funding and promoting research in critical areas, the big three have been able to exercise decisive influence over the growing edge of knowledge, the problems that are examined and by whom, and the uses to which newly generated information is put. Through the education programs they fund, foundations are able to influence the world views of the general public as well as the orientations and commitments of the leadership which will direct social change.

Foundations and their staffs represent neither retrograde reactionaries nor subversive radicals. Rather, as Fisher suggests in Chapter 8, they represent a sophisticated conservatism, supporting changes that help to maintain, and make more efficient, an international system of power and privilege. Their watchwords have been efficiency, control, planning. From the perspective of the foundations, those responsible for guiding and controlling change at home and abroad should be competent and pragmatic individuals —people much like the philanthropoids themselves.

The elitist and technocratic dimensions of foundations—their imperious and imperial stance—inhere in their belief that social change can occur and social ills can be redressed by highly trained professionals (scientists and technicians) who produce knowledge and proffer solutions. According to this technocratic perspective, quantification and systematic decision-making are viewed as the basis for purposive action.[56] And, as Schroyer has remarked, "a technocratic self-understanding of contemporary society—specifically, the ideal of rationally managed social change—now functions as both the principle of justice and the practice of domination."[57]

Intellectuals represent an important instrumentality of cultural domination as well as potential agents of revolutionary change. They may place their expertise at the service of dominant groups, working to legitimate the social order; or they can work with underclasses to enhance their understanding of everyday problems, assist them with different ways of viewing given social structures; and they can participate in collective struggles to transform an unjust society. The big foundations have effectively enlisted the support of some of the most promising and talented individuals in the United States and abroad. The foundations have channeled their energies and research activities in directions they have deemed important; and they have promoted modes of inquiry which circumscribe the examination of value questions and ideological issues.

The consequences of foundation support for the work of intellectuals are manifold. It cannot be argued that, in the absence of foundation funding, scholars, researchers, and academics would engage in militant action. More reasonably, it can be argued that foundation patronage has helped impede the formation of a critical scientific and intellectual community which examines basic mechanisms and thought systems of repression.[58] According to Horowitz, one far-reaching effect of the "foundation's pre-eminent role in financing academic research is namely the unbelievable dearth of organized information and systematic investigation of the men and corporate institutions that control the American economy, command the apex of the income pyramid, and dominate the strategic positions of power in the federal government."[59] Another far-reaching consequence is the striking absence of organized information on the crucial role foundations have exercised in the shaping of higher education and scholarly inquiry in the United States and overseas. Orville Brim, past president of the Russell Sage Foundation (a major source of funding for social science research in this century), made this observation: "Here is a major class of institution numbering in the tens of thousands, a more-than-billion-dollar-a-year enterprise, and yet there are hardly a half-dozen published reports on any substantial efforts at evaluation of foundation activities."[60]

A critique of domination must begin with an examination of the role of intellectuals and their connections to those groups which exercise hegemony in a society. This critique must examine their assumptions, languages, and modes of work as well as their funding sources and clients. This book has been dedicated to an elucidation of a principal source of patronage for those who work with ideas. It has examined past policy rationales for such involvements by foundations, the expectations held by foundations for researchers and academics, the funding patterns and modus operandi by which foundations elicited the support of and worked with the agents of cultural production and dissemination. It is hoped that the critiques contained in *Philanthropy and Cultural Imperialism* will lead to greater sensitivity on the part of academia to the ramifications, past and present, of foundation policies in the field of culture—and to greater awareness and understanding on the part of the public to the workings and consequences of these powerful institutions.

Notes

1. For the purposes of this introduction, "philanthropists" refers to those individuals who bequeathed the great fortunes constituting the endowments of foundations, and "philanthropoids" refers to the trustees, executive officers, and staff who design and implement foundation policies. Generally, the term philanthropists refers to those who both donate and administer the wealth of foundations.
2. Aileen D. Ross, "Philanthropy," in David L. Sills (ed.), *International Encyclopedia of the Social Sciences* (New York: Macmillan, 1968), Vol. 12, p. 78.
3. Edward C. Lindeman, *Wealth and Culture* (New York: Harcourt, Brace and Company, 1936).
4. It should be noted, however, that Lindeman focused on the role of philanthropic foundations in American society, and not on their activities overseas. Related critical works include Waldemar Nielsen, *The Big Foundations* (New York: Columbia University Press, 1972); Joseph Goulden, *The Money Givers* (New York: Random House, 1971); Benjamin Whitaker, *The Philanthropoids: Foundations and Society* (New York: William Morrow & Company, Inc., 1974). An excellent series of articles by David Horowitz with David Kolodney contains an essentially similar analysis of the role of the big foundations on an international scale: see "The Foundations [Charity Begins at Home]," *Ramparts* 7 (April 1969): 39–48;

"Billion Dollar Brains," *Ramparts* 7 (May 1969): 36–44; and "Sinews of Empire," *Ramparts* 8 (October 1969): 33–42. An in-depth analysis of the Russell Sage Foundation by Jay Schulman, Carol Brown, and Roger Kahn shares many of the themes of this book; see their "Report on the Russell Sage Foundation," *Insurgent Sociologist* 2 (Summer 1972): 2–33. Richard Colvard has written a useful essay that illuminates a number of similar issues; see his Risk Capital Philanthropy: The Ideological Defense of Innovation," in George K. Zollschan and Walter Hirsch (eds.), *Explorations in Social Change* (Boston: Houghton Mifflin, 1976 edition), pp. 864–885.

5. G. Orville Brim, Jr., "Do We Know What We Are Doing?" in Fritz Heimann (ed.), *The Future of Foundations* (Englewood Cliffs, N.J.: Prentice-Hall, 1973), p. 225, describes the background of foundation executives and trustees as "socially encapsulated" —over 90 percent being eastern males, Wasps who live surrounded by friends and colleagues from the same background.

6. Alan Bullock and Oliver Stallybrass (eds.), *The Harper Dictionary of Modern Thought* (New York: Harper and Row, 1977), p. 303.

7. John T. Zadrozny (ed.), *Dictionary of Social Science* (Washington, D.C.: Public Affairs Press, 1959), p. 77.

8. For further discussion of these concepts, see Martin Carnoy, *Education as Cultural Imperialism* (New York: David McKay, 1974); Philip G. Altbach and Gail P. Kelly, *Education and Colonialism* (New York: Longman, 1978); and John Liu, "Toward an Understanding of the Internal Colonial Model," in Emma Gee (ed.), *Counterpoint: Perspectives on Asian America* (Los Angeles: University of California, Asian American Studies Center, 1976), pp. 160–168.

9. Karl Marx and Frederick Engels discuss ideological hegemony in the *German Ideology, Part One*, edited by C. J. Arthur (London: Lawrence & Wishart, 1970).

10. Michael W. Apple, "The New Sociology of Education: Analyzing Cultural and Economic Reproduction," *Harvard Educational Review* 48 (November 1978): 500.

11. E. P. Thompson, "Eighteenth-Century English Society: Class Struggle without Class?" *Social History* 3 (May 1978): 158.

12. For further discussion of cultural hegemony see Antonio Gramsci, *Letters from Prison*, selected, translated and introduced by Lynne Lawner (London: Jonathan Cape, 1975); Alastair Davidson, *Antonio Gramsci: The Man, His Ideas* (Syndey: Australian Left Review Publications, 1968); Pedro Cavalcanti and Paul Piccone (eds.), *History, Philosophy and Culture in the Young Gramsci* (Saint Louis: Telos Press, 1975); Carl Marzani, *The Open Marxism of Antonio Gramsci* (New York: Cameron Associates, Inc., 1957); and Raymond Williams, "Base and Superstructure in Marxist Cultural Theory," *New Left Review*, No. 82, pp. 3–16.

13. Lindeman, *Culture and Wealth*, p. 24.

14. Ibid., p. 20.

15. Ibid., p. 26.

16. Based on data from the Foundation Center, John W. Nason, *Trustees and the Future of Foundations* (New York: Council on Foundations, 1977), p. 22, presents the following summary of expenditures for the period 1961–1973: 32 percent of foundation grants was spent on education; 15 percent on health; 14 percent, international activities; 13 percent, science and technology; 13 percent, welfare; 9 percent, arts and humanities; 4 percent, religion. According to *The Foundation Grants Index*, 1978 (New York: Foundation Center, 1979), p. xi, between 1975 and 1978 expenditures on education varied between 26 and 29 percent, and those on health, between 19 and 24 percent.

17. Donald Holsinger, "The Role of Philanthropy in Education," *UCLA Educator* 18 (Winter 1976): 12.

18. Ibid.

19. Ibid., p. 14. According to Holsinger, fellowship and scholarship awards "give the foundation a secure investment in the future careers of people who are going to be 'winners' in the course of life."

20. Ford Foundation, *Annual Report*, 1968 (New York: the same, 1969), p. xvii. For data on Ford Foundation investments in education, which totaled over $1.7 billion, between 1936 and 1977, see Richard Magat, *The Ford Foundation at Work: Philanthropic Choices, Methods, and Styles* (New York: Plenum Press, 1978), pp. 178–181.

21. F. Emerson Andrews, "Foundations," in David L. Sills (ed.), *International Encyclopedia of the Social Sciences* (New York: MacMillan, 1968), Vol. 5, p. 543.

22. Whitaker, *Philanthropoids*, p. 12.

23. Joseph C. Kiger, *Operating Principles of the Larger Foundations* (New York: Russell Sage Foundation, 1954), p.24.

24. Ibid., p. 118.

25. Ross, "Philanthropy," pp. 75–76.

26. Barry D. Karl and Stanley N. Katz, "Donors, Trustees, Staffs: An Historical View, 1890–1930," Proceedings of the Third Rockefeller Archive Center Conference, October 14, 1977, p. 6.

27. F. Emerson Andrews, *Philanthropic Foundations* (New York: Russell Sage Foundation, 1956), p. 11; also see the discussion of Thomas Parrish in *Future of Foundations*, pp. 10–11.

28. Kiger, *Operating Principles*, p. 25, thinks that philanthropy also accorded with American beliefs that it was morally proper for individuals to earn as much wealth as possible, and to dispose of it as they desired.

29. Karl and Katz, "Donors, Trustees, Staffs," p. 10.

30. Theodore H. White, "In the Halls of Power," *Life* 62 (June 9, 1967): 64.

31. John D. Millett, "Higher Education and the General Purpose Foundation," in *The Future of Foundations*, Final Report of the Great Lakes Assembly, Zion, Illinois, September 12, 1974, cosponsored by the American Assembly of Columbia University and the Institute of Government and Public Affairs, the University of Illinois (Urbana: University of Illinois, 1974), p. 33.

32. Adam Yarmolinsky, "Philanthropic Activity in International Affairs," in the

Commission on Private Philanthropy and Public Needs, *Research Papers*, Vol. II, Part I (Washington, D.C.: U.S. Department of the Treasury, 1977), pp. 775.

33. Ibid., p. 793.

34. Ford Foundation, "The Ford Foundation and the Less Developed Countries: The Decade of the Seventies" (New York: the same International Division, 1972), p. 41.

35. Ibid., p. 40.

36. Ford Foundation, *Annual Report*, 1973 (New York: the same, 1974), p. xii.

37. Jane H. Mavity and Paul N. Ylvisaker, Private Philanthropy and Public Affairs," in the Commission on Private Philanthropy and Public Needs, *Research Papers*, Vol. II, Part I (Washington, D.C.: U.S. Department of the Treasury, 1977), p. 797.

38. Whitaker, *Philanthropoids*, p. 118.

39. Wright Patman, "The Free-Wheeling Foundations," *Progressive* 31 (June 1967): 27; cited in Merrimon Cuninggim, *Private Money and Public Service: The Role of Foundations in American Society* (New York: McGraw-Hill Book Company, 1972), p. 74.

40. *The Foundation Directory*, 7th edition (New York: Foundation Center, 1979), p. xv.

41. Nason, *Trustees and Foundations*, p. 6, notes that the trustees of the Ford Foundation control "the largest single source of private philanthropy in the Western world."

42. *Foundation Directory*, 7th edition, p. xv.

43. Ibid., p. xvi.

44. Peter Schrag, "The Art of Giving," review of Warren Weaver et al., *U.S. Philanthropic Foundations: Their History, Structure, Management, and Record*, in *New York Times Book Review* (October 22, 1967), p. 3.

45. When the Ford Foundation was searching for a new president to succeed McGeorge Bundy in 1979, the final list of seven probable candidates included the presidents of Stanford, Princeton, and New York Universities. According to a program director at another New York–based foundation, the final list represented "the split personality of the Ford Foundation"—scholarly establishment types often found among the Foundation staff; and others identified with liberal causes involving social welfare for the deprived. The New York Times further noted that "each of the candidates has demonstrated a degree of administrative ability, either in current or past jobs. None could be considered a radical or an extremist on either end of the political scale. But they offer distinct, different talents." See Lesley Oelsner, "Ford Foundation Seeks a Skipper for Future Course," *New York Times*, January 3, 1979, pp. B-1, 8.

46. By contrast, the Russell Sage Foundation continued to manage many of its own research projects.

47. *Dedication Cermonies and Medical Conference, Peking Union Medical College, September 15–21, 1921* (Peking: PUMC, 1922), pp. 63–64.

48. "China Conference of the Rockefeller Foundation, January 19 and 20, 1921," China Medical Board files, Rockefeller Foundation Archives.

49. Andrews, "Foundations," p. 542.
50. Asher Brynes, *We Give to Conquer* (New York: W. W. Norton & Co., Inc., 1966), p. 81; also see Henry A. Bullock, *A History of Negro Education in the South* (Cambridge, Mass.: Harvard University Press, 1967), pp. 117–146.
51. Berdsley Ruml, "Recent Trends in Social Sciences," address at the University of Chicago, December 17, 1929; quoted by Raymond B. Fosdick, *The Story of the Rockefeller Foundation* (New York: Harper and Bros., 1952), p. 195.
52. For further discussion of these paradigms, see the introductory essay by Jerome Karabel and A. H. Halsey (eds.), *Power and Ideology in Education* (New York: Oxford University Press, 1977), pp. 28–40; Christopher J. Hurn, *The Limits and Possibilities of Schooling* (Boston: Allyn and Bacon, 1978), Chapter 2; and Rolland G. Paulston, *Conflicting Theories of Social and Educational Change: A Typological Review* (Pittsburgh: University of Pittsburgh, Center for International Studies, 1976).
53. The authors conducted their dissertation research under the same advisor at Rutgers University within two years of each other: Dennis C. Buss: "The Ford Foundation and the Exercise of Power in American Public Education," 1972; and David E. Weischadle, "The Carnegie Corporation of New York: A Study of Educational Politics," 1970.
54. The Carnegie "connection" to Washington continued throughout the 1970s. U.S. Commissioner of Education Ernest Boyer resigned in June 1979 to avoid a possible "conflict of interests" which might have arisen from the Ethics in Government Act. This act became effective in July 1979. Boyers, who was to become president of the Carnegie Fund for the Advancement of Teaching noted that the foundation and federal agencies had worked closely together on a number of studies.
55. The Ford Foundation expended $10 million in a multi-year grant action to facilitate the export of the California Master Plan to Chile in the 1960s.
56. *Trent Schroyer, The Critique of Domination* (New York: George Braziller, 1973), p.19.
57. Ibid., pp. 219–220; also see Robert F. Arnove, "The Ford Foundation and 'Competence Building' Overseas: Assumptions, Approaches, and Outcomes," *Studies in Comparative International Development* 12 (Fall 1977): 100–126.
58. Schroyer, *Critique of Domination*, p.248, and pp. 32–36. For further discussion, see Jürgen Habermas, *Toward a Rational Society*, translated by Jeremy J. Shapiro (Boston: Beacon Press, 1970); and his *Knowledge and Human Interests*, translated by Jeremy J. Shapiro (Boston: Beacon Press, 1971); Alvin Gouldner, *The Dialectic of Ideology and Technology* (New York: Seabury Press, 1976); Bruce Brown, *Marx, Freud, and the Interpretation of Everyday Reality* (New York: Monthly Review Press, 1973); Henri Lefebvre, *Everyday Life in the Modern World* (London: Penguin Press, 1971 edition).
59. Horowitz, "Billion Dollar Brains," p. 43.
60. Brim, "Do We Know?" p. 228.

Barbara Howe

The Emergence of Scientific Philanthropy, 1900–1920: Origins, Issues, and Outcomes

The American philanthropic foundation was not born with the republic, nor did it appear fully grown one day. The American foundation became an autonomous social institution during a twenty-year period in which it emerged, crystallized, was challenged, and survived in the form known to us today.

This chapter examines the economic, political, and social forces shaping the emergence and consolidation of philanthropic foundations during the first two decades of this century. It will focus on the wealthiest and most visible of the new millionaires, Andrew Carnegie and John D. Rockefeller, and the factors influencing their decision to systematize and institutionalize charitable giving.

Substantial attention will be given to the congressionally authorized Walsh Commission hearings of 1915, which served as a forum for debating the role of the general purpose foundations in American society. The debates focused on the potential contributions of foundations to the commonwealth as well as the dangers inherent in their concentration of wealth and power closely tied to corporate capitalism. The hearings highlighted issues concerning the ideology and processes of philanthropy. Not for another forty years would foundations be subjected to such critical examination and public scrutiny. The issues and patterns of foundation giving that emerged from the public debate during this period were to continue into the present.

Before discussing the benefactors, the setting, the issues, and the outcomes, it is first necessary to define the distinguishing attributes of the modern philanthropic foundation. Today there exists substantial consensus on the formal definition of the philanthropic foundation—a definition that distinguishes foundations from public charities, from endowments to extant institutions, and from other types of nonprofit organizations.[1] The modern philanthropic foundation is recognized as a separate organization; it is a grant maker as well as, or instead of, an operating research organization; and it possesses an endowment contributed by a small number of people.[2]

Formally, the foundation is often defined as "a nongovernmental, nonprofit organization having a principal fund of its own, managed by its own trustees or directors, and established to maintain or aid social, educational, charitable, religious, or other activities serving the common welfare."[3] Like earlier charitable instruments (corporations and trusts), American philanthropic foundations are based on large endowments and often established to exist in perpetuity. But unlike their predecessors, the great American foundations have been established for broad purposes and are dedicated to putatively preventive rather than palliative work. The latitude of purpose and freedom of operation in their charters is intended to prevent modern foundations from becoming obsolete, and their emphasis on sponsoring constructive projects and research reflects the twentieth-century American belief that philanthropic giving can and should be approached as a scientific endeavor.[4]

It is the notion of a "scientific" endeavor that distinguishes the United States philanthropic foundation from its precursors. And it is the appeal to "science" in the use of wealth that helps to explain the timing of the foundation's appearance: the first two decades of the twentieth century.

Situation of the New Millionaires

By the late nineteenth century the great capitalists of the United States and their associates began grappling with the problem of how to use their vast personal fortunes. The new millionaires had accumulated their resources in a booming industrial economy in amounts and at a rate previously unimaginable. By one estimate, the number of millionaires in the United States increased from 100 in 1880 to 40,000 in 1916.[5] Even more remarkable was the size of the fortunes earned by the most financially successful among the millionaires.[6] Marshall Field's (1834–1906) personal fortune was estimated to be $150 million.[7] Andrew Carnegie was worth approximately $300 million after he sold his steel company to J. P. Morgan in 1901.[8] When Morgan died in 1913, his net estate was valued at over $68 million. In that same year, John D. Rockefeller, at the height of his financial career, was said to have a personal worth of about $900 million.[9]

When the new millionaires of the turn of the century came to the point of deciding how to distribute their personal fortunes, they had unprecedented latitude. First of all, as citizens of the United States, the new millionaires were uniquely unencumbered by any direct governmental restrictions on their gift-giving or testamentary freedom. In addition, the first millionaires were unencumbered by indirect restrictions or influences on their estate planning decisions from federal taxation policies. A federal inheritance tax law had been debated seriously in the 1880s and 1890s and passed as part of the War Revenue Act of 1898,[10] but it was repealed in 1902.[11] There was no permanent income tax law enacted until after the ratification of the Sixteenth Amendment in 1913, and there were no amendments to it allowing for charitable deductions until 1917.[12] Although several of the states began to impose inheritance taxes early in the 1880s,[13] many of the more skeptical scholars agree[14] that tax-savings incentives could not have been the sole consideration for the millionaires of the early 1900s in their philanthropic decisions. As Barry Karl notes, "while public criticism and the threat of taxation probably played a part in their decisions to devote their fortunes to public use, neither really explains the degree of systematic organization and attention they gave to the process."[15]

The extreme amounts of attention and organization given by the first generation of U.S. millionaires is well documented in accounts of and by the John D. Rockefeller family and, to a lesser degree, by Andrew Carnegie. Consider first the Rockefeller account.

ROCKEFELLER: THE TEST CASE FOR SCIENTIFIC ORGANIZATION OF CHARITY

Frederick T. Gates was a minister, educator, and administrator with the Baptist Church when John D. Rockefeller first met him in the late 1880s, at which time both were involved in negotiations for the founding of a Baptist university. At the conclusion of those negotiations (1889), Rockefeller made an initial pledge of $600,000 to that school, the University of Chicago.[16] At the same time Rockefeller asked Gates to become his associate in charge of philanthropies. As Rockefeller told Gates: "I am in trouble. . ...The pressure of these appeals for gifts has become too great for my endurance. . . . I am so constituted as to be unable to give away money with any satisfaction until I have made the most careful inquiry as to the worthiness of the cause."[17] For the next twenty four years those inquiries were to be conducted by Gates.

Rockefeller himself was obviously concerned with making more systematic what he called his "haphazard" manner of giving.[18] However, Rockefeller and Gates, as well as their biographers, agree that it was Gates who conceptualized, extended, and implemented the principle of scientific benevolence for which Rockefeller became so famous.[19] Says Gates in his manuscript autobiography, "I gradually developed and introduced in all his charities the principle of scientific giving, and he [Rockefeller] found himself in no long-time laying aside retail giving almost wholly, and entering safely and pleasurably into what both referred to as the field of wholesale philanthropy."[20] Although the idea of "wholesale" philanthropy rather than "retail" philanthropy is not entirely synonymous with the corporate foundation approach, it does encompass the principle of channeling benevolence through an organization rather than giving directly to individuals.

From his memoirs we can see that Frederick Gates had considered the perils and benefits of the foundation idea that he was attempting to develop. As he watched Rockefeller's fortune accumulate, he wrote:

> Was it [Rockefeller's vast fortune] to be handed on to posterity as other great fortunes have been handed down by their possessors, with scandalous results to their descendents and powerful tendencies to social demoralization? I saw no other course but for Mr. Rockefeller and his son to form a series of great philanthropies. . .philanthropies, if possible, limitless in time and amount, broad in scope, and self-perpetuating. [21]

As early as 1901 Rockefeller's public pronouncements began to reflect Gates's influence. At a speech given at the University of Chicago in June 1901, he introduced to his wealthy audience the nascent concept of the Benevolent Trust, which he used at first as the name for corporations set up to manage the business side of benefactions:

> [Now], why not do with what you can give to others as you do with what you want to keep for yourself and your children: put it into a Trust? You would not place a fortune for your children in the hands of an inexperienced person, no matter how good he might be. . . .Let us erect a foundation, a trust, and engage directors who will make it a life work to manage, with our personal cooperation, this business of benevolence properly and effectively. And I beg of you, attend to it *now,* don't wait.[22]

After 1902 Gates reports that he began to read intensively about the origins and development of human civilization to find out the best means to use the foundations to promote human progress.[23] A 1908 article by Rockefeller reflects the outcome of Gates's reading. In describing the types of investment preferred by his benevolence and investment committees, Rockefeller listed six areas upon which the progress of civilization depended, categories identified by Gates elsewhere[24] as the work of historian William C. Morey: (1) the means of subsistence; (2) government and law; (3) literature and language; (4) science and philosophy; (5) art and refinement; (6) morality and religion.[25] In the case of the Rockefeller foundations, it is clear that Gates was largely responsible both for conceptualizing the idea of the flexible but perpetual entity as an approach to large-scale giving, and implementing it for his employer: "I knew very well that Mr. Rockefeller's mind would not work on mere abstract theories. He required concrete practical suggestions and I set about framing them."[26]

Gates proposed the establishment of a series of foundations, each of which would emphasize support for a distinct aspect of human progress similar to each of Morley's categorizations. As it turned out, Gates's proposal was modified somewhat by Rockefeller, who favored consolidation in philanthropy as well as in business.[27] Rockefeller had already established an Institute for Medical Research in 1901; the General Education Board (GEB) was incorporated by Congress in 1903, and his Sanitary Commission for the Eradication of Hookworm was established in 1909.[28]

Instead of many more separate foundations, therefore, Rockefeller, Gates, and Rockefeller, Jr. (who had now joined in the management of the family philanthropies), decided in 1909, after two years of consideration, to establish one great foundation. This foundation would be a single central holding company which would finance any and all of the other benevolent organizations, and thus necessarily subject them to its general supervision. Said Gates:

> We were to call this the Rockefeller Foundation and to secure a charter from Congress, thus giving it a national character and locating its principal office nominally in the District of Columbia.
>
> Its charter was to be perpetual, subject only to repeal by Congress. We thought repeal by Congress would be difficult if not practically impossible. The Congressional charter as planned by us was to permit limitless capital, to be national and international in scope, with its board of trustees to be wholly self-perpetuating and authorized to do anything whatever, anywhere in the world, within the legal definition of philanthropy as interpreted by our courts.
>
> It was true that such a charter would confer vast powers, but if they were abused, it could be revoked. It is true that no government at any time had conferred on corporations privileges so limitless, even for philanthropic purposes. But on the other hand, no fortune so great as Mr. Rockefeller's had ever before been accumulated by a private person, nor had any philanthropist ever arisen with aims so comprehensive in scope.[29]

The planned federal congressional chartering of the Rockefeller Foundation was never accomplished, mostly because of the refusal of several key U.S. Senators to support even an apparently rationally conceived benevolent organization as long as it bore the mark of the increasingly maligned John D. Rockefeller.[30] Instead, in 1913, the Rockefeller Foundation finally received its charter of incorporation from the State of New York, after an almost unanimous vote of the members of both houses of the state legislature.[31]

Like Rockefeller (who had begun at the age of sixteen to give a fixed percent of his income to charity), Andrew Carnegie had made a commitment to himself at a young age (thirty-three) not merely to accumulate wealth for himself and his heirs, "but [to] spend the surplus each year for benevolent purposes."[32] Unlike Rockefeller, however, Carnegie had no outstanding associate structuring his philanthropic credo for him, and he seemed to thrive on conceptualizing and implementing his own ideas for the systematic use of wealth.

In his famous article "The Gospel of Wealth," written and first published in 1889, when he was a fifty-four-year-old millionaire, [33] Carnegie specified exactly how he and other wealthy men could and should dispose of their fortunes. Carnegie said that there were three possible ways in which this could be done: by leaving one's wealth to family members, by bequeathing it for public purposes, or by administering it during one's own lifetime. [34] He rejected the first two available options. Leaving wealth to one's heirs was harmful both to the heirs and to the society. "The thoughtful man must shortly say," Carnegie wrote, "I would as soon leave to my son a curse as the almighty dollar."[35]

Somewhat surprisingly, perhaps, Carnegie also rejected the idea of leaving one's wealth at death for public purposes, such as in the charitable trust approach. He was well acquainted with previous cases in which this had been done:

> Knowledge of the results of legacies bequeathed is not calculated to inspire the brightest hopes of much posthumous good being accomplished by them. The cases are not few in which the real object sought by the testator is not attained. . . . Men who leave vast sums in this way may be thought men who would not have left it at all had they been able to take it with them. . .there is no grace to their gifts.[36]

Following this reasoning through, Carnegie commented favorably in the next breath on the virtues of recent proposals for an inheritance tax on large estates. "Of all forms of taxation," he said, "this seems the wisest. . . . By taxing estates heavily at death, the state marks its condemnation of the selfish millionaire's unworthy life."[37]

There was, Carnegie concluded, only one really constructive alternative for millionaires, and that was to give away their fortunes before they died, in ways which would benefit the community. Carnegie had definite ideas on what those ways should and should not be. "Of every thousand dollars spent in so-called charity today," he said, "it is probable that nine hundred and fifty dollars is unwisely spent—so spent, indeed," he said, "as to produce the very evils which it hopes to mitigate or cure," for "in alms giving, more injury is probably done by rewarding vice than by relieving virtue."[38] Nor would distributing one's wealth in small amounts among "the people" be advisable, since the good that can be done by amassed dollars is far superior to that which each individual could do with his small share even in the unlikely event it was put to its best use in each home.[39]

Carnegie concluded his essay by specifying seven types of projects which exemplified some of the ways in which millionaires could make good use of their surplus wealth: (1) founding or contributing to a university, (2) establishing community library buildings, (3) founding or contributing to medical institutions, (4) establishing public parks, (5) providing cities with meeting and concert halls, (6) providing public swimming baths, or (7) establishing community church buildings.[40]

It is clear that from his own reading and observations Andrew Carnegie had some well-researched, well-conceptualized ideas on philanthropy; it is clear also that he knew the philosophical and practical problems of the deadhand restrictions often found resulting from the charitable trust form.[41] However, at this point (1889) he had not publicly addressed himself either to the question of perpetuities or to the use of the *foundation* as a mechanism to institutionalize his scientific approach to giving.

Carnegie had provided funds to establish libraries since 1881 and by 1907 had contributed over $40 million toward more than 1,600 of them in the United States alone.[42] It was only after 1901, however, that Carnegie, richer by some $300 million from selling his steel enterprises to J. P. Morgan, began to implement his philanthropic philosophy on a wide scale. It was then that he began to create the first of his many foundations. In 1902 he established (with an initial endowment of $10 million) the Carnegie Institution of Washington, a District of Columbia and later (1904) a federal corporation, whose mission was "to encourage in the broadest and most liberal manner, investigation, research and discovery, and the application of knowledge to the improvement of mankind."[43] In 1904 he provided $5 million to establish the Carnegie Hero Fund Commission, an unincorporated association designed "to recognize those heroes of peace who had tried, successfully or unsuccessfully to save human life."[44]

During his tenure as a trustee of Cornell University, Carnegie had discovered and was dismayed at the low salaries paid to college professors and discussed this situation frequently with his friend Henry S. Pritchett, president of MIT. In 1904 Pritchett suggested that Carnegie provide $1 million to establish a college teacher-retirement plan—what Pritchett called "a Carnegie Foundation."[45]

Although rejecting the small amount Pritchett suggested, Carnegie, in 1905, did establish a $10 million foundation for the Advancement of Teaching. Another Carnegie advisor, Frank A. Vanderlip, urged that the foundation be incorporated, and it was—first in New York State, and soon after (1906) by the U.S. Congress. The initial purpose of the foundation was to provide pensions for college professors. However, the breadth of its charter statement ("to do and perform all things necessary to encourage, uphold and dignify the profession of teaching and the causes of education")[46] in the United States and Canada allowed it to aid many other educational projects later (1915), when the pension program became unworkable.[47]

The importance of having a broad purpose and flexible foundation charter was particularly important in the Carnegie incorporations because of his views on perpetuities. In a 1927 article on the question of perpetual endowments, Henry Pritchett recalls:

> This question [of perpetuities] did not escape Mr. Carnegie's keen vision. He frequently discussed with those who were associated with them in the development of his plans, whether such perpetual endowments as he proposed might in time become either useless or even injurious. He had an answer which is worth repeating. "No man of vision," he said, "will seek to tie the endowment which he gives to a fixed cause. He will leave to the judgment of his trustees, as times goes on, the question of modifying or altogether changing the nature of the trust so as to meet the requirements of the time."[48]

As far as the possibility that endowments in perpetuity eventually would become obsolete, Carnegie was reported to have said:

> I am willing to risk some slack periods in the fruitfulness of the foundations I have established in the confident belief that the service they will render in the fruitful years under able men will far counterbalance the mediocrity into which they may fall in other periods.[49]

Carnegie held consistent with these expressed views by designing all of his trusts to be perpetuities[50] and by establishing as his final memorial a large and potentially diverse foundation called the Carnegie Corporation. On

June 9, 1911, the New York State legislature chartered the Carnegie Corporation as a charitable organization designed "to promote the advancement and diffusion of knowledge and understanding among the people of the United States, by aiding technical schools, institutions of higher leaning [*sic*], libraries, scientific reserch [*sic*], hero funds, useful publications, and by such other agencies and means as shall from time to time be found appropriate therefor."[51]

The Debate over Scientific Philanthropy

The broad theme of "science in the service of society" can be seen as a central one both in the statements-of-purpose of the first great foundations, as described above, and in the approach that led their founders to develop the foundation mechanism itself. Rationality became the appealing means to justify the creation of the philanthropic foundation for wealth transfer and as the guiding principle for grant-making once the new foundations were chartered. Important broad social forces in the period of the founders' work provided potentially forceful support for this ideology, as charity organizations and social work leaders focused on a scientific approach to their own work. The leading social work journal, *Charities and the Commons*, renamed *the Survey* during this era, gave extensive editorial coverage to the proposed charterings of the Rockefeller, Carnegie, and Russell Sage foundations, expressing concern that there be controls on the foundations' leadership and potential perpetuity, but praising the concept of the new foundations because of their breadth, scope, and systematic approach to constructively alleviating the social ills of an urbanizing society.[52] As Barry Karl notes, progressives extended their notions of scientific social planning "well beyond the issues of job security and business cycles. . .to problems that educators, the new sociologists, social workers, and political scientists found important."[53]

Nevertheless, there were important counterforces that were suspicious of the foundations from the outset. There were some who viewed the new foundations as nothing more than corporate appendages that would serve to strengthen and prolong the resources and power of the great industrialists over American workers. And there were others who doubted whether the new foundations—even if initially well motivated—could maintain a semblance of scientific disinterest in funding individuals, institutions, or studies with potentially great influence on public policy.

The skepticism was given almost immediate credibility in the period 1913–1919 due to a series of events involving one of John D. Rockefeller, Jr.'s, corporations, the Colorado Fuel and Iron Company.[54] Dating from the early 1900s the Colorado Fuel and Iron Company had been the site of sporadic activities by the United Mine Workers; and in 1913 and 1914 the union's confrontation with the Rockefeller coal company and others had culminated in a civil war (the so-called "Ludlow Massacre"). This war, involving the national guard and federal troops, led to the death of numerous striking workers and the continued denouncement of the UMW by John D. Rockefeller, Jr.[55]

Meanwhile, the board of trustees of the newly incorporated Rockefeller Foundation had begun to investigate ways to carry out the founder's mandate "to promote the well-being of mankind throughout the world,"[56] and quoting from its 1913–1914 *Annual Report*):

> It seemed to the Trustees, especially in view of the industrial conflict in Colorado, that the Foundation could do no greater service than by instituting a careful and thorough inquiry into the cause of industrial unrest and maladjustment, with the object, not of passing judgment upon the merits of any particular controversy, but rather on assembling in a purely objective way, and with scientific accuracy, the experience of this and other countries, as illustrating both the evils inherent in modern industrial conditions, and the successful or promising experiments that had been made.[57]

Announcement of the industrial relations research project and the appointment of its director W. L. Mackenzie King, a distinguished labor negotiator from Canada, was made in the fall of 1914.[58]

At the same time, Frank P. Walsh and other members of a congressionally created citizens' Commission on Industrial Relations (CIR) were conducting traveling hearings on a broad spectrum of labor related issues in the United States.[59] Apparently as a result of questions raised during their sessions in Colorado, the Walsh Commission decided to include on its agenda a thorough probe of the Rockefeller Foundation. An announcement of this decision was made on December 2, 1914.[60] Then, less than two weeks later, the commission decided to extend its probe to include a "sweeping investigation of all of the country's great benevolent organizations": The Russell Sage Foundation, the Baron de Hirsch Fund, the Cleveland Foundation, and all of the Carnegie benefactions, as well as all of the Rockefeller foundations.[61]

Before the specifics of its hearings on the foundations are reviewed and interpreted, we might note in passing the dramatic aura surrounding the commission chairman's introduction of the foundation hearings. In announcements reported in the *New York Times* on December 17, 1914, for instance, Walsh said that charges had been made to the CIR that

> the creation of the Rockefeller and other foundations was the

beginning of an effort to perpetuate the present position of predatory wealth through the corruption of sources of public information . . .[and] that if not checked by legislation, these foundations will be used as instruments to change the form of government of the U.S. at a future date, and *there is even a hint that there is a fear of a monarchy*. [emphasis added].[62]

During January and February of 1915, the Walsh Commission called on professors, attorneys, social workers, socialists, and anarchists, as well as the well-known philanthropists and their associates. Almost every opinion ever voiced on the foundation idea before or since was stated and restated—as well as some that were never heard before or since: on the dangers of endowments in perpetuity; on the relationships between foundations and their parent industrial corporations; on the obligations between foundations and their academic recipients regarding freedom of inquiry; on the accountability of foundations to Congress and the public; on the goals of "constructive" philanthropy; on the legality of benevolent corporations; on the taxation of charitable corporations; on the sponsorship of research in the social sciences; and on the problems of accumulating assets and the power of the dead hand.

THE FOUNDATION FROM THE PERSPECTIVE OF THE CIR WITNESSES

After leaving Colorado, the Commission on Industrial Relations moved its traveling hearings to New York City in January 1915, to begin hearing testimony on the topic entitled "Centralization of Industrial Control and Operation of Philanthropic Foundations."[63] From January 18 through February 6, the commission received testimony from forty witnesses (twenty speaking directly on the foundation issue) and written statements from several others. As in previous sessions on various labor topics held by the commission, the commissioners' questions to the witnesses were often openly antibusiness in spirit. As commission chairman Walsh explained to one witness at the hearings, the questions were put in a "leading form" to reflect the types of suspicions people had about the foundations.[64] Although the motives behind Walsh's blunt and accusatory questioning are debatable, [65] the resulting testimony was and is a good source for determining the evolving norms regarding the philanthropic foundation. Among the issues raised were those pertaining to the perpetuity and accountability of foundations, the mechanisms through which they would work, the dangers of collusion through interlocking directors and self-serving grant-making, the implications for democracy of the inordinate concentration of wealth and power in the hands of an elite group of professional philanthropists tied to corporate industrial interests. The source of these issues is contained in the testimony of a series of notable witnesses representing both pro- and antifoundation interests, as well as some previously nonaligned spokesmen who expressed well-conceptualized positions on the foundation questions.

PROFOUNDATION REPRESENTATIVES

Many of the foundation associates discussed previously in this chapter were asked to appear at the Walsh hearings. Most notable among these foundation supporters were John D. Rockefeller, Sr., JDR, Jr., Jerome Greene, and Andrew Carnegie. Others closely associated with the foundations who spoke on their behalf were A. Barton Hepburn, prominent banker and a member of the board of trustees of the Rockefeller Foundation, and Charles W. Eliot, president of Harvard, past board member of the Carnegie Foundation for the Advancement of Teaching, and at that time a member of the General Education Board, the Rockefeller Foundation, and the Carnegie Peace Foundation.

John D. Rockefeller, Jr.

The questioning of John D. Rockefeller, Jr., was the longest of any of the witnesses at the foundation hearings.[66] Lasting more than twelve hours, it included detailed statements on topics ranging from Rockefeller's involvement in and attitudes toward the Ludlow Massacre and other incidents at Rockefeller-controlled Colorado mining companies, to the status of individuals like W. L. Mackenzie King on the Rockefeller payrolls, to the motives and functions underlying the institutionalized Rockefeller benefactions.

There were several suggestive questions that Walsh addressed to almost all the foundation witnesses, such as whether there should be a limit on the size or duration of foundations; whether there was danger in overlapping directorships among foundations; whether there should be mandatory reporting of foundation finances and activities; whether there should be special controls on investigations carried out by the foundation rather than by outside grantees; and whether capital used to endow foundations could better have been used to pay higher wages to industrial workers. Addressing the latter question first, Rockefeller, Jr., said that while his father believed that investment of capital directly into businesses was important, "there were certain things which could best be accomplished by gifts of sums to other organizations, educational and philanthropic."[67]

On the issue of public control over incorporated foundations, Rockefeller made a number of statements conveying his faith in the strength of public opinion combined with the legislature's power to repeal or modify any charter of incorporation. But, not unlike many businessmen, he combined that faith with the belief that the foundations would volunteer the reports, accounts, and publicity that would enable legislators and the public to do their vigilante work. Following that line of thinking, Rockefeller asserted also that there should be no limits on the size of foundations because

> the larger the foundation the safer it is, because the more sure it
> is to attract very general public interest, and there is nothing that
> could be so helpful in keeping any foundation directed along
> lines calculated to be of service to the recurring generations as
> that careful and critical and general public attention to the
> purposes and acts of such foundation.[68]

When pressed on the issue of the possible benefits of requiring foundations to make annual reports, Rockefeller said that although he did not think they should be mandatory, such a requirement might have some (unspecified) advantages.[69] He also conceded that the two-year-old Rockefeller Foundation had not published an annual report yet but planned to do so.

Another topic on which Rockefeller expressed a position, one that was endorsed by many other foundation supporters, was the matter of interlocking directors among the new foundations.[70] Rockefeller not only saw no dangers in such links, but stated that it might be advantageous to have such overlaps.[71] Finally, on the issue of grantee versus "in-house" research (undoubtedly provoked by the circumstances surrounding the study of industrial relations done by W. L. Mackenzie King for the Rockefeller Foundation), Rockefeller said that he saw no need for governmental restrictions on those foundations conducting their own investigations of, for instance, social conditions or other controversial topics.[72]

Jerome Greene

Further lengthy testimony on behalf of the foundation approach to wealth transfers was made by Jerome D. Greene, secretary of the Rockefeller Foundation.[73] He endorsed the interlock of directors among the giant American foundations, saying that because there was no individual profit to be made from the sale of some product or service among foundations, the possible dangerous conflict of interest in interlocking business directorships had no parallel in the case of foundations.[74] Like Rockefeller, Jr., Greene endorsed "the force of public opinion" in con-

trolling foundation activities,[75] especially as it was conveyed to the legislature via the press and in other forms for public debate,[76] and he disagreed
with the proposals to allow general inspections of foundation records.[77]

An important formulation introduced to the committee by Greene,
which was not provided by any of the other witnesses, was a statement of
principles. These principles comprised the unofficial guidelines by which
the Rockefeller Foundation had done its grant-making for the past two
years and which also had often been used in decision making by the
General Education Board as well. Drawn up by Greene for one of the
Rockefeller Foundation's early policy-making meetings, the previously
undisclosed memorandum provides an excellent demonstration of the
informal and gradual procedure by which policy was developed by the
first giant foundations, and it also illuminates the normative content of
that policy. As he presented the guidelines, Greene pointed out that
although the Rockefeller Foundation had never formally adopted them,
the seven guidelines outlined in his memorandum were "a fairly adequate
expression of principles that had been observed."[78] They were:

1. Individual charity and relief are excluded, except as the indirect
    result of aid given to other institututions well organized for such
    purposes.
2. Applications for the aid of institutions or enterprises that are
    purely local are excluded, except as aid may be given to these
    establishments as models to other localities and as part of a
    general plan for the encouragement or improvement of similar
    institutions. . . .
3. It may be said that when an individual or an institution goes into
    a community with the intention of making a contribution to its
    welfare, no gift of money, however large, and no outside agency,
    however wise or good, can render a service of unqualified good
    and permanent value except so far as the gift or the agency offers
    the means or the occasion for evoking from the community its
    own recognition of the need to be met, its own will to meet that
    need, and its own resources, both material and spiritual, where-
    with to meet it. . . .
4. In general it is unwise for an institution like the Rockefeller
    Foundation to assume permanently or indefinitely a share of the
    current expenses of an endowed institution which it does not
    avowedly control. . . .
5. On the other hand, the Rockefeller Foundation must carefully
    avoid the dangers incident to gifts in perpetuity. Having the
    qualities of permanence and universality it is better able than
    any private individual to adapt its gifts from generation to

generation . . . to the most urgent needs of the time. It should therefore be careful not to hamper its own trustees or the trustees of other institutions by gifts in perpetuity narrowly limited to particular uses.

6. As between objects which are of an immediately remedial or alleviatory nature, such as asylums for the orphan, blind, or crippled, and those which go to the root of individual or social ill-being and misery, the latter objects are preferred—not because the former are unworthy, but because the latter are more far-reaching in their effects. Moreover, there are many charitably disposed persons to whom remedial and alleviatory agencies make the more effective appeal.

7. As a general rule it is not expedient to entertain applications for the aid of projects, however meritorious, that have not been carefully thought out by their promoters, so that the purposes to be accomplished, the form or organization to be employed, the persons prepared to assume the permanent responsibility for the project, the precise programs to be followed and the amount of financial support already secured, may be stated with precision as to the basis of the application. . . .[79]

John D. Rockefeller, Sr.

It is apparent from the repeated "calls-to-order" by chairman Frank Walsh that are recorded in the CIR hearings of February 5, 1915, that the appearances by seventy-five-year-old JDR, Sr., and Andrew Carnegie were chiefly symbolic.[80] Rockefeller, Jr., and other foundation advisors had already testified on dozens of specific and general philosophic questions, but the appearance by Rockefeller, Sr., must be interpreted as lending credibility to the commission's inquiry.

After reading prepared answers to several of the commission's questions, Rockefeller extemporaneously answered several more questions from Frank Walsh.[81] Like his associates, Rockefeller pointed to the combined forces of American public opinion and foundation charter provisions allowing for legislative repeal or modification as sufficient safeguards against foundation abuses.[82] Referring to the more general issue of what constitutes the preferred method for the transfer of private wealth to public use, the following truncated interchange from the concluding section of Rockefeller's testimony is noteworthy:

Chairman Walsh. . . . It has been stated many times that it might be better for persons controlling very large industries, instead of devoting the excess profits to the dispensation of money along philanthropic and eleemosynary lines, that they should organize some system by which they could distribute it in wages first hand, or give to the workers a greater share of the productivity of the industry in the first place. Now, as one of the great givers of the world, Mr. Rockefeller, I will ask you kindly to comment upon that statement.

Mr. Rockefeller, Sr.   I will be very happy to see the laborers gradually become the owners of these same prosperous businesses to which you refer. I should be only too happy to surrender my holdings, in part, in any or all, that the laborers might come into the relation to the enterprise and have their representation on the boards of directors, according to their ownership, just the same as all other shareholders

Chairman Walsh.   I want to read you—

Mr. Rockefeller, Sr. (continuing).   Thus giving them the profits to which you referred, giving them in addition to their labor these handsome profits which you are having in mind. I should be very happy to have them get those profits, and feel that they were my partners.[83]

However, the means by which Rockefeller meant for workers to become stockholders remained ambiguous, as Walsh's probing merely yielded acquiesence by Rockefeller to the point that a person who had the money to pay for shares of company stock could and should become a shareholder.

Charles W. Eliot

Dr. Charles Eliot, president of Harvard University, appeared before the Walsh Commission on January 29, 1915.[84] Eliot commented on many of the commissioners' standard questions, but he also confronted some of the fundamental issues underlying the appearance of the foundation in American society. Eliot portrayed the foundation as "the corporation method of using large sums of money for the promotion of human welfare."[85] He viewed the chartered corporation as a structure that should be maintained alongside the rapidly growing public sector in promoting the public welfare.[86]

In his evaluation of the foundation Eliot expressed confidence in both the formal and informal normative structures which he saw as vital for maintaining the foundation's effectiveness as an American institution. "I hope for a prolongation of the great service of these corporations, dependent on public law and dependent also in a great many respects on publicity of their actions toward the public."[87] In concluding his testimony, Eliot strongly endorsed the foundation approach for wealth transfer. He volunteered special praise for the newly created Rockefeller Foundation, calling it "the most admirable charity" he had ever known. "And by admirable," he said, "I mean wise in its objects and effective in its organization."[88]

ANTIFOUNDATION SPOKESMEN

Testimony to be considered for inclusion in this section was made by representatives of organizations who had a well-established reputation for their antibusiness, prolabor stance. These interests were well represented at the CIR hearings in the persons of Edward P. Costigan and John R. Lawson of the United Mine Workers, Samuel Gompers of the American Federal of Labor, and Morris Hillquit from the Socialist Labor Party.

Morris Hillquit

The testimony given by Morris Hillquit on the foundation question is the most comprehensive expression of the antifoundation position available from the CIR hearings.[89] Hillquit, a leader of one of the Socialist factions of the progressive period and a lawyer, did not limit his analysis of the foundations to the Rockefeller Foundation and its alleged antilabor activities. In his testimony he said that the emergence of all of the large foundations of that era "represent[s] a very significant phase in modern development, and probably one that had not yet been fully appreciated by the people of the United States."[90] Hillquit compared the foundation's appearance in the field of philanthropy to the emergence of trusts in the world of business—from individual almsgiving, to organized charity, to the giant foundations.[91] He contrasted the earliest American approach to charity with the global, institutionally oriented, nonpalliative focus of the twentieth-century foundations. He spoke of the foundations' interest in international welfare as analogous to the approach to American missionaries: "[T]o my mind," he said, "they are both business enterprises," to advance the people of underdeveloped countries sufficiently to create new markets for American manufactured goods.[92]

Hillquit's critical analysis of the objects of American foundation philanthropy included education, social welfare, and even the Carnegie libraries program. In all cases he believed that endowments created obligations on the part of recipients not to use the monies in controversial ways. "...While it may be true that Mr. Carnegie does not make up the catalogues of those libraries," Hillquit said, "still we can hardly expect that a work which may be perfectly truthful and important, but which may oppose Mr. Carnegie's business interests in a pronounced way, will find its way among such books."[93]

Hillquit concluded his testimony by recommending that the government assume a greater responsibility for the education and social welfare functions, which at that time were supported by the private sector rather than government.[94] He further suggested that the foundations already in existence be subject to greater supervision by the state and that their charters be amended to restrict their functions.[95]

Costigan and Lawson

Two witnesses who appeared before the CIR on behalf of labor represented the United Mine Workers of America. Both had represented labor in the Colorado coal strike affair, and both were most concerned about the involvement of the Rockefeller Foundation in the Colorado situation. Costigan, an attorney,[96] spoke of the contradictions inherent in the fact that John D. Rockefeller, Jr., was at once a feudalistic absentee landlord and the president of a philanthropic organization.[97] Costigan was less critical of the foundations' work than Morris Hillquit had been and conceded the value of many of the works carried out by the Rockefeller Foundation. In fact, it was the effectiveness of the foundations' charitable work that Costigan saw as the greatest threat to society.

> In the investigations of the hookworm in the South, the vice districts in Chicago and New York, and in his donations to the Belgium fund, Mr. Rockefeller has shown the splendid side and possibilities of intelligent charity. For these beneficent acts he is entitled to and will doubtless receive proper public appreciation. The one danger in them in the light of the Colorado experience is that *these philanthropies may obscure the sordid practices of big business in Colorado and elsewhere* . . . [emphasis added].[98]

It is significant that Costigan at once celebrated and feared the effective manner in which the foundation was carrying out its altruistic work. However, he did not elaborate on the specific alternatives or controls he would place on the foundations but merely concluded by saying that public agencies rather than private ones should perform the society's charitable functions.

Nor did the testimony of a second United Mine Workers spokeman, John R. Lawson, include any specific alternatives to the foundation approach.[99] Lawson concentrated his attack on the foundation on the assertion that "it is not their money that these lords of commercialized virtue are spending, but the withheld wages of the American working class."[100] He also raised the criticism that the Rockefeller foundations were spending millions for health, education, and conservation throughout the world, but not a dollar for those suffering the effects of the Ludlow Massacre in Colorado.[101] He concluded his polemic by saying that "There are thousands of Mr. Rockefeller's ex-employees in Colorado today who wish to God that they were in Belgium to be fed or birds to be cared for tenderly."[102]

Samuel Gompers

When Samuel Gompers made his appearance before the CIR, he was sixty four years old and had been a leader in the American labor movement for over fifty years and president of the American Federation of Labor for almost thirty years.[103] Addressing himself to the committee's questions, he spoke on the mixed progress of the labor movement, the growth of industrial combinations and the problem of immigrant labor as well as the potential role of the new foundations in American society.[104] He was most critical of the Rockefeller Foundation, including, but not limited to, what he saw as their self-serving investigations of industry. However, it should be noted that Gompers did *not* extend his criticism of foundations to other large foundations such as Carnegie and Russell Sage; their worth he considered an open question. His overall opinion is perhaps best expressed by this statement.

> In so far as these foundations would devote their activities to the sciences, medical, surgical; to the laboratory, to the contributions toward history; for the arts, the sciences, they would be helpful. But in the effort to undertake to be an all-pervading machinery for the molding of the minds of the people . . . in the constant industrial struggle for human betterment . . . they should be prohibited from exercising their functions, either by law or by regulation.[105]

NONALIGNED SPOKESMEN

When studying the testimony given to the CIR, it is often easy to accurately predict a witness's basic posture and interpretation of the foundation merely by knowing his organizational affiliation. Therefore, it was not surprising to find general support for the foundation approach among philanthropists and their associates and a skepticism toward foundations by antibusiness spokesmen. In this concluding section on the CIR hearings, we will review briefly the interpretations of the new foundations provided to the commission by a few witnesses whose stance on the foundation question would not be predictable immediately from their affiliation or occupation, and whose statements enhance our description of the normative structure developing around the American foundations. In order of appearance before the Walsh Commission, they are Henry Ford, John H. Holmes, and George W. Kirchwey.

Henry Ford

At the time of the CIR hearings, Henry Ford was fifty one years old and had been in the automobile business for twenty five years. He had introduced the Model T in 1908 and was one of the few successful automobile manufacturers of the prewar period.[106] However, Ford was "strikingly different" from Carnegie and Rockefeller in his philanthropic style, according to William Greenleaf, expert on Ford's philanthropies.[107] "He [Ford] never mastered the art of systematic giving on a large scale; he never evolved a general plan or administrative mechanism for disposing of his surplus wealth; and he came to philanthropy late in life."[108]

What Henry Ford had done in January 1914—just one year before his CIR appearance—was to establish an innovative profit-sharing plan for Ford Motor Company employees. Ford's contemporaries considered the plan his vehicle for charity. But Ford abhorred charity. He viewed his plan as a way of justly compensating workers for their services.[109]

Probably because the Ford profit-sharing plan was such an innovative one, it became the main focus of the commissioners' exchange with Ford.[110] On the issue of philanthropic foundations, however, Ford was almost mute. In response to presubmitted questions on the role of great benevolent organizations such as the Rockefeller Foundation, Ford answered that he had not given enough thought to such questions to offer an opinion.[111] Finally, in answer to a question on the ability of private philanthropies to deal adequately with social problems, Ford responded:

> They may and probably do some good. Of course they are not adequate. But my idea is justice, not charity. I have little use for charities or philanthropies as such. My idea is to aid men to help themselves. . . .[112]

John H. Holmes

John Haynes Holmes, Harvard Divinity School graduate and pastor of the Church of the Messiah in Manhattan, was invited to testify at the hearings as "a student of industrial problems."[113] Holmes began his statement to the CIR by saying that the American foundation as a social institution was "essentially repugnant to the whole idea of a democratic society"[114] because of (1) the tainted origin of its funds, (2) the cliquishness of its administration, and (3) because the foundation impinged on people's opportunities to identify and attend to their own social needs without outside interference.[115] Holmes also objected to the foundations because of their potential to influence public debate on controversial issues and because foundations were autocratically administered organizations establishing themselves inside a society committed to democracy.[116]

Another issue raised by the Reverend Holmes was the potential influence of the foundations on American education. This general issue had been raised many times previously, both in and outside the CIR hearings.[117] But Clergyman Holmes's focus (although he identified himself as nonsectarian) was on the growing influence of the foundations on the option of sectarian higher education. The case in point was the Carnegie Foundation's stipulation that only nondenominational schools were eligible for the benefits of the foundation's pension program. Because of that restriction, Holmes said, many schools were divesting themselves of their established denominational character in order to qualify for the foundation's benefits.[118]

Throughout his testimony, Holmes emphasized that he was not criticizing the American millionaire foundation-creators or their motives;[119] rather, he decried a political economy that left to any individual the burden of deciding how to dispose of a great fortune. Holmes provided the committee with a sketch of an alternative "system" he advocated; but on the management of extant foundations he ruled out any drastic revisions. He proposed that legislative bodies currently overseeing foundation charters exercise their options to amend those charters and write in provisions for more public representation and greater control of foundation operations.[120] When questioned on the preferability of a total government takeover of the private foundations, Holmes replied that whereas he personally preferred such a move, he knew that "public opinion" would not yet support it.[121] In the meantime, he proposed that his millionaire contemporaries need not remain burdened by having to chose between "riotous living" or endowing a foundation. "There is a third way." The millionaire could use his money to help the government study how to handle and utilize great wealth, or, Holmes concluded, "he may turn it over to the government," just as Theodore Roosevelt had done (in 1907) with his $40,000 Nobel Prize.[122]

George W. Kirchwey

Among the issues with which the commission had been most concerned throughout its hearings was the potential legal latitude given the new American foundation to engage in crypto-political or crypto-business activities. From the testimony of Dr. George Kirchwey (professor of law, former dean of the Columbia University Law School, and expert on foundation law) the CIR hoped to clarify the legal latitude of the new foundations.[123] "Might a foundation circulate a presidential message or a party platform. . .?" the Commissioners asked. "Might it confine its benevolent service to the organization of business enterprises?" "Might it conduct a propaganda [sic] against trade-unions?"[124] What—the commission was asking Kirchwey—were the legal limits on the activities of an organization whose formal purpose was "to promote the well-being of mankind"?

In essence, Kirchwey said, each of the hypothetical cases raised by the commission could be judged only in court, where the question would be: is or is not the activity in question (say, the circulating of a party platform), an act which will promote the well-being of mankind? And, in making these decisions, Kirchwey believed that by and large the judgment of the court would reflect the state of public opinion on the activities and intent of the giant American foundations.[125] Although Kirchwey acknowledged that such a system might result in temporary discrepancies between the state of public opinion and the legal norms surrounding foundation activities, he supported the then popular legal realists' view that the judge-made law governing philanthropic foundations ultimately would be the "crystallization of what people think."[126]

In concluding his testimony, Kirchwey endorsed the foundation approach. "My own personal opinion," he said, "is that it marks a distinct advance in the direction of social well-being to have great wealth transferred from irresponsible private hands and placed in the responsible hands of a group of persons who are incorporated and supervised by the state."[127]

The Aftermath of Congressional Scrutiny of the New Foundations

In 1916 the Walsh Commission on Industrial Relations submitted to the 64th Congress its Final Report and Testimony, an eleven-volume, 11,224-page document prepared by the CIR's research director, Basil M. Manly.[128] Included in the Final Report were official recommendations as to what the commission should recommend on numerous labor-related issues. These recommendations were drawn up by Manly and signed by Commissioners Walsh, Lennon O'Connell, and Garretson.[129] Also included in the report was a "minority" report on a number of issues—including foundations—drawn up and signed by Commissioners Commons, Harriman, Weinstock, Ballard, and Aishton.[130]

The official (Manly) report included its findings and recommendations on foundations under the subject, "the concentration of wealth and influence."[131] It enumerated more than a dozen by-now familiar criticisms against the place of the foundation in American life.[132] In formulating its recommendations the Manly Report said that the giant, general purpose foundations were so "grave a menace" to society that "if they could be clearly differentiated from other forms of voluntary altruistic effort [,] it would be desirable to recommend their abolition."[133] The report concluded, however, that it was not yet possible "to devise any clear-cut definition upon which they [the menace foundations] can be differentiated," so that they could be abolished.[134] Therefore, the report recommended that the commission call for (1) legislation giving the Congress strict control over the foundations (including their size, financing, reporting procedures, and scope of operations); (2) a thorough congressional investigation of the finances and activities of all endowed charitable organizations holding substantial assets; and (3) increased federal appropriations to match, and thereby "counteract," the spending by foundations of social services.[135]

In its minority report, Commissioners Commons and Harriman and cosigners agreed with the majority's call for a congressional investigation of all types of foundations as well as an investigation of all other endowed organizations, including religious and educational ones.[136] They also agreed that federal funds should be appropriated to take over much of the work done by foundations. However, they did not agree with the majority's conclusion that the giant foundations were a menace to society. "We are convinced that many of these endowments in private hands have a beneficial effect," the minority report said.[137] And it recommended that no restrictive legislation be enacted against the foundation until Congress completed a thorough investigation into all aspects of endowed charities.[138]

Although the Walsh Commission recommended congressional investigation and regulation of the activities of American foundations, no such action was taken until after more than thirty years following the 1916 CIR report. Scholars disagree on the specific reason for that long hiatus; but the activities surrounding World War I, the waning strength of antibusiness forces, the growth of labor's power (despite the foundations' existence), and the highly visible contributions of the foundations in sponsoring effective medical research and war relief projects have all been mentioned as factors enabling the foundations to work unhampered after 1916.[139]

Additionally, it should be noted that the New York State charter received by the Rockefeller Foundation in 1913 (and the similar one granted to the Carnegie Corporation by the New York State legislature in

1911) did not include any of the restrictive amendments that had been agreed to by the Rockefeller representatives during their three years of charter negotiations with the United States Congress. There were no restrictions on the amount of principal or its accumulation, no suggested time limit for its liquidation, no provisions restricting selection of trustees. Even the requirement to submit an annual financial report—part of the original bill proposed to the U.S. Congress by Rockefeller—was omitted in the state charter.[140]

The outcome of the events of the first two decades of this century with regard to the philanthropic foundation is in some senses ironic. Because of congressional ambivalence toward the millionaires' foundation proposals—which on one hand fit well into popular models of rational social planning,[141] but on the other hand were seen as symbols of continued paternalism on the part of exploitive capitalists—the creators of the American philanthropic foundation were unable to gain either explicit credibility or open praise for their new institution. But, by surviving the congressional and Industrial Relations Commission challenges of the early 1900s and obtaining virtually unrestricted state charters, the millionaires and their associates had made a socially and politically significant gain. They had secured a level of public and legislative tolerance which enabled their foundations and others to flourish and function autonomously for decades to follow, both in the United States and abroad. Not until the 1950s was there to be any further congressional investigation of foundation activities;[142] and not until the Tax Reform Act of 1969[143] was the extraordinary latitude of action permitted to philanthropists and philanthropoids[144] threatened by governmental intrusion on their uniquely autonomous American institution.[145] Although many spoke of the tax-linked restrictions of the 1969 act as the death knell of organized philanthropy,[146] the foundation remained vital throughout the 1970s.[147]

Notes

1. The distinction between private foundations and public charities from the Internal Revenue Service's viewpoint has been reemphasized and operationalized in the Tax Reform Act of 1969. See John R. Labovitz, "The Impact of the Private Foundation Provisions of the Tax Reform Act of 1969: Early Empirical Measurements," *Journal of Legal Studies* 3 (January 1974): 63–105, especially pp.63–71.

2. For summary of diverging viewpoints on the distinguishing properties of a foundation, see Thomas Parrish, "The Foundation: 'A Special American Institution,'" pp. 7–42 in American Assembly, *The Future of Foun-*

dations (Englewood Cliffs, N.J.: Prentice-Hall, 1973), especially pp. 9–11.

3. The Foundation Libary Center, *The Foundation Directory*, Edition 1, Ann D. Walton and F. Emerson Andrews, editors (New York: Russell Sage Foundation, 1960), p. ix.

4. This characterization of the distinctive attributes of the modern American foundation is drawn from F. Emerson Andrews, "Foundations," in *The Foundation Directory*, Edition 1, pp. 542–543.

5. Richard L. Heilbroner, *The Making of Economic Society*, Third Edition (Englewood Cliffs, N.J.: Prentice-Hall, 1970), p. 100.

6. It should be noted that one 1910 dollar would be worth approximately six dollars in 1975. See William Manchester, "The Founding Grandfather," *New York Times Magazine* (October 6, 1974), p. 44.

7. Walter H. Page, "The March of Events: A Lesson from the Career of Mr. Marshall Field," *World's Work* 11 (March 1906): 7254.

8. Burton J. Hendrick, *The Life of Andrew Carnegie*, Volume II (New York: Doubleday Doran, 1932), p. 144.

9. Allan Nevins, *Study in Power*, Volume II (New York: Scribners, 1953), p. 300.

12. F. Emerson Andrews, *Philanthropic Foundations* (New York: Russell Sage Foundation, 1956), p. 41.

13. Ratner, *New Light*, pp. 47–51, 235.

14. For example, see Harace Coon, *Money to Burn* (New York: Longmans, Green & Co., 1938), pp. 332–333; also see Joseph C. Kiger, *Operating Principles of the Larger Foundations* (New York: Russell Sage Foundation, 1954), p. 25.

15. Barry D. Karl, "Philanthropy, Policy Planning, and the Bureaucratization of the Democratic Ideal," *Daedalus* 105 (Fall 1976): 146.

16. Allan Nevins, *Study in Power*, Volume II (New York: Scribners, 1953), pp. 179–182.

17. Ibid., p. 198.

18. John D. Rockefeller, "Some Random Reminiscences of Men and Events [Third Article]: The Difficult Art of Giving," *World's Work* 17 (December 1908): 11000.

19. See Nevins, *Study in Power*, Volume II, pp. 197–220; Frederick T. Gates, "The Memoirs of Frederick T. Gates," *American Heritage* 6 (April 1955): 71–86; and Raymond B. Fosdick, *Adventure in Giving* (New York: Harper & Row, 1962), p. 6.

20. Quoted in Raymond B. Fosdick, *The Story of the Rockefeller Foundation* (New York: Harper & Bros.), p. 7.

21. Gates, "Memoirs," p. 80.

22. John D. Rockefeller, "Some Random Reminiscences of Men and Events [Fourth Article]: The Value of the Cooperative Principle in Giving," *World's Work* 17 (January 1909): 11110.

23. Gates, "Memoirs."

24. Ibid.

25. Rockefeller, "Some Random Reminiscences [Third Article]," p. 11000.
26. Gates, "Memoirs."
27. Nevins, *Study in Power*, Volume II, p. 395; and Rockefeller, "Some Random Reminiscences [Fourth Article]," p. 11101.
28. Nevins, *Study in Power*, p. 302. It might be noted that the impetus to found the General Education Board probably came from JDR, Jr., rather than Gates. At first the GEB was envisioned by the Rockefeller associates as an organization that would be supported by many northern capitalists interested in southern education rather than by Rockefeller money alone. But when that support did not materialize, Rockefeller alone endowed it. See Raymond Fosdick, *Adventure in Giving*, pp. 6–9.
29. Gates, "Memoirs," pp. 84–85.
30. See John Lankford, *Congress and the Foundations* (River Falls: Wisconsin State University, 1964), for a detailed account of the failed negotiations for the Rockefeller Foundation Charter by the U.S. Congress.
31. New York [State] Legislature, *Journal of the Assembly of the State of New York at Their 136th Session* (1913), Vol. III, pp. 2931–2932; and *Journal of the Senate of the State of New York at Their 136th Session*, Vol. I, pp. 1314–1315.
32. Hendrick, *Andrew Carnegie*, Vol. II, pp. 146–147.
33. Andrew Carnegie, *The Gospel of Wealth and Other Timely Essays*, edited by Edward C. Kirkland (Cambridge, Mass.: Belknap Press, 1962).
34. Ibid., pp. 19–20.
35. Ibid., p. 21.
36. Ibid.
37. Ibid., p. 22.
38. Ibid., pp. 26–27.
39. Ibid., pp. 23–24.
40. Ibid., pp. 32–37.
41. Ibid., p. 24.
42. Robert M. Lester, *Forty Years of Carnegie Giving* (New York: Charles Scribner's Sons, 1941), p. 93.
43. Ibid., pp. 25, 29–30; also see Howard J. Savage, *Fruit of an Impulse* (New York: Harcourt, Brace & Co., 1953), pp. 5–6.
44. Lester, *Carnegie Giving*, pp. 36; 143–145; and Savage, *Fruit of Impulse*, p. 26. Also see *Autobiography of Andrew Carnegie* (Boston: Hougton Mifflin, 1924), p. 260.
45. Savage, *Fruit of Impulse*, p. 7.
46. Lester, *Carnegie Giving*, p. 155.
47. Hendrick, *Andrew Carnegie*, Vol. II, p. 26.
48. Quoted in Savage, *Fruit of Impulse*, p. 29.
49. Ibid.
50. Ibid., p. 26.
51. Lester, *Carnegie Giving*, p. 166. After 1906 Carnegie became a vocal and practicing advocate of the movement to reform spelling; see Hendrick, *Andrew Carnegie*, Vol. II, pp. 262–263.
52. For example, see editorial, "The Rockefeller Foundation," by Edward T.

Devine, *Survey* 23 (March 12, 1910): 901–903. For detailed account, see Slaughter and Silva, "Looking Backwards," Chapter 2 in this book.

53. Karl, "Philanthropy, Policy Planning," p. 132.
54. For an excellent account of these events in the context of the Rockefeller family's activities, see Peter Collier and David Horowitz, *The Rockefellers: An American Dynasty*, (New York: Holt, Rinehart and Winston, 1976), especially Chapter 8.
55. For a brief account of this episode, see any of the standard history texts, e.g., Arthur S. Link, *American Epoch: A History of the United States Since the 1890's*, 2nd ed. (New York: Alfred A. Knopf, 1963), pp. 60–61.
56. Raymond B. Fosdick, *The Story of the Rockefeller Foundation* (New York: Harper & Bros., 1952), p. 20.
57. The Rockefeller Foundation, *Annual Report 1913–14*, Second Edition (New York: Rockefeller Foundation, 1915), p. 18.
58. See *New York Times*, October 2, 1914, p. 7, and December 7, 1914, p. 1.
59. For discussion of the origins and composition of the Commission on Industrial Relations, see Robert H. Bremner, *From the Depths: The Discovery of Poverty in the United States* (New York: New York University Press, 1956), pp. 159–161; and Allen F. Davis, "The Campaign for the Industrial Relations Commission, 1911–1913," *Mid-America* 45:4 (1964): 211–228.
60. *New York Times*, December 2, 1914, p. 12.
61. *Ibid.*, December 17, 1914, p. 6.
62. Ibid.
63. United States Congress. Senate. 64th Congress, 1st Session, *Senate Documents*, No. 415, "Industrial Relations: Final Report and Testimony Submitted to the Congress by the Commission on Industrial Relations," Volume 8, p. 7427.
64. Ibid., Volume 9, pp. 8137, 8145, 8148.
65. For example, see Lankford, *Congress and Foundations*, p. 27. Lankford says that "in his selection and questioning of witnesses [for the CIR], Walsh betrayed his prejudices"—particularly concerning the goals and work of the Rockefeller Foundation.
66. "Industrial Relations: Final Report and Testimony," Vol. 8, pp. 7763–7895.
67. Ibid., p. 7850.
68. Ibid., p. 7856.
69. Ibid., p. 7877.
70. Ibid., pp. 7855, 7881.
71. Ibid., p. 7859. Rockefeller felt that having personnel experienced in handling questions that foundations often had to deal with would be desirable for a foundation. Hence, his lack of objection to interlocking directorates.
72. Ibid., p. 7863. Incidentally, the results of the study done by W. L. M. King were subsequently completed and published independent of Rockefeller Foundation sponsorship. See W. L. Mackenzie King, *Industry and Humanity* (Boston: Houghton Mifflin Co., 1918).
73. "Industrial Relations: Final Report and Testimony," Vol. 9, pp. 8137–8183.
74. Ibid., p. 8138.

75. Ibid., p. 8153.
76. Ibid., p. 8156.
77. Ibid., p. 8182.
78. Ibid., p. 8139.
79. Ibid., pp. 8139–8141. Note that several of the principles outlined by Greene (specifically numbers 2, 4, 6, and 7) are consistent with the risk of venture capital doctrine developed through the years by American philanthropists. As Andrews defines it "the funds of foundations were seen as the venture capital of philanthropy, best spent when invested in enterprises requiring risk and foresight, not likely to be supported either by government or the private individual." F. Amerson Andrews, *Legal Instruments of Foundations* (New York: Russell Sage Foundation, 1958), p. 12. For extensive analysis of development of this doctrine by the foundations, see Richard Colvard, "Risk Capital Philanthropy: The Ideological Defense of Innovation," pp. 728–748 in G. K. Zollschan and W. Hirsch (eds.), *Explorations in Social Change* (Boston: Houghton Mifflin, 1964).
80. Because Carnegie's testimony was almost entirely anecdotal, it is not reported here. See "Industrial Relations: Final Report and Testimony," Vol. 9, pp. 8286 –8297.
81. For the senior Rockefeller's testimony, see ibid., Vol. 9, pp. 8297–8304.
82. Ibid., pp. 8298, 8300.
83. Ibid., p. 8303.
84. Ibid., Vol. 8, pp. 7964–7986.
85. Ibid., p. 7982.
86. Ibid., pp. 7982–7983.
87. Ibid., p. 7983.
88. Ibid.
89. Ibid., pp. 8262–8286.
90. Ibid., p. 8263.
91. Ibid., pp. 8263–8265.
92. Ibid., pp. p. 8266.
93. Ibid., p. 8269.
94. Ibid., p. 8272.
95. Ibid., pp. 8273–8274.
96. For Costigan's testimony, see ibid., Vol. 9, pp. 8113–8126, 8126–8127.
97. Ibid., pp. 8116, 8118.
98. Ibid., p. 8119.
99. For Lawson's testimony, see ibid., Vol. 8, pp. 8003–8013, and ibid., Vol. 9, pp. 8014–8040, 8126, 8128.
100. Ibid., p. 8006.
101. Ibid.
102. Ibid.
103. Gompers began his labor activities as a young teenager. *Seventy Years of Life and Labor: An Autobiography by Samuel Gompers* (New York: Dutton & Co., 1957), pp. 17, 57.
104. Ibid., Vol. 8, pp. 7638–7657.
105. Ibid., p. 7647.

106. See Link, *American Epoch*, p. 262.

107. See William Greenleaf, *From These Beginnings: The Early Philanthropies of Henry and Edsel Ford, 1911–1936* (Detroit: Wayne State University Press, 1964).

108. Ibid., p. 7.

109. Ibid., pp. 7–8.

110. For Ford's testimony, see "Industrial Relations: Final Report and Testimony," Vol. 8, pp. 7626–7638.

111. Ibid., p. 7630.

112. Ibid.

113. Ibid., Vol. 8, pp. 7916–7933. Quotation from ibid., p. 7916.

114. Ibid., p. 7916.

115. Ibid., pp. 7916–7921.

116. Ibid., pp. 7917–7918.

117. For example, see Morris Hillquit's CIR testimony, discussed above in this chapter and Jacob Schurman's statement discussed in Chapter 3 or in "Quotations: Incorporated Benefactions," *Science* 30 n.s. (October 2, 1909): 564–565.

118. See Holmes's testimony in "Industrial Relations: Final Report and Testimony," Vol. 8, pp. 7918–7919.

119. For example, ibid., p. 7916.

120. Ibid., pp. 7917, 7931.

121. Ibid., p. 7923.

122. Ibid., pp. 7919, 7932.

123. For Kirchwey's testimony, see ibid., Vol. 9, pp. 8215–8229.

124. Ibid., p. 8217.

125. Ibid., pp. 8219, 8221.

126. Ibid., p. 8221. On legal realism, see E. A. Purcell, Jr., "American Jurisprudence between the Wars: Legal Realism and the Crisis of Democratic Theory," in Lawrence M. Friedman and Harry N. Scheiber (eds.), *American Law and the Constitutional Order: Historical Perspectives* (Cambridge, Mass.: Harvard University Press, 1978), pp. 359–374; also see Kirchwey's "Foreword" in A. Lief (ed.), *The Dissenting Opinions of Mr. Justice Holmes* (New York: Vanguard Press, 1929), pp. xi–xii.

127. Ibid., p. 8228.

128. "Industrial Relations: Final Report and Testimony," ibid., Vol. 1–11.

129. Ibid., Vol. 1. It should be noted that the commission members were unable to agree on conclusions to submit as official CIR recommendations. On this, see Bremner, *From the Depths*, p. 159.

130. "Industrial Relations: Final Report and Testimony," Vol. 1, pp. 169–230; recommendations for foundations on p. 220. One other "minority" statement on foundations (approved by Walsh, Lennon, and O'Connell) can be found on p. 269 of Vol. 1.

131. See ibid., Vol. 1, p. 80ff.

132. Ibid., pp. 81–84.

133. Ibid., p. 85 (emphasis added).

134. Ibid.

135. Ibid., pp. 85–86. At that time (1916)—according to the Manly Report—the philanthropic foundations of Rockefeller and Carnegie taken together had from their assets a total annual revenue of more than $13,500,000. The Report said that that amount was "at least twice as great as the [annual] appropriations of the Federal Government for. . .education and social service." See ibid., Vol. 1, 81.

136. Ibid., p. 220.

137. Ibid.

138. Ibid.

139. See Harold Keele, "Government's Attitude Toward Foundations," *Michigan State Bar Journal* 33 (October 1954): esp. p. 21; also see Eleanor K. Taylor, *Public Accountability of Foundations and Charitable Trusts* (New York: Russell Sage Foundation, 1953), p. 10; and Lankford, *Congress and the Foundations*, p. 32.

140. For a narrative account of this entire procedure, see Lankford, *Congress and the Foundations*, pp. 11–20; and Fosdick, *The Story of the Rockefeller Foundation*, pp. 16–20.

141. See Karl, "Philanthropy, Policy Planning," pp. 129–149; also see Robert Wiebe, *The Search for Order 1877–1920* (New York: Hill and Wang, 1967), esp. pp. 149–150; and Arthur A. Ekirch, Jr., *Progressivism in America* (New York: Franklin Watts, 1974), especially pp. 67–89.

142. Lankford, *Congress and the Foundations*, p. 33.

143. Labovitz, "Impact of Tax Reform Act of 1969," pp. 63–105.

144. "Philanthropoids" are those who manage the money-giving for each succeeding generation of the foundations. See Ben Whitaker, *The Philanthropoids: Foundations and Society* (New York: William Morrow, 1974).

145. For a review of the highlights of the 1960s congressional hearings leading to the passing of the Tax Reform Act, see Edith L. Fisch et al., *Charities and Charitable Foundations* (Pomona, N.Y.: Lond Publications, 1974), Section 43.

146. See, for example, John G. Simon, "Are Private Foundations an Endangered Species?" *Foundation News* 15 (January-February 1974): 11–18.

147. For evidence of the continued capacity of foundations to defend their interests, see U.S. Senate, Committee on Finances, *The Role of Foundations Today and the Effect of the Tax Reform Act of 1969 upon Foundations*, testimony submitted to the Subcommittee on Foundations, October 1 and 2, 1973 (Washington, D.C.: United States Government Printing Office, 1973). Further indication of the continued institutional resourcefulness of foundations is found in the workings of the Council on Foundations; and evidence that systematic grant making on a vast scale is still "alive and well" in the USA is found in the council's publication, *Foundation News*.

Sheila Slaughter and
Edward T. Silva

Looking Backwards: How Foundations Formulated Ideology in the Progressive Period

In looking backwards to the progressive period (1900–1920) and the part played by the first foundations in the systematic shaping of ideas, it is necessary to recall that the era was turbulent with a new material reality. In the years following the Civil War, radical changes in the mode of production shifted the United States from an agrarian to an industrial nation in which the exploitation of the technical developments that made industrialization possible depended on a landless, polyglot, urban proletariat whose only stake in existing social arrangements was the inadequate hourly wage. The resulting conflicts between capital and labor often flared into violence of such proportions that these struggles were referred to as labor wars and treated, with armed troops and martial law, as civil insurrections. Imperfect coordination of a newly national economy created frequent economic breakdowns—virtually half the years between the Civil War and World War I were beset with depression—that shook the confidence of the rapidly growing white-collar sector as to the stability of industrial capital. Finally, the emerging role of the farming hinterland as an internal colony—as a market for manufactured goods and a cheap food and fiber supplier for an increasingly urbanized labor force—gave rise to years of virulent and sustained regional opposition to the centralizing thrust of eastern finance capital.[1]

Rapid post–Civil War industrialization created a series of national crises as conflict followed conflict across the American political-economic stage. Continued crises called forth new ideologies to compete with established ones. Each ideology, new or old, was a more or less coherent set of ideas explaining the problematic issues of the day somewhat differently and offering its own solution to them. These ideologies helped organize their adherents' beliefs and hopes about their world's present and future, giving structure to citizen's perceptions in three ways.

First, each ideology outlined the way the political economy operated, clearly delineating who exercised power and on what grounds. This provided a framework for interpreting the wide variety of problematic social issues and conflicts encountered in daily life, in media, and in the political arena.

Second, ideology offered criteria for a moral evaluation of the ongoing political economy. In particular, it helped focus attention on the propriety of power arrangements and their consequences—on who got what, when, where, and how. Were these arrangements and their consequences basically just or fundamentally unfair? Were they good or bad?

Third, the descriptive and evaluative elements in these ideologies combined to supply citizens with imperatives to collective action. Ideologies mandated either a defense of the status quo—if it was seen as just and good—or an attack on those structures requiring change. Ideologies either inhibited or inspired social movements. In the progressive period, then, ideologies supplied a variety of solutions to the social problems that plagued industrializing America, explaining the way society worked and offering blueprints for the future.

While individual citizens were free to construct their own idiosyncratic analysis of current conditions and design programs for the future, they might also choose from those offered by a variety of groups—socialists, populists, urban reformers, business leaders, anarchists, conservative unionists, and radical workers—responding to the agreed-upon issues of the day: urban poverty, industrial concentration, the decay of the democratic process, and the role of state in mediating relationships between private capital and public welfare. How citizens constructed and chose blueprints for the future was of considerable interest to those satisfied with existing power arrangements and well rewarded by their consequences. Since ideologies supplied the social cement for collective political action, these satisfied resource holders concerned themselves with influencing the process of ideology formation—the production, dissemination, and consumption of ideas. Inasmuch as philanthropic foundations in the progressive period were created and controlled by satisfied resource holders, they vigorously intervened in the era's vibrant marketplace of ideas, putting their vast resources at the disposal of only some of the groups promulgating ideologies, furthering only these groups' capacities to produce and disseminate world-views supportive of the status quo. The foundations, in effect, subsidized the manufacture and distribution of some ideologies and not others, eventually to the extent of trying to create a consuming public for their subsidized wares.

In this chapter, we examine the work of three of the first foundations—Carnegie (1903), Russell Sage (1907), and the Rockefeller Foundation (1913). We present case studies of their deployment of resources to professionals and experts engaged in the examination and amelioration of social problems. By inspecting funding patterns, project expectations, and the product professionals and experts were able to deliver, we begin to understand how foundations attempted to shape ideas. Our last section shows the problems foundations faced when attempting to influence ideology formation in the progressive period.[2]

Russell Sage and Social Service

On July 22, 1906, Russell Sage, a noted robber baron,[3] died, leaving $65 million to his seventy-seven year old wife, Margaret Olivia Sage. During the last dozen years of her life, she donated $35 million and willed $36 million to charitable, educational, and religious organizations. One of her earliest and largest beneficiaries was the Russell Sage Foundation. Chartered in New York in 1907, the foundation began with $10 million and was heir to another $5 million. Its charter empowered the foundation to use its resources for "the improvement of social and living conditions in the USA" by "any means . . . including research, publication, education," and the support and creation of social service organizations. Equipped with vast resources and a broad mandate, the foundation invested in ideology production.[4]

Sage's involvement in ideology production is best seen through its founding personages and their common vision of social improvement. They shared, in the words of the foundation's official historians, "the fresh enthusiasm of the early years of the twentieth century for hunting down the causes of poverty, disease and crime, and discovering what could be done to eliminate or at least control those causes."[5] However, this enthusiasm and discovery was limited by a reluctance to explore to the left. Thus, the Sage's vision was blind to the many anticapitalist alternatives abroad during the progressive period. In general, Sage funded the tacit opponents of the left and helped them contain proponents of alternative ideologies, especially socialistic ideologies, by supporting social amelioration that took capitalist economic development for granted. In particular, the foundation joined hands with a "charity organization" movement that assumed industrial capitalism was a necessary framework for progress. Sage supplied resources to help nationally coordinate and centralize the charity organization movement and in so doing countered more radical approaches to social problems.

The charity organization movement arose after the Civil War. Before that war, the amelioration of social ills was often in the hands of individual citizens—the Lady Bountifuls—of the communities who took care of the poorly educated, the blind, the halt, and the lame as a matter of religious stewardship, ethical humanism, noblesse oblige, and the like. There was little sense of collective obligation for the "unfortunates" of the community. Indeed, given the laissez-faire ethos of the time, even such ad hoc amelioration was the due only of those who through no fault of their own could not compete in the Social Darwinian struggle of the fit.

After 1865, such unsystematic and unorganized relief began to reveal its limits in the face of accelerating, unplanned industrialization. In large urban areas, where social ills became most apparent, new charity organizations emerged to provide services beyond the scope of Lady Bountifuls. These local organizations, often headed by community political and economic elites, sought systematic and more efficient means to deliver "social improvement" to those they saw as deserving and worthy victims of misfortune. They concerned themselves particularly with economic poverty and its social and physical attendants: pauperism (the culture of poverty), family disruption, child labor, poor housing, lack of recreation opportunities, and so on.[6]

With such efforts, the local "charity organization societies" (COSs) began to modify their received laissez-faire ideologies in a reform direction. But their ideas of reform possibilities were limited by a strong and binding commitment to the very social process that underlay the poverty that so concerned them—accelerating industrial capitalism. Thus they saw poverty as an individual problem involving personal limitations—improper education, physical disabilities, bad work habits—and not as a structural problem inherent in capitalistic development. They did not see low wages as the other side of capital formation, nor did they view wageless unemployment as the result of widespread mechanization. Further, they were blind to the broader social problems that illuminated other movements. They did not see the problems inherent in the vast, socially irresponsible wealth such as that held in the hands of the robber barons, in the unprecedented concentration of social power in the corporate economy, and in the expression of that extraordinary wealth and power in rigged elections, purchased legislation, and, indeed, the wholesale corruption of liberal democratic political forms. In their selection of only some of the consequences of capitalist development as social problems worthy of efficient ameliorative reform, the COSs revealed their ideological commitment to capitalism per se.[7]

The charity organization movement spread rapidly across urban America. By the 1890s, ninety-odd local units were operating. COS representatives became dominant in the National Conference of Charities and Corrections (NCCC), asserting a claim to central leadership of the emerging profession of social work.[8] The NCCC, however, was unable to unify social service ideology and delivery because its internal coherence was limited by the persistence of strong factions, the inherently localistic focus of many participants, and a lack of resources. Thus, factions advocating working-class self-help organizations (workingmen's benevolent societies, five-cent savings banks, and the like) competed with those supporting limited union organization; and both these groups were opposed by champions of local and limited aid in crisis situations. Further, popular acceptance of professionally controlled social service was still tenuous. At this critical juncture, the newly organized Russell Sage Foundation put its resources behind professionalizing COS operatives, thereby tipping the scales toward a nationwide ideology of efficient, systematic social amelioration directed by trained social workers.

When Mrs. Sage decided to spend her husband's fortune on charity, her attention was turned to social work by her lawyers, one of whom—Robert W. deForest—had been president of the New York City COS for eighteen years as well as a past president of NCCC. DeForest drew heavily on his connections in the charity organization movement to help Mrs. Sage see the need for a foundation that would centralize and coordinate that movement. He was aided by Daniel Coit Gilman, a past president of the Baltimore COS and a founding Sage trustee, and John M. Glenn, another Baltimore COS leader, founding trustee, and Sage's chief executive officer. In fact, so successful was deForest that the foundation's self-perpetuating board was composed mainly of well-known charity movement activists.[9]

The Sage board, heavy with COS partisans, began immediately to support the movement's effort to disseminate its views. It granted the Charities Publication Committee of the New York COS sufficient funds to complete its efforts to establish a national journal. The initial grant to the committee was $20,000 in 1907, given in expectation of increasing the "circulation and educational influence" of its magazine. This level of support was continued over the next decade, during which $223,000 was advanced. This amounted to 12.4 percent—one dollar in eight—of the $1.8 million granted by the Sage in that first decade. Perhaps Sage's understanding of the need for such increased "circulation and educational influence" was made clearer by deForest, Gilman, and Glenn, who sat on both the New York City COS Publication Committee and Sage's board. Thus Sage helped *Charities and the Commons*, which was already a combination of Chicago and New York City COS-based journals, become *Survey*, a vehicle with a more nationally representative editorial board and audience. The charity movement then had a national periodical to spread an ideology of professionally directed reform aimed at solving problems within the parameters set by existing power arrangements.[10]

Beyond subsidizing *Survey* as a means of ideological dissemination for the charity organization movement, Sage funded various educational efforts whose activities were publicized in *Survey* and other social service journals. In effect, it funded the activities reported in these magazines, in a sense creating "copy" for their pages. These educational activities

offered detailed and continuing instruction in ameliorative reforms providing the emerging white-collar sector—the clerks and secretaries, state
officials and schoolteachers, managers and professionals—with a more
palatable solution to the problems posed by rapid industrialization than
the drastic structural solutions offered by socialism. They informed citizens that their part-time, volunteeristic efforts would solve their community's most pressing problems: "poverty, disease and crime."

The flavor of these well-publicized educational efforts is nicely captured
in Sage's own use of the community survey. Upon invitation from a
community's leaders, Sage would send staff to identify local needs. Then
the community leaders would supply local citizens to tramp about docu-
menting the exact extent of the identified ill, be it housing, TB, or loan-
sharking.[11] Finally Sage would help orchestrate a festival of publicity and
exhibits to more fully inform the populace about the unmet needs of their
locale.[12] The hoped-for outcome of such surveys, publicity, and exhibits
was a sense of informed social outrage which would be channelled into
"constructive" volunteer work to solve social ills as defined by Sage and
documented by the community.

At nub, both the educational efforts and Sage's own surveys were forms
of ideology-in-action. Participation concretized ideological commitment
to the notion that aroused citizens could and should solve the ills of the
day by ad hoc volunteer work directed by social service professionals.
Community mobilization was intended to create ideological consensus
among the white-collar middle strata then coming to some sense of self-
consciousness. Volunteer work with the urban poor confirmed the merit
of its donors and identified members of the emerging white-collar strata to
each other, while promising the perfection of industrial capitalism without
structural change. Thus Sage by its own efforts in its surveys as well as
through its broad support of other educational activities funded what
amounted to procapitalist agitation and propaganda. And what it supported at the local level, it also gifted at the state and national levels. In
sum, foundation sponsorship of these educational activities helped to
construct the curricula that filled the pages of the Sage-funded *Survey*, the
charity organization movement's self-conscious means of nationwide
ideological instruction.

In addition to providing resources for a national journal and educational activities that supplied copy for that journal, Sage helped create a
permanent work force to implement and maintain its ideology of ameliorative reform within capitalistic development by actively supporting the
professionalization of social work. Sage made direct grants to emerging
organizations engaged in creating social work, notably occupational
associations and the new urban social service schools linked to the COS
movement. Sage's contributions to social work occupational associations

included providing office space in its building and $1,000 to the Intercollegiate Bureau of Occupations in 1913 to establish a department placing social service graduates in professional positions, and continuing grants from 1914 forward to the National Social Worker Exchange, another employment bureau. Its support to urban social service schools, which later became major social work schools, included gifts to the Boston School for Social Workers ($70,100), the Chicago Institute of Social Science ($71,100), and the St. Louis School of Social Economy ($50,500), all between 1908 and 1915. Substantial aid was also given the New York School of Philanthropy. All told, some $246,700 was given the new schools—roughly one-eighth of the foundation's grants before World War I.[13]

Financial assistance was also given to agencies for demonstration as well as routine work. Innovative social service teaching and technical advances were fostered, results written up, and publications subsidized. Hundreds of pamphlets and books were produced with the aid of Sage resources, often with technical help from *Survey* staff. Particularly important innovators were put on foundation payrolls. Among them was Mary Richmond, who systematized social work's distinctive individualistic, not structural, case work theory and method. Sage also created a leading social work library in its ambition to become a national clearing house for professional social service information.[14]

The foundation, then, acted to facilate the growth and development of a profession that would control, even monopolize, employment opportunities in the sector the COSs had long tried to organize. Sage funds enabled COS leaders and professionals to manufacture and distribute an ideology that buttressed both their leadership in the field of social service and ameliorative reform as an alternative to more basic structural changes.

In sum, Mrs. Sage's foundation contributed to ideology manufacture in a variety of ways. *Survey* was a vehicle for the dissemination of a set of ideas purporting to offer solutions to the problem of urban poverty: data collection, education, mitigation of the eyesores of city life (unsanitary and overcrowded housing, the lack of recreational space, "street arabs"— apparently abandoned or improperly supervised children) through the volunteered effort of the emerging white-collar strata directed by professional social workers. Sage was concerned not only with dissemination of this ideology, but also with its pragmatic demonstration. Monies from the Sage coffers provided for community surveys, the results of which were used to inform the responsible classes of the issues at hand as well as to guide their efforts at amelioration. These projects served the additional purpose' of providing copy for *Survey* and other social service magazines. Finally, Sage contributed heavily to the establishment of social work, which supplied a permanent cadre of professionals to supervise implementation of the ideological line developed in *Survey*. Thus Sage funds worked to join together the COS's ideas and practice into a social work profession with an ideology that narrowly structured ways of thinking about the relation of social service to human needs in the progressive era. Some consequences of the structural poverty generated by industrial capitalism were treated, while fundamental problematics even within that system (socially irresponsible wealth, industrial concentration, political corruption) remained unchallenged.

The Carnegie Institute and the Economic History of the United States

The Carnegie Institute of Washington, D.C. (CIW) provides perhaps the earliest example of sustained resource support for a specific group of academics and public service professionals engaged in producing ideas that addressed clearly defined social issues. Founded in 1903, the business of the institute was to "conduct, endow and assist investigation" in all learned fields in conjuntion with formal agencies of higher education in order to secure for the United States "leadership in the domain of discovery and the utilization of new forces for the benefit of mankind."[15] The method by which the potential of original investigation would be unleashed was through "the substitution of organized for unorganized effort" in the domain of intellectual production.[16] Carnegie's general desire was to rationalize the production of new knowledge focused on a wide variety of problems confronting an industrializing society. By supplying resources for the production of knowledge to solve social and economic problems, the Carnegie Institute funded the construction of a pragmatic ideology of ameliorative reform that justified the perpetuation of industrial capitalism.

The successful construction of this ideology required locating and recruiting trained intellectual workers, and the CIW's board numbered among its trustees several university managers with a sense of such things. One such trustee was Carroll D. Wright, president of Clark University, who had helped select and train knowledge workers while serving as United States Commissioner of Labor (1885-1905). Another trustee, Andrew D. White, a past president of Cornell University, had acted as a foreign minister and diplomat who routinely evaluated knowledge and information producers. Finally, Daniel Coit Gilman had molded Johns Hopkins University while its president and had helped shape the Russell Sage Foundation as its trustee. Gilman became the CIW's first president.

The institute's main instrument of ideological production was its Department of Economics and Sociology. This department was concerned with the analysis of industrial production, the distribution of wealth, the relation of capital and labor, and the relation of private capital to the state.[17] These broad categories were broken down into a series of specific research problems that would yield solutions upon systematic investigation.[18] The institute trustees delegated the selection of manpower to advisory committees of experts chosen on the basis of shared friendship and acceptable past work. The chairman of the Economics Advisory Committee was Trustee Carroll D. Wright. The other two members of the institute's Advisory Committee on Economics were Henry W. Farnam of Yale and John Bates Clark of Columbia, both of whom shared the upper-class background of the majority of institute trustees, had worked with them in policymaking forums such as the Chicago Conference on Trusts, and would eventually act as foundation managers themselves.[19]

These three economists turned to an organization they themselves had helped create—the American Economic Association (AEA)—to recruit the manpower necessary to solve the problems identified by the Department. The Advisory Committee used the mediating efforts of AEA president E. R. A. Seligman, Columbia professor and son of the New York banking family, to secure recommendations from the AEA Council for personnel suitable to deal with the controversial subject matter under the department's investigation.[20] After expressing gratitude to the Carnegie Institute for providing research monies in the area of economics, the AEA Council nominated seven of eleven initial section heads from its own number.[21] Work in these eleven areas would result in a new, standard economic history of the United States, one drawing upon the past to create a future for the benefit of the "public welfare."[22] The project managers' understanding of the public welfare is suggested by a remark in Seligman's AEA Presidential Address: "the aim of economics is to show the reconciliation of private wealth with public welfare. . .."[23]

The Carnegie Institute, then, saw new knowledge as raw material that could be exploited for ideological purposes if producers of intellectual goods could be efficiently mobilized. To that end, the trustees turned through its advisory committee to a specialized national organization of competent academics—the AEA—with an offer for resource support. The particular economics professors with whom they then negotiated resource agreements were ideologically "safe." They shared with the trustees a definition of the parameters within which problems of power arrangements must be solved: the public welfare can be served while private wealth is preserved.

Although the general problems for investigation (development of industrial production, distribution of wealth, the relationship of capital and labor, the relation of private capital to the state) were set for them, the AEA economics professors were given wide latitude in mapping areas of study and in choosing the form of the final product. They divided the department into eleven sections: population and immigration, agriculture and forestry, mining, manufactures, transportation, domestic and foreign commerce, money and banking, labor movement, industrial organization, social legislation, and federal and state financing, including taxation. The results of investigation in each section would be packaged in books, the entire project in a set of volumes that would account for the economic history of the United States. They were also well funded. CIW doubled their first-year allocation request ($15,000), providing $30,000 in start-up funds. When the department's work was not completed in the initially projected five-year period (1904–1909), CIW continued support, granting a quarter of a million dollars over a dozen years (1904–1916).[24]

The arrangement between professors and trustees was mutually beneficial. Trustees chose professors with a shared sense of problem to investigate the ideologically relevant issues of the day, and provided them with resources and the autonomy to arrange their own work. Economists of the progressive period defined themselves as scientists able to intervene in the course of history if they could secure the opportunities necessary to full development of the discipline.[25] In return for such support, the institute expected organization of a data base that would permit "a forecast of American social and economic development," a reasonable expectation since institute president Gilman saw "the goal of science" as "a capacity for prediction" and held that "economic and social science are . . . plainly destined to play an increasingly important role in the progress of mankind."[26]

Social scientists, then, were asked to develop predictive capacity while organizing data in ways that pointed to solutions of current social problems. Knowledge of the future gave leverage for control. As E. R. A. Seligman said, "as the science itself becomes more complete, it . . . will be in a better position . . . to explain . . . the true method of making the real conform to the ideal." The application of theory to economic practice would result in stabilizing command; "industrial capital correctly analyzed and rightly controlled" would insure continued economic and social progress.[27] Moreover, as the Department of Economics and Sociology gathered data, it would "put the matter before the people in a way so much needed at the present time."[28] This would accomplish one of the ideological functions of CIW's social science research. It would show that U.S. capitalistic development was understandable, controllable, and reformable.

In sum, the research undertaken by the Department of Economics and Sociology was intended to serve several purposes: (1) the production of the tools for prediction; (2) the use of these tools in stabilizing an economy that was based on highly concentrated, privately controlled industrial capital; (3) the presentation of information to the public that legitimated an economic order based on a capitalism open to the process of incremental reform.

The project, however, was more easily negotiated than delivered. In the first several years, the economists began to appreciate the immensity of the task they had defined. No provision had been made for leaves of absence or permanent staff. Under the press of academic and civic duties, the eminent professors who functioned as section heads were forced to subcontract to graduate students in need of research support.[29] The graduate students in turn redefined areas of research to meet degree requirements; this fragmented a unified treatment of problem areas. Therefore, more professors and more graduate students were funded, with over 200 persons receiving subsidies at one point.[30] Yet by 1909, the date initially scheduled for project completion, there was not a single completed volume.[31]

During this period, CIW trustees developed a more systematic policy of resource support. The gentleman's agreement that had marked the inauguration of the Institute was replaced by more accountable management that was aimed at maximum knowledge production with minimum resource outlay. The CIW ceased funding individual researchers, concentrated capital in large programs, and selected projects that promised demonstrable, easily publicized results. The new resource disbursement policy of the trustee was restated in the metaphor of the marketplace: they wanted "sure returns."[32] Indeed, after the first general project audit in 1910, the department was very nearly disbanded. The economists had not produced the promised volumes, let alone a basis from which to predict the industrial future. The project was refunded on a temporary basis only when Henry Farnam of Yale, one of the original advisors, agreed to become project manager—department chairman—and made a pledge of reorganization, efficiency, and production.[33]

With the new resource policy, the trustee's expectation of the economic history of the United States changed. "A capacity for prediction,"[34] which President Gilman had recognized early on as the identifying mark of a science, was no longer mentioned as a project goal. Emphasis was placed on technical competence in designing ameliorative strategies of social and economic intervention: economists produced material on protective labor legislation, railroad and securities regulatory commissions, arbitration of capital-labor disputes.[35] As Farnam said in an annual report, "our studies in economic history . . . have an important bearing upon practical questions. In these days of rapidly increasing governmental regulation of business and labor, the one safe guide is the experience of the past."[36]

But while funding policy and some trustee project expectations shifted, the bedrock ideological function of the CIW's economic history continued as a vehicle for legitimating industrial capital by erecting a scientific bulwark against socialism. In expressing his conviction as to the importance and utility of the project, Farnam said, "Since we began our work, not a few books in American economic history have been published by writers under the influence of the Marxian doctrine of class conflict." After belaboring these writers for their undue emphasis on "material and egotistic motives," he offered instead, as the raison d'être of the department, "the scientific spirit . . . [that] will have an authority which cannot be possessed by the work of those who write with a theory to prove."[37] Farnam refused to recognize that Marxian economics made the same claim to science as did economists committed to incremental change. He ignored also the contradiction of a scientific social science that automatically rejected socialist solutions. Thus Farnam underscored the Carnegie Department of Economics and Sociology's commitment to the manufacture of an ideology justifying American capitalistic development while providing for the systematic and incremental amelioration of the social chaos and structural imbalances arising during industrialization. However, despite Farnam's sincerely given promises, his CIW Department of Economics and Sociology never did complete their new economic history. To understand fully why the history was not brought to fruition, we turn now to the Rockefeller Foundation's efforts at ideology manufacture.

Rockefeller and Industrial Relations

Limited and experimental foundation support of procapitalistic ideology manufacture and ameliorative reform, such as we have documented above, could not still industrial unrest. At the height of the progressive era, intense ideological conflict mirrored bloody clashes between capital and labor. According to the closest students of labor disorders, the years from 1911–1916 were "the most violent in American history except for the Civil War."[38] During these years, the Rockefeller Foundation (RF) was established and began planning to expend resources to combat the challenge militant labor presented to capitalist control of American industrialization in general and to the Rockefeller business group's antiunion stand in particular.

Both the Rockefeller industries and the RF held ideological and managerial positions at variance with many of their peers: the nation's largest corporations and foundations. The Rockefeller business enterprises, long led by John D. Rockefeller, Senior and Junior, were opposed to union recognition in principle and vigorously upheld the right of robber barons to control their industrial fiefdoms absolutely. This was a markedly more laissez-faire policy than that taken by many "enlightened" corporate leaders, such as the Morgan group and many financial and industrial leaders in the National Civic Federation. The more liberal corporate leaders held that recognition of conservative unions was not objectionable since it permitted organized labor and large-scale industry to negotiate a division of efficiently produced wealth within a framework of mutually accepted capitalism.[39]

As the Rockefeller group was at odds with many "corporate liberal" leaders on the labor issue, so the Rockefeller Foundation was operated differently than were other major foundations. Since Sage was dead and Carnegie had sold his steel-making operations to Morgan, their foundations could be offered to the public as gifts by principals putatively no longer active in finance or industry. It was therefore difficult to link up their foundations' granting to any financially interested Sage or Carnegie business enterprise. But the Rockefellers—JDR, Sr., and JDR, Jr.—were alive and well, running both their far-flung corporate empire and their philanthropic ventures. While the RF and the corporations were legally separated, the foundation shared offices, staff, and, most importantly, key decision-makers with the business group. Indeed, the foundation and the corporate empire were very closely interlocked at their tops, where all crucial resource decisions were made.[40] Accordingly, while Sage and Carnegie managers might argue with some plausibility that the separation of their funds from industrial production permitted them to deploy their resources in the widest public interest, the RF found it difficult to counter convincingly critics linking their grants to the private interests of its associated business group.

This lack of separable interests helped place the RF at the very center of major public debate on the proper role of foundations in United States life. In the fall of 1913, at about the time Rockefeller decision-makers began to discuss possible projects for their newly chartered foundation, miners in Colorado went on strike, in part for union recognition. The key firm was Colorado Fuel and Iron, an enterprise employing 6,000 of the 30,000 miners in the region and owned 40 percent by Rockefeller.[41] Interestingly, Jerome Greene, the foundation secretary, identified economic "research and propaganda," to quiet social and political unrest, as an area demanding philanthropic attention.[42] Apparently, public opinion on the labor question could be shaped through the foundation in order to counter leftist and populist attacks on both the Rockefeller business enterprises and on capitalism.

When looking for methods of approaching the public, Rockefeller Foundation officials had to contend with many other ideological producers, including an increasingly popular method of ideology manufacture—the nonpartisan investigating commission. The commission concept depended on the notion that social problems were technical problems. If the scientific facts on controversial subjects could be established, then the solution that best served the public interest would present itself and bring consensus to conflicting interest groups. Commissions were used in the progressive era by both government and business groups. In general, they operated through the appointment of representatives of capital, labor, and the public by a sponsoring agency: together these interest blocks investigated social problems with the support of professionals, often academics.[43] Both the process of investigation, which brought together contending groups, and wide publication of results were thought to resolve conflict over power arrangements in society.

In preparing to manufacture ideology on the labor problem, the Rockefeller Foundation had to take particular account of the U.S. Commission on Industrial Relations, or the Walsh Commission. This commission was the most popular, largest, and longest lived of the many commissions in the progressive era. It was conceived by a group of intellectual and social reformers (centered around the Sage subsidized *Survey*) after a 1910 dynamite blast destroyed the plant of the militantly antiunion *Los Angeles Times.* The *Survey* group helped President Taft draft a proposal for the commission which became part of his 1912 State of the Union message. Its commissioners were appointed days before miners struck in the Colorado coal fields on September 23, 1912.[44] The strike and the Rockefeller group's involvement became one of the Walsh Commission's broadest targets.

In fact, the Colorado coal wars and the part played by the Rockefeller group in fueling violence between capital and labor called forth a host of investigating groups, each bent on manufacturing and distributing its own variety of ideology. After state mediation efforts failed, a congressional (the Foster) subcommittee on mines and mining looked at the conflict in January 1914. Heightened violence culminating in the Ludlow Massacre stunned the nation in April 1914, leading President Wilson to appoint the Davis-Fairley Commission, which began work in May 1914. The Rockefeller Foundation itself presented plans for a study of Industrial Peace in October 1914, shortly after the Davis-Fairley Commission issued findings and recommendations that were extremely critical of, and unacceptable to, the Rockefeller enterprises. The Walsh Commission suspected the proposed Rockefeller Foundation study as a potential whitewash of the Rockefeller business group's role in the coal wars. It immediately subpoenaed the foundation officials involved and also intensified its own formal investigations in Colorado. With the Rockefeller Foundation and the Walsh Commission at odds over their investigations, President Wilson appointed a final commission headed by Seth Low to provide yet another viewpoint.[45] Thus a congressional committee, three federal commissions, and the RF were all engaged in competitive ideology formation, investigating violence between labor and capital in general and the Colorado coal wars in particular, between 1913–1916.

Putatively, these investigating groups were to articulate the national and the public interest, to make no prior assumptions about the rights and wrongs or possible solutions to the problem under investigation. In practice, interest groups engaged in elaborate manipulations of the appointment process, each striving to have appointments awarded to persons who accepted their frame of reference. For example, when Louis Brandeis was suggested by President Wilson as a possible head of the Industrial Relations Commission, Ralph Easley, director of the business-dominated National Civic Federation, exhorted Wilson to change his mind. Easley found Brandeis objectionable because Brandeis had suggested allowing representatives of the radical Industrial Workers of the World (IWW) to participate on the commission while Easley was prepared to tolerate only members of the more conservative American Federation of Labor (AFL).[46]

The four federal investigating groups—headed by Walsh, Foster, Davis-Fairley, and Low—were all led by people who accepted industrial capital as an economic system while recognizing a need for reform. These bodies, however, did take distinct positions on the degree of reform needed to establish peace in industrial relations. The Low Commission, for example, favored reforms wrought without benefit of union recognition. The Walsh Commission went so far as to solicit the testimony of Socialists and IWW representatives, and pushed, in its final report, for far-reaching reforms that anticipated the labor laws of the 1930s.[47] These federal bodies, then, produced and disseminated various brands of reform ideology, and suggest some of the "competition" the RF faced in its efforts.

The Rockefeller Foundation was a belated, privately sponsored entry into the ideological debate over industrial relations. The Rockefeller's most ideologically sensitive advisors, like Jerome Greene, were new recruits to the Rockefeller enterprises and worked closely with JDR, Jr., to modify the well-established conservative, even reactionary, image associated with JDR, Sr. Still, the small, closely knit staff was able to plot the foundation's ideological course with much greater control than the more democratically organized investigating bodies with whom the foundation would compete in presenting industrial ideology to the public.[48] And its $100 million resource base guaranteed a certain impact.

The foundation officials considered their options carefully. About the time that the Walsh Commission began operations, members of the Rockefeller group considered joining forces with other corporate leaders interested in ideology formation. They attended

> a conference. . .held between representatives of some of the larg-
> est financial interest of this country, in order to see whether
> something might be done to relieve the general unrest through
> some well-oranized agency of investigation and publicity.[49]

At this conference two approaches emerged, each designed to educate the citizenry in procapitalistic ideology and thus relieve unrest. One view saw the difficulty rooted in the poor quality of facts and interpretation available on social and economic issues. Accordingly, "what was needed was a constant stream of correct information, put before the public by a sort of publicity bureau" to reach "the middle and lower classes upon whom the demagogues chiefly preyed." This bureau would support prompt and detailed information on current topics of controversy: labor disputes, rail rates, tariffs, and the like.[50]

The Rockefeller representatives at the conference proposed an alternative strategy of public enlightenment. Although they accepted the usefulness of such a publicity organization, they also wanted a permanent research organization to manufacture knowledge on these subjects. While a publicity organization would "correct popular misinformation," the research institution would study the "causes of social and economic evils," using its reputation for disinterestedness and scientific detachment to "obtain public confidence and respect," for its findings. And, of course, the research findings could be disseminated through the publicity bureau as well as other outlets. However, the conference "came to naught because of the fundamental difference of opinion" among these large financial interests.[51]

Operating by themselves, Rockefeller Foundation officials continued to discuss plans for ideology production. In 1914 they considered a Department of Social Work that paralleled Sage efforts and an Institute for Economic Research similar to the Carnegie Institute of Washington.[52] However, events that touched the Rockefeller business operations suggested the project on which the foundation finally settled.

The Colorado strike lasted through the winter of 1913–1914. The miners endured the hardship and privation of life in tent cities after they were evicted from company towns. Violence between the coal firms' private armies and the strikers was without end. As a major owner, John D. Rockefeller, Jr., was called to explain to the Foster congressional subcommittee why his firm—Colorado Fuel and Iron—had not agreed to arbitration. In testimony he later compromised when confronted with documents subpoenaed by the Walsh Commission, Rockefeller argued that he had no personal part in his managers' actions. In effect, he took the position of an absentee owner out of touch with the local management, unable to influence them on a technical matter: arbitration.[53]

Two weeks after Rockefeller testified before the Foster subcommittee, the Colorado situation exploded into open warfare. On April 20, 1914, the Colorado militia called up by the governor to contain violence attacked a tent city, looted, and fired tents in what has come to be known as the Ludlow Massacre. Colorado's union leaders retaliated by asking its membership to move by force of arms against the coal companies' armies and the state guard. President Wilson declared a state of insurrection and sent in federal troops.[54]

With the Ludlow Massacre, the Rockefeller group found itself at the very center of a national ideological conflict for the violence repelled the nation and the insurrection threatened the social order. Further, many correctly suspected that JDR, Jr. had been less than forthright before the Foster subcommittee on his role in the Colorado coal wars. In fact, the eastern officials of the Rockefeller group had actively supported the strategy and tactics developed by the company's western managers, who had pressured the Colorado governor on the state guard's use, with Ludlow as the result.[55] To deal with the heated ideological climate, President Wilson appointed another commission, this one headed by Hywell Davis, a Kentucky coal capitalist, and W. R. Fairley, a former United Mine Worker (UMW) official, to ease the Colorado situation, if at all possible.[56] The Walsh Commission was also stepping up its investigations in Colorado. The Rockefeller interests at this point were clearly vulnerable to serious ideological attack.

To meet the crisis after Ludlow, the Rockefeller group planned an ideological offensive mounted by both the corporation and the foundation. They sought out experts to give the Rockefeller empire an image that stressed its concern with public welfare as well as private gain. Ivy Lee, one of the first professional public relations men, was paid out of corporate coffers. He was joined by William Lyon Mackenzie King, a Canadian labor specialist, who served initially as a consultant and later as an employee of the Rockefeller enterprises. But not the least of King's major contributions to meet the Ludlow crisis was his agreement to engage in a foundation-funded solo study presented to the public as an impartial "Investigation of Industrial Relations to Promote Industrial Peace," while doing what he could to defend the Rockefeller business interests.[57]

King and his industrial relations work were well known in the United States. Indeed, he testified as a labor expert before the Walsh Commission.[58] In Canada, King had served as minister of labor and had dealt with hundreds of labor disputes. His approach explicitly emphasized the structural depolarization of conflict between capital and labor, while implicitly limiting labor's strike strength and revolutionary potential. For example, he favored "compulsory investigation" which forbade employer lockouts or worker strikes until government investigators had found the facts of the dispute and offered them to the public for its advice and opinion. Compulsory investigation was designed to bring an informed public opinion to bear on the dispute, placing the economic struggle of worker and owner within the political order of the community. However, since industrial production continued while the facts were placed before the public, workers lost their most effective weapon—the strike.

Subjection of economic and potential class conflict to regulation in the name of the community's will was complemented by King's views on union recognition. He thought union recognition should not stand in the way of improving the workers' lot. He accepted company unions as potentially more realistic and democratic than autonomous unions, since they avoided the creation of "union tyrants." Of course, company unions also dampened the potential of autonomous unions to broaden any particular industrial dispute into wider class conflict. In sum, King favored defensive unions within capitalism to offensive unions testing the limits of the established economic order.[59]

After Ludlow, King was asked to join the Rockefeller group. During the summer of 1914, King was in close contact with Rockefeller, offering expert, confidential advice on how to resolve the conflict in Colorado without granting union recognition, a fact not widely known to the public at the time. In August of 1914, the Rockefeller Foundation voted to appoint King formally, effective October 1. King, who had earlier and privately advised Rockefeller on how to handle the Colorado conflict, was now to conduct his "Investigation of Industrial Relations" as an impartial third party representing the public and the foundation. [60]

In September, shortly before King's appointment was announced to the public, the Davis–Fairley Commission issued its report on the Colorado strike. The report viewed the strike as a war and called for a three-year truce, after which new negotiations would begin. The UMW accepted the Davis-Fairley scheme, even though it meant the union would not be recognized. However, Colorado Fuel and Iron Company rejected the Davis-Fairley report, indicating they had another plan. The announcement of King as director of Rockefeller Foundation's "Investigation of Industrial Relations" was made on October 1, 1914. Eight days later, Walsh subpoenaed JDR, Jr., King, and Greene, the foundation's secretary. He was convinced that King's investigation was being funded by the Rockefeller Foundation to whitewash the Rockefeller enterprises. Before the foundation even started its "Industrial Peace" work, it stood suspect of intent to produce ideology favorable to the Rockefeller empire. [61]

During the winter of 1914–15, King devoted his energies to helping the RF deal with the Walsh Commission's inquiries about the propriety of the foundations' project. He helped write the foundation's answers to the commission's many written questions. He also undertook the tutelage of

JDR, Jr., preparing him for his appearance before the commission. King "advised, and even preached, in season and out of season, at meal time, in the office, in walks along New York streets, in the subway and in the family car." He also supervised JDR, Jr.'s, series of appearances with union activists, designed to further the Rockefeller's liberalizing public image. JDR, Jr., was an apt pupil. He passed his examination before the Walsh Commission in January 1915 with flying colors.[62] It seemed that the Rockefeller ideological offensive was succeeding.

However, On April 23, 1915, one year after Ludlow, the Walsh Commission released subpoenaed Rockefeller papers to the press that documented JDR, Jr.'s close personal involvement in directing the events that led to Ludlow. In the furor that ensued, foundation operatives were called before the Industrial Relations Commission once again. Walsh—a maverick Wilsonian Democrat and an expert Kansas City trial lawyer—put JDR, Jr., King, and others into the witness box. Walsh was particularly interested in the relationship between the Rockefeller Foundation and the Rockefeller business empire. In his examinations of JDR, Jr., and Mackenzie King, he pointed out to the public the potential of the Rockefeller Foundation to produce ideology that defended the Rockefeller enterprises. Under questioning, JDR, Jr. maintained his position taken at the Foster subcommittee hearings, namely that the foundation was separate from the corporation, that it was established for the common good rather than Rockefeller's private interest, and that King was an impartial investigator. Walsh then produced correspondence from summer 1914 between King, now director of the Rockefeller Foundation Industrial Peace study, and Rockefeller, owner and director of the corporation, that spelled out King's plan for containing militant labor in Colorado without union recognition. While JDR, Jr., compromised his earlier testimony, Walsh hammered home the interlocking relationship between foundation and corporation again and again, pointing to the impossibility of the foundation's impartiality, and labeling the King project as an exercise in ideology rather than a scientific investigation.[63]

When King testified, he took the position that he had functioned as a technical expert advising Rockefeller on modern means of industrial peace in Colorado while conducting a more general study of the same phenomena worldwide. He argued that his work for Rockefeller was technical and did not affect his impartiality. However, when Walsh asked if the technical expert in a democracy should use his talents by placing the facts as he sees them before the public, or by advising those with power and influence, King indicated his preference for serving power: "More will come about" more quickly "than . . . years spent . . . trying to focus [popular] opinion" on "industrial conditions." King betrayed the propensity of the period's social science experts to serve power rather than public, and confirmed

Walsh's point that social scientists working for foundations might well have a proclivity for gathering facts most useful to the men and women who endowed the foundations.[64]

In its *Final Report*, the Walsh Commission addressed the issue of the service of experts and social scientists to their resource suppliers. The *Report* denounced foundation support for social science research. It questioned the researchers' ability to maintain scientific integrity while investigating social problems when their work was being paid for by those who had interests in the conclusions reached. The *Report* asked if foundations set up by corporate capitalists should fund research on socially controversial issues, issues that in a democracy should be decided by a public unswayed by interpretations manufactured by social scientists on foundation payrolls.[65]

The Walsh Commission's critique of social science funding culminated in recommendations for federal regulatory legislation for foundations; this was not enacted. However, the Walsh Commission seems to have had some effect on the manufacture of ideology in the progressive era. Shortly after the *Final Report* was issued, the CIW shut down the Department of Economics and Sociology, abruptly ending thirteen years of funding. Only a year previously the institute had seriously entertained plans to make the department permanent rather than issuing funds on an annual basis. At the RF, King continued on the foundation payroll, producing a highly personal book, *Industry and Humanity*,[66] at the end of four years. But his previously announced full-dress investigation of worldwide industrial conditions never took place.

The Walsh Commission, then, raised the question as to whether foundations magnificently endowed by great capitalists produced objective research or ideology. The *Final Report* suggested that ideology was more likely than objectivity. The principal foundations engaged in direct support of social research on ideology-determining issues (Carnegie and Rockefeller) seemed initially to withdraw their resources. However, they did not cease funding social research altogether. After the hiatus caused by the Great War, the learned foundations—perhaps taking their cue from Walsh's insistence that mixing funding with direct project management automatically invalidated results—began jointly funneling their resources through academic holding companies such as the Social Science Research Council (SSRC) and the American Council of Learned Societies (ACLS).

The SSRC was formed in 1924 and acted as a conduit for foundation funds to social science projects, fellows, conferences, and publications. Run by the disciplinary associations, the SSRC was granted $28 million between 1924 and 1960. Most of this funding came from three sources: $14.6 million from Rockefeller, $5.5 million from Carnegie, and $6.4 million from Ford (for further discussion see Seybold chapter). The ACLS was formed in 1919 to represent several learned societies in an International Union of Academics. It evolved into a mechanism for channeling foundation monies to support foreign language and area studies in the main. From 1925–1960 it received $20 million from foundations, of which $11.5 million came from the Rockefeller, the Carnegie, and the Ford.[67] By such arrangements, the foundations tacitly met one of the tests set out by the Walsh Commission: funds were now given through intermediaries. Whether such mediation answers the basic question of objective research versus ideology is a topic for another occasion.

Looking Backwards: Why the Foundations Experiments in Ideology Formation Failed in the Progressive Period

In the progressive era foundations such as Carnegie, Russell Sage, and Rockefeller tried to bring their resources to bear on ideology formation in the public sector. Foundation leaders and managers fully realized the problems presented by a free marketplace of ideas in a democratic society undergoing rapid capitalistic industrialization. Concentrated wealth and power coexisted uneasily with widespread poverty and alienation in a political democracy that gave the masses a voice in government. As representatives of capital, they clearly saw the potential threat posed to their control of the economy by popular, organized anticapitalist groups offering alternative ideological interpretations of power arrangements. Accordingly, they began using their resources to experiment with methods of producing, distributing, and, indeed, imposing an ideology that justified industrial capital.

Surely Jerome Greene, secretary of the Rockefeller Foundation, was speaking to such problems, when in a memo to the foundation's directors, he wrote:

> The early demonstration that the Foundation was seeking the best possible way of keeping alive its sense of responsibility to the people and of keeping in touch with the varied and changing needs of the country, would have a moral effect on the public that would greatly strengthen the Foundation's position and enlarge its influence. This is a vitally important consideration at a time when large aggregations of capital, even for philanthropic purposes, are regarded with suspicion—a suspicion which might lead to dissolution and the enforced distribution of funds in ways that might greatly injure their productiveness.[68]

Fears like Green's about the dissolution and enforced distribution of great aggregations of capital were not simply upper-class paranoia. The

Final Report of the Walsh Commission contained a full section devoted to what it styled "the concentration of wealth and influence." This section painstakingly and clearly linked together the large aggregations of capital so legitimate in Greene's mind and the enormous potential influence of foundations like the Rockefeller. It damned this link as corrosive to American democracy and called for further government investigation directed toward eventual popular control of philanthropic foundations via legislation.[69]

But as the Walsh Commission's Final Report recommendations fell on barren soil, so too did the foundations' first experiments at ideology formation during the progressive period. Looking backwards to understand this failure of serious and well-funded capitalists to realize their will, it is clear that foundation trustees and managers were fundamentally concerned with abolishing competition among political-economic ideologies. In a sense, the open and diversified marketplace of ideas mirrored the problems of inefficiency and instability industrial capitalists faced in the national economy. When the Sage, Carnegie, and Rockefeller Foundations entered into the process of ideology formation, they were faced with a threefold task: (1) the design and production of a new standardized industrial ideology, one justifying the power arrangements making possible the previously unthinkable accumulation of capital, such as that used to endow the foundations; (2) the marketing and dissemination of such an ideology; and (3) the creation of a unified public to consume that ideology.

Since the genius of industrial capitalists and their managers—men such as those who sat on the foundation boards—lay not in creation, whether technical or ideational, but in organization, they applied these talents to the tasks of ideological formation. Rather than attempting to invent ideology anew, the foundations initially used their resources to organize and rationalize existing knowledge production groups already engaged in approaching the issues of the day from a position favorable to their interests. Thus, the CIW provided funding for established AEA economists who had been working piecemeal on uncoordinated research that embodied wholehearted and shared acceptance of the newly emerging organizational forms of industrial capital. Russell Sage poured resources into those professionalizing groups able to convert local and idiosyncratic charity organizations into more systematic services. The Rockefeller Foundation, before the Ludlow crisis, hoped to orchestrate its proposed publicity bureau and research institute in a systematic counterpoint against socialist, populist, and other oppositional critics of capitalism, creating a great chord of ideological containment and consensus.

The foundations' initial approach to ideology manufacture was not formal. Trustees and managers were not interested in construction of a theoretical statement of a set of interrelated ideas that systematically explained and projected the dynamics of existing and future power arrangements in society. Formal development of ideology systems was elitist in tradition; foundation decision-makers recognized this was unsuited to the tenets and workings of a democratic society. Instead, foundation trustees and managers were pragmatic with regard to ideology. They looked for what worked and hoped to see a viable ideology emerge from this process.

To illustrate, the resources Carnegie and Russell Sage devoted to the support of economic research and social service were initially directed toward the examination and solution of controversial issues around which ideology coalesced. Thus in 1904 CIW-AEA economists began investigating the development of manufacturing, the organization of the economy, social legislation, and the role of the state in mediating between private capital and public welfare; all were issues that underlined power arrangements in society. Russell Sage in 1907 began engaging in a variety of practices designed to ameliorate poverty, an obvious manifestation of such power structures.

As the projects funded by these foundations materialized, the possibilities and limitations of expert intellectual and professional workers were revealed. The Russell Sage Foundation, from its 1907 beginning, emphasized word as well as deed, uniting its subsidized media—the *Survey*, books, pamphlets—with community action under the direction of professionals. The Carnegie Institute, after 1910, no longer asked economists to develop predictive capabilities. It accepted instead the economists' own union of ideology and technique; the experts who wrote on railroad regulation also served on the Interstate Commerce Commission. The Rockfeller Foundation, drawing upon these and its creators' previous philanthropic experiences, was able by 1913 to formulate demands upon intellectual workers with somewhat greater clarity and precision. As we have seen, the RF's managers were alive to the potential of expert professionals like Mackenzie King to shape public opinion. However, these managers also hoped their funded authorities would ground their efforts in practical problem solving. As John D. Rockefeller, Jr. said in his testimony before the Industrial Relations Commission,

> . . .merely scientific investigation, an academic study, simply the
> collection of facts would not seem . . . sufficiently worthwhile to
> the board of directors of the Rockefeller Foundation. Their hope
> is that under Mr. King's leadership [in the Industrial Peace
> study] something that will appeal to the labor interests of the
> country, to the capitalist interests of the country, may result. If it
> does not appeal to both these groups, if the result of the study is
> not something practical that both desire to try and many find to

work, that is the end of it; nothing will have been
accomplished.[70]

In sum, the foundations came to identify ideology manufacture as a
major purpose underlying resource deployment, and its production was
joined to the pragmatic solution of specific problems. This resulted in
three related but distinct modes of ideology manufacture. First, ideologies
of practice arose out of the confrontation and amelioration of actual,
concrete social problems within industrializing capitalism. This occurred,
for example, in social work. Second, ideologies of technique developed
from the concentrated energies of intellectual workers on the rationalization of technical problems within existing social arrangements. Such was
the case in academic economics. Third, ideologies of structure emerged to
describe and value a political economy, midway between the extremes of
laissez-faire capitalism and socialism. Typical producers included university-based sociologists and Protestant theologians sympathetic to, but not
deeply involved in, "the Social Gospel." Since each of these three modes
of ideology production created its own separate ideological content, the
foundations ended up subsidizing an overall ideology with two main
characteristics: (1) it was aggressively pragmatic and intellectually incon-
sistent, while (2) consistently defending capitalism. Foundations were not
concerned with theoretical elegance; they sponsored a tactical ideology
whose very lack of structure gave strategic advantage by rendering meaningful critiques extremely difficult.

Beyond production, foundations—through professors and other
professionals who claimed objectivity and value neutrality in their practice
and publications—marketed ideology that justified industrial capital.
Professionals were sought out to mediate the idea flow from corporate
capital to public in their role as experts representing no constituency other
than science, since, as Jerome Greene, a secretary of the Rockefeller
Foundation, noted, "this generation has, in large measure, accepted the
principle that exact knowledge of underlying facts must be the basis of all
movements looking toward betterment and progress."[71] Professionals
willing to serve foundation goals were not hard to find, for once industrial
capital was accepted by professionals as the framework in which betterment and progress would occur, social issues became technical problems
with these ideational assumptions embedded therein. Then the professions
could perform latent ideological functions while correctly claiming a
manifest value neutrality.

However, the foundations' efforts in manufacturing and marketing
ideology were not enough to eliminate competing products. The always
complex problems of ideology distribution were intensified because media
lagged behind other industries in terms of the technical sophistication,

centralization, and national integration that facilitate control by groups in possession of significant amounts of capital. In the progressive era, well before the advent of electronic media, almost any organized and determined group, sect, or party could command significant means of ideology production by running a printing press, renting a headquarters and meeting hall, speaking on the labyrinth lecture circuit, and otherwise moving into the marketplace of ideas. Ideological variety was manifested in the myriad daily and weekly newspapers and in the plethora of journals of the period, and fed by an ever-rising literacy level, most dramatically attested to by the growth of public high schools. In 1870 there were 500 secondary schools; in 1920, 10,000. Increasing ease of access to the means of ideology production combined with rising literary sophistication to enable competing groups both to proselytize and maintain their own internal cohesion. This sharpened rather than blunted ideological struggles, and also created a public of considerable diversity in taste, style, and thought. This diversity made it difficult to create a simple and direct ideology distribution mechanism.[72]

The creation of a unified public to consume ideology was a still more difficult issue. Given the decentralized media, the readily accessible means of ideological production, and the resulting diversity of publics, the foundations directed their efforts toward the increasingly self-conscious white-collar sector. An emerging consensus and common purpose might be strengthened by mobilizing the middle sector to pay attention to, and even participate in, ameliorative reforms sponsored by foundations. Further, such social action might also provide industrial workers with a sense that reform was a possibility. As we have seen, foundations created publications and filled them with copy oriented in this direction. In addition, the university classroom and the professional school were increasingly tied into this process. Professors disseminated and elaborated reformist ideas to a captive student audience already committed, by their very presence in college, to vaguely white-collar, even capitalistic, values and norms.

By the close of the progressive era with World War I, the foundations' experiment at pragmatic ideology formation had borne little fruit. While they did succeed at manufacturing some ideology, they could not solve the problems of distribution and consumption. The nub was that while they could deploy their own resources, they could not deny other groups the use of competing resources. Socialists, populists, and all sorts of oppositional anticapitalist groups continued their own ideological production, distribution, and consumption. In addition, a great variety of ideology poured out of investigating bodies where class-conscious representatives of workers' interests refused to endorse amelioration in which limits were set by industrial capital. For such reasons, as well as a desire to make a contribution to the war effort, the foundations by 1917 had temporarily withdrawn from ideology formation.

The Great War, however, served to create the unified public with some sense of consensus and common purpose that foundation leaders had earlier sought. After the war, while many Americans were still moved by nationalist sentiment, groups holding deviant ideologies were decimated through the use of wartime statutes (the Red Scare, the Palmer Raids, mass deportations).[73] In the 1920s foundations returned to funding research on social issues. However, this time foundations worked in a field from which many deviant ideologies had been uprooted, where the consensus of normality obtained, fostered by the rapid rise of centralized electronic media, and where the idea structure of professionals already supported industrial capital. Foundations were now able to direct their resources toward ideological formation unbothered by a free marketplace of ideas, and with a much greater probability of success.

Notes

1. For documentation of the period's economic turbulence, see Robert Wiebe, *The Search for Order, 1877–1920* (New York: Hill and Wang, 1967); and William Appleman Williams, *Contours of American History* (Chicago: Quadrangle, 1966); as well as the more specialized studies of Gabriel Kolko, *The Triumph of Conservatism: A Reinterpretation of American History* (Chicago: Quadrangle, 1967); Philip Foner, *A History of the Labor Movement in the United States*, Vols. 3 and 4 (New York: International, 1963, 1964); and James Weinstein, *The Corporate Ideal in the Liberal State, 1900–1918* (Boston: Beacon, 1968). Consult Samuel P. Hays, *The Response to Industrialism, 1885–1914* (Chicago: University of Chicago Press, 1957), on the farming hinterland as internal colony; and Michael Meeropol, "W. A. Williams' Historiography," *Radical America* (July-August 1970): 29–49, for a careful review of the period's depression statistics.

2. Our sense of "ideology" follows that advanced in Kenneth M. Dolbeare and Patricia Dolbeare, *American Ideologies* (Chicago: Markham, 1971). In selecting the Sage, Rockefeller and Washington Institute of the Carnegie Foundations for examination, we make no claim for statistical representativeness. Indeed, American foundations as they now exist were largely invented and institutionalized in the progressive period, and their explosive growth defies the usual sampling methodologies. See, for details, Barbara Howe, "The Emergence of the Philanthropic Foundation as an American Social Institution, 1900–1920," Ph.D. Thesis, Department of Sociology, Cornell University, 1976, and her chapter in this book; on growth, Ernest V. Hollis, *Philanthropic Foundations and Higher Education* (New York: Columbia University Press, 1938).

   However, we do claim that Sage, Rockefeller, and Carnegie were the leading creative foundations of the time. This view was common in the period itself. See, for example, the comments of the Socialist leader Morris Hillquit, *Industrial Relations: Final Report and Testimony Submitted to Congress by the U. S. Commission on Industrial Relations*, United States Senate, Doc. 415, 64th Congress, 1st Session (Washington, D.C.: USGPO, 1916), Vol. 8, pp. 8263–8275 (hereafter cited as *Final Report*) as well as comments in the *New York Times* by Rev. Joseph H. Rockwell, President of Brooklyn College, cited in " Summary of Criticism Directed against the Rockefeller Foundation," Dept. of Surveys and Exhibits, International Health Board, January 1919, pp. 2, 4 (available at the Rockefeller Foundation Archives, Hillcrest, Pocantico Hills, North Tarrytown, N.Y.; hereafter RFA). Accordingly, we present our analysis as not at all statistically representative of foundations operating in the period, but rather as an examination of the leading edge of their ideological work, work that cut the pattern for other foundations and later times.

3. For Sage as robber baron, see Matthew Josephson, *The Robber Barons* (New York: Harcourt, Brace & World, 1962), pp. 209–211 and elsewhere.
4. John M. Glenn, Lilian Brandt, and F. Emerson Andrews, *Russell Sage Foundation, 1907–1946* (New York: Russell Sage Foundation, 1974), pp. 3–13.
5. Ibid., p. 5.
6. On the organization of nineteenth-century social service, see Robert Bremner, *From the Depths: The Discovery of Poverty in the U.S.* (New York: NYU Press, 1956); and Robert Trattner, *From Poor Law to Welfare State* (New York: Free Press, 1974).
7. For analysis of the dilemma of consumption—and hence wages and poverty versus capital formation during industrialization, consult Karl de Schweimitz, *Industrialization and Democrary* (New York: Free Press, 1964), pp. 56–186. For data on wealth, power, and political corruption, see Wiebe, *Search for Order*, and Hays, *Response to Industrialism*.
8. Blanche D. Coll, *Perspectives in Public Welfare* (Washington, D.C.: USGPO, 1969), pp. 44–62 documents the growth of COSs in the late nineteenth century, and Trattner, *Welfare State*, p. 195, notes the COS takeover of the NCCC.
9. The founding board is listed in Glenn et.al., *Russell Sage Foundation*, pp. 9–10.
10. Ibid., pp. 27–28, 222–224, 685–701.
11. Ibid., p. 181. Apparently participation was not always voluntary, as when Prof. W. F. Willcox seems to have offered his students to the Ithaca Survey.
12. Ibid., pp. 177–196, 93–96.
13. Ibid., pp. 224–225, 685–686, 689–690.
14. For Sage support of the emerging social work profession, see ibid., p. 223ff., as well as pp. 685–691, which lists the Foundation's first fifty-six grants made between 1907 and 1920, almost all furthering the cause.
15. "Remarks by Mr. Carnegie on Presenting the Trust Deed," *Carnegie Institute of Washington Yearbook* (*CIWY* hereafter) 1 (January 1903): xiv.

16. "Proceedings of the Executive Committee," *CIWY* 1 (January 1903): xxxviii.
17. "Report of the Advisory Committee on Economics," Appendix A—Reports of Advisory Committees, *CIWY* 1 (January 1903): 1–2.
18. C. D. Wright, "Report of the Department of Economic and Sociology," *CIWY* 3 (January 1905): 55–64.
19. "Memorial—Carroll Davidson Wright, 1840–1909," *CIWY* 8 (February 1910): 13. Farnam's father was president of the Chicago and Rock Island Railroad; Clark's father was a manufacturer of milling machinery in Providence, R.I. Both were educated at Ivy League schools, received Ph.D.s in Germany, became economics professors at Yale and Columbia, respectively, leaders of the AEA, and served as foundation managers with Carnegie: Farnam as chairman of the Department of Economics and Sociology after Wright's death, and Clark as director of the Division of Economics and History of the Carnegie Endowment for International Peace, 1911–1923. Farnam was active in national Civil Service reform work at the time of his appointment to the Advisory Board of the CIW; Clark had recently served as Governor Theodore Roosevelt's representative to the Chicago Conference on Trusts.
20. For the importance of Clark and Seligman in the organization of the AEA, see Joseph Dorfman, *The Economic Mind in American Civilization*, vol. 3, 1865–1918 (New York: Viking, 1949), pp. 205–208. Wright was also a charter member (1885), while Farnam joined in 1890 and was active throughout the progressive era. See also A. W. Coates, "The First Two Decades of the AEA," *American Economic Review* 50 (September 1960): 555–574. For Seligman as negotiator between CIW and the AEA see "Report of the Secretary," *Publications of the American Economics Association* (hereafter *PAEA*) Part 1, 3rd ser. 5 (December 1903): 42.
21. For AEA expressions of gratitude, see "Report of the Secretary," *PAEA* Part 1, 3rd ser. 5 (December 1903): p. 42. The seven AEA leaders were Wright, W. F. Willcox, W. Z. Ripley, D. R. Dewey, J. W. Jenks, H. W. Farnam, and H. B. Gardner. Many other prominent AEA economists were assigned subsections of investigation under these section heads; see C. D. Wright, "Report of the Department of Economics and Sociology." *CIWY* 3 (January 1905): 55–64.
22. C. D. Wright, "An Economic History of the United States," *PAEA* Part 1, 3rd ser. 4 (May 1905): 390–409.
23. E. R. A. Seligman, "Social Aspects of Economic Law," *PAEA* Part 1, 3rd ser. 5 (December 1904): 73.
24. The original concept of the project is most clearly stated by H. W. Farnam, when he reviewed the department on taking over as chairman in 1909. See H. W. Farnam, chairman, "Department of Economics and Sociology," *CIWY* 8 (February 1910): 81–83. The estimate of total project cost is first given in "Report of the Advisory Committee on Economics," *CIWY* 1 (January 1903): 1–2. The total figure is cumulated from the annual amounts given in the yearbooks.
25. See for example, E. R. A. Seligman, " Economic and Social Progress," *PAEA* 3rd ser. 4 (February 1903): 70, 64.

26. D. C. Gilman, "Report of the President of the Institute," *CIWY* 4 (January 1906): 23.
27. E. R. A. Seligman, "Economic and Social Progress," p. 70.
28. C. D. Wright, "Economics and Sociology: Report of the Director," *CIWY* 5 (January 1907): 163.
29. H. W. Farnam, "Department of Economics and Sociology," *CIWY* 8 (February 1910): 81–93.
30. C. D. Wright, "Department of Economics and Sociology," *CIWY* 7 (February 1909): 74–85.
31. "Report of the President," *CIWY* 8 (February 1910): 30–31. The department did produce eight volumes of "Indexes of Economic Material in the Documents of the States of the U.S." by 1909. However, the department received a separate allocation for this project, which was not regarded as fulfilling the economic history of the United States for which the collaborators had contracted.
32. "Report of the President of the Institute," *CIWY* 4 (January 1906): 17, 23, 31.
33. See H. W. Farnam, "Department of Economics and Sociology," *CIWY* 8 (February 1910): 71–83, for his plans for organization. For the CIW's reaction see "Report of the President 1910," *CIWY* 9 (January 1911): 22, in which the president of the institute indicates the department will get no more funds. Due to Farnam's efforts, the institute reconsidered and plans for a permanent department were underway by 1913. See "Report of the President," *CIWY* 12 (January 1913): 18.
34. "Proceedings of Executive Committee," *CIWY* 1 (January 1903): xiv.
35. The same men who wrote with Carnegie funds on labor legislation, railroads and securities commissions, arbitration of capital and labor disputes also aided in implementing the intervention strategies they participated in designing. Indeed, one of Farnam's constant complaints was that his section heads were unable to complete their work because they were called to public service. See H. W. Farnam, "Department of Economics and Sociology," *CIWY* 8 (February 1910): 82. In brief illustration of the interrelationship of research and practice, the work done by D. R. Dewey, head of the CIW money and banking section, was slated to be published by the National Monetary Commission; H. W. Farnam, head of the section on social legislation as well as chairman of the department, was also president of the American Association of Labor Legislation; J. R. Commons, who took over the section on labor after Wright's death, pooled his Carnegie funds with other monies to support his ongoing work on labor history. He largely turned over this effort to Selig Perlman and other University of Wisconsin graduate students because his energies were occupied by his appointments to the U.S. Industrial Relations Commission and the Wisconsin Industrial Commission. B. M. Meyer, head of the section on transportation, was called to the Interstate Commerce Commission. V. S. Clark, head of the section of manufacturing, had to turn his work over to Francis Walker of the U.S. Bureau of Corporations because he was engaged on census work in Hawaii, and on government missions in Japan and Manchuria. Some also entered private service; E. Parker, head

of the mining section, gave up his U.S. Geological Survey position to become director of the Anthracite Bureau of Information for mining corporations in Pennsylvania. See H. W. Farnam, "Department of Economics and Sociology," *CIWY* 8–15 (February 1910–February 1916).

36. H. W. Farnam, "Department of Economics and Sociology," *CIWY* 15 (February 1916), pp. 101–102.

37. Ibid.

38. Philip Taft and Philip Ross, "American Labor Violence: Its Causes, Character and Outcome," in Hugh D. Graham and Ted R. Gurr (eds.), *A History of Violence in America* (New York: Praeger, 1969), pp. 281–395; quotation at p. 320.

39. On differences in corporate ideology and tactics in the period, see Weinstein, *Corporate Ideal*; Marguerite Green, *The National Civic Federation and the American Labor Movement, 1900–1925* (Washington, D.C.: Catholic University of America Press, 1956); Albert K. Steigerwalt, *The National Association of Manufacturers, 1895–1914* (Ann Arbor: University of Michigan Bureau of Business Research, 1964); and Foner, *History Labor Movement*.

40. "Testimony of John D. Rockefeller, Jr., *Final Report*, Vol. 8, p. 7776.

41. For a discussion of Rockefeller holdings in Colorado Fuel and Iron, see Peter Collier and David Horowitz, *The Rockefellers: An American Dynasty* (New York: NAL, 1977), pp. 106–107, 128n.

42. Jerome Greene, Secretary of the Foundation, Memo RFDR No. 12, October 22, 1913, "To the Members of the Rockefeller Foundation," p. 10ff. (RFA).

43. On the composition of such commissions, see Weinstein, *Corporate Ideal*, p. 7; and Foner, *History Labor Movement*, pp. 61–66.

44. Graham Adams, Jr., *Age of Industrial Violence 1910–1915: The Activities and Findings of the U.S. Commission on Industrial Relations* (New York: Columbia University Press, 1966). See also Weinstein, *Corporate Ideal*, pp. 172–213.

45. Fred A. McGregor, *The Fall and Rise of Mackenzie King: 1911–1919* (Toronto: Macmillan of Canada, 1962), pp. 121–130.

46. Green, *National Civic Federation*, pp. 349–350.

47. On the Low Report see McGregor, *Mackenzie King*; on the Walsh Commission see Weinstein, *Corporate Ideal*, pp. 211–212.

48. Collier and Horowitz, *Rockefellers*, pp. 95–133; and McGregor, *MacKenzie King*, pp. 143–144.

49. Jerome Greene, Memo RFDR, No. 12, p. 15. Such conferences were not unusual, at least so far as philanthropic funding was concerned. See, for example, the Anderson and Berman chapters in this book. Unfortunately, Greene's account of this conference does not name the "largest financial interests" it mentions.

50. Greene, Memo RFDR, No. 12, p. 16.

51. Ibid., pp. 16–17.

52. Jerome Greene, Memo DR 32, "Future Organization of the Rockefeller Foundation," 1914, pp. 2–9 (RFA).

53. Adams, *Industrial Violence*, pp. 154–167, contains an account of JDR, Jr's, conflicting testimonies before the Walsh Commission; McGregor, *MacKenzie King*, pp. 121–122.

54. Taft and Ross, *American Labor Violence*, pp. 330–332.

55. The fullest published narrative account of the role of the Rockefeller Eastern officials in the Colorado coal wars is George P. West, *Report on the Colorado Strike* (Washington, D.C.: U.S. Commission on Industrial Relations, 1915). It is based on subpoenaed documents.

56. McGregor, *MacKenzie King*, pp. 120–124.

57. Collier and Horowitz, *Rockefellers*, pp. 109–133; Henry Ferns and Bernard Ostry, *The Age of Mackenzie King* (Toronto: James Lorimer, 1976), pp. 187ff.

58. In addition, the Foundation knew King at least via Director Eliot and Secretary Greene. King was a favorite of Harvard's President Charles Eliot, who twice sought King for posts: first in the Economics Department and then as founding head of what evolved into the Harvard Business School. Jerome Greene, then Harvard advisor to Eliot, dissuaded the latter appointment, stressing King's Canadian citizenship. See Herbert Heaton, *A Scholar in Action: Edwin F. Gay* (Cambridge, Mass.: Harvard University Press, 1952), p. 67, and R. MacGregor Dawson, *William Lyon Mackenzie King: A Political Biography, 1874–1923* (Toronto: University of Toronto Press, 1958).

59. On King's approach to industrial relations, see Ferns and Ostry, *Age of MacKenzie King*; and Paul Craven, "An Impartial Umpire: Industrial Relations and the Canadian State, 1900–1911" (Ph.D. thesis, Department of Sociology, University of Toronto, 1978).

60. Dawson, *A Political Biography*, pp. 235–255.

61. McGregor, *MacKenzie King*, pp. 123–124, 129–130.

62. Ibid., pp. 130–143; quotation at p. 131.

63. Adams, *Industrial Violence*, pp. 161–168; Collier and Horowitz, *Rockefellers*, pp. 119, 123–125.

64. McGregor, *MacKenzie King*, pp. 165–174; quotation at pp. 169–170.

65. *Final Report*, Vol. 1, Section V.

66. William L. M. King, *Industry and Humanity* (Toronto: University of Toronto Press, 1973), contains a very useful "Introduction" by David Jay Bercuson, one that reviews reactions to the work, pp. v–xxiv.

67. On the return of the foundations to social science funding in the 1920s, see Ernest Victor Hollis, *Foundations and Higher Education*, p. 248 and elsewhere. For details on SSRC and ACLS funding, see Joseph C. Kiger, "Foundation Support of Educational Innovation by Learned Societies, Councils, and Institutes," in Mathew B. Miles (ed.), *Innovation in Education* (New York: Teachers College Press, 1964), pp. 533–561. For a brief account of the ACLS, consult Whitney J. Oates, "The Humanities and Foundations," in Warren Weaver (ed.), *U.S. Philanthropic Foundations* (New York: Harper and Row, 1967), pp. 300–303.

68. Jerome Greene, 1913, Memo RDFR, No. 12, p. 9.

69. *Final Report*, Vol. 1, Section V.

70. Ibid., Vol. 8, p. 7893.

71. Greene, 1913, Memo RFDR, No. 12, pp. 10–11.

72. For an account of the ways in which books could be published before the consolidation of the industry during and after World War II, see Bill Henderson, "Introduction: A Tradition of Do-It-Yourself Publishing," in the *Publish-It-Yourself Handbook: Literary Tradition and How-To*, ed. Bill Henderson (New York: The Pushcart Book Press, 1973), pp. 11–36; Bill Henderson, "Independent Publishing: Today and Yesterday," in *Perspectives on Publishing*, eds. Philip G. Altbach and Sheila McVey (Lexington, Mass.: Lexington Books, 1976), pp. 217–229; Scott Nearing discusses the great accessibility of media in the progressive era in his *The Making of a Radical: A Political Autobiography* (New York: Harper and Row, Torchbook Library Edition, 1972), especially Chapter 4, "A Teacher Must Communicate," pp. 52–75. On the growth of the public comprehensive secondary school, see Martin Trow, "The Second Transformation of American Secondary Education," in Sam D. Sieber and David E. Wilder (eds.), *The School in Society* (New York: Free Press, 1973), pp. 45–61.

73. For details on repression of this sort during World War I, consult Harry N. Scheiber, *The Wilson Administration and Civil Liberties, 1917–1921* (Ithaca, N.Y.: Cornell University Press); and Robert Justin Goldstein, *Political Repression in Modern America* (Cambridge, Mass., and New York: Schenkman and Two Continents, 1978), pp. 137–163, 547–574.

Russell Marks

Legitimating Industrial Capitalism: Philanthropy and Individual Differences

Dear Friend:
>   If you have any spare time at your command, will you kindly give me an answer to this question:—
>   If you had say five or ten millions of dollars to put to the best use possible, what would you do with it?
>   Prize given for best answer.
>
> Always very truly yours,
Andrew Carnegie[1]

A Paradox of the Protestant Work Ethic

At the dawn of the twentieth century, American industrial capitalism faced a distinct crisis. It was confronted with new challenges in legitimating industrial capitalism with its distinct class structure and unequal distribution of rewards. And the old wisdom for legitimating the social order no longer appeared appropriate. For generations, traditional wisdom proclaimed that the key to legitimating the social order and assuring worker productivity lay in the inculcation of the Protestant work ethic. The social order would be legitimated and an honest day's work would be secured if the worker were taught the dignity of all work, the promise of good fortune and social mobility for the deserving, and such virtues as honesty, punctuality, and frugality. In turn workers were assured they would be appropriately rewarded for their effort and character. The plausibility of the work ethic, however, was seriously undermined by the grim realities of the industrial workplace.

While early twentieth-century educators could drum in the virtues of hard work and efficiency, it was much more difficult for the worker to apply these virtues and his character and intellect to the challenge of the workplace. For factory work was characterized by menial, unskilled or semi-skilled, alienating labor.[2] To adequately adjust the worker to the industrial workplace, workers were taught middle-class work values and lower-class job skills. Yet this set up a paradox: given lower-class job skills the more the worker internalized the Protestant work ethic the more he realized it was an unrealistic ideal. Even the most skillful teaching of the Protestant work ethic could not overcome the inherent contradiction between the realities of the workplace and the dream of advancement. Menial, alienating factory work turned the belief that any work if well done was virtuous into a bad joke. At the same time, the plausibility of social mobility was undermined as unskilled laborers were locked into unskilled jobs that gave them neither the time nor the resources to improve their lot. And even deserving success through luck was seriously questioned since it was very unlikely a worker would see the boss's daughter let alone that she would marry him or even recognize his existence. Finally, the realities of the workplace no longer made it possible for rewards to be legitimated on the basis of effort and character. For great persistence, effort, and character were needed to perform these arduous, alienating, and oftentimes mindless jobs. Yet little reward was given for faithfully and efficiently performing one's job.

Bridging the gap between the middle-class work ethic and the practical realities of the workplace required that workers internalize ideas which rationalized their positions in the social order. To persuade workers that menial, alienating labor and minimal rewards were their proper condition in life required that workers internalize ideas of personal merit based on innate ability. The social construction of "individual differences" promoted a world view conducive to internalizing this sense of merit, a sense of personal inferiority and superiority, in many workers. Indeed individual differences seem to have provided the twentieth-century version of original sin: you were damned if you were innately inferior and elected if you were innately superior. The concept of individual differences, as the embodiment of original sin, played a dominant role in shaping the consciousness and institutional life of Americans; it was vital to the American social construction of reality.

Philanthropic foundations promoted, both theoretically and monetarily, a world view emphasizing individual differences. Closely cooperating with philanthropy were psychologists who articulated this world view and provided a rationale for programs for individual differences. This new emphasis on "scientific" individual differences not only reflected the perspective of philanthropists and psychologists, but also profoundly mirrored the outlook of the middle and upper classes. Indeed the reason philanthropists and psychologists were so successful was because the concept of individual differences neatly conformed to the social perspective of dominant groups in the society. This new world view that emphasized scientifically documented individual differences furnished a powerful rationale and legitimation of industrial capitalism. The conceptualization and institutionalization of programs for individual differences helped to legitimate industrial capitalism and made the American class system, unequal reward structure, and deadening workplace more palatable.

In order to perceive these developments it is first necessary to examine the role of psychology in constructing individual differences. In this process Edward L. Thorndike played a major role in constructing, articulating, and utilizing the concept of individual differences. Thorndike's formulation of individual differences reinforced philanthropy's view of the social order. In turn, Thorndike received generous financial assistance from the foundations for his efforts. Between 1922 and 1938 alone, for example, Thorndike received approximately $325,000 in grants from the Carnegie Corporation. These grants supported at least nine published books or monographs and nearly 100 scientific articles, doctoral dissertations and special reports. As we shall see, these studies and others showed that the interests and world view of Thorndike and the foundations were remarkably compatible. Indeed much of the strength of philanthropic foundations laid in their ability to finance people who held their world view. Given the proper world view, the outcome of many of these "scientific" studies was remarkably predictable. Such was the case with Thorndike's work.

Individual Differences and the Legitimation of the Social Order

In 1924, the officers of the Rockefeller Foundation met to discuss foundation policy. Playing a leading role in formulating foundation policy was Abraham Flexner. In these meetings, Flexner addressed himself to certain factors which seemed to affect foundation policy. Although he did not connect his remarks to the idea of individual differences, his remarks were very applicable. The first factor affecting foundation policy, Flexner noted, was that progress depended on neither money nor machinery but on ideas. Ideas were the basis of policy—foundations in effect were in the business of ideas. Ideas especially came from outside the foundation, in the case of the idea of individual differences from psychologists. Second, ideas must be within the context of a favorable environment if they were to achieve prominence. The idea of individual differences met this criterion; it reflected dominant ideas and to a certain extent the dominant mood of America. Third, foundation officers must be men of definite, feasible ideas who were capable of demonstrating that their programs would resolve particular social issues. As this chapter indicates, foundation officers with definite, feasible ideas would effectively utilize the idea of individual differences in this manner. Fourth, Flexner noted, it was generally unwise for foundations to engage in expensive programs if outside funds could not be secured.[3] More concretely, as Fred M. Hechinger has expressed it, "the ideal foundation-sponsored enterprise is one that blazes a new trail, thrives for a while on sponsored dollars, gathers momentum" and then "is quickly taken over as a permanent program by the local school board, the state education authority, or a university's own budget."[4] The idea of individual differences was effectively utilized in this manner.

Edward L. Thorndike was the dominant American psychologist in formulating the idea of individual differences. As a professor at Teachers College, Columbia University, Thorndike was recognized as a leading American educational psychologist. He wrote many of the standard textbooks on mental development and educational psychology; his prodigious efforts resulted in about fifty books and over 450 articles and monographs. Reflecting his involvement with the idea of individual differences, Thorndike in 1914 recorded the following dramatic breakthrough in the study of psychology:

> The differences in intellect, character and skill which separate individual human beings from the average or from the modal condition of man as a species seem to us now as obvious as the differences between species of animals, and as important for the understanding and control of nature as the common features of human action. Twenty-five years ago, however, the majority of psychologists neglected their existence and substantially denied their importance.[5]

The scientific discovery of individual differences for Thorndike was an enormously important achievement. Thorndike thought the scientific facts of individual differences provided both an accurate description of the characteristics of the individual and a principle for social reform. An alternative perspective however, is that individual differences did not simply exist but should be viewed as socially constructed.

This alternative perspective notes that the early twentieth-century conception of individual differences was rooted in several important valuative and empirical assumptions. It was based on the assumption that differences were essentially innate rather than acquired. What were the social-scientific and reform implications of viewing differences as a product of heredity rather than environment? Second, the concept of individual differences emphasized differences rather than similarities. While individual differences can be empirically established, so also can individual similarities. Whether differences or similarities were discerned depended largely upon the problem considered and the conceptual tools used in analyzing the problem. Why were differences rather than similarities emphasized in America? Third, the American social construction of individual differences stressed certain kinds of differences rather than others. While, for example, intellectual differences can be emphasized so also can artistic differences. Why were particular differences given priority in America? Fourth, the concept of human differences focused upon individual rather than social differences. The concept was psychological at its core; differences were rooted in the psychological makeup of the individual rather than in the social structure. What were the reform implications of this perspective? Finally, institutions providing for individual differences were structured on the basis of genetic and/or environmental differences rather than on the basis of genetic and/or environmental similarities. What were the implications of structuring institutions on the basis of differences rather than similarities?

In examining these and other questions, this alternative perspective defines individual differences as a concept that functions in and is a product of a particular social matrix rather than as a concept that simply describes, although it may, the characteristics of the individual. It focuses not on the alleged characteristics of the individual but rather on the definers of differences, analyzing who defines individual differences, how they are defined, and the social consequences of their definitions. From this perspective, it cannot be simply assumed that the facts of individual differences were necessarily valid or that they led to certain kinds of reform. Indeed, in Thorndike's case it will be argued that it was his view of reform and the social order that led him to emphasize individual differences, and that his perspective of individual differences in turn provided a powerful legitimation of the social order, and ultimately of industrial capitalism.

Thorndike believed that "every advance in the sciences of human nature will contribute to our success in controlling human nature and changing it to the advantage of the common weal."[6] In examining and controlling human nature, Thorndike believed that the "first duty" of the scientist was to "learn the constitution" of man and his "second duty" was to "learn each individual's variation from this common humanity."[7] In examining human variation, Thorndike thought the work of James McKeen Cattell and others in the 1890s had produced three important principles of method, which were

> to describe a quantity by its position on a scale of measurement,
> not by a classificatory adjective; to keep in mind the variable
> error of every determination that one uses; to study things,
> qualities and events by studying their relations.[8]

Adherence to these principles led Thorndike to his strong emphasis on measurement. By 1907, Thorndike was so pleased with the use of measurements in human affairs that he promised that accuracy was as possible in the humanities as in the exact sciences. He further observed that "there is no reason why we should not measure the merits of authors for literary style, for moral effect, or for interestingness as accurately as we measure the sun's distance."[9] In some respects, these remarks culminated years later in the famous observation of Thorndike and his student William McCall that "all that exists, exists in some amount and can be measured."[10] Measurement was the new key to unlocking the secrets of human variation.

In eagerly seeking to attain measurements of individual differences, Thorndike at times seemed to lose sight of what was being measured. While one might agree with Thorndike's view of reality that everything that exists can be measured, it is much more difficult to believe that everything that exists can be measured in a meaningful way. And it seems to be the case that Thorndike, and indeed many of his followers in the twentieth century, at times were more concerned about measuring something than about making sure it was a meaningful measure. Such was the case with tests of aesthetic appreciation that Thorndike proposed in 1916.

While he admitted in his initial publication on the topic that the tests were not "specially good" (an admission he dropped in subsequent works) he nevertheless felt they were useful until better tests of aesthetic judgment could be established. The tests included questions that asked the subject to rate the aesthetic merit of simple forms. This included ranking rectangles in the proper order, ranking the best-looking rectangle 1, the next best looking rectangle 2, and so forth. The same procedure was used with the crosses.

Thorndike gave these test questions to 200 judges (college juniors) and found that the correct aesthetic order for the triangles was from left to right 3, 4, 2, 5, 1 and for crosses 3, 2, 4, 1. Having established the correct order, these tests of aesthetic judgment could be easily used and scored by the simple method of counting the sum of displacements from the correct order.[11]

For Thorndike these tests represented an important step in measuring aesthetic appreciation. While measurements can of course be made of subjects' responses to crosses and rectangles, it's quite another thing to say that this is a measure, let alone a meaningful measure, of aesthetic judgment. It did not occur to Thorndike that perhaps what the tests really showed was Thorndike's view of aesthetic beauty. Any test used to measure individual differences can be viewed as an indicator of the subject's abilities, interests, and so forth, but can also be viewed as an indicator of the tester's or test constructor's values and beliefs. In these

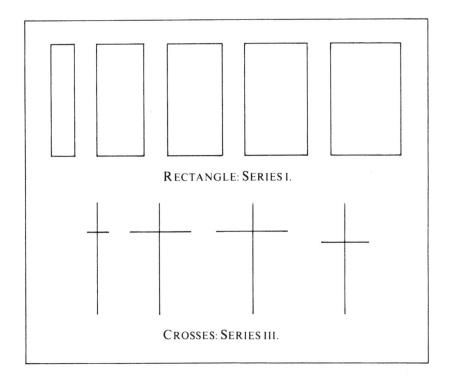

RECTANGLE: SERIES I.

CROSSES: SERIES III.

tests of aesthetic appreciation, much was learned about Thorndike's aesthetic judgment while little if anything was learned about the subject's aesthetic judgment.

More significant than aesthetic differences between persons, however, were intellectual differences. Regarding sexual differences, Thorndike reported that the central tendency of men and women was closely alike in innate intellectual ability. That left unanswered for Thorndike why most great achievements in the world were done by men rather than women. Thorndike's response was that the reason men excelled was because there was greater variability within the male sex. "The most gifted man," he noted, "may be superior to the most gifted woman even though the average man is equal to or below the average women, *if men vary widely from their central tendency*." This fundamental difference in variability, Thorndike noted, placed sharp limitation on what women could accomplish.[12]

Equally revealing were Thorndike's observations about racial differences. In his writings, Thorndike joked about the "negro's fetish" to go barefoot.[13] At the same time, he noted that although Negroes were genetically intellectually inferior to whites they could be improved through education:

> If it be true, for example, that the negro is by nature unintellec-
> tual and joyous, this does not imply that he may not be made
> more intelligent by wiser training or misanthropic and ugly-
> tempered by the treatent he now receives. It does mean that we
> should be stupid to expect the same results from him that we
> should from an especially intellectual race like the Jews, and that
> he will stand with equanimity a degree of disdain which a Celt
> would requite with dynamite and arson.[14]

While Thorndike believed that blacks were intellectually inferior to whites, he also observed that there was much overlapping between the races and that differences within the same race were many times as great as differences between the races.[15] Yet if this was the case, would it not be incompatible with Thorndike's hypothesis that the "negro is by nature unintellectual"? For this point would suggest that not only is the Negro by nature unintellectual but so also is much of mankind.

And indeed, one finds that Thorndike had a low regard for the intelligence of the masses. Thorndike believed the most critical intellectual differences for human welfare were not those between the races or sexes but those between the masses and the intellectual elite. And the gap between them was enormous. "People in general are stupid," Thorndike once observed.[16] Furthermore, the great majority of men are only half-educated. The danger of the half-educated man is that he does not "know his place intellectually" and that he is "likely to try (and fail) to understand the specialist instead of obeying him."[17]

Yet if Thorndike had low regard for the masses, he had utter disdain for those he labeled degenerates. He believed that a major problem of human welfare was to prevent "defectives, delinquents and worthless persons from wrecking the good life for the great majority."[18] Thorndike was particularly provoked when the welfare of the intellectual elite was placed in jeopardy. He would bemoan the fact that

> Our social arrangements are such, for instance, that Finlay, who
> first devised and tested the theory that yellow fever was caused
> by the bite of the mosquito, was left for twenty years unaided in
> the investigation which with sufficient authority and money he
> could have easily made absolutely demonstrative, and that La-
> zear and Carrol were allowed in crucial tests to risk their lives
> instead of those of some criminals whose risk would be
> harmless.[19]

If the risk of some criminals' lives was harmless, it was also the case that the nation took "great pains to care" for degenerates and gave little attention to its leaders:

Our nation takes great pains to care for its idiots, degenerates, and insane, but not for its leaders. It has an enormous outfit of legislation, personnel, and equipment to lessen the amount of harm done by its mean, brutal, and perverted citizens, but almost no laws, institutions, or persons at work to increase the amount of good done by its best. Yet, dollar for dollar, the latter will be far more profitable.[20]

In notable contrast to the masses and degenerates were the intellectual elite, who were relatively free from "ill will, cruelty, greed, injustice, etc." Since Thorndike believed there was a correlation of .40 to .60 between intellect and morality, persons of "superior intellectual ability" could be "trusted to average high in decency, dependability, good will and other social services." Such persons would act in the best interests of the world and could think impersonally, being led by the naked facts alone.[21]

In *Human Nature and the Social Order* Thorndike, supported by the Carnegie Foundation, further delineated his thoughts about degenerates and other groups in society. Thorndike sought to provide a system of weights for measuring each person's wants in society. He noted that while his system of weights may sound aristocratic and may be "opposed by the envious and brutish" it would be supported by the "able and good" men of the present and future. In creating his system of weights, Thorndike rejected any egalitarian system as unjust or unwise. Rather "more weight should be given to the wants of superior men than to the wants of inferior men." Able and good men are more likely to work for the general welfare than are stupid and bad men. Providing for the wants of able and good men, Thorndike noted, will "presumably enable them to do more of what they want to do; and this will improve the world and its customs for future residents."[22]

Utilizing this principle, Thorndike noted that the merit of wants ranged from the "noblest through the indifferent to extremes of every cruelty and meanness." Each person's wants should be weighted on the basis of merit. Although the scale should not be used "vindictively to torment human tigers, snakes, skunks and hogs" it nevertheless "will rate their happiness very low." More concretely this meant that the wants of human "skunks" and all persons were weighted according to the person's composite score in intelligence and other desirable abilities. Counting the ordinary or average man as 100, the person of the ability of Newton, Darwin, or Beethoven would count 2,000 and the "vegetative idiot" would count 1.[23]

These fundamental differences that separated the races, the sexes, and the elites from the masses were due to heredity rather than environment. Thorndike believed that the American social order essentially reflected the innate ability of the population. If, he noted, the "thousand babies born this week in New York City were given equal opportunity they would still differ in much the same way and to much the same extent as they will in fact differ." Man's original nature, Thorndike continued, gives him "large selective power over his environment." Thus, one of these thousand New York babies, "if of mean and brutal nature, can by pains avoid industry, justice and honor, no matter how carefully he is brought up; and that one of them of intellectual gifts can, if he cares enough, seek out and possess adequate stimuli to achievement in art, science, or letters, no matter how poor and sordid his home may be."[24] Failure on the part of the poor to succeed was not due to poverty and socioeconomic institutions that perpetuated poverty, but rather was attributable to genetic makeup. This explanation, in contrast to recent cultural deprivation theories, was a genetic rather than environmental version of "blaming the victim."

At the same time it is important to note the policy implications that Thorndike drew from innate individual differences. The implications were twofold: first he proposed eugenic measures to improve the human race and second he proposed institutional reform measures based on hereditary differences.

Regarding eugenic measures, Thorndike was confident that selective breeding could alter a person's capacity to be happy, to keep sane, to learn, and to cherish justice.[25] Selective breeding based on the "principle of eliminating bad genes," Thorndike noted, is so "thoroughly sound that almost any practice based on it is likely to do more good than harm." One such practice was eugenical sterilization. While Thorndike believed that much of the sterilization legislation was misguided, he thought that on the whole its operations were much more beneficial than would be an equal amount of time and skill spent on "social education." Indeed Thorndike continued,

> the first lesson in social education for an habitual criminal or a moral degenerate might well be to teach him to submit voluntarily to an operation which would leave his sex life unaltered but eliminate his genes from the world. The same would hold for dull and vicious sex perverts. The genes of a few of these persons might be up to the ordinary human level but on the average they would be exceedingly low.[26]

Yet if it was important to eliminate bad genes, it was many times more important to preserve and cultivate good genes. Thorndike noted that to add one man of the ability of, say, William James, to "the American stock is of greater advantage than to prevent the birth of a thousand feeble-minded or insane."[27]

More important in the immediate development of society, however, were the reform measures Thorndike proposed. Thorndike believed social institutions should be based on the innate capacities of the individual. Thorndike noted: "All the sciences and arts of controlling human nature must accept the original variety of human nature as a condition for thought and action." For education this meant that the "teacher who has not learned by ordinary experience that each child is to some extent a separate problem, demanding for his best interest an educational theory and practice to fit *him*, should learn it" from psychological theory.[28] Indeed the "competent teacher expects variety in human beings and examines each person to learn what he really is and needs."[29] By taking individual differences into account the school would double its effectiveness.[30]

Thorndike believed that whatever anyone became by education depended on what he was by nature.[31] Teaching then meant utilizing natural tendencies for ideal ends. Knowledge of the pupil's nature was vital to determining an appropriate curriculum. The fundamental mistake the schools made was providing the same highly intellectual curriculum for all students. Thorndike noted that it was not the fault of the schools or teachers that children failed to learn this curriculum, but rather was a result of the genetic makeup of the child. Schools must realize that "apparently you can lead certain minds to the springs of wealth and power but you can not make them drink."[32]

While Thorndike argued that human nature is diverse and does "not fall into sharply defined groups,"[33] his prescriptions for the curriculum lumped persons into narrowly defined categories. Thorndike's curriculum proposals were rooted in his assumptions about individual differences. At the same time his specific provisions for individual differences were built on the assumption that education should focus on developing special talents rather than the whole person. "The approved theory of education for any person," Thorndike noted, "is to fit him to respond well to the situations which he will meet."[34] More concretely:

> Each individual by sex, race, hereditary equipment and the circumstances of time and place in which he is born, is made likely to meet certain situations rather than others during life, and it is to be competent and happy in those situations that he particularly needs to be taught. It would be wasteful to train the Jews and the Negroes identically.[35]

Thus Thorndike would applaud the earlier efforts of certain Negro schools that changed from a predominantly literary curriculum to a "realistic and industrial curriculum."[36] And in educating women, he argued that women should not be trained so much for professions like administration and statemanship but rather for professions like nursing, teaching, and medicine where their average intellectual level was necessary. The female's intellectual level and her maternal, nursing instinct, which seemed to involve "unreasoning tendencies to pet, coddle and 'do for' others," made the women especially fitted for certain fields. Yet while for example women were fitted and might capture the teaching profession, they would not fill its most eminent positions.[37]

While women for Thorndike were more intellectual than blacks, there was a large body of women, blacks, and other groups who were incapable of abstract intellectual training. Indeed, "most people are not good thinkers or even good learners, and would not be under any provocation."[38] To provide for individual differences it was necessary to make different kinds of training available for different kinds of intellect. Thorndike expressed this well when he distinguished between idea thinkers and thing thinkers:

> Individual intellects can be divided roughly in to two classes: those able to work with ideas and those able to work with things. Some children manage numbers, words, parts of speech, chemical symbols and the like, but fail relatively in measuring boards, catching fish, cooking meals or making toys. They are the *idea thinkers*. Others make little headway with their arithmetic, grammar or textbook in chemistry but succeed in the shop, the woods and the laboratory. They are the *thing thinkers*.

The school, Thorndike continued, has provided primarily for idea thinkers. It has "left for shops, trades and the practical activities of life to give the other group the training which their natures crave." The school should give children what their natures crave, "the school should give opportunity" for both idea and thing thinkers. Thorndike believed the school "cannot afford to be unfair to those pupils whom nature has destined to be primarily not learners but doers."[39] Fortunately, vocational education was available for "doers." Even more fortunate was that it just so happened that the industrial world needed "doers" rather than "learners" to perform its labor. In proposing special training for blacks, women, and thing thinkers, Thorndike was rationalizing the existing social order and was assuring, through providing for innate individual differences, that these groups would be locked into their relative present positions in the socioeconomic order. By providing these groups an education that was compatible with their "nature," it was assured that these groups were locked into their existing place in the social order (see Anderson and Berman chapters on the education of blacks). Furthermore, the process was mystifying; while formerly, for example, industrial education for blacks was significantly promoted on the grounds of keeping Negroes in their place, now it was promoted on the grounds of providing for individual differences.

Finally, by understanding the needs of the individual, people in power could maintain their positions. According to Thorndike, employers must study the conditions which best promote the contentment of the worker without sacrificing productivity. Fortunately, this did not require increasing wages or reducing the work day but rather mastering the art of human relations. Thorndike described one successful attempt as follows:

> A factory superintendent who went through the war and post-war periods without labor troubles attributes his success in large measure to a number of simple rules treating workers as men and women. For example, the doorman is chosen partly for his cheerful voice and smile. He greets each worker by name, if he can. He takes pains to learn the name of each worker. . . .They are instructed to call workers by their names always. . . .

If the employer satisfied the psychological needs for recognition and social distinction, then economic and social grievances would largely disappear and the existing class structure would endure. "How much of an argument for turning over a share in the management of the shop to its workers," Thorndike asked, "is found in the satisfaction of the craving for personal dignity and importance which accrues thereby?" With proper manipulation of the worker, Thorndike assured employers they could not only promote the status quo but also find the "golden mean between a sullen gloom which depresses all workers" and one with "such cheerful sociability that work is neglected."[40]

Thorndike's work readily affirmed the world view of philanthropic foundations. Among the important advances in knowledge made by the grants he received from the Carnegie Corporation were the following:

> Proof that the variation among American cities in their provisions of a good life is caused much more by the personal qualities of their residents than by wealth, income and natural advantages. Very strong evidence that the equalization of wealth or income in and of itself will do no good to community—that equality in wealth and income is good in so far as it is a symptom and result of intelligence, morality, and those other desirable personal qualities in a population which, by raising the level of the poor, to that degree work toward equality.[41]

Here indeed was knowledge worth knowing for the wealthy; knowledge that both linked wealth with intelligence and virtue and suggested the folly of redistributing wealth for improving community life. And Thorndike was not ungrateful for these grants, which was perhaps evident in his following discussion of foundations:

> The funds of Harvard University or the Carnegie Corporation
> would probably be found to have done far more per dollar for
> the public welfare than the funds spent by any nation, or than
> the funds spent by all save a few municipalities, have done for
> their citizens. It is significant that the able and benevolent men of
> affairs who have made gifts to the public almost never give to a
> city, state or national government. Either they do not trust the
> public to decide what is for its welfare or they do not trust the
> elected representatives of the public to do what the public asks or
> to act for its welfare.

Not yet satisfied with the point he wished to make, Thorndike went on to say: "Indeed many a thoughtful lover of mankind must have wished that Carnegie and Rockefeller and Hayden could have been tax exempt so that their gifts could have been increased by that much!"[42] Happily also, philanthropic fortunes were justified because original capacity was the key to philanthropists' wealth. As Thorndike noted; "the fact that Mr. Rockefeller has amassed one of the great fortunes of the age is undoubtedly due almost exclusively to his original capacity, not to circumstances."[43] In supporting Thorndike, foundations were promoting and financing the social construction of individual differences. Foundations would be more intimately involved in this process in other ways.

Organizing Scientific Resources

Philanthropic foundations would actively promote reforms based on the idea of individual differences. Before turning to these specific reforms, it is important to briefly note the growing recognition by government, industrial capitalism, and philanthropic foundations of the importance of mobilizing scientific resources. Nowhere was this emphasis more evident than in the establishment of the National Research Council.

In April of 1916, when war appeared imminent, President Wilson requested that the research agencies of the nation be organized for war. The National Academy of Sciences responded by organizing the National Research Council, a federation of educational, governmental, philanthropic, and industrial research agencies. The financial resources of the NRC during the war years came largely from the federal government and the Engineering Foundation.

The success of the council in mobilizing the scientific and technical resources of the country for war led to its perpetuation in peacetime. The council was reorganized by the National Academy in 1919 and became independent from government support. Between 1919 and 1922 the council received approximately $8 million from foundations, industrial corporations, and individuals. Of this amount, $5 million came from the Carnegie Corporation of New York.[44]

A first task of the newly organized council was to promote a broader appreciation of "The National Importance of Scientific and Industrial Research." The first bulletin of the National Research Council addressed itself to this topic; it contained a series of short articles written by prominent members of the advisory committee of the council. Elihu Root, chairman of the board of trustees of the Carnegie Institute in Washington, emphasized the importance of organizing the scientific community for productive scholarship. "The effective power of a great number of scientific men may be increased by military discipline." For Root it was a "very interesting circumstance" that although the "long history of science exhibits a continual protest against limitation upon individual freedom," the impulse which necessitated American organization of scientific research was the German state's desire for world dominion—a desire supported by government-controlled research. The "immense value" of the German system of research gave a "tremendous impetus to effective organization of scientific power" in the United States. Root had no doubt that America under the guidance of the National Research Council could successfully combat her "traditions of separate private initiative" and organize "scientific research for practical ends as effectively as an autocratic government" could give "direction to a docile and submissive people."[45]

Henry S. Pritchett, president of the Carnegie Foundation for the Advancement of Teaching, also appealed to the German experience, which he felt operated on the right principle: "the research men of a nation are not isolated individuals but an organized and cooperating army." He was confident that the proper relationship between the scientific "army" and the "industrial and financial machinery" would "increase wealth, sustain human health and activity, and increase the comfort and security of human life." The scientific community and manufacturers must understand and cooperate with each other for the promotion of science and industry.[46]

George Eastman, an active philanthropist and President of the Eastman Kodak Company, also emphasized the importance of research in the advancement of industry. In the "reorganization and readjustment of industry" in the postwar years, Eastman noted, the "extension of scientific research must play a great part." The "effectiveness of industrial organization depends upon knowledge." Industrial research laboratories must "create and systematize the technical knowledge" so that this "knowledge may permeate all branches and sections of business life, raising the standard of aim and achievement alike in the manufacturing and commercial sides of industry, insisting on products of higher quality" while simultaneously "educating customers to make the best use of the products which are supplied to them."[47] The conviction that scientific organization and growth was an indispensable element of industrial productivity and national power was a powerful incentive to foundation donors and their trustees. It no doubt provided a basic rationale for the foundations' support of the NRC, and, as we shall see, for reform measures based on the idea of individual differences.

Providing for Individual Differences: Eugenic Reform

Philanthropic foundations actively supported eugenic reform and what might be called eugenic social engineering. While eugenic reform sought to control and modify the genetic makeup of the human race, eugenic social engineering sought to design institutions to fit the genetic makeup of the individual. Philanthropists especially promoted eugenic reform through their support of the eugenics movement, which sought the dual goals of increasing superior human stock and decreasing or eliminating undesirable human strains. In seeking both goals, philanthropists and eugenicists assumed that reliable information was available about the nature and correct treatment of individual differences.

Playing a dominant role in promoting and disseminating eugenic research and propaganda was the Eugenics Record Office. In 1910 Charles B. Davenport persuaded Mrs. E.H. Harriman, widow of the railroad tycoon, to establish the Eugenics Record Office at Cold Springs Harbor, New York. She spent over half a million dollars on the Record Office before the Carnegie Institute of Washington became the primary benefactor in 1918. The Record Office rapidly expanded its services and by 1929 was engaged in the following activities: (1) it served as a clearing-house and repository for thousands of records made by field workers of American families; (2) it built up an analytical index of over 1,200,000 cards on important traits of American families; (3) it trained about 220 field workers to gather data of eugenical importance; (4) it maintained an active field force to gather eugenical data for the Record Office; (5) it cooperated with other persons and institutions concerned with field work; and (6) it investigated the inheritance of specific human traits and other eugenical factors.[48]

For over twenty years, Charles B. Davenport served as director of the Eugenics Record Office. He early expanded the office's influence with the creation of the *Eugenical News* in 1916. This newspaper reported the latest eugenic reform activities and research findings in America and abroad. The *News* informed readers about the activities and findings of various eugenic committees like the Indiana Committee on Mental Defectives, the

Eugenics Survey of Vermont, and the Maryland Mental Hygiene Study; it reported the progress of immigration and sterilization laws; and it condemned the critics of eugenics and praised the works of Nordic advocates like Madison Grant, who feared "the passing of the great race." The *News* provided the latest research on the dominant or at least significant role of hereditary in epilepsy, hayfever, skin defects, migrains, manic-depressive insanity, nomadic-adventurous traits, exostoses, asthma, tongue-tie, and violent temper. It also described the activities and membership of such eugenic groups as the Eugenics Society of the United States of America, the Galton Society of New York, the Eugenics Committee of the United States of America, and the Eugenic Research Association. Included in the membership (on one or more of these committees) were such prominent educators and psychologists as Charles W. Eliot, David Starr Jordan, Robert M. Yerkes, Truman Lee Kelly, J. McKeen Cattell, Lewis Terman, and Thorndike. Also included were such prominent Rockefeller and Carnegie foundation spokespeople as Katherine B. Davis, general secretary of the Rockefeller-financed Bureau of Social Hygiene; Raymond B. Fosdick, a trustee and later president of the Rockefeller Foundation; Robert S. Woodward, president of the Carnegie Institute of Washington (1904–1920); and Charles H. Merriam, president of the Carnegie Institution of Washington (1921–1938).

Similarly, the *Eugenical News* applauded innovative methods used in promoting eugenics. The *News* enthusiastically reported that not only animal stock but also human stock was judged at the Kansas Free Fair in 1922. Mental, nervous, physical, and psychological examinations were given to all individual and family entrants at the fair. Young adults of marriageable age were given a eugenic exam to determine their marital fitness while all entrants were given a eugenic score of A, B, C, or below.[49] The *News* also reported the work of especially effective teachers of eugenics. They endorsed, for example, the ideas of a psychology professor from Pennsylvania who observed:

> I hope to serve the cause by infiltrating eugenics into the minds of teachers. It may interest you to know that each student who takes psychology here works up his family history and plots his family tree. He attempts to discover his own physical and mental traits as related to those of his family, and on the basis of this, work out his social vocation and maritial rights and duties. The insight thus gained throws new light on child-study and on the students' future teaching.[50]

Financed by philanthropy and other interests, the Eugenics Record Office and the *Eugenical News* played an influential role in the eugenics movement.

At the same time, the merging of the scientific community and business interests in the cause of eugenics was evident in the work of the National Research Council's Committee on Scientific Problems of Human Migration. Appointed in 1922, the Committee on Scientific Problems of Human Migration was financed by grants of over $130,000 from the Laura Spelman Rockefeller Memorial and a grant of $10,000 from the Russell Sage Foundation. Robert M. Yerkes chaired the committee, which included in its membership Raymond Dodge, chairman of the NRC's Division of Anthropology and Research; Miss Mary Van Kleeck, director of Industrial Studies at the Russell Sage Foundation; John C. Merriam, chairman of the Executive Board of the National Research Council and president of the Carnegie Institution of Washington; Davenport; and Thorndike.

The tasks of the committee were (1) to examine the complex migrational situation resulting from the war and the virtual elimination of space as a barrier to migration and race intermixture; (2) to prepare a research program that would provide reliable information about the characteristics, relations, and values of ethnic and racial groups; and (3) to initiate, promote, organize, coordinate, and support further important investigation.[51] Perhaps the most striking thing about this committee's discussions of racial and individual differences was that the importance of the individual as such was neglected. The individual was seen directly in relation to his/her social, economic, and political worth. This point was evident in the conferences and research projects of the committee.

In conference meetings, the question of race intermixture was vital. Charles Davenport, who had studied the problem at the Eugenics Record Office, was concerned about what happened in racial intermixtures. Davenport asked: "Does there result anything different than just a new combination of characters which may be just as good as any of the old combinations—perhaps different because new?" And he responded:

> We see the defects in the mixture of the negro-white—the off-
> spring often have the push and determination of the white but
> the intelligence of the negro; they are dissatisfied with themselves
> and with the world; they do not have the ability to better condi-
> tions. This constitutes a problem which we need to investigate
> more, first the inheritance of instincts, and secondly the problem
> of the relation of new combinations of instincts to society.[52]

For Davenport, racial intermixture of allegedly superior and inferior stocks posed an imminent danger to the social order.

Equally revealing were the findings of Raymond Dodge's subcommittee on primitive forms of human response. Using strength and skill as two criteria for judging the admissibility of an immigrant, Dodge noted that both criteria are important in estimating the "economic value of a human being." Lack of either strength or skill diminished social effectiveness. More concretely, in admitting immigrants, Dodge believed:

> Special skills increase the usefullness of an adult according to the need for each particular skill. Conversely skill without strength would be at a social disadvantage. From an economic stand-point, if I may venture upon that ground, I believe it would be a sound practical maxim that the adult skilled to perform some act for which there is a demand would be a more valuable immigrant than an unskilled adult, however strong; though strength with a minimum of skill would be better than weakness with a mini-mum of skill. A low grade of both strength and skill would render any prospective adult immigrant a social and economic liability unless he could be placed in a position to acquire one or the other.

Dodge believed these estimates of skill, strength, and other traits should not only be used to measure a man's fitness to enter society but also to give some indication of his "approximate place in that society." Further, he thought it was in the interest of society "to encourage the effective placement of the human material that it admits, by indicating lines of economically useful action that are open to each immigrant."[53]

These observations of Davenport and Dodge were in agreement with those of the committee's chairman, Robert M. Yerkes. In 1924 Yerkes stressed the importance of overcoming prejudice in working with the problem of immigration. He noted that "knowledge of human traits and potentialities—individual, occupational, ethnic—is tragically inade-quate." Wisdom, he continued, therefore dictates that reliable information be attained. Yet, Yerkes's own work maligned this goal, for one year earlier he reported that the results of the army tests clearly demonstrated the inferiority of Southern European immigrants. These new immigrants, Yerkes believed, were better understood as a national burden than as an industrial necessity. The army tests, he continued, "establish the relation of inferior intelligence to delinquency and crime, and justify the belief that a country which encourages, or even permits, the immigrations of simple-minded, uneducated, defective, diseased or criminalistic persons, because it needs cheap labor, seeks trouble in the shape of public expense." For Yerkes and many industrialists the need for cheap labor was secondary to the need for social stability and efficiency. Yerkes expressed this need for social stability when he noted that "it might almost be said that whoever desires high taxes, full alms-houses, a constantly increasing number of schools for defectives, of correctional institutions, penitentiaries, hospitals and special classes in our public schools," should, "by all means work for unrestricted and non-selective immigration."[54]

In promoting immigration restriction laws that discriminated against Southern Europeans, Harry H. Laughlin played a dominant role. As a prominent member of the Eugenics Record Office, Laughlin testified before the U.S. Congress on several occasions in the 1920s. Like the work of members of the Committee on Scientific Problems of Human Migration his testimony was important in the passage of the 1924 Immigration Act that discriminated against Southern Europeans. Laughlin delineated the historical significance of this act in his testimony before the House of Representatives in 1928 on "American History in Terms of Human Migration." He noted there were six major problems in American history in which the racial factor was dominant. They were:

> First, the effort of the white colonists along the Atlantic sea-board to prevent destruction by racial mixture with the American Indian. Second, the conflict for racial and institutional supremacy between the British colonists on the one hand and the French, Dutch, and Spanish on the other. Third, the introduction of negro slaves. Fourth, oriental migration. Fifth, the radical changes in racial and individual character of immigrants paralleling the great rise of American industry in the 1880's; and sixth, the entrance of colored races into the south-western part of the United States since 1920.

Laughlin's analysis of the problem posed by each of these groups was intriguing. For example, colonists, confronted by the Indians, faced the problem of maintaining their racial purity; Americans, confronted by the "involuntary immigration" of African blacks, faced the problem of assimilating inferior human stock; and now in the 1920s Americans, confronted with Mexican immigrants, faced the problem of closing the country to bad seed stock. To correct the Mexican problem of race mixture, Laughlin proposed an act whereby only Caucasians would be naturalized as American citizens. The purpose of the act was to keep out "those Mexicans who are of mixed Spanish and Indian or black blood, and the mixed blacks of the West Indies."[55] Perhaps most revealing about Laughlin's historical analysis was the absence of any discussion of white, Nordic oppression. Indians posed a threat to Nordic purity, inferior black "involuntary immigrants" posed a threat to Nordic community and values, and Mexicans provided another threat to racial dilution. It did not occur to Laughlin that Nordics posed a serious threat to the survival of each of these groups.

The survival of non-Nordics in America was indeed at issue with the passage of sterilization laws in America. While Laughlin in 1914 estimated

that 10 percent of the population was socially inadequate and recommended massive sterilization, his recommendations were not met. Nevertheless, between 1906 and 1938 over 27,000 people were sterilized in
America. California led the thirty states practicing sterilization with
12,180. Of the first 10,000 persons sterilized in California, two-thirds were
sterilized for insanity and one-third for feeblemindedness. Predictably, a
high percentage of those sterilized were either foreign-born or black.
Although only 20 percent of California's adult population in 1930 was
foreign born and 1.5 percent was black, 39 percent of the men and 31
percent of the women sterilized were foreign-born, while 4 percent of the
total number were black.[56]

Providing for Individual Differences: Eugenic Social Engineering

While eugenic reform achieved mild success with the enactment of sterilization and immigration laws, eugenic social engineering played a dominant role in shaping educational, industrial, legal, and military institutions. The theory of eugenic social engineering will first be examined in the
context of legal reform; then the theory and practice of eugenic social
engineering will be examined in the context of educational reform. The
underlying principle of eugenic social engineering was that institutions
should be structured on the basis of innate individual differences. Regarding legal reform, the theory of eugenical social engineering was evident in
the 1912 correspondence between John D. Rockefeller, Jr., and Charles
Davenport.

Rockefeller asked Davenport about the desirability of establishing a
"Criminalistic Institution" under the direction of Katherine B. Davis.
Davis's plan would suspend the sentencing of a convicted urban woman
until after the institute had made an extensive examination of her. At the
institute, the woman would be carefully studied by a trained corps of
experts who would determine her social, educational, physical, and moral
condition. Additionally, the experts would determine her industrial efficiency, which would be based on employer records and tests that determined how intelligently the woman "could use her hands." Presumably
the ability of the woman as a worker would influence the recommendations made by the institute. In any case, Rockefeller noted that after the
institute made these investigations it would refer her back to the judge as
follows:

> The Institute would then return the woman to the committing
> judge with the report of its findings, stating whether, if mentally
> and physically sound, she could safely be put on probation,

whether she would be a fit subject for reformatory treatment, whether she had been found to be an habitual offender, or on account of mental and physical defects was a candidate for a special institution. It would also recommend where she should be sent.[57]

In performing this function, the institute was providing for individual differences. As Rockefeller observed about his plan,

In this way, it would be possible to send the woman to the place best adapted to her needs and where she would either be kept from perpetuating her kind if she were mentally deficient and incapable of reform, or would be given every chance to rise above the criminal classes and return to normal society if that were possible. In any event the probability that she would ever again need to be dealt with by law would be reduced to a minimum.[58]

Rockefeller was confident that not only would Davis's plan meet the needs of the women but also would happily meet the needs of society. The plan, he believed, would mean an immense saving for the city and state "if it succeeded in lifting any large number of criminals out of the criminal class" or prevented "any considerable number of defectives and hardened criminals from being returned to society, if at all at least not until after the period of child rearing had been passed." In seeking Davenport's advice, Rockefeller noted that he believed the plan was immensely important, was equally applicable to men, and provided a "scientific way of escape from the evils which our courts are intended to correct."[59]

Davenport responded enthusiastically to the proposed plan for a Criminalistic Institution. He noted to Rockefeller that practically all crimes were related to weak innate social tendencies, although there were some criminals who had strong innate social tendencies but very bad training or especially strong temptations. The important principle, however, was that criminals be individually judged on their hereditary tendencies, their training, and the temptations afforded them. Davenport thought the motto of legal reform should be "All men are created unequal." Equality before the law, Davenport noted, reflects "cruelty and injustice." The *nature of the person*" should be "given no less consideration in determining treatment than the nature of the deed done." Davenport meant for example that for persons with altogether absent innate social tendencies that suitable treatment included "permanent segregation with useful employment and as much happiness as possible; but interdiction of reproduction."[60]

To claim that one knew the nature of a person was no less extraordinary than to claim one knew what was best for a person with that nature.

Nevertheless this claim, which was based on the existing science of individual differences, became a fundamental principle of the American legal system. Differentiated treatment and punishment of persons based on individual differences and the use of psychologists, psychiatrists, and other experts in determining individual differences increasingly became characteristics of the legal system.[61] Similarly, the theory and practice of eugenic social engineering, with philanthropic support, was applied to educational systems.

Throughout this century, enlightened and progressive American educators have maintained that providing for individual differences was the key to humane learning experiences and was essential to enhancing individuality, freedom, and equality. While, as we shall see, this point was debatable, there was no question but that the concept of individual differences played a vital role in defining the social reality of schooling. This concept influenced thinking about the curriculum, guidance, administration, supervision, the role and responsibilities of teachers and students, and the social functions of the school. It vitally influenced institutional structures and human consciousness by accentuating genetic and environmental differences rather than similarities.

In examining the role of individual differences in the educational system, we will focus on the differentiated curriculum. The growth of the differentiated curriculum was a triumph of eugenical social engineering, for the differentiated curriculum was based on eugenic institutional reform that altered the educational system to fit alleged innate individual differences. The differentiated curriculum was a key element of school reform promoted by the Rockefeller and Carnegie foundations. It permeated early twentieth-century foundation discussion of manual training, vocational education, the "Modern School," and general education.

At the dawn of the twentieth century, Henry S. Pritchett, president of the Massachusetts Institute of Technology and later president (1906) of the Carnegie Foundation for the Advancement of Teaching, delineated the relationship between education and work. Pritchett agreed with Aristotle that schools should train men for effective work in some station in life and should educate them for the best life in that station.[62] In promoting such schools, Boston, Massachusetts, and indeed America could learn much from Berlin, Germany. According to Pritchett, Berlin's system "rests upon an intelligent study of the whole question of the people," and "aims to meet in a rational way the varying wants of all classes." Pritchett believed that the American educational system had particularly failed the working classes. Although manual training was to provide a more relevant training, Pritchett thought it had not succeeded with the working class. "Instruction in manual training forms in this country practically a culture study: it contributes almost nothing to the betterment of those in trades."[63]

Pritchett noted the manual training school has "not reached down to serve the great mass of youth whom mechanical training and manual skill would mean most of all."[64]

Pritchett found the solution to this problem in Hampton Institute, a training center for Negroes, which offered "The Twentieth Century Type of Education." Hampton education looked to the "application of character and intellect in efficient work" and stood for "the idea that moral and intellectual and social efficiency can find complete expression in many callings." Pursuing this theme, Pritchett noted:

> The education for which you stand—a combination of character, intellect and economic efficiency—is peculiarly the type of education for the twentieth century. The eighteenth century school and university wrote over its doors the words, "I believe," as an expression for that for which its education stood; the nineteenth century school and university wrote over its doors the words, "I believe, but I think"; the twentieth century school, of which you are the representative, writes over its doors, "I believe, and I think, in order that I may work."[65]

Pritchett and Carnegie, who at the turn of the century were both concerned with economic efficiency and the proper utilization of human resources, fell back on nineteenth-century Social Darwinism to legitimate the inequalities of the social order. Yet these ideas were not internalized by a great majority of Americans. Indeed the growth of education and industrialization both posed significant challenges to the inequalities of the social system. For a primary impact of enforced compulsory schooling was to spread the Protestant work ethic to all classes and ethnic groups while industrialization led to the creation of menial, unskilled jobs. Given degrading factory conditions, the paradox of the work ethic, as noted, was that it led to greater alienation for the worker. For practice of the work ethic and its emphasis on character and effort did not lead to greater rewards for the unskilled laborer. Further complicating the matter was that both lower-class skills and middle-class values were essential for the factory to operate efficiently. Such conditions fundamentally challenged the justice of the social order. In order to bridge the gap between lower-class skills and middle-class values, workers had to internalize a sense of merit based on ability to legitimate their position in the social order. This challenge was in part met with the scientific discovery of individual differences and the institutionalization of educational provisions for individual differences.

While the concept of individual differences was popularized in the early twentieth century, widescale institutionalization of programs for individual differences in America did not occur until World War I. Many psychologists rallied together to ensure that programs providing for individual difference were adapted by the armed forces. These psychologists, led by Yerkes, Terman, Thorndike, Dodge, and others, were united by a common world view: they believed that significant innate individual differences existed, that programs were available to meet different abilities and needs, and that the consequences of these programs would be desirable for the armed forces and the nation. Reflecting this world view were the psychologists at the Division of Applied Psychology at the Carnegie Institute of Technology who devoted their full efforts to the war. According to a Carnegie Institute historian, the division's philosophy disavowed "the traditional theory of the Declaration of Independence, of Greek civilization, and of modern labor unions as to the equality of man" and proceeded on the "premises that all men are not equal, that there are enormous fundamental differences in individuals and that these differences can be tabulated to a workable degree by a rating scale."[66] This world view was especially realized with the use of army intelligence tests for classifying over 1.7 million soldiers.

The use of mental tests and homogeneous grouping grew rapidly after the war. While prior to the war Yerkes and Terman had been competing with each other for a grant from the Rockefeller General Education Board to design an intelligence test,[67] they discontinued their competition with America's involvement in the war. They joined forces with other psychologists to create the army tests. After the war, to maintain the momentum of testing, Yerkes and Terman requested that the General Education Board provide $25,000 for the peacetime revision of the army tests for public schools. Their request was met and Yerkes, Terman, and others designed the National Intelligence Tests. These tests sold over 400,000 copies in the first six months alone and by 1921 it was estimated that over 4 million school children had been mentally graded by various tests. These tests were widely used in elementary and secondary schools for homogeneous grouping.[68]

Perhaps one reason why the mental tests were so widely received was because in a particular way they expressed the disillusionment of the postwar period. As historian Vernon Parrington expressed it,

> Out of the muck of the war had come a great discovery—so it
> was reported—the discovery that psychology as well as econom-
> ics had its word to say on politics. From the army intelligence
> tests the moron emerged as a singular commentary on our Amer-
> ican democracy, and with the discovery of the moron the demo-
> cratic principles were in for a slashing attack. Almost overnight
> an army of enemies was marshaled against it. The eugenicist with
> his isolated germ theory flouted the perfectional psychology of

John Locke, with its emphasis on environment as the determining factor in social evolution—a psychology on which the whole
idealistic interpretation was founded.[69]

In any event, the new psychology based on mental tests and innate
individual differences was a primary instrument of eugenic social engineering. Between 1915 and 1938 alone, the Carnegie Corporation of New
York provided over $3 million to test over 13 million people in thirty-three
studies.[70]

In institutionalizing programs for individual differences, Abraham
Flexner played a significant role. After completing his influential study of
medical education for the Carnegie Foundation, Flexner in 1913 joined
the Rockefeller Foundation-funded General Education Board as a member and assistant secretary. As an influential member of the board, Flexner
proposed a plan for "A Modern School" that would provide a curriculum
for the needs and abilities of the individual. As Flexner noted, it was of
"fundamental importance to discover and direct to best advantage the
individual's motive capacity and bent." This meant that "definiteness,
thoroughness, and adjustment to personal capacity and opportunity"
should receive increasing attention in education. Consistent with this plan,
the Modern School provided only for the abilities and wants of a particular
group of children:

> The education planned for children who must leave school at
> fourteen necessarily differs in extent and thus to a degree in
> content from that feasible for those who can remain, say two
> years longer, so as to acquire the rudiments of a vocation. Still
> different are the possibilities for children who have the good
> fortune to remain until they are eighteen or twenty, reasonably
> free during this lengthened period from the necessity of deter-
> mining procedure by other than educational considerations. The
> Modern School of which we are now speaking contemplates
> liberal and general education in the sense last-mentioned.[71]

The Modern School was thus not designed for all children. Indeed, Flexner
wrote, "I should no more force a boy into a Modern School, if it is ill-
adapted to his needs and capacity, than I should force him into a classical
school, if that is ill-adapted to his needs and capacities."[72]

However, the classical school, Flexner cautioned, suited the needs and
abilities of fewer and fewer individuals. It failed to meet individual and
social needs because it was unable to help a person adjust to the social
order. On the other hand a Modern School education would give a student
a "firm grasp of the social world," which meant "a comprehension of and

sympathy with current industry, current science, and current politics."
Not only did formal, classical education fail to promote "sympathy with
current industry," but it also failed to meet individual abilities:

> A formal education, devoted to "training the mind" and to
> "culture" does little to connect capacity with opportunity or
> ambition. The more positive endowments, of course, assert
> themselves; but the more positive endowments are relatively
> scarce.[73]

In challenging the idea that learning the classics was necessary to be
educated, Flexner was attacking an elitist conception of knowledge.
However, in asserting that only a few possessed "more positive endowments," Flexner was suggesting perhaps a more damaging elitist conception of the nature of human beings. This conception, which was reinforced
by the new science of individual differences, suggested that many were
incapable of higher learning.

Flexner's plan for a Modern School would be enthusiastically received
by John D. Rockefeller, Jr. Rockefeller felt the Modern School represented the "dawn" for education and noted to Flexner that "if I only had
had such an education as is here outlined, it seems to be that I should be a
much more useful and valuable citizen today, and I naturally covet such
opportunities for my children."[74] As Rockefeller and Flexner hoped, the
philosophy of the Modern School was institutionalized with the establishment of the Lincoln School at Columbia University. Financed by the
Rockefeller-founded General Education Board to the tune of almost $6
million between 1917 and 1929, the Lincoln School provided a model for
educational reform.

Continuing this tradition, during the period of 1933–1940 the General
Education Board appropriated $8,446,264 to support research and exper-
imentation in general education. Included in these appropriations were
grants to the American Youth Commission, the National Education
Association, the Progressive Education Association, American Association of Junior Colleges, and numerous universities, colleges, and school
systems.[75] As originally formulated the operations of the general education project would include the following:

(1) Defining the aims of education in terms of individual and social
needs;
(2) Utilizing all valid results of recent studies bearing upon the
problems of general education through such means as the reconstruction of existing curricula so as to foster individual
development within an organized plan of general education;

(3) Promoting cooperative attack by school and college teachers and by productive scholars and scientists upon specific problems of general education.

(4) Indicating the desirable changes in institutional practice for putting the new programs into action.[76]

The purpose of the appropriations was, according to Edmund E. Day, director of General Education of the General Education Board, to provide a "program looking toward the reorganization of general education, chiefly in junior and senior high schools and junior colleges."[77] For Day, the need for reorganization of general education was directly tied to economic conditions. In 1936 Day very explicitly spelled out these economic conditions and the demands they made for reorganizing general education. He noted:

> It seems evident that, in the process of adjustment to changing
> economic conditions, we must contemplate for some time to
> come the elimination of workers at both ends of the age-scale,
> with provisions for an earlier retirement and a longer schooling.
> We must think in terms of some kind of educational program
> which will accommodate the great bulk of our population up to
> the age of eighteen or nineteen years.

But how were economic conditions to be met and students kept in schools for a longer period of time? Day responded that

> the schools which provide for the education of these young
> people over a more extended period must recognize more frankly
> than they have in the past the particular needs, interests, and
> capacities of their students. There must not be any inflexibility,
> or any undue retention of the purely academic tradition. We
> must not, by any means, fail to do justice to those young people
> with a definite academic bent, but it is also highly important that
> the schools get a more adequate understanding of the nature of
> the learning process, especially as it concerns those young people
> who are less verbally-minded and present all kinds of obstacles
> to the learning process.

But what kind of specific educational reform was required? Again Day had a ready response:

> I think we have to expect a fairly general overhauling of the
> whole educational program, looking, perhaps, toward a com-
> mon elementary school program of about six grades which will

provide a common educational experience for the whole population; a second unit—a high school—which again will be a common school, but one in which diagnostic treatment and differentiation of programs will be fully recognized and regarded as
fundamental; and over and above these two units, a battery of
different institutions—a junior college at one end and something
like a CCC camp at the other, and in between, manual or
industrial arts units, commercial units—a graduation from the
clearly nonacademic at one extreme to the clearly academic at
the other. Perhaps four or five different types of units will be
involved here, with curricula and teaching methods adjusted to
the variety of individuals in each school.[78]

This program indeed would provide for individual differences and socio-
economic needs; it would provide for both the "less verbally-minded" and
the college oriented; it would provide for changing economic conditions
and the needs of workers and employers. Operating from a world view
that defined and solved problems in a manner conducive to industrial
capitalism, this program assured the legitimation of the inequalities of the
economic order. Rather than attacking the distribution of wealth, this
program offered solutions that properly fit persons into their positions in
the economic order.

Day was also concerned about the failure of progressive educators to
instill democratic ideals. He felt very strongly that schools would have to
take a "more aggressive position in regard to American democratic
ideals." Day was "not fearful in this connection of appropriate indoctri-
nation" and advocated the development of "more positive and forceful
means of creating loyalty to democracy." Day was confident that if
progressive school people thought through their philosophies they would
decide to devise school procedures and classroom techniques which
"instill in young Americans an unswerving loyalty to the principles of
American democracy."[79] One such technique was articulated by the
Committee of the Social Studies on the Rockefeller-financed Progressive
Education Association Commission on the Secondary School Curriculum. The committee suggested that the development of a social vocabulary
could be used for organizing social action. This meant, the committee
noted,

that for a society to operate efficiently, there must be a great
number of words and phrases which will set up immediate responses in the minds of any group which is appealed to to act or
to refrain from action. Without such rallying words as "Democracy," "The Constitution," "Americanism," it would be impos-

> sible to organize masses into sufficiently integrated groups to
> produce social action. One definite task of the social studies
> teaching is to build up the *tone* of certain words, to place them in
> a series of contexts so that they come to have a fixed stimulus
> value in the mind of the listener. The tale of the martyr, the
> patriot, the hero, the narration of events as traitorous or despica-
> ble—all of these have this function.[80]

In an important sense this proposal for manipulating people with symbols
represented the new "realistic" assessment of human nature that viewed
people as socially plastic within sharply drawn genetic limitations.

Individual Differences and Social Reform

The concept of innate individual differences not only vitally shaped
eugenic reform and eugenic social engineering but furthermore influenced,
oftentimes subtly, discussions of environmental social engineering. For
innate individual differences furnished a conceptual framework for viewing human beings that emphasized not only innate rather than acquired
differences, but also individual (i.e., psychological) rather than social
traits, individual differences rather than individual similarities, and particular differences (e.g., intellectual differences rooted in the needs of the
social order) rather than other differences. Even though many later
educators and reformers viewed individual differences as essentially acquired rather than innate, the other issues surrounding individual differences tended to remain unexamined. Many educators and reformers,
regardless of their environmental and genetic assumptions about human
differences, ended up supporting very similar programs for social reform.
Thus, for example, the differentiated curriculum, whether based on innate
or acquired differences, often had very similar characteristics.
   Within the context of the differentiated curriculum, innate and acquired
differences had some important similar, as well as dissimilar, implications
in defining freedom and equality. Policy based on innate individual
differences defined freedom exclusively in terms of positive freedom.
Freedom meant freedom to act within the psychological parameters of
one's interests, abilities, wants, and needs. The area in which the individual
was free to act was determined by the boundaries drawn by the psychological expert. The psychological delimitations determined the boundaries of
individual freedom and choice. Positive freedom meant freedom to be
what one was psychologically; it did not include freedom to be something
else. Additionally, positive freedom entailed certain necessary restraints

on the individual that were grounded in one's nature. From this perspective, if one was by nature a mechanic, one was free to be mechanically trained, but not free to be professionally trained. It was not an unfair restraint not to be allowed to do something one could not by nature do.

On the other hand, negative freedom, freedom from restraints, was not present in this formulation. For individual differences prescribed the psychological parameters which in turn defined the boundaries of individual freedom and necessary restraints. Since only restraints that were necessitated by one's nature were required, it would be irrational to try to free the individual from such restraints. Thus, "thing thinkers," "doers," should be free to take shop courses, but it would be irrational to allow them to be free from the limits of their doer nature and take the classical curriculum. Freedom from restraints that allowed the individual to venture into areas beyond his psychological parameters was not freedom but irrationality.

Not only was the idea of freedom shaped by the concept of innate individual differences but so also was the concept of equality and its twentieth-century offspring, equality of educational opportunity. Ironically, the historical reason for promoting equality of educational opportunity was, as Paul Violas[81] suggests, to provide a rationale for unequal rather than equal treatment of individuals. Equal education, the common school ideal, was based on the principle that all children should receive a common education for a specified period of time regardless of intellectual ability. Opportunity, then, meant in theory an equal chance to develop one's intellectual capacities. At the turn of the century the idea of equal education began to be supplanted by the idea of equality of educational opportunity. This idea was fundamentally based on innate individual differences. Equality of educational opportunity meant that opportunities were first defined by one's innate makeup and then one was given an equal opportunity to succeed in areas compatible with one's nature. Equal opportunity entailed an equal chance to attend college only if one was by nature college material. If one was not by nature college material, then failure to provide training that was necessary for attending college was not a denial of equality of educational opportunity.

Ironically, although many educators rejected the hereditarian position, they embraced individual differences. Indeed the concept of individual differences defined the boundaries of discussions about the nature of human beings. Philanthropists and psychologists were able to effectively promote educational reform that was based on innate capacities under the slogan of "providing for individual differences." While one could argue for a differentiated curriculum based on innate individual differences, it was much more difficult to argue for a differentiated curriculum based on environmental differences. For if individual differences were essentially the result of nurture rather than nature, then to fit the child into a particular track was to limit the opportunity of the child to fully develop his/her capacities. Thus, no doubt unknowingly, many educators would contradict themselves: on the one hand they would oppose hereditarian explanations for student behavior, yet on the other hand they would support programs like a differentiated curriculum that were based on hereditary differences.

Yet even some educators who rejected innate individual differences still accepted the idea of developing particular talents and adjusting children to their likely work world through a differentiated curriculum. In this instance, freedom and equal opportunity were prescribed not by innate makeup but by acquired makeup consisting of one's existing environment and probable vocation. Again, as with innate abilities, acquired traits were rooted in the psychological makeup of the person. The rationale for the differentiated curriculum, then, was not based on innate differences but differences acquired from one's family, neighborhood, and culture. Providing for individual differences meant giving the person a curriculum that was appropriate for living within this environment. Whether based on innate or acquired makeup, a self-fulfilling prophecy was built into programs like the differentiated curriculum: for one received appropriate training grounded in innate or acquired differences that locked one into his existing position in the social order. In this context, providing for innate or acquired differences did not mean providing for different rates of learning but rather providing different subjects and materials for different innate or acquired abilities and interests. Practically, this meant that industrial capitalism and its unequal distribution of wealth and status could be legitimated on the basis of providing for acquired as well as innate individual differences.

One response to Andrew Carnegie's intriguing question, "If you had say five or ten millions of dollars to put to the best use possible, what would you do with it?" was to support the development of individual differences. Aided by foundation dollars and leadership, the conceptualization and institutionalization of programs providing for individual differences promoted a consciousness of reality based on the limitations rather than the possibilities of human nature. It created a secular version of original sin and a consciousness of society that encouraged self-fulfilling prophecies that perpetuated past inequalities and tended to lock people into their existing position in the social order. It generated a principle of social reform that decisively shaped eugenic reform and significantly influenced the parameters of dialogue on environmental social engineering. In the process, the concept of individual differences, the fundamental principle of early twentieth-century American reform, provided a fundamental legitimation of industrial capitalism.

Notes

1. Letter, A. Carnegie to H. S. Pritchett, January 14, 1908, Manuscript Division, Library of Congress, *Henry S. Pritchett Papers.*

2. See, e.g., David Brody, *Steelworkers in America; the Nonunion Era* (New York: Harper and Row, 1969) and Paul Violas, *The Training of the Urban Working Class* (Chicago: Rand McNally, 1978).

3. Abraham Flexner, "Foundations—Ours and Others," January 3, 1924, Library of Congress, *Abraham Flexner Papers.*

4. Fred M. Hechinger, "Education," in Warren Weaver et al., *U.S. Philanthropic Foundations* (New York: Harper and Row, 1967), p. 425.

5. E. L. Thorndike, "Professor Cattell's Relation to the Study of Individual Differences," *The Psychological Researches of James McKeen Cattell,* Columbia Contributions to Philosophy, Psychology and Education, Vol. XXII, No. 4, p. 92.

6. E. L. Thorndike, "The Contribution of Psychology to Education," *Journal of Educational Psychology* 1 (January 1910): 8.

7. E. L. Thorndike, *Individuality* (Boston: Houghton Mifflin, 1911), p. 25.

8. "Professor Cattell's," p. 93.

9. E. L. Thorndike, "Accuracy from the Viewpoint of the Psychologist," *Education* 27 (April 1907): 465.

10. See Geraldine Joncich, *The Sane Positivist: A Biography of Edward L. Thorndike* (Middletown, Conn.: Wesleyan University Press, 1968), pp. 282–283.

11. E. L. Thorndike, "Tests of Aesthetic Appreciation," *Journal of Educational Psychology* 7 (November 1916): 509–510.

12. E. L. Thorndike, *Educational Psychology*, Vol. 3 (New York: Columbia University, 1914), pp. 186–188.

13. E. L. Thorndike, "Sex in Education," *Bookman* 23 (April 1906): 214.

14. E. L. Thorndike, "Measurement of Twins," *Archives of Philosophy, Psychology and Scientific Methods* 1 (September 1905): 12.

15. *Educational Psychology*, Vol. 3, p. 220.

16. E. L. Thorndike, *Education* (New York: Macmillan, 1912), p. 23.

17. E. L. Thorndike, "The Psychology of the Half-Educated Man," *Harper's Magazine* 140 (April 1920): 667.

18. E. L. Thorndike, *Human Nature and the Social Order* (New York: Macmillan, 1940), p. 433.

19. E. L. Thorndike, "A Sociologist's Theory of Education," *Bookman* 24 (November 1906): 291.

20. E. L. Thorndike, "How May We Improve the Selection, Training, and Life Work of Leaders," *Teachers College Record* 40 (April 1939): 595.

21. E. L. Thorndike, "The Relation between Intellect and Morality in Rulers," *American Journal of Sociology* 42 (November 1936): 321, 329.

22. Thorndike, *Human Nature*, pp. 369–370.

23. Ibid., pp. 370–372.

24. E. L. Thorndike, "Eugenics with Special Reference to Intellect and Character," *Popular Science Monthly* 83 (August 1913): 127–128.

25. Ibid., p. 130.

26. Thorndike, *Human Nature*, p. 455.
27. Thorndike, "Professor Cattell's," p. 99.
28. Thorndike, *Individuality*, pp. 50–51.
29. Thorndike, *Education*, p. 70.
30. Thorndike, *Educational Psychology*, Vol. 3, p. 311.
31. E.L. Thorndike, Principles of Teaching (New York: A. G. Seiler, 1906), p. 34.
32. E. L. Thorndike, "Investigating the Curriculum. The Psychologists Dissect the Course of Study," *Journal of Adult Education* 1 (February 1929): 44.
33. Thorndike, *Principles*, pp. 68–69.
34. Thorndike, "Selection of Leaders," p. 597.
35. Thorndike, *Education*, p. 32.
36. Thorndike,"Investigating Curriculum," p. 41.
37. Thorndike, "Sex in Education," pp. 212–213.
38. E. L. Thorndike, "Psychology in Secondary Schools," *School Review* 10 (February 1902): 122.
39. Thorndike, *Principles,* pp. 87–88.
40. E. L. Thorndike, "The Psychology of Labor," *Harper's Monthly Magazine* 144 (May 1922): 804–805.
41. Carnegie Corporation of New York, *Report of the President and of the Treasurer,* 1937–1938 (New York: Carnegie Corporation of New York, 1938).
42. Thorndike, *Human Nature*, pp. 466–467.
43. E. L. Thorndike, *Measurements of Twins* (New York: The Science Press, 1905), p. 11.
44. See Albert L. Barrows, "A History of the National Research Council 1919–1933," *National Research Council Reprint and Circular Series*, No. 106, 1933, p. 9.
45. Elihu Root, "The Need for Organization in Scientific Research,'. *Bulletin of the National Research Council*, Vol. 1, Part 1, Number 1 (October 1919): 8–10.
46. Henry S. Pritchett, "The Function of Scientific Research in a Modern State," *Bulletin*, pp. 10–11.
47. George Eastman, "Concerning the Importance of Industrial Research," *Bulletin*, pp. 18–19.
48. Carnegie Institution of Washington, *Yearbook, 1929* (Washington, D.C.: the same, 1930), pp. 21–22.
49. *Eugenical News*, 1922, p. 111.
50. Ibid., 1917, p. 62.
51. Robert M. Yerkes, "The Work of Committee on Scientific Problems of Human Migration, National Research Council," *Reprint and Circular Series of the National Research Council*, Number 58.
52. "Report to Committee on Scientific Problems of Human Migration," Appendix March 8, 1923, Manuscript Division, Library of Congress, *John C. Merriam Papers.*
53. "Report on Raymond Dodge to the Committee on the Scientific Problems of Human Migration," November 29, 1924, *Merriam Papers.*

54. Yerkes, p. 189; Robert M. Yerkes, "Testing the Human Mind," *Atlantic* 131 (March 1923): 365.
55. Harry H. Laughlin, "American History in Terms of Human Migration," The Committee on Immigration and Naturalization, House of Representatives, March 7, 1928.
56. See Russell Marks, "Providing for Individual Differences: A History of the Intelligence Testing Movement in North America," *Interchange* 7: 3 (1976–1977).
57. Letter, J. D. Rockefeller, Jr., to C. B. Davenport, January 27, 1912, American Philosophical Society Library, *Charles B. Davenport Papers.*
58. Ibid.
59. Ibid.
60. Letter, Davenport to Rockefeller, February 1, 1912, *Davenport Papers.*
61. For the use of social scientific evidence in legal cases see especially H. H. Goddard, *The Criminal Imbecile* (New York: Macmillan, 1915).
62. Henry S. Pritchett, "The Part of the Manual-Training High School in American Education," *Proceedings of the National Education Association,* 1903, p. 71.
63. Henry S. Pritchett, "The Place of Industrial and Technical Training in Popular Education," *Technology Review* 4 (November 1, 1902): 27.
64. Pritchett, "The Part," p. 76.
65. H. S. Pritchett, "The Twentieth Century Type of Education," *Southern Workman* 38 (December 1909): 377–378.
66. A. W. Tarbell, *The Story of Carnegie Tech 1900–1935* (Pittsburgh: Carnegie Institute Press, 1937), p. 61.
67. See Letters, L. M. Terman to A. Flexner, January 8, 1917; A. Flexner to R. M. Yerkes, January 19, 1917; L. M. Terman to A. Flexner, January 31, 1917; A. Flexner to L. M. Terman, June 26, 1917, Rockefeller Archive Center, *Abraham Flexner Papers.*
68. M. E. Haggerty, "Recent Developments in Measuring Human Capacities," *Journal of Educational Research* 3 (June 1921): 241–253; W. S. Deffenbaugh, "Uses of Intelligence and Achievement Tests in 215 Cities," U. S. Bureau of Education, City School Leaflet No. 20, Washington, D.C., 1925.
69. Quoted in Arthur Mann, ed., *The Progressive Era: Liberal Renaissance or Liberal Failure?* (New York: Holt, Rinehart and Winston, 1963), p. 12.
70. Carnegie Foundation, *Twenty-Ninth Bulletin* (New York: The Carnegie Foundation for the Advancement of Teaching, 1937), p. xi.
71. Abraham Flexner, "A Modern School," *Occasional Paper,* No. 3 (New York: General Education Board, 1923), pp. xvii, 3.
72. Letter, A. Flexner to A. F. West, May 31, 1917, *Flexner Papers.*
73. Flexner, "Modern School," p. 17.
74. Letter, Rockefeller to Flexner, January 21, 1916, *Flexner Papers.*
75. "FMR to RBF," September 26, 1945, Rockefeller Archive Center, General Education.
76. "The Proposed Program in the Field of General Education," January 18, 1933, Rockefeller Archive Center, General Education.

77. Edmund E. Day, "Statement Made by Mr. Day to the Trustees," December 1936, Rockefeller Archive Center.
78. Ibid.
79. Edmund E. Day, "Heads of Schools Conference, Columbus, Ohio," October 22, 1936, Rockefeller Archive Center.
80. Margaret Mead, "Report to the Committee of the Social Studies of the Commission on the Secondary School Curriculum," October 26, 1935, Section 3, Rockefeller Archive Center.
81. See Paul Violas's penetrating study *The Training of the Urban Working Class* (Chicago: Rand McNally, 1978).

E. Richard Brown

Rockefeller Medicine in China: Professionalism and Imperialism*

Medical scientists gathered in September 1921 from eminent institutions around the world to help dedicate the Peking Union Medical College, the new "Johns Hopkins of China" and indeed the finest medical school in all of Asia. The autumn sun danced on the jade-green glazed title roofs of the fifty-nine buildings of the college, known to Peking residents as the "Green City."

Speaking for his father's philanthropy, which by then had spent nearly $11 million on the project, John D. Rockefeller, Jr., described the Peking Union Medical College (PUMC) as a vehicle through which China would absorb "the best that is known to Western civilization not only in medical science but in mental development and spiritual culture."[1]

Rich Standards in Poor Countries

This seemingly generous gift—eventually costing the Rockefeller philanthropy $45 million—did indeed bring "the best" in Western civilization to China by creating a medical education program based on the "highest standard" prevailing in the United States. Essentially the same entrance requirements, curriculum, and training objectives were introduced into China's traditional, agrarian, and economically underdeveloped society as were then being developed in the industrialized United States. In a country in which modern schooling was available to only a minute fraction of the population, three years of college-level premedical work was required in addition to graduation from the Chinese equivalent of high

*The old-style English spelling of Chinese names is used in this chapter, for example, Peking for Beijing and Mao Tse-tung for Mao Zedong. The author wishes to thank the Rockefeller Archives for permission to publish excerpts of documents in their files.

school. The four-year medical school curriculum emphasized individual diagnosis and treatment, virtually ignoring public health methods, and it had a strong hospital- and laboratory-based research orientation.

The PUMC was intended to train a small number of scientifically oriented medical doctors who would train other doctors and become the leaders of medical modernization in China. It was designed to supply a medical system in which Western-type physicians would provide the care. Doctors would be assisted by nurses, but only physicians would be autonomous practitioners.

Exported professionalism and medical "modernization," as exemplified by the PUMC, have been roundly criticized in recent years for not providing for the health needs of underdeveloped countries. Their emphases on technologically sophisticated care delivered by highly trained physicians have produced expensive curative medical care systems, serving only the small urbanized classes of these countries. "The rude facts are," reports John Bryant in a recent Rockefeller Foundation study, "that for most of Africa and Asia, the proportion of population to physicians and nurses in rural areas is seldom below 50,000, is usually in excess of 100,000, and frequently approaches one million."[2] Western models of medical education and medical care transplanted to underdeveloped countries are, according to Rockefeller Foundation officer Willoughby Lathem, "an unqualified disaster." "Whole segments of the population are excluded from access to health care, and a large proportion receive care inadequate to their needs," Lathem concluded.[3] Medical schools train too few physicians for the country's needs. Hospitals, doctors, and even clinics are usually available only in urban areas in which a fraction of the population lives. Nevertheless, expensive medical schools and hospitals consume an enormous portion of the scarce funds available for health care. This high-technology curative medicine has little or no impact on the major causes of death—mainly nutritional and infectious diseases—while public health measures, sanitation systems, and pure water supplies—which are more effective against the diseases of underdevelopment and less expensive than high-technology curative medical care—remain as malnourished as the majority population they would serve.

Underdevelopment and Professionalism

Why has health care in underdeveloped countries grown up as a caricature of health care in advanced industrial societies, with small high-technology, physician-dominated medical care systems—that absorb excessive shares of the national wealth—and with even smaller underdeveloped public health systems? One explanation focuses on the consequences of economic and political dependency, characteristic of underdeveloped countries in relation to industrialized nations. Based on a more general political economic analysis of underdevelopment, Vicente Navarro[4] argues that health care in underdeveloped countries, like other sectors of their economies, is drained by a net outflow of capital to the capital-owning and creditor advanced capitalist nations. In health care itself that outflow takes the form of a "medical brain drain," physicians emigrating to the wealthier countries,[5] and of money paid for the importing of drugs and other expensive medical commodities.[6] Navarro further argues that health care in underdeveloped countries serves the indigenous middle and upper classes of those countries by providing them with medical care that imitates the care available in the advanced industrial countries. The distribution of that care approximates the distribution of other goods and services, following the countries' extremely skewed class structures.

A second explanation for the distorted development of health care in poor countries is based on sociological studies of professions: the medical professions of underdeveloped countries, like those of the advanced industrial nations, obstruct progressive reforms in health care as they try to protect their control over medical education, their monopoly of medical practice, and thus their status and incomes. Placing the profession's and its members' interests above those of the populace's need for accessible health services, medical professions have generally tried to remain small elite strata within their national social structures. This pattern varies from country to country, depending upon the specific historical conditions of development and present political economic systems. Terence Johnson found that in countries that had been colonized by England, the professions have less autonomy and are more directly controlled by the government much as they had formerly served colonial authorities.[7] Michael Goldstein and Peter Donaldson found that, at least in Thailand, which had never been colonized but whose medical education system had been largely dictated by the Rockefeller Foundation, medical education development resulted in a profession similar in its autonomy, monopoly, and protectionism of its interests to professions in developed countries.[8]

In many respects, the development of a professional elite is quite consistent with the interests of foreign nations that dominate the economic and political affairs of underdeveloped countries. Just as old colonial powers found it expedient to develop a small class of native administrators, so have neocolonial* powers found it helpful in countries under their domination to have an indigenous class of managers, professionals, and

---

* "Neocolonialism" and "imperialism" are used interchangeably to refer to economic and political domination of less developed countries by more industrialized ones.

bureaucrats who (1) provide much of the expertise necessary to run a modern country and (2) tend to support whatever economic and political system maintains their class privileges.[9]

An elite medical profession performs both of these functions. First, its members provide modern technical care to the country's upper and middle classes, the military and police, and skilled workers in large industrial enterprises; and they largely run the health ministry, usually inadequately funded, which is charged with providing for the health needs of the majority population.[10] Second, medical professions typically support the differential status and material privileges they and other members of the upper classes receive from the inequitable class structures associated with underdevelopment and economic dependence. They are forces of conservatism.[11]

Although these functions serve the interests of the dominant neocolonial nations, the inaccessibility of medical care and the underdevelopment of public health systems (that derive from maintaining the medical profession as an urbanized elite) conflict with other needs of neocolonial powers. The industrial and commercial development and exploitation of a country require a work force that is healthy enough to labor day after day, and the maintenance of that work force requires that at least its members and their families receive adequate preventive and curative care. John C. Mc-Clintock, an assistant vice president of United Fruit Company, succinctly characterized the relationship between health and profits:[12]

> In the under-developed areas where American companies have gone, where they have brought great enterprises into fruition, where they are continuing, one of the primary factors was to establish conditions of health where people could not only exist but also could work.

Similarly, corporate economist Stacy May has observed that "where mass diseases are brought under control, productivity tends to increase—through increasing the percentage of adult workers as a proportion of the total population, [and] through augmenting their strength and ambition to work."[13]

Neocolonial powers thus have an interest in developing public health programs and in making medical care accessible to at least the working population and their families. Accordingly, the Rockefeller Foundation and other philanthropies, along with government foreign aid programs, have sponsored large public health projects designed to bring preventive and limited curative care directly to impoverished rural and urban populations.[14] Why then have they also sponsored apparently contradictory medical education aid programs that built high-technology, physician-dominated medical systems accessible more to elites than to the majority populations?

In this chapter we will see that the Rockefeller Foundation, in the era of unabashed American imperialism, provided foreign assistance for medical education in China in order to create an infrastructure it believed necessary for China's development along Western lines. Drawing on internal correspondence and memos culled from the Rockefeller Archives as well as on published materials, I will argue that the foundation officers expected their medical education program to help "modernize" China, to develop an elite professional stratum to transform Chinese society in ways suited to the needs of the industrialized, capitalist nations. Although this is a case study, it examines the foundation's premier program in foreign assistance for medical education, a program that developed the model that was replicated or adapted around the world for half a century to come by the Rockefeller Foundation, foreign aid programs of advanced industrial countries, and even international health organizations.

Missionaries, Philanthropy, and Imperialism

The earliest recipients of Rockefeller philanthropy in China were missionaries, not the PUMC. For years John D. Rockefeller, Sr., a seemingly pious Baptist, had given generously to missionary work throughout the world. In 1892 he hired Frederick T. Gates, an astute and energetic Baptist minister, to take charge of his philanthropies and a large part of his financial empire as well. Gates consolidated and expanded Rockefeller's contributions to missionary groups and other causes.

In 1905 Gates proclaimed the importance of missionaries—not for saving souls but for the economic prosperity of the United States. "Now for the first time in the history of the world," Gates explained to Rockefeller, "all the nations and all the islands of the sea are actually open and offer a free field for the light and philanthropy of the English speaking people. . . .Christian agencies as a whole have very thoroughly invaded all coasts, all strategic points, all ports of entry and are thoroughly intrenched where they are." For Gates, transforming heathens into God-fearing Christians was "no sort of measure" of the value of missionaries:[15]

> Quite apart from the question of persons converted, the mere
> commercial results of missionary effort to our own land is worth,
> I had almost said a thousand fold every year of what is spent on
> missions. . . .Missionary enterprise, viewed solely from a com-
> mercial standpoint, is immensely profitable. From the point of
> view of means of subsistence for Americans, our import trade,

traceable mainly to the channels of intercourse opened up by
missionaries, is enormous. Imports from heathen lands furnish
us cheaply with many of the luxuries of life and not a few of the
comforts, and with many things, indeed, which we now regard as
necessities.

Industrial capitalism, however, required not only raw materials and cheap
products. It also needed new markets for its abundant manufactured
goods. As Gates added to Rockefeller's receptive ear,[16]

our imports are balanced by our exports to these same countries
of American manufactures. Our export trade is growing by leaps
and bounds. Such growth would have been utterly impossible
but for the commercial conquest of foreign lands under the lead
of missionary endeavor. What a boon to home industry and
manufacture!

The missionary effort in China was effective for a time in undermining
Chinese self-determination. Missionaries were the velvet glove of imperialism frequently backed up by the mailed fist. Nevertheless, the missionary
effort was still a very transparent attempt to support European and
American interests. As J. A. Hobson, an English economist, noted at the
time, "imperialism in the Far East is stripped nearly bare of all motives
and methods save those of distinctively commercial origin."[17]

China ushered in the twentieth century with the "Boxer Rebellion"
against foreign domination, but the revolt was crushed and the Great
Powers penetrated deeper into China's resources, her society, and her
culture. In 1909 Rockefeller agreed to Gates's suggestion to finance a
special commission to China to study the possibility of founding a major
Christian university there under interdenominational control. Before a
university could be created, however, China's first republic was proclaimed
under Dr. Sun Yat-sen, an erudite and charismatic nationalist. The Chinese
government insisted that such a school must be controlled by individuals
selected by and accountable to the government—terms unacceptable to
Gates and the Rockefellers.[18]

Still determined to "help" China, the newly chartered Rockefeller
Foundation held an in-house conference on China in January 1914, bringing
together China scholars, leaders of the main missionary boards operating
programs in China, and academic advisors, including Harvard President
Charles W. Eliot and University of Chicago President Harry Pratt Judson,
both trustees of the two largest Rockefeller philanthropies. John Mott,
general secretary of the influential international committee of the YMCA,
spoke for all the conference participants as he answered the apparently
rhetorical question "whether in view of the unstable conditions in China

just now it is an opportune moment" for launching philanthropic programs. "This very instability" is the strongest argument for action now, he said, for "if we wait until China becomes stable we lose the greatest opportunity that ever comes in the life dealing with a nation."[19] All the conference participants agreed that China's political instability created an unparalleled opportunity for foreign intervention to help determine China's future development.

"I quite agree that the plastic hour is the hour for action," added Thomas C. Chamberlin, professor of geology at the Rockefeller-endowed University of Chicago, "but at the same time the work that shall be contemplated should be such as shall be least possibly affected by the plasticity. The changes that are imminent in China are likely to lie generally in the political field." What was most needed was a program that would influence the direction of future events in China but remain immune to political vicissitudes. "For whatever may be the political convictions or feelings of any party, whatever may be their socialistic views, they desire health, they desire their own personal well-being, and so an institution that is devoted primarily to this object will be likely to find support and sympathy."[20]

It was perhaps James H. Franklin of the American Baptist Foreign Mission Society who summed up the general sentiment of the conference most succinctly. They would undertake an education program "of the proper kind" to train "Chinese leaders who will do the things we have so long done for China," leaders "who will do the things we wish to see done."[21]

What were the objectives of the Rockefeller philanthropies and the missionaries in China? Gates's emphasis on the economic value of missionaries coincided with the aims of North American and European businessmen, statesmen, philanthropists, and missionaries. By the time of the Rockefeller China conference it had long been the explicit aim of U.S. foreign policy to create an *American* empire abroad. Articulated by McKinley's secretary of state, John Hay, the Open Door Policy declared the U.S. commitment to build an economic empire. The great prize was China and her immense wealth, insufficiently exploited by the European powers, Japan, and even Rockefeller's Standard Oil Trust. President Woodrow Wilson declared his intention for the United States to "participate, and participate very generously, in the opening to the Chinese and to the use of the world the almost untouched and perhaps unrivaled resources of China."[22]

If American capitalism was to continue to grow, it needed, as Gates had noted in his memo on missionaries, raw materials for its factories and markets for its agricultural and manufactured products. For China or any other country to provide resources and markets required an increasing level of industrial and economic development. Such development required a foundation of social organization, education of at least its technical and managerial workers, and a culture appropriate to an industrial society.

The more advanced industrial and economic development of the North American and European nations was evidence of their general superiority over agricultural and semifeudal countries like China. Corporate, political, and philanthropic intervention were clothed in ideological justification—as Gates put it, "our improved methods of production and agriculture, manufacture and commerce, our better social and political institutions, our better literature, philosophy, science, art, refinement, morality and religion."[23] Harvard president Charles Eliot more diplomatically related the difference in economic development between China and the West to the prevalence of inductive thinking in the West:[24]

> Since the Oriental, except recently in Japan, has been a student
> of the abstract he has never practiced inductive philosophy to
> which the West owes its remarkable progress in the last 400
> years—the inductive method of ascertaining truth. In contrast
> the Oriental has proceeded by intuition and meditation and has
> accepted his philosophy and religion largely from authorities.

With self-interest indistinguishable from humanitarianism, missionaries, teachers, medical workers, philanthropists, Standard Oil salesmen, and government representatives all took abroad the fervent belief that they were bringing the "blessings of civilization" to China and other "backward" peoples.

Western Medicine: The Trojan Horse

The moment for "civilizing" intervention was at hand, but the "unconcealed determination of the Chinese people to slough off foreign domination in every form"[25] made such transparently interventionist institutions as foreign-controlled universities unacceptable to the increasingly nationalistic Chinese. Gates, Rockefeller, Jr., and their China advisors all concluded that medicine was the uniquely appropriate vehicle for their philanthropic intervention. Gates, the architect of nearly all the early Rockefeller philanthropies, had been interested in medicine for nearly two decades. It was he who initiated the idea for the Rockefeller Institute for Medical Research, founded in 1901, and the public health programs in the southern United States, begun in 1909 and extended worldwide in 1913. And it was Gates who hired Abraham Flexner in 1911 to organize medical education programs for the General Education Board, the first Rockefeller foundation.

For Gates and other leaders of American industrial capitalism, scientific medicine was more appealing than mystical and traditional healing systems. The precise analysis of the human body into its component parts and the analysis of the dynamic processes within and between each part is analogous to the industrial organization of production. From the perspective of an industrialist, scientific medicine seems to offer the limitless potential for effectiveness that science and technology provide in manufacturing and social organization. Just as industry depends upon science for technically powerful industrial tools, science-based medicine and its mechanistic concepts of the body and disease would yield powerful technical tools with which to identify, eliminate, and prevent agents of disease, and to correct malfunctions of the body.

As Gates described this perspective to the senior Rockefeller, each of the body's cells is a "small chemical laboratory, into which its own appropriate raw material is constantly being introduced, the process of chemical separation and combination are constantly taking place automatically, and its own appropriate finished product is constantly being thrown off, that finished product being necessary for the life and health of the body." The liver, stomach, and other organs are "great manufacturing centers, formed of groups of cells in infinite number, manufacturing the same sorts of products, just as industries of the same kind are often grouped in specific districts."[26] Because it carries industrial world views and culture with its acceptance, scientific medicine was a valuable vehicle for industrial philanthropy. "The gift of Western medicine and surgery," Charles Eliot argued, is "one of the most precious things that Western civilization can do for the East. . . .There is no better subject than medicine in which to teach the universal inductive method."[27]

Of equal importance with its ideological functions, scientific medicine would promote a healthier population—and thus a healthier work force. For Charles Eliot, the constant advisor on most early Rockefeller philanthropies, scientific medicine would not only teach inductive reasoning, it would also help prevent "industrial losses due to sickness and untimely death among men and domestic animals."[28] Such benefits were especially likely from public health work, as demonstrated by the Rockefeller Foundation's International Health Commission and its hookworm control programs. A 1918 report on the "Economic Value of the Treatment of Hookworm Infection" demonstrated that for 320 laborers on two plantations in Costa Rica who were cured of hookworm infection, productivity increased dramatically. One plantation increased its acreage under cultivation by nearly 50 percent without the need of additional workers because healthier laborers could work harder and longer.[29] Virtually every annual report and every memo concerning the public health programs described the extent of hookworm infection, the resulting estimated loss in labor productivity, and the increased productivity following treatment. Improved health would increase the "economic efficiency" of the Chinese people and allow the development of all China's agricultural and mineral riches.[30]

In addition to the material and ideological benefits that were expected from scientific medical programs, the Rockefeller philanthropists understood that of all forms of foreign intervention, medicine was irresistible to peoples the world over. Its dominating and culture-transforming qualities were invisible compared with education or religion. Gates considered health "the most intimate, the most precious, the superlative interest of every man that lives." The desire for health is a unifying force "whose values go to the palace of the rich and the hovel of the poor." Medicine is "a work which penetrates everywhere."[31]

In the Philippines, for example, the foundation outfitted a hospital ship to bring medical care and the "benefits of civilization" to rebellious Moro tribes. Foundation officers were delighted that such medical work made it "possible for the doctor and nurse to go in safety to many places which it has been extremely dangerous for the soldier to approach." Their medical work paved "the way for establishing industrial and regular schools." As foundation president George Vincent put it, "dispensaries and physicians have of late been peacefully penetrating areas of the Philippine Islands and demonstrating the fact that for purposes of placating primitive and suspicious peoples *medicine has some advantages over machine guns.*"[32]

In summary, medicine was attractive to the Rockefeller philanthropies for several reasons. Although religious and educational programs were visible forms of foreign domination, medicine was less obvious. While the Chinese were attacking missionaries and insisting on controlling their own universities, Gates and the others correctly predicted that a medical program would be welcomed with humble thanks. Furthermore, they believed that scientific medical knowledge and medical care based on scientific findings would increase the health of the population. Such an investment in "human capital" would pay for itself through increased productivity of the Chinese work force, meaning more and cheaper raw materials for American factories and a growing market for American exports. Finally, and uppermost in the minds of the Rockefeller planners developing medical education programs abroad, scientific medicine would inculcate industrial culture. It would train an important segment of China's managerial and professional stratum to think "inductively," to adopt the perspectives, values, and world views that dominated similar strata in the Western industrial nations. Scientific medicine would thus contribute to the industrial development of China under the guiding hand of the Western powers.

China Medical Board

Having made the difficult policy decision—that the major Rockefeller philanthropy in China would be in medical education—what followed were the practical tasks. Gates sat down and drafted a plan for "The Gradual and Orderly Development of a Comprehensive and Efficient System of Medicine in China,"[33] a document that remained the program's blueprint for its first decade or more.

A new survey team was sent to China to report back detailed information on existing medical schools and training facilities and to recommend a specific plan for the character of their program and its location. This first China Medical Commission included University of Chicago president Judson, Francis W. Peabody of the Harvard Medical School, and Roger S. Greene, the American consul-general at Hankow whose brother Jerome was a trustee of the Rockefeller Foundation and of Rockefeller's General Education Board. The commission recommended that foundation resources should be concentrated at first in Peking and that the missionary-controlled Union Medical College become the Rockefeller philanthropy there.[34]

The commission's recommendations were adopted by the foundation as the basis for its future program, and on November 30, 1914, the foundation trustees voted to create the China Medical Board (CMB) as a subsidiary of the foundation to conduct all Rockefeller medical aid programs in China. Rockefeller, Jr., was the first chairman, and, at Gates's suggestion, Wallace Buttrick, the executive officer of the General Education Board, was made the first director. Roger Greene was appointed the resident director of the CMB in China.[35]

Secular Philanthropy

In order to accomplish its goals the foundation felt it was necessary to dispense with the missionaries. Missionaries in China were under frequent attack as agents of foreign domination. Moreover, whether in education or medicine, missionary programs were too concerned with religion to be effective in creating the secular industrial culture that was paramount in the Rockefeller programs. "China needs modern science but the missionary schools avoid science as leading to scepticism," Gates concluded disdainfully. "China needs modern medicine but the hospitals and physicians of the missionaries are merely proselyting agencies."[36] The missionaries may have been useful once for opening up all lands to trade with the industrialized countries, but the task at hand required a subtlety quite beyond their abilities.

Early in 1915, CMB director Buttrick, like Gates a former Baptist minister, was sent to England to negotiate with the London Missionary Society, the most influential of the six missionary societies that controlled the Union Medical College in Peking. With an offer of £25,000–30,000 and a sham assurance that the medical school "would be continued on its present lines as a Christian Missionary College," Buttrick easily won their support.[37] The other societies followed suit, and the prize belonged to the CMB. A separate board of trustees was created for the new PUMC, with the six missionary societies each getting one seat and the CMB appointing a seven-member majority and controlling the important committees.

Launching the PUMC

In order to gather more information, make more detailed recommendations on the development of admissions requirements and a curriculum, win complete cooperation from missionaries in China, and, perhaps most important, "win for the enterprise the confidence and respect of the leading medical men, officials and citizens" in America as well as in China, a second and even more illustrious China Medical Commission was sent on its way. William H. Welch, who had already achieved an international reputation as a medical education reformer, and Simon Flexner, the director of the prestigious Rockefeller Institute for Medical Research, were the luminaries. Wallace Buttrick went to "prepare the ground" by wooing the missionaries.[38]

Finally, the long and difficult task began—building the magnificent buildings of the college under wartime conditions, hiring faculty and other staff, admitting students, and conducting the education program. Although Gates never expressed anything but enthusiasm for the goals of the China medical program, he grew "disgusted" with the excessive costs of the building program and with inefficiencies and differences with the "local administrative officers in China." He resigned from the CMB in 1917, four and a half years before the formal dedication.[39] When the dedication was finally held in the fall of 1921, the PUMC was the realization of the idea conceived by Gates and implemented by a host of Americans committed to Westernizing China, to making China a fuller participant in the industrial and commercial "civilization" dominated by the great capitalist powers.

The "Highest Standards": Health Needs or Westernization?

The PUMC was conceived and actually created "on the highest practicable standard"[40] of medical education, modeled closely on the prevailing highest standards in the United States. Although many more practitioners could have been trained if entrance requirements were somewhat lowered and the length of training—and thus the cost—reduced, foundation officers and trustees rejected suggestions that large numbers of medical workers be educated to meet China's health needs.

At the foundation's conference on China in January 1914, Abraham Flexner urged that "the scheme of medical instruction [be] conceived at a greatly lower level" to meet China's pressing need for doctors. Although this attitude was prevalent among many missionaries, it was a surprising suggestion coming from Flexner. (Flexner had authored the Carnegie Foundation's famous report that attacked the low standards of American medical schools, and was hired in 1911 to head the General Education Board's program to upgrade medical education in the United States.) "An immense amount of medical treatment can be practiced with a very limited knowledge—or perhaps no knowledge in a wide sense—of chemistry, physics or biology," Flexner argued; "it is not very essential to put much emphasis on these subjects."[41] Forcefully opposing this heresy, Harvard president Eliot reiterated his perspective that a strong foundation in the sciences was essential if medicine were to be a vehicle for teaching "inductive" thinking. Flexner quickly backed down, and the argument was settled.

This rejection of proposals to accept lower entrance requirements and shorter training periods in order to produce large numbers of health workers dominated the foundation's medical education assistance programs for the next half century. Later in 1914, however, the foundation's first China Medical Commission dispensed with such proposals in three sentences:[42]

> This policy is not justified by its fruits. It does not fill the need for trained physicians because it does not really train physicians.
> The graduates are useful as hospital assistants, but are not fitted for the responsibility of medical practitioners.

Consistent with the objective of training a small number of physicians to lead China into scientific medicine, the PUMC conducted its classes in English. This was perhaps the most controversial policy decision the foundation had to make. It was opposed by nationalistic Chinese and by many faculty in missionary medical schools, who made meeting "the present needs of China in the shortest possible time" their highest priority. But the foundation and its advisors, together with Western-oriented

Chinese physicians and a minority of missionary medical faculty, believed that the use of English, while further limiting the number of Chinese students who would participate in the program, would make the most advanced medical texts, journals, and Anglo-American faculty available to these future leaders of Chinese medicine.[43] The goal of creating a Western-oriented medical elite, committed to the primacy of modern science, clearly justified this policy.

The foundation extended this policy of opposition to training large numbers of lower-level health workers to their other medical education assistance programs. In the very year the "Green City" was dedicated in Peking, the Rockefeller Foundation initiated support for medical education in Thailand. The foundation opposed the Thai government's desire to train large numbers of medical workers. Dr. Richard Pearce, the foundation's director of medical education, insisted that the foundation would support "financially and otherwise" only a " 'Class A' school with proper entrance requirements. . .to supply a small number of well qualified medical practitioners who will act as leaders in important questions."[44] With few exceptions, this policy remained the foundation's major emphasis in medical programs throughout the world into the 1960s.

Opposition to this narrow perspective arose from time to time within the foundation as well as from recipient countries. Dr. John B. Grant, the son of Canadian missionaries in China who joined the PUMC faculty in 1921, created the first community health center in Peking for training medical and nursing students and later established a rural training center, both ventures as part of the PUMC.[45] But Grant and his like-minded colleagues in and out of the foundation were unable to shift its major policies. Nevertheless, half a century after the policy was inaugurated, the foundation's own official studies finally supported the widely accepted view that the policy was a mistake. As foundation staff member Dr. John Bryant wrote in 1969, "for a health care system to work effectively requires that auxiliaries make the first decisions on most health care problems and that professionals be used as supervisors and consultants and for leadership functions that only they can fill."[46] Underdeveloped countries need training programs for auxiliaries at least as much as medical schools that train physicians according to the standards of advanced industrial nations.

But the rationale for the foundation's determination to train only small cadres of physicians was not primarily to meet the health needs of the population. It was rather to create a system of medicine ideologically and culturally conducive to the development of China and other countries as participants in economic relations with the industrialized Western nations.

Nowhere was medicine's use in cultural imperialism more evident than in the foundation's attitude toward China's traditional doctors. Although CMB director Wallace Buttrick observed that "we have much to learn from China," it was only China that was to do the learning. "Even her old time physicians can do some cures which transcend the powers of modern medicine," Buttrick wrote his New York colleagues from China, "as witness the testimony of every western doctor whom we meet."[47] Yet the CMB ignored traditional medicine and its approximately 400,000 practitioners—despite the small numbers of Western-trained doctors to serve China's 400 million people. By 1937, twenty-two years after the Rockefeller Foundation took over the medical college from the missionaries, the PUMC had graduated only 166 physicians, a tiny numerical contribution indeed to solving China's overwhelming health problems.[48]

The CMB rejection of traditional doctors found support within the ruling Nationalist party. The Nationalists' emphasis on developing China by Westernizing it was implemented in the health field by the Ministry of Health's efforts to restrict traditional Chinese medicine and promote Western medicine. This policy was undermined, however, both by the general ineffectiveness of the Nationalist government and by elements within the Nationalist party who supported traditional Chinese medicine as "an important part of Chinese culture."[49]

Recognition of any usefulness of Chinese traditional medicine had to await liberation in 1949. Chairman Mao Tse-tung and other leaders of the Communist party promoted traditional medicine because its half-million practitioners were needed to provide care to the people, because in many rural areas they were the only medical workers, and because the people, especially the peasants, believed in traditional medicine. But beyond these pragmatic reasons, Mao and the Communist party, while committed to modernizing and industrializing China, valued the political and economic independence that cultural autonomy helped nourish. Ending China's submission to and dependence on the West required independence from foreign capital, the development of its own road to socialism, and—in medicine—building on what is valuable in China's own healing traditions. "Chinese medicine and pharmacology are a great treasure-house," Mao proclaimed; "efforts should be made to explore them and raise them to a higher level."[50]

Chinese traditional doctors were given increased official status, and a modicum of integration of traditional and Western medicine was attempted. From liberation to 1966, China trained approximately 75,000 doctors of traditional medicine and about 100,000 doctors of Western medicine. In addition some 230 technical schools were established to train assistant doctors, nurses, midwives, and pharmacists. Finally, rural "barefoot doctors" and their urban equivalents were trained in large numbers since the beginning of the Cultural Revolution in 1965 to provide a veritable army of front-line medical workers to meet China's still pressing health needs.[51]

These innovations could not be accomplished so long as the guiding spirit of medical development was the creation of an elite profession dedicated to integrating China into Western industrial capitalism—the objective of the Rockefeller philanthropy leaders, the missionary societies, and the leadership of China's Nationalist party.

Discussion

From the establishment of the China Medical Board and its Peking Union Medical College in the 1910s up to the 1960s, the primary emphasis of the Rockefeller Foundation and other international medical education aid programs has been the development of high-technology medical care provided by physicians trained according to the "highest standards." Since the early 1960s the foundation, government, and international agency aid programs have encouraged the development of training programs for auxiliaries and more accessible care in rural areas, but the legacy of half a century is still reflected in the current training programs and patterns of health services in most underdeveloped countries.

The specific results have varied among countries depending on the particular political, economic, cultural, and historical contexts of each country. Yet there is a consistency among their results: small, urban, hospital-based medical care for the middle and upper classes; little or no modern medical care for the rural population or the urban poor; and woefully underdeveloped public health systems.[52]

Although the Rockefeller programs brought advanced scientific medicine to underdeveloped countries, they obviously provided very poorly for the health needs of the majority populations. In China, Thailand, and other countries there were numerous critics who argued that their countries needed large numbers of health workers distributed where the people live and work, not small numbers of highly trained, hospital-based physicians who were loathe to venture into the populated but poor countryside. It was certainly *not* the goal of the Rockefeller Foundation to create inaccessible medical care systems. The foundation leaders genuinely believed that their policies *would* serve China's health needs. But as the record of the creation of Peking Union Medical College demonstrates, improving the health of the Chinese people was a secondary goal. While Gates, Eliot, and the Rockefellers believed their programs would meet this goal, their judgments were strongly influenced by their primary goal. *The PUMC was chiefly a vehicle to lead China to modernization, to develop a culture and economy that would make her more useful to Western nations.*

The Rockefeller public health programs, which focused on reducing major epidemic and debilitating diseases, were aimed directly at improving the health of each country's work force. Foundation programs to reduce hookworm disease, yellow fever, and malaria in dozens of countries throughout the world brought medical treatment and sanitation campaigns to plantations, mines, and factories in each country.[53] Medical education programs, however, were more concerned with transforming cultures, although they too aimed ultimately at improving the health and "economic efficiency" of the laboring populations. Clearly guided by "trickle down" theories of cultural innovation, the foundation transplanted medical education programs to train elite medical professionals who would spread scientific medicine and "Western civilization" throughout their societies. They were thus willing to sacrifice China's health needs to this larger goal, fully believing that it was in China's and other countries' interests.

I am not suggesting that either the Rockefeller philanthropists or the missionaries lacked humanitarian feeling. Rather, their humanitarianism was shaped by their ethnocentrism, their class interests, and their support for the imperialist objectives of their own country. By the time their humanitarianism was expressed in programs, it was so intertwined with the interests of American capitalism as to be indistinguishable. In 1920, for example, Roger Greene, the PUMC resident director in China, urged foundation officers in New York to get U.S. bankers to offer a major loan to the Chinese government for famine relief. Undoubtedly motivated by sympathy for the widespread starvation in China, Greene also saw this as an opportunity to expand American intervention. "I believe," he wrote,[54]

> that the Chinese government would for this special purpose
> accept a very large degree of foreign control of expenditure. The
> practical experience gained under the operation of such a loan
> might be of enormous value in creating a better understanding
> between the bankers and the Chinese government. . . .

Thus the medical philanthropies wrapped imperialism in cloaks of humanitarianism.

The Rockefeller programs were the result not of dark conspiracies, but of simple recognition and articulation of the Rockefellers' and Gates's class interests. The Rockefellers, the very symbol of American corporate capitalism at the turn of the century, and Gates, a director or chairman of more than a dozen Rockefeller-controlled corporations and building a small fortune of his own, understood that advanced captialism needs free access to foreign markets, secure sources of raw materials, and opportunities for profitable investment of "surplus" capital. There is some evidence, according to the writer of the foundation's own historical record, that the philanthropic interest in China and other countries "may have grown out of the activities and responsibilities of the Standard Oil companies in different parts of the world."[55] Standard Oil representatives in Shanghai, Tientsin, Canton, and Hong Kong did assist China Medical Board representatives in their work.[56] However, Gates and the Rockefellers, whose financial investments spanned numerous industries and the entire globe, had much broader concerns than simply those of Standard Oil. They fully understood the unity of their personal fortunes with the longevity of capitalist society, and through their philanthropy and their political influence they articulated policies and programs for the larger corporate class and the very survival of capitalism.[57] China was a fertile garden for much of the American economy, and the Rockefeller Foundation proposed to cultivate it.

Ideological justifications enabled Gates, the Rockefellers, and other members of America's growing corporate class to view both medical education programs in recipient countries and corporate profits derived from these countries as beneficent transplantings of Western civilization. As we have seen, Gates and the Rockefellers understood and intended to make the Rockefeller Foundation health programs foster cultural, economic, and political dependence by recipient countries. Once these programs were launched by the foundation's top officers, however, the internal logic and historical conditions assured that the imperialistic ends would be served even if mid-level officers and professional personnel did not consciously promote imperialism through their programs.

First, the programs had a logic and momentum of their own. Acceptance of European and American medical theories and practices implied submission to the authority and technological superiority of these foreign cultures. As Frantz Fanon pointed out, colonized peoples also viewed Western medicine as inseparable from colonization.[58] In the social psychology of imperialism, to submit to the Rockefeller health programs was to submit to Rockefeller and American cultural, political, and—underlying it all—economic domination.

Second, historical reality coincided with these subjective perceptions of the Rockefeller philanthropists and the colonized. Then, as now, development capital was overwhelmingly possessed and tightly controlled by the advanced capitalist nations, eager to export their capital for the higher rates of return usually available in underdeveloped countries. In urging Rockefeller to buy into the Chase National Bank, Gates called his employer's attention to the international trust that had emerged among "the great financial houses of the world." "The liquid money of the world is like an ocean that laves all shores," Gates observed. "Today as never before, and increasingly, capital flows to any country, city or state in the world where capital is needed and which offers large returns."[59]

Medical schools as well as industrialization required outside capital, and the few countries able to export capital were in a position to "help."

Those who provided capital for medical education were able to dictate how their money was spent. The great foundations' wealth came from the giant financial and industrial corporations associated with the rise of imperialism. Their trustees and officers, by their material interests and ideological commitments, are part of the corporate class. Guided by their class and national interests, Gates and the Rockefellers applied their philanthropic funds where they felt they would reap "large returns." No conspiracy was needed to assure that these ostensibly humanitarian programs served the needs of imperialism.

Third, the Rockefeller and other medical education programs transplanted from industrialized to underdeveloped countries helped create politically conservative professional strata. Together with other groups in the indigenous upper classes, medical professions tend to oppose fundamental changes in their country's political, economic, and social systems. Wanting to retain their elite status, physicians in underdeveloped societies have seldom opposed their country's economic and political dependence on powerful creditor and capital-owning nations. Salvador Allende, Che Guevara, and the few prerevolution PUMC graduates who may have joined China's revolutionary struggle were indeed the exceptions.

The American and European health professionals who worked in these programs did not own or control the corporations that profited from foreign trade and investments, but they did share the material advantages that accrue to the "mother country." And they certainly shared the racist and ethnocentric ideologies that justify imperialism. William H. Welch, the dean of American medical education and a constant advisor to the many Rockefeller medical philanthropies, praised the facilitating role of medical science in European and American "efforts to colonize and to reclaim for civilization [sic] vast tropical regions."[60] Just as missionaries saw themselves promoting Christian civilization in their work, so too did health professionals join foundation programs to bring the "benefits of civilization" to "backward" peoples through their medical work.

Thus the development of an elite medical profession coincided with other Western goals of cultural, political, and economic domination of China. In that respect, medical "modernization" helped to perpetuate underdevelopment of the population's health and of the national economy in China and other dependent countries.

Conclusion

Medical education is inherently political. It helps shape a nation's culture, substantially determines its health resources, and, especially in underdeveloped countries, consumes a not insignificant portion of national income. Underdeveloped countries need modern medical science—developed to meet their needs for basic medical care, sanitation programs, and public health measures for all their people.[61] *The Rockefeller medical education programs*, guided in their conception and development by imperialist objectives, *were more concerned with building an elite professional stratum to carry out cultural and technological transformation than with meeting the health needs of each country.*

China's health care system today differs dramatically from those of other countries aided by the Rockefeller Foundation, despite the common influence of the Rockefeller policies. Of course many factors contribute to those differences, but among them some appear fundamental. China replaced foreign economic and political domination with self-determination. Economic exploitation and political ineffectiveness by China's own ruling class have been replaced by substantial economic equality of the population and effective leadership. These social changes have themselves contributed to improving the health status of the population,[62] and their principles have been applied to medical care. The denigration of Chinese traditional medicine has been officially abandoned and many of its techniques incorporated into scientific medicine, large numbers of doctors and auxiliaries have been trained, medical care has been distributed throughout the country, and public health programs have been very well developed.[63] It remains to be seen how well these advances will survive the political, economic and social redirection of China since Mao's death.

While such thorough-going reforms in medicine were, and probably must be, tied to broader social change, medical education may be a force for progressive change rather than an instrument of foreign domination and continued underdevelopment. If programs to educate health workers are to serve the health needs of underdeveloped countries, the people of those countries must not let the interests of foreign nations or the interests of their own medical professionals determine the purpose and character of their programs. Those who plan, develop, and teach in the fields of public health and medicine must consciously examine both the material interests that shape their programs and the social, political, and economic consequences of medical policies and practices. They must ensure that medical programs contribute to, and do not detract from, the goals of improving the health of the people.

Notes

1. *Dedication Ceremonies and Medical Conference, Peking Union Medical College, September 15–22, 1921* (Peking: PUMC, 1922), pp. 63–64.
2. John Bryant, *Health and the Developing World* (Ithaca, N.Y.: Cornell University Press, 1969) p. 315.

3. Willoughby Lathem, "Introduction," in W. Lathem and A. Newberry (eds.), *Community Medicine: Teaching, Research, and Health Care* (New York: Appleton-Century-Crofts, 1970), p. 2.

4. Vicente Navarro, *Medicine under Capitalism* (New York: Prodist, 1976), pp. 3–32.

5. Oscar Gish, *Doctor Migration and World Health* (London: G. Bell and Sons, 1971); and Gish, "Medical Brain Drain Revisited," *International Journal of Health Services* 6 (1976): 231–237.

6. Milton Silverman, *The Drugging of the Americas* (Berkeley: University of California Press, 1976); and Michael Bader, "The International Transfer of Medical Technology—An Analysis and a Proposal for Effective Monitoring," *International Journal of Health Services* 7 (1977): 443–458.

7. Terence Johnson, "Imperialism and the Professions," in P. Halmos (ed.), *Professionalisation and Social Change*, Sociological Review Monograph 20 (Keele, England: University of Keele, 1973), pp. 281–309.

8. Michael Goldstein and Peter Donaldson, "Exporting Professionalism: A Case Study of Medical Education," *Journal of Health and Social Behavior*, 20 (1979): 322–337. For the major development of this perspective on professions, see Eliot Freidson, *Profession of Medicine* (New York: Dodd, Mead, and Co., 1970).

9. See Andre Gunder Frank, *Lumpenbourgeoisie: Lumpendevelopment—Dependence, Class, and Politics in Latin America* (New York: Monthly Review Press, 1973).

10. See, for example, Milton I. Roemer, "Medical Care and Social Class in Latin America," *Milbank Memorial Fund Quarterly* 42 (July 1964): 54–64; and Roemer, "Organizational Issues Relating to Medical Priorities in Latin America," *Social Science and Medicine* 9 (1975): 93–96.

11. See, for example, the Chilean medical profession's opposition to President Salvador Allende and his Popular Unity government, as described in Howard Waitzkin and Hilary Modell, "Medicine, Socialism and Totalitarianism: Lessons from Chile," *New England Journal of Medicine* 291 (1974): 171–177; and Roberto Belmar and Victor W. Sidel, "An International Perspective on Strikes and Strike Threats by Physicians: The Case of Chile," *International Journal of Health Services* 5 (1975): 53–64.

12. Industrial Council for Tropical Health and Harvard School of Public Health, *Industry and Tropical Health, II*. Proceedings of the Second Conference, New York and Boston, April 20–22, 1954, p. 40.

13. Quoted in Introduction to *Tropical Health—A Report on a Study of Needs and Resources*, Publication no. 996 (Washington, D.C.: National Academy of Sciences–National Research Council, 1962).

14. See, for example, E. Richard Brown, "Public Health in Imperialism: Early Rockefeller Programs at Home and Abroad," *American Journal of Public Health* 66 (1976): 897–903.

15. F. T. Gates to J. D. Rockefeller, January 31, 1905, Letterbook No. 350, Record Group 1, Rockefeller Family Archives.

16. Ibid.

17. J. A. Hobson, *Imperialism* (London: George Allen and Unwin, 1938; first published, 1902).

18. John Z. Bowers, *Western Medicine in a Chinese Palace, Peking Union Medical College, 1917–1951* (New York: Josiah Macy, Jr., Foundation, 1972), pp. 30–31; Mary E. Ferguson, *China Medical Board and Peking Union Medical College* (New York: China Medical Board, 1970), pp. 13–14; and F. T. Gates, "China Medical Board," about 1917, memo in China Medical Board files, Rockefeller Foundation Archives.

19. "China Conference of the Rockefeller Foundation, January 19 and 20, 1914," China Medical Board files, Rockefeller Foundation Archives.

20. Ibid.

21. Ibid.

22. William Appleman Williams, *Contours of American History* (Cleveland: World Publishing Co., 1961), pp. 420, 368–369, 416–420.

23. F. T. Gates to J. D. Rockefeller, February 2, 1905, Letterbook No. 350, Record Group 1, Rockefeller Family Archives.

24. Charles W. Eliot, *Some Roads toward Peace* (New York: Carnegie Endowment for International Peace, 1912), p.1.

25. T. C. Chamberlin to F. T. Gates, January 22, 1914, Record Group 2, Rockefeller Family Archives.

26. F. T. Gates, "Notes on Homeopathy, No. 3," written as a memo to Rockefeller, Sr., and circulated approvingly within the Rockefeller philanthropies about 1911, Gates collection, Rockefeller Foundation Archives.

27. Eliot, *Roads toward Peace*, p.26.

28. Charles W. Eliot, "The Qualities of the Scientific Investigator," in *Addresses Delivered at the Opening of the Laboratories in New York City, May 11, 1906* (New York: Rockefeller Institute for Medical Research, 1906), p. 49.

29. G. C. Cox, "Economic Value of the Treatment of Hookworm Infection in Costa Rica," 1918, International Health Commission files, Rockefeller Foundation Archives.

30. China Medical Commission, *Medicine in China* (New York: Rockefeller Foundation, 1914), pp. 1–2.

31. F. T. Gates, "Address on the Tenth Anniversary of the Rockefeller Institute," 1911, Gates collection, Rockefeller Foundation Archives.

32. George E. Vincent, *The Rockefeller Foundation—A Review of Its War Work, Public Health Activities, and Medical Education Projects in 1917* (New York: Rockefeller Foundation, 1918); and "Hospital Ship for Sulu Archipelago," *Rockefeller Foundation* 1 (1916): 13–14 (emphasis added).

33. Published in *Rockefeller Foundation Annual Report, 1913–1914* (New York: Rockefeller Foundation, 1915), pp. 208–213.

34. China Medical Commission, *Medicine in China*.

35. CMB members included Rockefeller, Jr., Gates, Judson, Peabody, Starr J. Murphy (Rockefeller's business and philanthropy legal counsel), William H. Welch (dean of the Johns Hopkins medical school and a close adviser on all Rockefeller medical programs), Wickliffe Rose (director of the Rockefeller Foundation's International Health Commission), Simon

Flexner (director of the Rockefeller Institute for Medical Research), and Frank J. Goodnow (president of John Hopkins). *Rockefeller Foundation Annual Report, 1913–1914*, pp. 31–33, 163.

36. Gates, "China Medical Board."
37. Bowers, *Western Medicine*, pp. 41–43.
38. Ibid., pp. 47–61.
39. Gates, "China Medical Board."
40. China Medical Commission, *Medicine in China*, p. 91.
41. Quoted in Bowers, *Western Medicine*, p. 35.
42. China Medical Commission, *Medicine in China*, p. 81.
43. Ibid., pp. 81–85.
44. Goldstein and Donaldson, "Exporting Professionalism."
45. John Z. Bowers, "The Founding of Peking Union Medical College: Policies and Personalities (Concluded)," *Bulletin of the History of Medicine* 45 (1971), pp. 409–429.
46. Bryant, *Health and the Developing World*, pp. xi–xiii.
47. W. Buttrick to Rockefeller Foundation offices, October 28, 1915, China Medical Board files, Rockefeller Foundation Archives.
48. Ralph Croizier, "Medicine and Modernization in China: An Historical Overview," in A. Kleinman et al. (eds.), *Medicine in Chinese Cultures* (Washington D.C.: Fogarty International Center for Advanced Study in the Health Sciences, 1975), p. 24; and Victor W. Sidel and Ruth Sidel, *Serve the People* (Boston: Beacon Press, 1973), pp. 19–20.
49. Ralph Croizier, *Traditional Medicine in Modern China* (Cambridge, Mass.: Harvard University Press, 1968).
50. Quoted in Sidel and Sidel, *Serve the People* p. 157.
51. Ibid., pp. 153–172.
52. See Bryant, *Health in the Developing World*; Navarro, *Medicine under Capitalism*, pp. 3–32; Lathem and Newberry, *Community Medicine*; and Goldstein and Donaldson, "Exporting Professionalism."
53. Brown, "Public Health in Imperialism."
54. R. S. Greene to J. D. Greene, November 5, 1920, China Medical Board files, Rockefeller Foundation Archives.
55. Catherine Lewerth, "Source Book for a History of the Rockefeller Foundation," vol. 5, p. 1247, n.d., Rockefeller Foundation Archives.
56. J. D. Rockefeller, Jr., to R. S. Greene, June 8, 1915, China Medical Board files, Rockefeller Foundation Archives.
57. See Peter Collier and David Horowitz, *The Rockefellers—An American Dynasty* (New York: Holt, Rinehart, and Winston, 1976); and E. Richard Brown, *Rockefeller Medicine Men: Medicine and Capitalism in America* (Berkeley; University of California Press, 1979).
58. Frantz Fanon, "Medicine and Colonialism," in Fanon, *A Dying Colonialism* (New York: Grove Press, 1967), pp. 121–145.
59. F. T. Gates to J. D. Rockefeller, June 12, 1916, Record Group 2, Rockefeller Family Archives.
60. William H. Welch, "The Benefits of the Endowment of Medical Research," in

Addresses Delivered at the Opening of the Laboratories in New York City, May 11, 1906 (New York: Rockefeller Institute for Medical Research, 1906).

61. For the outlines of a model program and the costs of different alternatives, see Brian Abel-Smith and Alcira Leiserson, *Poverty, Development, and Health Policy*, Public Health Papers no. 69 (Geneva: World Health Organization, 1978).

62. See, for example, Bernard D. Challenor, "Health and Economic Development: The Example of China and Cuba," *Medical Care* 13 (1975): 79–84.

63. See Sidel and Sidel, *Serve the People*; and J. R. Quinn (ed.), *Medicine and Public Health in the People's Republic of China* (Washington D.C.: Fogarty International Center for Advanced Study in the Health Sciences, 1973).

James D. Anderson

Philanthropic Control over Private Black Higher Education*

This essay delineates the conflicting sets of values and interests that motivated northern mission societies and industrial philanthropic foundations to contribute millions of dollars and tremendous effort for the development of black higher education. It concentrates primarily on the ideology, power, educational policy, and methods of industrial philanthropy from 1915 to 1940, and the impact of such philanthropy upon the scope and thrust of black higher education during the post–World War I period and into the present. Inescapably, however, these concerns lead us back into the late nineteenth and early twentieth centuries when missionary and industrial philanthropists debated the role of higher education in the overall scheme of black education, and the relationship of educational socialization to larger issues of political and economic life. At the core of philanthropic interest in black education lay the central goal of preparing Afro-Americans for participation in the political economy of the New South. Each group, therefore, took as its point of departure a particular view of the "Negro's place" in the southern social order and shaped its educational policy and practices around that vision. Generally, missionary and industrial philanthropists were in sharp disagreement with one another over the ends and means of black education. Most visible were their divergent versions of the value of Afro-American higher education.

The Private Black College

The history of black higher education from the Reconstruction era to World War II is essentially a study of the origin and evolution of the

*An earlier version of this chapter was presented at the Conference on the Power Structure in American Education, sponsored by the Liberty Fund and the Center for Independent Education and the Institute for Human Studies, the University of San Francisco, November 1978.

private black college system. During this period the federal government gave scant aid to land-grant colleges, and the states followed a similar pattern in supporting black normal schools and liberal arts colleges. Between 1870 and 1890, nine black land-grant colleges were established and this number increased to sixteen by 1915. In that year there were also eleven black state normal schools or colleges. But nearly all of the black college students were enrolled in the private schools. This situation, albeit significantly improved, persisted into the 1930s. Arthur J. Klein's 1928 survey of black higher education demonstrated that the black private colleges were virtually the sole promoters of higher education for Afro-American students. In the academic year 1926–1927, there were 13,860 black college students in the United States and approximately 75 percent of them were enrolled in private black colleges. Not until after 1938, when the U.S. Supreme Court (in *Gaines* v. *Canada*) ordered the provision of "substantially equal facilities" within the states, did black state and land-grant colleges begin to compete with the private institutions of higher learning. Until this time, and for sometime thereafter, private philanthropy largely determined the shape and even survival of Afro-American higher education.[1]

From the Reconstruction era to World War II, northern mission societies (missionary philanthropy) and educational foundations (industrial philanthropy) represented the power structure in black higher education. To be sure, black church organizations led the movement to establish and maintain institutions of higher learning in the black community, but their sphere of control was very limited. By 1930, for example, only 14 percent of the black college students were enrolled in the colleges controlled by black church organizations, compared to the 61 percent that were enrolled in institutions controlled or identified with missionary and industrial philanthropy. Missionary philanthropy—the American Missionary Association, Methodist Episcopal Freedmen's Aid Society, Presbyterian Board of Missions for the Freedmen, and the American Baptist Home Mission Society—made the most important contributions to black higher education from the 1860s to 1915. By 1915, these mission societies had established over thirty colleges which enrolled the majority of Afro-American college and professional students. More importantly, the colleges founded and supported by Northern mission societies were and remain among the leading black institutions of higher learning. Talladega College in Alabama; Atlanta University, Clark University, Spelman and Morehouse Colleges in Georgia; Jackson, Rust, and Tougaloo Colleges in Mississippi; Bennett College and Johnson C. Smith University in North Carolina; Benedict College and Claflin University in South Carolina; LeMoyne College and Fisk University in Tennessee; Bishop and Wiley Colleges in Texas; and Virginia Union University were among the prominent black colleges founded and supported by mission societies. The educational foundations established exclusively to support black education were the John F. Slater Fund, the Julius Rosenwald Fund, and the Anna T. Jeanes Foundation. Other philanthropic foundations that gave considerable support to black education were the Peabody Education Fund, the General Education Board, the Phelps-Stokes Fund, the Carnegie Corporation and the Laura Spelman Rockefeller Memorial Fund. The industrial philanthropic foundations, established between 1867 and 1917, did not own or govern any black institutions of higher learning. In contrast to the mission societies, whose power originated mainly from their ownership of institutions, industrial philanthropic foundations derived their influence from their ability to provide resources that were absolutely essential to the survival and development of private black colleges. In the post–World War I era, as faculty salaries, retirement benefits, scientific equipment, laboratories, substantial endowments, libraries, and other material resources became necessary for colleges to be recognized as accredited institutions, black colleges became increasingly dependent on industrial philanthropy. Consequently, missionary philanthropy was soon replaced by industrial philanthropy as the dominant force in Afro-American higher education.[2]

Missionary Philanthropy

The missionary philanthropists, basically equalitarian in their views of civil rights and race relations, launched their campaign for black higher education as a means to produce a college-bred black leadership that would lead the black masses in their struggle for equal rights. Certainly, as has been pointed out, individual missionaries varied greatly in their sociopolitical and racial creeds. The dominant liberal leadership, however, held the mission societies to a belief in human equality, a concern for civil and social justice, and a faith in moral and cultural improvement through classical-liberal education. Hence, missionary ideology supported the struggle for black civil and political equality within the existing economic order. This ideology was shaped largely by such liberal missionary leaders as Thomas J. Morgan, Henry L. Morehouse, and Malcolm MacVicar of the American Baptist Home Mission Society and Joseph E. Roy and William Hayes Ward of the American Missionary Association. Morgan, a colonel of the Fourteenth United States Colored Infantry during the Civil War and former commissioner of Indian Affairs, served as executive secretary of the Baptist Home Mission Society from 1893 to 1902 and as editor of the society's influential *Home Mission Monthly* for the same period. Morehouse was the executive secretary of the American Baptist

Education Society. MacVicar, superintendent of the Home Mission Society's Educational Department from 1890 to 1900, headed the society's Virginia Union University from 1900 to 1904. Ward, one of the most vigorous defenders of black higher education, was for many years chairman of the American Missionary Association's executive committee. He was associate editor (1868–1870), superintending editor (1870–1896), and editor (from 1896 to 1913) of the *New York Independent*. His colleague, Roy, was field superintendent of the American Missionary Association. The status of these men in missionary activities and in the larger society enabled them to form a powerful vanguard that stood clearly and unswervingly for black higher education.[3]

These missionary leaders rallied their colleagues to support classical-liberal education for black Americans as a means to achieve racial equality in civil and political life. They assumed that the newly emancipated blacks would move into mainstream national culture, largely free to do and become what they chose, limited only by their own intrinsic worth and effort. It was supposed axiomatically, in other words, that the ex-slaves would be active participants in the republic on an equal footing with all other citizens. Education, then, according to the more liberal and dominant segments of missionary philanthropists, was intended to prepare a college-bred black leadership to uplift the black masses from the legacy of slavery and the restraints of the postbellum caste system. Thus the missionary philanthropists valued the higher education of black leaders over all other forms of educational work. "Neglect, if you will, the common school education in your missionary labor; neglect if you must, the industrial education," advised William Hayes Ward, "but never forget that it is your work to educate leaders." To Ward and other missionary philanthropists, black leadership training meant, above all, higher classical-liberal education. This view reflected, on the one hand, their paternalistic tendencies to make unilateral decisions regarding the educational needs of blacks. On the other hand, such enthusiastic support for black higher education expressed (making due allowance for exceptions) the missionaries' principled liberalism, virtually innocent of any inclination to doubt the intellectual potential of black Americans. As the Freedmen's Aid Society put it,

> this society (in connection with similar organizations) has demonstrated to the South that the freedmen possess good intellectual abilities and are capable of becoming good scholars. Recognizing the brotherhood of mankind and knowing that intellect does not depend upon the color of the skin nor the curl of the hair, we never doubted the Negro's ability to acquire knowledge, and distinguish himself by scholarly attainments.

Likewise, Henry L. Morehouse, speaking for his fellow missionaries in the American Baptist Home Mission Society, recognized "the thorough humanity of the black man, with devine endowment of all the facilities of the white man; capable of culture, capable of high attainments under proper conditions and with sufficient time; a being not predestined to be simply a hewer of wood and drawer of water for the white race." Convinced that the black race would progress largely through the wise leadership of a college-bred vanguard, Morehouse placed top priority on the higher education of the Afro-American "talented tenth." Thomas J. Morgan, a leading and most highly respected missionary, insisted that black Americans' social advancement depended upon the leadership of "noble and powerful minds raised up from their own ranks." It was the mission societies' duty, philosophized another philanthropist, "to educate. . .a number of blacks and send them forth to regenerate their own people." Malcolm MacVicar reasoned that black leaders could be educated for their task because their mental development followed "precisely the same laws in the case of the white man."[4]

To be sure, missionary philanthropists were not proposing revolutionary changes throughout the southern social order. Equality was carefully defined as political equality and equality before the law. They supported inequality in the economic structure, generally shied away from questions of social equality, and were probably convinced that blacks were culturally and religiously inferior to middle-class whites. Their liberalism on civil and political questions was matched by their conservatism on cultural, gious, and economic matters. Missionary philanthropists held that slavery had generated pathological religious and cultural practices in the black community. Slavery kept blacks from acquiring the important moral and social values (i.e., thrift, industry, frugality, sobriety) necessary to live a sustained Christian life, and prevented the development of a stable family life among Afro-Americans. Therefore, missionaries argued, it was essential for education to introduce the ex-slaves to the arts and morals of civilized life. Without education, they concluded, blacks would rapidly degenerate and become a national menace to American civilization. In vital respects, such views are easily identified with the more conservative retrogressionist ideologies of the late nineteenth century. Generally, retrogressionist arguments, as historians George Fredrickson and Herbert Gutman have shown, supported the advocacy of various forms of external control over blacks, including disfranchisement and increasingly rigorous legal segregation.[5]

But for the equalitarian missionaries, black cultural and religious conditions merely represented the debasing effects of slavery and had nothing to do with racial characteristics. They saw no reasons not to extend equal civil and political rights to black Americans. Moreover, since blacks possessed the same mental capacity as whites, only education was required to lift the ex-slaves to the same cultural and moral level as whites. In the words of the Freedmen's Aid Society,

> Let us atone for our sins, as much as possible, by furnishing schools and the means of improvement for the children, upon whose parents we have inflicted such fearful evils. Let us lend a helping hand in their escape from the degradation into which we have forced them by our complicity with oppressors. Justice, stern justice, demands this at our hands. Let us pay the debt we owe this race before we complain of weariness in the trifling sums we have given for schools and churches.

Consequently, the missionary philanthropists conducted a continual criticism of the political disfranchisement, legal segregation, mob violence, and poor educational opportunities which characterized black life in the American South. From this perspective, they supported the training of a black college-bred leadership to protect the masses from "wicked and designing men." The mission societies started their educational crusade by concentrating upon schools for rudimentary training, but by the late 1860s they had shifted their emphasis to the establishment and maintenance of higher educational institutions. From the outset, the missionaries named these institutions "colleges" and "universities," although most of their students were scarcely literate. However, these titles, as Horace Mann Bond has stated, "tell us that the founders took emancipation seriously, believing that the Civil War had settled, indeed, the issue of human inequality in the nation; they also tell us that the founders were applying, to the newly freed population, the ancient faith in the efficacy of higher education to elevate a people." Their efforts to establish a system of black higher education were enhanced greatly in 1888. At that time, the American Missionary Association was named custodian of a $2 million grant from the Daniel Hand Educational Fund for Colored People. By 1915 missionary philanthropists had established over 100 colleges and secondary schools for blacks, and these institutions enrolled the vast majority of black secondary, college, and professional students. Their efforts came at a critical time when public secondary schools for southern blacks were almost nonexistent, and there was virtually no public support for black higher education. Indeed, when most white Americans doubted blacks' ability to absorb even a common school education, missionary philanthropists offered the New England college curriculum as the key to Afro-American social progress. As historian Rayford W. Logan wrote, missionary philanthropists "assumed that the children of the freedmen were capable of grasping the 'glory that was Greece and the grandeur that was Rome,' that they could master Greek and Latin, comprehend Corneille, Shakespeare, Locke, Descartes. . . ." Euro-American chauvinism notwithstanding, such views were unusually liberal for nineteenth-century white America. The missionaries represented the most liberal vision of black participation in American society and showed the highest respects for Afro-American intelligence. This placed them on the fringes of northern white society and in direct confrontation with southern white society. Much of the opposition and criticism which missionaries encountered must be taken as conservative reactions to their liberal stance on equal rights and black higher education.[6]

Industrial Philanthropy

The growth of missionary philanthropy was paralleled by the gradual ascendancy of industrial philanthropy which had been struggling to become a powerful force in southern black education since the establishment of the Peabody Educational Fund in 1867 and the John F. Slater Fund in 1881. Not until the early twentieth century, however, did industrial philanthropy emerge as a contending force in southern black education. During the first two decades of the twentieth century northeastern capitalists and southern white school officials formed a powerful new force in the struggle to determine the scope and purpose of southern black education. This alliance was ratified by the creation of two major educational organizations, the Southern Education Board in 1901 and the General Education Board in 1902. The Southern Education Board, intersectional in membership and financed largely by northern industrial philanthropists, was a propaganda organization that concentrated primarily on arousing southern whites to control the development of the region's educational system. The General Education Board, established in 1902 by John D. Rockefeller, served as a clearinghouse for industrial philanthropy and disbursed grants to educational institutions and state departments of education. The membership of both boards was almost the same and, in 1914, the General Education Board absorbed the Southern Education Board. The General Education Board became a powerful philanthropic trust as Rockefeller supplemented his initial grant of $1 million by others amounting to $53 million by 1909. By 1921 Rockefeller had personally donated over $129 million to the board. Moreover, the board became an interlocking directorate of northern industrial philanthropy as its members directed the disbursements of old and new foundations. The Peabody and Slater Funds and the Anna T. Jeanes Foundation (1907) were under the direct control of the board. The board gained the cooperation of the Phelps-Stokes Fund, the Julius Rosenwald Fund, the Carnegie Corporation, and the Laura Spelman

Rockefeller Memorial Fund, all established between 1902 and 1917. As historian Louis Harlan aptly stated, the General Education Board acquired "virtual monopolistic control of educational philanthropy for the South and the Negro." The role of industrial philanthropy in shaping black education, then, is largely a story of the General Education Board, its trustees, agents, and cooperating foundations.[7]

The industrial philanthropists were more concerned with black education as a means to economic efficiency and political stability than with equal rights for southern blacks. They approached southern reconstruction from the point of view of active businessmen who were at ease with the region's racial hierarchy and who sought to increase the South's economic output while correcting some of its social shortcomings. Industrial philanthropists tended to think and act according to what was good to stabilize southern society, organize its industrial market, restore its agricultural prosperity, and achieve racial cooperation on southern white terms. In one sense, they were similar to other twentieth-century urban reformers who demanded an organized and efficient agricultural economy to supplement the emergent industrial nation. Their specific concern for southern agricultural prosperity, however, was inextricably bound to black farm workers, especially in a period of declining rural population and rapid urban growth. To the industrial philanthropists, the black farm worker was the last best hope to stimulate material prosperity in the South's agricultural economy. Thus New York philanthropist Robert C. Ogden, who served as president of the Southern Education Board (1901–1913) and the General Education Board (1905–1907), expressed the foundations' aims in these words: "Our great problem is to attach the Negro to the soil and prevent his exodus to the city." In Ogden's view, "the prosperity of the South depend[ed] upon the productive power of the black man."[8]

Industrial philanthropists viewed northern capital and cheap black labor as critical to southern economic reconstruction and reunion with the Northeast. This union, they believed, was hindered mainly by the South's political turmoil, racial conflict, and untrained labor which discouraged capital investments from the Northeast. In other words, the debate over black civil and political rights kindled the passions of racial warfare and blocked the swift return of southern economic prosperity and political stability. The industrial philanthropists viewed the return of political order and economic prosperity in the South as largely dependent upon the rapidity with which blacks could be removed from participation in politics, acknowledge the legitimacy of white domination and willingly perform unskilled and semiskilled domestic and agricultural labor. This view of the "Negro's place" in southern society, explicit in both educational and economic proposals, was best laid down by William H. Baldwin,

Jr., the first president of the General Education Board. Baldwin, one of the nation's rising railroad entrepreneurs, was appointed vice-president and general manager of J. P. Morgan's Southern Railway Company in 1894. The centrality of black labor in the railroad industry led him to consider the "Negro's place" in the larger social economy. He became a trustee of Tuskegee Institute in 1894 and, until his premature death in 1905, he worked closely with Booker T. Washington in addressing the South's racial and economic problems. In contrast to the missionaries' emphasis on equal rights, industrial philanthropists like Baldwin advised blacks to abandon their pursuit of equality. In 1899 he instructed black Americans to

> "face the music," avoid social questions, leave politics alone, continue to be patient, live moral lives, live simply, learn to work and to work intelligently, learn to work faithfully, learn to work hard, learn that any work, however, menial, if well done, is dignified; learn that the world will give full credit for labor and success, even though your skin in black; learn that it is a crime for any teacher, white or black, to educate the Negro for positions which are not open to him.

As to the occupational positions that were open to black workers, Baldwin was very explicit:

> The potential economic value of the Negro population properly educated is infinite and incalcuable. In the Negro is the opportunity of the South. Time has proven that he is best fitted to perform the heavy labor in the Southern states. "The Negro and the mule is the only combination so far to grow cotton." The South needs him; but the South needs him educated to be a suitable citizen. Properly directed he is the best possible laborer to meet the climatic conditions of the South. He will willingly fill the more menial positions, and do the heavy work, at less wages, than the American white man or any foreign race which has yet come to our shores. This will permit the Southern white laborer to perform the more expert labor, and to leave the fields, the mines, and the simpler trades for the Negro.

From Baldwin's vantage point, the agitation over equal rights prolonged the racial crisis in southern society which frightened away northern investors and kept the region's laboring classes preoccupied with political questions. He called for order and prosperity under white domination as the surest and most rapid means of making the South an important contributor to national economic development.[9]

Baldwin's opposition to the struggle for equal rights, and his ringing affirmation of black economic subordination, expressed values that lay at the core of industrial philanthropic ideology. Nearly all of the leading industrial philanthropists argued that blacks should serve as the cushion for southern capitalist development. Wallace Buttrick, the General Education Board's secretary and executive officer (1902–1917) and president (1917–1923), maintained that the Afro-American was destined to be "a producer—a servant—of his day in the highest sense." The wealthy investment banker and New York philanthropist George Foster Peabody, treasurer of the board from 1902–1909, was convinced that "the prosperity of the South and the world's supply of cotton" were dependent upon a subordinate black laboring class. These opinions were shared by trustees Walter H. Page (1902–1918), Andrew Carnegie (1908–1918), and others. Such views led naturally to a philosophy of "Negro education" which differed sharply from the missionaries' position.[10]

Baldwin and other industrial philanthropists were disappointed with the missionary educational system, believing that its influence "spoiled" black workers. In reviewing the missionary educational efforts from the Reconstruction era to the end of the nineteenth century, Baldwin commented:

> The days of reconstruction were dark for all. Their sting has not
> yet gone. Then appeared from the North a new army—an army
> of white teachers, armed with the spelling-book and the Bible;
> and from their attack there were many casualties on both sides,
> the Southern whites as well as the blacks. For, although the
> spelling-book and the Bible were necessary for the proper educa-
> tion of the negro race, yet, with a false point of view, the
> Northern white teacher educated the negro to hope that through
> the books he might, like the white man, learn to live from the
> fruits of a literary education. How false that theory was, thirty
> long years of experience has proved. That was not their opportu-
> nity. Their opportunity was to be taught the dignity of manual
> labor and how to perform it. We began at the wrong end. Instead
> of educating the negro in the lines which were open to him, he
> was educated out of his natural environment and the opportuni-
> ties which lay immediately about him.

Convinced that what Afro-Americans needed most to learn was the discipline of manual labor and the boundaries of their "natural environment," Baldwin advocated the Hampton-Tuskegee model of industrial education as the solution to the "Negro problem." This type of education aimed "to teach the negro boy or girl to be moral and religious, and how to make a living; to educate them in those lines in which the opportunity to make a living is open." Hampton, Tuskegee, and similar industrial schools educated black boys and girls "for their natural environment, and not out of it." Thus blacks were taught "to farm more intelligently, to keep the house cleaner, to cook better, to dress better, to be an influence for good in the community." Baldwin, Tuskegee's leading trustee, understood accurately the social purposes of the Hampton-Tuskegee model of industrial training. This model of black education was designed to develop habits of industry, instill an appreciation for the dignity of labor, and primarily to train a cadre of conservative black teachers or "guides" who were expected to help adjust Afro-Americans to a subordinate role in the southern political economy. The Hampton-Tuskegee program presupposed the existing racist social order and the inferior sociopolitical roles that it prescribed for black Americans. At best, the industrial education creed put a gloss on existing patterns of race relations. Black Americans would become better "educated" primarily to perform unskilled and semiskilled agricultural and domestic labor. They would accept uncomplainingly civil inequality, political disfranchisement, economic subordination, and cooperate with southern whites. This pattern of interracial cooperation would enable the South to overcome the political discord started as a consequence of Reconstruction abolitionist zeal. For the industrial philanthropists, the South would still have its racial customs, political disfranchisement, economic discrimination, and legal caste system. Yet, subsequent to industrial training, interracial cooperation, and economic prosperity, they believed that living conditions for the black population would be higher, more humane and responsible, thus giving the South greater social stability.[11]

Hence, the industrial philanthropist came to recognize "Negro industrial training" as the appropriate form of education to assist in bringing racial order, political stability, and material prosperity to the American South. Wallace Buttrick praised the Hampton-Tuskegee program as the most valuable "kind of education needed by the Negro." Robert Ogden, who served as president of the Hampton Institute Board of Trustees from 1894 to 1913, declared: "The main hope is in Hampton and Hampton ideas. Out first problem is to support the school; our second to make the School ideas national." For Baldwin, there was only one question concerning the race problem, "where shall we get another Booker T. Washington for these other schools?" It was the industrial philanthropists' task, said Baldwin, "to build up a secondary school system under the general control and supervision of the Hampton and Tuskegee that their influence may be far-reaching." Convinced that the Hampton-Tuskegee system would produce a conservative black leadership that would persuade Afro-Americans to remain in the South as efficient servants and agricultural laborers, he sought to make industrial training the dominant, if not exclusive, form of black education. "Except in the rarest of instances," remarked Baldwin, "I am bitterly opposed to the so-called higher education of Negroes." During the late nineteenth and early twentieth centuries, these views clearly won the day. The Peabody and Slater Funds carefully avoided giving support to black higher education. The General Education Board, making every effort "to develop industrial education in Negro schools," granted virtually no funds to black liberal arts colleges, except small donations to encourage industrial education departments at Atlanta and Fisk Universities. The Jeanes, Phelps-Stokes, and Rosenwald Funds, as part of the Board's interlocking directorate, were guided by the same educational policies.

These policies resulted in the establishment of a comprehensive system of black industrial education. At the bottom of the system were elementary industrial schools and county training schools, which provided industrial training from grades one through ten. This lower system of industrial education was crowned by a network of industrial normal schools such as Hampton and Tuskegee Institutes that were designed to train a corps of black industrial teachers. The industrial philanthropic foundations followed a policy of donating their funds almost exclusively to schools modeled on the Hampton-Tuskegee program of industrial training. As historian Louis Harlan stated, "northern members, who sat on all of the leading philanthropic boards interested in the South, channeled these funds into Negro industrial institutes and white colleges."[12]

The Crisis of Black Higher Education, 1900–1920

This missionary philanthropists' campaign to establish a solid system of black higher education fell far short of its goal. Though they plodded on persistently, preserving a modest system of black collegiate education, their nineteenth-century momentum declined sharply after 1900. By the turn of the century, the mission societies were virtually bankrupt and their campaign to develop black higher education was rapidly diminishing in scope and activity. In looking at the future of their black colleges, the missionary philanthropists had many reasons to be downhearted. By any standard, the material and financial status of black higher education was bad. Black colleges were understaffed, meagerly equipped, and poorly financed. The combined efforts of the missionary and black organizations could not raise sufficient funds to meet annual operating expenses, to increase teachers' salaries, expand the physical plant, improve libraries, or purchase new scientific and technical equipment. More importantly, almost all of the missionary black colleges were without sufficient endowments to insure their survival. Of the 110 black colleges in 1914–1915, two-thirds had no endowment funds; the endowment of the remaining institutions totaled $8.4 million. The vast majority of this sum represented the endowment of Hampton and Tuskegee Institutes, which had attracted large gifts from industrial philanthropists in support of industrial education. In 1926, the total endowment of ninety-nine black colleges had risen to $20.3 million, and more than $14 million of this belonged to Hampton and Tuskegee Institutes; the endowment of the ninety-seven remaining institutions totaled $6.1 million. As late as 1932, seventy-five black colleges had either a negligible endowment or none at all.[13]

The relative impoverishment of black "colleges" and "universities" made it difficult for them to increase their college-level enrollments, which were extremely small. In the academic year 1899–1900, only fifty-eight of the ninety-nine black colleges had any collegiate students. For these ninety-nine institutions, their collegiate and professional students totaled 2,624, and the precollegiate enrollment amounted to 27,869. The precollegiate students constituted more than nine-tenths of the total black college enrollment. This pattern had not changed significantly by World War I. In 1914–1915, Thomas Jesse Jones concluded that only thirty-three black private institutions were "teaching any subjects of college grade." Of the 12,726 students attending these institutions in 1915, only 2,637 were studying college subjects; the remaining 10,089 students (79 percent) were in the elementary and secondary grades. Many institutions were endeavoring to maintain college classes for less than 5 percent of their enrollment. The lack of good academic elementary and secondary schools for southern black students forced the black colleges to train pupils at lower levels in order to produce students qualified to enter collegiate work. Not having an adequate supply of high schoolers to enter the freshman course, the black colleges enrolled elementary and secondary students mainly as a means to feed their college departments. Thus, for sometime the enrollment patterns in black colleges differed significantly from the national pattern. In 1900, approximately one-quarter of all students enrolled in American colleges were in precollegiate programs. The black percollegiate enrollment, as late as the 1930s, represented about 40 percent of the total enrollment in black institutions of higher learning.[14]

Another important development, which threatened the survival of the missionary colleges and black higher education in general, was the establishment of national and regional accrediting agencies. In the late nineteenth century regional accrediting agencies like the Middle States Association of Colleges and Secondary Schools, the Southern Association of Colleges and Secondary Schools, the North Central Association of Colleges and Secondary Schools, and the New England Association of Colleges and Secondary Schools were formed to give more fixed meanings to the terms high school, college, and university. In the early twentieth century these regional accrediting agencies were joined by national stand-ardizing organizations such as the College Entrance Examination Board and the Carnegie Foundation for the Advancement of Teaching. Prior to 1913, accrediting agencies worked mainly to establish closer relations among institutions of higher learning, to standardize college admissions requirements, and to improve the academic quality of college and univer-sity education. Beginning in 1913, however, the North Central Association issued the first list of regionally accredited colleges and universities, which signaled the movement to define institutions of higher learning by specific, factual, mechanical, and uniform standards. This movement, financed by foundations like Carnegie, increased the pressures on black colleges to become full-fledged institutions of higher learning.[15]

In one sense, standardization or accrediting was voluntary action. No institution was surveyed for the purpose of accreditation except upon application. But despite the voluntary aspect of collegiate accreditment, it was virtually impossible for a college or university to exist as an important institution without the approval of these rating bodies. The nonattainment or removal of accreditation, whether by a regional or national accrediting agency, was a serious detriment to the welfare of an institution. The mere publication of lists of accredited schools had an adverse effect upon institutions which did not appear on the lists. Whether students were graduates of accredited or nonaccredited institutions figured significantly in job opportunities, acceptance to graduate and professional schools, and in the acquisition of required state certificates to practice various profes-sions from teaching to medicine.[16]

Although no formal accrediting agency took black colleges seriously until 1928, when the Southern Association of Colleges and Secondary Schools decided to rate black institutions separately, there were several evaluations of black higher education from 1900 to 1928. In 1900 and 1910, W. E. B. DuBois made the first attempts to evaluate and classify the black colleges. In 1900 DuBois listed thirty-four institutions as "colleges" with a total collegiate enrollment of 726 students. He concluded, however, that these 726 students could have been educated in ten institutions which he rated as first-grade colleges. In 1910 DuBois made a more careful evaluation of black higher education in which he attempted the classifica-tion of thirty-two black colleges. Institutions Like Howard, Fisk, Atlanta, Morehouse, and Virginia Union were classified as "First-Grade Colored Colleges." Lincoln, Talladega, and Wilberforce were examples of the "Second-Grade Colored Colleges," and schools such a Lane, Bishop, and Miles Memorial were included under the label "other colored colleges." DuBois's evaluation was, on balance, a friendly one designed to strengthen the black college system by concentrating college-level work in about thirty of the better black institutions. But in 1917 Thomas Jesse Jones, director of research for the Phelps-Stokes Fund (see Berman chapter), published a critical attack upon black higher education that questioned the legitimacy of nearly all black institutions of higher learning. From 1914 to 1916, Jones conducted a two-volume survey of black higher education for the Federal Bureau of Education. In the volume on black colleges he identified only two black institutions as capable of offering college-level work. These were Howard University and Fisk University. In Jones's words, "hardly a colored college meets the standards set by the Carnegie Foundation and the North Central Association." These rating agencies required, among other things, that accredited colleges maintain at least six departments or professorships with one professor giving full time to each department. The college's annual income had to be sufficient to maintain professors with advanced degrees and to supply adequate library and laboratory facilities. The rating agencies also held that the operation of a preparatory department was undesirable, and in no case could it be under the same faculty and discipline as the college. Finally, the North Central Association recommended that accredited colleges possess an endowment of at least $200,000. At that time, Hampton and Tuskegee were the only black institutions with substantial endowments, and they did not offer collegiate courses. For Jones, his findings strongly suggested only two or three black institutions were equipped to become accredited colleges. Hence, he recommended that the remaining "colleges" convert to secondary and elementary schools. Undoubtedly his views were harsh and unwarranted, reflecting significantly his bias toward the Hampton-Tuskegee model of industrial education. Still, Jones's survey, backed by the Federal Bureau of Education and northern philanthropic foundations, underscored a major crisis in black higher education. Black colleges, however segregated, could not exist apart from the power and control of white standardizing agencies. It had become apparent to missionary philanthropists and black educators that their institutions were compelled to seek admission to the society of standardized colleges and on terms defined by all-white regional and national rating agencies. Thus, as Harry Washington Green and Leland Stanford Cozart pointed out, for black institutions of higher learning, rating by accrediting agencies was the thing primarily worth striving for in the post–World War I era.[17]

The crucial threats to the survival of black higher education could not be met effectively by missionary philanthropists or black organizations, and the black colleges were forced to seek help from industrial philanthropists. As early as 1901, Thomas J. Morgan, then corresponding secretary for the American Baptist Home Mission Society, requested fellow Baptist John D. Rockefeller to "assume the expense of fully equipping" eight of the society's leading colleges. Writing to Wallace Buttrick, Rockefeller's advisor in philanthropic affairs, Morgan suggested several ways to support black colleges: "(a) by endowing each school separately; (b) by placing in the hands of the Home Mission Society a lump endowment sum; (c) the creation of a fund placed in the hands of trustees especially selected for the purpose, or (d) the donation of Mr. Rockefeller annually of such a sum of money as may be essential to carry on the work." Between 1901 and 1908, the Home Mission Society's leading members, Morgan, Malcolm MacVicar, Henry L. Morehouse, George Sale, and George Rice Hovey, wrote to Wallace Buttrick literally pleading for grants to keep their black colleges financially solvent. All requests were denied. Their correspondence reveals the growing impoverishment of missionary philanthropy. In 1901 Morgan wrote:

> Reflecting upon the future of our educational work it seems to me we have reached an actual crisis that demands very careful consideration. Suppose, for instance, that the Society is obliged to carry on the work as heretofore. What shall we do? It is exceedingly difficult to secure money to keep the schools up to their present degree of efficiency and it is uncertain whether the present interest in the schools can be kept up among the churches and individuals.

In Morgan's view, black colleges simply could "not expect too much of the Society in the immediate future with reference to enlargement, improvement, and increased costs." Likewise, George Rice Hovey, president of the Home Mission Society's Virginia Union University, said to Buttrick: "We, I fear, can never accomplish the work that we ought to do if we rely solely on the missionary society." Hovey's assessment aptly characterized the general state of missionary philanthropy. By the turn of the century, it had become a weak and ineffective force. Unfortunately, the missionaries became bankrupt at a time when black colleges depended almost exclusively upon private aid.[18]

Industrial Philanthropy's Rationale for Black Higher Education

Black higher education, after World War I, survived mainly within the limits imposed by industrial philanthropy. Indeed, as DuBois concluded in 1930, "not withstanding all of its past mistakes in attitude and personnel, there can be no doubt . . . the General Education [Board] in later years has been the salvation of *higher* education among Negroes." To those outside of philanthropic circles, the shift in industrial philanthropic attitudes toward black higher education indicated a fundamental change of ideology, a concession to the educational ideas advanced by missionary philanthropists. From the industrial philanthropists' vantage point, however, their response to black higher education in the post–World War I era was consistent with their long-term goals of limiting black access to collegiate work while making industrial education easily available.[19]

The main creed of the industrial philanthropists was the one expressed by Baldwin, that only "in the rarest of instances" should black youth pursue collegiate study. Yet, because industrial philanthropists appropriated virtually no money for black higher education prior to 1920, they were often perceived as committed exclusively to the idea of Negro industrial education. This was a misperception of the industrial philanthropists' view of black higher education. In 1907, Buttrick stated well his colleagues' attitude toward black higher education: "I am convinced that all the members of the [General Education] Board believes that there should be a sufficient number of thoroughgoing colleges for colored people in the Southern states." Further, he was inclined to agree with his associates of the board "that the matter of collegiate education for the colored people should be taken up as a whole by this Board." In fact, as Buttrick informed George Sale, superintendent of Negro education for the American Baptist Home Mission Society, the board had already designated one of its "School Inspectors" to make "a careful study of the whole question" of black higher education. This report, completed in May 1907 by W. T. B. Williams of Hampton Institute, set forth several reasons for developing a small number of strong black colleges in the South. First, these institutions would produce college-bred leaders to acculturate black Americans into white American values. The "farther the colored people are removed and kept from the more cultivated white people," said Williams, "the greater becomes their need for having considerable numbers of educated cultivated people of their own race among them." "Otherwise," he continued, "there must come a general retrogression from lack of ideals and competent leadership." Second, it was very important that black leaders be trained in the South by institutions "in touch with the conditions to be faced by the young people in later life rather than in the North by institutions. . .out of touch with Southern life." Third, and most importantly, the development of a few strong institutions was viewed as a strategic means to reduce the number of existing black colleges. Williams argued:

> If more strong men and good college courses, and better equip-
> ment both in the way of dormitories and apparatus could be
> added in a few places, and some scholarships or student aid in
> the college department, could be provided, as is common in the
> great Northern universities, the mass of Negro college students
> would congregate in these few institutions and their numbers

would steadily increase. This would render impossible many of
the weaker college courses and would make for strength in
organization and economy in the management of college training, for it would minimize duplication.

Williams expressed an interesting and noteworthy effect of standardization
which was not so marked and known. By establishing a few outstanding
black colleges, industrial philanthropists could use these institutions to
pressure the remaining ones into discontinuing their collegiate courses
because of their inability to keep pace with the rising standards of college-
level work. Buttrick regarded Williams's report as "so valuable that in my
judgement all the members of Board ought to read it just as it stands."[20]
  Williams's report impressed the board's trustees and spurred them to
develop a formal rationale for the support of black higher education.
Wallace Buttrick and Abraham Flexner were primarily responsible for
formulating the board's policy. In 1910 Flexner became nationally known
for writing Carnegie Foundation Bulletin No. 4, a detailed study of
"Medical Education in the United States and Canada." Flexner inspected
155 medical schools and reported their "appalling deficiencies," which led
him to conclude that all but thirty-one of them should discontinue. After
this report appeared, the Council of Medical Education of the American
Medical Association intensified its efforts to eliminate "inferior" medical
colleges. Much of the financial support for the medical reform movement
was provided by the General Education Board. In 1911 the board appropriated $1.5 million to Johns Hopkins Medical School for the purpose of
setting standards in American medical education. Flexner was placed in
charge of the board's medical reform program. His main goal was to
develop a model of medical education that would force weaker institutions
to shut down because of their inability to approximate the new standards.
Clearly, this policy followed closely the suggestions contained in the
Williams report, though there was no apparent relation between the two.[21]
  In 1914, Flexner became a trustee of the General Education Board and
assistant secretary to Wallace Buttrick. In this capacity, he began to apply
his medical model to the field of black higher education. Fortunately, for
Flexner, he did not have to conduct a study of black higher education
comparable to his investigation of American medical education. Both he
and Buttrick were actuely aware of the survey of black higher education
being conducted by Thomas Jesse Jones for the Federal Bureau of
Education. They were in close contact with Jones and realized, early on,
that they could rely upon his forthcoming survey as a "Flexner report" of
black higher education. Buttrick informed John D. Rockefeller, Jr., in
February 1914 that he was in "frequent conference" with Jones, and he
assured Rockefeller, Jr., that Jones's survey would "throw light" on the

whole question of black education. Though Jones's survey was not published until 1917, by December 1914 Flexner was already convinced that it would sound the death knell for many black colleges as his medical report had done for the vast majority of American medical schools. Writing to Oswald Garrison Villard about the value of the Jones's survey, Flexner proclaimed:

> Dr. Jones is a disinterested and competent outsider whose report will separate the wheat from the chaff. After its appearance the public will have a source of information the accuracy and impartiality of which cannot be discredited. The situation here is not different in principle from that which once existed in reference to medical schools. There was an association of American medical colleges that could enforce no standards just because it meant that the members, in order to do this, would have to legislate against one another. After, however, the Carnegie Foundation Bulletin appeared, an entirely new situation was created. Since then things have been run by the better schools and the others are rapidly disappearing.

Anticipating the impact of the Jones survey, the General Education Board held its first interracial "conference on Negro Education" in November of 1915. The invited participants represented the major parties that had to be confronted in any movement to reorganize and control black higher education. Presidents Fayette A. McKenzie of Fisk University and John Hope of Morehouse College represented two of the most outstanding black private colleges. Others included Principal R. R. Moton of Tuskegee Institute, Principal H. B. Frissell of Hampton Institute, Abraham Flexner of the General Education Board, Thomas Jesse Jones of the Phelps-Stokes Fund, W. T. B. Williams, field agent for the John F. Slater Fund, and James H. Dillard, president of the Anna T. Jeanes Foundation.[22]

Basically this conference brought together the forces which represented the industrial philanthropists' overall approach to the development of black education. On the one hand, Frissell, Moton, Williams, Jones, Flexner, and Dillard exemplified the movement to spread industrial education throughout the Afro-American South as the all-pervasive educational curriculum. On the other hand, McKenzie and Hope symbolized the industrial philanthropists' developing commitment to control and reorganize black higher education. First, the industrial philanthropists' advocates stressed the need for the continuing development of industrial education. But the conference shifted immediately to the question of black higher education. H. B. Frissell asked the central question: "What is sound policy in respect to the number, scope, support and development of higher academic institutions for Negroes?" Only John Hope questioned the relevance of industrial education and stated firmly that he stood for "modern sort of education" for black and white children. Flexner, speaking for the industrial philanthropists, insisted that black collegiate work was "very pretentious, and not calculated to get anywhere." Having tested some black college students in Latin, physics, and literature, he concluded that "if it had been Greek they could not have been more puzzled." Flexner then proceeded to get Hope's reaction to the General Education Board's scheme for reducing the number of existing colleges:

> Dr. Hope, what would be the effect of selecting four or five
> Negro colleges and building them up, making them good, hon-
> est, sincere, effective colleges so far as they went, and letting the
> others alone, not try to suppress them or consolidate them, but
> just let them "sweat," would that tend in the long run, to
> stigmatize the inferior institutions that they would give up, the
> way the poor medical schools are giving up?

Hope admitted that such a policy might pressure weaker colleges to discontinue, but he did not sanction this approach.[23]

Shortly after this conference, the board formed a special committee to review its overall policy for the development of black education, paying particular attention to the question of higher education. This committee made formal the board's desire to reduce the number of black institutions of higher learning, and to influence the aims of the remaining ones. According to the board's committee, there were "far too many Negro colleges and universities," and not one was "well equipped and manned on a sensible, modest scale." Therefore, the committee reported, "wise cooperation with one or two institutions would be the most effective way of bringing order out of chaos, of distinguishing the real from imitation."

The following year, Jones published his survey of black education. Like the board's private report, he recommended the development of "two institutions of university grade" and three colleges for Afro-American students. At that time, there were over 10 million Afro-Americans, with a college-age population of over 250,000. As noted earlier, only 2,637 of these students were enrolled in college and professional courses. However, there was an increasing desire for higher education among black youth. Historian Monroe Little, Jr., studied Afro-Americans' growing demand for college education between 1900 and 1920. Controlling for population growth, he discovered that "only 9.81 percent of the increase in school attendance can be attributed to black population growth; while 48.96 percent of the increase for whites of the same age group is attributable to this factor." Little concluded that early twentieth-century black communities were characterized by an all-pervasive desire for higher education. The industrial philanthropists, however, viewed such tendencies as a general contradiction to their campaign to stabilize southern society and to retain black Americans in the region largely as domestic and agricultural laborers. For industrial philanthropists, blacks' widespread desire for education indicated a disdain for hard labor and an unwillingness to cooperate with the southern racial hierarchy. Hence, in pursuing their own interests in shaping the New South, they set out to make black higher education more conservative and less accessible.[24]

The Ascendancy of Industrial Philanthropy

The industrial philanthropists' first major attempt to control black higher education originated in 1915 when the General Education Board decided tó "take hold" of Fisk University and develop it as a model institution of black higher education. Indeed, the Fisk University case illustrates the role of industrial philanthropy in shaping black higher education on the eve of World War I. Fisk, like most prominent black colleges was founded by missionary philanthropists (American Missionary Association) during the Reconstruction era. The industrial philanthropists regarded it as the "capstone" of private black higher education. Wallace Buttrick said: "Perhaps the most promising of the academic institutions for the higher education of the Negro is Fisk University." Outside of Howard University, Fisk had nearly 20 percent of the black college students enumerated in Thomas Jesse Jones's 1917 survey of black higher education. Fisk enrolled 188 of the 737 college students in private black colleges and Virginia Union University, with fifty one, had the next largest enrollment. Thus, when the General Education Board held its 1915 conference to discuss the reorganization of black higher education, Fisk University's president, Fayette Avery McKenzie, was invited as a key representative of black higher education. Convinced that McKenzie was sympathetic to the board's policy, the industrial philanthropists selected him to spearhead their campaign to reshape black higher education.[25]

McKenzie, a sociologist at the Ohio State University before coming to Fisk in 1915, was quickly regarded by industrial philanthropists as the kind of leader that would help make Fisk a more conservative institution. More than any of his predecessors, McKenzie sought to make Fisk acceptable to the white South and urged its graduates to concentrate on the economic development of the region. In his inaugural address McKenzie paid homage to Fisk's liberal-arts tradition but introduced a new concept of "service" education which promised that the college would help restore the South to economic prosperity. He maintained,

> It was the function of Fisk to increase the material wealth of the nation. . ..Fisk University claims the right to say that it will be one of the chief factors in achieving larger prosperity for the South. Every dollar spent here in the creation of power may mean a thousand dollars of increase in wealth of the South within a single generation.

McKenzie attempted to persuade Fisks' students to forsake equalitarian principles and to work within the southern racial hierarchy to improve the region's industrial efficiency and maintain interracial cooperation. This policy pleased the industrial philanthropists and they hailed McKenzie's inauguration as a new and wise departure from the missionary tradition.[26]

Consequently, as Raymond Wolters has demonstrated, McKenzie set out to convince the industrial philanthropists that "Fisk students were not radical egalitarians but young men and women who had learned to make peace with the reality of the caste system." To this end, McKenzie disbanded the student government association, forbade student dissent, and suspended the *Fisk Herald*, the oldest student publication among black colleges. He would not allow a campus chapter of the NAACP and instructed the librarian to excise radical articles in the NAACP literature. Student discipline was rigorously enforced, special "Jim Crow" entertainments were arranged for the white benefactors of the university, and Paul D. Cravath, the president of the Fisk Board of Trustees, endorsed complete racial separation as "the only solution to the Negro problem." McKenzie would not allow certain forms of social intercourse such as dancing and holding hands, and he justified his code of discipline on the grounds that black students were particularly sensuous beings who needed to be subjected to firm control. In short, McKenzie attempted to repress student initiative, undermine their equalitarian spirit, and control their thinking on race relations in order to produce a class of black intellectuals that would uncomplainingly accept the southern racial hierarchy.[27]

From the outset, industrial philanthropists reinforced McKenzie's behavior by contributing their economic and political support to his regime. Philanthropist Julius Rosenwald, who visited Fisk at McKenzie's installation, was initially ambivalent about the possibility of transforming the college into an accommodationist institution. In revealing his "mixed feelings" about Fisk students to Abraham Flexner, Rosenwald stated, "There seemed to be an air of superiority among them and a desire to take on the spirit of the white university rather than the spirit which has always impressed me at Tuskegee." To Rosenwald and other industrial philanthropists, Tuskegee was training black leaders to maintain a separate and subordinate Negro society. They were primarily interested in supporting black institutions committed to this mission. Thus Flexner assured Rosenwald that McKenzie, with the help of industrial philanthropy, was working to transform Fisk into an institution more acceptable to southern white society. Toward this end, the General Education Board began appropriating in 1916 about $12,000 annually to help Fisk pay its yearly operating expenses. In 1917 the board contributed $50,000 to Fisk for endowment and building purposes and persuaded the Carnegie Corporation to give the same amount. Still, Fisk had no substantial endowment, was deeply indebted, its physical plant was deteriorating, and its faculty was poorly paid. According to Hollingsworth Wood, vice-chairman of the Fisk Board of Trustees, "$1,600 has been the maximum salary of a professor at Fisk University. This has meant lack of food in some cases." Fisk authorities knew that the college could not really survive without a sizable endowment, and sufficient money could be raised only from the industrial philanthropists. Under these circumstances however, a certain amount of compromise was required. As McKenzie put it, "intimation has been made to me from several sources that if we continue to behave ourselves, if we are efficient in teaching and administration and continue to hold the right relationship to our environment, we can expect large and highly valuable financial aid in carrying out a great program at Fisk."[28]

The philanthropists' financial assistance to Fisk University was accompanied by a new coalition of Negro accommodationists, southern whites, and northern businessmen who took control of the university's administration from the old alliance of black and white equalitarians. McKenzie and the philanthropists restructured the Fisk Board of Trustees to reflect the new power realities. In October of 1915 Thomas Jesse Jones informed Flexner of the new changes:

> The Board of Trustees is being strengthened. Governor Brumbaugh and two influential colored men have been added in the last few weeks. With Mr. Cravath and Dr. Washington as trustees and the constant attention which I can give to the institution, we have at least a guarantee of fairly sound educational policy.

By 1919 Jones was executive secretary of the Fisk Board of Trustees and one of five members on the Executive Committee. In 1920 the philanthropists, acting through the General Education Board, agreed to spearhead a campaign to obtain for Fisk a $2 million endowment, and their strength on the university's Board of Trustees increased. William H. Baldwin, son of the General Education Board's first chairman, was appointed by the board to chair the endowment committee. He was immediately appointed to the Fisk Board of Trustees and became in 1924 the chairman of the trustees' executive committee. Other conservatives were added as the philanthropists moved in a quiet and forceful manner to reorganize the school's administration. In May of 1920 Hollingsworth Wood notified the president of the General Education Board that

> Dr. Moton of Tuskegee is now on the Board; Miss Ella Sachs, daughter of Samuel Sachs, and a close friend of the Rosenwalds, is an eager new member; and Mrs. Beverly B. Mumford of Richmond, Virginia adds an excellent influence from the Southern viewpoint.

The traditional missionary equalitarians were gradually pushed off the Fisk Board of Trustees. They were replaced mainly by northern businessmen and a few conservative Negroes who were virtually hand-picked by industrial philanthropists. The philanthropists were actually raising an endowment for a new Fisk that was largely controlled by their agents and supporters.[29]

The philanthropists no doubt hoped that their economic and firm political hold on Fisk would squelch the school's equalitarian tradition and allow them to develop a more conservative black professional class. In 1923 the General Education Board generated a memorandum on the Fisk endowment campaign which emphasisized the urgent need to train "the right type of colored leaders" who would help make the Negro "a capable workman and a good citizen." Industrial philanthropists, as the memorandum stated, aimed primarily at "helping the Negro to the sane and responsible leadership that the South wants him to have." To the white South, "sane" Negro leaders were the type who encouraged blacks to "stay in their place."[30]

By June 1924, the industrial philanthropists had successfully conducted a campaign for Fisk's million-dollar endowment. The following pledges were then in hand: $500,000 from the General Education Board; $250,000 from the Carnegie Corporation; and $250,000 secured elsewhere, including sizable pledges from such philanthropists as Julius Rosenwald and George Peabody. This endowment fund was not, however, collectible until the deficits, which Fisk had accumulated, were met. The outstanding indebtedness of that date was $70,000. To meet this indebtedness a special campaign by Nashville's white citizens for $50,000 was successfully completed by June 1924. This campaign was led by Nashville's Commercial Club, which included Tennessee's governor, Nashville's mayor, and many of the city's leading businessmen. From 1915 to 1924, Fisk had become so conservative that the Commercial Club was inspired to call Fisk "the key" to interracial cooperation and understanding in the South. "He came into our midst unknown," the Commercial Club said of McKenzie, "and by his wise administration and official methods won our hearty co-operation." With such backing, plans were perfected for raising the money to eliminate the school's deficits and thereby secure the endowment for Fisk's financial rehabilitation.[31]

At thus juncture, however, McKenzie's conservative administration was attacked by black students, intellectuals, and community organizations. Led by W. E. B. DuBois, the Fisk alumni attacked McKenzie's Draconian code of student discipline and were outraged by the humiliation and insults perpetrated on the student body. DuBois openly challenged the school's administration in 1924 when he was invited to give the commencement address. He especially criticized the administration's campaign to suppress Fisk's equalitarian tradition in order to obtain economic support from industrial philanthropy. The students, long dissatisfied with McKenzie's regime, were reinforced by alumni support and escalated their protest against the school's repressive policies. In January of 1925, the *New York Times* reported that Fisk's alumni were organizing in "all sections of the United States to agitate for the removal of Dr. Fayette McKenzie, the white president of the University." The following month the students went on strike against McKenzie's administration, and as Wolters has shown, they were backed in their protest by the alumni, the black press, and the local black community. On the day following the student rebellion more than 2,500 black citizens of Nashville convened and formally declared that McKenzie's "usefulness as president of Fisk is at an end." This protest forced McKenzie to resign in April of 1925.[32]

DuBois praised the students' victory over McKenzie and hailed them as the new breed of black intellectuals necessary to challenge the power of industrial philanthropy:

> God speed the breed! Suppose we do lose Fisk; suppose we lose
> every cent that the entrenched millionaires have set aside to buy
> our freedom and stifle our complaints. They have the power,
> they have the wealth, but glory to God we still own our own
> souls and led by young men like these at Fisk, let us neither
> flinch nor falter, but fight, and fight and fight again.

But many black intellectuals, especially those responsible for black colleges, could not easily afford to attack the policies of industrial philanthropy. After the Fisk rebellion, the General Education Board withheld the endowment pledges on the grounds that they were not collectible until Fisk eliminated all its deficits. The Nashville Commercial Club, which was expected to raise the capital to cover the deficits, withdrew from the campaign following McKenzie's resignation. Convinced that McKenzie's successor, Thomas Elsa Jones, did "not conceive himself to be a leader or an emancipator of the Negro group," the philanthropists eventually granted Fisk the endowment. Fisk, however, was still dependent on industrial philanthropy. From 1915 to 1960, the General Education Board alone disbursed over $5 million to Fisk. During the same period it also granted over $5,800,000 to Atlanta University; $1,900,000 to Morehouse; $2,250,000 to Dillard University; $3,500,000 to Spellman; and $1,100,000 to Clark College. In all the General Education Board's expenditures to black higher education, from 1902 to 1960, amounted to $41,410,399. Consequently, as previously stated, even critics like DuBois were forced to recognize that industrial philanthropists represented "the salvation of education among Negros."[33]

Between 1915 and 1940, the industrial philanthropists pushed southern black education into two divergent directions. Through an elaborate system of industrial normal schools and county training schools, they financed the development of a widespread industrial noncollegiate curriculum. By the early 1930s, when more than two-thirds of all southern blacks lived in rural areas, fully 66 percent of those attending high schools were enrolled in industrial training schools. This school system was financed and presided over primarily by industrial philanthropists and their educational agents. At the same time, industrial philanthropists were supporting a few select black colleges in order to establish models for black higher education, to pressure the weaker colleges into discontinuing, and to gain more influence over the training of the college-bred Negro. This program of educational development was consistent with the industrial philanthropists' long-standing goals, to train the vast majority of black students for domestic and agricultural work and to provide higher education for the "rare exceptions."[34]

The Philanthropic Legacy

In vital respects black higher education, after World War I, survived mainly within the limits imposed by industrial philanthropy and its underlying structure of financial power and political prestige. While many blacks and white equalitarians were quite capable of recognizing and rejecting the industrial philanthropists' vision of black America's "place" in the southern social order, college presidents and faculty members were vulnerable to the power and status of the philanthropic foundations. Few, if any, black college leaders could afford, as DuBois asked them, to challenge the "power in high places, white power, power backed by unlimited wealth." The General Education Board's policy of concentrating funds in select institutions did not cause many institutions to discontinue. However, since the great majority of private black colleges did not participate equally in this endowment development, they were unable to build up a solid financial base. In 1958, F. D. Patterson, president of the

United Negro College Fund (UNCF), and W. J. Trent, Jr., executive director, reported: "Of the 33 member colleges in the United Negro College Fund, 4 have endowment in the excess of $5,000,000, 10 have endowment of $1 to $5,000,000, 6 have endowment from $500,000 to $1,000,000, and 13 have endowment of less than $500,000." It is important to point out that these endowments included the grants of $4,653,000 to colleges by the Ford Foundation for endowing teachers' salaries. Even the "wealthiest" black colleges were not sufficiently endowed to rely upon endowment dividends as a major portion of their annual income. In 1958, the combined endowment of UNCF colleges was less than the endowment of Northwestern University. The black colleges remained dependent on industrial philanthropy. According to Trent and Patterson, in 1958, "fully one-third of the money raised by the UNCF comes from corporations. This source of gifts for the private Negro college—will become increasingly more important." Gradually, the industrial philanthropic foundations of the early twentieth century were replaced by the Ford Foundation, Sloan Foundation, Taconic Foundation, Duke Trust, and Mellon Charitable Trust. This recent philanthropic interest in black higher education is a story in its own right. However, industrial philanthropy remains a major force in the shaping of black higher education. Since the General Education Board phased out its activities in the 1950s, there have been virtually no significant grants for endowment funds to black colleges. Hence, the private black college administrators have adapted to surviving on gifts for annual income, or what they have titled "living endowments." In this sense, the private black college has come full circle. In the day-to-day struggle to survive, industrial philanthropy is still a controlling force in the power structure of black higher education.[35]

Notes

1. Rayford W. Logan, "The Evolution of Private Colleges for Negroes," *Journal of Negro Education* 27 (Summer 1958): 216; Thomas Jesse Jones, *Negro Education: A Study of the Private and Higher School for Colored People in the United States*, Vol. I (Washington, D.C.: U.S. Government Printing Office, 1917), p. 310; Arthur J. Klein, *Survey of Negro Colleges and Universities* (Washington, D.C.: U.S. Government Printing Office, 1929); Dwight Oliver Holmes, *The Evolution of the Negro College* (College Park, Md.: McGrath Publishing Company, 1934), p. 201.
2. Klein, *Survey of Negro Colleges and Universities*, pp. 5–33; Holmes, *The Evolution of the Negro College*, pp. 163–177.
3. James D. Anderson, "The Hampton Model of Normal School Industrial Education, 1868–1900," in Vincent Franklin and James D. Anderson

(eds.), *New Perspectives on Black Educational History* (Boston: G.K. Hall, 1978), p. 86.

4. Missionary Philanthropists quoted from Dwight Oliver Holmes, *The Evolution of the Negro College* (New York: Arno Press, 1934), p. 69; C.T. Wright, "The Development of Education for Blacks in Georgia, 1865–1900" (Boston University, Ph.D. Dissertation, 1977), p. 31; Franklin and Anderson (eds.), *New Perspectives on Black Educational History*, pp. 84–89.

5. Ronald Eugene Butchart, "Educating for Freedom: Northern Whites and the Origins of Black Education in the South, 1862–1875" (State University of New York at Binghamton, Ph.D. Dissertation, 1976) p. 353; George M. Fredrickson, *The Black Image in the White Mind: The Debate on Afro-American Character and Destiny, 1817–1914* (New York: Harper and Row, 1971), p. 244; Herbert G. Gutman, *The Black Family in Slavery and Freedom 1750–1925* (New York: Pantheon, 1976), p. 532.

6. Freedmen's Aid Society quoted from Holmes, *The Evolution of the Negro College*, p. 69; Horance Mann Bond, "A Century of Negro Higher Education" in William W. Brickman and Stanley Lehrer (eds.), *A Century of Higher Education: Classical Citadel to Collegiate Colossus* (New York: Society for the Advancement of Education, 1962), p. 187; Butchart, "Educating for Freedom," pp. 453–490; Wright "Education for Blacks in Georgia," p. 29; Logan, "The Evolution of Private Colleges for Negroes," p. 216.

7. Raymond B. Fosdick, *Adventure in Giving: The Story of the General Education Board* (New York: Harper and Row, 1962); Louis Harlan, *Separate and Unequal: Public School Campaigns and Racism in the Southern Seaboard States 1901–1915* (Chapel Hill: University of North Carolina Press, 1958; 1968 Atheneum edition), pp. 86–87.

8. For an excellent treatment of urban interest in organizing American agriculture see David Byers Danbom, "The Industrialization of Agriculture, 1900–1930" (Stanford University, Ph.D. Dissertation, 1974); Robert C. Ogden to Mrs. Arthur Gilman (May 23, 1903), Box 6, Robert C. Ogden papers; Library of Congress, Washington, D.C. (hereafter listed as Ogden Papers); Ogden, "Speech on Negro Education" (1900), Box 22, Ogden Papers; see especially James D. Anderson, "The Southern Improvement Company: Northern Reformers' Investment in Negro Cotton Tenancy," *Agricultural History* 52 (January 1978): 111–131.

9. William H. Baldwin, "The Present Problem of Negro Education in the South," *Journal of Social Science* 37 (December 1899): 52–60; James D. Anderson, "Education for Servitude: The Social Purposes of Schooling in the Black South, 1870–1930" (University of Illinois, Ph.D. Dissertation, 1973), pp. 208–216.

10. Industrial Philanthropists quoted from James D. Anderson, "Northern Foundations and the Shaping of Southern Rural Black Education, 1902–1935," *History of Education Quarterly,* 18 (Winter 1978): 371-396.

11. Baldwin, "Problem of Negro Education in the South," pp. 53–54; for the

social purposes of black industrial education, see Anderson, "The Hampton Model of Normal School Industrial Education, 1868–1900."

12. Confidential Report of Wallace Buttrick to the Trustees of the John F. Slater Fund, 1902, Box 260, General Education Board Files in Rockefeller Foundation Archives (hereafter listed as GEB Files); Baldwin quoted from Louis P. Harlan (editor) *The Booker T. Washington Papers*, Vol. 4 (Urbana: University of Illinois Press, 1975), pp. 141–145; Ogden quoted from Henry S. Enck, "The Burden Borne: Northern White Philanthropy and Southern Black Industrial Education, 1900–1915" (University of Cincinnatti, Ph.D. Dissertation, 1970), p. 52; Baldwin "Problem of Negro Education in the South," pp. 54–55; Baldwin quoted from Raymond B. Fosdick, *Adventure in Giving: The Story of the General Education Board* (New York: Harper and Row, 1962), p. 11; Henry S. Enck, "Black Self-Help in the Progressive Era: The Northern Campaigns of Smaller Southern Black Industrial Schools, 1900–1915," *Journal of Negro History* 41 (January 1976): 73–87; Harlan, *Separate and Unequal*, p. 94.

13. Meyer Weinberg, *A Chance to Learn: A History of Race and Education in the United States* (Cambridge: Cambridge University Press, 1977), p. 280.

14. Weinberg, *A Chance to Learn*, pp. 267, 280; Henry C. Badger, "Negro Colleges and Universities 1900–1950," *Journal of Negro Education* 21 (Winter 1952): 89–93; Thomas Jesse Jones (ed.), *Negro Education: A Study of the Private and Higher Schools for Colored People in the United States* Vol. I (Washington, D.C.: Government Printing Office, 1917), p. 59.

15. William K. Selden, *Accreditation: A Struggle Over Standards in Higher Education* (New York: Harper and Brothers Publishers, 1960), pp. 32–37; Harry Washington Green, "Higher Standards for the Negro College," *Opportunity* 9 (January 1931): 8–11; Leland Stanford Cozart, *A History of the Association of Colleges and Secondary Schools 1934–1965* (Charlotte, N.C.: Heritage Press, 1967).

16. Selden, *Accreditation*, pp. 35–37.

17. W. E. B. DuBois, *The College-Bred Negro* (Atlanta: Atlanta University Press, 1900); W. E. B. DuBois and Augustus Dill (eds.), *The College-Bred Negro American* (Atlanta: Atlanta University Press, 1910); Jones, *Negro Education*, pp. 58, 64; Green, "Higher Standards for the Negro College"; Cozart, *History of the ACSS*. Hampton and Tuskegee, the two black educational institutions most favored by industrial philanthropists, were excluded from consideration because they were normal schools and it was their mission to provide precollegiate education for the training of common school teachers.

18. Thomas J. Morgan to Wallace Buttrick (January 25, 1901); Morgan to Buttrick (January 29, 1901); George Sale to Buttrick (December 23, 1909); Sale to Buttrick (January 8, 1908), Box 716; Malcolm MacVicar to Buttrick (June 7, 1902), MacVicar to Buttrick (August 12, 1902); Buttrick to MacVicar (August 18, 1902); George Rice Hovey to Buttrick (March 30, 1908), Box 170, GEB Files; Jones, *Negro Education* pp. 7–8.

19. W.E.B. DuBois, "The General Education Board," *Crisis* 37 (July 1930): 230.

20. Wallace Buttrick to George Sale (Mary 29, 1907), Box 59; Report of W.T.B. Williams to Buttrick (May 22, 1907), Buttrick to the General Education Board (May 22, 1907), Box 716, G.E.B. Files.
21. Fosdick, *Adventure in Giving*, pp. 151–155; Darlene Clark Hine, "The Pursuit of Professional Equality: Meharry Medical College, 1921–1938, A Case Study," in Franklin and Anderson (eds.), *New Perspectives on Black Educational History*, pp. 176–177.
22. Wallace Buttrick to John D. Rockefeller, Jr. (February 5, 1914), Box 203; Abraham Flexner to Oswald Garrison Villard (December 1, 1914), Box 203; The General Education Board's Conference on Negro Education (November 19, 1915), GEB Files.
23. The General Education Board's Conference on Negro Education (November 29, 1915), pp. 130–138, 149–152, 162–164.
24. General Education Board, "Negro Education" (January 24, 1916), Box 722; Jones, *Negro Education*, p. 64; Monroe Henry Little, Jr., "The Black Student at the Black College, 1880–1964" (Princeton University, Ph.D. Dissertation, 1977), p. 28; James D. Anderson, "Philanthropy in the Shaping of Black Industrial Schools: The Fort Valley Case, 1900–1938," *Review Journal of Philosophy and Social Science*, 3 (Winter 1978):184–209.
25. Jones, *Negro Education*, pp. 310, 314–315; The General Education Board's Conference on Negro Education (November 29, 1915), GEB Files.
26. Fayette A. McKenzie, *Ideals of Fisk* (Nashville: Fisk University Press, 1915), p. 7; Herbert Aptheker (ed.), *W.E.B. DuBois: The Education of Black People* (Amherst: University of Massachusetts Press, 1973), pp. 52–57; DuBois, "Fisk," *Crisis* 28: 251–252; Raymond Wolters, *The New Negro on Campus: Black College Rebellions of the 1920s* (Princeton: Princeton University Press, 1975), pp. 35–39.
27. The most thorough study of McKenzie's repressive educational practice is Wolters, *The New Negro*, chapter 2, "W.E.B. DuBois and the Rebellion at Fisk University," pp. 29–69.
28. Julius Rosenwald to Abraham Flexner (January 15, 1917), Box 138, GEB Files; Flexner to Rosenwald (January 17, 1917), Box 138, GEB Files; Flexner to Harold H. Swift (April 2, 1917); Stewart B. Appleget to H.J. Thorkelson (June 12, 1928), "Appropriations Made by the General Education Board to Fisk University"; for endowment contributions see report of William H. Baldwin to General Education Board (October 6, 1924); L. Hollingsworth Wood to the General Education Board (May 6, 1920); Box 128, GEB Files; *Fisk University News*, December 1924, p. 20.
29. *Fisk University News*, April 1923, p. 7; *Fisk University News*, October 1920, p. 21; Thomas Jesse Jones to Abraham Flexner (October 4, 1915); L. Hollingsworth Wood to Wallace Buttrick (May 6, 1920); H.J. Thorkelson to L. Hollingsworth Wood (November 5, 1926), Box 138, GEB Files. For the philanthropists' role in actively recruiting trustees see Abraham Flexner to Julius Rosenwald (January 8, 1917); Rosenwald to Flexner (January 13, 1917); Flexner to Rosenwald (January 17, 1917); Flexner to Harold H. Swift (April 2, 1917); Flexner to Harry Pratt Judson (March 27, 1917);

Judson to Flexner (March 30, 1917); Judson to Flexner (April 13, 1917), Box 138, GEB Files.

30. Flexner, Memorandum on the Fisk Endowment Campaign (May 25, 1923), Box 23, GEB Files.

31. "Fisk University," a 1926 Memorandum in Box 138, GEB Files; "Fisk Endowment Drive in Nashville," *Fisk University News*, May 1924, pp. 31–32; "First Million-Dollar Endowment for College Education of the Negro in the History of America," *Fisk University News*, October 1924, pp. 1–13; The Commercial Club of Nashville to the General Education Board (January 24, 1920), Box 138, GEB Files. Jones (ed.), *Negro Education*, pp. 314–315, 320–321.

32. Wolters, *The New Negro on Campus*, pp. 34–40, 49; *New York Times*, February 8, 1925, 2: 1.

33. DuBois quoted in Wolters, *The New Negro on Campus*, pp. 62–63; "Fisk University," a 1926 memorandum in Box 138, GEB Files; for General Education Board's contributions see Fosdick, *The General Education Board*, pp. 329–332; "Fisk University," Report by Thomas E. Jones to the General Education Board (September 27, 1928) and (September 28, 1928), Box 138, GEB Files.

34. Anderson, "Northern Foundations and the Shaping of Southern Rural Black Education"; Anderson, "Northern Philanthropy and the Training of the Black Leadership, 1915–1930," in Franklin and Anderson (eds.), *New Perspectives on Black Educational History*, pp. 97–111; Anderson, "Philanthropy in the Shaping of Black Industrial Schools."

35. Henry C. Badger, "Colleges That Did Not Survive," *Journal of Negro Education* 35 (Fall 1966): 308; W.J. Trent, Jr., and F.D. Patterson, "Financial Support of the Private Negro College," *Journal of Negro Education* 27 (Summer 1958): 401–402; Rufus E. Clement, "The Historical Development of Higher Education for Negro Americans," *Journal of Negro Education* 35 (Fall 1966): 301.

Edward H. Berman

Educational Colonialism in Africa: The Role of American Foundations, 1910–1945

Early in the twentieth century the idea became popular in influential circles that the common racial origins and similar dependent statuses of American Negroes and Africans justified—or perhaps even dictated—an identical educational policy for both groups. That the educational policy devised by the colonizers for their dependents, whether in America or in Africa, would benefit the former more than the latter was a significant factor in its formulation.

Support for this policy came from a number of American philanthropic foundations created as a result of the immense wealth amassed during the Gilded Age. Several of these—e.g., Rockefeller's General Education Board, the Jeanes Fund, the Rosenwald Fund—directed much of their largesse toward the nonacademic training of southern American Negroes. Personnel from the Phelps-Stokes Fund, frequently utilizing funding from the Carnegie Corporation and several Rockefeller foundations, facilitated the transference of the theory and practice of nonacademic education designed for southern Negroes (the so-called Tuskegee philosophy) to their African counterparts. This policy was clearly designed to perpetuate the dependent status of the African and the concomitant hegemony of the European colonial powers and settlers, thereby replicating the socio-economic relationships linking blacks and whites in the American South.

This chapter examines the evolution of and implementation of this policy from its inception late in the nineteenth century in the American South and discusses how the policy was transferred to English-speaking Africa in the period from 1920 to 1940. Much of the discussion focuses on the role played by the Phelps-Stokes Fund of New York, whose officers facilitated the exportation to dependent Africa of the Tuskegee variety of educational colonialism. The ability of the Phelps-Stokes Fund to garner funds for its African work from the Carnegie Corporation, the Laura Spelman Rockefeller Memorial, and the Rockefeller-created International

Education Board suggests a commonality of viewpoints regarding the direction of African education among these several foundations, whose interactions will be examined briefly.

The Planning of Negro Education: Background to the Phelps-Stokes Fund

By the time the Phelps-Stokes Fund was chartered in New York in 1911, with its primary purpose "the education of Negroes both in Africa and the United States," a differentiated and restricted educational system for southern Negroes had been institutionalized.[1] Beginning in 1898, a group of northern philanthropists—led by Robert C. Ogden of the New York department store chain of John Wanamaker; George Foster Peabody, a Wall Street banker; and William H. Baldwin, Jr., of the Southern Railway—met with selected northern and southern clergy and southern educators at Capon Springs, West Virginia, to coordinate southern Negro education.[2] These men had long before accepted the wisdom of the Tuskegee educational philosophy, with its emphasis on vocational and agricultural, nonacademic education and its depreciation of liberal-arts, academic education for southern Negroes. The proponents of the Tuskegee philosophy argued not only that a narrowly utilitarian education would win acceptance among southern whites, who would not feel threatened by Negro restiveness growing out of a literary education, but that such educational provision would greatly increase the labor value of the Negro race for the benefit of southern development and northern capitalist investors (see Anderson chapter).

There was little sentimentality and scant evidence of humanitarianism in these attempts to design an educational program for the southern black masses.[3] The tone for the decisions emanating from the several Capon Springs conferences was set by the 1898 keynote address, delivered by J. L. M. Curry, agent for the Peabody and Slater Funds, both long active in black education in the South. Curry asked his fellow conferees to remember that "the white people are to be the leaders, to take the initiative, to have the direct control in all matters pertaining to civilization and the highest interest of our beloved land. History demonstrates that the Caucasian will rule, and he ought to rule."[4] William H. Baldwin, Jr., a conference organizer, was very explicit about the relationship between Negro education and the economic development of the South. At the second Capon Springs Conference in 1899 he noted that "in the negro is the opportunity of the South. Time has proven that he is best fitted to perform the heavy labor in the Southern states. . . . He will willingly fill the more menial positions, and do the heavy work, at less wages, than the

American white man or any foreign race. . . . This will permit the Southern white laborer to perform the more expert labor, and to leave the fields, the mines, and the simple trades for the negro."[5] Baldwin was no less specific about the type of training necessary to inculcate the appropriate attitudes and skills into southern Negroes. Tuskegee, he said, not only taught black youngsters to work with their hands and the dignity of hard labor (a common refrain throughout the nineteenth-century literature on colonial and dependent peoples) but the experience there also taught the student "to have simple tasks [*sic*] and few wants . . . that can be satisfied."[6]

The conferees at Capon Springs arrived at three major decisions regarding Negro education by 1901. First, they decided that since Negroes did not have access to the mass systems of cultural diffusion as did the whites—and since the conferees did not intend to lobby for integration of the larger society to make these facilities available to all—it was necessary that provision be made to train a Negro leadership cadre. For this purpose, then, it was concluded that certain Negro colleges would be strengthened to educate a strong professional class—doctors, lawyers, ministers—which would be responsible for raising the general physical and moral level of the race in the segregated black communities. Second, it was agreed that slavery had shaped within the Negro mind some undesirable attitudes which had been reinforced under the influence of northern educators (during the Reconstruction period). These educators had led the freedmen to hope that through books they could enjoy the fruits of a literary education like white men. Consequently, it was decided that the Negro had been educated away from his natural environment and that his education should concern only those fields available to him. This key decision marked the formulation of the concept of a special Negro education. Third, it was decided that this special education—vocational and agricultural in focus—of the Negro had to be directed toward increasing the labor value of his race, a labor value which, not surprisingly, would see the white capitalist class as chief beneficiary.[7]

At the fourth Capon Springs Conference for Education in the South in 1901 a resolution was passed creating the Southern Education Board, formed to advocate public opinion in behalf of public schools for black and white southerners. The creation the next year of John D. Rockefeller's General Education Board alleviated any financial concerns which the planners of southern Negro education might have experienced. In addition, the General Education Board became, in Harlan's words, "a sort of clearing-house for Southern education and a permanent 'steering committee' for Northern sentiment interested in the educational advancement of the South."[8]

One of the more remarkable aspects of this campaign to design an education befitting the "special" condition of southern Negroes was the power wielded by the small and cohesive group of individuals who were involved. Harlan comments on the interlocking directorate which took control, noting that "eleven members of the Southern Board were also members of the General Education Board in its first decade, Baldwin and Ogden being successive presidents of the latter board and Peabody treasurer of both."[9] Ogden had been instrumental in the evolution of the concept of a special education for southern Negroes from the time of the Civil War. Indeed, it had been in the parlor of his Brooklyn residence that a few men had met in 1867 to consider Samuel Chapman Armstrong's plan for a vocational institute for freedmen in the tidewater Virginia village of Hampton. Ogden was associated with the resultant Hampton Institute for forty-five years, as trustee, as financial supporter, and finally as president of the board. Baldwin had a long and similar involvement with Hampton's sister institution at Tuskegee, Alabama.

The creation in 1907 of the Jeanes Fund, dedicated to the improvement of the rural life of southern Negroes through education, provided another link in the evolving network of northern philanthropic involvement in black education in the South. Established with the enthusiastic cooperation of the principals of Hampton and Tuskegee, the Jeanes Fund's first president was James H. Dillard, a member of the Southern Education Board, the General Education Board, and the agent of the Slater Fund (which supported vocational education for southern blacks). In 1923 Dillard became an active trustee of the Phelps-Stokes Fund, thereby formalizing a relationship that had proven mutually advantageous for the Jeanes Fund and the Phelps-Stokes Fund from 1911, the year in which the latter was incorporated.[10]

Like Booker Washington, whom he knew well and admired, Dillard wanted the southern Negro to inch forward, utilizing those resources at hand, gradually moving toward that Utopia which had been expected since 1863. And for Dillard one of the most efficacious means to this end was the Jeanes teacher, a local Negro who could make contact in the rural communities as no one else could and who could adapt the school curriculum to the conditions of these communities. Hygiene, home economics, and industrial and agricultural training were to form the backbone of the curriculum for Jeanes rural schools. In 1925 the Jeanes school concept was transferred to Kenya, largely owing to the vigorous advocacy for such a transplantation by representatives of the Phelps-Stokes Fund.[11]

Anson Phelps Stokes, the first and influential president of the Phelps-Stokes Fund, had close links to the northern philanthropist-capitalists who planned the "special" education for southern Negroes. In addition to being the secretary of Yale University and later canon of Washington Cathedral, Stokes was a longtime member of the General Education Board, the Rockefeller-created International Education Board, the Rockefeller Foundation itself, and Tuskegee Institute. He was joined at the fund in 1912 by Thomas Jesse Jones, who had spent seven years at Hampton Institute as part-time instructor, chaplain, and director of the research department. By the time he became associated with the Phelps-Stokes Fund, the Welsh-born Jones shared the social, political, and economic viewpoints of the northern philanthropists who had designed the system of southern Negro education. Although he would spend his next thirty-two years at the Phelps-Stokes Fund arguing that his educational philosophy was based solely on objective data (he was trained as a sociologist) and the best interests of black people in America and Africa, Jones's antiegalitarian and white supremicist views were always close to the surface. Subscribing to the theory that the industrialization of the South and the mechanization of the region's agriculture could best be carried forward through the physical efforts of the black man, Jones could write as late as 1939 that "the Southern States require the Negro at least for his services as a laborer."[12] In view of these sentiments it is not surprising that his educational philosophy was an extension of this sociopolitical pronouncement.

It should be emphasized that Jones's viewpoint was not an aberration among those responsible for Negro education from 1900 to 1945. Rather, it was the representative view of the philanthropists and their agents. In the context of American social thought throughout the period, these philanthropists were considered to be liberals or, in Harlan's words, "moderate progressives." They acquired this designation because they were "moderate in the North on the delicate racial and sectional issue, and progressive in the South in the limited sense that . . . they offered education as a key to regional progress."[13] But the moderation, or liberalism, of this period did not include an egalitarian approach to the role of the black man in American society any more than it did when Thomas Jefferson wrote of universal rights and privileges while excepting Negroes.

In 1917 a two-volume survey of Negro education in the American South was published.[14] Authored by Jones and sponsored partly by the Phelps-Stokes Fund, of which he was by then the educational director, the study maintained that the only education appropriate for the black man was that with a strong vocational/agricultural bias. Academic/literary education was perceived as dysfunctional for the black man because it (1) would open vistas that he could not attain in the rigidly segregated American social structure, (2) would fail to provide the appropriate skills that would make the black man a more productive worker or agriculturalist (significantly, there were no data to indicate that training along lines epitomized by the Tuskegee philosophy actually did improve the laborer's market value), and (3) would seriously undermine the ability of the white ruling oligarchy to maintain its political hegemony in the face of demands for equality, which it was feared an academic/literary education would engender. In brief, Jones was espousing the Tuskegee philosophy of education, which sought to ensure that the black man in the southern United States would be trained as a semiskilled, semiliterate, and cooperative member of a burgeoning work or agricultural force, and whose manpower would be utilized to help industrialize and modernize the economy of the reconstructed South.

Jones's recommendations flowed logically from the series of events which began with the opening of Hampton Institute in 1869, led to the founding of Tuskegee in 1881 in its image, necessitated the codification and institutionalization of the theory of a "special" education for southern Negroes at the Capon Springs Conferences after 1898, and elevated Booker T. Washington to the position of spokesman for all things pertaining to Negro Americans. Jones's survey lent an aura of intellectual respectability to these events by encompassing them within the framework of an educational philosophy (that of educational "adaptation" or educational "essentials"), thereby providing a pedagogical rationale for a basically discriminatory educational policy.[15] It also legitimated these events by cloaking his recommendations and the policy predating them in the mantle of objective social science survey data. His study "proved," he argued, that Negro children were gaining more from an applied educational experience than from one which stressed liberal arts subjects and had no immediate applicability. Jones's recommendations were given additional credence by the fact that the study was published by and partly funded by the United States Office of Education, thereby providing at least the appearance of the official imprimatur.

Not everyone, however, concurred with Jones's recommendations or the sociopolitical-economic philosophy supporting them. By arguing "that sound policy requires white management and white teachers to have some part in the education of the [Negro] race,"[16] Jones opened the door for a spate of virulent criticism regarding his motives and those of the organization he represented. W. E. B. DuBois asked if Negroes were going to be content "to have our interests represented in the most important councils of the world—missionary boards, educational committees, in all activities of social uplift—by white men who speak for us, on the theory that we cannot speak for ourselves?"[17] Carter G. Woodson, Negro historian and social critic, objected that "no school was considered ideal by these 'controllers' [Jones, Stokes, the Phelps-Stokes Fund, and those foundations supporting the Fund] unless it followed the usual industrial lines and emphasized domestic arts, domestic science, gardening, and home nursing. Schools which concentrated on developing the power of the Negro to think and do for himself were not desirable and were classified as unworthy of philanthropic support."[18] Both DuBois and Woodson were concerned that Jones's main interest, and that of the foundations supporting him, was in developing a pliable, obedient, self-effacing Negro populace which would not question the existing social order or the Negro's place in it and would defer to white dictates. They argued loudly that the perpetuation of the Tuskegee philosophy would indeed create a permanent Negro underclass. Their fears were justified of course, not only for the American South but for Africa as well.

The Africanization of the Phelps-Stokes/Tuskegee Philosophy

Despite these criticisms of Jones's motives by DuBois and Woodson, the publication of the Negro education survey catapulted the Phelps-Stokes Fund into a leadership role among those organizations concerned with the education of the so-called "backward" peoples (read colonial subjects, who were almost exclusively black, brown, or yellow). The Africanization of the Phelps-Stokes/Tuskegee policy dates from a visit to Tuskegee in 1912 by J. H. Oldham and Alek Fraser, both influential British missionary-educators, who immediately sensed the possibilities for the adaptation of Booker T. Washington's educational activities to Britain's African colonies. The British interest in the Tuskegee concept was not new; it had been expressed in one way or another since the mid-nineteenth century.[19] What was novel, however, was that for the first time British colonial policymakers were searching seriously for a coherent educational policy to implement in their dependencies. The Negro education survey, which articulated British sentiments of long standing, provided a rallying point for those British officials who wanted to codify colonial educational policy.[20]

J. H. Oldham was one of the most persuasive and influential advocates of the applicability of the Tuskegee concept for Africa in British public life. From 1908 to 1910 he was secretary of the World Missionary Conference at Edinburgh and secretary of its Continuation Committee from 1910 to 1921. In addition to his position as secretary of the International Missionary Council, he edited the *International Review of Missions*, which under his guidance became the quasi-official journal of the Protestant missionary societies in Great Britain from its inception in 1912.[21]

From his London headquarters Oldham, described by one observer as "that arch intriguer for good,"[22] began to exert influence over members of Parliament, primates of England, and, more importantly for our purposes, the general direction of British colonial and missionary education policy. Early in the 1920s, just at the time that the Phelps-Stokes Fund was undertaking its initial work in Africa, Oldham began to devote more attention to the problems of African education. He introduced Thomas

Jesse Jones to those British officials most responsible for African educational policy, as well as to missionary and colonial officials in Africa. In 1924 Oldham became the Phelps-Stokes Fund's representative in the United Kingdom and intensified his vigorous lobbying efforts to have Phelps-Stokes Fund/Tuskegee concept incorporated into official mission and colonial educational policy.[23]

British missionary groups had been agitating, with Oldham's encouragement, for a survey of British African education since 1914, but first official parsimony and then the Great War interceded. Heeding a call from their coreligionists in Britain, the American Baptist Foreign Missionary Society called for a survey of African education in 1919, a survey which it was felt would provide the data enabling the Protestant mission societies in Africa to better coordinate and plan their work. J. H. Oldham saw the proposed survey as just the instrument required to bring some semblance of order to a disjointed African educational policy on the parts of both the British government and British and Continental mission societies. Thomas Jesse Jones viewed the survey as a logical extension of his work in Negro education, as well as being the vehicle to spread his gospel of a restrictive educational franchise in the service of the British empire he so admired.

Because of the wide publicity given to Jones's survey of Negro education, as well as the semimissionary character of the Phelps-Stokes Fund, it was not surprising that the request from the American Baptist Foreign Missionary Society to conduct the survey of African education should be directed to the Phelps-Stokes Fund. By 1919, when this official request was considered by the Committee of Reference and Counsel of the Foreign Mission Conference of North America, there was general agreement by missionary policymakers on both sides of the Atlantic that the fund's expertise in the problems of the education of the underdeveloped peoples was unparalleled. The final details for the survey of African education were worked out in a meeting including Stokes, Jones, Oldham, and Robert R. Moton, who had succeeded to the principalship of Tuskegee upon Washington's death in 1915. It was agreed that Jones would be chairman of the forthcoming educational commission and that Oldham would provide Jones with introductions to British government and missionary officials both in London and in Africa.

The report of the African Education Commission, which toured eight countries in western and southern Africa during 1920 and 1921, reads remarkably like the earlier survey of Negro education.[24] As in the Negro education report, that of the African Education Commission stressed the importance of agricultural education and simple manual training, the need to establish a differentiated educational system for African leaders and for the masses, and the necessity of adapting education to local conditions. Jones argued strongly for increased emphasis on character education, noting that an emphasis on vocational rather than literary education was the surest way to achieve the formation of a malleable and docile African worker.

Jones's report was published just as policymakers in London were searching for elements to include in a uniform educational policy for British Africa. J. H. Oldham was the key figure among this group, and in 1923 he approached representatives of the Colonial Office with the suggestion that he draft a memorandum on education in British Africa.[25] The result was the creation, several months later, of the British Advisory Committee on Native Education in Tropical Africa. This committee, which was charged with coordinating British African educational policy during the remainder of the 1920s and the 1930s, was in total agreement with the need to transfer the Tuskegee/Phelps-Stokes Fund policy to Britain's African colonies. In fact, committee members felt so strongly about the appropriateness for Africa of this policy that they dispatched the committee's newly appointed chairman, Hanns Vischer, on a three-week "study" tour of southern Negro educational institutions. The Phelps-Stokes Fund office coordinated Vischer's schedule, which, not surprisingly, featured visits to Tuskegee Institute and several schools in its orbit.[26]

The Colonial Office, enthusiastic about the work of the first Phelps-Stokes African Education Commission, later in 1923 prevailed upon the officers of the fund to dispatch a second survey team to Africa, this time to eastern, central, and southern Africa. The problems there were more intractable for the British government than those in its West African colonies because of the presence in eastern, central, and southern Africa of significant numbers of white settlers. Rather than viewing the settler presence as a problem, however, Jones felt that the white minority groups in Kenya, Malawi, the Rhodesias, and South Africa rendered the situation in those territories more akin to that in the American South, where of course blacks greatly outnumbered whites in many areas, particularly in the rural locales. Accordingly, Jones included among the personnel for this second African survey team James H. Dillard, president of the Jeanes Fund and by this time a Phelps-Stokes Fund trustee. His reasons for doing so were simple: the good works performed by Dillard and his colleagues in other foundations and agencies in institutionalizing the Tuskegee philosophy had provided an appropriate educational system for the southern Negro. Since the situations of the American South and colonial Africa were so similar, Jones reasoned, surely the model so successful in the former locale could be transferred to the other.

Given the background to the second commission and its personnel, it could hardly have produced a novel document.[27] Once again Jones gave primary emphasis to his four essentials of education—health and hygiene,

appreciation and use of the environment, the effective development of
home and household, and recreation and culture. Additionally, he stressed
the importance of offering the African masses only the most restricted
vocational training and, citing the overwhelmingly rural nature of African
societies, particularly agricultural education. Implicit in his pronouncements was the assumption that African societies would remain rural
indefinitely, while at the same time providing the European-dominated
sectors with the requisite raw materials and labor to support industrialization.

Having once established the justification for the primacy of agricultural
instruction, Jones introduced Dillard and the concept of the Jeanes
teacher, an important instrument in the furtherance of the Tuskegee
concept of a rurally based and restricted educational franchise. The Jeanes
school concept in the southern United States had been nurtured pedagogically by Booker T. Washington and Hollis B. Frissell, Hampton Institute's principal, and by James H. Dillard. Financial support to implement
the concept came from these institutions, but more particularly from the
General Education Board, the Southern Education Board, and the Phelps-
Stokes Fund.[28]

The colonial officials and white settlers in eastern, central, and southern
Africa immediately sensed the political implications of the Phelps-Stokes
Fund's recommendations, recognizing, as their American white southern
counterparts had earlier, that such a restricted educational offering would
insure, in the words of Kenya's colonial secretary, ". . . an intelligent,
cheerful, self-respecting, and generally docile and willing-to-learn African
native. . . ."[29] Another colonial educationist, upon whom Jones's proposals made a favorable impression because they paralleled his own, felt that
the only way to minimize the African's ". . . annoying conceit and self-
assertiveness . . ." was by training him to a due appreciation of his
industrial and agricultural potential.[30] That such an education would
perpetuate the African's status as a drawer of water and a hewer of wood
was fully understood by Jones, the members of his team, and the white
settlers and colonial officials with whom Jones discussed his plans.[31]

Jones's reasons for establishing the Jeanes school in Kenya, and for
negotiations over the next several years for others in white-ruled eastern,
central, and southern Africa, were two-fold. On the one hand, he believed
unequivocably that non-European peoples were unsuited for a literary
education and, consequently, a reasonable alternative must be sought for
them—an alternative beneficial to the dependent peoples and to their
European benefactors as well. This belief grew out of Jones's southern
American experience and was related to the perceived "civilizing" effects
of the superior European culture on the more primitive African culture,
whether in America or in Africa. In this vein, he wrote to the British

Under-Secretary of State for the Colonies in 1925 regarding the necessity of British settlement for the "development of Africa and Africans. Intimate acquaintance with interracial problems in America and some knowledge of Africa convince me that there is sufficient similarity between the two continents to warrant forecast and judgments on the basis of comparison."[32] Secondly, his great regard for the civilizing and uplifting impact of British colonialism led him to recognize that the Tuskegee philosophy implemented in Africa would provide a pedagogical creed to complement the Colonial Office's political philosophy of indirect rule and a tool to enable the colonial administrators to control the Africans under their jurisdictions, while at the same time providing a social service that *appeared* beneficial to the Africans.

While the Phelps-Stokes Fund was still accepting the accolades of British policymakers who in 1925 offered up a slightly Anglicized version of the fund's program as official British African educational policy,[33] Jones was negotiating with the Carnegie Corporation for financial aid to place a Jeanes training school in Kenya. In 1925 his efforts succeeded, capping negotiations which had begun two years earlier, when the corporation agreed to appropriate $37,500 for the Kenya venture.[34]

The Phelps-Stokes Fund's influence with the Carnegie Corporation was not limited to winning support for the establishment of a Jeanes school in Kenya. In 1927, armed with letters of introduction and advice from Jones, President Keppel and Secretary Bertram of the corporation traveled to Africa to assess the possibilities for substantial grants to British territories. Upon their return they noted that "education and culture [in Africa] generally suffer from too slavish an imitation of British institutions and practices, whereas the actual conditions of life are much more similar to Canada and the United States, and suggestions as to how African problems can most effectively be solved are in many instances more likely to be found in these countries."[35] Jones had even persuaded President Keppel of Carnegie to allow his close collaborator, Charles T. Loram of South Africa, to arrange Keppel's itinerary. Loram, who was born of British parents in South Africa and who at the time served as *the* African representative of the Phelps-Stokes Fund, had been a key figure on the 1920 and 1924 African Education Commissions.[36]

The Carnegie Corporation's programs in black Africa (from initiation in the 1920s until their practical cessation caused by the outbreak of war in 1939–1940) fell into three categories, all of which revolved around the Phelps-Stokes Fund/Tuskegee "conventional wisdom" of the period. These included (1) aid to support Jeanes training schools in eastern and central Africa; (2) visitors' programs enabling prominent white educators from southern and eastern Africa to travel to the United States, where they "investigated" firsthand the southern Negro and his network of mission-supported schools; and (3) a shortlived attempt to devise intelligence tests adapted to African conditions, such as those which by this time had come into vogue in the United States.[37]

Because the income from the Phelps-Stokes Fund was quite limited, and because his ideas about exporting to Africa the Tuskegee concept were quite grandiose, Jones was forced to look to other American foundations in addition to Carnegie for support for his African programs. Here he met with only limited success. One of the Rockefeller philanthropies, the International Education Board, of which Anson Phelps Stokes was a trustee, partially underwrote expenses incurred in mounting the second African Education Commission in 1924. In 1925 Jones sent a long memorandum to the acting president of the Laura Spelman Rockefeller Memorial, detailing the need for immediate action by America on behalf of Africa. He argued that intervention in African affairs was warranted by the applicability to Africa of the American experience in the development of her great rural areas and in the education of southern Negroes. Several projects, with emphasis on "learning by doing," were outlined. Among these were (1) study and observation of American activities by colonial officers, mission educators, and native educators; (2) financial aid and redirection of African education institutions for the training of Jeanes visiting teachers; and (3) the encouragement of his essentials of education and of other activities relevant to the special conditions of Africans. Within the year the Laura Spelman Rockefeller Memorial responded with a grant of $35,000 for this exploratory scheme.[38]

This grant enabled Jones to push ahead with an even larger scheme. His chief collaborator was Loram, and during 1926 they hammered out details of a plan which they were certain would give direction to African education in eastern, southern, and central Africa for the forseeable future. At the core of the design was the Jeanes supervisory teacher, an individual whose appropriateness for Africa neither Jones nor Loram doubted for a moment. The plans were ambitious: Loram suggested the establishment of Jeanes training centers in Northern Rhodesia, the Transvaal, Bechuanaland, Natal, Basutoland, Cape Province, Nyasaland, Portuguese East Africa, Tanganyika, Uganda, Zanzibar, and Southern Rhodesia. These would supplement the pioneer school funded by the Carnegie Corporation at Kabete, Kenya. To accomplish this task, Jones submitted another and significantly larger proposal to the Laura Spelman Rockefeller Memorial.[39] But even as he was working on this task, Phelps-Stokes Fund personnel were heavily involved in yet another manifestation of the Tuskegee philosophy in Africa—the establishment in Liberia of the Booker Washington Agricultural and Industrial Institute.

As early as 1909 Olivia Eggleston Phelps Stokes, Anson Phelps Stokes's aunt, had won the enthusiastic endorsement of Booker T. Washington for a school in Liberia modeled after Tuskegee.[40] It was not until Jones had led the first African Education Commission to Liberia in 1920, however, that the idea of founding an agricultural and industrial school there began to take definite shape. Jones concluded that Liberia was a mess. Part of the reason for this situation was that even the little education given was inappropriate for the students. "The type of education in which they are interested," he noted, "is so exclusively concerned with preparation for clerical pursuits and government service of a literary character as to exclude any effort to prepare youth to deal with hygenic, agricultural, industrial, and social needs. . . ."[41] The typical remedy for this unsatisfactory state of pedagogical affairs lay in curricular revision: "the work will be much strengthened if provision is made for more instruction in cooking and sewing and some work in simple industries.[42]

Jones's recommendations for Liberia led, in 1923, to the creation of the Advisory Committee on Education in Liberia, a consortium of Protestant mission societies dedicated to implementing Jones's educational essentials.[43] The first educational advisor to this group, James L. Sibley, was selected by Jones after demonstrating his belief in the applicability of the Tuskegee philosophy for Africa. The work of this Advisory Committee, orchestrated by Jones from the Phelps-Stokes Fund's New York office, was the catalyst which rekindled Olivia Eggleston Phelps Stokes's interest in the dormant Tuskegee-in-Liberia idea. In mid-1927 the educational advisor met with representatives of the mission societies, Tuskegee Institute, and Anson Phelps Stokes (representing his aunt and the Fund), to discuss final arrangements for the opening of a Tuskegee-in-Liberia. A year later the Liberian legislature chartered the Booker Washington Agricultural and Industrial Institute at Kakata, Liberia, with administrative offices located at the Phelps-Stokes Fund in New York.

From the beginning and despite considerable time, effort, and financial support from the Phelps-Stokes Fund and from Tuskegee Institute itself, the project experienced difficulties. These included financial problems, the removal from the scene by disease and death of crucial institute personnel, the affiliation with the institute of an outspoken white supremicist, and the links between the institute and the Firestone Company at a time when the company's name was anathema to many Liberians. By the mid-1930s, however, there were a few signs of success. For example, in 1936 thirty-one acres were under cultivation, a like amount had been prepared, and over 100,000 bricks had been fired toward the construction of the pumphouse, the woodwork shop, and the powerhouse. Additionally, there were over 100 student boarders and some twenty-five day pupils. But the struggle was uphill continually, and for each step forward during the 1930s the institute seemed to lose two. Toward the end of the 1930s there was outspoken criticism of the curriculum, the principal noting that the youngsters had no interest in the narrow industrial and agricultural course, showing a preference for "strictly academic work." At the same time the motives of the Phelps-Stokes Fund and its representatives in Liberia were increasingly questioned by the Liberians themselves. In 1939 the American minister to Liberia sent a report to the State Department, detailing some of the problems of the Booker Washington Institute. The Liberian government was concerned, he noted, that the head of the institute was not a Negro, that there was discrimination in salary schedules between black and white workers, and that the curriculum at the institute derived from a colonial model.[44]

Perhaps the most telling criticism of all was leveled in 1943 by Liberia's president, Edwin Barclay. President Barclay was angered because many Americans affiliated with the institute "appear to look upon Liberia as they would upon a Negro community in the southern United States." He echoed the sentiments of many of his countrymen when he noted that "because I feel that the Liberian point of view has been ignored [with regard to curriculum and organization of the Institute], I have taken very little interest in it. . . ."[45] Although it was obvious as early as 1931 that Liberians had little interest in a vocational and agricultural education laced with strong Christian overtones, the Phelps-Stokes Fund continued to promote this educational fare as the most appropriate for them.

Jones and the Phelps-Stokes Fund were indeed viewing the Liberians as "a Negro community in the southern United States," but they were surprised, and not a little chagrined, to discover that the Liberians—and other Africans as well—refused to accept their dictates. The Booker Washington Agricultural and Industrial Institute was planned by those of a common philosophy and implemented by them after only token consultation with the prospective clientele. The Liberian point of view was indeed ignored. Considering that Jones and his colleagues did not bother to consult with their southern Negro constituency before deciding what kind of education it should have, it is not surprising that the same modus operandi was followed in Liberia. This total disregard for the opinions of the Liberians stands in vivid contrast to the close consultation which characterized the relationships between Jones and fund personnel and the white leadership of South Africa, where the Phelps-Stokes Fund was engaged in a series of projects.

Jones first visited South Africa in 1921 with the African Education Commission. By this time, of course, the Union was well on its way toward the evolution of a policy of apartheid. Not surprisingly, the recommendations of the African Education Commission, which paralleled theory and practice not only within the Union but in Rhodesia and Kenya as well, were well received as vindications of a prudent course of development. Jones's recommendations for Bantu education in the Union paralleled those for Negro education in the United States as suggested in his 1917 survey.

Those South African institutions with strong vocational and/or agricultural emphases, e.g., Tsolo Agricultural School, Marianhill Institute, Amanzimtoti Institute, and Inanda Seminary, were accorded high praise by Jones because they provided institutional confirmation of the efficacy of his theory of a narrowly applied education for dependent peoples.[46] Although Lovedale Institute was often referred to as the Hampton of Africa, Jones noted important and disappointing differences between the two. One of these was the very limited instruction in gardening, hygiene, and handiwork related to simple needs (one of Jones's pet phrases), while another was the slight relationship of the school to the community.[47] Put another way, the child had failed to follow in the parent's proven footsteps. The one institution of higher education for Africans was the South African Native College at Fort Hare. Jones disapproved of the institution's emphasis. The work of the college was based on the requirements of the University of South Africa, which, Jones noted, "has courses of a non-practical type. . . ." He considered the difficult course of study at Fort Hare unsuitable for native students because of its literary orientation.[48] It would be better to have courses in gardening techniques than in Roman history at Fort Hare, Jones argued. Significantly, he had advocated a similar program for Howard University in Washington, D.C. in the 1917 survey of Negro education.

It was during this 1921 trip that Jones first met Charles T. Loram, then Natal's chief inspector of native education, whose role was central to the southern African educational activities of the Phelps-Stokes Fund and the Carnegie Corporation. Although this was the first time Jones and Loram had met, they knew of one another. Loram's educational/political philosophy was remarkably similar to Jones's. Vocational and agricultural education, adapted to local conditions, were at its core. He argued that "the course of study should take account of the peculiar experience of the Natives. . . . From the beginning the education given should be meaningful to the Natives, and to this end should lead up to the future occupations open to them."[49] Loram's educational ideas regarding the Bantu had been reinforced during his residence in the United States, where he came into contact with the Tuskegee philosophy and practice during his graduate study at Columbia University's Teachers College. Jones was impressed with Loram even before their initial encounter. He noted that "his [Loram's] splendid book, *Native Education in South Africa*[sic], is undoubtedly the best summary of Native education in any part of Africa. . . ."[50] Jones could identify particularly with Loram's assessment that the fundamental problem of the existing system of African education was that it was "very much a bookish affair and almost entirely tinged with the white man's outlook." Additionally, it was "too academic and too little related to the everyday needs of the African."[51]

That the fund would conduct its work in South Africa through the established political order, which happened to be white, was never questioned. Jones, Stokes, and Loram assiduously courted the white establishment. The canvassing of black African opinion was carried out largely by Africans who had won grudging acceptance in the white man's world, e.g., D. D. T. Jabavu of the South African Native College, and who did not question the existing political and social arrangements. Africans such as John L. Dube, who labored successfully with Jones's concepts and methods but who were considered independent and thus politically unsafe, were never considered worthy of support by the fund.[52]

Jones believed that black South Africans were to play subordinate roles to the ruling whites indefinitely. This paralleled his belief regarding the role of the black man in America. Black South Africans, like their black American counterparts, could actively partake of the best of their respective societies just so long as they were content to remain, in Stokes's words, "junior partners in the firm."[53] Jones counseled that the Phelps-Stokes Fund and other American philanthropic foundations should continue to support South African activities because the Union "is destined to become more and more the determinant of all Africa. . .because of the splendid types of whites. . .there."[54] American philanthropy could help "the whites make the best possible use of their opportunities [and then] . . . they will be able to continue their society successfully, and [the] development of the native should not endanger that success."[55]

The provision of a specific type of schooling was, of course, viewed as an important factor in retaining a segregated society. Loram perceived that "racial strife was against the best interests of the white community in South Africa . . . ." Consequently, he likened himself to one "going round with an oil can reducing race friction wherever he could. Schools run along. . . [Tuskegee] lines constituted part of the oil that would reduce the friction and thus make the white minority in South Africa more secure."[56] The increasingly institutionalized forms of inequality and discrimination were no more important to Loram than to his friend Jones; rather, they were viewed as part of the natural order of things.

Conclusions

From its incorporation in 1911 until 1945 the Phelps-Stokes Fund based its actions on several premises: (1) that the experience of the Negro South was directly relevant to black Africa; (2) that neither the African nor the

American Negro would be self-governing, or even have a large say in his welfare, in the foreseeable future; and (3) that a narrowly defined vocational education could be used to train American Negroes and Africans to become productive, docile, and permanent underclasses in their respective societies. These premises were logical outcomes of the historical processes that had led Samuel Chapman Armstrong to launch Hampton Institute in 1869, Booker T. Washington to create Tuskegee in 1881 while eschewing political equality, the Capon Springs Conferences for Education in the South between 1898 and 1901 to institutionalize a "special" education for southern Negroes, and the agreement of British and American policymakers in the first quarter of the twentieth century that education was important in helping to maintain stratified societies.

Jones and Stokes were direct descendants and participants in these historical events, and their influence was greatly augmented by the visibility of the Phelps-Stokes Fund, the cooperation of other American philanthropic foundations, the Colonial Office's Advisory Committee on Native Education in Tropical Africa, and mission groups in Great Britain and North America. During the 1920s and 1930s Jones and the Phelps-Stokes Fund could not accept that Africans should have a voice in their educational future. Consequently, they clung tenaciously to the concept of "adapted" education, Jones's educational essentials. Ranger has noted the perversity of this disdain for African aspirations. The Africans, he points out, "were not demanding white restriction of educational form and content in the interests of the preservation of what whites thought to be valuable in African life." And yet, "these were the years of the Jeanes teacher-training centres where Africans were instructed how to impart educational essentials in a relevant manner."[57] The limited success of the Booker Washington Agricultural and Industrial Institute in Liberia and the failure to implement the major recommendations of the two African Education Commissions demonstrate that imposition of educational concepts and practices incompatible with African aspirations was destined to fail.

Notwithstanding the ultimate failure of most of his recommendations, Jones's work in Negro education and on the African Education Commissions projected him and the Phelps-Stokes Fund into the forefront of British African educational planning until the outbreak of World War II. With the fund as their institutional base, Stokes and Jones used their contacts and influence to solicit aid from American philanthropic foundations for support of approved forms of American Negro and African education. There is no doubt that Jones's influence was important in the allocation of the $500,000 which the Carnegie Corporation appropriated for its African work in 1927. The General Education Board and the Carnegie Corporation made grants to southern Negro education largely on the recommendations of individuals affiliated with the Phelps-Stokes Fund, e.g., Jones, Dillard, Stokes.

The members of the boards of trustees of the several foundations concerned with Negro education—the General Education Board, the Southern Education Board, the Jeanes Fund, the Phelps-Stokes Fund, to mention only the most prominent—shared the belief that the position of the Negro in the American social order necessitated an education commensurate with his predetermined and immutable status as a member of the laboring class. American political realities, however, dictated that public pronouncements assure all groups of equal access to society's social benefits—one of which was schooling. At the same time, the requirements of an expanding system of corporate capitalism, to whose basic tenets the trustees of the foundations under discussion subscribed without reservations, necessitated an educational system that would (1) provide the requisite skills for a burgeoning work force to perpetuate the capitalist system, and (2) socialize the working classes to the belief that they were receiving their fair share of society's educational benefits. It was this basic contradiction between the public rhetoric of democracy and corporate necessity that explains the lengthy public defense of nonacademic education as an "uplifting" force for a previously deprived race. The requirements and realities in Africa were considered so similar by foundation, missionary, and Colonial Office personnel that the transference of the ideology and educational practice from the southern United States to Africa appeared eminently reasonable to these policymakers.

It was this commonality of outlook among these interested parties regarding the black man's permanent place that enabled Phelps-Stokes Fund personnel to successfully solicit funds to implement the Tuskegee educational policy both in the United States and in Africa. The small grants voted by the Phelps-Stokes Fund trustees to support a vocationally oriented school in southern Africa or to finance the program to bring carefully selected British colonial educators and missionaries to examine the schools within Tuskegee's orbit were not nearly so important as the catalytic effect that the fund's advocacy had on larger donor foundations, e.g., the Carnegie Corporation.[58] The message articulated so cogently by Thomas Jesse Jones was well received as the most prudent course to follow in the boardrooms of some of America's most important foundations. The success of the Phelps-Stokes Fund lay at least as much in its articulation of an ideology whose general tenets were already commonly accepted in influential American (and British) financial and political circles as in any inherent merits of the policy itself. The Phelps-Stokes Fund/Tuskegee philosophy was, in short, an idea whose time had arrived, and representatives of several major foundations provided the largesse to implement the credo.

Large-scale implementation of the Phelps-Stokes/Tuskegee concept of education would have altered the course of African history radically (as it did of American history), and not in the African's favor. For a long time the Phelps-Stokes Fund advocated a policy which not only was pedagogically questionable, but which was strongly racist as well. Phelps-Stokes Fund policies in Africa were intended to perpetuate indefinitely the unequal relationships characteristic of the colonial situation, a situation in which Africans were confronted with policies beneficial primarily to the metropolitan powers and their representatives in the colonies.

Notes

1. Many of the details concerning the work of the Phelps–Stokes Fund can be found in my unpublished doctoral dissertation, "Education in Africa and America: A History of the Phelps-Stokes Fund, 1911–1945" (unpublished Ed.D. dissertation, Columbia University), 1969.
2. A good discussion of the social and political ideologies of these men can be found in Louis R. Harlan, *Separate and Unequal: Public School Campaigns and Racism in the Southern Seaboard States, 1901–1915* (New York: Atheneum, 1968).
3. Indeed, Harlan, p. 80, quotes editor Lyman Abbott of the reasonably enlightened publication *The Outlook* as saying that "we have to get rid of our more or less vague idea that all men are created free and equal." This was not an atypical sentiment shared by most of the "liberal" elements of eastern society at the turn of the twentieth century.
4. *Proceedings of the Second Capon Springs Conference for Education in the South, 1899* (Capon Springs: n.p., 1900), p. 38.
5. Quoted in James D. Anderson, "Education as a Vehicle for the Manipulation of Black Workers," in Walter Feinberg and Henry Rosemont, Jr. (eds.), *Work, Technology and Education* (Urbana: University of Illinois Press, 1975), pp. 33–34.
6. Ibid., p. 34.
7. For an analysis of the Capon Springs conferences, see Henry A. Bullock, *A History of Negro Education in the South from 1619 to the Present* (Cambridge, Mass.: Harvard University Press, 1967).
8. Harlan, *Separate and Unequal*, p. 85. See James D. Anderson's chapter in this volume for a discussion of the influence and *modus operandi* of the General Education Board.
9. Harlan, *Separate and Unequal*, pp. 85–86. Again, see Anderson's chapter cited above for details.
10. The Jeanes Fund's origins are described in Arthur D. Wright and E. R. Redcay, *The Negro Rural School Fund, Inc. (Anna T. Jeanes Foundation, 1907–1933)* (Washington, D.C.: The Rural School Fund, Inc., 1933). The first educational allocation made by the Phelps–Stokes Fund was in the sum of $2,500 for the Jeanes Fund. See the Minutes of the Executive

Meeting and Trustees of the Phelps–Stokes Fund, November 15, 1912, at the Phelps–Stokes Fund office, New York.

11. For details see pp. 187–189 below.

12. Thomas Jesse Jones to H. L. West, May 6, 1939, American Colonization Society Papers, Library of Congress, Washington, D.C. Details of the backgrounds of Jones and Stokes can be found in Berman, "Education in Africa and America," pp. 64–69.

13. Harlan, *Separate and Unequal*, p. 75.

14. Thomas Jesse Jones, *Negro Education, a Survey of the Private and Higher Schools for Colored People in the United States*, 2 vols. (Washington, D.C.: Government Printing Office, 1917).

15. Jones's philosophy of education is elaborated in his *Four Essentials of Education* (New York: Charles Scribner's Sons, 1926).

16. *Negro Education*, I, p. 7.

17. W. E. B. DuBois, "Thomas Jesse Jones," *Crisis* 12 (October 1921): 253.

18. Carter G. Woodson, review of *Progress in Negro Status and Race Relations, 1911–1946: The Thirty-five Year Report of the Phelps–Stokes Fund*, in *Journal of Negro History* 24 (1949): 368.

19. As early as 1847 the Education Committee of the Privy Council to the Colonial Office had issued a report detailing the importance of industrial training for the colored races in the colonies. The text of this 1847 report is summarized in H. S. Scott, "The Development of the African in Relation to Western Contact," *Yearbook of Education, 1938* (London: Evans Brothers, 1938), pp. 698–739.

20. Kenneth King, *Pan-Africanism and Education: A Study of Race Philanthropy and Education in the Southern States of America and East Africa* (Oxford: Claredon Press, 1971), indicates other early manifestations of these sentiments. See especially pp. 43–57.

21. For more on Oldham's influence on education in Africa and on the work of the Phelps-Stokes Fund, see George Bennett, "Paramountcy to Partnership: J. H. Oldham and Africa," *Africa* 30 (October 1960): 353–361; and K. J. King, "Africa and the Southern States of the United States of America: Notes on J. H. Oldham and American Negro Education for Africans," *Journal of African History* 10 (1969): 659–677.

22. R. E. Wraith, *Guggisberg* (London: Oxford University Press, 1967), p. 146.

23. Shortly after his return from Tuskegee in 1912 Oldham persuaded the principals of Hampton and Tuskegee, H. B. Frissell and Booker T. Washington, respectively, to contribute articles to the *International Review of Missions*, detailing the applicability of the educational model developed at their institutions for African conditions. See, for example, Booker T. Washington, "David Livingstone and the Negro," *International Review of Missions* 7 (1918): 420–431.

24. Thomas Jesse Jones, *Education in Africa: A Study of West, South and Equatorial Africa, by the African Education Commission* (New York: Phelps-Stokes Fund, 1922).

25. This is detailed in a memorandum entitled "Educational Policy in Africa," and dated April 3, 1923, from Oldham to W. G. A. Ormsby-Gore, Ar-

chives of the Conference of Missionary Societies in Great Britain and
Ireland (Edinburgh House), Box 219, London. These papers have now
been transferred to the archives of the World Council of Churches in
Geneva.

26. For specifics, see J. H. Oldham to C. T. Loram, June 28, 1923; and H. Vischer
to Oldham, November 19, 1923, Edinburgh House Box H-15.

27. Thomas Jesse Jones, *Education in East Africa: A Study of East, Central and
South Africa by the Second African Education Commission under the aus-
pices of the Phelps-Stokes Fund, in Cooperation with the International
Education Board* (London: Edinburgh House Press, 1925).

28. See Anderson's chapter in this volume for details of this support by the
General Education Board.

29. Edward B. Denham to Thomas Jesse Jones, June 4, 1924, Edinburgh House
Box 232.

30. H. S. Keigwin, "Native Development," n.d., but c. 1921, Edinburgh House
Box H-21.

31. In fact, the Governor of Northern Rhodesia, after entertaining Jones and his
party, wrote that Jones had urged "very strongly that the direction of
Native Education should not be in the same direction as European, and he
convinced me of the correctness of that view." H. J. Stanley to J. H.
Thomas, September 25, 1924, Edinburgh House Box 230.

32. Jones to W.A. Ormsby-Gore, September 8, 1925, Phelps-Stokes Fund file L-7,
New York.

33. *Educational Policy in British Tropical Africa*, London, His Majesty's Station-
ery Office, 1925, xxi, cmd. 2374. J. H. Oldham and the British Advisory
Committee on Native Education in Tropical Africa played crucial roles in
the formulation of this document.

34. For details, see Richard D. Heyman, "The Role of Carnegie Corporation in
African Education, 1925–1960" (unpublished Ed.D. dissertation, Columbia University, 1970), pp. 49–59.

35. Quoted in Heyman, "The Role of Carnegie Corporation in African Education," p. 19.

36. See pp. 190 and 193–194 below for a discussion of Loram's work on behalf of
the Phelps–Stokes Fund.

37. For additional details, see the chapter in this volume by Russell Marks; and
Clarence J. Karier, "Testing for Order and Control in the Corporate
Liberal State," in Clarence Karier, Paul Violas, and Joel Spring (eds.),
Roots of Crisis: American Education in the Twentieth Century (Chicago:
Rand McNally, 1973).

38. Jones to Colonel Arthur Woods, June 1, 1925; Beardsley Ruml to Anson
Phelps Stokes, April 9, 1926; Anson Phelps Stokes to Beardsley Ruml,
April 7, 1926, Phelps–Stokes Fund file C–5.

39. Loram to Jones, August 14, 1926; Jones to Beardsley Ruml, February 19,
1927; Jones to Leonard Outhwaite, March 3, 1927; Jones to Raymond
Fosdick, May 18, 1927; Anson Phelps Stokes to John D. Rockefeller, Jr.,
May 21, 1927, Phelps–Stokes Fund file C–5. Jones's proposal for a network
of Jeanes schools was not funded by the Laura Spelman Rockefeller

Memorial, probably because by this time the memorial was devoting most of its money and interest to the social sciences. For details, see Donald Fisher's chapter in this volume.

40. Booker T. Washington to Olivia Eggleston Phelps Stokes, December 2, 1909, Phelps-Stokes Fund file S-0.
41. Jones, *Education in Africa*, p. 298.
42. Jones, "Diary of the African Education Commission," typescript copy at Phelps–Stokes Fund, p. 15.
43. For details, see Berman, "Education in Africa and America," pp. 173–229.
44. Lester B. Walton to Secretary of State, January 7, 1939, copy in Phelps-Stokes Fund file S-4 (3).
45. Edwin Barclay to Anson Phelps Stokes, July 8, 1943, Phelps-Stokes Fund file S-2 (1).
46. Jones, *Education in Africa*, pp. 208–212.
47. Jones, "Diary of the African Education Commission," pp. 240-247. A discussion of the work at Lovedale can be found in Robert H. Shepard, *Lovedale, South Africa* (Lovedale: Lovedale Press, 1940).
48. Jones, "Diary of the African Education Commission," p. 248. The role played by Fort Hare in nurturing several generations of African nationalists who would challenge South Africa's *apartheid* policy and the reasons for the institution's eventual demise are discussed in R. Hunt Davis, Jr., "Fort Hare: The Rise and Decline of an African University in South Africa, 1916–76," a paper presented at the Ninety-Second Annual Meeting of the American Historical Association, Dallas, Texas, December 1977.
49. Charles T. Loram, *The Education of the South African Native* (London: Longmans, Green and Company, 1917) p. 225.
50. Jones, "Diary of the African Education Commission," p. 195. Jones was so impressed with the book's contents that he forgot the correct title.
51. Quoted in R. Hunt Davis, Jr., "Charles T. Loram and an American Model for African Education in South Africa," *African Studies Review* 19:2 (September 1976): 91. For additional details on Loram's career, see Richard D. Heyman, "C. T. Loram: A South African Liberal in Race Relations," *International Journal of African Historical Studies* 5:1 (1972).
52. In his unpublished diary, Jones noted that although Dube's leadership of the Ohlange Institute created some problems the European authorities in Natal should remain on friendly terms with him. The clear implication was that problems arose because Dube refused to act the way an African was "supposed" to act, i.e., subservient. Needless to say, these sentiments were omitted from Jones' published version of his diary, *Education in Africa*. For more on Dube: R. Hunt Davis, Jr., "John L. Dube: A South African Exponent of Booker T. Washington," *Journal of African Studies* 15 (Winter 1975/76): 497–529.
53. Quoted in Davis, "Charles T. Loram and an American Model for Education in South Africa," p. 90.
54. Jones, *Education in Africa*, p. 179.
55. Jones as quoted in *The Rand Daily Mail* (Johannesburg), May 4, 1931.

56. Quoted in Davis, "Charles T. Loram and an American Model for African Education in South Africa," p. 97.

57. T. O. Ranger, "African Attempts to Control Education in East and Central Africa, 1900–1939," *Past and Present* 32 (December 1965): 68.

58. Specifics of two annual educational budgets voted by the Phelps–Stokes Fund trustees will indicate just how limited were the financial appropriations made by the fund. The 1927–1928 educational budget, voted at the trustee's meeting of November 15, 1927, appropriated $74,865 for the fund's educational work. Of this total $29,780 was for general administration, including staff salaries; $10,360 for Negro educational institutions and scholarships, including $2,500 for the Hampton–Tuskegee endowment campaign and $460 for support of an Alabama Jeanes Teacher; $4,850 for interracial work in the United States, including $500 for the discretionary fund of Tuskegee's principal, R. R. Moton; $19,875 for African educational work, including $2,500 to support visits of educators from Africa to America, $1000 to support the work in Liberia, and $7,000 for the work in South Africa; $9,000 was earmarked for work on the Indian educational survey and support of the Penn School, a satellite of Hampton. The depression–year budget of 1931–32 reflects similar priorities, only at a slightly reduced scale. The educational budget, voted at the trustees' meeting of November 19, 1931, appropriated the funds as follows: $31,274 for general administration and salaries; $11,200 for support of Negro education in the United States; $3,150 to support interracial work in the United States; $20,750 for African education, including $2,000 for the Liberian venture, and $4,000 for the educator fellowship program; and $7,250 for work in South Africa.

Edward H. Berman

The Foundations' Role in American Foreign Policy: The Case of Africa, post 1945*

The major American foundations—Ford, Carnegie, Rockefeller—have played important roles in the furtherance of American foreign policy objectives since 1945. By that time it was obvious to all but the most recalcitrant colonialist that it was only a matter of time before the British, French, and Dutch colonial empires would be dismantled. At the same time, the division of the world between the two superpowers, the United States and the Soviet Union, signaled the beginning of the scramble to align the colonial territories to one or other of the emerging power blocs.

Washington policymakers viewed a strong American influence in the former colonies necessary for several interrelated reasons. First, measures had to be taken to insure that raw materials required to fuel the economies of the Western bloc be kept available for Western interests. Second, since the American corporate system requires an ever expanding market for its continued economic health, it was perceived that constraints diminishing that market by however small a factor were threatening to the total system. According to this analysis, any newly independent nation in Africa or Asia that fell under the influence of the Communist bloc was lost to American capitalist markets, thereby threatening not only the American corporate and financial system but worldwide capitalism as well. The advent of the Cold War, with its increasing McCarthyite hysteria in the United States, was fortuitous for American policymakers and business leaders for two reasons. On the one hand, it provided a justification for the increasingly expansionist tendencies of the American military establishment, as policymakers cited the Communist threat to the Western and American way of life posed by Soviet expansionism. Second, this continually cited threat served to deflect domestic attention from the fact that

* An earlier version of this chapter appeared in the *Harvard Educational Review*, 49 (May 1979): 145–180.

military expansionism primarily served the interests of American corporations and financial institutions with international operations.

Since 1945 the trustees and officials of the Carnegie Corporation and the Ford and Rockefeller foundations have shared with Washington policymakers and corporate and financial leaders the belief that the future of the American economic and political system required a strong American presence in the nations of the developing world. This commonality of viewpoint linking the foundations to the American political and business structure is explained by the fact that foundation officers and trustees often double as, or previously served as, Washington policymakers as well as business leaders. Indeed, the boards of trustees of the Ford, Carnegie, and Rockefeller foundations represent, according to Nielsen, "a microcosm of what has variously been called the Establishment, the power elite, or the American ruling class."[1]

In this chapter I shall indicate how, in the post–World War II period when overt colonialism was no longer acceptable to the world community, the foundations devised strategies to bind the newly independent African nations to the United States to insure that the vested economic and strategic interests of this country were not threatened. The most important way in which foundations accomplished this was by devising programs linking the educational systems of the new African nations to the values, modi operandi, and institutions of the United States. Foundation officials have stressed the nonpolitical, technocratic nature of this involvement in African education, noting that their interests lay solely in the provision of educational models and institutional support designed to help the developing African nations modernize their societies and thereby provide more benefits for their populations. Below I shall also examine this rhetoric of altruism and the assumptions undergirding the technocratic approach and shall suggest that these are merely smokescreens behind which the economic and strategic interests of the United States were/are furthered.

The Foundations as Part of the Ruling Class

The major foundations were creatures of nineteenth- and twentieth-century capitalist accumulation, and by mid-twentieth century they sought to perpetuate that form of corporate capitalism that brought them into existence. Since the American Cold War mentality of the post–World War II period viewed a monolithic Communist threat directed against the economic and political hegemony of the worldwide capitalist structure, it should come as no surprise that the foundations sought to create the circumstances in the developing world that would insure change that was predictable, manageable, and consonant with their interests. We could hardly expect otherwise from institutions that are "overwhelmingly passive, conservative, and anchored to the *status quo*."[2] Several examples illustrating the ties linking foundation boards of trustees to the American economic and political hierarchy will help to explain the foundations' attachment to the status quo from which their principals benefit.

John J. McCloy, who served at various stages of his career as Assistant Secretary of War, chairman of the board of the Rockefellers' Chase Manhattan Bank, High Commissioner to Germany in the postwar period, chairman of the board of trustees of the Ford Foundation, trustee of the Rockefeller Foundation, and president of the World Bank, is the archetypical member of this establishment. Robert S. McNamara's career parallels McCloy's in its broad outlines: he has served as the president of the Ford Motor Company and the World Bank, as secretary of Defense and an architect of the Vietnam war, and as a trustee of the Ford Foundation. The list goes on, of course, and includes, for example, Stephen Bechtel, president of the corporation which bears his name and which is one of the world's largest building concerns. In addition to his position as director of several large corporations, Bechtel serves as a trustee of the Ford Foundation and of Stanford University, the latter having received considerable financial support from the former. Indeed, so intertwined are the corporate leaders with the activities of the major foundations that Nielsen, onetime Ford Foundation executive, cites as "incontestable fact" that "the boards of the big foundations are controlled by members of the American business elite."[3] These links do not, ipso facto, guarantee that foundation board members with corporate interests will use foundation activities to further their vested interests. However, it strains credibility to assume that foundation policies set by these people "are neutral as regards social change and controversy."[4]

The strong links between the American business elite and the boards of the major foundations insure that the foundations will not pursue policies inimical to the best interests of the business community. One could even argue, of course, that it would be likely that the foundations favor policies which actively further these interests. In fact, data presented below indicate that because the large American foundations—particularly Ford, Carnegie, and Rockefeller—are linked so closely through board memberships to the American corporate and financial structure and to the governing establishment of the United States, that they pursue policies both at home and abroad which further the interests of both the American business community and the American government. This comes about, according to Prewitt and Stone, because of "the perceived mutuality of interest between high government officials and . . . big business." This in turn means that big business "is extremely influential in the exercise of political power in the areas of business concern."[5]

Foundation officials share with business leaders and with Washington policymakers a concern for the political stability of the territories in which they have programs. This mutual concern with stability has led to the overriding assumption on the parts of foundation officials, business leaders, and implementors of American foreign policy that change in the newly independent African nations must be evolutionary rather than revolutionary. Packenham notes that the consensus among American foreign policy and aid architects holds that "radical politics, including intense conflict, disorder, violence, and revolution, are unnecessary for economic and political development and therefore are always bad."[6] In short, the measured and gradual development of African nations serves the best interests of world stability, as defined by American interests, and, at the same time, provides an international context within which the major foundations play crucial and influential roles in developing national polities. This involvement has the further advantage of binding leaders of the new African nations to political doctrines which, at the very least, are not overtly antagonistic to corporate capitalist development.

Given the commonality of interests and outlook and the overlapping memberships that characterize the boards of the major corporations and financial institutions, the major foundations, and Washington policymakers it is little wonder that American foundations made concerted efforts in the late 1950s and early 1960s to be in positions to influence the direction taken by newly independent African nations. The repeated references by foundation spokesmen during the 1950s to the economic importance of Africa, Asia, and Latin America further help to explain the American foundations' interest in the underdeveloped world. As Carnegie's Alan Pifer noted, American industry could ill-afford the loss of cheap sources of raw materials which could only be secured in the nations of Africa, Asia, and Latin America.[7] Paul Hoffman, the first president of the Ford Foundation, one-time president of Studebaker Corporation and of the influential Committee for Economic Development, and director of the Marshall Plan spoke to this point bluntly, noting that ". . . our own dynamic economy has made us dependent on the outside world for many critical raw materials."[8] Any actions threatening American industrial access to the sources of raw materials so vital to the continued expansion of the American economy were viewed as a threat to the United States. Philip E. Mosely—then a staff member of the Rockefeller Foundation and formerly of the Council on Foreign Relations' influential War-Peace Studies project—had made the same point as early as 1949 when he remarked that "the resources which the United States needs are not located in Europe, but are in the underdeveloped areas of the world. This is a significant reason why we can't concentrate all our efforts on Europe."[9]

The almost pathological fear that the national leaders in the developing nations would deny American access to sources of raw materials led the United States government to appraise national leaders in terms of their favorable disposition toward the American free enterprise system and the concomitant American access to raw materials. While on the one hand American democracy demanded lip service to the ideals of national independence and territorial integrity in the developing nations, the dominant thinking of the period, as Kolko succinctly concludes, held that ". . . the future of American economic power [was] too deeply involved for this nation to permit the rest of the world to take its own political and revolutionary course in a manner that imperil[ed] the American freedom to use them."[10] Appropriate measures, consequently, had to be taken to assure American access to resources deemed important to the United States. These measures could be subtle, in the form of influencing important individuals through training, economic assistance for institutional development, or even bribes. Or the measures could be brutal, as, for example, in the American interventions in Guatemala, the Dominican Republic, and ultimately Vietnam. Whatever the means, many important policymakers subscribed to the sentiments of W. W. Rustow, who wrote ". . . that the security and well-being of the United States, even its very survival as a free nation, was dependent upon the utilization and application of its power to shape the international environment in a manner compatible with American interests and security."[11]

Foundation Programs in Africa

By the mid-1950s, then, a consensus had emerged among foundation officials, business leaders, and Washington policymakers regarding the importance of the developing world for the United States. The mutual concern for controlled development which did not threaten American interests in Africa, Asia, and Latin America led the Carnegie, Ford, and Rockefeller foundations to support educational projects and developmental models which would bind foreign nationals and their institutions to the dominant values of the American corporate state. In Africa these program emphases led to (1) the creation of lead universities located in areas considered of geo-strategic and/or economic importance to the United States; (2) an emphasis within these institutions on social science research and related manpower planning programs; (3) programs to train public administrators; (4) teacher training and curriculum development projects; and (5) training programs which shuttled African nationals to select universities in the United States for advanced training and returned them home to assume positions of leadership within local universities, teacher training institutions, or ministries of education. Of no less significance was the training made available by foundation programs to help American scholars understand various aspects of selected African societies. At the Ford Foundation this latter concern took the form of the International Training and Research Program, the purpose of which was, as a Ford vice-president wrote to his Carnegie counterpart in 1954, "to put such knowledge [of world affairs as is gleaned by the scholars through this program] more effectively at the disposal of those who are responsible, in government and private life, for representing the United States in international affairs. . . ."[12] A few words about each of these program thrusts will help to understand the attempts by foundation personnel (1) to train a generation of African leaders sympathetic to the interests of the United States, and (2) to train a generation of American scholars who would place their knowledge at the service of the American corporate state.

LEAD UNIVERSITIES

By the mid-1950s, after extended discussion, the officers of the Rockefeller Foundation determined to increase the Foundation's activities in the developing world. Late in 1955 the trustees voted to appropriate $5 million annually for five years to further this work. The focus immediately turned to building up university centers of excellence in selected developing countries.[13] These lead universities would play important roles in the creation of a leadership cadre, which, in the words of foundation president Dean Rusk, would help to sustain "the orderliness of economic growth. The objective is one that engages directly the self-interest of the economically more advanced peoples and calls for their understanding and assistance."[14]

The Ford Foundation's concern with the developing world crystallized during the early 1950s also. The most immediate catalyst, coupled with the prevading economic and strategic concerns, was a Ford study in the early 1950s which confirmed the suspected "abysmal lack of knowledge" about the underdeveloped areas of the world on the part of policymakers in the United States.[15] This was of particular concern because foundation personnel felt that one of the primary responsibilities of the foundation was to insure that "the training [provided by Ford] . . . advance, either directly or indirectly, United States interests abroad."[16] The foundation's decision to undertake programs in India and South Asia had been made for similar reasons.[17]

The decision of the Ford Foundation to concentrate its African programs (with a few notable exceptions) on the training of elite cadres in public administration, agricultural economics, the applied sciences, and the social sciences, and to strengthen African universities and other postsecondary institutions for this purpose, was a logical extension of similar emphases in the foundation's domestic work. The foundation's concern for nurturing an academic and intellectual elite which would play the leadership role in the evolving domestic policy found its best expression in the work of the Ford-created and -supported Fund for the Advancement of Education.[18]

Ford and fund officials felt that they could nurture, through training offered in elite American universities, a cadre of potential leaders whose outlook and values would insure their support of the dominant American social, economic, and political institutions. These Ford-nurtured leaders would then assume their places in the upper managerial levels of major American institutions, where they would continue to uphold the interests of society's dominant classes. The assumption was that those trained in a particular way at specific institutions were the best fitted to run the key institutions of this society. Ford policy held that this approach was technocratic, nonideological, and only designed to assure that society's future leaders received the most appropriate training for the onerous tasks before them. From Ford's perspective there seemed little reason to doubt the efficacy of exporting a similar theory and modus operandi to developing nations.

The concern with world stability and the need to incorporate peripheral areas into the American-dominated world capitalist system led the foundations to concentrate their university programs in African areas considered of strategic and economic importance to the United States government and American corporations with African investments.[19] To this end, the Ford Foundation's most significant postsecondary educational undertakings were in Nigeria, Ethiopia, Congo/Zaire, and in a combined university scheme linking the East African nations of Kenya, Uganda, and Tanzania. Rockefeller funds were concentrated on the East African interterritorial scheme, in Nigeria, and, more recently, in Zaire.

The strategic, economic, and political importance of Nigeria for West Africa, indeed for all of Africa, is the result of her population base (almost one-quarter of Africa's total), her rich mineral resources (today Nigeria is the world's sixth leading oil exporter), and her geopolitical mass (bestriding the Bights of Benin and Biafra and spreading to the reaches of the Sahara). Ford Foundation personnel early recognized Nigeria's importance in terms of regional stability and as an area for potential investment by American corporations. This is evident from the fact that between 1958 and 1969 Ford spent approximately $25 million there, a figure representing almost two-thirds of its total West African expenditure during this period. Of this amount, almost $8 million went to underwrite university development, and some $5 million of that was concentrated at the University of Ibadan. If we include in this total the $2.3 million designated for economic development and planning (most of which was sponsored by the University of Ibadan) and the $3.9 million spent on training in public administration (most of which also took place within a university context), the total expenditure on university education in Nigeria by Ford was approximately $15 million, by far the most significant share of the total Nigerian expenditure.[20] The Rockefeller Foundation, on the other hand, allocated some $9 million to the University of Ibadan in the decade from 1963 to 1972.[21] The concentration of Rockefeller money in the University of Ibadan and in its other University Development Centers around the world (one of which was the University of East Africa scheme) meant, in the words of a high foundation official, that "our dollars will . . . be able to exert an extraordinary leverage."[22]

THE FOUNDATION EMPHASIS ON SOCIAL SCIENCE RESEARCH

Both the Ford and Rockefeller foundations placed great emphasis on the development of the social sciences at the lead universities they supported in Africa. They did so because of the belief in the efficacy of the social sciences to bring about, in Schroyer's words, "rationally managed" social change.[23] The conventional wisdom regarding development in the Third World during the 1960s held that the key lay in the creation of technocratically oriented elites with social science competencies which could be applied to the alleviation of the problems of underdevelopment. Arnove's comments on the orientation of the Ford Foundation are significant in this context, and no less so to the Rockefeller than the Ford Foundation that he discusses. "The Foundation's fascination with social science research in large part has consisted of support for a certain breed of economists whose quantitative approach to development is safe and respectable. This favoring of economists, particularly in the early sixties, has accorded with the Foundation's approach to treating development 'in terms of economic growth, technological competence, and improved managerial competence.' "[24] At the University of Ibadan both Ford and Rockefeller invested heavily in the development of the Nigerian Institute of Social and Economic Research and its related departments of economics, political science, and sociology. At the University of East Africa, generously supported by both foundations, the institutional bases for social science research were the East African Institute of Social Research in Uganda and the Institute for Development Studies in Kenya. In East Africa as in Nigeria there was a heavy emphasis on the development of the departments of economics, political science, and sociology.

Related to the foundations' emphasis on the development of the social sciences in the lead African universities was the equally strong concern with the manpower planning approach as the key to development. It was through the strengthening of the social sciences and the application of the manpower planning approach that the major foundations hoped to achieve the orderly growth of educational systems and subsequently of nations in Africa. In the late 1950s the Carnegie Corporation sponsored the much heralded Ashby Commission study of educational needs in Nigeria.[25] A crucial aspect of that study was a manpower projection forecast for the period 1960–1980. This manpower projection section was the work of Princeton University economist Frederick Harbison. His estimates of the high-level manpower requirements for Nigeria during the 1960–1980 period were followed by estimates of the kinds and quantity of schools required to fulfill these needs. The evident success of the manpower planning schema in the Ashby report led this human resources theory of development to win numerous adherents during the next few years.

Ford Foundation personnel were supportive of this approach because of their addiction to the application of social science research techniques, which they claimed were value-free, to developmental problems. Also, Harbison's work seemed marked by rigorous social science methodology. Not only did the Ford staff accept the efficacy of the manpower planning approach as related to educational development, but they soon became the champions of the gospel and attempted to spread it among the unconverted. To this end, the foundation teamed with the Carnegie Corporation in 1960 to underwrite a major research project, based at Princeton University, whose purpose was to study the role of education and high-level manpower in the modernization process. The book emanating from this research, *Education, Manpower, and Economic Growth*, was presented by its foundation sponsors as incontestable evidence supporting the new conventional wisdom embodied in the manpower planning approach to development.[26]

Educational reform posited on a theory of human resource development and elite mobilization is basically conservative, since its primary task is, according to Paulston, "to facilitate investment in personal development and to produce 'better' workers within the context of the existing educational and social system."[27] This emphasis on human resource development and technocratically oriented elites assumes, in short, that change can only flow from the top down, that change should be led by and orchestrated by an elite with the appropriate and approved training supportive of the existing social order. This view, so often passed off as nonideological, is, according to Barber, "pervaded by instrumental values such as stability (homeostasis) and efficiency ('good functioning' per se) that give it a static and politically conservative temper."[28] It hardly need be emphasized that African national leaders who subscribed to this viewpoint were more likely to be bound to the developmental perspectives and the political and economic institutions of the United States than were those who did not so subscribe.

It was an article of faith that the Ford Foundation's value-free development expert would carry with him to Africa the appropriate technology to help further the development effort. This American-produced technology often had not proven successful at home; however, it was assumed, ipso facto, that its application in Africa would hasten social development. Melvin J. Fox, long a Ford representative in West Africa, noted how "the technicians around Ford . . . believed that we could transfer the techniques necessary for modernization and that once we did transfer them . . . modernization would flow like water over the dam automatically. . . . In areas like Africa . . . it was generally believed that by transferring through expatriate advisors . . . some of our know-how we would enable these countries to at least begin the climb toward modernization."[29] It is instructive that, for all Ford's emphasis on empirical social science research methodologies and data aggregation in both its domestic and overseas work, so little attention was paid to the data collected on the efficacy, or lack thereof, of particular educational innovations at home before they were exported.[30]

Even those closest to Ford's work have expressed serious reservations about its African accomplishments. Despite Ford's professed rationality and logical planning in "the building of public services, education, and research on social and economic problems"[31] in Africa, "there was no overall plan or strategy." The foundation's massive educational efforts in Nigeria have been characterized by a Ford official as having grown haphazardly.[32] Farrell contends that the exportation to developing nations of educational gadgetry untested in the United States is a blatant manifestation of "intellectual colonialism." He argues that "one of the greatest mistakes of the last decade was the tendency of many Western academics to use the poor nations as laboratories for testing out theoretically interesting educational novelties which they have been unable to sell completely in their own societies . . ." and that "it is time that we got out of the business of peddling untried universal nostrums once and for all."[33] The Ford Foundation, of course, often facilitated the peddling of these nostrums in Africa and in the rest of the world as well.

If some few Ford field representatives had reservations concerning the efficacy of the foundation's emphasis on the social sciences and human resource development theory as the panacea for underdevelopment, Rockefeller personnel did not seem to manifest these qualms. The Rockefeller Foundation assured the orientation toward the corporate-capitalist development model by (1) placing its African fellowship recipients in the social sciences in elite American universities, whose proclivities toward the system-maintaining, structural functionalist view of society and the human resources theory of development were pronounced;[34] and (2) employing as faculty, during the formative periods of the universities of Ibadan and East Africa, only those expatriates whose academic approach subscribed to these viewpoints. The ability of the Rockefeller Foundation to mold an intellectual perspective is suggested by Kenneth W. Thompson, one-time vice-president of the foundation, who notes that "66 percent of all East African faculty have been Rockefeller Foundation scholars or holders of Special Lectureships established with Rockefeller Foundation funding for returning national scholars. . . ." And if the sample is limited to only professors and deans, the percentage of university personnel beholden to the Rockefeller Foundation for part or all of its training rises to 80.[35]

David Court, a Rockefeller Foundation representative in East Africa, has noted how "the desire of the University of East Africa to produce research-based policy recommendations and its faith in a value-free social science technology led to a willingness to rely on large numbers of expatriates as the best available practitioners."[36] The social science technology was not, of course, value-free. Nor were the expatriate faculty. Both technology and faculty subscribed to a structural-functionalist view of the world which presumed certain things. Such a *Weltanschauung* presumed, for example, that equilibrium is the normal state; change, consequently, "will generally appear to be pathological; where efficiency is regarded as the only acceptable value-neutral utility, it will quickly come to play the role of real values and goals. Functionalism, finally, 'banishes' values by disguising and renaming them."[37]

The foundations' heavy reliance on "value-free" social science research techniques, and the topics that interested them, precluded the examination of the fundamental structures, workings, and norms of the societies they supported. In effect, the foundations contributed substantial sums of money to programs and approaches that promised evolutionary, elite-directed change as opposed to revolutionary, mass-directed change.

PROGRAMS IN PUBLIC ADMINISTRATION

The foci of the Ford Foundation programs in public administration were at Ahmadu Bello University in Nigeria, the University of East Africa, and, most importantly, at the National School of Law and Administration in the Congo. In terms of strategic location, mineral wealth, and political potential the Congo loomed large in the eyes of Ford officials during the late 1950s and early 1960s. The relationships linking the foundation to State Department policymakers and to the CIA in the exercise of American foreign policy stand in clear relief through an examination of Ford's public administration program there.

Consultations in 1959 and early 1960 between the United States ambassador to Brussels and the director of Ford's International Affairs program resulted in a foundation grant in late 1960 to support the visit to the United States of carefully selected and prominent Congolese. The Ford funds were supplemented by the State Department. This initial Ford interest, on the eve of Congolese independence, soon led to a more substantial endeavor in the Congo itself. Again the initiative for Ford involvement came from the State Department, and this time concerned the establishment of a center for the training of Congolese leaders in Leopoldville, the Center for Research and Socio-Political Information.[38]

Significant though the center was at the time, it was not nearly as important for the subsequent political development of the Congo as Ford's next undertaking there, the establishment in 1961 of a National School of Law and Administration. Designed to train an elite cadre of public administrators, the National School concept grew out of Ford's interest in training limited numbers of administrators in elite institutions who would rule their polities. The success of the National School in performing this function is suggested by Ashley, who notes that "by 1968, the 400 odd graduates of the school made up an elite corps of civil servants who are now holding important administrative and judicial posts throughout the Congo." It is of more than just passing interest that the first and influential secretary-general of the National School was James T. Harris, who, according to Ashley, was "a Foundation specialist who had formerly served with the American Society of African Culture and had been president of the United States National Student Association."[39] What Ashley neglects to tell us is that allegedly Harris was long an important and valued CIA operative who was an active agent at the time he administered the Ford-organized National School in the early 1960s.[40]

Between 1961 and 1970, when it phased out its program, the Ford Foundation granted over $3 million for the work of the National School of Law and Administration. Because of the influence it exerted in American foreign policy matters, the foundation could also exert leverage on the International Cooperation Agency (the precursor of the Agency for International Development) to allocate funds for the work there. In this connection the comments of a high Ford official are germane: after noting that foundation representatives regularly consulted with federal agencies regarding the foundation's overseas work, James L. Morrill commented that the United States government and the foundation "had, of course, very similar objectives. . . ."[41]

Ashley, a one-time Ford program officer and a sympathetic observer of the foundation's overseas activities, sums up the relationship between the foundation and American foreign policy nexus during the 1960s. He notes:

> From the standpoint of the United States government, Ford activity in the Congo has been useful in furthering foreign policy objectives. The United States has been successful in its main political objectives of helping create an independent Congo not subject to Communist influence. It has been able to do this by relying on the United Nations for peacekeeping and on the Ford Foundation for helping initiate the key institutions for the training of administrators. . . . Ford assistance has therefore been an important element in furthering United States interests in Africa.[42]

Robert I. Fleming, one-time director of the Rockefeller Brothers Fund program in West Africa, elaborates on the role performed by the major foundations overseas. He notes that since World War II the government's and the foundations' assistance programs have been "striving to thwart communism, sell America's producers' goods, raise foreign living standards, or all three at once." In order to further the trade relationships between West African nations and the United States producers, Fleming suggested a number of ways in which foundations could facilitate this endeavor, including having the foundations support an economic advisor to each of the host governments and by helping to establish "investment promotion centers."[43]

The Ford Foundation consistently has stressed that its interest in training administrative cadres in Africa derives solely from its concern to educate public servants capable of providing basic administrative services in areas woefully lacking in any semblance of an independent civil service. Given the economic interests of the United States in the developing nations where Ford (and Rockefeller and Carnegie) programs have been concentrated and the role of the U.S. government in furthering these interests, one wonders if perhaps Gouldner's assessment may not be closer to the mark. "It is central," he notes, "to the effectiveness of a society using a system of 'indirect rule' that its organizational instruments be reliably controllable from the outside. The society thus depends greatly on appropriate socialization and education of the *administrative* and political classes. These develop expert skills, and create a readiness to credit the hegemonic class, to define it as a 'responsible' and effective stratum dedicated to the commonwealth; they define its role as legitimate and also generate loyalty to the social system."[44] The outside interests, of course, are American (and other Western) corporate and financial institutions with significant (and increasing) investments in developing areas. The "expert skills" are learned in foundation-sponsored programs, and the new administrative and political classes indicate to the society at large the benevolence of their rule while minimizing the debts they as a class owe to the outside interests, who benefit more than do the local nationals (see Arnove chapter).

The work of the Carnegie Corporation in Africa moved along different but complementary lines to that of the Ford and Rockefeller foundations during the 1950s and 1960s. The corporation's emphasis on higher education, which became noticeable after Alan Pifer joined the staff in 1953, was further delineated to focus on teacher education. The available evidence suggests that this focus resulted from the discovery in the late 1950s of an American institution not only heavily involved in teacher education, but which was desirous of exporting to Africa some of its accumulated expertise in this field.[45] In 1960 Columbia University's Teachers College received the first of several sizeable grants from Carnegie for a cooperative Afro-Anglo-American programs in teacher education. The purpose of the program was (1) to facilitate training opportunities for African teacher educators at Teachers College; (2) to provide a vehicle whereby Americans desirous of teaching in Africa could be prepared for this task at Teachers College and at the University of London's Institute of Education; and (3) to provide a wedge whereby Teachers College, and by extension American pedagogical principles and the values implicit in these, could gain entry into the evolving network of teacher training institutions in ex-British Africa.[46]

The cooperative relationships which the corporation had evolved with British officialdom from the 1920s soon paid handsome dividends (see my chapter on the Phelps-Stokes Fund). Without the cooperation of representatives of the British African colonial establishment, the rapid expansion of Carnegie's teacher training program in Africa could not have been realized. An important individual who helped to facilitate Carnegie's large scale entry into African teacher education institutes via the Teachers College Afro-Anglo-American program was L. J. Lewis, formerly a colonial official in Nigeria, one-time head of the department of education at Ghana's University College, and from the late 1950s the head of the influential department of Education in Tropical Areas at the University of London's Institute of Education. His counterpart and close friend at Teachers College was Karl W. Bigelow, who in 1952 had traveled to Africa courtesy of the Carnegie Corporation to familarize himself with the English education system there. In mid-1958 a Ford Foundation official chatted with Carnegie's Alan Pifer about the corporation's evolving teacher training emphasis in Africa. Later that year another Ford official, aware of Bigelow's association with the Carnegie people, met with the Teachers College professor in London and was impressed enough to recommend that the foundation support some of his African travel.[47]

Shortly thereafter the Ford Foundation decided to leave teacher education projects, with the exception of a sizable project in northern Nigeria during the mid-1960s, for the Carnegie people to coordinate.[48] A Carnegie-sponsored meeting in London in 1960, attended by representatives of Teachers College, the Colonial Office, the Carnegie Corporation, and the colleges or universities in Ibadan, Zaria, Ghana, Sierra Leone, Rhodesia, Nyasaland, and Uganda, assured a continuing and significant role for the Carnegie Corporation in African education.[49]

The influence of the Carnegie Corporation in an evolving teacher training network in Africa is suggested by the amount of money, totaling some $1.3 million, the corporation granted to Teachers College between 1960 and 1972.[50] This amount represents only the grants given directly to Teachers College to administer agreed-upon programs and does not include the sizable amounts granted to the African colleges and Institutes of Education which were linked to Teachers College and Carnegie through curriculum development projects, fellowship and teacher training schemes, and a common ideology.

A fuller understanding of Carnegie involvement in African education can only come through an examination of the Afro-Anglo-American Program in Teacher Education and related projects at Teachers College. As Carnegie officials recognized that American ties to the newly independent African nations needed to be strengthened, they began to search for ways, perceived by Africans as being nonpolitical, to insure these connections. The Afro-Anglo-American program, which eventually linked the educational systems of the new nations to the educational concepts, practices, and institutions of the United States, increasingly was viewed as the vehicle to accomplish this end. The significance of this program was profound, for, as I have noted elsewhere:

> By 1975 personnel from institutes of education at most universities in most formerly British colonies had been exposed to (if not influenced by) American pedagogical concepts as practiced at the influential Teachers College, Columbia University. Movement of personnel between African institutes and Teachers College for advanced degree work was an integral part of the program. In this way large numbers of influential African educators

were exposed at first hand to American pedagogical concepts
and practices, as well as to the values implicit in the corporate-
capitalist system. These educators also were made beholden to
American benevolence and largesse for their graduate training,
upon which rested so much of their status, prestige, and power at
home. Thus, through directed institutional development in Africa and through the influences exerted on those who directed
and served in these educational institutions, American influence
on Africa and African education systems was exerted.[51]

The foundations' links to American foreign policy, as articulated
through support for various African teacher education programs coordinated by carefully chosen American colleges and universities, is further
illustrated by the outcome of a 1960 meeting held at Princeton, New
Jersey. Representatives at that gathering included the Ford, Carnegie, and
Rockefeller foundations, the Department of State, the International Cooperation Administration, the British Colonial Office, the African-American Institute, and representatives of the three East African territories of
Uganda, Kenya, and Tanzania. The conferees noted especially the lack of
qualified secondary school teachers available to the area during a period
when it was hoped that school enrollments would increase significantly.
Consequently, it was suggested that the foundations and the International
Cooperation Administration pool their resources, identify a significant
American teacher training institution as their agent, and support that
institution's efforts to train a large cadre of American teachers to work in
the rapidly expanding secondary school network in East Africa.[52] Because
of its previous contacts with both the Carnegie Corporation and the Ford
Foundation, it was not surprising that Teachers College, Columbia University, was designated as the training institution, and that Karl W.
Bigelow (long a Ford and Carnegie protégé) was the chief negotiator in
securing the contract. The awarding to Teachers College of this contract
for the training of teachers was a guaranteed way of assuring that change
in East Africa, at least that articulated through the educational system,
would not be revolutionary.[53]

AMERICAN UNIVERSITY TRAINING PROGRAMS FOR AFRICAN STUDENTS

In the previous section mention was made of the influence of one institution, Teachers College, in forging a common outlook among African
students studying in the United States. An elaboration of this point is
provided by the comments of Karl W. Bigelow, the architect of the
Teachers College-Carnegie Corporation liaison for African teacher edu-

cation, in his report on the 1972 conference of the Association for Teacher Education in Africa. The association was the successor of the Afro-Anglo-American program and Bigelow was the chief executive officer. Bigelow noted that of the twenty-seven official African participants at the 1972 conference, 33 percent had Teachers College associations, primarily through earlier fellowship provisions. He further noted that Teachers College was associated with all twenty African institutions comprising the association's membership.[54]

Arnove's comments on the recruiting and training patterns which mark the Ford Foundation's Latin American programs are no less relevant when the focus is turned to Africa. In the case of Latin American students and Ford, three institutions—Harvard, Chicago, and Stanford—train a significant proportion of Ford-sponsored Latin American educational researchers, planners, administrators, and faculty. But, as he comments in his chapter, "the power of the foundation is not that of dictating what will be studied. Its power consists in defining professional and intellectual parameters, in determining who will receive support to study what subjects in what settings."

A perusal of the Rockefeller Foundation list of fellowships in the social sciences awarded to Nigerians and East Africans, the foci of Rockefeller African educational efforts from 1955 to 1975, reveals a concentration of awards for study at a handful of elite American universities. Awards to study economics were most frequently made for students attending Stanford, Harvard, Michigan, and Chicago; Columbia University's Teachers College garnered the majority of awards for the study of education.[55]

While there can be little doubt that African students educated at Stanford, Chicago, Michigan, or Columbia received high levels of instruction, there is evidence to suggest that they were also being trained in methodologies and ideologies grounded in the Western, capitalist-oriented theory of development. This in turn has led to a restricted view of the "right" and the "wrong" way of looking at particular problems. Such a perspective, long encouraged by foundation policies, precluded the possibility of formulating a truly revolutionary approach to developmental problems susceptible to no other solutions. Consequently, the typical African approach to development tends to be cautious, modest, and, as a result, ineffectual in accomplishing anything other than perpetuating the status quo.[56] The restricted *Weltanschauung* which so characterizes African development experts trained in Western, or in Western-influenced, institutions may indeed serve the best interest of the United States, but there is scant evidence that African development is being enhanced commensurately. Development programs and investment policies that involve foreign corporations and result in large outflows of scarce capital can hardly be judged as beneficial to Africans. However, there are very few African developmental economists who advocate the complete nation-alization of foreign properties or a more equitable distribution of scarce resources as panaceas for underdevelopment. When considering the source and ideological orientation of their training, this reluctance is perhaps understandable.

As argued previously, the foundation emphasis on education fitted into the larger view that held that stability and the orderly and controlled growth of independent African nations were in the best interests of the United States and of the Africans themselves. Education was deemed important in giving African leaders an intellectual framework which would make them sympathetic to capitalist development and the demo-cratic west as opposed to the Communist bloc. Select American universi-ties were chosen by foundation representaties to perform this task.

Post–World War II foundation policies in education and leadership training have their roots in the earlier activities of American philanthropy in Africa. During the 1920s and 1930s officials of the Phelps-Stokes Fund attempted to bring to America Africans who were considered sympathetic to the Tuskegee philsophy and who would then implement the philoso-phy's principles upon returning home. The cultivation and recruitment of the "safe" African during the period from 1920 to 1945 has by now been well documented.[57] The evidence cited above strongly suggests that there were comparable attempts after World War II to bring to the United States the latter-day "safe" African, an individual who had accepted the necessity of incorporating into African educational systems American pedagogical principles, content, and sociopolitical perspectives. If all went according to plan, these educators would train future African leaders who would be sympathetic to the viewpoints of the American government and to those American businesses with interests in Africa.

THE TRAINING OF AMERICA'S AFRICANISTS

From the mid-1950s both Ford and Carnegie attempted to build up a cadre of competent and trusted Africanists in the major universities, to whom they could turn for the resolution of problems and the design of field projects. This pattern emerged as early as 1952, when the Ford Foundation sponsored a conference at Northwestern University to discuss the needs and directions of African studies in the United States and how training programs could be developed for the benefit of African develop-ment and to remedy the lack of knowledge about Africa within the United States. This, in turn, led to the creation of several major centers of African studies in the United States, including Northwestern, Boston University, Columbia, Wisconsin, Indiana, and UCLA.[58] Africanists from these institutions were frequently involved in foundation sponsored projects in Africa, be they feasibility studies for proposed programs, as members of or consultants to the Africa Liaison Committee, or through the actual implementation of field projects themselves. At the same time, these same individuals were instrumental in creating a formal academic organization for the burgeoning field of African studies, the African Studies Association, which owed its creation to largesse from the Ford Foundation and the Carnegie Corporation.

A 1951 Ford report led to the conviction "that one of the first things the Foundation should do was to train, to devise ways to build up more competence in the United States about these areas that in the post-war world we had to relate to in one way or another."[59] This concern led to the growth of the Foreign Area Fellowship Program, whereby apprentice American social scientists would have their overseas field research subsidized by prestigious (and lucrative) grants from the Ford Foundation.

It was assumed from the beginning that these fellows would make available to Washington policymakers their assessments of local Third World situations considered of strategic geopolitical importance to the defense of the United States.[60] Indeed, so strongly did Ford officials feel about the potential service which returned fellows could offer through established channels to policymakers that they were concerned over attempts by the agents of the Central Intelligence Agency to extract random bits of information from the fellows. When CIA overtures to Ford fellows surfaced, Ford officials were furious. According to one of the latter, foundation president Heald "went down [to Washington] and he raised hell. . . . We just said, Jesus Christ! If the cover blows on any one of these things everything we're doing will be jeopardized. . . . The whole notion that we tried to impress on the CIA was that . . . it was much more in the national interest that we train a bunch of people who at later stages might want to go with the CIA . . . than it was for them to have one guy that they could call their source of information."[61]

While the Ford Foundation was initiating its program to train American Africanists who would provide assessments important to American strategic and economic interests in Africa, the Carnegie Corporation was encouraging well-placed American individuals to undertake study tours of Africa. Carnegie's officers felt that a greater understanding of Africa by Americans was required for the interests of the United States and for an American contribution to post-independent African development. To this end the Carnegie trustees in 1957 appropriated funds to enable the Council on Foreign Relations to identify and to encourage important Americans to go to Africa. Included among those traveling to Africa at Carnegie expense between 1959 and 1961 were David Rockefeller of the Chase Manhattan Bank; Paul Nitze, who in 1962 became Assistant Secretary of

Defense for International Security Affairs; and Thomas Finletter, former Secretary of the Air Force.[62]

The influence of the major foundations in shaping the intellectual parameters within which American Africanists function is suggested by a 1967 study conducted by the State Department. That report noted that 107 of the 191 university centers of foreign affairs research depend primarily on support from the Ford Foundation; included in this total were most of the African institutes at the prestigious American universities. Horowitz elaborates on this, noting that "in 11 of the 12 top universities with institutes of international studies, a single foundation, Ford, is the principal source of funds."[63] Equally significant, however, is the fact that when foundation support for area studies began to be withdrawn during the mid-1960s, it was replaced by funding from Title VI of the National Defense Education Act, administered by the Office of Education. Those who administered these funds for the United States government certainly did not view the world in a way which would have jeopardized the African interests of the United States as defined by the business and foundation leaders and Washington policymakers.

Foundation Cooperation for African Education and Political Development

The Ford Foundation, the Carnegie Corporation, and the Rockefeller Foundation as a matter of policy established or supported institutions and/or individuals capable of implementing programs desired by the foundations.[64] Oftentimes, as in the case of the Afro-Anglo-American program based at Teachers College, one of the foundations was looking for an agency to implement its policy just as an educational institution was searching for a sponsor for a particular project. A marriage of convenience then resulted, whereby the foundation subsidized the institution while the latter implemented foundation programs. Frequently the large foundations jointly supported African-related projects, e.g., the Northwestern University African studies program grew out of efforts by personnel there who, over a period of years, worked closely with officers of the Carnegie Corporation and the Ford Foundation.[65]

This cooperation which marked the Africa-related activities of the large foundations after 1958 was not always the case. Ford's Melvin Fox notes that, in the early days of the foundation's international activities, ". . . we were very chary . . . about consorting with other foundations. Now we do this as a matter of deliberate policy. . . . Something like our international institutes are made possible by the kind of consorting we do with other foundations."[66] This "consorting," as Fox terms foundation collaboration, extended to the difficult situations as well as to those which augured well for program development. Particularly when one of those difficult situations threatened to prove embarrassing did the foundations work together.

This was the case with the African-American Institute (AAI) in the early 1960s. The institute had been heavily funded by the CIA during the 1950s.[67] In 1961, the recently appointed president of the AAI, Waldemar Nielsen, persuaded its board of directors to break with the intelligence agency. It was important to the foundation community to secure a more respectable base of funding for the AAI. The institute had served as a major clearing house for African students coming to the United States; and the Carnegie Corporation and the Ford and Rockefeller foundations were closely identified with the institute through board memberships and program subsidies. Without undue delay representatives of the corporation, the Ford Foundation, the Rockefeller Foundation, and the Rockefeller Brothers Fund agreed to underwrite the budget of the African-American Institute. They were subsequently joined in this effort by the Agency for International Development and the State Department's Bureau of Educational and Cultural Affairs.[68]

Coordination of the resources and activities of the foundations as they relate to Africa is perhaps no better illustrated than with the convening in 1958 of a conference at the Greenbrier Hotel in White Sulfur Springs, West Virginia. The conference, organized on the initiative of Carnegie's Alan Pifer, brought together twenty-three representatives of some of the most important institutions concerned with Africa. The institutions included the Ford Foundation, the Rockefeller Brothers Fund, the Department of State, the British Colonial Office, the International Cooperation Administration (the precursor of AID), the International Bank for Reconstruction and Development, several commercial firms with African interests (e.g., Mobil Oil, Unilever, American Metal Climax), and several American and British universities. In the words of one observer, the assemblage represented "the most relevant American foundations, the key U.S. government aid agencies, and important American business and individual interests, as well as a number of key Britons concerned with Africa."[69]

Heyman notes that the primary purpose of the gethering was to devise programs which "themselves were to be based on the common interests of the African states and the free world nations, which interests the Greenbrier participants saw as new African states with political and economic viability, and friendship, or dependency on, the west."[70] Carnegie personnel claimed that the corporation's interest in the conference was simply that of a facilitator, that its impartial sponsorship of the gathering was "free from the motives other than a desire to serve the best interest of the Africans."[71] This expression of disinterested humanitarianism was somewhat difficult to reconcile with Pifer's statement several months earlier, in a background paper for another Carnegie sponsored conference, that ". . . the basis of our [American] concern with Africa in the future is going to be self-interest."[72] As noted above, this self-interest was defined by Pifer in ideological and especially in economic terms.

Of the immediate outcomes from the Greenbrier conference perhaps none was more significant than the creation of the Africa Liaison Committee, designed to serve as the agency through which many American proposals for work in higher education in Africa would be processed. Representatives of the Ford Foundation and Carnegie Corporation frequently met in New York and Washington with key individuals from the committee to coordinate their evolving plans for African education. These cooperative efforts, which occasionally included the Rockefeller Foundation as well, resulted in numerous joint foundation activities in African education during the late 1950s and 1960s.

One of these was the creation of an organization called Education and World Affairs, which originated in a 1959 meeting of the presidents of the Ford Foundation, the Carnegie Corporation, the Rockefeller Foundation, and representatives of the Department of State's Bureau of Educational and Cultural Affairs. The primary purpose of this organization was to be the initiation of "research, conferences, publications, and other activities, all designed to strengthen the international dimensions of American universities." Africa loomed large in the plans of Education and World Affairs, most of whose funding was eventually assumed by the Ford Foundation.[73]

Another example of foundation cooperation for African education involved the creation of the University of East Africa. During the summer of 1963 representatives of the Agency for International Development, the Africa Liaison Committee, and the Carnegie, Ford, and Rockefeller foundations met in New York to discuss a common American strategy to present to the representatives of the three constituent East African institutions and other, particularly British, donor agencies. The conference on the needs of the University of East Africa was held at the Rockefeller Foundation villa at Bellagio, Italy, later that same year. Representatives of the Africa Liaison Committee, the Agency for International Development, and the foundations were determined to force the creation of a regional university of East Africa, even in the face of indications from the three governments concerned that they preferred to have autonomous universities within their own countries, discussions about political federation notwithstanding.[74]

Although the federated University of East Africa concept eventually foundered because of political problems among the three territories, the role played by the foundations in forging an outlook sympathetic to

American interests at the independent institutions was significant. Carnegie's main emphasis was in the field of teacher education; Rockefeller's, in the biological and social sciences; and Ford's, in the social sciences and public administration. The leverage afforded the foundations by virtue of their areas of concentration and funding patterns is suggested by Thompson's comment, cited above, that approximately 80 percent of the upper-level administrative and professorial personnel at the University of East Africa had been supported by the Rockefeller Foundation for part or all of their professional training.

Conclusions: The Foundations and Constraints on African Development

There can be little doubt but that the Ford Foundation, Carnegie Corporation, and Rockefeller Foundation have used their largesse since 1945 to insure the controlled growth and development of African societies through the strengthening of strategic cultural and political institutions. The primary means to accomplish this end has been through support for African education, as well as complementary social science research and public administration training institutes. The emphasis on education has had two advantages over a comparable concern with other areas. First, the quantitative expansion of education in Africa has enabled foundation personnel to spread their common ideology across a greater range of local societies than heretofore. Second, the emphasis on the provision of a commodity which ostensibly has no political overtones and which is in great demand has enabled foundation personnel to appear in the guise of disinterested humanitarians. As the above has made clear, there was little humanitarianism in these foundation attempts to develop educational systems in Africa, despite the proclivities of random foundation personnel in this direction. Education was perceived as the opening wedge ensuring an American presence in those African nations considered of strategic and economic importance to the governing and business elite of the United States. The contention that American foundation expenditures in Africa were designed primarily to benefit the recipients cannot be sustained. Rather, it was through African education that American foundation personnel hoped to exert leverage on the direction of African development, development which would follow lines acceptable to American interests.

Foundation personnel had no trouble justifying programs that furthered American interests at least as much as African interests because, from their perspective, the two were inseparable. This identification of African needs in terms of American interests derived from the manner in which the major foundations defined their functions. For example, the Rockefeller Foundation's charter stated broadly that the purpose of the foundation was the promotion of human progress.[75]. If African needs could be served while American interests were furthered, then certainly foundation officers would keep faith with the intent of the charter, at least as they interpreted it. Likewise, the Ford Foundation's statement of purpose, as drafted in 1949, delineated the strengthening of democracy and the establishment of peace as two cornerstones of foundation activity.[76] Thus the Ford Foundation could justify its involvement overseas by appealing to American patriotism, by arguing that it, together with other bastions of the American Establishment, was developing programs to thwart Communist aggression while strengthening American-style democracy around the world. This was a persuasive argument during the 1950s and well into the 1960s.

The overriding concern of the "philanthropoids" in Africa has been to train elite cadres capable of running their nations in ways guaranteed to maximize internal growth and political stability, desiderata from the American perspective. Funds have been used to train Africans in the techniques of administering their recently independent nations, be they as public servants, educational planners, or teachers. At the same time, foundation grants for training programs at select American universities have been made available to African leaders in an attempt to bind them to the principles of the American democratic-capitalist development model, thereby assuring overseas fields for American corporate investment. Socialization in American institutions would discourage, it was thought, African flirtation with the socialist, Soviet model of development.

The many and tangible benefits which did accrue to Africans as a result of foundation expenditure were incidential outcomes of a policy which held that support for educational networks in Africa should be beneficial primarily to American foreign policy planners and corporate interests. There is at present increasing concern among Africans that the priorities encouraged by the outside donor agencies have had a negative impact on African cultures as well as on the long-range prospects for meaningful development. Mazrui, among others, recognized that "African universities were capable of being at once mechanisms for political liberation and agencies of cultural dependency." This is so because "university graduates in Africa, precisely because they were the most deeply Westernized Africans, were the most culturally dependent."[77] While the African university has indeed produced trained manpower to forward the development effort—albeit along lines acceptable to and articulated by Western interests—at the same time it has helped to expand markets available to Western corporations by altering the consumption patterns of the African student. In Gershenberg's words, "a very impressive feature of the relationship between the expatriate multinational firm and the economically-underdeveloped country is that the multinational has been able to socialize the indigenous to the norms and values of the metropolitan center."[78] The question now facing the independent African nations is, according to Mazrui, "whether modernization can be decolonized without being destroyed."[79] That the contemporary African situation has to be stated in such stark terms is to a significant degree a testimony to the success with which the major American foundations have pursued their work in African education since 1945.

Notes

1. Waldemar Nielsen, *The Big Foundations* (New York and London: Columbia University Press, 1972), p. 316.
2. Ibid., p. 406.
3. Ibid.
4. Ibid., p. 407.
5. Kenneth Prewitt and Alan Stone, *The Ruling Elites: Elite Theory, Power, and American Democracy* (New York: Harper and Row, 1973), pp. 68–69.
6. Robert A. Packenham, *Liberal America and the Third World: Political Development Ideas in Foreign Aid and Social Science* (Princeton: Princeton University Press, 1973), p. 132. Cf. Barrington Moore, Jr.'s, analysis of the efficacy of the revolutionary as opposed to the evolutionary path of development in his important *Social Origins of Dictatorship and Democracy: Lord and Peasant in the Making of the Modern World* (Boston: Beacon Press, 1966).
7. Alan Pifer, background paper, May 14, 1957. Carnegie Corporation archives (hereafter CC): folder: Columbia University–American Assembly Conference on "The U.S. and Africa."
8. Quoted in Gabriel Kolko, *The Roots of American Foreign Policy: An Analysis of Power and Purpose* (Boston: Beacon Press, 1967), p. 50.
9. Interoffice Memorandum from Philip E. Mosely to Rockefeller Foundation staff, February 3, 1949, folder 900: Program and Policy, Underdeveloped Areas, Rockefeller Foundation archives, New York City. Papers pertaining to the activities of the Foundation are located in the Rockefeller Foundation Archive Center (hereafter RFAC) at Pocantico Hills, Tarrytown, New York, and at the Foundation offices at 1133 Avenue of the Americas, New York City (hereafter RFNYC).
10. Kolko, *The Roots of American Foreign Policy*, p. 53.
11. Quoted in Philip Green, "Necessity and Choice in American Foreign Policy," in Irving Howe (ed.), *A Dissenter's Guide to Foreign Policy* (New York: Praeger Publishers, 1966), p. 132.
12. Don K. Price to John W. Gardner, March 24, 1954, Ford Foundation International Training and Research Papers, Administration, Board of Overseas Training and Research Meeting, March 31, 1954, Ford Founda-

tion archives (hereafter FF). An internal consensus had been reached on this point some six months earlier. See FF International Training and Research Papers, Administration, Board of Overseas Training and Research Meeting, September 15, 1953.

13. The justification for this step is provided by Rockefeller Foundation President Dean Rusk in his "Background for Proposal of Increased Program in Non-Western Underdeveloped Areas, Memorandum to the Trustees," November 29, 1955. Folder 900, Pro, Unar-6, RFNYC.

14. *Rockefeller Foundation Annual Report, 1958*, p. 128.

15. The survey was undertaken by Carl Spaeth and focused primarily, although not exclusively, on the state of knowledge in the United States about Asia. See his "A Survey of Asian Studies," FF archives report 001066, 1951. The actual quote is from Melvin J. Fox, Oral History transcript, FF, p. 5.

16. FF International Training and Research Papers, Administration, Board of Overseas Training and Research Meeting, September 15, 1953.

17. John B. Howard, Oral History transcript, FF, p. 5.

18. For details of the work of the Fund for the Advancement of Education, see Dennis C. Buss's chapter in this book and his "The Ford Foundation and the Exercise of Power in American Public Education" (unpublished Ed.D. dissertation, Rutgers University, 1972).

19. For an elaboration of the relationships linking peripheral areas to metropolitan economic and political centers, see Johann Galtung, "A Structural Theory of Imperialism," *Journal of Peace Studies* 2 (1971); and Paul A.Baran, *The Political Economy of Growth* (Harmondsworth, Middlesex: Penguin Books, 1973).

20. Melvin J. Fox, "Education: Goals and Achievements, Future Prospects," paper prepared for Ford Foundation Staff Conference, June 9–11, 1970, pp. 1–10 of Appendix. FF archives report 002387.

21. "The Rockefeller Foundation University Development Program, University Development Centers, Expenditures, Allocations and Appropriations, 1963–72." Folder 900: Pro, Unar-14, RFNYC.

22. Robert S. Morison to George Harrar and Staff, January 26, 1961. Folder 900: Program and Policy, Underdeveloped Areas, 1961–63, RFNYC.

23. Trent Schroyer, *The Critique of Domination* (New York: George Braziller, 1973), p. 220.

24. Robert F. Arnove, "The Ford Foundation and 'Competence Building' Overseas: Assumptions, Approaches, and Outcomes," *Studies in Comparative International Development* 12 (Fall 1977): 108.

25. The document was entitled *Investment in Education: The Report of the Commission of Post–Secondary School Certificate and Higher Education in Nigeria* (Lagos: Federal Government Printer, 1960), but is generally referred to as the Ashby Commission Report, after its chairman, Eric Ashby.

26. For details, see E. Jefferson Murphy, *Creative Philanthropy: Carnegie Corporation and African Education, 1953–1973* (New York: Teachers College Press, 1976), pp. 86–87.

27. Rolland G. Paulston, *Conflicting Theories of Social and Educational Change: A Typological Review* (Pittsburgh: University Center for International Studies, 1976), p. 15.
28. Benjamin R. Barber, "Science, Salience and Comparative Education : Some Reflections of Social Scientific Inquiry," *Comparative Education Review* 16 (October 1972): 435.
29. Fox, Oral History transcript, p. 217.
30. Apropos this, see Arnove, "The Ford Foundation and 'Competence Building' Overseas."
31. Francis X. Sutton, "Africa Ten Years Later," typescript prepared for the Board of Trustees, December 1970, FF archives report 002710, p. 4.
32. Fox, FF archives report 002387, p. 19.
33. Joseph P. Farrell, "A Reaction to 'The Micro–Planning of Education: Why It Fails, Why It Survives, and the Alternatives,' " *Comparative Education Review* 19 (June 1975): 208–209.
34. For specifics on the placement on Rockefeller–funded students, see *The Rockefeller Foundation Directory of Fellowships and Scholarships, 1917–1970* (New York: The Rockefeller Foundation, 1972).
35. Kenneth W. Thompson and Colleagues, "Higher Education and National Development: One Model for Technical Assistance," in *Education and Development Reconsidered: The Bellagio Conference Papers*, F. Champion Ward (ed.) (New York: Praeger Publishers, 1974), p. 201.
36. David Court, "Higher Education in East Africa," in *Higher Education and Social Change: Promising Experiments in Developing Countries, vol. 2: Case Studies*, Kenneth W. Thompson, Barbara R. Fogel, and Helen E. Danner (eds.) (New York: Praeger Publishers, 1977), p. 471.
37. Barber, "Science, Salience and Comparative Education," p. 435.
38. Walter E. Ashley, "Philanthropy and Government: A Study of the Ford Foundation's Overseas Activities" (unpublished Ph.D. dissertation, New York University, 1970), ch. 6; and communications from F. X. Sutton.
39. Ibid., pp. 94–95.
40. For an indication of Harris' activities on behalf of the CIA and its friends, see Dan Schechter, Michael Ansara, and David Kolodney, "The CIA as an Equal Opportunity Employer," *Ramparts* 7 (June 1969): 25–33.
41. James L. Morrill, Oral History transcript, FF, p. 20.
42. Ashley, "Philanthropy and Government," p. 97.
43. Robert I. Fleming, "Program for Accelerating Private Foreign Investment in Less Developed Countries," FF archives report 000358, 1966, pp. 1–2.
44. Alvin W. Gouldner, *The Dialectic of Ideology and Technology: The Origins, Grammar, and Future of Ideology* (New York: The Seabury Press, 1976), p. 233. Italics added.
45. As early as 1948 personnel at Teachers College, Columbia University, began laying plans for the College's future involvement in international educa-tion projects. The strategy to be followed is mentioned several times in materials contained in Box 11, folder 11/12 of the Karl W. Bigelow Papers, Teachers College Archives, New York City.

46. Murphy, *Creative Philanthropy*, pp. 133–136, provides some details of the evolution of the Afro–Anglo–American Program in Teacher Education.

47. F. X. Sutton, memorandum to files, November 10, 1958, FF General Correspondence 1958, file Africa.

48. This project involved the School of Education, University of Wisconsin, in a teacher training project in northern Nigeria. See Lindley J. Stiles, "A Proposal for the Improvement of Teacher Education in Northern Nigera," FF archives report 001951, June 1964. Although the exact reasons behind the Ford decision to abandon the area of teacher training to the Carnegie Corporation are not spelled out, it may simply have resulted from a foundation decision not to get further involved in an area in which it had little interest or expertise. Part of the reason may also have related to the fact that Ford personnel felt that ". . . we have not been in a position to directly influence total education planning or curriculum development [in Nigeria]." Information Paper: Middle East and Africa Program, FF archives report 001327, December 1966, p. 18. The most favored outside agency administering Ford–funded education projects in Africa was the Cambridge–based organization Educational Services Incorporated.

49. Murphy, *Creative Philanthropy*, ch. 8.

50. See ibid., pp. 245–266, for details of Carnegie appropriations for work in Africa.

51. Edward H. Berman, "American Philanthropy and African Education: Toward an Analysis," *African Studies Review* 20: 1 (April 1977): 80–81.

52. Murphy, *Creative Philanthropy*, pp. 107–112.

53. By this time Teachers College had received sizable grants from both the International Cooperation Administration for educational projects around the world and from the Peace Corps for training programs in New York. In order to insure the continuing flow of outside funding, which had become an important component of the college budget as well as a source of prestige within the academic world (and which was to become significantly larger), the Teachers College approach to educational change in developing nations was identical to that of the funding agencies themselves, i.e., gradual, moderate, and controllable. Details can be gleaned from a perusal of the Bigelow papers at Teachers College.

54. "Report on the ATEA 11th Conference in Addis Ababa, 26–31 March, 1972," by K. W. Bigelow, p. 2. Typescript copy in Bigelow Papers, Teachers College Archives.

55. These data are culled from "Rockefeller Foundation Fellowships in Social Sciences, East Africa, 1969–1976," and "Rockefeller Foundation Fellowships in Social Sciences, Nigeria, 1962–1976," both documents generously made available by officers of the Rockefeller Foundation.

56. For an explication of this, see Francis J. Method, "National Research and Development Capabilities in Education," in *Education and Development Reconsidered*, pp. 128–140. The argument in Barrington Moore, Jr.'s, *Social Origins of Dictatorship and Democracy* is worth recalling once again at this juncture.

57. See, for example, my chapter entitled "Educational Colonialism in Africa: The Role of American Foundations, 1910–1945," in this volume; and Kenneth James King, *Pan–Africanism and Education: A Study of Race Philanthropy and Education in the Southern States of America and East Africa* (Oxford: Claredon Press, 1971).

58. F. X. Sutton and David Smock, "The Ford Foundation and African Studies," Ford Foundation archives report 002168, November 1975, details these initial efforts.

59. Fox, Oral History transcript, p. 72. This was the so-called Spaeth Report referred to above.

60. Howard, Oral History transcript, pp. 109–110.

61. Ibid.

62. Richard D. Heyman, "The Role of Carnegie Corporation in African Education, 1925–1960" (unpublished Ed.D. dissertation, Columbia University, 1970), p. 201

63. David Horowitz, "Sinews of Empire," *Ramparts* 6 (October 1968): 33.

64. See, for example, Alfred Wolf's memorandum to Francis X. Sutton, July 23, 1958, about the former's discussion of Carnegie's African program with Alan Pifer. FF General Correspondence 1958, file Carnegie Corporation.

65. Some indication of the early foundation interest in the creation of African studies program can be gleaned from Murphy, *Creative Philanthropy*, pp. 28–29; and "Ford Foundation Conference on Africa, Evanston, Illinois, August 18–23, 1952: Findings and Recommendations," FF archives report 1146, General Correspondence file 1958, Africa.

66. Fox, Oral History transcript, p. 25.

67. The links between the CIA and the AAI were corroborated in a conversation between the writer and William Cotter, past President of the African-American Institute, in his office on May 18, 1976.

68. Fox, Oral History transcript, p. 205.

69. Murphy, *Creative Philanthropy*, p. 60.

70. Heyman, "The Role of Carnegie Corporation in African Education," pp. 177–178.

71. Ibid., 178.

72. Pifer, background paper, May 14, 1957.

73. On the origins and some of the problems of Education and World Affairs, see Murphy, *Creative Philanthropy*, pp. 94–98.

74. Correspondence between Karl W. Bigelow and Carnegie's Alan Pifer, as well as communications among several individuals in the other foundations and the Agency for International Development, corroborates this. See especially Bigelow to Pifer, August 12, 1963, and other materials contained in file at Carnegie Corporation and entitled: East Africa, University of, 1961–63.

75. This purpose was cited repeatedly in interoffice memoranda during the 1950s when Rockefeller Foundation officers were discussing the expansion of their programs into developing areas.

76. These areas are first specified in the so-called Gaither report of 1949, *Report of the Study for the Ford Foundation in Policy and Program* (Detroit: The

Foundation, 1949), and repeated with some regularity in subsequent foundation publications.

77. Ali A. Mazrui, "The African University as a Multinational Corporation: Problems of Penetration and Dependency," *Harvard Educational Review* 45 (May 1975): 194.

78. Ibid., p. 200.

79. Ibid.

Donald Fisher

American Philanthropy and the Social Sciences: The Reproduction of a Conservative Ideology

In recent years social scientists have renewed their interest in the role of American philanthropic foundations in Western industrialized societies. Some authors have provided brief descriptions of Carnegie and Rockefeller involvement in the development of educational testing,[1] while others have attempted to give us an overview of the relationship between philanthropy and society.[2] Yet thus far this work has remained at the descriptive level and has simply provided a number of enticing images that stimulate new questions and attract further research. This work appears to be based on the following untested assumptions. First, that foundations, past and present, have occupied a mediating role between the economic structure of capitalistic societies and the other social institutions. Further, that their mediating influence has tended to reproduce the existing social structure rather than alter it. What follows is an attempt to provide concrete evidence for the above assumptions by explicating the mediating role that American foundations have adopted with respect to the development of the social sciences in Britain[3] during the interwar period, 1919 to 1939.

In this chapter, the writer has three interrelated objectives. First, to describe the impact of American philanthropy[4] on the development of the social sciences in Britain. Second, to demonstrate what Lewis Coser has called the "Gatekeeper" function[5] that these foundations have served with respect to the development and distribution of knowledge in the social sciences. Specifically, in Britain, the Rockefeller foundations have determined to a great extent not only "what" should be studied in the social sciences but also "how" these studies were conducted. This in turn led to the institutionalization of certain subject areas and of certain methodological approaches. Finally, this chapter will show that the direction in which the social sciences developed in Britain tended both to serve and to perpetuate the ideological perspective of American philanthropy.

The Impact of American Philanthropy on the Development of the Social Sciences in Britain

This section will begin with a description of the policy that the various Rockefeller foundations developed with regard to the social sciences during the interwar period. This will be followed by an account of how this policy was implemented in Britain during these years. Finally, the writer will describe the overall impact of Rockefeller involvement on the development of the social sciences in Britain.

A POLICY FOR THE SOCIAL SCIENCES

During the 1920s, interest in the social sciences, on the part of Rockefeller philanthropy, was almost exclusively limited to the Laura Spelman Rockefeller Memorial (LSRM). While the Rockefeller Foundation (RF) had made excursions into the field during the prewar years, it had opened itself to a barrage of criticism and had subsequently withdrawn to the safer fields of medicine and public health. The most notable example was the Mackenzie King affair in 1914, over which the RF was severely criticized by the United States Commission on Industrial Relations (see Chapter 2 in this book). The investigation by the commission was headline news for weeks and resulted in a tremendous amount of bad publicity both for the family and the foundation. It followed that the RF's policy toward social issues and the social sciences generally was so conservative that at least during the 1920s they avoided this area like the plague. The fact that the LSRM took over this field as a major interest was primarily due to Dr. Beardsley Ruml.[6]

The original interest of the LSRM had been social welfare, particularly child study and parent education. Ruml took over as director in 1922 and decided that the foundation should concentrate on the social sciences and public administration. This move occurred largely because of Ruml's faith in the potential of the social sciences to solve society's problems. For Ruml, the route to advancing human welfare was through scientific social research. This meant that means had to be devised to bring the social scientist into intimate contact with social phenomena. For, as Ruml observed in 1929, "the impingement of the phenomenal world on the observer, is the beginning of things scientific."[7]

With Ruml as the architect, the LSRM developed a clear policy with regard to the social sciences. The basic tenet was that the social sciences should be brought into a more equal relationship with the natural sciences. Essentially, Ruml believed that as the social sciences became more "scientific" in the natural science mode, so they would be more efficient in helping to solve the "real", "practical" problems that society faced.

The policy that developed in these early years was based on two general scientific objectives. The first objective was ". . . to increase for the scientist and scholar the possibilities of immediate personal observation of the social problems or social phenomena which were under investigation."[8] When in 1930 Edmund E. Day (director of Social Sciences for the RF, 1928–1937) was summarizing the early history of the LSRM, he laid particular emphasis on the fact that social studies had traditionally been "philosophical, historical and dialectical," which meant there was plenty of theory but no facts. He described how the memorial set out to increase the number of "facts" by focusing on "realistic" factual research.[9] The second objective was the promotion of collaborative research between the various disciplines in the social sciences.[10]

To achieve these objectives Ruml concentrated on two main approaches. First, the creation of institutional centers in various parts of the world that would with Rockefeller money embody scientific teaching and research. Collaborative research was to be encouraged through the specific research grants to these institutions. These centers would therefore not only be creative institutions but would also serve as a model for the development of the social sciences generally. Second, Ruml began an extensive fellowship program which was designed to complement the training provided by the institutional centers and increase the number of able people working in the field.

From the beginning of his association with the LSRM, Ruml wanted to strengthen and develop major universities as institutional centers of social research. As Day put it in 1930,

> There has been from the start a definite regional plan, the idea of
> developing within each country of any importance some center
> which would fructify the local situation and influence other
> institutions within the same sphere of scientific influence, then
> within the larger regional centers.[11]

The LSRM focused exclusively on the United States and Europe and by 1926 had decided that the support of these centers was its principal activity. As the LSRM's Final Report noted,

> The development of twelve or fifteen well rounded centers of
> social science research throughout the world with possibilities of
> easy interchange of faculty and students was undertaken.[12]

In Europe, the emphasis was on developing a specific center in each country, the most prominent examples being the University of Stockholm, Deutsche Hochscule für Politik in Berlin, and the London School of Economics.

This was indeed a "grand strategy." The idea was to construct, in Day's words, ". . . a framework of institutional centers, the influence of which will radiate to establish a fresh tradition as to the character of social science research."[13] The policy of the LSRM and indeed the RF, after the memorial was included in the foundation in 1929, had a general and overriding objective. As Day noted in 1930, this objective had been clearly defined from the beginning:

> It involved an attempt to acquire a better understanding of the
> nature of social phenomena, social institutions, social behaviour;
> along with that the direct cultivation of a scientific approach to
> social problems.[14]

In Ruml's view, if the social sciences were going to help achieve improvement in the conditions of life then they should genuinely reflect, both in method and ethos, the physical sciences.

The second main approach to the fulfillment of Ruml's objectives was the provision of fellowships for advanced students. The fellowship program began in 1923 and had as its major aim the coordination and stimulation of scientific research in the social sciences. In Ruml's words, the provision of fellowships ". . . will tend to place the social sciences in a more equal relation to the physical sciences."[15] The memorial itself ran the program in Europe and Australia, bringing students usually to the United States, although the fellowship was tenable in any country or countries where the foundation was represented.[16] It was envisaged that fellows from countries throughout the world would move between the institutional centers, where they would receive training in scientific methods and be allowed the freedom to conduct their own research. As economics was the most developed social science with regard to a natural scientific approach, the subject was chosen for major emphasis both through the fellowship awards and in the funding of research generally.

In 1928, Edmund E. Day took over from Ruml as director of the Social Sciences in preparation for the memorial's incorporation into the RF.[17] The RF continued with the same overall policy as the LSRM until the early 1930s. On the surface it was hard to discriminate between the two programs. Yet some changes were taking place. First, the new division, like its three counterparts in medicine, natural science, and the humanities, was a "formal organization." This structure naturally pervaded the negotiations and agreements that the division undertook and one can observe a new formality in the relations between the RF officers and the recipients of grants. While Ruml's approach was definitely in the entrepreneurial tradition, the new division was unquestionably professional. Second, and even more important, was the increased emphasis on the "scientific approach."

Day had no doubt about the direction in which the social sciences should go. As Day put it in 1930, "what we have to do is to establish in the social sciences the scientific tradition and the scientific habit of mind." There was a need to recognize academic work by strengthening ". . . certain types of interest and certain habits of thought . . ." so as to coordinate the scientific attack upon social problems.[18] In the social sciences, Day saw the potential for "human engineering" and referred to the program as one in social science and social technology. The results of research had to be tried out in the social situation, for as he said, ". . . the validation of the findings of social science must be through effective social control."[19] Day noted that economics was in the lead in the use of scientific quantitative methods and felt that the RF should focus on economic stabilization. Significantly, Day also picked out anthropology as having acquired a technique which would stand scientific examination better than the technique employed in sociology.[20] This was a reference to B. Malinowski's "functional theory,"[21] which posited that social phenomena should be studied with regard to the contribution that a particular institution made to the survival and well-being of a society. The theory assumes that any society or culture is composed of parts which are interrelated and interdependent, each performing a function necessary to the life of the group. For Malinowski, the functional view involved the search for definite laws of social process. Day did not exclude other social science disciplines from the program but obviously intended to focus on those that best fitted his notion of the scientific approach. Finally, Day mentioned that specific attention should be given to research in international relations.

The aim was still to increase the amount of "scientific" research, but now the focus was on clearly defined areas. The notion of collaborative research between different disciplines was dropped and institutional development began to move into the background. The RF's 1930 Annual Report laid the foundation of what was to become the major emphasis in their social science program. "Industrial Hazards and Economic Stabilization"[22] was described as one of the most important fields of research. The RF felt that this research should be concentrated upon the hazards of the economic enterprise as these hazards ". . . relate to uncertainty of competitive outcome in such ways as to raise issues of general economic stability."[23] The report then declared that the

> . . . alteration of activity and idleness, of prosperity and depression, with which the business enterprise is afflicted, constitute a social problem of the first order, to which all the forces that science and administration can bring to bear to resolve the difficulties, should be marshalled as rapidly as possible.[24]

Yet while the decision to support "cultural anthropology," the RF's label for "functional social anthropology," had been operationalized by 1931,[25] it was not until 1932 that they specified their other interests. In the RF's 1932 Annual Report, "international relations" and "the planning and control of economic structures and economic process" were described as "Special Research Programs."[26] Using language very similar to that used when they discussed "Industrial Hazards and Economic Stabilization" the RF gave detailed reasons why they felt that research in "Economic Planning and Control" was so important:

> Events of the past three years have made strikingly evident the tremendous social losses occasioned by the ups and downs of modern business enterprise. Much physical suffering, illness, mental disorder, family disintegration, crime, and political and social instability trace their origin to economic reasons.[27]

The RF felt this area of research was not only "highly important" but also well adapted to research methods and mentioned some of the studies that they had already funded.[28] The foundation believed

> ... that a more complete knowledge of the working of our present economic system—e.g. of conditions as revealed by realistic, statistical studies of unemployment; the characteristics, methods, and hazards of specific industrial society in a number of specific situations—must supply the necessary basis for planning an effective economic organization.[29]

Under the heading "International Relations" the RF described their endeavor to improve such relations ". . . by extending the area of objective analysis of controversial subjects." Through their program they sought ". . . to promote understanding among nations and to reduce the friction which may lead to warfare."[30] The two programs, "economic control" and "international cooperation," were of course interrelated. The aim was to create the knowledge which would prevent any future "crisis of capitalism." Throughout the 1930s the officers of the RF seemed genuinely to believe that the salvation of the system of capitalist democracy could be achieved by wise investment in social research.

In 1934, a committee of RF trustees produced a report[31] which recommended that the Social Science Division should place all its emphasis on the special fields of research and no longer look toward the development of institutional centers. The committee felt the efforts to establish in the universities an empirical base for the social sciences had been reasonably successful and therefore it was time to concentrate their efforts on applied research and social amelioration. As they put it, ". . . we now have the opportunity to see whether we cannot assist in applying to concrete problems of our social, political and industrial life some of the ideas and data which research all over the world is rapidly developing."[32]

The new policy went into operation in 1935. This change was summarized by Raymond Fosdick (president of the RF) in the 1936 report when he noted that the RF was ". . . particularly interested in problems relating to social security, international relations and public administration. . . ."[33] While the label for economic research had been changed from "economic planning and control" to "social security," the objective remained the same. Fosdick went on to repeat in almost the same words as the 1932 Report, the description of how the economic ills of the world were at the base of ". . . the most pressing problems of the present social order."[34] He felt there was something "fundamentally wrong" with a society that had an abundance of raw materials yet could not control poverty or unemployment. He then immediately described the situation as ". . . unmistakably one of maladjustment . . ."[35] for which the remedy or at least some amelioration could be found through research. This research came under the heading of "social security" and had two objectives:

a) Research directed to the description and measurement of cyclical and structural change and to the analysis of the causes of instability.
b) Research directed to the question of protection against the main hazards that confront the individual such as sickness, accident, old age, dependency, and unemployment.[36]

In the 1930s the RF was particularly concerned to see an increase in the cooperation between social scientists and the business community. Rockefeller officers had no use for abstract theorizing: they wanted the social sciences to be harnessed to solving Western capitalism's problems and to providing on-the-spot service to "men of affairs."

The funding of the social sciences in Britain naturally reflected the policy objectives outlined above. During the 1920s attention was focused upon the establishment of a major social science institution and the provision of fellowships. The 1930s are characterized by the move toward the support of specific subject areas—namely, anthropology, economics, and international relations—which were considered useful in the analysis and selection of the immediate problems of the period.

GIFTS TO BRITISH SOCIAL SCIENCE[37]

During the period 1919 to 1940, Rockefeller, Carnegie, and Harkness philanthropy provided approximately £690,000 ($3,180,000)[38] for the social sciences in British universities (see Table 2). In addition, approximately £360,000 ($1,660,000) was provided to independent organizations which were closely tied to the universities. Academics usually staffed these organizations and invariably benefited from the research funds that were received. The two Rockefeller foundations, the LSRM and the RF, were responsible for approximately 95 percent of the total expenditure during this period. While at first sight the sum of approximately £1 million ($4,840,000) spread over a period of twenty years ($250,000 a year) may seem small, it was in fact very important. There was no government research council like the Medical Research Council that dealt with the social sciences, and government departments made very few research grants during this period. While some of the University Grant Committee's recurrent grants did of course support social science departments the proportion was extremely small. As Table 1 illustrates, even as late as 1938–1939 the total departmental maintenance of these subjects in Britain's universities only amounted to £116,000 ($550,000). The amount spent on such maintenance in the 1920s and early 1930s was certainly much less, so that a rough estimate of the total spent during the same twenty-year period was probably in the region of £1,350,000 ($4,900,000). This amount represented what all British universities spent on the social sciences between 1919 and 1940. When one turns to nonrecurrent grants[39] Rockefeller philanthropy provided approximately £180,000 ($830,000) during this period (see Table 2) while the University Grants Committee almost certainly spent less than £100,000 ($460,000), a major portion of which went to the London School of Economics. It becomes apparent that the contributions from American philanthropy, far from being small, were the mainstay of the support that social science received.

Table 1
Total Departmental Maintenance in British Universities 1938–1939 (Including Scotland but Excluding Certain Outlays at Oxbridge)

	£	%
Arts	1,084,873	28.2
Pure science	986,663	25.6
Medicine	885,964	23.0
Technology	533,224	13.9
Agriculture	241,625	6.3
Social science	115,909	3.0
Total	3,848,258	100

Source: The Clapham Report, *Report of the Committee on the Provision for Social and Economic Research* (London: HMSO., Cmd. 6868, July 1946), p. 15.

Just as government paid little attention to these subjects so it was with British philanthropy. The major contributor was the Cassel Trust, but even then the endowment provided was small in comparison to the Rockefeller contributions. Other foundations like the Leverhulme Trust, the Halley Stewart Trust, the Ratan Tata Foundation, the Beit Trust, and Sir Montague Burton all provided grants, but they were usually modest and often went to independent organizations. It was not until the late 1930s when Lord Nuffield announced his enormous grant to Oxford that British philanthropy began to take over the responsibility from the RF. Even then, as late as 1947, the RF was providing approximately £45,000 a year for the social sciences in England while the Nuffield Foundation was providing approximately £20,000.[40] In addition, Rockefeller grants drew approximately £160,000 ($740,000) to the social sciences in the universities either because of conditional clauses in their grants or merely because of the example they set. This amount does not take account of either the University Grants Committee capital grants to the London School of Economics (LSE) or the large increases in that school's University Grants Committee (UGC) recurrent grant, which came about largely because of the continuing Rockefeller interest in that institution.

INSTITUTIONAL DEVELOPMENT AND THE FELLOWSHIP PROGRAMS

With respect to their policy of developing institutions, Rockefeller money was the key factor in the development of the LSE. The fact that, in the words of Lord Simon of Wythenshawe, "the LSE had become an important world centre of the social sciences"[41] was largely due to Rockefeller involvement. The LSE was chosen for three reasons.

First, in the early 1920s it was the most developed center of the social sciences in Britain[42] and could therefore be expected to be more valuable as a model for the rest of Britain than any other institution. Only at the LSE could a student be exposed to the whole range of social science subjects. In addition, the school began publishing *Economica* in January 1921, and in 1922–1923 established, in cooperation with Cambridge, the London and Cambridge Economic Service.

Second, William Beveridge (Lord), the director of LSE, shared with Rockefeller philanthropy the same conception of the way in which the social sciences should develop. Beveridge, an economist by training, believed that the social sciences must utilize the natural scientific approach.[43]

Third, as the school was located in London, it was in a position to influence the whole world, especially through the British Empire. It

Table 2 Rockefeller, Carnegie, and Commonwealth Fund, Social Science Grants to the Universities of England and Wales, and to Various Independent Organizations, Between 1914 and 1940 [a]

Year	£ Capital Building and Equipment		£ Endowment Including Teachers' Salaries		£ Research Including Fellowships		£ Total	
	Universities	Other	Universities	Other	Universities	Other	Universities	Other
1920	—	—	—	—	—	—	—	—
1921	—	—	—	—	—	1,000	—	1,000
1922	—	—	—	—	—	2,000	—	2,000
1923	—	—	—	—	—	—	—	—
1924	6,100	—	—	—	15,300	—	21,400	—
1925	600	1,000	—	—	16,300	4,700	16,900	5,700
1926	7,300	—	200	3,000	18,050	5,150	25,550	8,150
1927	12,750	—	30,550	—	16,700	6,050	60,000	6,050
1928	38,000	4,000	145,150	7,000	16,650	10,450	199,800	21,450

Year								
1929	5,900	—	3,650	7,000	19,850	7,050	29,400	14,050
1930	2,200	—	2,650	7,000	10,950	3,200	15,800	10,200
1931	1,600	—	2,000	7,000	8,450	6,450	12,050	13,450
1932	38,300	—	7,400	7,000	13,050	23,050	58,750	30,050
1933	57,000	—	6,800	7,000	16,650	31,350	80,450	38,350
1934	3,050	—	6,050	7,000	12,950	30,150	22,050	37,150
1935	1,100	—	5,900	7,000	19,550	32,000	26,550	39,000
1936	1,100	—	28,650	7,000	18,850	29,250	48,600	36,250
1937	2,050	—	6,500	7,000	19,950	20,350	28,500	27,350
1938	—	—	6,500	7,000	17,250	21,100	23,750	28,100
1939	—	—	2,300	7,000	13,450	16,050	15,750	23,050
1940	—	—	3,500	7,000	4,050	14,000	7,550	21,000
Total	177,050	5,000	257,800	94,000	258,000	263,350	692,850	362,350

Source: D. Fisher, "The Impact of American Foundations on the Development of British University Education, 1900-1939." Ph.D. dissertation, University of California, Berkeley, 1977, Table 23, pp. 560–61. For a detailed account of how this money was spent, see Thesis, Chapter 3, pp. 322–575.
[a] The writer has rounded these figures to the nearest 50. Each year represents the expenditures in the academic year, that is for example, 1920 represents 1919/20.

followed that after a series of meetings between Ruml and Beveridge in September 1923 a partnership was formed that was to have a lasting influence on the development of the LSE. In Beveridge's words, they had formed "a new alliance," which ". . . opened a new chapter in the history of the school and of the University of London."[44]

During the period 1923 to 1939 the memorial and the RF gave approximately £430,000 (over $2 million) to the LSE.[45] During this same period the school expanded rapidly and came to be regarded as ". . . the leading centre of research in the Social Sciences . . ." for ". . . Great Britain and for the British Empire. . . ."[46] The percentage of space occupied by the library doubled[47] and it became the leading research library for the social sciences in Britain. An RF grant in 1931 was in large measure responsible for this expansion. The total amount of space occupied by the school increased from 51,000 square feet in 1923–1924 to 134,000 square feet in 1936–1937.[48] The total amount spent between 1923–1924 and 1936–1937 on the acquisition of land, building extensions, and equipment, including the library, came to £403,000. Rockefeller philanthropy provided approximately 40 percent of this total.[49]

The number of full-time teachers rose from twenty-six in 1923–1924 to seventy-six in 1936–1937. Whereas there were five full-time professors and five full-time readers in 1923–1924, by 1936–1937 these numbers had increased to nineteen and fifteen, respectively.[50] Once again the subventions from the memorial and the RF for research and teaching contributed substantially to this development.[51] This was particularly true for anthropology, international relations, and social biology[52] while the teaching staff in mental health and child guidance had received support from the Commonwealth Fund.[53] Just as the numbers of teachers and subjects increased, so student enrollments rose substantially. Indeed, as the *Review* commented, the UGC figures showed that ". . . the percentage increase of full-time students between 1923–1924 and 1935–1936 is markedly higher at the School than at any other university or college of which particulars are available in the reports of that Committee."[54] The number of students increased from 818 in 1923–1924 to 1,439 in 1935–1936.[55] As part of this general increase in enrollments, the number of students reading for higher degrees had risen from eighty-four in 1923–1924 to 293 in 1936–1937. The RF could take particular credit for this aspect of student enrollment because of its large grants for postgraduate teaching and research. Between 1931 and 1938 the RF provided $210,000 to support postgraduate teaching and research.[56] The LSE had by the end of the 1930s become an international center training many foreign students[57] and was still the only institution in Britain at which undergraduate teaching was devoted exclusively to the social sciences.

One reason for the school's prominent position in the social sciences was the publication record of its faculty. A major factor in the productivity of the faculty was the continuous research grants provided by the Rockefeller foundations.[58] The list of books and articles that emerged as a result of this funding is enormous.[59] The RF was also actively involved in other research projects at the school, including the International Price History Investigation[60] and the Survey of London Life and Labour.[61] Finally, the school itself published an *Annual Survey of English Law* and the journal *Politica*, while other members of the faculty had either created journals or were active as editors.[62]

The school's effect on the development of the social sciences in Britain and abroad was enormous. Of the students and teachers at the LSE between 1924 and 1937, ninety-three held academic positions in universities or university colleges in Britain.[63] Similarly, ex-students and teachers were holding academic positions throughout the world: India (52), United States (31), Africa (18), Canada (13), Australia (9) and China (9).[64] The school's staff had been actively involved in advising and conducting research for the British government as well as various foreign governments. With regard to the curriculum of other university institutions the *Review* noted that there had been ". . . a considerable extension of the number of institutions and university colleges in Great Britain and throughout the Empire, preparing students for the external degrees in Economics, Commerce and Law . . ." of the University of London.[65] The staff at the LSE had considerable representation on the university boards that supervised these degrees and therefore had an important responsibility in developing the syllabi at the institutions preparing external students. Finally, as the *Review* noted, it seemed that there could ". . . be little doubt that the very considerable extension of departments of Economics, Economic History, Sociology and Social Science in the Universities of Great Britain and the Dominions, and, in some cases, in Continental Europe, has received some impetus from the example of the School."[66] It seemed clear that the LSE was not only providing teachers but was also controlling to some extent the direction of curriculum development.

The record of achievement during the period 1923 to 1938 had indeed been phenomenal. In its *Review*, the school evaluated the influence of Rockefeller grants and came to the conclusion that

> . . . the great increase of the activities of the School which has been recorded in the historical section, is due in very large measure to the subventions of the Foundations. The physical extension of the School and the growth of its teaching activities, have been materially helped in this way; and the growth both of the teaching body and of the research activities of the School have been greatly assisted.[67]

The *Review* continued to note that the grants had "considerably assisted" the raising of other funds. After commenting on the difficulty that always arose when one tried to associate particular developments with particular grants, the school still felt that in the case of the Rockefeller subventions this was not a problem. They referred specifically to the ". . . growth of the central activities of the School's Economics, History, Law, Political Science and Sociology . . ." which had ". . . all received material assistance. . . ."[68] In addition,

> . . . new experiments and developments in less familiar fields on the borderland between the natural and the social sciences have also been made possible. The generosity of the Foundation has enabled the aspirations of the Founders of the School to be realized with a rapidity and to an extent would have been otherwise almost impossible.[69]

The RF was justifiably proud of its record at the LSE. The trustees were provided with a summary of the *Review* in a confidential bulletin in which the developments at LSE were described as ". . . a panorama of distinguished and progressive change almost unprecedented in the history of educational and research institutions devoted to the social sciences."[70] While the RF noted that evolution and sound planning at LSE had played a part in creating this "unique institution" it was also apparent that this evolution ". . . was energized and speeded by the aid granted by the Memorial and the Foundation, and certainly the assistance came at a strategic time."[71] Rockefeller philanthropy had achieved its central objective of creating an international center for the social sciences, a center that was a model for other universities to follow because of its commitment to "scientific" research.

The reasons that caused Ruml to choose the LSE were used by Day in the early 1930s to create a broad program in the social sciences at Oxford University. Even though the RF had changed its policy with respect to institutional development before it received a request from Oxford, the foundation decided to make this application a "special case." As the RF noted in 1938, ". . . it was felt that the development of the social sciences at Oxford was of such importance as to warrant support."[72] Indeed the grants to Oxford were the only other contributions made by the RF toward the development of institutional social science in Britain.[73]

Without Rockefeller influence Oxford would probably have limited itself to the much smaller project of creating an institute of statistics. As it was, the relatively small grants to Oxford[74] were used to develop a whole program in the social sciences. Apart from some capital expenditures on the newly formed Institutes of Statistics and Experimental Psychology the rest of the RF grants were split evenly between the provision of research lectureships and research projects. Research lecturers were appointed in Human Geography, African Sociology, Colonial Administration, Public Administration, and Public Finance. Coordinated research groups were formed in Economics, Colonial Administration, and Studies of Native Populations, around the development of an Oxford Survey and a program of training for the social sciences.[75] This funding eventually led to the major benefaction of £1 million by Lord Nuffield and the permanent establishment of the social sciences at Oxford.[76]

Throughout the period, Rockefeller philanthropy used its fellowship program to develop not only the LSE and Oxford but also scientific work in every British university. Between 1924 and 1940 the LSRM and the RF awarded 108 fellowships to British citizens in the social sciences. As one would expect, by far the largest number were awarded to economists, who accounted for approximately 40 percent (forty-two fellowships) of the total.[77] Political Science, including international relations, was the second most numerous category, with fifteen fellowships, while sociology and history had eleven and twelve representatives, respectively. Surprisingly, only eight anthropologists received fellowships. In addition, during the 1920s B. Malinowski and A. M. Carr-Saunders made study visits to the United States at Rockefeller expense. Both men were to play critical roles in the development of the social sciences in Britain.[78]

The LSE was responsible for nominating the largest number of fellows (nineteen) while the rest of the University of London nominated a further fifteen. Next in order was Oxford with sixteen, Cambridge with seven, and Manchester with five. Taken together, these two factors, that is, the focus on specific institutions and subject areas, demonstrate admirably Rockefeller philanthropy's intention both to further institutional development at LSE and Oxford and to provide scientific training in economics. Leading young economists were chosen from LSE (R. G. D. Allen, N. Kaldor, J. W. F. Rowe, F. B. Whale, A. B. Lerner), Oxford (Phelps Brown, E. D. Hugh-Jones, J. Marschak), and Manchester (C. D. Campbell, J. Jewkes, J. Stafford) to come to the United States to benefit from the empirical advances being made on that side of the Atlantic. In anthropology, the provision of fellowships was funneled through the International Institute of African Languages and Cultures, so the foundation list was limited. Even so, it should be mentioned that the list of those chosen for foundation fellowships did include four individuals who were to become very famous in the "functional" or "structural functional" school of anthropology. In 1931–1932 Lucy Mair received a fellowship to work in Uganda; Meyer Fortes held a fellowship for two years, 1932–1934; Audrey I. Richards held a fellowship in 1933–1934 for her work in Northern Rhodesia; while Geoffrey B. Wilson received fellowship support for three years (1934–1935 and 1936–1938) for his work in Tanganyika. Furthermore, social science fellowships were awarded to three other anthropologists to study in England as well as other countries. These men were Christoph von Furer-Haimendorf, Ralph O. Piddington, and S. F. S. Nadel. The latter two were also destined to become leading figures in the above-mentioned school of anthropology.

A NATURAL SCIENTIFIC BASE FOR THE SOCIAL SCIENCES

The central objective of making the social sciences more "scientific" was translated into action in almost all the grants made to British institutions. While it is true that much of the research conducted by the teachers at the LSE did not fit tightly into the mode, it is also true that the essential thrust of the development of the school was toward more practical, more empirical, and more scientific study. Certainly, the RF was responsible for the two major innovations of the period, that is, the Institute of Statistics at Oxford and the Economic Research Section at Manchester.[79] Furthermore, their support of social surveys at London, Liverpool,[80] Oxford, and Manchester;[81] the funding of economic research through the LSE, Oxford, Manchester, the Economic Foundation,[82] the London and Cambridge Economic Service,[83] the National Institute of Economic and Social Research,[84] and the Geneva Research Center;[85] and extensive support for "functionalist" anthropology—all served to further their general objective.

The prospect of grants for research proposals that emphasized "practical and realistic" research also drew the right response. This emphasis on the practical ties was especially apparent in the funding of colonial research projects; the close linkages between the Manchester section and the local industries of the area; and the inclusion of "men of affairs" in the cooperative research at both Oxford and the Royal Institute of International Affairs.[86] Similarly, the funding of psychological research and training by both Rockefeller philanthropy and the Commonwealth Fund, at the National Institute of Industrial Psychology[87] and in child guidance,[88] respectively, was also intended to bring social scientific knowledge to bear on practical problems. While no major break with tradition occurred in that there was a complete shift to scientific social research, the general trend during the interwar period was in that direction. As the RF itself commented in 1941 when looking back on the last two decades, "the shift in emphasis from deductive theory to empirical investigation has been marked."[89] Both the size and pace of that shift in Britain had been largely due to Rockefeller influence. As the Clapham Report noted, it was to foundations rather than the universities themselves that ". . . we owe what provision exists already for organized research institutes or divisions."[90] Furthermore, the report recounted how "many of the most important publications of those years [the interwar years] in the field of the social sciences bear an acknowledgment that they were made possible by a grant from the Rockefeller Foundation."[91]

From the middle of the 1920s Rockefeller philanthropy provided the major support for "functional anthropology." The partnership between Malinowski and the LSRM led to the whole series of major grants in both anthropology and the allied subject of colonial administration. Rockefeller philanthropy provided grants to support research and teaching in anthropology and colonial administration at the LSE, Oxford, the Royal Anthropological Institute, the International Institute of African Languages and Cultures, and the London School of Oriental Studies. These grants were part of one scheme whose design was aimed at establishing the "functionalist" school of anthropology as the preeminent school in Britain which would then provide detailed scientific knowledge about native African societies and thereby help solve the problems of colonial administration. One example of the extent of this involvement is the fact that the RF between 1931–1932 and 1938–1939 provided approximately 65 percent (£44,000) of the total running expenses of the International Institute of African Languages and Cultures.[92] The "functionalist" school of anthropology could not have developed or achieved the prominence that it had by 1939 but for Rockefeller help. Similarly, the tremendous outpouring of publications based on economic empirical research, particularly on the "business cycle," was also largely dependent on Rockefeller funds. Until the late 1930s British money was simply not available for this type of project and often only became available because of the stimulus provided by Rockefeller. The fellowship program was also used extensively to support economic research. Finally, in international relations, the RF's grants to the Royal Institute of International Affairs, and their influence at the LSE, Oxford, and Aberystwyth[93] did much to establish this subject as part of the university social science curriculum.

THE SOCIAL SCIENCES IN BRITAIN AFTER THE SECOND WORLD WAR

Let us now turn to an evaluation of these gifts from American philanthropy with respect to their impact on the development of the social sciences in Britain. The key document is the Clapham Report, which was published in 1946. This committee was appointed by the government to consider ". . . whether additional provision is necessary for research into social and economic questions."[94]

While the committee was specifically asked to focus on the provision of research funds in the social sciences it did also discuss the general provision of facilities and teaching. The report began by stating that they doubted whether ". . . the great practical value of knowledge in these various fields is generally appreciated."[95] They compared the provision of research funds in the social sciences to the position in the natural sciences and commented that with regard to the former the position was most unsatisfactory. As they put it,

> . . . the universities are under-staffed and under developed; the idea that provision for research in these fields by way of libraries, calculating machines, computers, and research assistants, is as important as provision for laboratories and experimental stations seems still to present an appearance of novelty and paradox.[96]

The committee reflected admirably the changing mood of the time by noting that ". . . the prospects of tangible return in national welfare are at least as great in the social as in the natural sciences."[97] As an example of this they referred specifically to the *New Survey of London Life and Labour*, which as they pointed out, had cost only £22,000. As they saw it, progress with regard to the provision for social research in the universities during the interwar period had been extremely slow and had suffered from the lack of adequate financing. Where progress had been made it had depended almost exclusively on private benefactions and although the committee did not say so directly, they indicated that this private money had come mainly from the Rockefeller foundations.

As the committee described the situation, apart from economics, every other subject in the universities was inadequately staffed and received a minimum of resources. When they compared the number of chairs and readerships in the social sciences with the other major curricula groups they found the numbers to be woefully small (see Table 3). The committee wished to see a large increase in the number of faculty positions in all the subjects. They particularly stressed the paucity of statistical training and noted that "an adequate supply of statistical competence is quite fundamental to the advancement of knowledge of social and economic questions."[98] They continued to say that there were ". . . few more urgent needs today than the increase of the supply of first class statisticians."[99] In addition, they recommended that more money should be provided for equipment, libraries, and travel. For, as they saw it, "the more realistic and practical the work becomes, the more it involves processes of collection and analysis which necessarily involve considerable outlay."[100] In view of the obvious contributions that the social sciences could make to the "national interest" the committee recommended that the State should provide much larger subsidies. They realized that foundation money had been the mainstay of social science in the previous decades and in general felt that this involvement was positive. Yet they also pointed to the danger

Table 3
Faculty in Great Britain's Univerities and University Colleges

	Professors	Readers
Social science	35	17
Arts	373	90
Medicine	144	32
Pure science	234	62
Technology	84	23
Agriculture	19	3
Total	889	227

Source: The Clapham Report, *Report of the Committee on the Provision for Social and Economic Research* (London: HMSO, Cmd. 6868, July 1946), p. 14. These figures include Scotland.

of the applicant tailoring his research to suit the research program of the foundation. Therefore the committee recommended that the University Grants Committee (UGC) should set up a subcommittee for the social sciences to survey universities' needs and to locate the gaps in the existing programs. The UGC was recommended to take the initiative by offering grants to stimulate the universities to repair these deficiencies. The Clapham Committee were convinced that money must be provided on a permanent and routine basis. Their final recommendation was that the UGC should provide an additional £250,000 to £300,000 a year for the social sciences.

In the summer of 1947 the UGC appointed a subcommittee to advise them upon matters relating to the social sciences.[101] After consultation with the universities the UGC began distributing a grant of £250,000 ($1,007,500)[102] in 1947–1948. Even so, the UGC still felt this estimate was on the low side and had decided in 1948 to increase the annual amount to £400,000 ($1,120,000) in the year 1951–1952.[103] By the middle of the 1950s the social sciences in British universities could truly be said to be experiencing a boom. Nuffield College, Oxford, was fully operative and the UGC grants were creating new teaching posts and providing research grants and materials in all the universities. The social sciences had become a recognized part of the university curriculum.

Rockefeller philanthropy and to a lesser extent the Carnegie foundations and the Commonwealth Fund played a critical role in the development of the social sciences in Britain. The fact that these subjects had become an established part of the university curriculum and were to receive government funds was almost entirely due to the persistent efforts of Rockefeller philanthropy. The emphasis upon the natural science approach and upon "practical and realistic" research demonstrated the clear utility of these subjects. Indeed, the very fact that the British government had begun to recognize the value of social research—as evidenced by the appointment of the Board of Trade surveys in the early 1930s and by the appointment of the Clapham Committee—was due in large part to the continuous funding by Rockefeller philanthropy of such research during the interwar years. The LSRM had introduced in the early 1920s the almost revolutionary idea that social research should be funded and placed on a permanent footing. The enormous number of Rockefeller grants and the large number of fellowships in economics all served to establish this subject in British universities. The fact that the number of graduate economists from British universities rose from sixty in 1925–1926 to 115 in 1938–1939[104] was almost entirely due to grants provided by the Rockefeller foundations. Similarly, the grants for statistics at the LSE and Oxford helped to establish this subject. Forty-six students gained degrees in this subject between 1925 and 1939;[105] all were graduates from the University of London and mainly the LSE.[106] With regard to postgraduate research the total number of students in British universities had increased from 1,800 in 1922–1923 to 2,800 in 1938–1939.[107] The increase in the number of postgraduates at the LSE in the same period accounted for 25 percent of this total increase across all subjects.

In 1950 there were five major university centers for the social sciences: LSE, Oxford, and to a lesser extent Cambridge, Manchester, and Liverpool. Rockefeller philanthropy had established the LSE and provided the impetus for the developments at Oxford. Similarly Rockefeller money had been used either to endow chairs or support social research at the other three institutions. In 1949–1950 there were fifty-six chairs in British universities in the social sciences, of which number eighteen were occupied by former prewar fellows, while a further fifteen were occupied by individuals who had received research grants from Rockefeller philanthropy.[108] Of the 108 prewar Rockefeller fellows appointed from Britain in the social sciences forty-three held academic positions in British universities.[109] Three other British[110] fellows held ministerial posts in the 1950 Labour government while nine more held senior positions in the Civil Service.[111] Finally it should be noted that, by 1950, 137 foreign Rockefeller fellows had spent time working in British universities. While many decided to return to their own countries or settle in the United States, a few had decided to make their careers in Britain.[112]

It is clear that the Rockefeller fellowship programs had exerted a substantial influence on the development of the social sciences in Britain. Indeed Rockefeller philanthropy prepared the way for the post–World War II developments in Britain not only in terms of the increased spending by government but also with respect to what was regarded as important in the social sciences. Rockefeller philanthropy had determined which subjects should be studied, which research questions should be answered, and which methods should be utilized to answer these questions. Rockefeller philanthropy had made sure that research in the social sciences was for the most part tied to "practical" and "real" concerns rather than theoretical issues.

FOUNDATIONS AS GATEKEEPERS

The relation between foundations and the recipients of foundation grants is complex and diverse. While it is reasonable to describe this process of influence with the "gatekeeper" analogy one also has to locate this process within its historical setting. The development of the social sciences before the First World War had proceeded without Rockefeller interference and to some extent these subjects continued to develop along the established lines during the interwar period. The trend toward empiricism and "scientific" study was general and reflected to some degree the changing social and economic conditions of Western industrial society. Similarly, Rockefeller policy reflected this broader societal trend and was itself affected by the results of its own involvement. In other words, the writer is not positing a linear causal model but is attempting to describe the most important characteristics of this particular social process.

Before further explication of the "gatekeeper" relation it is necessary to clear up a potential misunderstanding. This misunderstanding is the myth that foundations do not actively pursue policies and objectives. The ideology of philanthropy presents foundations as basically reactive institutions. In other words, while admitting their interest in some areas rather than others, they have consistently guarded against giving the impression that they have influenced, let us say, a university or a university department to develop one way rather than another. In an attempt to preserve the image of impartiality, foundations have insisted that the proposal must be seen to have come from the institution or the individual. Further, during the 1920s and particularly in the social sciences, the Rockefeller groups insisted that their grants be given almost no publicity and invariably refused having their name attached to a new building or department. The emphasis has been on working behind the scenes rather than openly for all the world to see. But while the process of influence has often been devious and indirect, it has nonetheless been based on definite policy objectives.

Rockefeller philanthropy had, during the interwar years, clearly defined policies. The officers had implicit objectives which were pursued unremittingly, objectives that emerged from discussions in New York rather than negotiations in London, Oxford, or Cambridge. This fact is clearly demonstrated in almost all the projects that have been discussed in this chapter. Rockefeller philanthropy was not impartial, did not react to proposals that emerged independently. Instead, its officers pursued explicit goals and were actively involved in preparing the proposals that were made to the foundations.

In this context it is important to modify the "gatekeeper" analogy, for it becomes clear that we are not simply describing a control mechanism that deals with quantity and direction. In addition, foundations as "gatekeepers" in the social sciences have served a filtering function both actively and passively with respect to the type of proposal that reaches them. Furthermore, they have served to concentrate the support for the proposals they let through the gate by conditioning grants so that support from other funding agencies became a condition of receiving the foundation grant. The "gatekeeper" has therefore extended its influence so that the flow of proposals is limited and the subsequent flow of research, teaching time, etc., is more concentrated than before. In any event, this modified conception of the "gatekeeper" function represents admirably the social control that the Rockefeller foundations have exercised over the development of the social sciences.[113]

When the social relations between the Rockefeller foundations and the recipients of grants in this chapter are examined it becomes abundantly clear that a great deal of control was exercised. Rockefeller funds were almost the only available source for the social sciences in Britain during the 1920s and for most of the 1930s. This was true for all types of support but was especially true when one refers to the availability of research funds. The Rockefeller foundations had explicit policy objectives which were pursued in the field by either contacting recipients and/or cooperating in the writing of the subsequent proposal. Finally, during the 1930s the RF increasingly used the conditional grant.

From an examination of the impact of Rockefeller funding upon the development of the social sciences in Britain it becomes clear that these foundations determined to a significant extent who would teach and conduct research in the social sciences; where this teaching and/or research took place; what was to be taught and which research questions were to be answered; and finally, how all this work was to be done. First, the control over individuals was demonstrated in the fellowship programs and in those cases where academics were defined as allies because of their potential to exert a national influence on the social sciences. For example, Beveridge, Malinowski, Carr-Saunders, and Jewkes all fit into this second category. Second, the control over institutional development was demonstrated by the support given to the LSE, Oxford, and Manchester rather than to other universities. Third, the control over the content of the social sciences was illustrated throughout the interwar period because of foundation emphasis upon research and training that was "scientific" and "practical" rather than what they perceived to be the more traditional theoretical and philosophical approaches. Further, within this broad framework the Rockefeller foundations exerted enormous control over the expansion of some subjects rather than others, that is, economics, statistics, anthropology, and international relations. Fourth, the control over methodology was apparent in almost all the funding relations discussed above but was especially noticeable in the emphasis upon empirical economics and functional anthropology. In the late 1920s Rockefeller philanthropy made a choice between the two conflicting schools on British anthropology. The traditional "diffusionist" school as represented by Elliot-Smith and Perry was refused support while Malinowski's "functionalist" school was given extensive support.[114] This support provided the launching platform (publications, positions, conferences, etc.) which led to the dominance of the functional school. Finally, it should be noted that recipients, both individuals and institutions, have at their own discretion consistently utilized either the promise of Rockefeller funds or the grant itself to raise other support. If one takes into account the interplay of all the factors it becomes apparent that the Rockefeller foundations were the archetypical "gatekeepers" when it came to the development of the social sciences in Britain.

THE IDEOLOGY OF AMERICAN PHILANTHROPY

The two Rockefeller foundations referred to in this chapter, the LSRM and the RF, were controlled by a board of trustees and a group of foundation officers. Key officers like Beardsley Ruml and Edmund E. Day were responsible for not only formulating policy, but to a large extent controlled how these policies were put into effect. This is not to say that the trustees or the particular donor's family did not have some input into the process, for indeed they did consistently exert their influence upon the operation of the foundations. Yet their influence was indirect and implicit, so that while Rockefeller officers had a large degree of freedom, they were also constantly aware of presenting policies and programs that would be acceptable to the trustees. In other words, the trustee's role was once of setting the broad parameters within which the foundation could operate.

According to Edward C. Lindeman, the trustees of American foundations in the 1920s were characterized by ". . . social prestige, financial success and middle aged respectability."[115] Just as the foundations were created by the most successful sons of American capitalism, so the trustees were a selection of the most successful men operating in a competitive economy. These men had a vested interest in the present organization of society and consequently tended to be conservative and unprogressive. The writer is then arguing that, on the one hand, the foundation officers had an enormous amount of freedom and, hence, power, but that they were controlled by the fact that any policy or program had to be consistent with the ideological viewpoint of their trustees. Within those set boundaries the Rockefeller officers were essentially more progressive and change-oriented than the trustees. These men usually had an academic or professional background and were employed because of their expertise in their chosen fields. They often brought with them to the job definite ideas about the way in which they thought the social sciences should develop. Even so, the officers invariably shared the same overall conservative orientation that their trustees held. What tension existed between these two groups of foundation personnel tended to revolve around specific items of a program, rather than the overall view of the foundation's role in the world.

Both groups can be labeled as "sophisticated conservatives" who, unlike "practical conservatives," were not against change in principle. On the contrary, changes that contributed to a more efficient, industrial productive system; to a more efficient functioning of colonialism; to ways of controlling the trade cycle; and to the preservation or spread of free, democratic political systems were welcomed and encouraged. The watchwords of this brand of "sophisticated conservatism" were "efficiency," "control," and "planning."

This ideology was made explicit in the early 1950s when the RF was ironically accused by the U.S. Congress of being subversive.[116] To answer the charges of subversion the RF noted that they refrained ". . . as a matter of policy from making grants to known communists."[117] This fact was confirmed by the Cox Committee, who found that out of 26,753 grants made by the RF only twenty-three had gone to individuals and two to organizations, which appeared on the inclusive lists of the House Un-American Activities Committee.[118]

Under a heading "social implications" the RF commented:

> A further impulse behind the interest in social studies was a conviction that the strengthening of our own free institutions required a better understanding of the processes of a free society and the framework within which a citizen enjoys the privileges and bears the responsibilities of liberty itself. At a period when free institutions came under challenge from totalitarian ideology of both the left and the right, it was felt that penetrating studies of our own free economic and political institutions would help them to withstand assault.[119]

In the same report, beneath the heading "Public Responsibility and Free Enterprise in Philanthropy" the president of the RF, Dean Rusk, defined the foundation in the following way:

> It is private in that it is not governmental; it is public in that its funds are held in trust for public rather than private purposes. As a social institution, it reflects the application to philanthropy of the principles of private initiative and free enterprise, under public policies which have long recognized the benefits of such activity to a free society.[120]

Finally Rusk noted that "we believe that a free society grows in strength and in moral and intellectual capacity on the basis of free and responsible research and scholarship."[121] This writer interprets "free society" to mean capitalist democracy and therefore contends that the underpinning of Rockefeller policy has been the intention to preserve that economic and political form of organization in Britain.

One essential component of Rockefeller ideology was the concept of education as an investment in human resources. These foundations were among the first organizations to apply a theory of human capital to education. Throughout the interwar period, the Rockefeller foundations and to a lesser extent the Carnegie and Harkness foundations all defined education as a form of "investment." Education, as represented by the institution or the individual, was seen as a form of capital investment, the capital being the "knowledge," "the brains," "the leadership" that education produced. This view of education received expression consistently in the Rockefeller negotiations with the LSE and Oxford, but has been especially noticeable when foundation officers have referred to either the larger institutional grants or their fellowship programs. Education, in these contexts, becomes almost a special "means of production" that will solve all society's problems. As the RF Annual Report put it in 1941,

> no amount of pressure can suddenly create a supply of thoroughly trained and broadly experienced physicists, mathematicians, chemists, biologists, economists and political scientists. These men represent the trained intelligence without which a war cannot be won, or a lasting peace achieved. They emerge spontaneously, unpredictably, but irresistibly out of long, patient, and sustained effort.[122]

In the 1950s when the RF reviewed their fellowship programs they labeled the total scheme as one of "investment in people."[123] The Rockefeller foundations invested in people through fellowships, research grants, and through their grants to universities and research institutes.

The product of this process was knowledge. In turn, the RF equated knowledge with power. As they put it, again when reviewing the fellowship scheme, "knowledge is power, and power which cannot escape the calculus of political rivalry."[124] That the Rockefeller foundations had objectives which pertained to the distribution of power in American society and served the interests of the economic elite should not come as a surprise. If one assumes that the interests of philanthropic foundations and business are not merely similar, but, to quote Lindeman, are "identical,"[125] then it becomes inevitable that in a capitalist economy their activities will be directed toward preserving the system of capitalist democracy. Philanthropy becomes capitalism's way of distributing surplus wealth, which might otherwise go to the state in taxes, in its own interest. With respect to the development of the social sciences in Britain, the Rockefeller foundations used this surplus to produce knowledge that would help preserve the economic structure of Western society. Economic stability was the objective, and consequently the vast majority of British economic research focused on studies that would explain why depressions occurred. Similarly, with anthropology their aim was "social security": consequently the vast amount of anthropological research focused on British African territories and almost certainly helped make the system of "Indirect Rule," whereby the British governed these territories through their traditional leaders, that much more efficient.[126] Stable African territories of course contributed to strong economies in Europe and therefore helped to stabilize Western capitalism.

Conclusion

Rockefeller philanthropy had an enormous impact on the development of the social sciences in Britain. Insofar as the Rockefeller foundations wished to make the social sciences more "scientific"—that is, in their terms, more empirical, more realistic, more practical—then this was achieved. Insofar as they wished to make the social sciences utilitarian and respectable, then this also was achieved. The LSRM and the RF were the "gatekeepers" who determined that the social sciences in Britain should help preserve the economic structure, and the resulting social inequality, in British society and its overseas empire.

Notes

1. See Samuel Bowles and Herbert Gintis, *Schooling in Capitalist America* (New York: Basic Books, Inc., 1976), pp. 197–198; and Clarence J. Karier, "Testing for order and control in the corporate liberal state," in Roger Dale, Geoff Esland and Madeleine MacDonald (eds.), *Schooling and Capitalism* (London and Henley: Routledge & Kegan Paul in association with the Open University Press, 1976), pp. 128–141.

2. See Ben Whitaker, *The Foundations, An Anatomy of Philanthropy and Society* (London: Eyre Methuen, 1974).

3. In this chapter Britain refers to England and Wales.

4. While some reference will be made to the Carnegie foundations and The Commonwealth Fund (Harkness) the major emphasis will be upon two of the Rockefeller foundations, specifically the Laura Spelman Rockefeller Memorial and the Rockefeller Foundation. This limitation is justified because it was the Rockefeller foundations who spent approximately 95 percent of the total funds expended on the social sciences by American foundations during the period under discussion.

5. See Lewis A. Coser, *Men of Ideas* (New York: The Free Press, 1970), Chapter 25, "Foundations as Gatekeepers of Contemporary Intellectual Life."

6. Ruml, who was only in his late twenties, had been trained in psychology. Before coming to the LSRM he had been associated with James R. Angell, President of the Carnegie Corporation.

7. Beardsley Ruml, "Recent Trends in Social Sciences" Address at the University of Chicago, December 17, 1929. Quoted by Raymond B. Fosdick, *The Story of the Rockefeller Foundation* (New York: Harper and Bros., 1952), p. 195.

8. LSRM, Final Report, 1933, p. 11.

9. Edmund E. Day, "Verbatim Notes on Princeton Conference of Trustees and Officers," 10/29/30, pp. 120–121, File, Program and Policy, Reports 900, 1926–1930, Rockefeller Archive Center. It should be noted that this depiction of social studies was somewhat misleading. During the latter half of the nineteenth century social scientists were themselves debating the desirability of moving from the older "classical" studies toward empirical social science. By 1920, leading U.S. economists were well established in empiricism, for example, W. C. Mitchell of business cycle fame.

   The papers of both the Laura Spelman Rockefeller Memorial and the Rockefeller Foundation are stored at the Rockefeller Archive Center (Henceforth referred to as RFA). Hillcrest, Pocantico Hills, North Tarrytown, New York, 10591.

   Before joining the Rockefeller Foundation, Edmund E. Day had been a professor of economics at Harvard and the dean of the School of Business Administration at the University of Michigan. In addition, Day had also been the treasurer of the Social Science Research Council since 1924.

10. See LSRM, Final Report, 1933, p. 12.

11. Day, "Verbatim Notes on Princeton Conference of Trustees and Officers," 10/29/30, pp. 123–124, File, Program and Policy, Reports 900, 1926–1930, RFA.

12. LSRM, Final Report, 1933, p. 13.

13. Day, "Verbatim Notes on Princeton Conference of Trustees and Officers," 10/29/30, p. 124. File, Program and Policy, Reports 900, 1926–193 0, RFA.

14. Ibid., p. 115.

15. Ruml, General Memorandum, 10/22. Quoted by Fosdick (1952), *Story of Rockefeller*, p. 198.

16. The memorial appointed a "national advisor" for each country in which they were interested, who then essentially supervised the selection of candidates as well as acting as host to the fellowship holders who selected his country for study. Advisors were appointed in England, France, Germany, Austria, Czechoslovakia, Italy, Holland, Norway, Sweden, Denmark, and Australia.

17. In 1929, Rockefeller philanthropy consolidated most of its separate interests under the one organization, the Rockefeller Foundation.

18. Day, "Verbatim Notes on Princeton Conference of Trustees and Officers," 10/29/30, p. 115, File, Program and Policy, Reports 900, 1926–1930, RFA.

19. Ibid., p. 118.

20. Ibid., p. 135.

21. Earlier that year Day and Malinowski had met in London to discuss the activities and aims of the International Institute of African Languages and Cultures, London. See the "Memorial Presented to the Rockefeller Foundation," 3/30, p. 3. Enclosed with a letter from Lord Lugard, 3/27/30. File 475s, International Institute of African Languages and Cultures, 1930, RFA.

22. Reference was made particularly to the National Institute of Industrial Psychology, London, who the RF described as having ". . . rendered important service in dealing with problems of personnel and scientific management in British commerce and industry, and in developing more effective methods of individual vocational guidance." RF, *Annual Report, 1930*, pp. 220, 224.

23. Ibid., pp. 220, 221.

24. Ibid.

25. RF, *Annual Report, 1932* (New York: the same, 1933), pp. 249–250.

26. Ibid., p. 274.

27. Ibid., pp. 274–275.

28. One such study was done through the "Economic Foundation" of New York and will be referred to later.

29. Ibid., p. 276.

30. Ibid., pp. 277, 278.

31. "Report of the Committee on Appraisal and Plan," 12/11/34. Referred to by Fosdick (1952), *Story of Rockefeller*, p. 207.

32. Quoted by Fosdick, Ibid.

33. "Presidential Review," RF, *Annual Report, 1936* (New York: the same, 1937), p. 5.

34. Ibid., p. 34.

35. Ibid., p. 35.

36. Ibid., p. 36.

37. Under this heading the writer includes economics, economic history, sociology, political science, anthropology, demography, social psychology, and statistics, as well as certain aspects of commerce, public administration, and law.

38. To provide an indication of the equivalent in American dollars the author calculated these dollar amounts using average exchange rates. These rates from American dollars to pounds sterling are as follows:

1916–1920	4.57
1921–1925	4.38
1926–1930	4.85
1931–1935	4.54
1936–1940	4.72

39. Nonrecurrent grants are given outright and therefore require no renegotiation. The grants for endowment or building purposes usually come under this heading.

40. Figures quoted by F. S. Stone (Secretary, National Institute of Economic and Social Research), "Research in the Social Sciences," *University Quarterly* 2 (May 1948): 277.

41. Lord Simon of Wythenshawe, "A Survey," *University Quarterly* 2 (May 1948): 260.

42. Britain's other universities gave scant attention to these subjects. Traditionally, the only subjects that had been part of the university curriculum were economics, economic history, and anthropology. By the early 1920s only Cambridge with its long-standing focus on economics could be regarded as a competitor to the LSE. Oxford had only just recognized the importance of the social sciences when it created in 1922 the Honour School of Philosophy, Politics and Economics. Most of the Redbrick universities, had some representation in economics, though only Manchester appeared to be taking a strong lead. Birmingham was known for its Commerce Department and Liverpool was beginning to focus on Social Studies.

43. For an account of Beveridge's philosophy, see Beveridge, "Economics as a Liberal Education" (first address at LSE), January 1921, No. 1, p. 7, Section V, Universities Files 4–2, "Rockefeller LSE." Beveridge Papers, London School of Economics.

44. W. H. B. Beveridge (Lord), *Power and Influence* (New York: The Beechhurst Press, 1955), p. 276.

45. See Donald Fisher, "The Impact of American Foundations on the Development of British University Education, 1900–1939," Ph.D. dissertation, University of California, Berkeley (henceforth referred to as Thesis), Table 18, p. 353.

46. London School of Economics, *Review of the Activities and Development of the London School of Economics and Political Science (University of London) during the Period 1923–1937* (London: LSE, 1938). p. 19 (henceforth referred to as the *Review*).

47. Ibid., p. 8.

48. Ibid., Appendix 1, p. 53.

49. Ibid., pp. 30–31.

50. Ibid., pp. 9–10.

51. Ibid., pp. 33–34.

52. The involvement of Rockefeller philanthropy in the development of this new

262 Philanthropy and Cultural Imperialism

subject, social biology, is particularly interesting. This new departure was
first suggested by Beveridge in 1924 as part of a proposal the "Natural
Bases of the Social Sciences." (See "Memorandum from the London Scool
of Economics and Political Science," from Beveridge to the Trustees,
LSRM, 7/15/24. File 593, LSE, Building Fund, 1923–1926, RFA.) The
aim was to bridge the gap between the natural and the social sciences and
be a means of importing the methods of the former into the latter. (see
ibid., p. 2) Subsequently, Lancelot Hogben was appointed to the new chair
and this department between 1930–1931 and 1936–1937 published nine
books and approximately fifty articles. (See *Review*, Appendix 6, pp. 113–
115.) This work focused on genetics, population statistics, heredity, eugenics, and dysgenics.

53. See Fisher, *Thesis*, pp. 380–385.
54. *Review*, p. 13.
55. Ibid., Appendix 3, p. 63.
56. See Fisher, *Thesis*, pp. 435–436. The LSE was in 1931 the first university
    institution to appoint a Dean of postgraduate studies.
57. In 1936–1937, 145 of the postgraduate students came from abroad. The
    leading countries were China, India, and the United States. Between 1931–
    1932 and 1936–1937 American students had chosen the LSE as the place to
    pursue advanced studies. See *Review*, Appendix 3, pp. 64–65.
58. Apart from the many grants for specific departments or research projects,
    Rockefeller philanthropy provided approximately £59,000 in yearly grants
    between 1924 and 1940 to support research in the school. See ibid., pp. 32–
    33.
59. Among the most important book titles resulting from Rockefeller funding
    are the following: *Economics*: Sir W. H. Beveridge, *Causes and Cures of
    Unemployment* (1931) and *Tariffs* (ed.), (1931 and 1932, Two Editions); A.
    L. Bowley and M. H. Hogg, *Has Poverty Diminished* (1925); A. L. Bowley
    and Sir J. Stamp, *The National Income 1924 (1927); A. L. Bowley and R. G.
    D. Allen, Family Expenditure* (1935); T. E. Gregory, *Gold, Unemployment
    and Capitalism* (1933). F. A. von Hayek, *Prices and Production* (1931 and
    revised 1935), and *Collectivist Economic Planning* (ed.) (1935); L. C. Rob-
    bins, *The Nature and Significance of Economic Science* (1932) and rev.
    1934), and *The Great Depression* (1934); *Anthropology*: R. W. Firth, *We,
    the Tikopia* (1936); L. P. Mair, *Native Policies in Africa* (1936); B. Mali-
    nowski, *Crime and Custom in Savage Society* (1926), *Myth in Primitive
    Psychology* 1926), *The Father in Primitive Psychology* (1927), *Sex and
    Repression in Savage Society* (1937), *Courtship and Marriage in N.W.
    Melanesia* (1929), *Coral Gardens and Their Magic* (2 volumes, 1935); C. G.
    Seligman, *Races in Africa* (1930), and *The Pagan Tribes of the Nilotic
    Sudan* (1932); E. Westermarck, *Ritual and Belief in Morocco* (2 volumes,
    1926), and *Wit and Wisdom in Morocco* (1930); *Political Science*: H. Finer,
    Theory and Practice of Modern Government (1932), and *English Local
    Government* (1933); W. I. Jennings, *Local Government in the Modern Con-
    stitution* (1931); H. J. Laski, *Studies in Law and Politics* (1932), and

Nationalism and the Culture of Civilization (1933). A. Meyendorff, *The Background to the Russian Revolution* (1929); <u>*Sociology*</u>: M. Ginsberg, *Studies in Sociology* (1932), and *Sociology* (1934); <u>*Economic History*</u>: L. Knowles, *Economic Development of the Overseas Empire, 1924–1936* (1936); R. H. Tawney, *Religion and the Rise of Capitalism* (1926), and *Equality* (1930 and second ed. 1931); <u>*International Relations and Law*</u>: W. A. Robson, *Civilization and the Growth of Law* (1935). For a full listing of all the publications, refer to the *Review*, Appendix 6, pp. 88.

60. This study was funded separately through the "Economic Foundation" of New York.
61. This survey was begun in 1929 and by 1934 had been published as a nine-volume study. *New Survey of London Life and Labour*, 9 volumes (London: University of London, 1930-1934).
62. This list included *Economic History, Local Government Population, Modern Law Review, Sociological Review,* and *Review of Economic Studies.*
63. Review, pp.26, 126–127, 132–133.
64. Ibid., p. 27.
65. Ibid., p. 24.
66. Ibid., p. 25.
67. Ibid., p. 34.
68. Ibid.
69. Ibid.
70. "Confidential Bulletin for Trustees," 4/38, p. 1. File 401S, LSE, 1938, RFA.
71. Ibid., p. 4.
72. Document, "Oxford University—Social Sciences," n.d., p. 2, File 401S, Oxford University, Social Science, 1938, RFA.
73. The only other attempt to create an institutional center occurred at Cambridge. In 1927 the LSRM endowed a Chair of Political Science and made it very clear that more substantial support would be forthcoming if the right sort of plans were presented. Cambridge did not build upon this foundation, and the social sciences as a whole remained relatively undeveloped until after the Second World War.
74. Between 1935–1940 the university received £3,600 per year for three years. The focus of this latter project was an analysis of the various factors which had influenced trace cycle developments in Great Britain from 1926 to 1937.
75. For a detailed account of the research and resulting publications, see Fisher, *Thesis*, pp. 476–498.
76. In 1937 Lord Nuffield announced his gift for a postgraduate college devoted to research in the social sciences. For details of the connection between Nuffield's grant and the previous Rockefeller funding refer to Fisher, *Thesis*, pp. 490-501.
77. All the statistics relating to these fellowships are calculated from the *Rockefeller Directory of Fellowship Awards*, 1917 to 1950 (New York: The Rockefeller Foundation, 1950).
78. A. M. Carr-Saunders was the professor of Social Science at Liverpool

University before he took over from Beveridge as Director of the LSE in 1937. Beveridge became the Master of University College, Oxford.

79. Between 1933 and 1940 the Rockefeller Foundation provided a total of £7,200 to the Economic Research Section at Manchester. This represented one-quarter of their total income during this period. For further details, see Fisher, *Thesis*, pp. 539–548.

80. Between 1929 and 1934 the LSRM provided approximately £5,200 for the Liverpool Survey. This amount represented 80 percent of the total expenditure. For further details, see Fisher, *Thesis*, pp. 395–402.

81. As part of the research program the Economics Section at Manchester had undertaken a survey of industrial trends in Lancashire. This survey, entitled "Readjustment in Lancashire, was published in 1937. See Memorandum, "Program of Economic Research Section, University of Manchester," T. B. Kitteridge to S. M. Walker (RF, Officers) and SM (not sure who these initials refer to), 5/21/38. File 401S, University of Manchester, 1938, 1939, RFA.

82. William Beveridge and Professor Edwin F. Gay of Harvard were joint directors of an international study of prices which the RF funded through the Economic Foundation of New York. Between 1929 and 1938 the RF provided $325,000 for this study which covered the history of prices in the United States and Seven European countries. See Fisher, D., *Thesis*, pp. 538–539. Beveridge received a further grant of £1,500 in 1938 to complete the section on England. It is interesting to note that during this period at University College, Oxford, Beveridge obtained money from the RF funds which were going directly to Oxford to employ a research assistant, J. H. Wilson. Harold Wilson later became prime minister of Britain.

83. Between 1937 and 1940 the RF provided £300 to the London and Cambridge Economic Service to develop research on problems of the business cycle. These grants effectively doubled the income of the Service. See File 401S, London and Cambridge Economic Service, 1936-1941, RFA.

84. The RF guaranteed to provide the income (£5,000) of the newly formed National Institute of Economics and Social Research beginning in 1937 for a period of seven years. For further details see Fisher, *Thesis*, pp. 549–555.

85. Professor J. B. Condliffe (Commerce, LSE, and Chairman of the Geneva Research Center) received grants totaling $56,000 in 1937 and 1938 from the RF. This money was used to organized international economic research programs and for an international trade regulation study. The National Institute of Economic and Social Research was responsible for the research in Britain. See "Report on the New Program of Liaison," 3/10/38. File 100, Geneva Research Center, June-December 1938, RFA.

86. Between 1932 and 1939 the RF provided approximately £66,000 to the Royal Institute of International Affairs. This funding represented the major thrust of Rockefeller support for the newly emerging field for international relations. For further details see Fisher, *Thesis*, pp. 534–537. The Institute

was the sister organization of the American Council on Foreign Relations.
87. Between 1921 and 1936 the LSRM, the RF, and the Carnegie United
Kingdom Trust provided £35,700, £21,000, and £14,700, respectively, to
support the National Institute of Industrial Psychology. See Fisher, *Thesis*, Table 19, p. 408. The Rockefeller money had been used specifically to
support research in three general fields: industrial psychology, vocational
psychology, and industrial output.
88. During the 1930s the Commonwealth Fund was almost entirely responsible
for the course in mental hygiene that was offered at the LSE. They
provided approximately £25,000 for this purpose during these years. See
File 272-2-T, English Mental Hygiene, 1 LSE Statistical Data, Commonwealth Fund. By the Second World War the fund had provided approximately £83,000 for the running of both the Child Guidance Council and
the Child Guidance Clinic in London. See files 272–2C, 1, 2 and 3; English
Mental Hygiene, Child Guidance Council, Financial Material, Commonwealth Fund Archives, New York.
89. RF, *Annual Report, 1941* (New York: the same, 1941), p. 42.
90. The Clapham Report, *Report of the Committee on the Provision for Social
and Economic Research* (London: HMSO, Cmd. 6868, July 1946), p. 10.
Besides Sir John Clapham, who chaired the committee, there were seven
other members. They were Sir Alan Barstow, Sir Hector Hetherington, Sir
Walter Moberly, A. M. Carr-Saunders, Henry Clay, Lionel Robbins, and
R. H. Tawney. The last four members had all been in intimate contact
with Rockefeller philanthropy and had each received financial support
from that quarter.
91. Ibid.
92. See Fisher, *Thesis*, table 20, p. 518. Yet this is not the place to explore the
details of this process. The writer will simply provide a partial list of those
individuals who received support for their research or who occupied
teaching positions that were endowed by Rockefeller philanthropy. This
list includes B. Malinowski, R. W. Firth, I. Schapira, E. Evans Pritchard,
Lucy P. Mair, Reginald Coupland; M. F. Perham, Meyer Fortes, Audrey I.
Richards, Geoffrey B. Wilson, Ralph O. Piddington, S. F. S. Nadel, and J.
R. Firth. Finally, it should be noted that Carnegie philanthropy also
provided funds to the International Institute and specifically provided the
funds for Lord Hailey's mammoth *African Survey* (1938).
93. There was a concentration of ex-Rockefeller fellows (international relations)
at this university.
94. Clapham Report, p. 3.
95. Ibid.
96. Ibid., pp. 3-4.
97. Ibid., p. 4.
98. Ibid., p. 8.
99. Ibid., p. 9.
100. Ibid.
101. This subcommittee of sixteen included five academics who had received

substantial support from Rockefeller philanthropy. They were H. Clay, R. W. Firth, J. Jewkes, L. Robbins, and R. H. Tawney.

102. Exchange rate:£1 = $4.03.

103. UGC, Report, 1948. p. 73.

104. Figures quoted by Michael Sanderson, *The Universities and British Industry 1850–1970* (London: Routledge and Kegan Paul, Ltd., 1972), p. 271.

105. Ibid., p. 268.

106. The only other place where statistics could be studied for a degree with the university was at University College. Egon Pearson founded a department in the mid-1930s.

107. Refer to UGC, Annual Returns, 1922–1923 and 1938–1939.

108. These and later figures were calculated from the *University Year Book*, 1949–1956, and the *Rockefeller Directory. . .1917–1950*.

109. This group included eighteen professors, two senior administrators, eleven readers, senior lecturers, or fellows, and twelve lecturers. Because of space limitations the writer will simply provide a partial list of the chair holders by institution: LSE: C. A. W. Manning, International Relations; K. B. Smellie, Political Science; R. G. D. Allen, Statistics; E. H. Phelps Brown, Economics of Labour; L. D. Stamp, Social Geography, D. V. Glass, Sociology. University of London: G. S. Graham, Imperial History; P. E. Vernon, Educational Psychology. Oxford: J. Jewkes, Economic Organization. Cambridge: D. M. Brogan, Political Science; M. Fortes, Social Anthropology; For complete details see Fisher, *Thesis*, pp. 387, 510–512.

110. Hugh T. N. Gaitskell, Chancellor of the Exchequer; H. A. Marquand, Minister of Pensions; and Eric Roll, Minister, U.K. Delegation to the Organization for European Economic Cooperation. It should be noted that all three were awarded fellowships under the heading economics.

111. This list included John M. Fleming, Deputy Director, Economics Section, Offices of the Cabinet; Margaret F. W. Hemming, Economic Advisor, Economics Section of Cabinet Office; and Harry Campion, Director, Central Statistical Office, Cabinet Offices.

112. Included in this group were Thomas Balogh, Fellow of Balliol, and senior Research Associate in the Institute of Statistics at Oxford; and Karl Maiwald, Senior Researcher in the Department of Applied Economics at Cambridge.

113.   *Diagram of the Gatekeeper Function
as applied to Philanthropic Foundations*

Foundations   Recipients

Social Control

Input Elements   Output (control) elements[a]
Availability of funds in relation to   individual (who)
  other funding agencies
                                          geographical/institutional (where)
Foundation has explicit policy   content (what)
  objectives
                                          methodology (how)
Foundation officers actively pursue
  objectives

Foundation uses its funding to draw
other money by conditioning its
grants[b]

Recipient uses foundation grant
to draw other funds

---

[a] Because foundations serve to concentrate the flow of knowledge so one would
   predict a fair degree of interdependence between these elements.

[b] This reference to the practice of promising to fund a proposal on condition that
   the recipient can obtain other funds (usually an equal amount) from another
   funding agency.

114. See Fisher, *Thesis,* pp. 415–416. It was of course no accident that anthropology and later sociology should have taken the "functional " or "struc-
   tural-functional" route toward scientific respectability. It is impossible not
   to draw the connection between the conservative bias in the functionalist
   approach, the intimate linkage with colonial administration, and the
   conservative ideology that ruled Rockefeller philanthropic interests. By

contrast the British School of Diffusionism adopted an extreme historicist position that was antiscience. As G.E. Smith put it in 1928, ". . . the distinctive fact in human behavior is the impossibility of predicting the nature of the response to any set of circumstances. . . " [G.E. Smith, *In The Beginning: The Origins of Civilization* (New York: Morrow, 1928), p. 19.] This view of the world was counter to everything that the RF hoped to achieve in the social sciences.

115. Edward C. Lindeman, *Wealth and Culture: A Study of 100 Foundations and Community Trusts and Their Operations during the Decade 1921–1930* (New York: Harcourt, Brace and Co., 1936), p. 161.

116. Two committees were created during the McCarthy era to investigate tax-exempt foundations. The Cox Committee, U.S. Congress, *"U.S. Select Congressional Committee on Tax Exempt Foundations" Hearing and Report,* (Washington, D.C.: U.S. Government Printing Office, 1953); and the Reece Committee, U.S. Congress, House, *"Tax-Exempt Foundations"* House of Representatives, 83rd. Congress, 1954, House Report, No. 2681.

117. RF, *Annual Report, 1953* New York: the same, 1954), p. 27.

118. Cox Report, quoted by Ben Whitaker, *The Foundations, An Anatomy of Philanthropy and Society* (London: Eyre Methuen, 1974), p. 106.

119. RF, *Annual Report, 1953,* p. 18.

120. Ibid., pp. 7—8.

121. Ibid., p.17.

122. RF, *Annual Report, 1941* (New York: the same, 1942), pp. 7–8.

123. RF, *Annual Report, 1955* (New York: the same, 1956), p. 11.

124. RF, *Annual Report, 1957* (New York: the same, 1958), p. 9.

125. Lindeman, *Wealth and Culture,* p. 160.

126. It should be noted that toward the end of the Second World War the British government established the British Colonial Development and Welfare Fund. This fund was used to establish a Colonial Social Science Research Council, with Raymond Firth as its first secretary. This council was established to formulate and supervise a program of social research in the colonies, and anthropology was given a prominent place. Large amounts of money were spent during the next ten years financing this research. Just as Nuffield and the USC took over the responsibility for the social sciences generally from the RF, so the Colonial Office took over their role as backers of anthropological research. For more details refer to C.D. Forde, "Applied Anthropology in Government: British Africa," in A.L. Kroeber (ed.) ,*Anthropology Today* (Chicago: University of Chicago Press, 1953).

Peter J. Seybold

The Ford Foundation and the Triumph of Behavioralism in American Political Science*

From 1948 to 1961 a revolution took place in American political science. The traditional institutional approach to the study of politics was replaced by the "new" behavioral political science. Prior to the behavioral revolution, political science was basically confined to the formal-legal study of institutions such as the legislature, the courts, and the presidency.[1] In traditional political science, the state was a major organizing principal of political inquiry and knowledge. Borrowing heavily from classical political philosophy (Plato, Aristotle) the theory of the state in traditional political science provided the basis for discussion of the nature of the ideal policy and the relationship between the state and its citizens.[2]

In the 1950s this political philosophy was replaced by what David Truman has called "the new realism." The result has been the eclipse of political theory, classically understood, and the triumph of the behavioral approach. The long-term decline of political theory and the general disappearance of the notion of the state are for all practical purposes synonymous with the rise of the "scientific" attitude toward the study of politics.[3] The long-standing tradition of political philosophy has been pushed into the background and replaced by a tradition of thought barely half a century old in the United States. Political theory thus fell victim to "political science" in the post–World War 11 era.

Prior to 1950, a well-defined subfield of political sociology did not exist in the United States. But in the 1950s the field gradually began to take

*This chapter is a summary of a more extensive study by me entitled "The Development of American Political Sociology: A Case Study of the Ford Foundation's Role in the Production of Knowledge" (Ph.D. Dissertation, SUNY–Stony Brook, 1978). A more general discussion of the behavioral sciences can be found in "The Ford Foundation and the Rise of the Behavioral Sciences," February 1979. Paper presented at the Third Annual Marxist Scholars Conference, Cincinnati, Ohio.

shape, largely as a result of the successful institutionalization of the behavioralist approach to politics. However, the rise to prominence of the behavioral sciences and the behavioralist approach to politics was not a simple process, for it involved the confluence of many distinct forces within academic social science. The authors of a recent voting study have summarized the complex merger of social forces which resulted in the behavioral revolution in political sociology:

> The flowering of large scale survey studies in the 1950s depended on the availability of scholars with training and inclination in that direction, on the development of the technical apparatus needed for such studies and on the willingness of foundations to supply the large sums of money required for such work. That the personnel, the technical apparatus and the funding all came together during the Eisenhower years was fortuitous.[4]

Nevertheless, it is not enough to say that the behavioral revolution was a fortuitous occurrence, for it involved too many complicated processes. To argue that all of this occurred simply by chance is to obscure a genuine understanding of the process by which scientific disciplines change. In the 1950s, despite a wide range of possibilities for research in political sociology, the bulk of the research was dominated by the behavioralist perspective. The rise to prominence of behavioralism in political sociology then had important consequences for defining the substance and the research strategies of social scientists working in the area, for the political behavior approach soon became political sociology.

Indicators of the success of the behavioral revolution in political science can be found on a number of different levels. The results of a 1962 survey of American academic political scientists clearly demonstrated the extent of the change in the general orientation of the field. Asked to specify the area within which the most significant work in political science was taking place, they gave more weight to "comparative government" and "political behavior' than to the more traditional "public law" and "political theory." The political scientists most frequently mentioned as making the more important contribution to the subject since World War II were all behavioralists: Robert Dahl, Harold Lasswell, Herbert Simon, David Truman, and V. O. Key.[5]

Another indicator of the success of the behavioral revolution has been the control of the presidency of the American Political Science Association. From 1927 when Charles Merriam, an early proponent of behavioralism, was elected president, until 1950, none of the presidents was prominently identified as an advocate of the behavioral approach. The election of Peter Odegard in 1950 might be regarded as the turning point. Since that time no fewer than six of the political scientists who served on

the Social Science Research Council's Committee on Political Behavior
have been chosen president of the association. Moreover, of its twenty
three presidents chosen from 1950 to 1973, at least thirteen are generally
identified as behavioralists.[6] Behavioralists then have been able to show
their strength in their professional activities.

There is also direct evidence of the impact of the postwar "behavioral
revolution" in political science in the proportions of different age cohorts
in various fields of specialization. In the newer "behavioral" specializations such as political psychology, political socialization, methodology,
judicial, legislature and voting behavior, revolution and violence, and
empirical theory more than 70 percent of the respondents in a 1967 survey
were thirty-seven years old or younger.[7] On the other hand, specializations
like administrative law, government regulation of business, and personnel
administration seem to be attracting few young people. Traditional political science areas such as normative and historical political theory, constitutional law, and political history have witnessed a decline in interest as
behavioral political science theories and methods have established their
dominance.

The continued prominence of behavioralism has also been documented
in a more recent study by Walter Roettger:

> Although there is clearly a circulation of elites within the profes-
> sion, the data suggest a rather stable and relatively homogeneous
> "learned discipline" whose principle concern is with American
> political phenomena and whose preferred mode of inquiry is
> *behavioral.*[8]

By the middle 1960s the behavioralists were in firm command of the
field and they have continued to exert tremendous influence on the
development of political science. How do we account for the success of the
behavioralists' campaign? As this chapter will argue, a complete understanding of the behavioral revolution must involve an analysis of the
impact of the Ford Foundation on the development of American political
science.

Why should the Ford Foundation be singled out as an entry point for
studying the rise of the behavioral sciences? The answer is simple: foundations in general, and Ford in particular, were the main force behind its
development. The words of Bernard Berelson, a major figure in political
sociology and former head of the Behavioral Science Division at Ford,
probably best illustrate this:

> What happened to give rise to the term (behavioral sciences)?
> The key event was the development of a Ford Foundation pro-
> gram in this field. The program was initially designated "individ-

ual behavior and human relations" but it soon became known as the behavioral sciences program and, indeed, was officially called that within the foundation. It was the foundation's administrative action, then, that led directly to the term and to the concept of this particular field of study. . . .

It was in this way that an administrative decision having to do with the programming and organization of a large foundation influenced at least the nomenclature, and probably even the conception, of an intellectual field of inquiry.[9]

Robert Dahl, another leader in the "behavioral revolution," echoes Berelson's assessment of the foundations' role:

A sixth factor that needs to be mentioned is the influence of those uniquely American institutions, the great philanthropic foundations—especially Carnegie, Rockefeller, and more recently Ford—which because of their enormous financial contributions to scholarly research, and the inevitable selection among competing proposals that these entail, exert a considerable effect on the scholarly community.

If the foundations had been hostile to the behavioral approach, there can be no doubt that it would have had very rough sledding indeed. For characteristically, behavioral research costs a good deal more than is needed by the single scholar in the library— and sometimes, as with the studies of voting in presidential elections, behavioral research is enormously expensive.[10]

The effort to restructure political science required a substantial financial investment in graduate departments, individual scholars, research institutes, and professional associations. During the crucial decade of the 1950s, it was the Ford Foundation which played the key role in supporting the behavioral sciences. Between 1951 and 1957 the Behavioral Science Division of the Ford Foundation granted over $23 million for support of the behavioral science movement.[11] This was clearly the largest investment made by any institution and was particularly significant since the federal government had not yet become involved in supporting the social sciences. Thus, for a considerable period of time, grant money from private foundations was the only source of funding for research. This gave Ford and other foundations tremendous leverage in shaping the behavioral sciences.

The Ford-funded Foreign Area Fellowship Program probably illustrates best its great influence on the field. This program represented the extension of behavioral political science into studies of comparative politics. As George Beckmann has argued, the activities of Ford in this area were crucial in its formation:

> A few more statistics will demonstrate just how successful this program has been in strengthening American higher education. Of the 984 former fellows, 550 hold faculty positions in 181 colleges and universities in 38 states. . . .

> Some twenty-nine universities have employed five or more fellows, and ten universities have employed ten or more. In addition to academic and teaching careers, eighty-two former fellows are now in government service, thirty-eight have joined philanthropic or non-profit organizations, and forty-five are in business or professions. Many former fellows have added to our knowledge of the non-Western world through the publication of results of research. Altogether they have published some 373 books and over 3,000 articles and short monographs; moreover, they have edited or contributed to another 516 volumes.[12]

The creation of foreign area specialists was just one part of a larger movement to develop a practical understanding of human behavior. It is in this context that Ford's involvement in the behavioral sciences and its support for the behavioral revolution should be understood. For as Bernard Berelson makes clear, the foundations were not interested in supporting academic disciplines, but instead pushed for usable results:

> The foundations have always been interested in improving man's estate, and from the beginning they hoped for and wanted practical returns that could be directly applied to the solution or amelioration of human problems.[13]

The Ford Foundation's support for the behavioral revolution can likewise be seen as an attempt to retool political science in the post–World War II era. In order for political scientists to contribute to a practical understanding of human problems, they would first have to be encouraged to do empirical research and to transcend the boundaries of a traditional political science which was preoccupied with normative questions.

To accomplish this dramatic transformation of the field, Ford concentrated its efforts on building an institutional structure which would insure the victory of the behavioralists. This required involvement at a number of different levels: support for the individual scholars, elite universities, research institutes, capturing of professional journals, domination of intermediary organizations such as the Social Science Research Council, and the training of younger scholars in behavioral techniques. By the middle 1960s, the behavioral approach to political science was firmly entrenched in a network of institutions which assured its dominance. As a consequence, a "mobilization of bias" prevailed which severely limited the possibilities for the emergence of alternative approaches which could challenge behavioralism.[14] By definition, traditional political science, constitutional law, political history, and radical political science research were not part of the "new political science." This perspective stressed survey research as the dominant technique in the field, which in turn placed further limits on the topics which could be investigated. In short, a narrow, pragmatic orientation became prominent which excluded other possible perspectives.

Thus the Ford Foundation was able to set the tone for research in political science by promoting the behavioral revolution. In the next sections, we will look at the specific mechanisms which Ford utilized to shape research and professional training in the field. As a case study, the analysis of Ford's involvement in political science illustrates many of the ways in which Ford and similar foundations have shaped the development of research in areas critical to the corporate elite. Crucial to this process is the foundation's capacity to build university programs, create academic stars within disciplines, influence intermediary organizations, and create "think tanks" to promote practical research. Ultimately, it is this ability to build institutions and dominate the network of organizations which are involved in the production of knowledge which allowed Ford to set the agenda for social science research in the United States.

The Behavioral Science Division—Defining and Organizing the Field

As the Ford Foundation emerged as a national entity in 1950 it entered into a period of real uncertainty both at home and abroad. The world historical situation had changed substantially and new nations were beginning to develop. As the Report of the Study Committee of the Ford Foundation (1949) reveals there was great concern with the rapid pace of social change and the potential for social disruption:

> Our advisers recognized the importance of the fact that our entire social structure is undergoing profound change. We are now well along on the transition from a rural, agricultural, and relatively simple society to one which is urban, industrial, and highly complex. The pace of social developments has been hastened by the extraordinary speed and range of economic growth and by the impact of two wars. The slowness of people to adjust themselves to such vast and rapid changes is of considerable

significance. In such a period of change, dislocations and break-downs occur, with resulting political, economic and social unrest. And at various points during the transition basic political and moral principles are subjected to re-examination and challenge. . . .[15]

It is in the context of this fear of social disorganization that the foundation sought to develop the practical aspects of the behavioral sciences. Rather than promoting fundamental social change to meet problem areas that were emerging, the foundation attempted to remap the world at the level of ideas and to update the dominant ideology. The 1949 report, for instance, viewed "internal conflicts in a democratic society" as subject to accommodation and the "millions of Americans who remained confused in their analysis of crucial problems" as correctable once the people are given a viable definition of democracy.[16] It was the foundation's task to develop such a definition of democracy in order to cure the confusion of the masses. Those individuals who fail to accept this formula for "democracy from above" and go beyond reasonable disagreement were seen by the study committee as pathological or maladjusted, for they have violated the basic norms of democratic society.

From the foundation's perspective, it was very important to develop an understanding of social disorganization. With this in mind, it turned to the development of the behavioral sciences and to a redefinition of democracy:

The timing of the program may well be strategic . . . . In the past fifty to seventy-five years has developed what might be called a new approach to the understanding of man. It is not new in the sense that it has identified new problems, but rather in its application of the principles of scientific method to the study of human behavior. As with other such ambitious enterprises, this approach has experienced certain defeats, distortions, and excesses. But at the same time, it has produced a body of technical, verified knowledge which is not unimpressive. While it is not yet a "mature" science, it is certainly more than "promising.". . . The Foundation has a real opportunity to further this movement.[17]

It is with this general orientation that the Behavioral Sciences Division embarked on a program of development which ultimately would profoundly influence the organization of the social sciences. The first step was taken in the summer of 1950 when the foundation, as part of its interim program, provided a total of $3 million for a "program of support for the further development of university resources for research in individual behavior and human relations." Grants of $300,000 each were made to seven universities (California, Chicago, Columbia, Cornell, Harvard,

Michigan, Yale); grants of $100,000 each, to six universities (Illinois, Minnesota, North Carolina, Pennsylvania, Princeton, Stanford); and a grant of $300,000, to the Social Science Research Council. The announcement of these grants stated the objectives as follows:

> The purpose of the grant is not the support of research projects, as such, but rather the development of the personnel and the improvement of the conditions and facilities for effective research. Success is, therefore, not to be measured so much by research findings *per se* as by an increase in the number or capacity of the research workers, the improvement of their methods and the enhancement of their facilities and resources. Through emphasis on effective manning and "machine tooling" for research, rather than upon specific projects, it is hoped that the underpinning will be strengthened for subsequent activity in all the various and specialized segments of the broad area of individual behavior and human relations.[18]

Shortly thereafter the behavioral sciences program began to take shape as the formal plans for the division were approved by the trustees. The 1953 report summarizes the early organization of the division:

> In early 1951, at the request of Paul G. Hoffman, then President and Director of the Foundation, H. Rowan Gaither, Jr., then an Associate Director, took direct responsibility for the development of Program Five. He appointed Donald Marquis, Chairman of the Department of Psychology at the University of Michigan, and Hans Speier, Chief of the Social Sciences Division of the RAND Corporation, as his consultants in this task. In the summer of 1951, Bernard Berelson was named senior staff member for the development of this program, and later became Director of the Behavioral Sciences Division. Two deputy directors were subsequently appointed: David McClelland, Chairman of the Department of Psychology at Wesleyan University, in the summer of 1952, and Waldemar Nielsen, Director, Office of Information, Mutual Security Agency, Paris, in the fall of the year.

> During the fall of 1951, a proposed plan for developing this program of the foundation was drawn up by Mr. Gaither and his associates. It was approved by the officers in December 1951 and by the trustees in February 1952. Following thes actions, the Behavioral Sciences Division was organized to carry forward the work of Program Five.[19]

In the overall plan of the foundation the Behavioral Sciences Division was given the responsibility for developing research that could be applied to the problem areas specifically assigned to the other divisions such as international relations and metropolitan government. In organizing this program the foundation coined the term "behavioral sciences" as a way of separating itself from the present organization of the social sciences and to stress the interdisciplinary orientation of the program. In the proposed plan for the development of the behavioral sciences (December 1951) the foundation's meaning of the term "behavioral sciences" is clarified:

1) It refers primarily to a program of research.
2) It refers to the scientific approach.
3) It refers to the acquisition of basic knowledge of human behavior and thus it is considered as a comparatively long-range venture.
4) It refers to the interest of the Foundation not in knowledge of human behavior as such but rather in knowledge which promises at some point to serve human needs.
5) It refers to an interdisciplinary approach and not to any single conventional field of knowledge or a single combination of them; traditional academic disciplines as such are not included or excluded.
6) It refers to a broad and complex subject matter, since the program aims at a scientific understanding of why people behave as they do.
7) Finally, it is definitely not considered as a cure-all for human problems but rather as a contributor to their solution, along with other sources of knowledge and judgement.[20]

As defined by the foundation, the behavioral sciences became an applied program. The task of the division was to develop research which could contribute to the understanding of human behavior. Implicit in this conceptualization of the field was the hope that the behavioral sciences could suggest ways in which individuals could adjust to changing social conditions and therefore limit social disorganization. However, this approach was heavily weighted toward the preservation of the status quo for it takes the existing social arrangements as given and then seeks to explain why individuals feel alienated. The stated goal of the program was to reduce social disorder by proposing practical steps to aid personal adjustment rather than fundamentally altering the social structure.

The development of this kind of behavioral science was not an easy assignment. It was the division's task to evaluate how the foundation could effectively contribute to the behavioral sciences. Simply providing additional funds to the behavioral sciences would not necessarily result in improvement.[21] The 1951 proposed plan attempted to analyze the problems in the behavioral sciences in order to clarify the kinds of activities the division should support. Among the internal problems of the behavioral sciences noted by the report were

1) Too few highly qualified and competent personnel.
2) Tendency toward diffuseness, unorganized specialization, insufficient cumulation and integration.
3) Lack of cooperation with related approaches to the understanding of man.
4) Deficiencies in institutional arrangements.[22]

Outside the behavioral sciences various problems were also noted:

1) Too much pressure for immediate results and applications.
2) Ideological barriers
3) Skepticism, misunderstanding, and ignorance on the part of public and administrative leaders.[23]

The division was then faced with the problem of reorganizing the social sciences to meet the challenges of the post–World War II era. This meant a more concerted emphasis on practical research. Up until this time the social sciences had been lacking this orientation. In developing a behavioral science program the division had to build from the ground up. An infrastructure supportive of this new, practical, interdisciplinary approach would have to be constructed. The problems which the foundation faced in entering this area were extensive, as is indicated above. Not only were there internal difficulties, but there was also the problem that the social sciences had lacked legitimacy in the past. In the foundation's view, these problems were significant, but they were overshadowed by the perceived need for a practical behavioral sciences program that could aid in promoting social stability.

The reconstruction of the behavioral sciences began on a large scale once the division had evaluated the findings of its program of grants begun in 1950 on "Individual Behavior and Human Relations." This series of grants and three other early grant programs—a 1952 inventory of several major research areas which Ford wanted to investigate (social stratification, organizations, political behavior, socialization and child development, communications, and economic development and cultural change); a 1953 grant to encourage institutional self-surveys in the behavioral sciences; and a 1953 Behavioral Sciences Fellowship Program—provided the basic information which guided Ford's intervention in the field.

Assessing and Preparing the Field

The goal of the 1952 inventories was to evaluate the research which had been done previously in these areas and assess the direction the field could take as well as the current level of methodological sophistication. The selection of areas of interest is itself instructive, as they mirror the concerns of the 1949 study group report and represent vital areas in understanding the dynamics of a rapidly changing society. The inventories, then, were part of Ford's initial efforts to locate areas in which it could most readily intervene and which promised practical payoffs. In particular, the areas in which Ford expressed interest in promoting research constitute significant sectors that were undergoing transformation (the family, political order, stratification system, industrial order) and thus could be subject to "social maladjustment".

In 1953 Ford began two other programs which contributed to the assessment of the needs of a national behavioral science program. First, it began its own Behavioral Sciences Fellowship Program by spending $450,000 to attract qualified people to do research in the behavioral sciences. This program thus addressed the problem of the lack of qualified behavioral scientists and was aimed at strengthening the personnel. Second, the foundation funded a series of grants to major universities to undertake self-surveys of their training and research programs in the behavioral sciences. In 1953, $50,000 each was given to the University of Chicago, Harvard University, the University of Michigan, Stanford University, and the University of North Carolina for this purpose. A committee formed from the universities' own faculty and staff was to carry out the basic work and was to be assisted by a visiting committee selected jointly by the institution and the foundation.

The program of self-surveys is a further example of the foundation's attempt to evaluate the needs of the behavioral sciences at various universities. The thrust of this program was to encourage "a small group of American universities to take a systematic look at the state of the behavioral sciences at their institutions and express their needs in terms of detailed plans for development and improvement."[24] This program, then, represented an attempt by Ford to evaluate the needs of elite universities as a first step in building an institutional base for the behavioral science movement. If the behavioral sciences were to become established they would have to take hold in the major universities. This program had an additional advantage in that these universities could then provide examples of the kind of work which was gaining favor to other universities and colleges; this would help promote Ford's definition of this field.

The Case of Political Sociology—Defining Political Behavior

At the very same time that this general process of assessment of the needs of the behavioral sciences was occuring, a specific evaluation of the field of political behavior also took place. Between 1950 and 1954 an identical pattern of intervention happened in political sociology. Just as Ford had begun its initial involvement with the general field of the behavioral sciences with a series of exploratory grants, it likewise adopted this same strategy in political sociology. This was followed by an extensive inventory of the field, more general institutional support, and assistance of individual scholars.

The first step in organizing the intervention into the field of political sociology, as in the general consideration of the behavioral sciences, was defining the field. The division defined political behavior in the following manner:

> This topic refers not only to behavior involved in the operation of formal governments, domestic and international, but also to behavior in power relations generally. It includes such questions as the causes and consequences of political participation and apathy in democratic society, the distribution of political values and doctrines, and the characteristics and codes of political leaders.[25]

Other important questions in this area which the foundation was concerned with included:

> How is public opinion formed on political issues? When and how is public opinion brought to bear on policy formation?

> How are political values and doctrines distributed throughout the community, what is their present status, and how do they change?[26]

As was characteristic of the conception of the behavioral sciences, the definition of political behavior reflects an applied approach. As the foundation's definition of the key questions in the field make clear, there was a need to understand the formation of public opinion. This focus on the process of forming political attitudes fit in directly with the earlier concerns expressed in the 1949 report about apathy and political alienation. For instance, area two of the foundation's overall organizational setup (1949 report) was entitled "Strengthening Democracy." It was in this context that Ford embarked on a program to reorganize political science. The development of a research capacity was a key part of this process.

Two additional steps were taken to develop the field of political behavior which also paralleled the general involvement of the foundation in the behavioral sciences. First, as a result of Ford grant money, initial programs in political behavior were started at major universities. At Columbia University a committee was set up to address the problems in behavioral research and the training of behavioral scientists. At the University of Chicago a graduate seminar in research and research training in political behavior ran through the school year of 1951–1952. At the core of this program was a series of research fellowships awarded to exceptional students to do research in political behavior. At the University of North Carolina a political behavior committee was formed to formulate a program of research in this area. The impact of this committee was crucial in building support for behavioral research:

> The committee has fixed political behavior research in the minds
> of students, faculty, and administration as an appropriate and
> continuing part of graduate training and faculty research pro-
> grams of the university. Before the creation of the political
> behavior committee there were no voluntary applications from
> political science students for research assistantships in the Insti-
> tute for Research in Social Science. The work of the committee
> led directly to the initiation of a substantial research program in
> political behaviors. It was also instrumental in helping the de-
> partment to recruit new faculty members who were interested in
> political behavior.[27]

At the University of Michigan the Political Behavior Program was established in the spring and summer of 1951 after discussions with the university's Committee on Individual Behavior and Human Relations. This committee was set up after a grant had been made to the university by the Ford Foundation for training and research in the behavioral sciences.

The major achievement of these early efforts at various universities was to plant the seeds which ultimately resulted in the development of large-scale graduate programs in political behavior. As the progress reports from a number of programs make clear, the foundation's grant went a long way in legitimating the existence of political behavior research programs and was the starting point for a number of programs which later built a national reputation.

In addition to this series of grants, the foundation moved even more directly to evaluate the needs of the field of political behavior by sponsoring an inventory of the field in 1952 by a group at Columbia University consisting of Seymour Martin Lipset, David Truman, Richard Hofstadter, Herbert Hyman, and William McPhee.[28] The Political Behavior Committee was asked to review the state of the field during this period and consolidate the present research findings so that an evaluation could be made as to what would be fruitful research topics to pursue and what developments looked especially promising. In short, this was an attempt to take stock of the field and to plan future work in behavioral political sociology. Even at this early stage, it is important to note that the focus was on political behavior and representatives of other approaches were excluded from a process that was crucial in shaping the development of the field.

Support for this inventory was continued in 1955 and it resulted in a number of publications which were crucial in giving direction to the field. Quite clearly this team of experts represented the emerging political behavior wing of the field led by Truman, whose book *The Governmental Process* (1951) was one of the linchpins of the attack by the postwar behavioralists.

The movement to establish a behavioral political science was thus aided by the work of this influential group and the support for political behavior programs at major universities. The foundation continued to give support in later years to political behavior programs at the University of Michigan, the Institute for Research in Social Science at the University of North Carolina, and to the Bureau of Applied Social Research at Columbia. In subsequent years the major support for the behavioral revolution shifted to Ford-funded programs at the Social Science Research Council and to more specific practical programs such as grants for research in metropolitan government.

Expanding the Program

The initial grants to major universities for behavioral science programs and the more specific grants in political behavior, along with the inventories and self-study grants, provided the basis for an expanded program of support. In the middle 1950s the foundation tried to address other areas which were fundamental in restructuring the social sciences and to reach smaller universities and colleges. Attention was also focused on improving methodology and supporting outstanding individuals in the field. Several major programs were started during this period which followed the guidelines set down by earlier grants.

Based largely on the results of the self-surveys and previous experience in funding the behavioral sciences at major universities, the foundation embarked on a program of grants in 1955 under the title of "development and improvement of the behavioral sciences." Included among the universities supported were Harvard ($474,000), Michigan ($220,000), Stanford ($408,500), North Carolina ($246,000), Minnesota ($133,000), Illinois ($75,000), and Columbia ($54,650). These grants were basically designed to begin the work of building a solid underpinning for the behavioral sciences at the leading universities.

In addition to the funding of university programs, the foundation also supported training programs and research institutes. The foundation gave grants to the Bureau of Applied Social Research at Columbia for a variety of activities, including an international center of survey research materials and a case book on applied social research. It also gave support to the National Opinion Research Center ($36,000) at the University of Chicago for research in the behavioral sciences and to the Russell Sage Foundation for a program on the practical utilization of the behavioral sciences. The grant to Russell Sage, $750,000,[29] was especially significant since it was used to promote the behavioral sciences through two major types of programs: (1) appointment of postdoctoral scholars to residencies in operating agencies or professional schools; (2) support to professional schools for the development of their work in the behavioral sciences by providing funds for the appointment of behavioral scientists to the faculty, for fellowships for advanced students and for research planning. The goal of this program was made clear by Donald Young, president of Russell Sage: "Little provision has been made in our educational system for the training of personnel equipped to apply behavioral science in any practicing profession. . . . If we had more money, we would expand and speed up our efforts to increase the number and quality of such persons."[30]

In extending its program of support to include research institutes, the foundation exhibited an awareness that it could not limit its activities to the universities. It would also have to develop other parts of an infrastructure in order to promote the behavioral sciences and behavioral political sociology. Moreover, the foundation derived the fringe benefit of placing these organizations in a state of perpetual financial dependence. This increased the foundation's influence due to its financial clout and also started a process which forced organizations to seek support from other sources to insure their survival. In much the same way as universities came under the broad influence of the foundation, research institutes also found themselves in a position of accommodating their interests to the foundation. A complex division of labor, then, was beginning to develop in the knowledge producing sector which was linked to the activities of the Ford Foundation and could be mobilized to accomplish various tasks.

The general support for the behavioral sciences by the Ford Foundation was continued in 1956 with a series of grants made predominantly to universities under the title of "Grants in Aid to Facilitate Research in the Behavioral Sciences." Included among the grantees were twenty-three universities in the United States and abroad as well as such organizations as the London School of Economics, the International Social Science Council located in Paris, and the RAND Corporation. This program provided support for both institutions and individual scholars and represented a branching out of Ford Foundation support for the behavioral sciences by including other major state universities within the United States. Thus, once successful programs had been established at select universities, the foundation then moved to extend its support to other universities.[31]

Two other programs which were initiated in 1957 (the final year of operation for the Behavioral Sciences Division at Ford) constituted further attempts to bolster elite departments in the behavioral sciences as well as prominent individual social scientists. In a series of grants entitled "Research in the Behavioral Sciences," $75,000 each was given to Berkeley, Chicago, Columbia, Cornell, Harvard, Michigan, and Yale for support of research in the behavioral sciences over a period of five years. The grants were to be matched by $50,000 from each institution for the same purpose. As the description of the grant indicates, these institutions were selected because of the concentration of behavioral science research. This general program of grants to select universities was conceived to provide flexibility in the foundation's overall program of support and was generally seen as a way of providing initial modest support for pilot and exploratory studies as well as a response to individual universities' pleas for free research funds for local allocation in small amounts.

The second foundation program, which began in 1957, was entitled "Basic Research in the Behavioral Sciences." This series of grants was given to individual scholars and was administered by the university with which the individual was affiliated. The logic behind this program was very simple: it was thought that the key to good research was the support of the best people in the field. The grants were flexible, to be used for whatever purposes the designated scholars thought could advance their own studies, and they were to be given a five-year period to provide continuity for research planning and execution. This series of grants marked a return to the foundation's attempt to support elite scholars within various fields in order to augment its more general institutional and training programs.[32]

By the late 1950s the foundation had created an institutional base which promoted the behavioral sciences. It had built behavioral science programs at major universities, supported research institutes engaged in behavioral sciences, and given grants to key individuals in the field. The outcome of this massive program of support was to institutionalize the behavioral sciences and to foster the behavioral revolution in political science. Yet, the fundamental restructuring of the social sciences was not simply a product of Ford's benevolence. It was rather a part of their effort to enlist the social sciences in the struggle to promote social stability. In order to contribute to this effort, it was essential that a practical problem-solving orientation be promoted in the behavioral sciences. This necessarily placed limits on the development of other perspectives which did not share this preoccupation with what C. Wright Mills called "liberal practicality."[33]

The Use of Intermediaries

The task of promoting the behavioral sciences and the behavioral revolution was not handled exclusively by direct grants from the Ford Foundation. The foundation also made use of intermediary organizations to tackle problems it had difficulty addressing through its own programs. The two most important intermediaries utilized by Ford during this period were the Ford-built (1954) Center for Advanced Study in the Behavioral Sciences and the Social Science Research Council.

THE CENTER FOR ADVANCED STUDY IN THE BEHAVIORAL SCIENCES

One of the major problems which confronted the Ford Foundation when it moved into the behavioral sciences was the general lack of legitimacy which plagued the social sciences. To remedy this situation the foundation set up a planning group to develop a center committed to the behavioral sciences. The planning committee submitted its report in June 1952 and in July the trustees appropriated $3,500,000 for one year of planning and five years of operation. In the spring of 1953 the board announced the appointment of Ralph Tyler, dean of the Division of Social Sciences, University of Chicago, as director of the center. In 1954 the Center, which was built exclusively by the Ford Foundation, was opened at Palo Alto. The 1953 report outlines the purposes of the center:

> The major purpose of the Center is to develop the general field of the behavioral sciences as fully and as richly as possible over a relatively short period of time by concentration upon the advanced study of highly creative and productive behavioral scientists of established reputation and of highly promising young scholars with their professional careers ahead of them. If the

level of competence of a considerable number of behavioral scientists can be markedly improved in this way, the program will make a major contribution to the universities, which over the long run must bear the responsibility for developing the behavioral sciences. More specifically, the objectives of the Center are these: 1) to provide a greater number of highly qualified scholars in the behavioral field for the staffs of the universities where they are now urgently needed; 2) to increase the competence of present faculty members, help them broaden their vision, and stimulate fresh endeavors; 3) to help in the development of more comprehensive and better integrated content and methods in the behavioral sciences, and thus to a fuller understanding of human behavior; and 4) to provide new designs and materials for advanced research training.[34]

The founding of the center signaled the coming of age of the "Behavioral Sciences." The center was significant for several reasons. First, it bolstered the claims of legitimacy of the behavioral sciences since it was founded by the Ford Foundation, the largest and soon to be the most prestigious of the philanthropic foundations. Second, especially during its early period, the center became a gathering point for social scientists who were disenchanted with traditional studies of politics and who advocated the change to the behavioralist approach to politics. Third, the center not only was an example of successful institution-building but also was extremely important in the development of younger scholars trained in the behavioral approach who could solidify the behavioralists' hold on the field. The significance of the center in promoting the behavioral sciences and establishing their legitimacy has also been noted by Robert Dahl:

In the newest and richest foundation, Ford, the short-lived Behavioral Sciences Program probably increased the use and acceptability of the notion of behavioral sciences as something born more behavioral and more scientific than the social sciences. The most durable offshoot of the Behavioral Sciences Program at Ford is the Center for Advanced Study in the Behavioral Sciences at Palo Alto.[35]

The Social Science Research Council

The problem of prestige was not the only one confronting the foundation. While the Ford Foundation had a number of direct programs which tied it to the major universities, it was not equipped to carry out the overall job of restructuring the study of politics, for this was an extremely complicated venture that required involvement on a number of different levels. Through its support for the general activities of the council and for the Council's committees on Political Behavior and Comparative Politics, the Ford Foundation was able to launch a major organizational campaign that was crucial in the behavioralist's efforts to capture the field.

One of the earliest joint efforts was the council's program of undergraduate stipends and first-year graduate study fellowships in the Behavioral Sciences which was funded by the Ford Foundation. This program was designed to encourage qualified students to consider a career in the behavioral sciences by giving them the opportunity to be involved in research projects. The recruitment of qualified undergraduates was the first step in building-up a cohort of behaviorally trained new Ph.D's that could then make their mark on academic social science.

More directly relevant to the task of reformulating political sociology was the council's Ford-funded 1954 Summer Seminar in Political Behavioral Research, which was sponsored by the University of Michigan, Department of Political Science, and the Survey Research Center. The purpose of the seminar was to stimulate interest in the quantitative study of political behavior. To this end, the postdoctoral fellows from political science who attended the conference were given access to the Social Science Research Council files, including materials from the 1952 Survey Research Center election study. Seminars were held that particularly focused on research methodologies and were supervised by the major figures involved in the voting studies at Michigan, such as Angus Campbell, Philip Converse, Donald Stokes, and Warren Miller. A second summer seminar on the analysis of electoral behavioral was held in 1958 at the University of Michigan under similar circumstances and was also funded by the Ford Foundation. This seminar placed particular emphasis on the analysis of survey data.

These seminars attempted to encourage research on electoral behavior as well as teach participants how to go about doing this kind of research. Notably, these training programs were carried out at the University of Michigan where the Survey Research Center had established its reputation as the leading center for voting studies. Thus the SRC and the Michigan political scientists working in this area were essentially trying to extend their influence to a broader contingent, within the profession by providing models of behavioral research for post-doctoral fellows.[36] The concentration on the post-doctoral level is also significant because it represents the building up of another level of the academic hierarchy.

Further evidence of the Ford Foundation's continued interest and support for the behavioral science revolution can be found in the Foundation's 1957 grant to the SSRC of $860,000 for a varied program of support for the behavioral sciences. This was part of the Behavioral

Sciences Division terminal grant program, which was designed to continue support for important areas after the division within the foundation was dismantled. This grant, which was to last for approximately five years, was the division's last step in the institutionalizing the behavioral focus, although support continued through programs that originated out of other divisions of the foundation. Included within this grant was a provision for four types of programs of support, all of which had been previously approved by the foundation at one time or another. First, there was $200,000 allocated to small flexible research grants to individual scholars. Second, $250,000 was used for a program of terminal-year predoctoral fellowships which would support doctoral candidates in their last year so that their degrees could be completed quickly. Third, $150,000 was used for a number of small grants in the behavioral sciences to smaller institutions not covered under the foundation's program of support for major universities. Finally, $260,000 was to be made available for committees, conferences, and other activities.[37]

In summary, the foundation demonstrated with this grant an awareness that to maximize its influence on the social sciences it had to do more than just support a few elite scholars and universities—that would have a "trickle down" effect. Support was given not only to big-name scholars and large universities, but also to smaller institutions, to scholars who did not have national reputations, and to graduate students. By working through institutions like the SSRC the foundation was able to directly influence a wider audience.

A crucial part of the foundation's efforts to restructure political science centered on the council's Committee on Political Behavior and the Committee on Comparative Politics. The activities of these committees represent one of the most important forces in the successful campaign to reorient research in political sociology, for it was these committees which served as an institutional base for the behavioral revolution and which provided early models for behavioral research in political sociology on the national, state, and local levels.[38] The cumulative impact of these committees can hardly be overestimated. The publications that resulted from their work make up a large part of the literature of the behavioral revolution, and the members of these committees form a roster of the key figures in the postwar behavioral movement.[39]

THE COMMITTEE ON POLITICAL BEHAVIOR

The committee was expecially active during this period. One of its most important contributions was the administration of a grant of $340,000 from the Ford Foundation for awards to individuals for research on

American governmental processes at the federal, state, and municipal levels. Support was given for research in a variety of areas including (1) urban politics— Robert Dahl, Peter Rossi, Edward Banfield, Norton Long, James Q. Wilson; (2) state politics—Avery Leiserson, Heinz Eulau; (3) federal politics—Lester Milbrath, Richard Fenno, Nelson Polsby, Raymond Wolfinger; (4) voting—Warren Miller, Phillip Converse; and (5) other areas such as legal processes, civil rights regulatory process, and federal administration. The work of these individuals was crucial in defining these areas of study.

While the primary focus was on research grants, the committee also worked on identifying and analyzing new and developing areas of interest to social scientists. As part of its concern with law and social science, the committee held two institutes which were centered around law and social relations and the second on the judicial process.

THE COMMITTEE ON GOVERNMENT AND LEGAL PROCESSES

In 1964 the Committee on Political Behavior's long involvement in the field was ended and was replaced by the Committee on Government and Legal Processes. It was given responsibility for the administration of the program of grants previously awarded by the Committee on Political Behavior as well as its other functions. This committee thus represented a continuance of the political behavior committee's focus, as its membership attests:

> Four of the new committee's 6 members and 9 of the total of 13
> who served on it at some time had received financial support
> from its predecessor. And all 13 members, as graduate students
> and young scholars in the late 1940s and 1950s, were the prod
> ucts of the "behavioral revolution" in political science that the
> Committee on Political Behavior had done so much to bring
> about.[40]

The Committee on Government and Legal Processes not unexpectedly concentrated its attention on political behavior. However, it modified its focus to include two other kinds of research. First, it stimulated studies of the substance of public policies which differed somewhat from the Political Behavior Committee's concern with policy and processes. Second, it encouraged the development of "impact studies" which traced the consequences of particular policies for the life situations of the people affected by them.[41] For example, the impact of urban renewal on the community and voter registration laws on political participation were studied. The work of this committee represented a firmer commitment to practical research that could contribute to the formation of public policy.

COMMITTEE ON COMPARATIVE POLITICS

Before concluding this section on SSRC programs supported by the Ford Foundation, it is important to review briefly the activities of the Committee on Comparative Politics, which was the other crucial committee in the effort to restructure political sociology. It was through the work of this committee that the broad area of comparative government was reformulated so that the primary focus became the study of the non-Western world and the problems of political development of the new states that emerged after World War II.

Before this orientation emerged, comparative government almost exclusively concentrated on the major powers of Europe. Adopting the behavioral perspective to comparative politics, the committee tried to look beyond the formal institutions of government and study the groups and interests that provided the dynamics of politics in different settings.[42] Following this approach, the first summer seminar sponsored by the committee (1955) was concerned with Western leadership.

However, it was soon realized that looking solely at isolated institutions and groups was inadequate and that to understand political development fully one needed a concept of the total political system. Gabriel Almond, then chairman of the committee and formerly a member of the Committee on Political Behavior, was very instrumental in the formulation of a systems approach. With this new perspective the committee went on to studies of political culture and modernization. These studies in turn led to the investigation of historical processes in political development. In addition, the committee, in an effort to develop more dynamic theories, sought to identify the principal crises or problems that arise in political development and to trace the enduring consequences of the particular order or sequences in which the crises are experienced.[43] The goal of this research was to develop a better understanding of the historical dynamics of social change in order to develop better predictive ability. Crises were then studied from the perspective of how to control and channel conflict. This information might then contribute to the restoration of social stability.

The need for a wider historical perspective also led the committee to look again at Europe in light of the questions that came out of the studies of the development of new nations. The committee sponsored two kinds of work in this area. First it sponsored the work of a group of scholars under the leadership of Raymond Grew of the University of Michigan who were reviewing the separate histories of European states in terms of patterns of sequences of crises that were experienced in their national development. Second, the committee sponsored a workshop on state- and nation-building in Western Europe which was held from June 15 to August 7, 1970, at the Center for Advanced Study in the Behavioral Sciences. This workshop looked at a number of different variables associated with the conditions under which strong or weak, centralized or decentralized, stable or unstable states came into being.[44]

The committee's activities represent a thorough reworking of the study of comparative government along behavioral lines. Even more than the Committee on Political Behavior, the work of the Committee on Comparative Politics reflects the need for up to date information and practical knowledge about the emerging nations. It was the task of this committee as well as other programs to produce the necessary information on the political and economic conditions in developing countries in the post–World War II period.

But knowledge was not the only thing that was needed; an ideology was needed which promoted the Western view of development to the emerging countries. In response to this need the committee along with other parts of the research apparatus produced what has been called "an ideology of developmentalism" which argues that developing countries face similar problems as the United States did in modernizing and that definite stages of growth exist.[45] In this view, the United States is seen as the "First New Nation" and thus provides a model for modernization to emerging countries. However, this theory of development has been criticized because it fails to recognize that the historical situation differs greatly at the present time for modernizing countries, due to the existence of a complex world economy which distorts the economies of Third World countries. The decidedly Western bias of this model has been challenged by a view which suggests that the underdevelopment of the Third World is the result of the overdevelopment of advanced capitalist countries.[46]

These questions notwithstanding, the committee and the other organizations involved in the network which makes up the research apparatus of the United States were able to affect profound changes in the structure of research in comparative government. The field of comparative politics was reformulated so as to include the entire contemporary world rather than just Western Europe. The focus on development ultimately yielded an array of area specialists that could provide valuable information to government officials and corporate leaders. Furthermore, it provided a literature which would dominate the field of comparative politics and insure that another large area of political sociology would come under the reign of the behavioral revolution. The accomplishments of this committee, then, and of the other programs, are especially significant in the history of the transformation of political sociology.

DIRECT SUPPORT OF UNIVERSITY PROGRAMS—SOLVING PRACTICAL PROBLEMS

Although the Ford Foundation's efforts to construct a behavioral political sociology were channeled to a large extent through intermediary organizations such as the SSRC, it could not simply rely on this approach to shape the direction of the field. A more direct involvement was necessary in order to guarantee its dominance. Direct intervention by the foundation was essential to guide research in this area and make certain that it retained a practical focus. This was especially the case in the early stage of field development, when a network of institutions was lacking which could be counted on to define a problem congruent with the foundation's interest.

Ford was particularly well suited for the task of establishing hegemony over the knowledge-producing sector because of its financial support for research planning agencies and universities and its ability to define areas through its own programs of support. It should also be remembered that during this period the federal government was not involved in supporting social science research which increased further Ford's influence.

The foundation's impact on the field transcended its ability to directly influence various institutions. Its importance was extended considerably by the fact that it was a trend setter in the educational network. By developing model programs at select universities it clearly indicated what the largest and most prestigious foundation considered to be innovative and promising research. Consequently, at some smaller universities which may not have come directly into the Ford Foundation's orbit, similar behavioral political research programs were initiated. To some extent a "trickle down effect" did reach other institutions. The shift in the orientation of the vast majority of political scientists away from traditional political studies to behavioral research in a decade is just one example of the cumulative effect of Ford's programs.

Three factors contributed to the foundation's influence on the field. The first was its financial clout. Second was its ability to confer prestige, and third was its capacity to set the tone for research in an area. While in many cases Ford responded to requests from researchers, it was not the researchers who defined the program. It was only after Ford had given direction to an area that it could rely at all on receiving proposals that reflected its views. Even then, the foundation directly intervened and suggested programs in metropolitan government and community development as well as in other areas. This was the case in the grant program which established rotating research professorships in governmental affairs at several major universities. In this instance, grants were given to Columbia, Harvard, Yale, Chicago, Princeton, and Berkeley prior to receiving a proposal.[47] Quite clearly, the foundation took the initiative by selecting the universities it wanted in the program.

INTERNATIONAL STUDIES PROGRAMS

The foundation's involvement in establishing an international affairs program at major universities was a microcosm of its entire involvement in political science. This program illustrated clearly the overlapping of mutual interests. Ford was able to construct institutes that would do practical research in this area and the universities' prestige was heightened by its involvement in an emerging field. The logic of the development of this program was nevertheless shaped by the foundation's definition of the field.

Along with its efforts to train foreign area specialists and reconstitute the field of comparative politics, the foundation acted to build a network of centers which concentrated on international affairs and international communications research. The foundation's International Training and Research program was instrumental in creating various centers at American universities which specialized in foreign areas; international relations and foreign policy; and economic, political, and social development. Under this program substantial grants were made to Columbia (largest single grant: $1,275,000 in 1956), MIT, Cornell, Berkeley, Harvard, Chicago, Princeton, Stanford, and Washington, among others. The fundamental goal of these grants was to foster specialization in a number of areas relating to international studies.

At Princeton, for example, the Ford Foundation gave $200,000 (1957) for support of the Center for International Studies for five years. This money was used primarily to finance faculty associates who would spend most of their time doing research for the center. With the money from this grant it was then possible to have eight faculty associates in the center at any one time. In order to qualify for this money, programs in international relations had to meet four tests applied by the staff of the Foundation: (1) an effective relation between teaching and research; (2) interdisciplinary cooperation; (3) a contribution of area studies to international relations; (4) useful research on international problems. At the end of the five-year program the Foundation hoped that the university would have long-range plans to integrate the international program into its structure and budget.[48] Obviously the incentives for the university to comply with the Foundation's suggestions were quite overwhelming.

At Harvard, the foundation embarked on a similar program of support for the Center of International Affairs. Of the $1 million granted by the foundation to Harvard (1958) for this program, $500,000 went to the center, $75,000 to a training program in economics and political development at the Graduate School of Public Administration, $300,000 for training and research on the economy of modern China, and $125,000 for a program of training teachers in East Asian studies. All of these programs were concerned with the twin problems of producing knowledge concerning foreign affairs and training additional skilled personnel. For instance, the center was to engage in research and training in five major fields: political-military strategy, the Atlantic community, problems of underdeveloped countries, Far Eastern problems, and problems of international order.[49] As a result of Harvard's numerous personnel in the field of international relations, it was particularly well suited to address specific problem areas in international studies. For instance, during this period it was singled out to train specialists on China, who were sorely needed. To accomplish this task, the Ford Foundation provided funds to endow a professorship in modern China studies. This was the beginning of an extensive training program to meet the need for knowledge on the Chinese economy.

Two other programs were especially important in the network of international studies programs. The Ford Foundation made two grants (1952 and 1956) to the Massachusetts Institute of Technology, totaling $1,425,000, to develop the Center for International Studies, which concentrated on international communications research. These grants enabled MIT to undertake major studies dealing with important leadership groups in a number of countries, how they get their information about international affairs, and what they did about it, and to establish a long-term program of teaching and research in international communications at MIT.[50] In a short time the Center at MIT became the leading site for research in the area and provided a model for other universities which wanted to concentrate on this field.

The other major program which the Ford Foundation supported in this area was at Stanford, where it funded the Institute for Communications Research, directed by Wilbur Schramm. Schramm, who was a leading government advisor in this area, received a grant of $100,000 in 1958 from the Ford Foundation for this institute's program of basic research. This program was to supplement and build on the work done at MIT by concentrating on (1) a detailed analysis and comparison of communications systems in a number of different countries and (2) the flow of information across national boundaries in order to discover the structure and operating characteristics of the international system of communications. As was pointed out in the summary of the grant, research on communications abroad was not nearly comparable to public opinion research at home. This grant was designed to assist in furthering the understanding of communications abroad and to integrate its research into other research being conducted at other universities. Again, most of the money went toward logistical support for the institute.[51]

Looking back over the foundation's efforts in the field of international relations, we find many of the same strategies employed for developing a previously disorganized and undefined area. The primary activity of the foundation was institution-building. Selected elite universities were encouraged to develop programs in the area which maximized their resources. At all of the universities, specific centers for international affairs came into being with the help of Ford Foundation funds and ultimately became integrated into the structure of the university. Each of these centers addressed the problems of training specialists and contributing needed research in the field. Activities at these centers included a mixture of basic research and practical issue-oriented work. During their early period of operation most of these centers utilized the Ford Foundation money to attract prominent scholars to head their programs. It was the work of these scholars and the general orientation of these centers which set the tone for research in this area. Soon an ongoing network of institutions concerned with international relations and communications had been established and the process of institutionalization of specialty areas characterized by a renewed emphasis on practicality was well on its way.

The ultimate routinization of this process and the "domination of the social outlook" which it entailed marked the point of departure of the foundation from general activities in the area. Once the overall institutional structure was in place, the foundation concentrated on specific problem areas such as the lack of specialists on the Chinese economy. By adopting this approach, the foundation insured that other financial backers would also be drawn into the area to finance the needs of the emergent network of programs in international relations.

The most concrete effect which the foundation had on the field was through its *institutional support*, but its influence was not limited to this area. Its strategic position within the knowledge-producing sector and its role as coordinator of research magnified its influence and permitted it to establish a loose kind of hegemony over research in the area. Over time, its mechanisms of control became increasingly subtle and unobtrusive as the institutional base, which it was instrumental in establishing, matured and gained some autonomy. Its influence nonetheless continued, for it had basically shaped the larger environment in which these research programs operated and the publications which were produced from its early grants soon came to define the field of international studies.

In this one example we have many of the dynamics which characterize the Ford Foundation's overall efforts in shaping research in the behavioral sciences. In the case of international affairs research, the logic of the Foundation's intervention is particularly explicit. Foundation support for research in this area was a direct response to corporate and governmental needs. Unlike other areas of research which the foundation supported, there was no institutional structure available that the foundation could utilize to organize its efforts. Consequently, it had to develop an entire apparatus which was oriented to the various aspects of international affairs research.

Conclusions and Reflections

By the end of the 1950s an array of organizations and programs were established which provided the institutional support for the behavioral revolution. As in the specific case of international studies, the foundation was directly involved in the initial stages of this process. Gradually, as the institutional base matured, the foundation's involvement diminished and it then concentrated its efforts on specific problem areas. In merely a decade the foundation had redefined political research in the United States, restructured studies of comparative politics, trained foreign area specialists, and established programs in international studies and metropolitan government. In other words, it had totally revamped the study of politics so that it could meet some of the major problems that were emerging in the 1950s.

Although the foundation continued to exert considerable influence on the behavioral sciences the Behavioral Science Division itself was discontinued in September of 1957.[52] Money continued to be granted by the division up until 1961 as a result of a terminal grant which allowed existing programs to be completed. Significantly, the more practical aspects of the behavioral science program were retained and taken up by other divisions.

During its relatively short period of operation the Behavioral Sciences Division made its mark on the field by radically restructuring the organization and the orientation of the social sciences. Its most important accomplishment was the creation of an entirely new concept, "the behavioral sciences," which was quickly institutionalized. The division helped to train and recruit personnel to this perspective, contributed significantly to anchoring the behavioral approach in leading universities, and supported the work of outstanding individuals along these new lines. It was on the institutional level that the division had its greatest impact.

The coining of the term "behavioral sciences" by the foundation was only the most superficial representation of the foundation's influence. More importantly, the term did not die when the division ended—rather an institutional network was in place that assured the continued importance of the "behavioral sciences." This network continued to produce new behavioral scientists and new behavioral research long after the division was inactive. In short, the behavioral sciences had become firmly entrenched within an institutional nexus which perpetuated its existence.

A complete understanding of this process must also include the social context in which the institutionalization of the behavioral sciences and the behavioral revolution took place. Excerpts from the 1949 study report make clear the problems the foundation was attempting to address:

> The belief of a number of Americans that the principles of democracy are a collection of cliches.[53]

> The struggle of thoughtful and informed persons to find a meaningful, contemporary, and usable definition of democracy.[54]

> The processes of government are seriously affected by public apathy and lack of citizen participation. Research, for example, will be required to analyze public apathy in order to understand its causes and the ways which it may be lessened.[55]

> Intergroup hostilities weaken our democratic strength by dissipating important resources of energy in internal conflicts and swelling the ranks of malcontents who constitute the seed bed for undemocratic ideologies.[56]

The immediate problem was the legitimation crisis, reflected in the questioning of the classical democratic image and the low voter turnouts. This problem was soon incorporated into the foundation's agenda for research. Most of the foundation's efforts in political science during this time were directed toward developing a *realistic* understanding of the political behavior of Americans and the construction of a revised democratic theory which could replace the idealistic and seemingly outdated classical view. It should come as little surprise, then, that the foundation's efforts in political science were focused on the analysis of electoral behavior and the creation of a revised and much more sophisticated legitimating ideology (elite democratic theory which ultimately yielded elite pluralism).

The foundation's stress on understanding electoral behavior was part of the assessment of the depth of the legitimation crisis, for, as Piven argues, elections can be seen as a "signal or barometer of discontent and disaffection" in a society.[57]

At stake for the Ford Foundation was the possibility that elite concessions would have to be made to the poor, for, citing Piven again, "under conditions of severe electoral instability, the alliance of public and private power is sometimes weakened, if only briefly, and at these moments a defiant poor may make gains." Thus the foundation's interest in developing sophisticated methods to analyze electoral behavior was linked closely to its efforts to judge the level and form of political protest in the United States and to develop strategies to structure that protest.

Rather than attempting a program of far-reaching social reform, the foundation focused instead upon the legitimacy of existing social arrangements. It did so by remapping the world at the level of ideas and providing practical support for extremely limited social reforms. In place of programs which might have encouraged genuine political participation by the citizenry and thus bolstered the legitimacy of institutions, the Ford Foundation tried to develop new justifications for the social order. The hidden agenda of its involvement in political science during this period was an attempt to reform the field. In its view, a new political science could contribute to the effort of stabilizing a social structure which was experiencing "disequilibrium due to social disorganization." The foundation ascribed the problems of this era to an outdated ideology. It sought therefore to reestablish ideological hegemony rather than restructure fundamentally social institutions.

The task of the foundation was to promote a better understanding of the system through the definition of new social norms. In a broad sense, the ultimate goal of the foundation was to preserve the status quo by promoting its definition of social problems—a definition which was overwhelmingly influenced by the interests of elite members. In the final analysis, the foundation's activities can be seen as critical to the struggle to establish cultural domination.

Notes

1. For a discussion of the orientation of traditional political science in the United States prior to the behavioral revolution, see Anna Heddow, *Political Science in American Colleges and Universities 1636–1900* (New York: Octagon Books, 1969); Bernard Crick, *The American Science of Politics—Its Origins and Conditions* (Berkeley: University of California Press, 1959); Joseph Tannenhaus and Albert Somit, *The Development of Political Science* (Boston: Atherton Press, 1967); and Heinz Eulau, "Understanding Political Life in America; the Contribution of Political Science," *Social Science Quarterly* 57 (June 1976): 113–153. It is also very important at the outset to note the *behavioralist* movement in political science and sociology is quite different from behaviorist psychology. See

Eulau, "Understanding Political Life," p. 119, for a discussion of this distinction.

2. See the forthcoming dissertation by Robert Higgins, Department of Political Science, University of Massachusetts at Amherst, which is concerned with competing models of legitimacy in political science. The first section of this chapter draws heavily from his work and I am grateful for the opportunity to share the preliminary findings.

3. See Higgins, Ch. 1. Also Crick, *American Science of Politics*, "The Growth of Political Science," Ch. 6.

4. Nie, Verba, and Petrocik, *The Changing American Voter* (Cambridge, Mass.: Harvard University Press, 1976), p. 5. For a critical review of this book and the weaknesses of the behavioral approach to politics, see Peter Seybold, "The Changing American Voter," *Contemporary Sociology: A Journal of Reviews* 6 (November 1976): 791–793.

5. Albert Somit and Joseph Tannenhaus, "Trends in American Political Science," *American Political Science Review* 62 (May 1963): 933–947. It is interesting to note that of the six people listed only Hans Morganthau does not have a behavioral orientation and that both Key and Truman served as the first chairmen of the Social Science Research Council's Committee on Political Behavior.

6. Austin Ranney, "The Committee on Political Behavior, 1949–1964 and the Committee on Governmental and Legal Processes 1964–1972," Social Science Research Council *Items* 5 (September 1974): 39. For instance, in the mid-1960s the behavioralists Pritchett (1964), Truman (1965), Almond (1966), and Dahl (1967) held the presidency of the APSA.

7. Heinz Eulau and James G. March (eds.), *Political Science* (Englewood Cliffs, N.J.: Prentice-Hall, 1969), p. 81.

8. Walter Reottger, "Strata and Stability of Reputations of American Political Scientists," *Political Science* 4 (Winter 1978): 10.

9. Bernard Berelson, "The Behavioral Sciences," in David Sells (ed.), *International Encyclopedia of the Social Sciences* (New York: Macmillan and Co., 1968), pp. 42–43.

10. Robert Dahl, "The Behavioral Approach to Political Science: Epitaph for a Movement to a Successful Protest," *American Political Science Review* 55 (December 1961): 765–766.

11. Ford Foundation, *Final Report of the Behavioral Science Division, 1957* (New York: the same, 1958), p. 10.

12. George Beckmann, "The Role of Foundations," *Annals of the American Academy of Political and Social Science* 4 (November 1964): 18.

13. Bernard Berelson, "The Place of Foundations," paper delivered at American Sociological Association meetings, 1960, p. 6.

14. The concept of the mobilization of bias is discussed by E. E. Schattschneidder in his book *The Semi-Sovereign People* (New York: Holt, Reinhart and Winstop, 1961). It is also a central concept in Bachrach and Baratz, "The Two Faces of Power," *American Political Science Review* 56 (December 1962): 947–952; and Stephen Lukes, *Power—A Radical View* (New York: Humanities Press, 1975).

15. Ford Foundation, *Report of the Study for the Ford Foundation on Policy and Program* (New York: the same, 1949), pp.44–45.
16. Ford Foundation, *Study Committee Report* (New York: the same, 1949), p. 64.
17. Ford Foundation, *Behavioral Sciences Division Report* (New York: the same, 1951), p. 5.
18. Ford Foundation, "Behavioral Sciences Division Report" (New York: the same, 1953), p. 2.
19. Ibid.
20. Ibid. pp. 3–4.
21. While additional support surely would have been welcomed, there was a consensus that the foundation would have to do more than this. The behavioral sciences were conceived as just entering into the scientific stage and it was in the area of organization and training of personnel that the foundation could best assist the field. Berelson throughout the division's reports assumed the fundamental unity of the sciences and the cumulative nature of scientific growth. Thus, the behavioral sciences were seen as entering an era where major developments and breakthroughs would occur just as they had in an earlier period for the natural, more "mature" sciences.
22. Ford Foundation, *Behavioral Sciences Division Report* (New York: the same, 1951), pp. 14–15.
23. Ibid., pp. 15–16.
24. Ford Foundation, *Behavioral Sciences Division Report* (New York: the same, 1953), p. 37.
25. Ibid., p. 10.
26. Ford Foundation, *Behavioral Sciences Division Report* (New York: the same, 1951), p. 18.
27. Ford Foundation, Grant File No. 50–266, "University of North Carolina."
28. In addition to this group, Paul Lazarsfeld and Ithiel de Sola Pool wrote memoranda on desirable research directions in the area of political behavior. Significantly, the foundation did not solicit the advice of more traditional political scientists or critics of recent trends in sociology. Representatives of a comparative historical approach to politics, for instance, were excluded from the discussion of developments in the field.
29. Ford Foundation, Grant File #55–118, "Russell Sage Foundation".
30. Ibid.
31. This grant supported, for example, the work of Lipset at Berkeley (Grant File #56–53), Robert Lane and Harold Lasswell at Yale (Grant File #56-66). S. N. Eisenstadt also received support for his work at Hebrew University (Grant File #56-148). The case of Eisenstadt is most interesting because the foundation wrote to him asking if he needed any research funds while he was a fellow at the Ford-supported Center for Advanced Study in the Behavioral Sciences in Palo Alto. This example differs from what people believe usually happens, that is, someone applies to the foundation for funds. In fact, foundation inquiries to leading scholars are not that unusual.

32. The most notable of the individuals supported under this grant who worked in the area of political sociology was S. M. Lipset (Grant File #57–385, Berkeley), who received $40,000 from the foundation. This money was used to support the work which went into Lipset's *Political Man* (New York: Doubleday, 1960) and *The First New Nation* (New York: Doubleday, 1963) as well as other related publications. *Political Man* was cited as the most important book in the field since 1945 in a survey of political sociologists conducted by the author as part of the research involved for the dissertation.
33. See C. Wright Mills, *The Sociological Imagination* (New York: Oxford University Press, 1959), Chapter 4, for a critical analysis of this perspective.
34. Ford Foundation, *Behavioral Sciences Division Report* (New York: the same, 1953), pp. 16–17.
35. Robert Dahl, "The Behavioral Approach," pp. 765–766.
36. The degree of Ford Foundation involvement in this process is especially significant, for in 1950 the foundation gave a grant to the University of Michigan's Political Science Department that enabled the establishment of a specific graduate training program in political behavior research. The later grants for summer training sessions reflect the further nurturing of behavioral political science by the foundation and the realization that successful institutions like the Survey Research Center are crucial to institutionalization of the behavioral focus.
37. Ford Foundation Grant File #57–378, "Social Science Research Council Varied Program of Support for the Behavioral Sciences."
38. Eulau discusses the transformation of political science by looking at the landmark books in each specialty area. The overwhelming dominance of the Ford Foundation working in concert with the SSRC is thoroughly demonstrated by the fact that all but three of the books mentioned by Eulau in his discussion of the period between 1952–1959 were supported either by the Ford Foundation or through the SSRC. Ten of the twelve books which fall into this category were directly supported by Ford, including

   1. Berelson, Lazarsfeld, and McPhee, *Voting* (Chicago: University of Chicago Press, 1954).
   2. Campbell et al., *The American Voter* (New York: Wiley, 1960).
   3. Heard, *The Costs of Democracy* (Chapel Hill: University of North Carolina Press, 1960).
   4. Neustadt, *Presidential Power* (New York: Wiley, 1960).
   5. Peltason, *Fifty-eight Lonely Men* (New York: Harcourt, Brace & World, 1961)
   6. Eulau et al., *The Legislative System* (New York: Wiley, 1962).
   7. Bauer, Pool, and Dexter, *American Business and Public Policy* (New York: Atherton, 1963).
   8. Sayre and Kaufman, *Governing New York City* (New York: Russell Sage Foundation, 1960).
   9. Dahl, *Who Governs?* (New Haven: Yale University Press, 1961).

10. Banfield, *Political Influence* (New York: Free Press, 1961).

39. The Committee on Political Behavior during this period included such figures as David Truman, 1949–1964; Angus Campbell, 1949–1958, 1963–1964; Robert Dahl, 1955–1962; Oliver Garceau, 1949–1964; Alexander Heard, 1954–1958; V. O. Key, 1949–1963; and Avery Leisersen, 1949–1964. Heard is presently Chairman of the Board of Trustees of the Ford Foundation.
40. Pye and Ryland, Social Science Research Council, *Items* 5 (September 1974): 40.
41. Ibid.
42. Pye and Ryland, Social Science Research Council, "Report of the Committee on Comparative Politics," 1971, p. 2.
43. Ibid., p. 3.
44. Ibid., p. 5.
45. For criticisms of this research see Suzanne Bodenheimer, "The Ideology of Developmentalism: American Political Science's Paradigm—Surrogate for Latin American Studies," *Berkeley Journal of Sociology* 15 (1970): 95–137; and Mark Kesselman, "Order of Movement?—The Literature of Political Development and Ideology," *World Politics* 5 (October 1973): 139–154.
46. For an overview of these criticisms see Andre Gunder Grank, *Latin America: Underdevelopment or Revolution* (New York: Monthly Review Press, 1969), Ch. 2; K. T. Fann and Donald Hodges (eds.), *Readings in U.S. Imperialism* (Boston: Porter Sargent Publishers, 1971); and Charles Wilber (ed.), *The Political Economy of Development and Underdevelopment* (New York: Random House, 1973).
47. Ford Foundation Grant File #56–83, "Rotating Research Professorships in Governmental Affairs."
48. Ford Foundation Grant File #56–152, "Princeton University."
49. Ford Foundation Grant File #58–48, "Harvard University."
50. Ford Foundation Grant File #56–104, "Massachusetts Institute of Technology."
51. Ford Foundation Grant File #58–374, "Stanford University."
52. A case study of the rise and fall of the Behavioral Sciences Division would be an interesting enterprise in itself. Clearly, Henry T. Heald's appointment as president of the Ford Foundation in 1956 was the most important immediate factor in the division's demise, but it is not the whole story. Tensions between the division and the trustees over the division's contribution had been present much before Heald's appointment. The announcement of the division's end went against the advice of many prominent scientists and educators. Berelson himself in his final report on the division clearly could not fully understand why the division was ended and presents his case for continued foundation involvement in the behavioral sciences. To some extent the division was also undermined by the fact that other programs within the foundation adopted the more practical aspects of the division's work thus leaving area five increasingly as a research division with declining practical payoffs to the foundation.

53. Ford Foundation, 1949 Study Group Report, p. 64.
54. Ibid.
55. Ibid., pp. 67–68.
56. Ibid., p. 46.
57. Frances Fox Piven, "The Social Structuring of Political Protest," *Politics and Society* 3 (Fall 1976): 320.

Robert F. Arnove

Foundations and the Transfer of Knowledge*

United States philanthropic foundations (Ford, Rockefeller, and Carnegie) have played an important role in shaping higher education at home and abroad. In the post–World War II period, they have been a principal source of funding for institutional innovation, research, and advanced training in the emerging universities of Africa, Asia, and Latin America. Throughout the 1950s and 1960s, these foundations emphasized institutional development as the key to the strengthening of higher education in Third World countries. But by the 1970s, with the increasing sensitivity of Third World nationals to outside intervention in their education systems, with the failure of past aid policies and modalities, and with the bankruptcy of aid paradigms based on liberal notions of development, the foundations turned to new forms of assistance to higher education and to related research organizations. This new form of aid, as elaborated by the Ford Foundation, focuses on competency-building and the creation of regional and international networks of individuals and agencies conducting research and training activities.

This chapter is a speculative essay on the origins and implications of these newly forged networks of academic institutions and scholars. Among the questions asked are the following: Do these new technical assistance arrangements strengthen the capacity of individuals and institutions in developing countries to understand and resolve societal problems free of outside determination? Who benefits from the knowledge generated by these networks?

*An earlier version of this essay was prepared for "The Conversations in the Disciplines: Universities and the New International Order," State University of New York at Buffalo, March 23-25, 1978; parts of the chapter also appeared in, "The Ford Foundation and 'Competence Building' Overseas: Assumptions, Approaches, and Outcomes," *Studies in Comparative International Development* 12 (Fall 1977): 100-126.

Before discussing the evolution and consequences of these new arrangements for the transfer of knowledge and competencies from North to South (from advanced industrial to less-developed countries), I believe it is desirable to provide background information on the scope and significance of Rockefeller, Ford, and Carnegie involvement in higher education overseas.

Scope and Significance of Foundation Involvement

Foundations have been key investors in the development of universities, think tanks, and research institutes throughout the world. They have provided the necessary funds by which academic programs flourished and unknown scholars gained international prominence.

The Rockefeller Foundation—which prior to World War II concentrated its higher education efforts in the field of medicine—has been a prime mover in the creation and modernization of a dozen "lead" universities overseas. Former Rockefeller vice-president Kenneth Thompson notes:

> Beginning in the early 1960's, the Rockefeller Foundation undertook to provide technical assistance for overall university development to a few selected institutions in the developing countries. . . . Institution-building is at the heart of the Foundation's tradition. The rationale of university development was rooted in this tradition plus the belief that, for the developing countries the missing factor was educated people or trained leadership.[1]

Rockefeller's program of university development was initiated in 1961 and has involved expenditures of approximately $5 million per annum on some fifteen universities in Latin America, Africa, and Asia. These institutions include the University of Valle in Colombia; the National Agrarian University, la Molina, in Peru; the University of Bahia in Brazil; Mahidol University, Kasetsart University, and Thammasat University in Thailand; the University of Ibadan in Nigeria; the national universities in Uganda, Tanzania, and Kenya; the University of Yaounde in Cameroon; the University of Zaire; the University of the Philippines; and Gadjah Mada University in Indonesia.

One example of the influence Rockefeller has wielded in university development is that of East Africa. According to Thompson, "66 percent of all East African faculty have been Rockefeller Foundation scholars or holders of Special Lectureships established with Rockefeller Foundation funding for returning national scholars for whom an established post was not yet available. If the sample is limited to East Africans who are full professors and deans, 80 percent have had assistance."[2] Not only the East African university leadership, but that of Asian and Latin American universities, according to Thompson, is a testimony to the efficacy of over fifty years of Rockefeller Foundation involvement, and over 10,000 fellowships and scholarships awarded by the foundation.[3]

The Ford Foundation, as Dean Rusk once noted, is "the fat boy in the philanthropic canoe."[4] The magnitude of its investments eclipses that of all other foundations. Colvard, who has recently established a data bank on foundation investments at home and abroad, estimates that between 1971 and 1975, Ford funds, in four out of the five years, amounted to nearly two-thirds of all the money for foreign grants of the leading 200 foundations studied.[5] From its inception in 1936 through 1977, the foundation allocated $919.2 million to "less-developed countries"; overall expenditures on both domestic and foreign programs during this period amounted to $5 billion.[6] During the 1960s and 1970s, the International Division of Ford was spending roughly $50–60 million per annum on overseas technical assistance.[7] And at least one-fourth of these monies was directed in one way or another to the strengthening of higher education institutions—often the same universities selected by Rockefeller—by improving curricula, university administration, and extension services, and building up research facilities in such areas as economics, agriculture, nutrition, public health, and fertility. In Latin America, the foundation has not only been a major source of funding for alternative models of a university—such as the Monterrey Institute of Technology in Mexico, and the University of the Andes in Colombia—but the principal supporter of social science research ($50 million in grants since 1959).[8]

Until the 1970s, Ford Foundation institution-building grants, like those of Rockefeller, were aimed at replicating within the Third World setting the organizational patterns, professional acitvities, and criteria of academic excellence which prevailed within the donor country. As it had done in the United States, the foundation selected key academic institutions as models of what a university should be, and millions of dollars were poured into strengthening them as "centers of excellence."

The Carnegie Corporation, the third most important philanthropic foundation engaged in international activities, has been spending approximately $1 million annually on international activities. According to its charter, these grants must be made overseas to members of the British Commonwealth. What the Carnegie Corporation lacks in magnitude of funding is compensated for by its focus and leverage. Since 1945, it has played a pivotal role in supporting the development of teacher training institutions in Africa. Throughout the 1960s, Carnegie, with Ford Foundation support, worked closely with Columbia University's Teachers

College in facilitating training opportunities for African teacher-educators at Teachers College, and in preparing American teachers to work in Africa.[9] Carnegie also has served as the sponsor of a number of important conferences to determine the future involvement of America and Great Britain in African development efforts (see Chapter 7).

Despite the manifestly political overtones of foundation involvement in strategic Third World countries (e.g., India, Pakistan, Thailand, the Philippines, Indonesia, Nigeria, Zaire, Brazil, and Mexico), philanthropic foundations have been able to function effectively where governmental agencies could not.[10] In a doctoral dissertation on "Philanthropy and Government: A Study of the Ford Foundation's Overseas Activities," Ashley reaches the conclusion that from the U.S. government viewpoint, the foundation has sometimes filled a gap between what the State Department would like to do and what Congress would have it do.[11] For example, following the 1967 Egyptian-Israeli War, the Ford Foundation sponsored an exchange program for Egyptian scholars to come to United States universities which, according to Ashley, helped "provide an additional window to the West for an Egypt subject to greatly expanded cultural influences."[12]

More significantly, the Ford Foundation—"despite highs and lows in the political weather"[13]—has helped maintain a steady stream of scholarly exchange with the Soviet Union and other countries of Eastern Europe since 1956, and with the People's Republic of China since 1973. The principal conduit for exchanges with the Soviet Bloc, the International Research and Exchange Board (IREX), received over $10 million in grants between 1968 and 1978.[14] According to the special 1978 Ford Foundation report, "Bridges of Scholars—East and West,"

> Because it is funded by private as well as government sources, IREX has been able to steer an independent course between immediate diplomatic interests and the long-term intellectual concerns of the scholarly community.[15]

That such "long-term intellectual concerns of the scholarly community" might also have direct bearing on strategic concerns is noted in the case of exchange programs with the People's Republic of China—a nation which, in the foundation's words, had been "virtually closed to Americans for twenty-five years." Between 1973 and 1978, the foundation provided $450,000 to the Committee on Scholarly Communications with the People's Republic of China. While early exchanges were predominantly in scientific and technological fields, the committee increasingly has been able to arrange for the exchange of scholars in the social sciences and humanities.[16] The "payoff" to U.S. national security interests resides in the comprehensive reports that the committee requires of each American delegation. According to the Ford Foundation, "the fifteen published [reports] to date provide a remarkably systematic view of China in key areas."[17]

In addition to their ability to function in politically sensitive areas, such as the exchange of scholars between ideologically opposed nations, foundations like Ford have often been able to operate within politically volatile institutions, notably, universities. They have been able to do so because they have projected an institutional image of professionalism and political independence. When compared with other sources of support, both domestic and foreign, foundation funding is often considered the least objectionable to many academics and intellectuals. As a case in point, the Ford Foundation has supported radical researchers and, following military coups in Argentina in 1965 and Chile in 1973, the relocation of displaced scholars. In 1977 the foundation approved a grant of $390,000 to the Latin American Social Science Council in Argentina; the bulk of these funds were to be used to assist Argentine scholars who had been removed from their academic posts for political reasons and to provide individual research rewards for social scientists in the Southern Cone countries (Argentina, Chile, Paraguay, and Uruguay), where the climate of support for open inquiry has been described as "fragile." According to Horowitz and Horowitz, foundations like Ford represent the most liberal arm of foreign technical assistance.[18] For these reasons, foundations may be a *persona grata*, where the U.S. government is not.

Changing Environment for Aid

Despite the generally greater acceptability of foundation assistance to overseas university administrators and academics, these funds also have been a source of controversy. Particularly in Latin America, foundation involvement in certain universities has been violently resisted by radical university students and faculty. One example is the violent student and faculty demonstrations which took place in 1971 at the University of Valle in Cali, Colombia,[19] a favored recipient of Ford and Rockefeller monies. Moreover, those institutions and departments favored by the foundations often have been bitterly resented by those who were neglected. Scherz-Garcia over a decade ago observed that "assistance, in the measure to which it is considered unfairly discriminatory, thus assumes an unexpected and unfavorable role for the harmonious relations between the different units which comprise the institutions of higher education."[20]

By the late 1960s, students of aid generally were pointing to the inadequacy of extant modalities of technical assistance and the difficulties faced by North American and European agencies (whether public or private) and academics working in overseas universities. Referring to the institution-building program of USAID, a high-ranking education officer noted that the existence of U.S. advisors in a particular country implies criticism, for their presence indicates inadequacy, whether financial or intellectual.[21] The AID official, Newbry, further observes that Third World nationals "want change, but they do not want simply to be observers of change in their own country."[22] Moreover, a Ford-funded Conference on Professionals in Developing Countries concluded:

> Governments in developing countries have in the past few years become increasingly impatient of American or European researchers who take up the time of officials with requests for data and access to confidential documents, who sometimes upset local communities in which they may be mistaken for spies, and who then produce nothing useful. . . . Similar ambivalence can arise in relationships with overseas scholars. They may be suspicious of the ideological motives underlying American research and resentful of the presumption of foreign scholars in tackling problems of their own society without long experience of its culture and language.[23]

North American university contract programs also were coming under fire as ineffective mechanisms of assistance to overseas higher education institutions. John Gardner, former Carnegie Corporation president, reviewed the USAID program of sister university relations. He found this program to be a creative invention for institution-building which suffered in its implementation: the program was plagued by misunderstandings, mediocrity, and inflexibility.[24]

Fellowship programs similarly were found lacking. A principal criticism, drawing widespread attention, was the "brain drain" of high-level human resources occasioned in part by North American and European training programs which imparted professional expectations and orientations incapable of being satisfied by working conditions in Third World public bureaucracies and academic institutions.[25] Unless satisfactory support facilities could be provided for returning Third World scholars and researchers, it was highly unlikely that the flow of talent from the Third World to the North American and European metropolitan centers would abate.

At the same time that the institutional arrangements for delivering technical assistance were found wanting, students of overseas development were criticizing the prevalent social science assumptions and paradigms concerning the nature of social change in the Third World. Packenham, in his book *Liberal America and the Third World*, found the liberal assumptions which characterized technical assistance and social science research to be too optimistic, too parochial, and too rigid.[26] Such assumptions failed to explain, for example, the debacle of Vietnam, why countries could demonstrate rapid economic growth but not political stability and democratic forms of government, and why countries which were considered politically developed could undergo political decay.[27] Interestingly enough, according to Packenham, "the vast majority of research that led to the major political development theories were privately financed"—by Ford, Rockefeller and Carnegie.[28]

If, as according to Thompson of the Rockefeller Foundation, "for everything there is a season" and "in the 1960s it was a time for institution building,"[29] by the 1970s a new set of responses was required on the part of philanthropic foundations to the changing international milieu. The Rockefeller Foundation's response was to expand the service outreach activities of the universities where it was heavily committed[30]—gearing teaching-learning and research activities of higher education institutions to the so-called "development needs" of their societies. The Carnegie Corporation by the late 1960s similarly began to shift its attention, but on a smaller scale, to helping universities in Africa (Ibadan, Ahmadu Bello, Nairobi, Makere, Sierre Leone) build greater capabilities in educational research and evaluation.[31] The Ford Foundation's response was competency-building and networking.

In the following section I will focus on the case of Ford Foundation involvement in educational and social science research in Latin America to illustrate the general functioning of this new form of knowledge transfer.

Ford Foundation, Competency-Building, and Networking

Over the past decade a consensus has emerged among the foundation's hierarchy as to what constitutes development and what roles Ford can best play in development processes.[32] As reiterated in the *1976 Annual Report*, "in general the Foundation's overseas program seeks to help poor countries develop the ability to recognize, understand, and solve their own problems. The International Division works increasingly with international networks of scholars, managers, and planners through associations established and run by nationals of the developing countries."[33]

The Ford Foundation's present involvement in education in other countries is tantamount to developing the research competencies of educators cum social scientists. In effect the Ford Foundation has set out to train "a new generation of educational researchers."[34] As first defined by the Office for Latin America and the Caribbean (OLAC), the foundation should "concentrate its education program . . . on strengthening the capacity for what we call 'educational research and development.' We include by this phrase the actual organization and performance of research and analysis, and also the process of making greater contributions to decision-making and patterns of implementation."[35]

Due to the difficulties involved in working in the large national universities in capital cities, the foundation has gradually focused on assisting selected individuals and independent organizations (e.g., the Center for Educational Studies in Mexico and the Foundation for Higher Education in Colombia) or, if within higher education, working with private and provincial universities (the Pontifical Catholic Javeriana University in Colombia, the Pontifical Catholic University of Peru and Cayetano Heredia Peruvian University, the Pontifical Catholic University of Chile, and the University of the Valley in Guatemala). Due to the political repression in Brazil and the countries of the Southern Cone of South America, the Ford Foundation recently has tended to concentrate its support there on behalf of private research organizations. Examples of such private organizations, which conduct research in the areas of education and the social sciences, include the Center for Educational Research and Development, and the Academy of Christian Humanism in Chile; the Foundation Center for Research and Social Action, and the Center for Studies of the State and Society in Argentina; the Getulio Vargas and the Carlos Chagas Foundations, and the Center for Analysis and Planning in Brazil.

In Brazil the foundation also has supported a research and fellowship competition designed to "stimulate the application of social science methods to educational problems."[36] The foundation relies on a panel of Brazilian referees to select the projects which will receive grants. "Since 1972," according to the 1976 Annual Report, "forty-three research projects and thirty doctoral fellowships for training have been funded. The program has led to the emergence of a community of education researchers whose work is proving increasingly useful to educational policy makers."[37]

The foundation's self-perceived role has not only been to support training and research activities of such scholars and centers, but to facilitate their coming together in "networks." The concepts of "linkage" and "networking" are not new to foundation terminology and operations. And references to regional research centers linked together appear as early as 1961 in the writings of the prominent social scientist Edward Shils, who noted that "the emergence of a coherent intellectual community in an Asian or African country or region will involve the emergence of metropolitan intellectual centers in these areas. These centers will be linked across national boundaries in the way in which they are now linked in the West, as a linkage of peers."[38]

Historically, foundations have worked through international networks of training and research organizations which connected talented individuals and their institutional bases to one another as well as to their benefactors.[39] The foundations have used these networks to cultivate and utilize brain power.

Moreover, since the 1960s, the foundations themselves, together with national and international technical assistance agencies, have formed networks of decision-makers to determine development priorities in education and other fields for Third World countries. Notable examples include the 1962 meeting at the Rockefeller villa in Bellagio of the Agency for International Development, the Africa Liaison Committee, and the Carnegie, Ford, and Rockefeller foundations to discuss the needs of the University of East Africa. In May of 1972 and November of 1973 an expanded set of donors met in Bellagio to discuss education for national development.[40] The group attending the 1972–1973 Bellagio conferences consisted of the Canadian International Development Agency, Ford Foundation, French Ministry of Foreign Affairs, Inter-American Development Bank, International Bank for Reconstruction and Development, International Development Research Centre, Ministry of Overseas Development (United Kingdom), Organization for Economic Cooperation and Development, Overseas Economic Cooperation Fund (Japan), Rockefeller Foundation, Swedish International Development Authority, United Nations Children's Fund, United Nations Development Programme, United Nations Educational, Scientific and Cultural Organization, and the United States Agency for International Development. One principal outcome of these conferences was the study of higher education and social change sponsored by the Ford- and Rockefeller-funded International Council for Educational Development and directed by former Rockefeller vice-president Kenneth Thompson.[41]

Organizationally the Ford Foundation had a prototypical model of networking in its series of international research institutes in tropical agriculture.[42] But the foundation's Office for Latin America and the Caribbean, through its education and social science research program, [43] apparently stimulated the International Division to think of regional activities in a different light: "Not as support of supra-national organizations, but as the development of mutually-supporting linkages among mostly national organizations, which together can form a strong network serving regional as well as national objectives."[44]

By 1978 the foundation had helped establish ten educational research centers studying the educational problems and needs of the region.[45] The foundation envisions such centers as the Centro de Estudios Educativos (CEE) in Mexico, the Center for Educational Research in Argentina, and the Federal University of Minas Gerais and the Carlos Chagas Foundation in Brazil as regional training centers for advanced study and work in educational and social science research. Prior to the advent of the Pinochet military regime in Chile (and the ensuing difficulties of working in that country because of human rights violations), the Latin American Faculty for the Social Sciences (FLACSO) with United Nations and Ford funding had played such a role. The foundation has provided support for Latin American scholars from selected universities and research institutes to visit these centers for varying lengths of time, to attend regional conferences, and to work on collaborative research projects within the context of Latin America. The Center for Educational Studies (CEE), which has received over $500,000 from Ford, also publishes a prestigious Spanish-language research journal which contains articles by Latin Americans who are working on Ford-funded projects or who have received advanced degrees in special U.S. programs, such as that of the Stanford School of Education, where Ford has provided major support.

The research focus of the Latin American education program has diffused over the past five years to other regional offices—in particular, the Office for Francophone Africa.[46] The 1976 annual report of the International Division, in the section pertaining to projects in Africa, notes that "for many years, the Foundation has supported efforts to train social scientists to analyze development problems and to improve scholarly communication across disciplinary and national lines."[47] The report goes on to state that assistance was provided for research awards and regional conferences in the social sciences. In 1976–1977, a more effective instrument—AWAREC—was fashioned with foundation assistance to develop research competencies and facilitate intercountry collaboration in West Africa. The Anglophone West African Regional Education Research Consortium provides support for (1) individuals who pursue postgraduate training in traditional social sciences—but with an orientation to the study of educational phenomena; and (2) workshops on data analysis in education using "modern methods of computerized manipulation and analysis of survey data for social scientists and educators. . . ."[48]

Foundation support of research by Third World nationals could conceivably lead to the generation of important insights into how education systems function within poor countries to perpetuate existing stratification systems and social relations of production; and, under certain conditions favoring larger social change, research might provide a basis for decision-making geared toward helping the most neglected groups within the society. However noble the intentions of the Ford Foundation may be, the policies it pursues to strengthen research competencies in the nationals of other countries run counter to professed aims. In the following sections, I will examine some of the limitations and implications of these training and technical assistance modalities.

APPROACHES TO COMPETENCY-BUILDING

The approaches followed by the foundation tend not to open up new perspectives and methodologies for studying the problems of development on the part of Third World researchers, but work instead to induct them into regional and international networks of individuals and institutions conducting the type of research the Ford Foundation thinks is appropriate and useful.

The modalities the foundation employs to develop research and analytic competencies consist of (1) postgraduate training in education and social sciences at a few select universities, usually in the United States; (2) institutional grants, which also contain budgetary items for overseas study; (3) visiting consultants and travel grants; (4) grants to national planning offices for education and human resource development; (5) pilot projects; and (6) individual research undertakings—usually research efforts of foundation personnel or North American graduate students and scholars, sometimes in combination with host country nationals.

Of these different modalities, to date, the single most important has been postgraduate training in the United States. Individuals who are selected for these fellowships usually come from universities, research centers, and planning offices considered to be of strategic importance by foundation staff. They are in many cases institutions which have received foundation assistance to develop research and training activities. In the case of Latin America, individuals selected for doctoral study are often those who have already received a master's degree in one of the U.S. universities receiving foundation support as a "resource base." These resource bases in education are Stanford, Chicago, and Harvard, which between 1969 and 1978 were awarded close to $1 million to provide advanced training in education and the social sciences to some 150 Latin American educational researchers, planners, administrators, and faculty. By 1978 the Stanford Program in International Development Education alone had trained some eighty-two Latin American graduate students at the master's level in the concepts and methods of educational research and planning; and, with Ford funding, Stanford also had trained some sixty-six Southeast Asian educators (principally from Malaysia, Indonesia, Thailand, and the Philippines) at the master's level.[49]

The foundation also recruits its education program advisors from these resource bases. Since 1969, 90 percent of the education program advisors or assistants have either received their doctorates or taught at one of these three institutions.

IMPLICATIONS AND CONSEQUENCES

Stanford, Harvard, and Chicago form part of the elite system of "lead universities" built by Ford, Rockefeller, and Carnegie. These three, plus another twenty-two, have produced, according to Horowitz,[50] 75 percent of all doctorates awarded in the United States. Together with think tanks, like Brookings, and the national research and learned councils—all heavily funded by the big foundations—these institutions frame for the different academic disciplines the guiding assumptions concerning the questions which will be examined and the methodologies employed to study social, physical, and natural phenomena.

The foundation traditionally has preferred to send nationals from "less-developed countries" to such North American universities because the training they will receive accords with its notions of professionalism and scholarship. At the resource bases in the United States the students learn the respectable ways of viewing and analyzing development problems. While students in these universities might be exposed to divergent interpretations of development and to a number of radical faculty members, these divergent and radicalizing tendencies must be weighted against the entire process of graduate education which works to socialize students into a profession or learned tradition. Students, whether foreign or not, are groomed to be responsible scholars—to be acquainted with the dominant domain assumptions[51] of their disciplines, the standard literature, and the appropriate research methodologies.[52]

One likely outcome of this training is that overseas nationals will tend to view development problems from the same perspectives as their North American and European counterparts—which is to say they will be more pragmatic and less ideological. As early as 1968, Gustav Papanek of the Harvard-based and Ford-funded Development Advisory Service[53] commented on such outcomes for development economists who had received the "appropriate training":

> As a result of progress towards a professional consensus, foreign economists working in many less developed countries have immediate and national allies in their national colleagues, who share their professional language and often their goals. The differences between foreign and national economists are disappearing. The universities' future training, research and institutional involvement in the less developed world needs to take this development into account.[54]

Along these lines, it is interesting to note that the Ford Foundation in 1976 awarded International House of Japan a $179,000 grant to administer a fellowship program. The program will provide up to 100 awards over a seven-to-eight-year period for Japanese social scientists to pursue graduate study in the United States and other countries. According to the *1976 Annual Report*,

> with the world's second largest economy, Japan plays a significant international role in business, in the arts, and natural sciences. But in the social sciences only a few senior Japanese scholars are able to keep in touch with their counterparts or professional developments in the rest of the world. To help stimulate communication and to broaden the orientation of Japanese scholarship in the social sciences, a fellowship program for young Japanese scholars has been launched with the support of the Foundation, the Toyota Foundation, and other Japanese donors.[55]

By contrast, a distinguished Asian social scientist, Pieris, observes that "in Japan alone, a long tradition of sociology dates from about 1879, when the word *shakaigaku* first appeared in print."[56] What the Ford Foundation terms a "broadening" may be instead a circumscribing of perspectives, a process of substituting the behavioralism and "hard-nosed" quantification,[57] which it has long supported, for the Asian tradition of humanistic scholarship.

According to Pieris, "sociology proper, in so far as its main task is the discovery of new analytic truths hitherto unknown, requires a different kind of training calculated to foster creativity, inventiveness, and ingenuity."[58] From this perspective, the goal of sociology is to help stimulate social awareness on the part of the many. By contrast, Pieris believes that Western academics and their funding agencies have promoted "the most dehumanized forms of sociology and economics" involving fragmentation of scholarly efforts and a narrow focus on quantifiable facets of reality.[59]

The Ford Foundation has been well aware of these different social science traditions and at times has agonized over its funding a technocratic approach to social problems. The late Kalman Silvert, Ford Foundation Social Science Advisor for Latin America, repeatedly urged the foundation to view the social sciences as a means of multiplying meanings and enhancing the capacity of individuals, from all strata of society, to understand the social forces impinging upon them.[60] But the Ford Foundation also found itself tending to support the social sciences for their instrumental value in solving problems faced by government bureaucrats and technicians, those who would plan for and manage the affairs of the general public. And in certain Latin American countries—particularly those that have turned authoritarian—there has existed what Manitzas describes as a schizophrenic situation: "The Foundation could find itself training economists to perform technocratic tasks for a military regime and training sociologists whose natural bent was to oppose, criticize, and question the military authorities."[61]

The case of Japan, a developed country, is suggestive of what the foundation is endeavoring to accomplish in developing countries. In effect, the overseas training programs may serve to socialize and induct Third World educators and researchers into what Gouldner calls an international "occupation of experts and technicians who constitute a *specific status group* with *status interests* they wish to protect and advance."[62] These technicians and experts, according to Gouldner, turn to more powerful allies to support their endeavors. (And it should be noted here that some of these experts are neo-Marxist researchers who nonetheless are willing to receive funding from foundations like Ford to engage in the type of research that interests them and have intercourse with an international audience.)

More specifically, the "ego-identities" of the sponsored students in time become anchored in their profession and in an international community of scholars the philanthropic foundations (Ford, Rockefeller, and Carnegie) have been instrumental in shaping. Their behaviors and attitudes eventually are shaped by expectations as to what professionals with North American graduate degrees should know and how they should act. Rewards and gratifications as professionals derive from publishing in international or regional journals, in attending conferences forming part of the international peer network, and in engaging in scholarly activities for which they have been trained.

Whether or not the Ford Foundation intentionally attempts to shape the "ego-identities" of fellowship and grant recipients—a term which derives from the sociology of disciplines—the effects of foundation sponsorship are such that individuals become increasingly attached to viewing themselves in certain ways and conducting research which accords with Ford views of appropriate scholarship. The foundation looms large as a principal source of funding for the professional activities mentioned above. The ties of dependency on the foundation are difficult to sever. The returning student often will be employed in an institution or program receiving substantial foundation support. In numerous other cases, the returning students—dissatisfied with their work situation or denied the opportunity to work in the national universities—turn to the foundation to support their research or find them employment. Ironically, some of these individuals are denied employment in the national universities of certain countries like Colombia because their colleagues and students refuse to work with professionals trained in the United States; and in some instances, the radical orientations they have developed abroad lead to conflict with their governmental employers.

The foundation willingly plays the role of benefactor. As described in its *1975 Annual Report*, ". . . young educational research specialists have been sent abroad for graduate training, mostly in the social sciences rather than in traditional pedagogy or philosophy. Several have now returned to their countries, often to be employed in an emerging network of Foundation-supported research centers."[63] The foundation provides the endowment funds and start-up costs for research centers and programs where like-minded individuals can assemble and engage in scholarly inquiry; and it also supports the journals which will publish their work.

The power of the foundation is not that of dictating what will be studied. Its power consists in defining professional and intellectual parameters, in determining who will receive support to study what subjects in what settings. And the foundation's power resides in suggesting certain types of activities it favors and is willing to support. As Laski noted, "the foundations do not control, simply because, in the direct and simple sense of the word, there is no need for them to do so. They have only to indicate the immediate direction of their minds for the whole university world to discover that it always meant to gravitate swiftly to that angle of the intellectual compass."[64]

Variations in funding patterns are unlikely to minimize foundation influence. Innovative practices overseas, such as the use of panels of host-country referees to select which projects will be funded, remain under foundation guidance. In the first place, the foundation selects the referees. According to foundation criteria, these will be individuals with impeccable credentials and sound judgment. Similarly the more recent efforts by the foundation, in Latin America, to train increasing numbers of individuals at home or within the region are unlikely to result in what the foundation calls "intervention without undue influence." The national and regional centers are usually staffed by individuals who have the appropriate graduate credentials (often acquired under foundation sponsorship) from reputable U.S. and European institutions, or who have taught in such institutions and work within well-established scholarly traditions. And these are Latin American centers where the foundation, through its generous support, has been able to shape the direction in which they develop.

The replacement of North American and European university-based centers by regional local centers of Latin American countries began in the early 1970s. According to rough estimations, as much money was awarded in 1973 ($1.5 million) and in 1974 ($2 million) for the North American and European research communities to study Latin America as was directly awarded to Latin American scholars and institutions for research in the fields of education and the social sciences in their respective countries.[65] In 1975, for the first time, grants awarded to Latin American institutions and individuals for research activities in the above fields exceeded those awarded to North American bases and individuals.

WHO BENEFITS?

The activities of an emerging network of centers engaged in educational and social science research and training raise some provocative issues. Conceivably, these centers could constitute the bases for an independent Latin American tradition of scholarly inquiry. Some of the research funded by the Ford Foundation is highly critical of U.S. economic, political, and cultural penetration of the Southern Hemisphere. Yet the intriguing question remains as to who benefits from the critical analysis.

My speculation is that these overseas networks of research centers and individuals are gradually replacing the North American and European university-based centers of research on the Third World and development problems. The North American centers, which have received some $1 billion in foundation support since 1950, were expected, according to the International Division, to provide the United States "with a continuing flow of able young scholars thoroughly grounded in the realities of the developing countries."[66] McGeorge Bundy, Ford Foundation president from 1966 to 1979, stated the expected payoff from such funding activities more bluntly when he was national security advisor: "It is still true today, and I hope it always will be, that there is a high measure of interpenetration between universities with area programs and information-gathering agencies of the government of the United States."[67]

But because of the increasing obstacles encountered by U.S. nationals conducting research in such regions as Latin America, the foundation, as one critic has observed, finds surrogate researchers. These foundation-supported scholars and research agencies in Latin America and elsewhere not only are gathering data which would be extremely difficult for outsiders to collect, but they are generating alternative paradigms which are likely to provide more realistic and accurate assessments of events overseas. A number of the researchers who are socialist in their political orientations combine both rigorous quantitative methodologies with a conflict model for interpreting social phenomena.[68] As Paulston has noted,

> it is, moreover, no accident that educational agencies such as the World Bank, the Ford Foundation, the Rand Corporation et al., have recently sought the aid of neo-Marxist scholars in efforts to diagnose what went wrong with reforms grounded in the liberal

world view, a perspective that by definition avoids recognition of power and conflict and is thus unable to explain its failures, and is increasingly under attack from both the left and the right.[69]

As a case in point, dependency theory, with its empirico-analytical interpretation of underdevelopment in relation to the specific historical context of a country, has emerged as a source of insight to academicians and policymakers. Fernando Henrique Cardoso (a leading dependency theoretician who has received Ford Foundation support to teach in the United States) is not unmindful of the utility of this perspective:

> The protest of American blacks, the war in Vietnam and the movement in opposition to it, the counterculture, the student movement, the feminist movement, etc., all demanded paradigms that were more sensitive to the historical process, to social struggles, and to the transformation of systems of domination. In such a perspective, analyses of dependency correspond better to this search for new models of explanation, not only to comprehend what is happening in Latin America, but also what is happening in the U.S.A.[70]

Whatever the intentions of the Ford Foundation, the research generated by Latin Americans and researchers in other regions is flowing back to U.S. academic communities and governmental agencies.[71] This information enables the United States to understand better and, perhaps, respond more effectively to Latin American thinking and actions. What the foundations have consistently done at home and abroad is to cultivate and employ talented scholars and professionals: individuals whose studies provide the means for more insight into the problems affecting our own and other societies; and researchers who are likely to point up emerging issues and areas of concern.

A Kafkaesque situation exists where information, produced by Latin Americans on situations of internal and external domination, is flowing to the alleged sources of oppression—rather than toward those who need the information to defend themselves against exploitation. It is a curious situation that regimes like those of Brazil tolerate the writings of radical social scientists whom the foundation is helping to support. Either the regimes are ignorant of this literature, which has received international recognition—an unlikely case—or the writings of these individuals pose no serious threat to the political system. The research is not threatening probably for two reasons: (1) it is not intelligible to the masses, for certainly, if the same sentiments were expressed not in academic journals but from a street corner or as part of a political movement which mobilized large numbers, the individuals would be jailed or exiled; and (2) the regime itself benefits from the knowledge generated, while simultaneously enhancing its international image by permitting academic freedom. This situation is further suggestive of Gouldner's observation that "revolutionary solutions remain mythical so long as ideological elites and their cultural apparatus can reach masses only by going through the consciousness industry."[72] In this case, the consciousness industry consists of those agencies which shape the mass media as well as the channels of publication and communication for intellectuals and academics.

In developing countries an infrastructure is generally lacking not only for integration of research into policy formulation, but also for widespread dissemination of knowledge in terms understandable to the general public. Within the existing international context, scholarly publications and communications are controlled by and flow through the metropolitan centers of Europe and North America, rather than within and among the developing countries. This variant of imperialism has been described by Altbach as "literary colonialism."[73] The people who consume the excellent and highly critical literature on such topics as dependency are a restricted circle of Latin American, North American, and European academics and policymakers.

The regional networks supported by the foundation contribute to facilitating the movement of ideas among nationals of a region and between the metropolitan centers and the periphery. This is precisely one of the stated objectives of such networks: to connect the leading institutions and brightest individuals working on the most pressing problems to one another, wherever they may be located.[74] Through these networks, ideas and programs which have revolutionary potential—such as Paulo Freire's consciousness-raising approach to the adult literacy process—circulate with greater rapidity. But these networks also make ideas more readily available to technical assistance agencies and other governmental entities concerned with development. Divorced from grassroots movements, these ideas become domesticated and another means of fostering what Paulston and LeRoy call "incremental improvements in resource production and allocation, to make existing societies, even if characterized by gross structural violence, more viable." [75]

What foundation money does is to engage the interests and efforts of some of the most talented Third World intellectuals, researchers, and reformers. They become involved in attempting to tamper with and change, through evolutionary processes, existing societal structures so that, hopefully, greater social justice and human welfare results. The absence of foundation support does not necessarily imply that radical revolution or fundamental structural changes would then occur. But foundation support often prevents Third World activists from coping with their domestic problems in their own terms and addressing them with a level of resources consonant with their level of development. Foundation-induced reform efforts, then, tend to divert Third World nationals from more realistic, and perhaps revolutionary, efforts at social change.

Foundations like Ford—and the networks through which they work—are the brokers, the disseminators of innovations. They are the agencies for introducing the sweeping new ideas; they are the sponsors of the panaceas—such as the "green revolution" or "contraceptive technology"—which will enable the "less-developed countries" to overcome the crushing problems of poverty, unemployment, and malnutrition. As soon as one approach to change is seen to accomplish less than expected, the foundation is there, working on the frontiers of knowledge and innovation, to fund the next "comprehensive" or "best" strategy for reform. Through the funds they allocate, the foundations determine where energies will go, what issues will next be studied, and what individuals will be mobilized to examine the emerging issues of our time.

What are the outcomes of such unprecedented expenditures of money and mobilization of talent to study the problems of development? Basically, the foundation does not know. According to Frank Sutton, deputy director of the International Division of Ford, "there has not been a scholarly analysis of foundations' range of engagements with developing countries in the years since 1945."[76]

Areas for Further Study

The above discussion has merely touched upon several provocative issues which merit further study. To test the propositions advanced in preceding sections on the implications and consequences of competency-building and networking, the following related sets of studies are recommended:

> What competencies are developed in whom, and where; and what pattern of continuing relationship is maintained between fellowship recipients and the foundations after they return from study abroad?

> The self-definitions, membership and reference groups of those individuals sponsored by foundations. What rewards and incentives do they consider to be critical to their continued commitment to and satisfaction with their professional work?[77]

> Who consumes the research: in which language and countries? To what extent are disadvantaged or oppressed groups viewed as the intended recipients of information generated by foundation-sponsored inquiry?[78] Through which channels are research findings published? Further research along the lines of Altbach's studies[79] of book publishing in the Third World is recommended.

Which policymakers, in which countries, are aware of the research and literature produced by foundation-funded organizations and individuals? How is this research used? Packenham, for example, believes that social science research may serve only to legitimate the policies of top decision-makers.[80]

The communication patterns, activities, and internal workings of the networks themselves. Who interacts in what ways with whom on what issues, and with what outcomes? The role of the foundations and other technical assistance agencies in funding and shaping these activities.

The interactions between the constituents of the donor networks. The means by which these agencies come together, decide upon, and implement programs in the Third World. The special tasks these networks perform for the donor agencies.

The relations between the investments and engagements of foundations and other technical assistance agencies (public, private, national, and international) and those of economic institutions (such as multinational corporations) and ideologically similar blocs of nations.

Summary

In this chapter I have speculated on the origins and consequences of foundation involvement in universities and research institutions overseas. In particular, I examined the activities of the Ford Foundation in competency-building and networking in education and the social sciences. I conjectured that this new approach to technical assistance has its origins in the political difficulties of previous university institution-building programs and the inadequacy of American social science paradigms of development based on liberal assumptions. I proposed that, in the changing international environment, the Ford Foundation develops the research competencies of Third World nationals to undertake investigations which would be extremely difficult for American and European researchers to conduct. I suggested that the networks of research and training institutions established by Ford (as well as Rockefeller and Carnegie) presently serve as mechanisms for the generation of knowledge and conduits for the transmission of information—not only from North to South, but also in the opposite direction. Third World researchers and scholars are presently providing policymakers and academics in the metropolitan centers of North America and Europe with alternative theoretical frameworks and more accurate assessments upon which to make informed judgments. What Chase-Dunn has said about a world-system appears to be applicable to foundation involvement abroad in education, culture, and science: along with economic and political institutions, these foundations constitute an important element in the flow of resources between previously unconnected societies in order to achieve and maintain "control structures, which link the superordinate to the subordinate in the same interactive system."[81] Such speculation merits further attention as do, more generally, the activities of the philanthropic foundations at home and abroad.

Notes

1. Kenneth Thompson, "Higher Education and National Development: One Model for Technical Assistance," in F. Champion Ward (ed.), *Education and Development Reconsidered* (New York: Praeger Publishers, 1974), p. 195.

2. Ibid., p. 201.

3. Kenneth Thompson, *Foreign Assistance: A View from the Private Sector* (South Bend, Ind.: University of Notre Dame Press, 1972), pp. 56–57.

4. Cited from Philip Coombs, *The Fourth Dimension of Foreign Policy* (New York: Harper & Row, Publishers, 1964), p. 70.

5. Richard Colvard, "Foreign Grants by U.S. Philanthropic Foundations," paper prepared for presentation at Pacific Sociological Association Annual Meeting Spokane, Washington, April 1978, mimeo, p. 8.

6. Richard Magat, *The Ford Foundation at Work: Philanthropic Choices, Methods, and Styles* (New York: Plenum Press, 1979), pp. 188–189, 193; also see Lally Weymouth, "Foundation Woes: The Saga of Henry II," *New York Times Magazine*, March 12, 1978, p. 24.

7. See, for example, "The Foundation and the Less Developed Countries" (New York: Ford Foundation, 1972), Appendix II; and Peter Bell, "The Ford Foundation as a Transnational Actor," in Robert O. Keohane and Joseph S. Nye, Jr. (eds.), *Transnational Actors and World Politics* (Cambridge, Mass.: Harvard University Press, 1972), p. 117.

8. *Magat, Ford Foundation at Work*, p. 157; Aldo Solari, "Obstacles to the Institutionalization of Sociology in Latin America," *International Social Science Journal* 21:3 (1969): 448; and Bell, "Ford as Transnational Actor," p. 116.

9. For further discussion, see E. Jefferson Murphy, *Creative Philanthropy: Carnegie Corporation and Africa, 1953–1973* (New York: Teachers College Press, 1976), pp. 123–151, 264–266.

10. For further discussion, see Coombs, *Fourth Dimension of Foreign Policy*, pp. 70–71; and Bell, "Ford as Transnational Actor."

11. Walter Ashley, "Philanthropy and Government: A Study of the Ford Foun-

dation's Overseas Activities," unpublished Ph.D. dissertation, New York University, 1970, p. 8.

12. Ibid., p. 84.

13. "Bridges of Scholars—East and West," Ford Foundation Letter 9 (December 1, 1978), p. 3.

14. IREX was established in 1968 by the American Council of Learned Societies and the Social Science Research Council. The Rockefeller, Carnegie, Russell Sage, and Ford Foundations have been principal supporters of the ACLS and the SSRC who, in turn, have served as mechanisms for distributing foundation grants to individuals and institutions. For example, in 1978 the Ford Foundation provided the SSRC with $1 million for a consolidated program of dissertation and postdoctoral awards for research on various areas of the world. For further discussion of foundation support for such councils, see Philip E. Mosely, "International Affairs," pp. 375–394; and George M. Bechmann, "Non-Western Studies," pp. 374–401, in Warren Weaver et al., *U.S. Philanthropic Foundations* (New York: Harper and Row Publishers, 1967); Joseph C. Kiger, "Foundation Support of Educational Innovation by Learned Societies, Councils, and Institutes," in Mathew B. Miles (ed.), *Innovation in Education* (New York: Teachers College Press, 1964), pp. 553–562; Barry D. Karl, "Philanthropy, Policy Planning and the Bureaucratization of the Democratic Ideal," *Daedelus* 105 (Fall 1976): 138–141. For a critical analysis of the relationship between the Russell Sage Fund and the SSRC see Jay Schulman, Carol Brown, and Roger Kohn, "Report on the Russell Sage Foundation," *Insurgent Sociologist* 2 (Summer 1972): 2–34. For an analysis of Ford Foundation involvement with the SSRC, see Peter Seybold's chapter in this book.

15. "Bridges of Scholars," p. 3.

16. The American Council of Learned Societies and the Social Science Research Council assisted the Committee on Scholarly Communications with the Peoples' Republic of China in its efforts to include social scientists and humanities in the scholarly exchanges.

17. "Bridges of Scholars," p. 3; As early as 1969, the Ford Foundation commissioned Professor John M. H. Lindbeck, Director of the East Asian Institute at Columbia and Chairman of the Committee on Scholarly Communication with the Peoples' Republic of China, to prepare an assessment of American scholarly resources on China. The report was published as *Understanding China* (New York: Praeger Publishers, 1971). For further discussion on the Ford Foundation's role in developing the field of China Studies, see Moss Roberts, "How the Foundations Bought a Field," *Bulletin of Concerned Asian Scholars* 3 (Summer-Fall 1971): 113–137; and in the same issue of the *BCAS*, David Horowitz "Politics and Knowledge: An Unorthodox History of Modern China Studies," pp. 139–168.

18. Irving Louis Horowitz and Ruth Leonora Horowitz, "Tax Exempt Foundations: Their Effects on National Policy," *Science* 168 (April 10, 1974): 224; see also Adam Yarmolinsky, "Philanthropic Activity in International Affairs," in Commission on Private Philanthropy and Public Needs, *Re-*

search Papers (Washington, D.C.: U.S. Department of the Treasury, 1977), Vol. II, Part I, pp. 773–777.

19. Kenneth Thompson, Barbara R. Fogel, and Helen E. Danner (eds.), *Higher Education and Social Change* (New York: Praeger, 1977), p. 354.

20. Luis Scherz-Garcia, "Some Disfunctional Aspects of International Assistance and the Role of the University in Social Change," *International Social Science Journal* 19 (1967): 399.

21. Burton Newbry, "AID Education Efforts: A Critque," *Journal of Developing Areas* 3 (July 1969): 490.

22. Ibid., p. 491.

23. Guy Benveniste and Warren F. Ilchman (eds.), *Agents of Change: Professionals in Developing Countries* (New York: Praeger, 1969), pp. 21–22.

24. John William Gardner, *AID and the Universities* (New York: Education and World Affairs, 1964), cited from Thompson, *View from Private Sector*, p. 47.

25. Lester B. Pearson, *The Crisis of Development* (New York: Praeger, 1970).

26. Robert A. Packenham, *Liberal American and the Third World* (Princeton, N.J.: Princeton University Press, 1973).

27. See, for example, Samuel P. Huntington, *Political Order in Changing States* (New Haven, Conn.: Yale University Press, 1968).

28. For further discussion, see David Horowitz, "Billion Dollar Brains," *Ramparts 7 (May 1969): 36–44*.

29. Thompson, *View from Private Sector*, pp. 15–16.

30. Kenneth W. Thompson, "Higher Education for Development," paper presented at the Annual Meeting of the Comparative and International Society, Toronto, Canada, February 25, 1976, pp. 13–14; and Kenneth W. Thompson and Barbara R. Fogel, *Higher Education and Social Change* (New York: Praeger, 1976).

31. For further discussion, see Murphy, *Creative Philanthropy*, pp. 197–202. A second principal thrust of the Carnegie Corporation in the late 1960s and early 1970s continued to be the sponsorship of exchange programs bringing African educators to the U.S. and Canada, principally through the good offices of the African-American Institute, the Overseas Liaison Committee of the American Council on Education, and Columbia University Teachers College.

32. Ford Foundation, "Foundation and Less Developed Countries," 1972, p. 24.

33. Ford Foundation, *1976 Annual Report* (New York: same, 1977), p.36.

34. Ibid., p. 44.

35. Reuben Frodin with R. Drysdale, K. N. Rao, R. Sharpe, K. Silvert, and P. Strasburg, "Toward a Policy for Foundation Assistance to Latin American Education in the Seventies" (New York: Ford Foundation, Office for Latin America and the Caribbean, 1971), pp. 11–12.

36. Ford Foundation, *1976 Annual Report*, p. 44.

37. Ibid.

38. Edward A. Shils, "Metropolis and Province in the Intellectual Community," in V. M. Dandakar and N. V. Sovani (eds.), *Changing India* (Bombay and London: Asian Publishing House), pp. 375–394; cited from his *The Intel-*

lectuals and the Powers and Other Essays (Chicago: University of Chicago Press, 1972), p. 371.

39. For the use of such networks by one prominent family of philanthropists, see Peter Collier and David Horowitz, *The Rockefellers* (New York: Holt, Rinehart and Winston, 1976), p. 500.

40. Papers presented at these conferences are found in F. Champion Ward, *Education and Development Reconsidered* (New York: Praeger, 1974).

41. The results of this study are published in Thompson and Fogel, *Higher Education and Social Change*, 1976; and Thompson, Fogel, and Danner (eds.), *Higher Education and Social Change*, 1977; for a review of these studies see Robert F. Arnove, *Higher Education* 7 (November 1978): 471–474.

42. For further discussion, see Thompson, *View from Private Sector*; and Vernon W. Ruttan, "The International Institute Approach," in Benveniste and Ilchman, *Agents of Change*, pp. 220–228; also "The President's Review," *1977 Annual Report* (New York: The Ford Foundation, 1978), pp. v–xiv.

43. The foundation's Office for Latin America and the Caribbean was the first to staff systematically its field offices with professional educators, who also were expected to have advanced training in the social sciences. The foundation particularly has favored educators with a strong training in economics.

44. Ford Foundation, "The Ford Foundation and the Less-Developed Countries," draft paper (New York: same, 1971), p. 6; and 1972 revised version with the same title, p. 36.

45. Ford Foundation, *1977 Annual Report* (New York: same, 1978), p. 37.

46. Ford Foundation, *1975 Annual Report* (New York: same, 1976), p. 51.

47. Ford Foundation, *1976 Annual Report* (New York: same, 1977), p. 48.

48. Ralph W. Harbison, "Anglophone West African Regional Education Research Consortium" (Ford Foundation: Abidjan, Ivory Coast, November 10, 1978). According to its *1977 Annual Report*, p. 40, the Ford Foundation set aside during the 1977 fiscal year the sum of $360,000 for graduate training of West African educational researchers and for studies of educational policy and assessment in the region.

49. "The Stanford Educator," *Stanford University School of Education News* 17 (Autumn 1977): 2.

50. Horowitz, "The Foundations [Charity Begins at Home]," *Ramparts* 7 (April 1969): 39–48.

51. For discussion of domain assumptions, see Alvin Gouldner, *The Coming Crisis of Western Sociology* (New York: Basic Books, Inc., 1970), pp. 27–35.

52. Horowitz, "Billion Dollar Brains," p. 40.

53. The Ford-funded Development Advisory Service (DAS), throughout the 1960s and early 1970s, provided technical assistance to national planning offices overseas. For a critical analysis of the role of Papanek and DAS in Indonesia, see David Ransom, "Ford Country—Building an Elite for Indonesia," in Steve Weissman, *The Trojan Horse* (Palo Alto, Calif.: Ramparts Press, 1975 edition), pp. 93–116.

54. Gustav Papanek, "Training Economists for Service in Developing Countries," in Benveniste and Ilchman, *Agents of Change*, p. 183.
55. Ford Foundation, *1976 Annual Report*, p. 39.
56. Ralph Pieris, "The Implantation of Sociology in Asia," *International Social Science Journal* 21 (1969): 440.
57. For further discussion, see Horowitz, "Billion Dollar Brains."
58. Pieris, "Implantation of Sociology," p. 439.
59. Ibid., p. 438.
60. Kalman Silvert, "Ethics and Programmatic Thinking about Rural Welfare" (New York: Ford Foundation, Office for Latin America and the Caribbean, October 1972).
61. Nita Manitzas, "The Ford Foundation Social Science Program in Latin America" (New York: Ford Foundation, Office for Latin America and the Caribbean, 1973), p.6.
62. Alvin W. Gouldner, *The Dialectic of Ideology and Technology* (New York: The Seabury Press, 1976), p. 241.
63. Ford Foundation, *1975 Annual Report* (New York: same, 1976), p. 93.
64. Harold Laski, "Foundations, Universities, and Research," in his *Dangers of Obedience and Other Essays* (New York: Harper & Brothers, 1930), p. 174.
65. These figures are based on a review of the Annual Reports of the Ford Foundation. They are rough estimates, due to the difficulty of separating out funds allocated for general institutional support and those directly for research purposes. Furthermore, the summary budget statements in the Annual Reports do not indicate what proportion of the funds allocated to the North American and European bases actually went to support efforts of Latin American institutions and researchers.
66. Ford Foundation, "Foundation and Less-Developed Countries," 1971, p. 29.
67. McGeorge Bundy, in E. A. Johnson, *The Dimensions of Diplomacy* (Baltimore: Johns Hopkins Press, 1964), pp. 2–3; cited from Steve Weissman, *The Trojan Horse*, p. 21.
68. An interesting side note is that in 1975, Ralf Dahrendorf, director of the London School of Economics, became a member of the Ford Foundation Board of Trustees. Dahrendorf had long been one of the most articulate critics of the limitations of American social science research, due to its failure to study such basic phenomena as violence, revolution, and class. See, for example, his "European Sociology and the American Self-Image," *Archives Europeenes de Sociologie*, 11 (1961), pp. 324–366. Another trustee who has distinguished himself by realistic research on political processes is Alexander Heard, Chairman of the Board. Heard, according to Domhoff, has conducted "one of the most thorough studies ever done of campaign finance" and the candidate-selection process in the U.S. See G. William Domhoff, "State and Ruling Class in Corporate America," *Insurgent Sociologist* 4 (Winter 1974): 10–11. Heard is a political scientist by training and chancellor of Vanderbilt University.
69. Rolland G. Paulston, "Ethnicity and Educational Change: A Priority for Comparative Education," *Comparative Education Review* 20 (October 1976): 275.

70. Fernando Henrique Cardoso, "The Consumption of Dependency Theory in the United States," *Latin American Research Review* 12:3 (1977): 17.
71. The flow of information is obviously not one way. But this essay concentrates on the less studied ramifications of competency- and institution-building overseas—those instances where the donor countries benefit, perhaps to a greater extent than the recipient countries, from the research results generated by this technical assistance.
72. Gouldner, *Dialectic of Ideology and Technology*, p. 177.
73. Philip G. Altbach, "Literary Colonialism: Books in the Third World," *Harvard Educational Review* 45 (May 1975): 226–236.
74. See, for example, "Ford Foundation, Foundation and Less-Developed Countries," 1971, p. 19.
75. Rolland G. Paulston and Gregory LeRoy, "Strategies for Nonformal Education," *Teachers College Record* 76 (May 1975): 587.
76. Francis X. Sutton, "The Foundations and Governments of Developing Countries," *Studies in Comparative International Development* 12 (Summer 1977): 97.
77. See, for example, Gouldner, *Dialectic of Ideology and Technology*, p. 269.
78. For a critical discussion of the dissemination policies and beneficiaries of social science research projects financed by an influential foundation, see Schulman, Brown, and Kahn, "Report on Russell Sage Foundation": 28–23.
79. Altbach, "Literary Colonialism," and his "Servitude of the Mind? Education, Dependency, and Neocolonialism," *Teachers College Record* 79 (December 1977): 187–204.
80. Packenham, *Liberal America*, p. 253; see also Gouldner, *Dialectic of Ideology and Technology*, pp. 255–257.
81. Christopher Chase-Dunn, "Dependence, Development and Inequality," *American Sociological Review* 40 (December 1975): 721.

Dennis C. Buss

The Ford Foundation in Public Education: Emergent Patterns*

The Ford Foundation has played a powerful and significant role in American public education. When its record of grant-giving is examined, a set of characteristic approaches to educational change and reform emerge. This chapter seeks to demonstrate that the Ford Foundation strategy of giving has consistently (1) favored elitist policies and cooperated with elitist institutions to induce change; (2) used a technocratic approach to the delivery, management, and financing of educational change; (3) used promotional techniques rather than empirical studies as a means to advance preferred programs; and (4) reacted to rather than anticipated important developments in public education despite an image as an innovative philanthropy. The impact of these strategies has been the attempt by Ford to control and manage the direction of educational change in America. By carefully exercising various forms of power and influence, the foundation has engaged in a policy of social engineering designed to avoid significant structural change in the schools and society.[1] These observations about the Ford style of educational philanthropy will be discussed by focusing on representative programs over the last thirty years for teacher education, gifted students, school management and organization, educational technology, and equal educational opportunity.

The foundation began funding these projects for public education in 1951 through the Fund for the Advancement of Education (FAE). The latter served as a separately funded agency of the foundation proper in order to concentrate on the problems of public educational reform. Between 1951 and 1967, when the FAE was reabsorbed into the foundation, the FAE expended just under $71 million on educational programming.[2] In the meantime the foundation itself was spending hundreds of

*This essay is based in part upon the author's Ed.D. dissertation, "The Ford Foundation and the Exercise of Power in American Education: 1951–1971" (unpublished Ed.D. dissertation, Rutgers University, 1972).

millions primarily in the areas of higher education and international education. Between 1965 (when the phasing out of FAE programs began) and 1977, the foundation spent over $146 million on projects related to public education.[3]

These figures are significant when we consider the fact that philanthropic foundations as a group, after the federal government, are the largest single source of funds for the financing of educational research and experimentation. Foundations themselves consider education their most important priority.[4] Since Ford is the largest of these foundations and gives more to educational programming than any other foundation, its influence, at least in monetary terms, is enormous.[5]

Knowing the wealth of the Ford Foundation, what then does it seek to accomplish as a national influence in public education? Officially, the FAE and the foundation have sought to use their power and influence in the pursuit of the following objectives:

1. The improvement of the preparation and recruitment of teachers and administrators.
2. The improvement of the utilization of teaching resources.
3. The improvement of the curriculum.
4. The improvement of educational opportunities for all students.
5. The clarification of the functions of education in relation to the obligations of citizens to education.[6]

The foundation has used its vast financial resources and a collaborative strategy with other powerful agents of change to implement these ambitious programs. In so doing, Ford has become a major formative influence on national policy for public education. Careful scrutiny of the goals, operations, and modes of influence of the Ford Foundation is therefore necessary, especially since there has been relatively little public control or evaluation of its activities.

Leadership by Elites

Before analyzing the Ford programs and the concerns they raise, it is important to note some basic characteristics of Ford leadership and of the American educational establishment. Such an examination will reveal that the foundation has sought to cooperate with and support a network of like-minded establishment collaborators in an effort to direct the course of educational innovation. In the years after World War II a new pattern of leadership emerged in American education which was distinctive from the traditional power structure. In the past, the educational establishment consisted primarily of state education officers, school administrators, and professors of education. This establishment was distinguished by the fact that most of its members developed their careers entirely within the public schools as professional teachers. Its influence was essentially local in nature.

Although this "old" establishment still has considerable influence, a "new" establishment has challenged its prominent position. This new establishment is characterized by a career pattern which is not exclusively confined to the public school area. Increasingly, the new leaders in education have served in varying capacities such as holding high positions in the federal government, philanthropic foundations, major universities such as Harvard, and large business corporations. Frequent movement among these institutions is characteristic of the new establishment. In effect, they comprise a national educational elite because they are closely affiliated with some of America's most prestigious institutions and hold high positions within those bodies. They have become a nationalizing influence upon the public schools in their attempt to formulate and control educational policy and change.[7]

Examples of this establishment are not hard to find. For instance, John Gardner was president of the Carnegie Corporation of New York before leaving the foundation to become Secretary of Health, Education and Welfare in 1965. After this experience he headed the Urban Coalition and later the national lobbying group Common Cause. Gardner has never held an elective office.

James B. Conant was president of Harvard from 1933 to 1953. In 1953 he became high commissioner to West Germany and later ambassador to that country. In 1958 he was invited by the Carnegie Corporation to conduct a series of studies on the status of American public secondary education and teacher education. In this capacity he exerted enormous influence on the schools at a time when Cold War pressures for academic excellence were strong.

Another example has been the career of Francis Keppel, whose father once served as president of Carnegie before Gardner. Keppel became dean of Harvard's Graduate School of Education in 1947. During his stay there he became closely involved in foundation-supported projects including those of the Ford Foundation. After his Harvard position he became Commissioner of Education from 1962 to 1965. Upon completing his government career he assumed leadership of the newly created General Learning Corporation, which was set up as a result of a merger between the General Electric Corporation and Time, Inc. In that capacity he became a key figure in the growing "industrial-education complex."

The career patterns of important figures in the Ford Foundation are illustrative. Paul Hoffman served President Truman as director of the

European Recovery Program before coming to the foundation as its president in 1951. After his short stay at Ford he concentrated on his duties as chairman of Studebaker-Packard. McGeorge Bundy, who was appointed president of the foundation in 1966, was dean of Harvard's Graduate Faculty of Arts and Science before he became a chief foreign policy advisor to Presidents Kennedy and Johnson. Harold Howe, current vice-president in the Division of Education and Research of the foundation, initially achieved a reputation as superintendent of schools in the wealthy New York City suburb of Scarsdale, where he was the recipient of numerous Ford grants. In 1965 Howe was tapped as new Commissioner of Education, replacing Francis Keppel (a former dean of the Harvard Graduate School of Education) in that capacity. In 1968 he went to the Ford Foundation as head of its India office.

It is quite apparent that the Ford Foundation has served a strong institutional role in the support of this new national establishment. What is especially significant is that most of its leaders have served in appointive positions rather than elective positions. Consequently, their leadership role has been maintained regardless of the institution with which they were affiliated. Moreover, they have promoted basically the same educational policies and programs regardless of their particular institutional role. This is significant in that as the interests of the foundations, universities, corporations, and federal government converge into a basic consensus, fewer alternative and competing educational programs or proposals are able to survive. The management of educational change becomes centralized.

Teacher Education

According to the widely circulated document *A Decade of Experiment*, published by the FAE, "about half of the money granted by the Fund in its first decade of operation" was for the recruitment and training of teachers. "Second to this interest is the Fund's concern with the more efficient use of teachers' time and energy."[8] In another pamphlet, *Teachers for Tomorrow*, published in 1955, the FAE graphically outlined the problem of the national teacher shortage.[9] Dealing with such questions as how many young people will be attending school and college, how many school and college teachers will we need, what are our chances of getting enough good teachers, and so on, the FAE concluded: "It will be impossible under the present pattern of teacher recruitment and teacher utilization to secure anywhere near enough good teachers for our schools and colleges over the next 15 years."[10]

As a result, the FAE recommended that a concerted effort be made to make teaching a more attractive profession. This could be done in three ways: (1) increase the prestige and status of teaching; (2) modify the salary structure; and (3) redefine the teacher's job. In this way the schools could hold on to the teachers they already had, recruit students already in college, and attract college-educated adults in the community.[11] In effect the FAE was saying that "if we are to improve the supply we must also improve the utilization of teachers, for the two are inseparable."[12]

The Ford funds were also concerned with the quality of education received by teachers as they prepared for their profession. FAE leaders were convinced of the inadequacy of the conventional four-year teacher education program offered in most state colleges and universities where the vast majority of teachers were prepared. As Clarence Faust, president of the FAE, put it, "since the beginning of the century there has been a tendency in the preparation of public school teachers to increase the attention to professional education rather than to the substance of teaching."[13]

The FAE believed that teaching had declined relative to other professions because it lacked the advanced educational requirements these other professions possessed. As a result, teaching lacked prestige as well as higher salaries. Presumably, by increasing the liberal or general education component relative to professional education courses, these difficulties could be overcome. A more demanding (time-consuming) professional preparation program would enhance the prestige of the teaching profession which, in turn, would justify claims to higher salaries. Moreover, such a development would tend to attract more and brighter students to the profession, it was assumed.

This could be accomplished, claimed the FAE, through the concept of the fifth-year approach to teacher education. This approach would "reduce the emphasis on professional courses and increase the emphasis on liberal education, on supervised teaching, and on the subjects to be taught."[14] In this way, students from better liberal arts colleges who found professional courses "incapable of interesting them or capturing their imagination"[15] could find an alternative route to certification.

The FAE's most notorious attempt at implementing the fifth-year concept was through the so-called "Arkansas Experiment."[16] Convinced of the efficacy of its liberal arts bias, the fund in 1951 approached the University of Arkansas to help plan a statewide "experiment" which would eliminate the four-year approach to training teachers. All Arkansas colleges, public and private, which had teacher training programs would no longer provide the four-year certificates but instead offer a four-year liberal arts program capped by a fifth professional year at the University of Arkansas or Arkansas State Teachers College.

According to the FAE, the "major purpose [of the Arkansas experiment] is to improve the quality of preparation for teaching, although, it too is expected to prove fruitful in opening new sources of supply for teachers."[17] This statement is important because the essence of the Arkansas program was to *extend* the number of years in college required to receive the initial teaching certificate and bachelor's degree from four to five. Apparently the FAE was more interested in demonstrating the theoretical assumption that there could be a drastic reduction in professional education course requirements without any decrease in the quality of teachers.

This operating assumption led to a clash with professional educators. The American Association of Colleges for Teacher Education claimed that the plan was not an experiment at all since no alternatives were to be compared with the Ford project approach.[18] Others argued that the teacher education component of the plan amounted to little more than an apprenticeship.[19] A compromise was reached. It was agreed that the notion of separating liberal from professional education should be treated as a testable hypothesis and that existing four-year undergraduate teacher education programs would not be eliminated but left open as an option to those students who wished to pursue this route.[20]

According to Colvard, the program demonstrated that fifth-year graduates were able to teach as well as conventional four-year graduates. Nevertheless, after the Ford grants were terminated, the program virtually died. In 1955, the peak year, the program graduated sixty-four students; by 1959, the last year, the number had declined to seven.[21] Apparently, the traditional four-year program of teacher education proved more attractive to students, given the minimum time and costs involved.

Nevertheless, while the Arkansas proposal "aroused more controversy and brought the Fund more criticism than any other program in its entire history,"[22] the FAE persisted in promoting the fifth-year concept. What was needed was a more effective means to make the program self-sufficient. Scholarship aid to support graduate students enrolled in these programs was expensive. As a result of this problem, the FAE sought a breakthrough in the fifth-year teacher education concept.

The answer came from Francis Keppel, dean of the School of Education at Harvard University, who suggested to the FAE that a cooperative relationship be formed between colleges and universities training teachers and the surrounding school districts that employed them. The fifth year would include a paid "internship" in the local school which would give the teacher trainee the equivalent of a student teaching experience. This would provide the teaching intern with financial support to complete a Master of Arts in Teaching (M.A.T.) degree. Known as the "breakthrough program," the foundation itself supported the concept with an investment of $29 million in grants to some fifty-two colleges and universities to develop and/or maintain M.A.T. programs.

The paid internship was seen as a means to integrate teacher training with organizational innovations in the local school districts which the Ford funds were also supporting. Thus the intern would become part of a hierarchically organized team of teachers, each having different role responsibilities within the school. As the FAE put it:

> It [team teaching] carries the old principle of the division of labor into the schools. . . . Besides this mobility and better division of talent, the team principle arranges for the highly gifted teacher to be assisted by other teachers, trainees, and aides. . . . Schools reorganized so as to employ several different levels of skill and competence would be able to pay teachers according to their clearly differentiated roles, as it is done in business and the professions. And this prospect . . . would attract the more talented people and thus greatly aid the recruitment effort.[23]

In order to promote the "breakthrough" concept Ford carefully avoided involving the traditional state teachers colleges and university schools of education in the program. Instead, they involved a select group of elite institutions compatible with the Ford liberal arts bias:

> These particular "Ivy League" institutions were selected as the instigators of needed change in teacher education because they were generally recognized as the institutions of higher education in America, and there would be considerable "rub-off" from their programs on those of the less influential colleges and universities. . . . It might be logical to expect the state colleges of the nation, which produce the overwhelming majority of new teachers, to be the most strategic spot for the investment of risk capital as a stimulant for innovation, but, in the Foundations' eyes, these colleges lacked a dynamic, experimental climate or the high visibility and fame that would make them valuable as pacesetters. Strategic investment, then, in prestigious institutions whose innovations would be assured of a serious hearing by educators, became a guiding principle of the Foundation's "Breakthrough" efforts.[24]

Two divergent tendencies characterized Ford efforts in teacher education. One was to view teacher education as a problem of numbers—how to recruit more teachers and use them more efficiently in light of the exploding student population. The other was to increase the amount of time a teacher would have to spend in his own education from four to five years in order to become a fully certified classroom teacher. The FAE chose to extend the length of time a teacher needed in his formal preparation even though a teacher shortage existed.

What explains this contradiction? Initially, the FAE seemed more interested in proving a point in educational theory than it was in fulfilling its intentions of solving the teacher shortage. The FAE was convinced that teacher education was illiberal and overly professionalized. Moreover, it was sure that this situation was caused by the entrenched powers of a self-seeking professional education "establishment." This establishment needed breaking up and its programs needed radical change. The Arkansas experiment and the M.A.T. programs reveal this inherent anti-educationist bias of the FAE and the Foundation. These Ford programs were characterized by their intention to discredit the traditional four-year teacher education institution, while promoting a relatively few eastern Ivy League liberal arts institutions as models for five-year teacher education programs. Moreover, the antieducationist values of these institutions could be viewed as more compatible with the values of the emergent national elite which the foundation represented.

The Ford programs in teacher education failed to radically alter the pattern of teacher education in America. The vision that the Arkansas plan would serve as a model for all other states was soon spoiled as it became apparent that the five-year model could not compete with the traditional four-year program without draining the FAE's financial resources through supportive scholarships. Moreover, the M.A.T. program never graduated even 1 percent of the total teacher education majors in any given year since its revival by Ford.

As these failures became apparent, the foundation and the FAE concentrated on proposals for the efficient utilization of teachers. The Arkansas controversy convinced the FAE of the powers of the local educational establishment when directly confronted; therefore, a less direct approach was taken. If the liberal arts bias could not be implemented perhaps the efficiency programs could. Thus there occurred the transformation of the fifth-year program from one designed to demonstrate the efficacy of the liberal arts emphasis to one designed to demonstrate how new ways of utilizing teachers in more efficient organizational and technological patterns could be implemented. This latter emphasis became a major focus if not the motivating force behind the "breakthrough" programs.

The Pursuit of Excellence

A prime example of the foundation's collaborative strategy with the elite establishment institutions was its involvement in the "pursuit of excellence" during the Cold War period. The national mania for competition with the Russians reached its climax with the so-called *Sputnik* crisis. It was then the schools became the scapegoat for the national failure in the space race. The foundation responded to these pressures by developing a series of programs to encourage the gifted student in his school and college career. These involved academic acceleration through curriculum compression and a nationwide testing and scholarship program. If the most talented students in the schools could be identified and then allowed to proceed through their academic careers at a rapid pace, the benefits to the nation's pool of "brainpower" would be obvious.

By 1967, both the FAE and the foundation had allocated a total of nearly $45 million to these programs.[25] The Ford Foundation sought to make the schools more effective instruments of national policy by developing cooperative strategies with the federal government and other foundations. Thus the Ford projects must be viewed as part of a massive national effort to upgrade the schools by emphasizing programs for the talented. The curriculum reforms in the sciences and mathematics sponsored by the National Science Foundation (NSF) and the National Defense Education Act (NDEA) were all compatible with Ford Foundation efforts. The bright student would be able to take these more enriched offerings if identified and appropriately guided by school counselors. Consequently, a more intense meritocratic academic elitism was promoted in the schools.

The FAE denied it was promoting such policies:

> Preoccupation with the manpower aspects of education, however statesmanlike, runs into the fundamental question whether the individual exists for society or society for the individual. On this question, the American commitment would seem to be clear, that the individual is not primarily to be regarded as a resource of the state but the state as a means for assuring the full flowering of the individual.[26]

Despite protestations to the contrary, a number of actions more accurately reveal the foundation's role in this period. While critical of the excesses of NDEA, officers of the FAE and the foundation nevertheless earnestly supported the creation of the NDEA scholarship and loan program for "all" students going to college.[27]

For example, in testimony before the House Education and Labor Committee, Philip Coombs, secretary and director of the FAE, asserted his support of a federal scholarship and loan program by reiterating the familiar Cold War message:

> By honoring excellence of performance in education and by honoring quality in education the Federal Government can do much to help expand the Nation's total supply of well-developed

talent for all uses, not merely scientists and engineers. This is
vital because a major key to our Nation's future development
and progress, whether in relation to peace or to defense, is our
supply of well-educated manpower. Our natural resources are
not likely to be our major bottleneck; our main limiting factor
will be brainpower. Therefore, as a Nation we must help every
young person develop his potential to the full, whatever his
potential is.[28]

Despite his initial disclaimer that he was not speaking for the FAE or
the Ford Foundation, Coombs in that same testimony urged the committee not to create legislation which would compete with the FAE-sponsored
early college admissions program, the advanced placement program, and
the National Merit Scholarship program.[29] This testimony clearly illustrates the FAE's desire to carefully coordinate its programs with federal
efforts as well as Ford's acceptance of the premises upon which the NDEA
was based. Its own programming was "serving" the nation's manpower
needs by encouraging the gifted student. These actions also confirm the
uniformity of thought and purpose that existed between the federal
government and the philanthropic establishment as they attempted to set
an agenda for national educational priorities.

QUALITY CONTROL THROUGH NATIONAL TESTING

The foundation's activities in national testing provide an interesting case
study in how it created an elitist program in order to adjust to Cold War
pressures. In responding to these pressures, Ford collaborated with those
forces—the federal government, other foundations, business corporations, and testing agencies—which viewed talented American youth as an
undeveloped national resource.

In 1955 the foundation embarked on a project creating a national
testing program to identify and grant bright students scholarships to
pursue a higher education. This program, funded with the cooperation
and financial aid of the Carnegie Corporation, was administered by the
National Merit Scholarship Corporation (NMSC). The NMSC was created with an initial grant of $20.5 million ($20 million from Ford and the
remainder from Carnegie), to administer what became known as the
National Merit Scholarship Qualifying Test (NMSQT). The foundation
was concerned that many qualified students were not applying to college
either because of lack of interest, lack of financial resources, or unaware-
ness of their ability to succeed in college. Thus, the Ford Foundation
considered it "essential that top quality students among nonapplicants

also be identified and encouraged, and their further education supported, as part of the process of insuring maximum development of the nation's resources of talent."[30]

Of the $20.5 million granted, $18 million was allocated for scholarships over a ten-year period; the other $2.5 million was for administrative and operative costs over that same period. The program also included a provision for the matching of grants given by other donors in order to encourage outside support. The Ford Foundation continued its support of the program with a grant of $14.5 million in 1962[31] and a $4 million grant in 1967 which carried funding through to 1973.[32]

Given this source of funds, the Corporation turned over the development of NMSQT to the College Entrance Examination Board (CEEB). Later, Science Research Associates (SRA), a private test and textbook publishing firm, took over this function. The program is now part of the Preliminary Scholastic Aptitude Test given to second-semester junior and first-semester seniors in public, private, and parochial high schools. Semi-finalists are chosen from the highest scorers within each state. These semifinalists then take the follow-up test, the Scholastic Aptitude Test of the CEEB, to determine those who qualify as finalists and who are eligible to become Merit Scholars. A committee of evaluators then study the finalists' school record, recommendations, and other data. Once the winners are selected, solely on the basis of merit, their financial needs are determined and the size of each scholarship is set.

What was the impact of all of this massive testing? LaVigne notes that the program has led to invidious comparisons between schools, "encouraged the awarding of scholarships on the basis of standardized test results rather than school records and local school recommendations," turned the attention of guidance personnel from terminal students to the college bound, and has raised the general issue of local control versus nationalizing influences (in this case private influences).[33]

In addition, the results have not been what the foundation anticipated. As early as 1958, John M. Stalnaker, then president of the National Merit Scholarship Corporation and a consultant to the FAE, testified in a House Education and Labor Committee hearing on the NDEA bill that well over 90 percent of the top 15,000 students taking the NMSQT go on to college regardless of their receiving a Merit Scholarship or not.[34] Apparently, the NMSQT did little to influence the college aspirations or plans of bright students.

Despite this admission by Stalnaker, his real purpose in appearing before the House committee was to convince Congress that a federally administered testing and scholarship program was not needed. The Ford Foundation already had in operation the NMSQT, which would serve quite well in identifying the talented youth needed by the nation in the

Cold War and space race. NMSQT, in effect, would operate as a national instrument of quality control whereby the elite students would be sorted out from the mass to serve the nation's brainpower requirements.

This bias was noted by LaVigne in her study, which found that "ability to attain success in the National Merit Scholarship Program is related to the socio-economic background of the students."[35] In apparent response to this kind of criticism, the foundation created the National Achievement Scholarship Program (NASP) in 1964, some nine years after the formation of the NMSQT. NASP was designed to identify through testing approximately 200 black students per year who could qualify for scholarships comparable in amount to those given under the NMSQT program. Compensatory in nature, the program allowed talented black youth some means of making up the difference that their educational and economic handicaps imposed on them.[36] The foundation allocated $8.1 million to this program.[37]

A further example of Ford's efforts to control the quality of the educational product was its involvement in another testing enterprise, the National Assessment of Educational Progress (NAEP). NAEP is designed to assess student performance outcomes in a number of fields: reading, writing, literature, science, mathematics, social studies, citizenship, art, music, and career and occupational development. Through the use of criterion-referenced tests given periodically to four age groups, NAEP is able to monitor national trends in the knowledge, understanding, skills, and attitudes scores in the ten subject areas. The results of these test findings can be used to identify subject attainment variations among various subgroups of the tested population. Thus the NAEP program becomes a diagnostic instrument which provides data on national educational performance.

The role of the Ford Foundation in creating NAEP was less known and subordinate to that of its sister foundation, the Carnegie Corporation of New York. The FAE and the foundation provided financial support totaling $1,336,000 to the Carnegie Corporation (headed by John Gardner) which initiated the idea in 1964 in cooperation with the U.S. Office of Education (headed by Francis Keppel).

When the idea of national assessment was first proposed, there was considerable opposition. Originally, Forrest H. Connor, executive secretary of the American Association of School Administrators, was alleged to have "held that the committee devising the assessment was a foundation-sponsored 'closed corporation' without clear responsibility to the public or representation by superintendents."[38] Furthermore, a federally sponsored assessment program was subject to dispute since education is legally decentralized. In response to such criticism, the Carnegie Corporation first decided to expand the exploratory committee which was originally created to study the feasibility of national assessment. The reconstituted committee was formed in 1968 and included representatives from all sectors of the educational world chosen by the institutions they represented.[39] As opposition to assessment decreased on the organizational front, the move was made to solicit the Education Commission of the States (ECS) to oversee the project. In 1969 the ECS, which was created and financed by the Ford and Carnegie foundations with additional aid from state legislatures, agreed to oversee the project. This nonfederal quasi-governmental body was of particular strategic importance to Carnegie and Ford as it became a primary means of coopting school administrators opposed to the NAEP program.

While national assessment has been a story of the political maneuverings of the Carnegie Corporation, the participation and support of the Ford Foundation was of no small consequence. The program was in accord with the efforts of the FAE and the Foundation to seek some measure of control over the quality of the American educational product. According to Woodring, the program offered an opportunity for the nation "to say with confidence just what or how much American children are learning or have learned."[40] But, perhaps of even greater significance, Woodring noted:

> The history of this program provides an excellent illustration of the value of philanthropic support of innovative projects. Although the need for a national assessment had existed for many years, the nature and extent of the opposition to it makes it apparent that it could not have been started without the support and encouragement of philanthropic funds.[41]

Ford funds contributed to this process of eliminating the opposition. The strategies used encompassed various sources of power available to influence the opposition. Both Carnegie and Ford collaborated to provide funds and machinery to set up the national assessment program. They created the Education Commission of the States to seek more cooperation from the various states as well as the American Association of School Administrators. Moreover, advocates of national assessment sought federal funds for their foundation-supported venture. These funds were received from the U.S. Office of Education.

In sum, the establishment of the NAEP was a result of cooperative strategies among foundations and the federal government, facilitated by the collaboration of members of the new educational elite (Gardner and Keppel) and the clever use of the ECS as a cooptive mechanism to overcome opposition to a national testing program. The object of all this maneuvering is the management and control of educational programs.

Promoting Efficient Schools

The Fund for the Advancement of Education and the Ford Foundation have had a long and continuing fascination with innovations designed to make the schools operate more efficiently. Over the years, the surface motivations for Ford programming in educational efficiency have been twofold. Originally, the FAE and foundation were concerned with the utilization of teachers during the teacher shortage of the 1950s and 1960s. More recently, the concern has been with making the schools cost-effective given declining enrollments, inflation, and taxpayers' reluctance to support school programs. Regardless of the reasons for these Ford projects, the innovations themselves took two forms. First, there was a series of managerial and administrative innovations designed to utilize teachers and facilities more efficiently. Second, there were technological innovations promoted as examples of educational automation.

The managerial and administrative innovations were numerous. The FAE sponsored projects between 1951 and 1961 on the use of teacher aides, team teaching, differentiated staffing, flexible modular scheduling, the nongraded school, and the "Trump Plan"—a combination of the above.

For example, the FAE promoted the use of teacher aides as a means of relieving the classroom teacher of more mundane clerical duties, thereby improving teacher performance. The FAE envisioned such staffing arrangements as being more efficient with the added bonus of solving the teacher shortage of an earlier decade. In order to demonstrate this assumption, it sponsored a teacher-aide program in Bay City, Michigan, in 1952. The results encouraged the FAE to make the following statements: "If further experimentation with the use of aides confirms these results and an adequate system of teachers' aides comes to be general practice, the school systems of the United States might possibly be operated with one-fourth to one-third fewer teachers than are now thought necessary. . . ."[42] Despite the rhetoric, the claim was never realized. Ford's strategy of using aides primarily as a labor-saving device—rather than to improve the quality of classroom experience aroused the opposition of teachers' groups who feared the loss of jobs.[43] In the end, aides have generally served to enrich the classroom environment.

Undaunted in its efforts to bring about the more efficient utilization of staff, Ford, beginning in 1956, gave funds to promote what became known as the "Trump Plan." The National Association of Secondary School Principals (NASSP) was selected to conduct a series of "experiments" using a variety of organizational innovations in over 100 junior and senior high schools. These innovations entailed teams of teachers differentiated according to function, rank, and salary; the organizing of students into large-group, small-group, and independent modes of study; the flexible use of time for classroom meetings and the flexible use of space and facilities to accommodate these staffing and grouping arrangements.

J. Lloyd Trump, an officer of the NASSP, served as chairman of the project and coauthored a widely circulated report on the various innovations adopted by the participating schools. The report, entitled *Focus on Change: Guide to Better Schools*, contained no experimental evidence regarding the impact of the innovations on student learning. The real motivation of the project was revealed through a caption on the front cover of *Focus on Change*: "How your tax dollar can go further."[44] Surprisingly, there was no evidence in the book to support the latter claim, either.

The role of the foundation and FAE in the above cases was largely promotional rather than experimental. The Ford philanthropies were convinced of the self-evident need to attack traditional patterns of school organization. As Woodring admits, "the Fund preferred whenever possible to give its support to action programs. . . . It was less prone than most foundations to solve problems by sponsoring research."[45] When describing its educational programs as "experimental," the Ford funds meant this "in the sense of trying something new." They supported few programs which could be characterized as carefully designed experimental (scientific) studies.[46] This promotional approach to educational change is summarized in the FAE published report *Decade of Experiment*, which reviews the work of the FAE in public education from 1951 to 1961:

> Those who insist on maintaining the status quo of school organi-
> zation—the self-contained classroom, the egg-crate school-
> house, the hallowed ratios—are clinging to external forms rather
> than preserving the essence of the pupil-teacher relationship. In
> meeting the emergency [teacher-shortage] in orthodox ways,
> they jeopardize the quality of education. . . .[47]

The attack on orthodoxy was not based on providing scientifically proven alternatives. The tactic was simply that of saying that if one could not be convinced of the efficacy of an FAE-promoted innovation such as team teaching, one might be moved to change in order to avoid the label of educational traditionalist.

The FAE merely *assumed* that a new organizational pattern will somehow serve as a solution to the teacher shortage or result in good teaching and better learning. But as Shaplin observes, the "organization itself is unimportant and guarantees nothing."[48] Essentially, this is the same point Silberman makes in regard to team teaching: "By itself, however, putting teachers together in teams does not necessarily mean that the curriculum or the teaching will be improved, only that a new kind of division of labor

will be put into effect. . . ."[49] The point, of course, is that the foundation
preferred to use shallow promotional rhetoric rather than substantive
experimental evidence to advance its programs.

The programs described above—teacher aides, the Trump Plan, and
team-teaching—typify the FAE approach to educational innovation as
the "experimental wing" of the foundation. In most cases these projects
were small-scale, piecemeal attempts at stimulating change. Later when
the foundation became responsible for funding programs in public education, the amount of money increased in accordance with the greater
resources of the parent body. This move was exemplified by the foundation's organizing and coordinating all of the separately developed FAE
innovations into what it called its Comprehensive School Improvement
Program (CSIP). In this program more than $30 million was invested in
twenty-five projects between 1960 and 1970, nearly twice the amount spent
by the FAE between 1951 and 1961.[50] According to the foundation, CSIP
was designed to bring

> together a sufficient number of the new practices to create a
> *critical mass*—a chain reaction of change that would overcome
> the inertia of school systems and produce significantly different
> educational institutions. The new program was to provide a
> capstone for the projects of the past decade, consolidating gains
> and encouraging large-scale implementation.[51]

In spite of these intentions, the results were less than encouraging, as
the CSIP report admits. Many of the projects suffered from both conceptual and operational errors. Conceptually, CSIP tended to focus upon the
manipulation of variables within the school rather than including outside
factors such as parental and financial support from the community. In a
systems sense, CSIP was not comprehensive enough. In the same vein, the
program's "preoccupation with efficiency and new teaching styles" initially avoided broader social issues such as equality of opportunity,
educational philosophy, curriculum relevance, public accountability,
etc.[52] Operationally, many of the programs had difficulty with high
turnover rates among project directors, failure to specify project objectives, inability to diffuse innovations within school districts, and an
inability to succeed in urban compared to suburban districts.[53]

Indeed, the foundation may have been victimized by its own promotional rhetoric and cavalier approach to educational experimentation.
"Since the emphasis was on implementing new practices," the report
concedes, "evaluation and research did not receive high priority, even
though sizable amounts of money were spent for these purposes."[54] The
report then goes on to state:

> Project objectives were stated in such vague and global terms
> that it was impossible to say with any certainty whether or not
> they had been reached. Goals were often stated in *input* or
> *process* terms, on the assumption that changes, *per se* would
> produce better education. Relatively little emphasis was placed
> on the actual outcome of the projects.[55]

The conclusion seems all too obvious. The FAE and Foundation
embarked on a series of heavily funded organizational innovations for the
public schools in response to the teacher shortage of the 1950s and 1960s.
Instead of presenting these innovations as testable alternatives to existing
practices, they were simply promoted as self-evidently superior to them.
Although FAE officers were skeptical of the need to encourage educational research as part of their innovative programming, in retrospect this
seems to have been a mistake. Their programs might have gained greater
legitimacy even if the research findings indicated no significant difference.
Whatever the results of such studies, Ford could thereby promote the
cause of both educational research and meaningful educational change. In
the absence of research evidence, why should public monies be spent on
costly innovations the foundation promoted?

Moreover, by continuing to cultivate an image as an "experimental"
change agent, the expectation was that research was an integral part of
Ford programming. But as Woodring admits, this expectation was not
intended. At best one could say this experimental image was confusing; at
worst, deceptive.

A more recent example of Ford support of organizational reform in
education has been its funding of alternative school programs. Because of
the inherent instability of private alternatives, the foundation has concentrated on promoting alternatives within the public school system. In a
report entitled *Matters of Choice*, the foundation details the variety of
programs it supported. Promoted on the basis "of their ability to correct
mistakes and respond rapidly and directly to the needs of their constituen-
cies," the foundation claims the overall record of alternative schools is
one "of success and vitality in providing a wide range of educational
experiences and options."[56]

The report characterized the public school system as an intransigent
bureaucracy: "it bends, absorbs, and springs back to its original form."
Noting that the CSIP had failed to make substantive changes in the
education system, the report hopes that improvement will occur by
providing choices and options for students and their parents.[57] Interestingly, the report did not note the failure of the Ford experiments with
school decentralization and community control in Oceanhill-Brownsville,
New York, to be discussed below. Apparently, alternative education is

safer, if not less controversial, than community control of the schools in large urban areas.

Typical of Ford, the *Matters of Choice* report is not clear on what improvements alternative education will bring: will choices improve student learning or will choices serve to make the educational bureaucracy more responsive? The report gives a few isolated examples that the latter goal is occurring with some difficulty in a few schools. However, virtually no evidence is given as to whether the academic performance of students is improved as a result of enrolling in alternative as opposed to traditional school programs. With this, as with other programs it has sponsored, the foundation has demonstrated its interest to be in cosmetic rather than in substantive changes in the schools.

Arnove and Strout indicate two principal results of the alternative school movement. One has been the creation of a new tracking system whereby alternative schools have been used to "dump" troublemakers or "cream" the talented and gifted from the regular school program. In many cases, alternative schools have served to resegregate previously integrated schools. The second result has been to use the alternative schools as magnet schools with special programs and facilities to attract children from different ethnic, racial and socioeconomic groups. However, school systems have used the magnet schools as a delaying tactic to forestall the eventuality of mandatory busing to achieve system-wide integration. Many magnet schools do not attract racially balanced student bodies, and those that do often isolate students by race within the school.[58]

THE TECHNOLOGICAL SOLUTION

Educational technology represents another programmatic area the foundation entered without a clear conception of the limitations and implications of the innovation it was promoting. The clearest example of misguided enthusiasm for technology is that of instructional television (ITV). In 1957 the FAE published Alexander J. Stoddard's *Schools for Tomorrow: An Educator's Blueprint*.[59] It describes how instructional television could be utilized in softening the impact of the teacher shortage. Stoddard, who was former superintendent of schools in Los Angeles and former chairman of the Educational Policies Commission of the National Education Association, was given funds by the FAE to study how to alleviate the critical shortage of teachers and buildings. In his FAE published report, Stoddard advocates the widespread use of ITV to solve these problems.

Anticipating the fears of some who believe television in education endangers the teacher's job, Stoddard asserts:

> Already there are those who talk of television in education as
> putting teachers out of jobs. Is it likely that multiplying means of
> communication will make teachers less necessary? It should en-
> hance their importance. One purpose of television is to help
> enrich teaching—to bring something worthwhile into the class-
> room or school that might not be possible otherwise.[60]

Despite this reasonable statement regarding television usage, Stoddard's
proposals contradict his stated purpose of proposing a plan whereby
classroom television would eliminate a sizable number of teaching positions. His plan seeks to determine "whether a high level of teaching
efficiency can be attained with fewer trained teachers than would be
involved in the usual school organization."[61]

For example, on the secondary level he proposes that a regular teacher
teach two televised classes a day to 250 to 300 students, followed by two
small group discussion classes. An assistant would teach in both regular-
sized and small-group classes. Through this plan, Stoddard predicts a
saving of six teachers on this level per school.[62]

In looking at the savings on a national level, Stoddard feels that 50,000
elementary and 50,000 secondary teachers might be absorbed through his
plan: "It is thrilling to contemplate what could be done to improve the
profession of teaching, to raise the level of school efficiency, to provide
badly needed augmented services for young people in the schools, with
approximately $500,000,000 that would be involved in the absorbed
positions at all school levels."[63] The Stoddard plan represented another in
a long line of promotions by the FAE and the foundation to solve the
teacher shortage.

Instructional and educational television became a major commitment
for the Ford philanthropies. The amount committed to educational and
instructional television in all its varieties came to over $100 million.[64]
Television was promoted not on the educational basis of enriching the
content of the curriculum but on the technocratic basis of increasing the
efficient utilization of teachers and staff.

What was the impact of this enormous investment in instructional
television? In a study commissioned by the FAE, Murphy and Gross,
respectively consultant to and staff member of the FAE, were asked
whether ITV made a worthwhile contribution to education:

> The short answer to such a sweeping question would probably
> probably have to be "No." Whether measured by the numbers of
> students affected, or by the quality of the product, or by the
> advancement of learning, televised teaching is still in a rudimen-
> tary stage of development. The medium can take credit for

helping understaffed schools to cope with ever increasing enrollments. But television has not transformed education, nor has it
significantly improved the learning of most students. In short,
TV is still far from fulfilling its obvious promise. Television is *in*
education all right, but it is still not *of* education.[65]

Yet what is omitted from these insights is a frank assessment of the Ford
role in promoting ITV for the wrong reasons. Ford conceived ITV as an
automation device to increase educational efficiency in a time of increasing
school enrollments. This approach was exemplified by John K. Weiss,
former treasurer and assistant vice-president of the FAE, who testified
before the Senate Labor and Welfare Committee in 1958 that

[ITV] can. . . provide quality education with less teachers than
we had previously believed; that we can obtain quality learning
results with less school classrooms and less college classrooms
than were once thought necessary; and that we can get more and
better educational results per dollar than is possible through
conventional teaching methods.[66]

By encouraging ITV in this narrow technocratic sense, Ford miscon-
ceived its potential as a "window to the world," as a means to enrich and
expand the quality of curricular offerings in the schools. As Murphy and
Gross concede, it "might have been better if greater attention and resources had gone, first, into programming that incorporated new ideas in
curriculum and methods. . . ."[67] Doubtless, this conceptual flaw contributed to the failure to implement ITV on a broad scale and to use it as an
effective teaching device.

Equality of Opportunity

During the 1950s and 1960s, the Fund for the Advancement of Education
and the Ford Foundation were primarily concerned with responding to
Cold War pressures for manpower development. The schools came under
attack by critics who believed the schools were not providing enough well-
trained manpower, especially in the sciences and mathematics. The FAE
and the foundation reacted to this criticism by developing programs to
promote academic excellence and by introducing technological innovations to relieve the critical teacher shortage. Focusing on the schools as
the means of solving Cold War and space race problems, the FAE and the
foundation ignored other more significant social trends and problems that
were clearly emerging. Ignored were the growing demands of blacks
seeking greater equality of educational opportunity. Also ignored were

the problems of the so-called "educationally disadvantaged." Significant recognition and reaction to these problems did not occur until after destructive outbreaks of social unrest occurred in the late 1960s. Thus, despite the claims that the FAE and the foundation were "innovators" in education, they largely made belated moves to "solve" fully developed social problems once they affected the schools.

Beginning with the foundation's first policy report of 1949, which stated as a goal "the reduction of economic, religious, and racial barriers to equality of educational opportunity at all levels," [68] the foundation demonstrated at least a verbal interest in this cause. After the Fund for the Advancement of Education was created it was not until the second report in 1954 that an effort to secure equalization of educational opportunity was described as one of the five major educational goals of the FAE.[69] These concerns, however, must be interpreted as mere lip-service if one compares FAE funding of programs in other areas with its stated concern for minorities in education. From the standpoint of major financial commitment on the part of Ford, minority programs did not receive priority status until after 1967. For example, during its existence, Woodring reports, the FAE granted $4,549,800 for "fellowships and other programs designed primarily for the purpose of improving the educational opportunities of negroes." The figure compares favorably with the $4,939,483 expended on the early admission and advanced standing programs by the FAE during the same period.[70] These were programs which benefited mostly bright middle-class white students from prestigious private and public schools. But when these expenditures for expanding Negro educational opportunities are compared with the overall grants of $60,778,145 made between 1955 and 1966 by the FAE, they constitute only 6 percent of the total.[71]

What these figures indicate is that in spite of a continuing verbal commitment to equal educational opportunity on the part of the FAE, the financial commitment was by no means as impressive. Perhaps anticipating this criticism, the FAE noted that no philanthropic foundation could have a large and immediate impact on the problem of equal educational opportunity without rapidly dissipating its funds: ". . . the Fund could, however, and did undertake pilot studies and demonstrations to point the way to large-scale solutions."[72] This statement was written in 1961 and therefore probably represents an uneasy recognition of a decade of neglect by the FAE in failing to make equality of educational opportunity a more important priority in its programming. For example, even when the FAE was phased out in 1967, education of disadvantaged minorities was still not the most important priority of the foundation's programs in public education.[73] In that year $15,042,027 was granted for public education projects including $5,100,000 to support the National Merit Scholarship

Corporation. Approximately $607,000 was granted for programs affecting disadvantaged minorities.[74]

The choice made by the FAE and the Foundation to give less priority to the problems of disadvantaged minorities seeking equality of educational opportunity was made in the face of considerable efforts by civil rights groups to agitate for enforcement of the Supreme Court decision of 1954 in the South and to expand their efforts in the North in a battle against *de facto* school segregation. While Ford chose to respond to the more sensational criticism of the schools generated by the launching of *Sputnik*, the more fundamental question facing America was whether racial integration could be achieved in our public schools. This problem literally entailed a basic social reconstruction of our society. Yet the Ford Foundation and the FAE, self-proclaimed leaders and innovators of educational change, chose to ignore this issue in favor of promoting the more popular causes of "excellence" and "efficiency" in public education. When an independent and critical voice was most needed, the FAE and the Foundation followed the prevailing forces which accused the schools of failing the nation in the military and space races with the Soviets.

Initially the FAE seemed committed to the goal of racial integration for the schools. It was responsible for the publication of Harry S. Ashmore's report *The Negro and the Schools*, issued on May 16, 1954, the day before the Supreme Court decision of *Brown* v. *Topeka*.[75] The book attempted to survey the status of biracial schools in both the South and the North. However, instead of serving as a prod to Ford action in this area, the book was left to stand by itself, i.e., an information source for those concerned about racial segregation. The FAE continued with this reportorial approach by creating the Southern Education Reporting Service in 1954 in order "to provide accurate and objective information on developments in southern schools resulting from the Supreme Court decision."[76] This cautious approach to the problem allowed Ford to appear to be concerned about the issue, while avoiding the more difficult task of helping to promote racial integration in the schools.

It was not until the mid-to-late 1960s that Ford began to renew its concern with the problems of racial minorities and the disadvantaged. This was, of course, a delayed response to the civil rights activism in the South and the outbreak of violence in northern urban ghetto communities. It was at this point that the foundation shifted what little commitment it had toward school integration to a strategy of compensatory education.

For example, after the Comprehensive School Improvement Program had been in operation for three years, the foundation began to realize the needs of the disadvantaged and shifted the focus of CSIP to these concerns. Thus the program began to fund projects in "school systems with large concentrations of disadvantaged students and less financial resources, rather than the districts already considered to be the leaders in education."[77] This shift in emphasis, however, was mitigated by the CSIP projects in the South. Rather than choose black colleges and universities as fiscal agents for these programs, southern white universities were chosen. Even though the programs were intended to help black school children, the foundation conformed to "existing political and organizational realities." [78] What were these realities? The low prestige and administrative inexperience of black colleges and the fear of alienating moderate white leaders led Ford to grant $12 million to the white colleges. As the CSIP report concedes, there were grounds for criticism:

> . . . the decision was also partly out of habit, partly a judgement of which organization seemed to hold the power of educational change. Clearly, the black institutions could not develop the necessary resources without outside aid. And almost as clearly, leaders of the white institutions . . . often lacked vigorous commitment to the goal of equal educational opportunity.[79]

Whether the programs were in the North or South, or in urban or rural districts, the approach was to compensate students for their disadvantaged background by enriching their experiences through the various managerial and technological innovations the foundation had been promoting up to that time. More important, the compensatory nature of the CSIP projects reveals an underlying bias. As Kenneth Clark observed, such programs assume the minority child to be culturally deprived or inferior. Such an assumption "might be the controlling fact which restricts the educational responsiveness of children to the alleged educational experience."[80] In other words, the victim is blamed in a program of compensatory education rather than the institutional structures, which are in greater need of change.

By 1967 the foundation had entered a newer phase in its programming for equality of educational opportunity:

> For several years, the Foundation has supported a variety of approaches to widespread educational failure of children in deprived urban and rural sections—remedial programs and team teaching, for example. This year, the Foundation turned to another aspect of the problem: more direct and effective parent and community participation in school affairs.[81]

Thus began a series of highly controversial events culminating in the New York City teachers' strike of 1968. In effect, the foundation moved farther away from integration as a goal for the schools, and it now believed that community control was a more productive strategy than compensatory education for achieving the goal of equality of educational opportunity.

Mario Fantini, then a program officer of the foundation and chief architect of its programs to support decentralized schools in New York City, provides the rationale for this shift. He repudiates both compensatory education and integration as a means to overcome equality of educational opportunity. He reiterated Clark's argument that

> ... compensatory education is a prescription that deals with *symptoms*, with strengthened doses of prescriptions that have been ineffective before—more trips, more remedial reading, etc.—without differences. . . . The assumption is that the schools need to do somewhat more for disadvantaged pupils, but it does not presume that the school itself is in need of wholesale reexamination.[82]

In regard to integration as a solution, he asserts:

> In most urban settings, integration has proved elusive, if not impossible. The failure to achieve integration to any significant extent was due, first, to massive white resistance. Now, it is even less likely to occur in this generation because of the growing concentration in the inner city of blacks and other minorities.[83]

Fantini claims that there was an ideological shift among many blacks in regard to the efficacy of integration. Many blacks despaired of continuing the integration fight because of the intransigence of whites. Moreoever, many perceived the integration movement as clothed in condescension—with integration the option of the white community. Finally, a dependent status for blacks was perpetuated by the notion that the way to help black school children was to sit them beside white children. By contrast, community control, participation in decision-making, entails a desire by blacks to develop a collective identity and to seek control of their own destiny.[84] In effect, this movement toward local determination of education is seen as a means toward separate black self-development and the eventual reconnection with the white community on equal terms.

Fantini's rationale misrepresents the motives of large segments of the black urban community. For example, it was apparent that the black separatist movement represented a militant black power wing of the black community. There were many black moderates such as A. Philip Randolph and Bayard Rustin, as well as followers of the NAACP, who were committed to school integration. Furthermore, by catering to the separatist demands of black militants, this rationale played into the hands of white racists who were also resisting integration. Rather than exerting leadership to appeal to moderate influences in both black and white communities, the foundation overreacted to the racist appeals of extremists from both sides.

Moreover, Fantini's arguments at that time amount to a repudiation of the 1954 Supreme Court decision. After having taken credit for anticipating that decision with the Ashmore report, the foundation then committed itself to compensatory education. When it was found that this alternative did not have the desired results, it moved to a form of community segregation by promoting school decentralization and community control of the schools. In both programs the foundation never confronted the implications of the 1954 court case or the implications of the Coleman Report[85] to end inferior education for minority students and to end racial isolation through effective school integration.

The foundation refused to make any distinction between the separatist and integrationist positions. As foundation president McGeorge Bundy put it, "the Ford Foundation will work with Negro leaders of good will and peaceful purpose without any anguished measurement of their position on the issue of a separated power of blackness as against the continuing claim to integration."[86] Apparently using this statement as its guiding rationale, the foundation in 1967 initiated a series of grants to three "experimental" school districts in New York City neighborhoods where residents (mostly black and Puerto Rican) were dissatisfied with the quality of their local schools. The grants were designed to aid the organization of locally selected governing boards and the planning of improved school programs.[87]

Also in 1967, Mayor John Lindsay of New York appointed Bundy to head a panel of private citizens to prepare recommendations. Its purpose was to decentralize the entire school system of New York. Later that year the panel submitted a report to the mayor entitled *Reconnection for Learning: A Community School System for New York City.*[88] The report contained detailed recommendations for decentralization as well as a draft of a bill to be submitted to the Albany legislature for that purpose. In 1969 the state legislature voted to decentralize the schools into thirty-one local districts. The state version was more cautious than the Bundy draft with respect to delegating power to the local districts, especially in the areas of budget, the hiring of teachers, and the governance of secondary schools. Control of the latter was retained, for the most part, by the central board of education.

The foundation's activities in New York City school decentralization raised many questions. For example, its support of anti–teachers' union activities in one of its funded demonstration districts and its attempt at influencing legislation by writing a draft for the decentralization bill were highly criticized.[89] The latter activity would now be in clear violation of federal statutes which prohibit foundations from lobbying to influence legislation.

Since its involvement in the New York City decentralization controversy, the Ford Foundation has continued to vacillate on the question of promoting equality of educational opportunity. Between 1970 and 1977, it was only in 1974 that the foundation allocated more funds to this problem than to any of its other projects in public education.[90] Except for 1974, a more important priority has been a series of grants to improve the leadership training of school administrators and policymakers. Apparently such programs may create a corps of administrators more disposed toward accepting and/or implementing educational "innovations."

Despite these priorities, the foundation has nevertheless made a perceptible shift in its programming for equal educational opportunity. In 1970 and 1971 the primary interest was still in the area of school decentralization and community participation in school decision-making. However, in 1971 the foundation began supporting efforts to reform school financing in order to promote its version of greater equality of opportunity. This long-standing problem[91] came to the attention of the foundation as a result of the California Supreme Court decision of *Serrano* v. *Priest*. In that case, the Court found the state school funding scheme to be discriminatory because poorer districts could not support schools on the same financial basis as wealthier ones. Using this case as a stimulus, "the Foundation has sought to strengthen the intellectual resources focusing on school finance problems, to improve understanding of public policy alternatives, and to assist various national organizations engaged in reform activities."[92] Specifically, the foundation has funded various legal groups and law schools throughout the country (such as the Education Law Center, Lawyers' Committee for Civil Rights under Law, Stanford University, University of California-Berkeley) in order to challenge the inequitable distribution of both tax burdens and educational services.

Between 1973 and 1977 Ford funded these programs at a higher level than any of its other projects dealing with equal educational opportunity. As measured by allocations of funds, projects related to school desegregation and discrimination were of lesser importance.[93]

Ford efforts to make school finance and the delivery of educational services more equitable have produced unanticipated outcomes. The emerging role of state educational bureaucracies in monitoring these reforms has increased their authority relative to that of local school districts. Consequently, it has become more difficult for parents and citizens to have a voice in school governance and policymaking on the local level. As Kirst suggests, "in many ways school finance reform is an elitist movement. It was not galvanized by an overwhelming bottom-up demand from the populace or professional educators. It came from an alliance of educational finance scholars, lawyers, foundation officers, the USOE and the NIE." [94] Thus Ford has found it necessary to support projects which help to improve relations between the schools and the public.[95] From this perspective, the need for corrective action to involve citizens becomes necessary only to affirm and support the initiatives taken by the foundation and its allies.

School finance reform programs have a progressive ring. As a matter of fact, school finance reform may become coopted by those who do not seek equity in the distribution of school funds but rather seek the reduction of educational spending and the elimination of "frills." This has become clear in New Jersey, where the foundation supported school finance reform through the courts. Hailed as a means to redress the inequities between poor urban districts and the more affluent suburbs, the *Robinson v. Cahill* decision has not accomplished this end. Local school taxes have been cut or "capped" as the state has assumed greater responsibilities for school finance. But there has not been a redistribution of school aid from wealthy to poorer districts. It appears that cutting taxes is more appealing to the public than equity in school aid.

The policies of the Ford Foundation in regard to equality of educational opportunity have been marked by a general avoidance of promoting racial integration in the schools. Not that the foundation has been opposed to such efforts (it has always given integration some token support over the years); rather, it has found other policies more attractive. Compensatory education, decentralization, and school finance reform, all heavily supported by Ford, do not represent direct attempts at desegregating the schools. In each case, the racial composition of the schools remains intact. It is quite apparent that the Ford Foundation has been more interested in exploring and demonstrating alternatives to school integration while appearing committed to the cause of equality of educational opportunity.

Conclusion

Although this chapter touches upon a sample of the many programs developed by the FAE and the Ford Foundation, some basic patterns to their funding in public education clearly emerge. Foundation officers are a part of an elite educational establishment which has had a powerful impact on the formation of national education policy. The FAE systematically favored elite universities in granting funds for the reform of teacher education, the most important priority of the FAE in the 1950s and 1960s. Moreover, the foundation contributed to the formation of an academic meritocracy when it created and funded the National Merit Scholarship Program.

Throughout their existence, the Ford philanthropies have strongly supported the use of managerial and technological innovations as solutions to substantive educational problems. In all cases—including ITV, teacher aides, and team teaching—programs were promoted on the basis of their being cost efficient. Efficiency became the goal of educational reform. The result was a technocratic approach to educational management.

Moreover, when the FAE and the foundation supported educational innovations, they tended to be more interested in promotion than in finding an empirical basis for change. One promotional tactic was to ridicule existing practices. At the same time, the foundation employed its substantial resources to line up prominent spokespersons on its side to promote its brand of change in public education.

Finally, despite the rhetoric, promotionalism, and publicity generated by Ford, the FAE and the foundation have not played a forward-looking role in educational programming or policy. Their roles may be powerful and significant, but in all cases they have *responded* to larger sociopolitical developments rather than *anticipated* them. Thus they succumbed to Cold War pressures which favored programs for the gifted in science and mathematics. When the civil rights movement and urban crisis finally erupted, the foundation abandoned its old priorities and sought to find new programs. Yet these new programs all avoided a direct confrontation with the issue of racial integration.

As the foundation itself concedes, many of its most heavily funded programs failed, including the fifth-year teacher education program, instructional television, and the Comprehensive School Improvement Program. Rather than blame an unyielding educational bureaucracy for these failures, Ford should examine its own assumptions, modes of operation, and the implications of its stances. Whether such a self-examination will prove beneficial is problematic given the relatively unaccountable position of the Ford Foundation itself.

The recent appointment of Franklin A. Thomas, a black, as president of the foundation has generated considerable euphoria both within and outside of the foundation. As Kenneth B. Clark said, "this may be the Ford Foundation's most significant and important demonstration project."[96] Thomas comes from the Bedford-Stuyvesant Restoration Corporation, a Ford-funded community rehabilitation organization in Brooklyn, which he headed for nearly ten years. He is a graduate of Columbia College and Columbia Law School in New York. Just what direction the foundation will take as a result of the appointment is open to speculation. According to Alexander Heard, president of the foundation's board of trustees, Thomas was chosen for his intellectual and leadership capacity rather than for his identification with any foundation program objectives.[97]

With new leadership comes the opportunity for the Ford Foundation to pursue new—possibly less elitist and technocratic—directions. But fundamental change in foundation ideology and modes of operation is unlikely in the light of past funding patterns. Substantial change in Ford Foundation policies is likely to occur only when its prominent role in maintaining the existing power structure in America is effectively curtailed.

Notes

1. Gordon N. Mackenzie, "Curricular Change: Participants, Power and Processes," in Mathew Miles (ed.), *Innovation in Education* (New York: Teachers College Press, 1964), pp. 399–424.
2. Paul Woodring, *Investment in Innovation: An Historical Appraisal of the Fund for the Advancement of Education* (Boston: Little, Brown and Company, 1970), p. 211.
3. *Annual Reports* of the Ford Foundation, 1965–1977 inclusive.
4. Thomas H. Buckman, *The Foundation Directory*, 5th ed., edited by Mariana O. Lewis (New York: The Foundation Center, 1975). p. xxiii.
5. Ibid.
6. These purposes are defined in the *Reports* of the FAE since 1951 and in the *Annual Reports* of the Ford Foundation.
7. Patricia Cayo Sexton, *The American School* (Englewood Cliffs, N.J.: Prentice-Hall, Inc., 1967), p. 33.
8. The Fund for the Advancement of Education, *A Decade of Experiment: The Fund for the Advancement of Education 1951-1961* (New York: FAE, 1961), p. 19.
9. The Fund for the Advancement of Education, *Teachers for Tommorrow*, Bulletin No. 2 (New York: FAE, 1955).
10. Ibid., p. 21.
11. Ibid., pp. 32–33.
12. Ibid., p. 31.
13. Fund for the Advancement of Education, *Annual Report, 1951–1952* (New York: FAE, 1952), p. 21.
14. Fund for the Advancement of Education, *Decade of Experiment*, p. 28.
15. Ibid.
16. For a thorough study of the Arkansas controversy see Richard Colvard, "The Colleges and the 'Arkansas Purchase' Controversy," in Miles, *Innovation in Education*, pp. 117–155.
17. Fund for the Advancement of Education, *A Report for 1952-1954* (New York: FAE, 1954), p. 26.

18. "The Ford Foundation Teacher Education Proposal to Arkansas, A Statement by the American Association of Colleges for Teacher Education, Chicago, February, 1952," in *Progressive Education* 29 (March 1952): 174–175.
19. I. L. Kandel, "An Experiment or a Revival?" *School and Society* 76 (August 2, 1952): 75.
20. C. M. Clarke, "The Ford Foundation—Arkansas Experiment," *Journal of Teacher Education* 3 (December 1952): 260–264.
21. Colvard, "The Colleges and the 'Arkansas Purchase' Controversy," pp. 119–120.
22. Woodring, *Investment in Innovation,* p. 125.
23. Fund for the Advancement of Education, *Decade of Experiment*, pp. 37–38.
24. James C. Stone, *Breakthrough in Teacher Education* (San Francisco: Jossey-Bass, Inc., Publishers, 1968), p. 15.
25. Woodring, *Investment in Innovation*, p. 216; Ford Foundation, *Annual Reports* for 1955, 1962, 1967.
26. Fund for the Advancement of Education, *A Report for 1957–1959* (New York: FAE, 1959), p. 5.
27. U.S. Congress, Senate, *Science and Education for National Defense*. Hearings before the Committee on Labor and Public Welfare, 85th Cong., (Washington, D.C.: U.S. Government Printing Office, 1958), pp. 1247–1269.
28. Ibid., p. 1163.
29. Ibid., pp. 1170–1171.
30. The Ford Foundation, Annual Report, 1955 (New York: the same, 1956), p. 14.
31. The Ford Foundation, *Annual Report, 1962* (New York: the same, 1963), p. 11.
32. The Ford Foundation, *Annual Report, 1967* (New York: the same, 1968), p. 28.
33. Lorraine LaVigne, "The National Merit Scholarship Program," in Ronald F. Campbell and Robert A. Bunnell (eds.), *Nationalizing Influences on Secondary Education* (Chicago: Midwest Administration Center, University of Chicago, 1963), pp. 54–56.
34. U.S. Congress, House, *Scholarship and Loan Program*, Hearings before the Committee on Education and Labor, 85th Cong. (Washington, D.C.: U.S. Government Printing Office, 1958), pp. 1481–1484.
35. LaVigne, "The National Merit Scholarship Program," p. 53.
36. The Ford Foundation, *Annual Report, 1964* (New York: the same, 1965), p. 11.
37. Ibid., and the Ford Foundation, *Annual Report, 1967*, p. 28.
38. *New York Times*, February 11, 1969, p. 68.
39. David E. Weischadle, "The Carnegie Corporation of New York: A Study in Educational Politics" (unpublished Ed.D. dissertation, Rutgers University, 1970), pp. 308–311; also see his chapter in this book.
40. Woodring, *Investment in Innovation*, p. 168.
41. Ibid., p. 171.

42. The Fund for the Advancement of Education, *A Report for 1952–1954* (New York: FAE, 1954), p. 29.
43. Woodring, *Investment in Innovation*, p. 149.
44. J. Lloyd Trump and Dorsey Baynham, *Focus on Change: Guide to Better Schools* (Chicago: Rand McNally, 1961).
45. Woodring, *Investment in Innovation*, p. 236.
46. Ibid., p. 237.
47. The Fund for the Advancement of Education, *A Decade of Experiment: The Fund for the Advancement of Education 1951–1961* (New York: FAE, 1961), p. 47.
48. Judson T. Shaplin, "Description and Definition of Team Teaching," in Judson T. Shaplin and Henry F. Olds, Jr. (eds.), *Team Teaching* (New York: Harper and Row, Publishers, 1964), p. 12.
49. Charles E. Silberman, *Crisis in the Classroom: The Remaking of American Education* (New York: Random House, 1970), p. 161.
50. Ford Foundation, *A Foundation Goes to School* (New York: the same, 1972), pp. 8, 13.
51. Ibid., p. 9.
52. Ibid., p. 40.
53. Ibid., pp. 40–43.
54. Ibid., p. 12.
55. Ibid.
56. The Ford Foundation, *Matters of Choice* (New York: the same, 1974), p. 4.
57. Ibid.
58. Robert Arnove and Toby Strout, "Alternative Schools and Cultural Pluralism: Promise and Reality," *Educational Research Quarterly* 2 (Winter 1978): 74–95; also their "The Evolution, Uses, and Implications of Alternative Education," mimeo (Bloomington: School of Education, Indiana University, 1977).
59. Alexander J. Stoddard, *Schools for Tomorrow: An Educator's Blueprint* (New York: The Fund for the Advancement of Education, 1957).
60. Ibid., p. 30.
61. Ibid., p. 43.
62. Ibid., pp. 48–50.
63. Ibid., p. 51.
64. Judith Murphy and Ronald Gross, *Learning by Television* (New York: The Fund for the Advancement of Education, 1966), pp. 11–12.
65. Murphy and Gross, *Learning by Television*, p. 9.
66. U.S. Congress, Senate, *Science and Education for National Defense*, p. 1252.
67. Murphy and Gross, *Learning by Television*, p. 65.
68. The Ford Foundation, *Report of the Study for the Ford Foundation on Policy and Program* (Detroit: the same, 1949), p. 79.
69. Fund for the Advancement of Education, *A Report for 1952–1954*, pp. 5, 8–13.
70. Woodring *Investment in Innovation*, p. 216.
71. Ibid., p. 211.

72. Fund for the Advancement of Education, *A Decade of Experiment*, p. 19.
73. The Ford Foundation, *Annual Report, 1967*, pp. 90–94.
74. Ibid.
75. Harry S. Ashmore, *The Negro and the Schools* (Chapel Hill: University of North Carolina Press, 1954).
76. Fund for the Advancement of Education, *Decade of Experiment*, p. 78.
77. Ford Foundation, *A Foundation Goes to School*, p. 11.
78. Ibid., p. 28.
79. Ibid.
80. Kenneth Clark, *Dark Ghetto* (New York: Harper & Row, Torchbooks, 1965), p. 147.
81. Ford Foundation, *Annual Report, 1967*, p. 27.
82. Mario D. Fantini, "Alternatives for Urban School Reform," A Ford Foundation Reprint from *Harvard Educational Review* 38 (Winter 1968): 4.
83. Mario Fantini, Marillyn Gittell, and Richard Magat, *Community Control and the Urban School* (New York: Praeger Publishers, 1970), p. 35.
84. Ibid. pp. 40–41.
85. James Coleman *et al.*, *Equality of Educational Opportunity* (Washington, D.C.: U.S. Office of Education, 1966).
86. Ford Foundation, *Annual Report, 1967*, p. 4.
87. Ibid., pp. 27, 91.
88. Mayor's Advisory Panel on Decentralization of New York City Schools, *Recommendation for Learning: A Community School System for New York City* (New York: The Mayor's Panel, 1967).
89. Martin Mayer, *The Teachers Strike New York, 1968* (New York: Perennial Library, Harper & Row, Publishers, 1969); and U.S. Congress, House Committee on Ways and Means, *Tax Reform, 1969, Hearings*, 91st Cong. (Washington, D.C.: U.S. Government Printing Office, 1969), p. 445.
90. See Ford Foundation, *Annual Reports* for 1970 through 1977 inclusive.
91. See Patricia Cayo Sexton, *Education and Income: Inequalities in our Public Schools* (New York: Compass Books, The Viking Press, Inc., 1961); and Charles S. Benson, *The Cheerful Prospect* (Boston: Houghton Mifflin, 1965).
92. The Ford Foundation, Paying For Schools and Colleges (New York: the same, 1976), p. 4.
93. See Ford Foundation, *Annual Reports* for 1973 through 1977 inclusive.
94. Michael Kirst, "The New Politics of State Education Finance," *Phi Delta Kappan* 60 (February 1979): 428.
95. Ford Foundation, *Annual Report, 1977* (New York: The Foundation 1977), p. 8.
96. *New York Times*, February 4, 1979, p. B4.
97. *New York Times*, January 30, 1979, p. B3.

David E. Weischadle

The Carnegie Corporation and the Shaping of American Educational Policy

It is the purpose of this chapter to examine the origins, evolution, and implications of Carnegie Corporation participation in public education. Particular attention will be given to the Cold War era, 1945–1970. The study will illustrate that the corporation funded projects in accordance with technocratic and elitist assumptions which reflected Carnegie concern with U.S. national strength. The corporation used its financial resources and organizational prominence to capture a national policymaking role. In this role it set forth and helped implement policies which responded to the concerns and vested interests of Carnegie leadership.

In the past three decades, Ford, Carnegie, Rockefeller, Sloan, Markle, Kettering, and Danforth have become key watchwords in the vocabulary of educational change. These philanthropic organizations—trust funds enjoying special tax privileges—are often viewed with great public respect. For many, a foundation name attached to a project signifies independence, reliability, and truth.[1]

However, as I will suggest in this chapter, public esteem often unwarranted, grows out of a general lack of knowledge about how these organizations function. Few realize that far more is involved than just the symbolic appearance of a credit line; philanthropic participation in a project can also have great influence on shaping the direction and outcomes of a project. Through their funding efforts, foundations exert undue influence and promote adoption of policies which are primarily in the interest of the American corporate class.

As one of the largest philanthropic organizations in the country, the Carnegie Corporation of New York now has assets of over a quarter of a billion ($250 million) dollars and awards grants of approximately $13 million annually. Carnegie is controlled by a self-perpetuating board of publicly active, wealthy, and prominent people. The corporation is generally recognized for its high caliber performance which "sets a model for all other foundations."[2]

The corporation's purpose, as stated in its charter, is "the advancement and diffusion of knowledge and understanding among the people of the United States and the British Dominions and Colonies."[3] Under the guidance of this charter, through the means of a multimillion-dollar trust, the foundation has been able to wield an alarming measure of power. Since Carnegie money began to flow in 1901, the corporation has influenced national decision-making by using wealth, prestige, and important political connections.

The Birth and Consolidation of Carnegie Power

The Carnegie name has been so long associated with education that many fail to recognize that Andrew Carnegie, the "Ironmaster," was the wealthy baron of the United States Steel Corporation. By the end of the nineteenth century, however, Carnegie interest in steel waned in favor of philanthropy, where his zeal was reflected in the establishment of a large number of charitable trusts. For his native Scotland, Carnegie founded the Carnegie Trust for Universities of Scotland (1901) and the Carnegie Dumferline Trust (1903). In 1902 he created the Carnegie Institute of Washington. The Carnegie Hero Fund was founded in 1904, and in 1907 he endowed the Carnegie Institute of Pittsburgh. The Carnegie Endowment for International Peace was organized in 1910, and in 1913 the Carnegie United Kingdom Trust was established. But the endowment which would have far-reaching impact on American educational policy at all levels was the Carnegie Foundation for the Advancement of Teaching, established in 1905.

This foundation was essentially a $10 million trust which financed pensions for aging college and university professors in a number of elite private east coast institutions.[4] Carnegie's first impulse was to subsidize the salaries of MIT faculty when he found out that the institute's learned scientists earned less than the clerks at his steel company. He was persuaded against this approach by Dr. Henry Pratt, MIT president, who advised Carnegie to subsidize instead a pension plan which would allow professors to retire with dignity and security.

Soon after its establishment at MIT, the Carnegie pension plan attracted widespread attention. Similar arrangements were demanded by faculty and supported by trustees at other leading public and private universities.[5] Once established, the plan worked to insure loyal service from grateful faculty and thus encouraged stability, compliance, and conservatism on the part of the academic labor force.

As the pension plan was requested by more and more institutions, Carnegie officers found themselves in a position to grant a college or university the right of participation. Membership in the plan came to depend upon the institution's meeting certain standards set by the foundation. This definition of acceptable standards resulted in the designation of the so-called "Carnegie Unit" of academic credit, which most American (and Canadian) secondary students have pursued for over half a century. Those institutions which had initially resisted the new standards would simply have to forgo participation in the pension fund. Subsequently, however, the unit achieved such widespread acceptance (largely due to the appearance of Carnegie money in the form of pension stipends) that most were forced to accept Carnegie norms in order to provide their students with transferable credits and recognized degrees.

Carnegie involvement was a key factor which coerced acceptance of the standard unit. Since the mid-1880s, several important groups—the Committee of Ten, the Committee on College Entrance Requirements, the American Association of Universities, and the College Entrance Examination Board—had encouraged the professional community to support such a standard. But it was not until presidents of prestigious universities like Charles W. Eliot of Harvard, Nicholas Murray Butler of Columbia, and Woodrow Wilson of Princeton held key positions on both the Carnegie Foundation's board of trustees *and* the College Entrance Examination Board that the necessary impetus was provided for its acceptance.

The corporation's early success with such interlocking networks introduced a highly suitable model which was to be further refined, and repeated, by postwar trust efforts. This model operated on the premise that groups who were acting independently could not effectively achieve their goals. Rather, diverse organizational efforts could be coalesced, using key people with membership on one or more policymaking boards (for further discussion see Colwell chapter). In terms of foundation operations, the acceptance of the Carnegie Unit represented the initial test of power of a philanthropic trust to employ its financial resources and prominent personnel to bring about educational change.

By 1911, Carnegie had literally exhausted names for his philanthropic organizations, yet the bulk of his fortune was still without a suitable tax shelter. With the remaining millions, the Ironmaster established one final trust, the Carnegie Corporation of New York. Assisted by close advisors, friends like Elihu Root, Carnegie directly managed the corporation. When he died in 1919, the corporation was passed on to public trustees initially picked by the founder, who, in turn, selected new members; an elite future leadership of the corporation was thus insured.

While the new leadership expanded corporation funding to include higher education, medicine, and the arts, the years between the wars were generally careful and conservative. In addition to the obvious pressures created by the Great Depression, the foundation's pension program was all but depleting the endowment. By 1931 the drain was so obvious that Carnegie financial advisors shifted the program to a contributory plan administered by the Teachers Insurance & Annuity Association (TIAA).

In contrast, the years following World War II brought increased earnings for Carnegie stock holders, providing the corporation with more grant money. Furthermore, Frederick Paul Keppel, one of the corporation's prewar presidents, assured Carnegie a viable existence by granting monies only from accured interest, rather than from the foundation's stock portfolio. The war also furnished Carnegie leadership with the reins of strategic power, as many of the corporation's top executives were participants in military and civilian, national and international, war efforts.

Carnegie trustees and staff included General George C. Marshall, a leading military figure and appointee of Harry Truman as Secretary of State; Vannevar Bush, the director of the Office of Scientific Research and Development during the war; Charles A. Thomas, who played a crucial role in the Manhattan Project; Frederick W. Osborn, deputy American delegate to the U.N. Atomic Energy Commission; a young psychologist named John W. Gardner, who was a key member in the Office of Strategic Services during the war; Clyde Kluckhorn, who after the war headed the Russian Research Center at Harvard; Whitney W. Shepardson, a former intelligence officer who, upon retiring from Carnegie, became president of the National Committee for a Free Europe, the overseer of Radio Free Europe; C. D. Jackson, who served as chief advisor on Soviet propaganda to President Eisenhower; Charles M. Spofford, the former chairman of the Council of Deputies of NATO; and many others.

The postwar board of trustees at Carnegie was replete with men of national prominence. During World War II and in the succeeding Cold War period these individuals continued to hold prestigious positions in government and business. Their interest in both national and global affairs eventually led them to be concerned with the development of human resources as an important factor in maintaining national strength.

The Carnegie Philosophy

Simultaneous with the consolidation of Carnegie money and power in the post–world War II years was the development of an overriding philosophy which would dictate the nature of corporation funding for the next quarter century. Couched in neutral, scientific terms, this philosophy was characterized by a number of basic assumptions. These included a belief in technical solutions for social problems and the faith that these solutions could be uncovered through research. Most important, Carnegie policy was characterized by a commitment to finding the most competent, talented people in order to assign them to the most pressing issues.

By 1946, corporation officers were very much aware of the Cold War, a preoccupation which continued to dominate their thinking in subsequent years. Over a decade later, James Bryant Conant, president of Harvard, expressed a fear felt by many of Carnegie's executives:

> I do not have to remind the reader that the fate of freedom in the world hangs very much in balance. Our success against the spread of Communism in no small measure depends on our successful operation of our free society.[6]

What evolved out of this fear was a meritocratic view that society depended on talent in order to buttress itself against outside threats to survival. Given this ideological stance, Carnegie officers pursued a series of policies designed to identify and produce an academic elite who would develop the technology needed to maintain a strong national posture.

The need to identify and train the talented then characterized corporation policy from the post–World War II period into the 1970s. In the spirit of Jefferson, who identified one task of popular schooling to be instruction that would insure that ". . . the best geniusses [sic] will be raked from the rubbish,"[7] James B. Conant, a favored recipient of corporation funding, suggested that American education

> must endeavor to combine the British concern for training the "natural aristocracy of talents" with the American insistence on general education for all future citizens.[8]

In particular, it was John W. Gardner who became most closely identified with the "great talent hunt."[9] While president of the corporation (1953–1968), Gardner formalized the Carnegie emphasis on talent by suggesting that

> unused talents lead to personal frustration, but they also deprive a society of the mainspring of vitality. . . .. A society must learn to regard every instance of misuse of talent as an injustice to the individual and an injury to itself. And it must cultivate the idea and exercise of excellence in every man at its disposal.[10]

Gardner clearly was establishing what he thought should be a national policy. Elsewhere, he describes education as a "sorting out process." The task of the schools was one of identifying the talented and training them in special programs which would enable them to assume a leadership role in an emerging postindustrial, technological society. Schools, suggested Gardner, must enter into a form of "triage," a sorting out of the talented from the disabled or disadvantaged, and from the great "middle."[11]

Schools could then more effectively administer scarce resources. Conant, in agreement with Gardner's view, proposed the following:

> My feeling is that in the best interests of all students, there should
> be ability grouping in grades 7 though 12 in such subjects as
> English, social studies, mathematics, and science. . . . In these
> subjects there ought to be subject-by-subject grouping in three
> groups—fairly small top and bottom groups and a large middle
> group.[12]

To facilitate this identification and training process, Carnegie mounted an effort designed to redirect the goals of public education. Up to the end of World War II, the corporation funded very few projects which had direct impact on public primary and secondary schools. Abraham Flexner, a longtime Carnegie aide, noted the problem of making such grants:

> The public schools exist by the thousands; they are almost
> wholly tax supported; they are organized in systems; teachers
> and curriculums can change only with great effort; so that even a
> successful experiment makes its way only slowly.[13]

Not surprisingly, the very tendencies identified by Flexner made public education an important focus of Carnegie postwar funding with its need to forge national educational policy in critical areas. While the task of influencing public education was a challenging one, changes were essential if the talented were to be identified and trained. Carnegie funding was designed to redirect school practice toward national goals rather than local ones (similar efforts by the Ford Foundation are discussed in the chapter by Buss). Only in this way, it was thought, could the schools provide the talented leadership needed by the country.

The initial corporation effort was begun by Roy E. Larsen, then president of Time, Inc. A longtime associate of Henry Luce, Larsen approached the corporation with the embryo of a national effort to improve the public schools. Larsen's plan centered around a group of influential private citizens who would work to sensitize the nation toward the problem of changing the schools. In 1948, the National Citizens Commission for the Public Schools was awarded a $12,000 grant from the corporation's discretionary fund; and a year later, a grant of $200,000 provided this group with the funds needed to develop a staff and national headquarters.[14] Support of the Larsen Commission signaled to the professional educational community that a new funding source was available.

Carnegie Policies

In order to carry out the massive talent search identified as basic to the country's security, Carnegie trustees directed funding to three areas: a program of national testing and assessment; an effort to introduce curriculum reform; and a series of fellowship programs for talented youth, including those from minority groups.

NATIONAL TESTING

Needing a means to identify and isolate the talented from the large masses of students attending the public schools, the corporation invested substantial resources in a program of standardized testing. There was great faith in the notion of national testing. As Gardner observed, while standardized tests perform an unpopular job, e.g., deciding who does or does not go to college,

> the best achievement and aptitude tests are remarkably effective
> in sorting out students according to their actual potential per-
> formance in the classroom."[15]

To further the coordination of national efforts in academic assessment, James B. Conant was asked in 1946 to chair a special committee established to determine how four existing testing programs—the College Entrance Examination Board, the Testing Service of the American Council on Education, the National Teachers Examination, and the Graduate Records Examination of the Carnegie Foundation—could be merged into one effective organization. The result was the creation of a single nonprofit agency, the Educational Testing Service of Princeton (ETS). Founded on January 1, 1948, the service's first president was Henry Chauncey, the head of the College Entrance Examination Board. Under Chauncey, a former assistant dean at Conant's Harvard, the service expanded from being simply a testing agency serving education to a multi-service educational agency with a specialty in evaluation.[16]

ETS itself was to become a giant in the testing field. In 1977, its total revenue reached $70 million,[17] making it one of the major educational organizations in the country. Initially created by the Conant committee, ETS later became an intermediary in a Carnegie grant to the Harvard president to study the American high school; and Conant was to serve on the ETS board of trustees as well. In subsequent years, Carnegie and ETS were to coordinate frequently their program efforts to engineer change.

CURRICULUM REFORM

Once the talented were identified through a program of national assessment, it became necessary to design academic programs which would meet their needs. The corporation responded rapidly to the impetus to improve elementary and secondary education by assuming a national role in the development of "new curricula," which supported the notion of a basic subject discipline and an emphasis on math and science. By 1955 Carnegie had already entered the "math wars"[18] with a grant of $227,000 to Max Beberman of the University of Illinois Committee of School Mathematics.[19] Over the next five years, the corporation continued to fund a variety of math projects, investing $1 million in 1959 alone. Most of these programs involved the use of computers, programmed instruction, and other technological devices (also see Buss chapter on the Ford Foundation).

In an attempt to lay a solid foundation of support for widespread curriculum reform, Carnegie President John Gardner

> appointed the now famous Commission on Mathematics in 1955 at a time when the professional educational establishment still denied that sweeping curriculum reforms were needed. The Commission set in motion a reform trend that gained political and educational popularity only after the first Soviet space satellite was launched.[20]

Gardner found it important to focus direct public attention on the schools. To this end, Carnegie awarded a grant to Conant, returning from an ambassadorship in the Federal Republic of Germany, to undertake a survey of the American high school. The result was a best-selling publication.[21] In this study, Conant corroborated the Carnegie emphasis on basic subject disciplines by calling for the talented to have four years of mathematics at the secondary level. Pleased with these findings, Gardner then alerted his staff to seek other similar efforts which could be funded by the corporation. As one Carnegie executive noted,

> . . . the officer involved was continuing his task of becoming acquainted with the professor and teachers who saw the need most clearly. As the same time he was letting it be known in these circles that the Carnegie Corporation would be receptive to significant ideas for constructive action. Such ideas were soon forthcoming, and the Corporation was launched upon a new program.[22]

If the Cold War provided a cause for Carnegie support of curriculum change, then it was Jerome Bruner who provided the rationale. In 1959, Carnegie provided assistance in planning a conference of academics held at Woods Hole, chaired by Bruner, a Harvard psychologist. The conference led to the publication of Bruner's well-known book, *The Process of*

Education. In this text, Bruner suggested that students learn the structure of disciplines and become fledgling scientists making discoveries.

Bruner also noted that the rise of technology as an instructional process was now possible as a result of money being made available by the National Defense Education Act. Bruner concluded his book by stating that

> ... the intelligent use of [NDEA] money and of other resources now available will depend on how well we are able to integrate the technique of the filmmaker or the program producer with the technique and wisdom of the skillful teacher.[23]

Thus the Harvard psychologist recognized the need to use technology as part of the new curriculum in order to take advantage of available government funding.

FELLOWSHIP FOR TALENTED YOUTH

Tied to the identification of talent through a national testing program, and to a curriculum effort which was designed to structure learning, was an effort to reward the talented with scholarships and enriched learning opportunities. The budding National Merit Scholarship fund, which combined standardized testing, identification of the talented, and the award of cash stipends to those talented students who were going to college, was aligned with the Educational Testing Service through a grant to John N. Stalnaker, an ETS research psychologist. Under this grant, the National Merit Scholarship Corporation was enlarged to become a non-profit agency but maintained its founding purpose:

> To identify, honor, and encourage academic excellence in a way that draws attention to the extent and importance of academic attainment of students, both for themselves and for the nation.[24]

As part of its effort to fund special projects for the talented, the corporation awarded a $225,000 grant to the State of North Carolina to operate the Governor's School, a special eight-week institute for highly gifted youngsters.[25] Governor Terry Sanford, adopting the idea from a member of his personal staff, worked to obtain state support, especially when the project was enlarged under the aegis of the Learning Institute of North Carolina (LINC). LINC's director was Harold Howe II, who as a Newton, Massachusetts, school administrator worked with Harvard dean Francis Keppel. Later, Howe served as superintendent of schools in Scarsdale, New York, where John Gardner resided. (Subsequently he became a high-level officer of the Ford Foundation.)

In danger of losing state funding for the project for the talented, Governor Sanford approached Carnegie and the U.S. Office of Education. He sought to obtain a special grant to cover the operation of the school until the legislature could be persuaded to fund the effort.[26] It was the beginning of a close relationship among Gardner, Keppel, Sanford, and Howe, one that would lead to overlapping influential roles in national policymaking.

By 1965, the Carnegie Corporation had firmly established a program based on meritocratic principle. Its president, John Gardner, was to become a leading proponent of—and in fact would build a national image based on—the "pursuit of excellence." In doing so, Gardner and the corporation followed a vested interest, a cause which it promoted and developed with its prestigious funding program.

MINORITY YOUTH

During the same period, tension created by the civil rights movement was causing the trustees and officers at Carnegie to review their efforts. As Conant noted in his second major Carnegie report, *Slums and Suburbs*,

> . . . we are allowing social dynamite to accumulate in our large cities. . . . In some slum neighborhoods I have no doubt that over a half of the boys between sixteen and twenty-one are out of school and out of work. Leaving aside human tragedies, I submit that a continuation of this situation is a menace to the social and political health of our large cities.[27]

If American values in the cities, and the nation as a whole, were endangered by riots and similar disruptions, then national leadership had to guide the country toward calm. The fear of an explosion of "social dynamite" then led to a new Carnegie funding thrust which was aimed at minority youth.

The character of these Carnegie grants was very much in keeping with its philosophy of talent, and its belief in talented leadership. By focusing on minority youth, Carnegie was developing leadership for the minority community. Not surprisingly, in 1963, Carnegie awarded a grant of $250,000 to the United Negro College Fund and to six black colleges to improve current programs.[28] Later that year, and in 1964, Carnegie grants went to Educational Services Incorporated (later the Education Development Center) to develop special materials for black college students.[29] Subsequent grants went to the Carnegie Institute of Technology and the Bank Street College of Education to help prepare and counsel minority students for college.[30] In addition, the corporation made grants to Brandeis University to recruit minority students, to Yale and the University of Wisconsin to provide assistance to black colleges, and to the National Urban League college fellowships program.[31] Indeed, the corporation was attempting to follow its philosophy of meritocracy, and develop in the minorities a talented elite supportive of mainstream values (also see Anderson chapter).

It was obvious to both the corporation and others that, in order to develop this talented leadership, easy access to educational opportunities had to exist. In his presidential address in 1964, Gardner wrote:

> The most important task facing American education today is to remove the remaining barriers to educational opportunity; whether the barriers are due to race prejudice, urban slum conditions, economically depressed rural life, or just plain bad education.[32]

At the same time, U.S. Commissioner of Education (Francis Keppel) was ordered by the 1964 Civil Rights Act to conduct a survey of educational opportunity in the nation's schools. The law called for the determination of any lack of equal opportunity in public educational institutions at all levels, by reasons of race, religion, or national origin.[33]

Seminal documents resulted from the requirement. First, a Carnegie grant to the American Academy of Arts and Sciences produced two issues of its periodical *Daedalus* on "The Negro American."[34] More significant, a second study was conducted by James S. Coleman, a Johns Hopkins sociologist. The Coleman et al. study of *Equality of Educational Opportunity* was supported by the Office of Education and the Educational Testing Service.[35] The conclusions of the Coleman report became the subject of widespread discussion and debate. As a result of the ensuing controversy, Carnegie, to assist Keppel, made a $25,000 grant available for a seminar at Harvard.[36] The agenda of this meeting of prominent educators was to examine and explain Coleman's findings to the public.[37]

Implementing Carnegie Policies

Among the many ways in which the corporation fostered acceptance of its policies, three particular strategies were used with repeated success. The first of these has already been noted: the placing of Carnegie officers in policymaking positions in Washington, or the selection of those who already held such positions as corporation trustees. Established early, this strategy recognized that corporation and national efforts could be successfully coordinated through key people with membership in two or three prominent organizations. A second approach centered around the use of "seed" money to initiate new projects which would eventually be assumed by other sources of support. A third major technique was to publicize and widely distribute the results of Carnegie projects and reports in an effort to create a climate of support for corporation policies. (See Darknell chapter for discussion of Carnegie's strategy of funding and publishing reports that advocated its point of view.)

THE "WASHINGTON CONNECTION"

It is interesting to note that no matter which party—Republican or Democratic—was in power in Washington, there was heavy reliance on Carnegie advisors. Eisenhower, Kennedy, Johnson, and Nixon all made use of Carnegie leadership in either an advisory capacity or via appointment to national-level posts.

Toward the end of his administration President Eisenhower wanted to establish some direction for educational policy in the 1960s. He turned to the American Assembly, an organization he had established while president of Columbia University and a member of the Carnegie Foundation's board of trustees. Members of the American Assembly included James B. Conant, James R. Killian, Jr., who also served as special assistant to Eisenhower for science and technology, and Clark Kerr, president of the University of California and chairman of the Carnegie Commission on Higher Education (for further discussion of Kerr and the commission, see the Darknell chapter).

With the election of John F. Kennedy, a new era of federal activism began. Kennedy established a series of task forces, with one on education directed by Frederick L. Hovde, president of Purdue University and a Carnegie Foundation trustee. The job of this task force was to identify the ways in which the federal government could aid public schools. John Gardner (who had earlier participated in a project launched by the Rockefeller Brothers Fund to examine the future of America in the Cold War era) and Francis Keppel (son of the former president of the Carnegie Corporation and dean of the Harvard Graduate School of Education) were task force members.

The influence of Carnegie on that task force was reflected in Kennedy's first education message to Congress:

> . . . Our twin goals must be: A new standard of excellence in education—and availability of such excellence to all who are willing and able to seek it.[38]

The following year, Gardner edited a special book containing Kennedy's speeches.[39] In 1963, Kennedy chose Carnegie associate Francis Keppel as the new U.S. Commissioner of Education.

With much of Kennedy's program tied up in congressional committees, educational changes failed to materialize. But after the Kennedy assassination, Lyndon Johnson was prepared to take decisive action. In 1964 Johnson appointed John Gardner to chair a new task force on education, and Keppel to serve in an ex officio capacity as Education Commissioner. The work of this task force was directly translated into legislation, as the landmark Johnson education bill became the Elementary and Secondary Education Act (ESEA).[40]

The basic impact of ESEA was to enlarge and strengthen the U.S. Office of Education. In effect, the Keppel-led agency began to function very much like a foundation, awarding grants to initiate special programs and projects. Groups such as the Education Development Center, the Educational Testing Service, and other nonprofit corporations became direct recipients of ESEA-created programs. To some measure, this new federal act reduced their dependency on grants from foundations, thus enabling organizations like Ford and Carnegie to concentrate funding activites in other areas. Even more important, ESEA could be effectively used by an enlightened administration to shape educational policy from the executive branch. Through such funding sources as Title III of ESEA, local districts could be persuaded to try innovative programs and then adopt them with additional grants. Carnegie's initial efforts to redirect local goals were being implemented by national government programs.

Two months after President Johnson signed ESEA, he convened the White House Conference on Education. Its chairman was Carnegie president John Gardner, and vice-chairmen included Terry Sanford, James Conant, and Ralph Tyler, a major figure in the national testing movement. Lawrence Cremin of Teachers College, who was writing a history of American education under a Carnegie grant, was also a participant. In fact, many of the conference participants were current or former Carnegie grant holders. Cynically, the White House Conference could be called a "Carnegie Convention," in that the corporation funded much of the preliminary research and writing. A *New York Times* article reported:

> . . . An even subtler change could be detected in the nature of conference leadership. Mr. Gardner is at the unofficial control center of power in the world of education, not because of the widespread trust in his sense and sophistication. He represents something new in national educational influence. He has, in the White House Conference, provided a working model of the "new men" who are likely to call the tune increasingly in the future.[41]

A month after the White House Conference, Johnson appointed John Gardner as the new Secretary of Health, Education, and Welfare. As one observer noted, the groundwork for the Great Society was laid by the foundations, and some of their best men have gone to Washington to develop it, notably, Mr. John Gardner."[42] Gardner soon promoted Keppel to Assistant Secretary for Education and completed a powerful triumvirate with Harold Howe II as the new U.S. Commissioner of Education.

The ascent of the Gardner-Keppel-Howe team to the executive branch of government represented what seemed to be the capstone of a twenty-year effort to establish the Carnegie Corporation in a solid national-level policymaking role. Through a funding program which promoted the academically talented, the corporation gained a national reputation. Through leadership provided by its president, the corporation became a major national-level influence. As an outside force, the corporation was able to bring about change in policy and, as a result, gained for its chief executive officer, Gardner, an inside role in the official machinery which made federal educational policy.

Perhaps one could argue that the presence of these three men in senior policymaking roles was coincidental, a twist of fate bringing them to Washington at the same time. However, it must be recognized that the careers of Gardner, Keppel, and Howe were intertwined with the development of policy at Carnegie. Howe in North Carolina and Scarsdale with grants for the talented; Keppel at Conant's Harvard, using Carnegie money, and with a strong family connection at Carnegie; and Gardner, whose professional life up to this point was largely spent in Carnegie pursuits. The arrival of all three in Washington was the completion of the chain of Carnegie power-brokering in education.

Clearly there is evidence that, with its "Washington connection," the Carnegie Corporation had reached the apogee of its influence on national educational policy. As the Gardner-led triumvirate moved through Washington circles, it was able to reaffirm several of the Carnegie programs, shifting their support to new financial sources. In reviewing the Carnegie funding pattern it is apparent that the corporation wanted to fund, or "seed," a project, maintaining it only until it could acquire other funding. Carnegie money enabled new ideas to develop—and occasionally flourish, if other sources of funding were forthcoming, or if the project could become self-supporting.

FUNDING KEY AGENCIES

Several alternative funding patterns evolved. In some instances, Carnegie-initiated projects like ETS became nonprofit organizations with their own identities, enlarging to seek other grants and charging customers for their services. In other cases, the size of the projects involved made it necessary to establish totally new funding sources, particularly in the federal government. In still other cases, projects introduced by the corporation were turned over to public tax monies.

The Carnegie Corporation recognized early the value of the nonprofit corporate structure suggested by the Educational Testing Service. A similar organization was the Education Development Center in Massachusetts. An MIT faculty member, Jerrold Zacharias, located his Physical Science Study Committee (PSSC) at the school. But the PSSC soon outgrew the available facilities and in 1958 was relocated at Watertown, Massachusetts, as Educational Services Incorporated (ESI). ESI was developed as a financially independent agency which could publish its own work, produce materials, and receive grants without involving MIT. By 1965, Carnegie had awarded over $1 million in grants to ESI projects, including an offshoot of the Illinois math project.[43]

In 1965, ESI merged with another nonprofit corporation to form the Education Development Center (EDC). EDC's great efficiency in production of curriculum materials resulted in its characterization as the "General Motors of curriculum reform."[44] Later that year, the center became a regional laboratory under the Elementary and Secondary Education Act. The following year, Arthur L. Singer, an executive associate at Carnegie, was appointed executive director.[45] In this case, an organization that was "seeded" by Carnegie funding was developed as an independent nonprofit corporation, and was later utilized as a regional center by the federal government, with Carnegie influence remaining intact.

Another influential Carnegie-created agency was the Education Commission of the States (ECS), an interstate agency comprised of governors, legislators, and educators. In 1964, the Carnegie Corporation supported a Conant study on *Shaping Educational Policy*. In this book, Conant suggested that an interstate compact should be formed in order to avoid fragmented educational change.[46] Carnegie asked Terry Sanford, then working under a Ford Foundation grant, to determine the feasibility of such a project.[47] With corporation grants of $175,000[48] and $200,000, [49] Sanford established offices to study the problem. In 1967 Sanford wrote:

> The Education Commission is enabling the states to unite in the
> resolve to meet their responsibility to the quickening interest of
> the American people in the pursuit of excellence. The Compact
> for Education places the states in the forefront of that pursuit.[50]

The ECS, not coincidentally, provided Carnegie with a means to gain suport for one of its most important policies. The establishment of a large-scale testing effort, seen by Carnegie as basic to its search for talent, was never popular with professional educators. Such groups as the National Education Association and the American Association of School Administrators were quick to criticize national assessment. The unpopularity of its testing programs led Carnegie to enlarge a special committee, headed by Ralph Tyler, a major figure in measurement and evaluation, to include almost all those professional groups that were opposed to it.

However, it was not until the Education Commission of the States agreed to oversee national assessment that the testing program was finally accepted.[51] The seemingly broad-based involvement of the ECS both reduced criticism and cleared the way for a Carnegie-sponsored program. In retrospect, the appearance of ECS merely coalesced Carnegie interests. Carnegie's use of the commission to further its own programs had become a familiar theme by the mid-1960s.

The establishment of the Corporation for Public Broadcasting represents another way in which projects initially funded by Carnegie seed money were passed to other sources—in this case, public taxes. Carnegie's support of technology in the classroom led its officers to turn toward television as an efficient way of reaching large numbers of people. In 1965, under a $500,000 grant, the Carnegie Commission on Educational Television was established.[52]

The commission, chaired by James R. Killian, Jr., president of MIT and member of the board of the Education Development Center, included two other old Carnegie friends, Terry Sanford and James B. Conant. The widely distributed commission report was recognized as the impetus that led to the passage of key legislation which created the Corporation for Public Broadcasting in 1967. Killian was appointed to chair the newly created corporation.

What we see here is a familiar pattern of Carnegie involvement: initial funding or "seeding" of a nonprofit corporation or commission; working through powerful connections to assure the takeover of funding of that corporation (in this case by the federal government); maintaining involvement in that corporation, despite relinquishing the purse strings; and using the prestige and influence of the newly created organization to further Carnegie ends.

Carnegie into the 1970s

As I have noted, the Carnegie presence in Washington, both official and unofficial, was not a single-party phenomenon. Indeed, Carnegie trustees, officers, and associates participated in influential positions in the Eisenhower, Kennedy, and Johnson administrations. The Carnegie influence in Washington political affairs continued under Nixon and Carter, but certainly with far less force in the absence of John Gardner. Under a new chief executive officer, Alan J. Pifer, the Carnegie Corporation altered its operational style, but continued many traditional foundation program thrusts.

The Carnegie influence notwithstanding, a renewed interest and awareness of foundation activity and abuses centered in Congress.[53] The Tax Reform Act of 1969 only slightly altered the course of foundation affairs at Carnegie, but caused its leadership to think inwardly about the organization's function. While Carnegie continued to fund educational efforts, these were conducted much less publicly. This change in style, not substance, allowed the corporation to continue as a force in educational policymaking.

When Pifer took over as Carnegie president in 1968, he began, in the Gardner style, by commissioning a study of the nation's graduate schools. The resulting effort, conducted by Charles Silberman, was instead, at Silberman's design, a study of open education.[54] A second stumbling block occurred at the hand of President Nixon. Like his predecessors, Nixon made use of Carnegie talent by appointing Pifer to chair a task force which would prepare an educational agenda for the Nixon administration. Unlike Eisenhower, Kennedy, and Johnson, however, Nixon (for whatever reasons) discarded many of the recommendations.

Pifer, finding that the Gardner approach of working through Washington was not an appropriate one, developed new modes of action as well as a different style of management. (It should be noted, however, that both the Silberman study and the Pifer task force, while they failed to achieve the desired ends, were well received by the professional community and gave the corporation continued prestige.[55]) In addition, Pifer was becoming extremely successful as a public spokesperson for foundations generally. His presidential essays in the Annual Reports discussed how foundations should operate, their special tax privilege, and their role in society. In 1969 he wrote:

> The assault this year on foundations, if it reveals anything, tells
> us that the safety of all types of private charitable
> organizations—religious, educational, medical, and philan-
> thropic—may now be in serious doubt. . . . From what I have
> seen in Washington in recent months, it is my sad conclusion that
> the role played by free, private institutions as a bulwark of the
> American democratic system may be in jeopardy.[56]

Furthermore, Pifer's urbane manner and conservative appearance made him a very acceptable representative during the congressional hearings which threatened to impose harsh reforms on tax-exempted philanthropy. Pifer's style appeared in sharp contrast to that of Ford Foundation

President McGeorge Bundy, who seemed to irritate the investigating legislators.

By 1970 Pifer had begun to formulate his own style of running Carnegie. He initiated a wide variety of studies and seminars which examined the operation of philanthropic trusts.[57] He changed the style of Carnegie management to a corporate management scheme, with more responsibility for grant development placed with the staff associates. The staff itself, however, was carefully selected from those organizations and institutions which were longtime Carnegie grant recipients. For example, three Carnegie executive associates came from the funded projects of Conant, Sanford, and Bruner. Other sources for staff were nonprofit organizations such as the Educational Testing Service, the Institute for Educational Development, Aspira, the Institute for Community Studies, the College Entrance Examination Board, and the Education Commission of the States. Staff were also hired from other foundations—Ford and Russell Sage—and foundation-related groups such as the Foundation Center. In selecting staff, the corporation practiced "pathological professionalism," in an effort to maintain its past character through inbreeding. Indeed, the corporation did maintain the same philosophical orientation, as newly hired staff shared many of the Carnegie values.

The conservative orientation guided the officers and staff in selecting their agenda or selecting future grants. They sought to support projects where the outcomes had known qualities. Observations by researchers at agencies like the Center for Analysis of Public Issues at Princeton suggest that foundations tend to be uninterested in funding research studies whose findings are unpredictable. Its director noted:

> When we go into a study, we're not sure whether we're going to come out for or against something. Ninety-five percent of the foundations in this country will walk away from you if you have that attitude. They want to know what it is you're pushing, because if it's what they're pushing, then they'll give the money.[58]

While the style of the corporation may have changed, there is strong predictability in funded projects. From 1966 to 1977, Carnegie continued to fund its major program areas through key organizations. During those years, Children's Television Workshop received grants for $2.1 million; Educational Testing Service, $2.4 million; Education Development Center, $2.1 million. In addition, Carnegie granted during those years $.8 million to National Assessment; $.8 million to the Education Commission of the States; $.5 million to National Educational Television; $.4 million to the New York Urban Coalition; and $.8 million to the National Urban Coalition (of which Gardner was a founder and past president).[59]

The Carnegie Legacy: Implications for Democracy

The corporation's continued interest in education at the elementary and secondary levels is a legacy of the Cold War period of national activism. This era witnessed the corporation's earnest efforts to carry out what it saw as the means of maintaining and strengthening a society which produced it. The corporation built upon a Social Darwinism, according to which the talented would succeed to the benefit of society. Carnegie coopted the Jeffersonian elitism of Conant to structure its funding program around two main tenets: a discipline-oriented curriculum of standard units, and the use of standardized tests to sort out the talented and to measure the quality of education.

Of course, the belief that corporation trustees knew what the country (and its state public educational systems) needed was based on an arrogant view of the philanthropoids that their vision was essentially correct and superior to that of the general public. The corporation, under the stewardship of its wealthy and prominent trustees, selected a corps of managers to operate the foundation; they in turn selected worthy recipients. In effect, these college-trained managers made selections according to their perception of the trustees' biases. The corporation was the living embodiment of what the corporation thought society ought to be. Accordingly, the Carnegie officers and staff were enfranchised with the Ironmaster's wealth to choose perennial advisors, make vested grants, and seek national roles. They were indeed an educational "power elite." The final words of C. Wright Mills's treatise may well characterize the "elite" corporation:

> The men of higher circles are not representative men; their high position is not a result of moral virtue; their fabulous success is not firmly connected with meritorious ability. Those who sit in the seats of the high and mighty are selected and formed by the means of power, the sources of wealth, the mechanics of celebrity, which prevail in their society. They are not men selected and formed by civil service that is linked to the world of knowledge and sensibility. They are not men shaped by nationally responsible parties that debate openly and clearly the issues this nation now so unintelligently confronts.[60]

The above comment by Mills cogently describes the men at the Carnegie Corporation. This management class of professional foundation personnel hold no special talent, ability, education, or competence. They do, however, have a unique quality of influence—namely, access to Carnegie wealth. This access enhances their public image as well as social perceptions of their credibility—for, what they propose they can also finance. Thus people listen and follow their advice.

During the period under examination the corporation was in no sense a benevolent, impartial, independent broker of innovation and experimentation. Carnegie had a cause and sought to establish that cause as national policy for the schools. Without public debate, national referenda, or other means during the post–World War II era, the corporation sought to achieve dominance in policymaking. And, indeed, it was able to exercise a substantial measure of influence on public education. As is the case with other general-purpose foundations, the corporation's combination of wealth and prominence endowed it with the power to do essentially what it wished, when it wished.

While foundations are undoubtedly creatures of capitalism, the question remains as to whether they are institutions appropriate to a democracy. Based on the Carnegie experience, it is evident that the big philanthropic foundations invest tremendous power in a small minority, who in turn exercise inordinate influence over the majority. The power is not placed there by vote, but by means of money and prestige. Such elitism has grave implications for the workings of a democratic system. Not only did Carnegie attempt to alter a basic institution of society, it deposited power with a small group of men insulated from majority influence and wisdom. It is clear that there is a continuing need for systematic, critical scrutiny of foundation activity and the effects of organized philanthropy on American democratic institutions.

Notes

1. See, for example, Robert J. Havighurst, "A Comparison of Foundations and Government as Supporters of Experimentation," *Phi Delta Kappan* 59 (June 1978): 179–181.
2. Ibid., p. 181.
3. *A Manual for the Public Benefactions of Andrew Carnegie* (Washington, D.C.: The Carnegie Endowment for Peace, 1919), pp. 211–212.
4. See Henry S. Pritchett, *A Comprehensive Plan of Insurance and Annuities for College Teachers* (New York: The Carnegie Foundation for the Advancement of Teaching, 1916), Bulletin No. 9; and Abraham Flexner, *Henry S. Pritchett: A Biography* (New York: Columbia University Press, 1943).
5. Howard J. Savage, *Fruit of an Impulse: Forty-Five Years of the Carnegie Foundation, 1905–1950* (New York: Harcourt, Brace and Company, 1953), Chapter 1.
6. James B. Conant, *Slums and Suburbs* (New York: McGraw Hill, 1961), p. 34.
7. Thomas Jefferson, *Notes on the State of Virginia* (1782: London, 1787), Query XIV, Laws.
8. James B. Conant, *Education and Liberty* (New York: Vintage Books, 1953), p. 87.

9. John W. Gardner, "The Great Talent Hunt," in Carnegie Corporation of New York, *Annual Report, 1956* (New York: the same, 1957), p. 12.

10. John W. Gardner, "Special Studies Project Report V," in Rockefeller Brothers Fund, *The Pursuit of Excellence* (New York: Doubleday, 1958), p. 38.

11. John W. Gardner, *Excellence* (New York: Harper & Row, 1961), p. 34.

12. Conant, *Slums and Suburbs,* p. 64.

13. Abraham Flexner, *I Remember* (New York: Simon and Schuster, 1940), p. 252.

14. Carnegie Corporation of New York, *Annual Report, 1949* (New York: the same, 1950), p. 55.

15. Gardner, *Excellence,* p. 57.

16. Henry Chauncey, "A Shift in Focus," in Educational Testing Service, *Annual Report 1966–1967* (Princeton, N.J.: the same, 1968), pp. 12–14.

17. Educational Testing Service, *Annual Report, 1977* (Princeton, N.J.: the same, 1978), p.24.

18. Benjamin DeMott, "The Math Wars," *American Scholar* 31 (Spring 1962): 296–310.

19. Carnegie Corporation of New York, *Annual Report, 1956* (New York: the same, 1957), p. 66.

20. *New York Times*, July 28, 1965, p. 18.

21. James B. Conant, *The American High School Today* (New York: McGraw Hill, 1959), p. 57.

22. Frederick H. Jackson, "The Private Foundation," an address at the National Conference on Curriculum Experimentation, September 26–30, 1961. See Paul C. Rosenbloom (ed.), *Modern Viewpoints in Curriculum* (New York: McGraw Hill, 1964), p. 212.

23. Jerome Bruner, *The Process of Education* (Cambridge, Mass.: Harvard University Press, 1960).

24. *Guide to the National Merit Scholarship Program* (Evanston, Ill.: National Merit Scholarship Corporation, 1972), p. ii.

25. Carnegie Corporation of New York, *Annual Report, 1963* (New York: the same, 1964), p. 9.

26. Terry Sanford, *But What About People?* (New York: Harper & Row, 1966), p. 165; the Carnegie grant was for $500,000.

27. Conant, *Slums and Suburbs*.

28. Carnegie Corporation of New York, *Annual Report, 1963*, p. 26.

29. Carnegie Corporation of New York, *Annual Report, 1964* (New York: the same, 1965), p. 18.

30. Ibid., p. 67.

31. Ibid., p. 73.

32. Ibid., p. 15.

33. Sec. 402 of the Civil Rights Act of 1964.

34. "The Negro American", Vols. I & II, *Daedalus* (Fall 1965 and Winter 1966).

35. James S. Coleman et al., *Equality of Educational Opportunity* (Washington, D.C.: U.S. Government Printing Office, 1966).

36. Carnegie Corporation of New York, *Annual Report, 1967* (New York: the same, 1968), pp. 23–24.

37. For a compilation of the papers delivered at this seminar see, Frederick Mosteller and Daniel Moynihan (eds.), *On Equality of Educational Opportunity* (New York: Random House, 1972).
38. U.S., 87th Congress, 1st session H.R. Document No. 92, "American Education—Message from the President Relative to American Education," February 20, 1961.
39. John F. Kennedy, *To Turn the Tide* (New York: Harper Brothers, 1962).
40. Stephen Bailey and Edith K. Mosher, *ESEA: The Office of Education Administers a Law* (Syracuse, N.Y.: Syracuse University Press, 1968).
41. *New York Times*, July 25, 1965, p. 9E.
42. "Back to the Foundations," *Economist* 221 (December 31, 1966): 1391.
43. Carnegie Corporation of New York, Annual Reports 1962–1966.
44. James D. Koerner, "EDC: General Motors of Curriculum Reform," *Saturday Review* 50 (August 19, 1967): 56–58, 70–71.
45. Carnegie Corporation of New York, *Annual Report, 1966* (New York: the same, 1967), p. 69.
46. James B. Conant, *Shaping Educational Policy* (New York: McGraw Hill, 1964).
47. Ibid., p. 123.
48. Carnegie Corporation, *Annual Report, 1966*, pp. 50—52.
49. Ibid., p. 78.
50. Terry Sanford, *Storm over the States* (New York: McGraw Hill, 1967), p. 119.
51. *New York Times*, February 23, 1969, p. 9E.
52. Carnegie Corporation of New York, *Annual Report, 1965* (New York: the same, 1966), p. 45.
53. See *Tax-Exempt Foundations and Charitable Trusts: Their Impact on Our Economy*, Six Installments, Subcommittees Chairman's Report to Subcommittee No. 1, Select Committee on Small Business, House of Representatives, 90th Congress (Washington, D.C.: U.S. Government Printing Office, March 26, 1968).
54. Charles E. Silberman, *Crisis in the Classroom* (New York: Random House, 1970).
55. James Cass, "Education in America: The New Guard Takes Over", *Saturday Review* 52 (March 15, 1969): 55.
56. Alan J. Pifer, "Foundations and the Unity of Charitable Organizations," in Carnegie Corporation of New York, *Annual Report, 1969* (New York: the same, 1970), p.3.
57. For example, see *Philanthropy in the 70s: An Anglo-American Discussion* (New York: The Council on Foundations, 1972), pp. vii–xi.
58. Interview with John Kolesar, quoted in David E. Weischadle, "Carnegie: A Case Study of How Foundations Make Decisions," *Phi Delta Kappan* 59 (October 1977): 110.
59. Carnegie Corporation of New York, *Annual Reports*, 1966–1977.
60. C. Wright Mills, *The Power Elite* (New York: Oxford University Press, 1956), p. 361.

Frank A. Darknell

The Carnegie Philanthropy and Private Corporate Influence on Higher Education

Following the initial work of C. Wright Mills, a number of writers have documented the ways in which a very small segment of the American population controls the major part of the industrial wealth of the country.[1] They have also shown how this segment forms a surprisingly interconnected and cohesive social class linked by business, family, friendship, educational, and cultural ties.[2] More importantly, they have attempted to demonstrate how this capital-holding upper class, through its control of the corporate structure, seeks to influence and control the course of general public business, including government policy in key spheres of national and local activity.[3]

Many social scientists prefer not to use "elitist" or "ruling-class" sociological theories or models to explain the development of public policy in the United States. Further, they frequently ask those who do use them to show how the alleged ruling class of private corporate interests actually rules. They wish to know through what obvious routines or subterfuges such a ruling class controls, makes policy, or takes action. As a consequence, certain power structure analysts have focused on the composition and activities of private, high-level public-policy formation groups and their links to ruling-class economic interests.[4]

These policy formation groups—comprised of leading businessmen, academics, and other prominent citizens—are funded by large, private, corporate-controlled foundations. Together with the foundations, they constitute, according to Karier, a "fourth branch" of American government.[5]

As documented by Karier, this unofficial branch of government developed in the Progressive Era before World War I and represented the essentially *liberal* corporate forces of newly developing monopoly-capital interests, rather than the rigid conservativism characteristic of the American small business world. The new philanthropic foundations maintained the interests of corporate wealth by underwriting studies and solutions designed to maintain the flexibility and hence the stability of the liberal state in the face of massive social problems that developed with the expansion of modern industry. Well-known examples of philanthropic concern with issues of the day were work in Negro education and civic affairs, by the various Rockefeller foundations, the Russell Sage Fund in welfare, Carnegie in medical education, and so on.[6]

However, the range of public issues for which the American corporate ruling class has taken long-term responsibility through satellite policy-formation groups, supported by private tax-exempt foundations and direct corporate grants, has been far wider. It includes the nation's foreign affairs, the special purview of the Council on Foreign Relations;[7] political and economic policy, the concern of the Business Council,[8] whose advisory role to presidents is generally noted in national newspapers and by the wire services; and the more general areas of social and economic concern monitored by the Committee for Economic Development, the American Assembly, and the National Planning Association, among others.[9]

Domhoff[10] argues that these private policy groups help (1) facilitate a consensus within the corporate ruling class on important issues which affect the country or threaten the established social and economic order and (2) provide the means of resolving these pressing issues via public and private institutions.

According to Domhoff, one of the most useful ways to trace the influence of the corporate ruling class is to study the funding patterns of the large private foundations which consistently provide the monetary support for these private policy groups.[11] Large, corporate ruling-class controlled foundations such as the Carnegie Corporation of New York, the Ford Foundation (the largest), Rockefeller, Sloan, Mellon, and others in effect serve as special tax-exempt "banks," providing credit and money flow to the various private committees, commissions, institutes, university research centers, and think-tanks that make up the unofficial ruling class policymaking network.[12]

The Carnegie Corporation of New York provides an example of one such private policy agency, operating with notable success in the field of education and particularly in higher education. Since Carnegie money began to flow in 1901, public authorities have, for a variety of reasons, adopted and implemented many Carnegie-sponsored policy proposals which in turn have become standard procedures in education.[13] The Carnegie Corporation is an endowed foundation with holdings of approximately $250 million;[14] it is controlled by a self-perpetuating board of publicly active, wealthy, and eminent people, and a staff of foundation specialists. The board of trustees is made up mostly of high-level corporate business people and highly paid professionals who serve the corporate world. Most of the trustees also serve on other boards of directors of other corporations, both profit-making and nonprofit in nature.[15]

This chapter contends that the Carnegie Corporation, through its various subsidiary agencies—committees, commissions, councils, or the Carnegie Foundation for the Advancement of Teaching—has consistently developed and promoted higher education policies primarily in the interests of the American corporate ruling class. These policies over the years have served to direct, contain, and channel the flow of students within higher education. In the short run, these policies have helped provide a trained and ideologically prepared work force in sufficient numbers to meet corporate needs; in the long run, they have maintained the organization and stability of the system of higher education by controlling supply and demand for its services. Excessive demand (however and whenever that might be defined) could be seen in ruling-class circles as leading to increased public expenditures and higher taxes, possibly triggering the kind of financial instability characterized by O'Connor[16] as a "fiscal crisis" of the corporate capitalist state.

The chapter will further show that Carnegie's role as a private developer of public policy has been to foster a system of classification and channeling of students in higher education which parallels the system of testing and tracking in the lower schools.[17]. These systems, inherently biased by class and race, have led to a stratification of the structure of education at all levels in America. Higher education, formerly seen as the stairway to higher class status, now serves to consolidate and strengthen castelike tendencies within the corporate capitalist society itself.[18]

Mass Higher Education: Its Beginnings in California

Mass higher education was born in the rich, exuberant, pace-setting state of California between the first and second world wars (1920–1940). A peculiar mix of conditions there had led to what a 1932 Carnegie study characterized as unusual educational "unrest," following from ". . . the advanced position which the state has taken in educational matters."[19]

California, like other states or regionally based subsocieties in nineteenth-century America, had developed a local business and industrial elite, culturally and technologically centered around the land grant university. For many of the members of these local or regional elites, the state university was often the socially prestigious finishing school, as well as the center for professional education in law, medicine, engineering, economics, and commerce. More accurately, California's peculiar "advanced position" stemmed from the fact that it had developed a chain of two-year junior colleges throughout the state. California had also taken the lead in upgrading its state normal schools to four-year teachers colleges, giving the bachelor of education degree. (These degrees, however, were widely viewed as less prestigious and less marketable than the bachelor of arts.)

By the early 1930s a broadening demand for higher education was causing concern among the traditional upper-class supporters of the university. The proliferation of junior colleges and extensive dissatisfaction with limited programs at teachers colleges were whetting the appetites of many upwardly mobile or job-seeking Californians. Throughout the state there was a rising demand for access to four-year colleges offering a full B.A. program.

In the midst of the Great Depression, then, significant popular pressure was exerted on the state department of education, through the legislature, to upgrade the available opportunities in higher education. Because this pressure represented a threat to the educational and financial position of the University of California, the Carnegie Corporation—already recognized as an expert agency in higher education policy—was commissioned to study and make recommendations on the future of higher education in California.

In 1932, the Carnegie Commission of Seven[20] presented a plan for controlling the growing demand for college degrees in California. It proposed that jurisdiction over the state teachers colleges be transferred from the state department of education to the constitutionally independent jurisdiction of the regents of the University of California. This move, presumably, would decrease the chances of the state legislature's conferring full degree-granting status on the teachers colleges. Additionally, the commission devised a new mechanism for neutralizing any future demands for broadened access to higher education: a permanent independent state board to "impartially" study such questions and advise the legislature and the general public accordingly. Recommendation #47 of the Carnegie study reads:

> The Commission recommends that in order to avoid the premature or unwarranted expansions which have in the past been the costly product of enthusiastic local or group aspirations, and to avoid wasteful duplicate operations. . . all matters involving educational finance be referred before action to the State Council for Educational Planning and Co-ordination.[21]

This recommendation illustrates the direction of the Carnegie Corporation's initial venture into higher education policy development in California. Directly solicited by the University's president, the corporation's proposals were from the start slanted toward restricting access and preserving the elite nature and structure of higher education—a theme to be repeated in subsequent policies it would propose for American public higher education.

The California legislature, however, did not see fit to adopt the commission's 1932 proposals. Responding to local pressures, they moved instead to upgrade teachers colleges into B.A.-granting state colleges.[22] Thus, prior to World War II—with a network of twenty or more two-year junior colleges, and in addition seven state colleges and two university campuses offering full college degrees at nominal cost—California had initiated a statewide system of mass higher education.

Mass Higher Education: After the GI Bill

After World War II, the Servicemen's Resettlement Act of 1944 (the GI Bill) dramatically spread the demand and opportunity for higher education among masses of people throughout the United States. The large numbers of ex-servicemen and women who chose to go to college surprised even the early sponsors of the legislation.[23] Millions of veterans reached for the chance of a United States government-supported college education. The "seeding" effect of the GI Bill in stimulating further college attendance among lower-middle- and working-class communities and families is worthy of careful historical and sociological study. It does seem clear that the various GI bills after World War II and Korea were the primary reason why many sons and daughters of Americans of the lower ranks of society continued education beyond high school.

All of this gave higher education monitors and would-be gatekeepers, like those at the Carnegie Corporation, several things to worry about. The first of these was the changing social class composition of people desiring higher education. Increasing numbers of lower-class students and their parents began to see a college degree as the surest way to improved economic and social status, and to see government support as a legitimate means of getting it. A second worry was the expected demographic "tidal wave" of college-age young people resulting from dramatic increases in national birth rates in the 1940s and 1950s.[24]

Both these trends called for an expanding number of university and college places, and even the development of new institutions of mass higher education. These developments led to a third concern: the problem of preserving the established hierarchy of universities and colleges, which sorted out and allocated individuals to different roles in the society. This established hierarchy—from low-status junior and teacher training colleges through the state and private universities to exalted Harvard—could become scrambled if old campuses expanded and new ones were set up indiscriminately.

Southern Illinois University at Carbondale was an example from the early GI Bill days which apparently became a nightmare for the higher education establishment. SIU began as a humble downstate normal school and grew to challenge the established land-grant school, the University of Illinois at Champaign-Urbana, by the 1950s. In 1964 James Bryant Conant, former president of Harvard and Carnegie's main observer and elder statesman of the period, described SIU as an example of runaway development in higher education, threatening the financial stability of the established university:

> The line dividing the University of Illinois and Southern Illinois University, is not an academic one. Rather, it is political. For more than a decade the two have fought, sometimes quite bitterly, over definitions of role and function. Southern Illinois, having shaken off its former normal school status, became after World War II the state's most rapidly growing (proportionately) and politically aggressive university.[25]

Describing how an alert and quick moving administration was able to rally sufficient support in the state legislature, Conant explained SIU's politically supported academic expansion:

> In recent years, its president has bundled up all of the educational appeals—the nation's need for teachers and engineers, the lack of opportunity for youngsters in southern regions of the state, shortage of qualified Ph.D.'s—for presentation to the Governor and the state legislature.[26]

As a consequence, the University of Illinois was hard put to remain strong in the competition for state and—once SIU had doctoral programs—the most lucrative federal grants.

Conant went on to point out that the State of Illinois had no way of controlling or rationalizing a phenomenon like SIU:

> The educational decision-making in this state reflects a fragmented pattern and a lack of overall direction and planning. . . . Illinois has had no machinery with the legal authority or the prestige and status necessary to make decisions based on a comprehensive evaluation of the state's educational problems and needs.[27]

In summary, Illinois had not yet moved "toward the development of a master plan"[28]—unlike California, where with the considerable assistance of the Carnegie Corporation, such a statewide plan was already in operation.

The California Master Plan 1960: Building-in the Class System

> When I was guiding the development of the Master Plan for
> Higher Education in California in 1959 and 1960, I considered
> the vast expansion of the community two year colleges to be the
> first line of defense for the University of California as an institu-
> tion of international academic renown. Otherwise the University
> was either going to be overwhelmed by large numbers of stu-
> dents with lower academic attainments or attacked as trying to
> hold on to a monopoly over entry into higher status.
>
> —Clark Kerr[29]

Dr. Kerr (president of the University of California from 1958 to 1967, chairman of the Carnegie Commission for Higher Education from 1967 to 1974 and of the Carnegie Council for Policy Studies in Higher Education from 1975 to 1979) here notes the dilemma facing ruling elites who wish to hold on to their privileges in an egalitarian democracy. Mass higher education, however, came to be adopted in California, not only because of popular demand for it, but also because it eventually appeared beneficial to the interests of the corporate ruling class. Further, in the process the ruling elites were able to retain a higher education structure designed to maintain their social prerogatives and their class hegemony.

By the late 1950s California had developed into an industrial region of considerable potential in high technology. Aerospace, electronics, and related industries were given a major stimulus by Soviet space achievements in 1957. These industries also grew upon a base of wealth already established by agriculture and food-processing, mining and refining, light manufacturing, tourism, entertainment—and, notably, extensive facilities for education and training.

Because the expansion of industry based on sophisticated technology required a more highly educated work force, California's corporate business interests began to support middle- and lower-class aspirations for schooling beyond high school.[30] Building the "human capital" value of working-class people came to be seen as a legitimate task of the state, and the taxpayers.[31] Cheap high education and training for those who wanted and could use it became a solution for high technology's growing need for masses of technicians and more highly trained experts and administrators. As the historic "space race" with the Soviet Union got underway after *Sputnik* in the late 1950s, new plants demanding these kinds of specially trained workers proliferated up and down the state, and in nearby states where higher education systems were still relatively undeveloped.

In the face of this demand and with concern for the attendant costs, the California legislature in 1959 established a Master Plan Survey team, consisting of representatives from the California state colleges, the junior colleges, the University of California, and the independent colleges and universities.[32] The final report,[33] which was to shape higher education in California for the indefinite future, essentially reflected a model proposed in 1955 by T. R. McConnell. McConnell was an experienced university administrator and acknowledged expert on academic selection processes. He had been invited to California by the president of the university, and managed to function simultaneously as (1) professor in the School of Education at the University of California, Berkeley; (2) director of the Center for the Study of Higher Education, which had been set up on the Berkeley campus through a grant from the Carnegie Corporation; and (3) major consultant to a liaison committee established between the University of California Regents and the State Board of Education (acting for the state colleges) to study higher education needs in the state.[34]

Basically, McConnell's model[35] involved a stratified system of tiers or ranked segments, offering an assortment of "good," "better," and "best" quality in higher education. The nonelite, nonselective, locally financed two-year colleges occupied the bottom tier, providing limited programs in most communities throughout the state. The subelite, semiselective, state-financed four-year colleges, situated in most urban and certain rural areas, made up a large middle tier. At the top level were the handful of highly selective elite University of California campuses, situated in key areas of the lower two-thirds of the state, and richly funded by state and federal money.[36] Selection of students for the four-year programs would be based on merit, as measured by standardized tests and previous school performance. Articulation or transfer between the tiers allowed upward mobility for late-blooming scholars, or those whose merit had previously been obscured by lower class position.[37]

In terms of output of graduates, the plan proposed a "differentiation of function."[38] The two-year colleges would provide terminal technical instruction or academic transfer programs leading to the state colleges or the University. These latter programs would be controlled by a screening and counseling program to keep a brake on "unrealistic" transfers by students who were not "college material."[39] The four-year state colleges would offer academic programs leading to the bachelor's and some limited master's degrees, as well as semiprofessional and vocational education. Exclusive to the University of California would be academic programs leading to the doctoral degree, as well as education for the major professions. The university, furthermore, would carry the primary responsibility for state-supported research. The fact that it had exclusive monopoly on doctoral degrees meant that it would automatically qualify for the largest share of federal research support. Essential to the Master Plan as a means of bringing mass higher education and its development under control was the California Co-ordinating Council for Higher Education. Bearing an obvious resemblance to the "State Council for Educational Planning and Co-ordination" recommended by the Carnegie Commission of Seven study of 1932, this non-elected, state-wide "super-board"—largely dominated by the University of California—effectively took out of the hands of local communities and the legislature the power to respond to popular demand for equal access to top quality higher education in California after 1960.

It should be noted that the master plan provided what a great many established interests and a great many ordinary people wanted: (1) it absorbed the greatest number of students into two-year colleges and graduated them as employable technicians; (2) it provided liberal and inexpensive training opportunities at the four-year colleges for semiprofessionals and lower-level administrators; and (3) it restricted to the University of California the preparation of major professionals, experts, and high-level administrators, all generally destined for the upper levels of the corporate hierarchies and the California class system.

This was the first comprehensive system of mass post-secondary education to be developed in the United States, and it was clearly tied to the social class system. It allowed everyone to enter the higher education system, but encouraged the applicants to line up at different entrances. That is, it tended to take students in at the level—junior college, four-year college, or elite university—where a class- and race-biased selection system had deposited them. In other words, the master plan became an extension of the lower school tracking system. Students from less affluent social backgrounds, already trapped for the most part in lower-class schools, tended to be channeled into terminal programs at two-year colleges. Such students would not, as a rule, go on to four years of higher education, but would instead be passed through the system to emerge at the same social class level. Thus, although everyone would go to college, everyone would stay in place and move up one square. Those at the fringes of society unable to move up—illegal immigrants, "guest-workers," and declassed whites and nonwhites of all kinds—would simply fill in at the bottom of the new social ladder. What the master plan meant, then, as a public policy for higher education, was the institutionalization of what Bowles and Gintis[40] later called the "reproduction" of the existing class hierarchy within the structure of a new monopoly capitalist social order—a new social order with mass higher education as a major social institution.

As the California legislature moved in 1960 to enact the state master plan for higher education, the Carnegie Corporation began to promote the master plan concept as an appropriate policy for any state coping with

expanding demand for higher education. In the early 1960s, the corporation put out a series of nearly two dozen volumes[41] which had resulted
from studies supported by Carnegie grants. The corporation financed the
studies

> to provide facts and recommendations which would be useful to
> all those who make or influence the decisions which shape Amer-
> ican educational policies and institutions.[42]

Many of the volumes in this series directly or indirectly supported the
master plan concept. The series included Conant's widely read treatise on
educational policy, cited above.[43] This work clearly argued for the adoption of master plans, on the grounds of orderly allocation of resources and
preservation of established elite institutions. A key volume in the series
was *A General Pattern for American Education*[44] by T. R. McConnell, who,
as we have noted, devised the major outlines of the California master plan.
His book offered a general blueprint for state master plans, to cope with
the impending "deluge" of college-age Americans expected in the next
decade. The publisher's description of McConnell's book is worth noting
in this connection:

> The author discusses the problems involved in the statewide
> organization of public higher education and analyzes the ways in
> which it can be organized more efficiently, *and proposes ways of
> maintaining the primacy of the major state universities* [emphasis
> added].[45]

Much of the research for the Carnegie studies was conducted through
the Center for the Study of Higher Education, which the corporation had
funded at Berkeley. The research there was largely concentrated in three
areas: (1) statewide coordination of public higher education, (2) the junior
college as a sorting and distributive agency, and (3) the diversity of student
bodies in American higher education.[46] This latter project identified
"academic," "collegiate," and "vocational" student cultures,[47] which, not
surprisingly, correspond to values deemed appropriate to the differing
levels of a stratified system of higher education. This research in turn was
used to bolster an emerging meritocratic ideology that helped to change
the mix of students at established state universities. Where collegiate
values had reigned at these socially elite schools, now academic values
were actively promoted, to provide an appropriate climate for institutions
of the new meritocracy.[48]

The meritocracy could be characterized—and was probably viewed by
Carnegie planners—as an essentially rational, class-free system of allocat-
ing educational resources. But the basic class nature of the master plan,
which was the means developed to achieve such an order in California, in

reality left the higher education system there subject to unanticipated disruption. In 1962, the student population at San Francisco State College was 12 percent black. By 1967, it was 3 percent black, in a city which had fewer than 40 percent white students in its school system.[49] Barlow and Shapiro[50] document how a combination of test scores, counseling, and high-school experiences combined to direct blacks away from San Francisco State to the local junior college. To the extent that what happened to blacks there also happened to other nonwhites and working-class whites generally, it can be seen how the master plan served to channel such categories of students away from the four-year institutions to the two-year colleges, with their emphasis on vocational and terminal programs.

This of course did not pass unnoticed by the socially aware and politically active student generation of the 1960s; and at San Francisco State by the mid-1960s they had initiated their own action to rectify the obvious imbalance of race and class.[51] When ultimately this led to conflict, and hundreds of students battled with riot police in the rainy fall and winter of 1968–1969,[52] the vast majority of Californians had no idea that the trouble stemmed in part from the master plan passed by their own legislature in 1960.[53]

The Carnegie Commission and Council, 1967–1979: Nationwide Masterplans

According to Alan Pifer, president of the Carnegie Corporation, the Carnegie Commission on Higher Education was established in 1966 to study the costs of expanding higher education in America.[54] While the commission's focus was later broadened to include future structure and functions of higher education, the issue of costs and methods of containing them nevertheless remained an underlying theme of the commission. It continued as a focal concern of the Carnegie Council for Policy Studies in Higher Education, which succeeded the commission after 1974.

It should come as no surprise that the Carnegie Corporation was preoccupied with financing in the middle and late 1960s; popular demand for higher education and other welfare state programs was rapidly increasing, along with the costs and the inflationary effects of the war in Southeast Asia. No doubt there was concern in a great many business boardrooms over the possible effects of expanding government programs, civil and military, on federal and state tax structures, which had been generally favorable to corporate profit-making.

The work of the Carnegie Commission provides a dramatic illustration of the power of independent, private funding to create a private policy-making network. During its six years of existence, the commission spent more than $6 million.[55] It was one of the corporation's largest investments in research, ideas, ideology, and public policy proposals for higher education since its establishment early in the century. With this kind of money flow,[56] Carnegie was able to swamp the previously arcane field of higher education studies; to monopolize discussion; identify basic problems; and set agendas for public policy development, implementation, and further research.

The commission's library of more than 100 newly published books and documents was itself a large and up-to-date information resource.[57] But further, the commission's money soon supported and linked together most of the established specialists in the field; and it attracted and helped develop newer and younger scholars, thus adding an incoming generation of experts to the policy network. Given the vital importance of publishing in the definition of scholarly status, the commission's publications helped establish or confirm the credentials of Carnegie specialists as reputable scholars in the field of higher education. At the same time, by consciously pursuing what Clark Kerr characterized as a "liberal moderate" line,[58] the commission in effect excluded Marxist, conservative, countercultural, or any "extreme" ideas and proposals.

As with other privately funded policymaking bodies with links to the corporate ruling class, Carnegie policy groups like the commission operate on two levels. First, they function as quasi-academic research agencies, sponsoring scholarly work which is compatible with a corporate liberal orientation. On another level, they work as subtle and indirect lobbies in government and legislatures. (See the Weischadle chapter for the more direct ways in which the Carnegie Corporation has shaped policy from Washington.) Both the research and policy development, and the lobbying capability, arise from the fact that Carnegie has the money and the time to develop and pursue its goals.

To illustrate the process: the Carnegie policy group monitors developments in higher education and publicly defines what issues merit national attention. It then funds investigations into problems arising out of such issues. The resulting conclusions, arrived at by reliable scholars at leading elite universities, are published, often under Carnegie sponsorship. The results are then directed toward key people in higher education and concerned members of the lay public, reaching the latter via the press and serious opinion journals and magazines. Finally, study results and new policy proposals dealing with the problems earlier identified are directed toward government decision-makers, who now find a mobilized constituency supporting Carnegie's proposals in the apparent absence of anything else.

In other words, by using its extensive resources and established position, the Carnegie Corporation has been able to largely control the parameters of recent serious public debate over higher education in America. While open lobbying by private foundations is illegal, Carnegie through its policy groups has apparently managed to exert influence within the law. Clark Kerr[59] has described the substantial input made by the commission to policy discussions in Washington, when the Higher Education Amendments of 1972 were passed.[60] Carnegie's unique position of strength in the sometimes stormy congressional process that produced the 1972 amendments stemmed from the extensive range of studies that had been previously funded by the commission. As Kerr puts it, the Carnegie Commission, in its "little office out in Berkeley,"[61] had more information, and was able to reach people in the official apparatus *with* more of it, than anyone else:

> We got a lot of requests because we have a lot of information. We
> had people calling . . . from the staffs; people in the House and
> Senate—and I must say not just those friendly to our
> approach—saying: "Will you run it through and see how this will
> affect such-and-such an institution?"[62]

Reflecting upon the "effectiveness" of the commission, and by implication, the long-term Carnegie policy study network, Kerr noted:

> Solid information is a form of power. We had the information
> and it's surprising the impact it has when people get down to the
> hard decisions![63]

The extent to which information is "solid" or accurate varies according to the points of view of those who ask the questions or develop the data. Carnegie's information, essentially, was derived from studies generated by a corporate liberal concern about higher education. As such, it may not have been as "solid" as Kerr assumed. But in the often turbulent process where new legislation is being drafted and debated, any information is frequently in short supply, and whatever information is available can become a usable commodity.

By the time the Carnegie Commission had completed its formal assignment in 1973, it was evident that the main policy theme emerging from its work—clearly outlined in its final report[64]—was the continued promotion of the state master plan concept, but with significantly greater emphasis on controlling enrollments in all public four-year institutions than was advocated in the previous decade. The commission recommended that public higher education in all states follow the California model: large numbers of two-year community colleges should be established within commuting distance of most people; and the various levels of higher education institutions should be clearly differentiated by academic function—community colleges to be primarily concerned with technical and vocational education, state colleges with occupational programs, and the established universities with doctoral and major professional programs.

In addition, the commission recommended that restrictions such as higher tuition charges be implemented at four-year public institutions, ostensibly to help private colleges and universities survive, but in effect to curb enrollment growth at four-year public institutions. Marxist critics Bowles and Gintis[65] emphasize the significance of cutting enrollment in the sector that produces "college graduates." They suggest that Carnegie is attempting to "restrict the size of the reserve army of unemployed white collar workers to politically acceptable levels."[66] In other words, a concentration of unemployed college graduates is a potentially volatile element in a depressed economy. (By contrast, unemployed workers who are "not qualified" would be more likely to blame their failure on themselves than on the economic system.) Bowles and Gintis also see the creation of types of campuses effectively differentiated by social class as an effort to fragment the higher education communities, reducing the chances that students and faculties from all levels might mobilize for common action.[67] They contend that the end result of the commission's work is generally to reinforce and reproduce the existing class sytem.[68] Sociologist Norman Birnbaum,[69] another critic of the commission, has also noted this aspect of the postsecondary structure proposed by Carnegie:

> . . . in proposing a stratified system of higher education, the Commission effectively proposes to continue the stratification of the present one.[70]

Although the Commission formally ended its work in 1973, the Carnegie Corporation's interest in higher education policy continued. By 1974, over 9 million students—more than half of all high-school graduates—were attending postsecondary education institutions, and the total was expected to grow.[71] At the same time, expenditures for higher education had passed $30 billion per year, and were also expected to grow.[72] As Clark Kerr observed, higher education had become such "an enormous enterprise" that it ". . . warrants continuous study."[73] Consequently, the Carnegie Council on Policy Studies in Higher Education was established to maintain the Carnegie Corporation presence in the monitoring and development of higher education policy. Subsequent administrative changes in the late 1970s, however, removed these functions to the venerable Carnegie Foundation for the Advancement of Teaching.[74]

In all, it is clear that the Carnegie Corporation, through its policy groups, will continue to dominate the area of higher education policy. By spending the money to coordinate scholarship, amass information, develop policies, and encourage their adoption, Carnegie has established itself as an important, ostensibly independent, authority to be consulted whenever changes in the structure of American higher education are contemplated.

Master Plan Malfunction: A Case for the Doctor of Arts

This chapter has argued that the Carnegie Corporation of New York has supported the development and promotion of policies for higher education which are primarily in the interests of the American corporate ruling class. These policies have generally followed two main lines during the expansion of mass higher education since World War II. First, Carnegie has favored policies which preserve the elite status of the established major universities in the face of competition from rising institutions with more humble origins such as the public state colleges. Second, Carnegie has played an instrumental role in developing state master plans and in encouraging their adoption. These plans were intended to restrict the development of popular higher education and keep the costs of higher education low enough to avoid disturbing the existing state tax structures which usually favor corporate wealth—the basis of the Carnegie Corporation's constituency.

The extent to which Carnegie pursues these kinds of policies can be illustrated by its persistent efforts to promote and popularize a new doctoral degree—the doctor of arts (D.A.)—designed especially for faculty in four-year state colleges. The corporation's determination to promote the D.A. has been all the more surprising to observers in view of the fact that since the late 1960s many authorities have agreed there is a surplus of men and women with the Ph.D., the degree usually seen as most suitable for college teaching throughout the world.

Our discussion to this point might suggest that the Carnegie Corporation, with its considerable resources, always succeeds in developing higher education policies in line with the views and interests of its corporate ruling class constituency. That is not the case, of course. Carnegie policy proposals, like most others, can have problems or "bugs," and sometimes these are discernible only after the proposals have been implemented as public policy. The master plan model, which Carnegie promoted over two decades, has been subject to such defects. Ironically, a major problem emerged from the internal logic of the master plan concept itself.

By the end of the 1960s, graduate schools at elite-level research universities were overproducing Ph.D.s in all fields. This was not surprising, given the prior demand for large numbers of skilled and specialized experts in the active military, the competitive aerospace race with the Russians, and the generally high-riding economy, as well as demands for fully qualified faculty from new and expanding colleges and universities throughout the country. But when the war in Southeast Asia failed, when the space program succeeded, and the economy stumbled, all at more or less the same time, overproduction occurred in the elite university Ph.D. "factories"—as it did in other American industries at the time.

A few Ph.D.s had found their way into the state colleges before the 1960s, but they were usually a minority among the Ed.D.s remaining from the teachers college days. After 1965, however, Ph.D.s began to appear in greater numbers and make up larger proportions of faculty, particularly as four-year state colleges developed traditional academic undergraduate departments.[75] Inevitably they began to change the tone and level of these "second-tier" state colleges in ways unintended by master plan developers. Their elite Ph.D. preparation had left them with elite notions and tastes; and, relegated to a nonelite setting, they became restless. Ultimately, their activity threatened to destabilize the master plan system of stratification.

In 1970, E. Alden Dunham, a rising executive associate of the Carnegie Corporation, first drew public attention to the problem of the Ph.D. in the state college.[76] Speaking at the annual National Conference for Higher Education, he complained that Ph.D.s at state colleges were not content with teaching the nonelite students assigned to them, but instead were pressuring their colleges to upgrade research. (He implied that the first sign of such pressure was often a concerted effort to change the name "state college" to "state university.") As a result, more graduate programs were being added and more emphasis put on the production of knowledge through research rather than its distribution through teaching. Finally, Ph.D.s on state college faculties were even pushing for doctoral programs (an apparent reappearance of the Southern Illinois syndrome).

That same year, in *Colleges of the Forgotten Americans: A Profile of State Colleges and Regional Universities*,[77] Dunham specifically identified the elite research university graduate schools and their Ph.D. products as "culprits" in this disruption of the newly established hierarchical structure of higher education:

> It is perfectly clear that research-oriented Ph.D.s from these graduate schools will do all they can to transform their employing institutions into what they have just left as students.[78]

This apparently follows from the tendency of state college faculty with Ph.D.s to take the wrong "reference groups":

> A Ph.D. at a state college will always compare his status with that of a colleague at the state university and will seek to do the same kind of things and want to receive the same kind of rewards.[79]

According to Dunham, very few of the 300 or more state colleges in the country could realistically expect to lift themselves to the level of research universities, no matter what the hopes of their faculty. They could not expect to get enough money, or attract "top-flight research faculty" and "academically oriented students."[80] Noting that there are only about fifty truly elite research universities in America, Dunham warned:

> To fight one's way into this group of institutions will be impossible for most. They are doomed to failure if they persist down the current road.[81]

To cope with the problem Dunham advocated replacing the Ph.D. with the Doctor of Arts as the desirable degree requirement for teaching positions at state colleges. He describes the preparation for the D.A. as "taking as much time" as the Ph.D. program,[82] and covering a wider range of substantive areas of knowledge. But the D.A. candidate is not asked to demonstrate ability to carry out independent research; instead, the doctoral project requires candidates to develop materials for courses which they are likely to teach. The program is designed to impart broad subject knowledge and the ability to relate more effectively to students who do not have an academic vocation, the supposed constituency of the state colleges. Such college teachers would be trained to accept "large numbers of students who are less than brilliant"[83]—presumably the "forgotten Americans"—and devote their lives to serving as members of ". . . a faculty really concerned about the personal lives of students and the role of higher education in their development."[84]

The important outcome of all this is that faculty members holding D.A. degrees would have motives and goals different from those with Ph.D.s from elite research programs. Consequently, they would not create problems for systems based on the master plan concept by generating pressures for the upward mobility of their nonelite state colleges.

The higher education master plan maintains existing stratification systems intact even though Clark Kerr advocated that students be permitted "easy transfer on merit"[85] from the less selective segments to the elite layer of institutions.[86] Consigning the D.A. teachers exclusively to the less prestigious, undergraduate teaching levels tends to obstruct articulation between the institutional ranks. One reason for this is that when faculties at both elite research universities and nonelite state colleges have pursued the traditional Ph.D. program, some common ground exists between them—those who have earned the Ph.D., in most cases, have earned it from the same fifty research university graduate schools.[87] State college faculty with the Ph.D. function as a strategic link for students from lower class levels who want to attend graduate school.[88] The master plan with the D.A. faculty in the state colleges could curtail this linkage.

Dunham has admitted that Ph.D. faculty at research universities would be hesitant to accept D.A.s as colleagues, even as teaching faculty in their departments.[89] In a similar vein, Dressel and Thompson, two Carnegie-sponsored researchers, have observed that the D.A. degree is inappropriate for highly selective undergraduate institutions which send large numbers of students to graduate schools.[90] Clearly, then, it becomes questionable whether the research university faculty, who control entrance to graduate programs, would readily accept students of state college teachers with the D.A. on an equal basis with students prepared by faculty of their own academic standing. The resulting loss of bridges between institutional ranks could effectively block the upward mobility—regardless of "merit"—of poor-but-talented or late-blooming state college students.

Invidious distinctions of this kind would not likely remain restricted to academic circles. State college graduates could find themselves regarded as much less desirable by a wide range of employers, both public and private. Thus the doctor of arts policy advocated by Carnegie seems likely to increase the chances of educational class becoming educational caste in American society. Such issues become increasingly important as more and more students from all social class levels come under pressure to attend college in order to compete in a more highly schooled labor force. (An earlier generation went to college to get ahead; now students go to institutions of mass higher education, and go longer, to keep from falling behind.)

Notwithstanding the probable deleterious consequences of such stratification in higher education for a democratic "open class" society, the Carnegie Corporation has vigorously pushed for widespread training and utilization of teachers with the doctor of arts degree. After funding a pilot project at Carnegie-Mellon University in 1967,[91] the corporation by 1970 had given "planning grants" totaling nearly a million dollars to a broad range of institutions.[92] From that date the cash has continued to flow into D.A. programs across the country, so that by 1975 more than $2 million had been disbursed.[93] Carnegie has also spent money to bring the disparate programs together and to encourage joint institutional efforts. For example, a 1970 grant to the Council of Graduate Schools (created by a Carnegie grant in the early 1960s)[94] underwrote a conference at which representatives of the scattered campuses with new D.A. programs could exchange ideas and provide mutual moral support.[95]

For a time, the alleged "Ph.D. surplus" of the early 1970s appeared to threaten the D.A. campaign. In addition, both federal and state money for new graduate programs was being cut everywhere, and a number of states stopped development of all new degree programs. But the new doctor of arts program was kept moving: as some campuses dropped the program,

Carnegie simply funded others eager to receive outside money to replace shrinking local funds.[96] In 1977, Carnegie sponsored a survey of the progress of the D.A. program, and the new degree was pronounced "here and here to stay"[97]—despite previous stories to the contrary in the higher education trade press.[98] The survey showed over twenty institutions across the country which were offering the degree, with 482 doctors of arts already graduated and another 740 candidates in current programs.[99]

Probably the most decisive move towards possible general adoption of the D.A. at four-year state colleges has come with the decision by the Regents of the State of New York to have one of the research universities in the State University of New York system, together with the private Syracuse University, prepare D.A. degree faculty for the four-year and two-year colleges in the New York state system.[100] This decision by the regents was underwritten by a three-year Carnegie grant of $347,000. The implications of the decision are illuminated by these lines from the corporation's 1976 *Annual Report*:

> The Regents of the State of New York is the first state governing board to endorse and actively encourage the Doctor of Arts degree. Since it awards 11 percent of all doctorates in the nation, *this breakthrough could have considerable impact in other states* [emphasis added].[101]

It is easy to speculate on the consequences if California—with an even higher output of doctoral students—were to adopt a similar arrangement, with the elite University of California awarding D.A. degrees, which in turn would become the standard teaching requirement at the "second tier" state universities and colleges. Projecting the anticipated round of retirements in the 1980s (of faculty hired en masse in the 1950s and early 1960s), it is conceivable that Carnegie's proposal to phase out Ph.D.s from most state colleges might very well prove feasible and succeed. At this time, no sensible person would rule out Carnegie's chances for eventual success, given the long-term resources and perspectives with which the corporation and its staff are accustomed to working.

The Carnegie Corporation of New York: Who Does It Represent?

The simple question of what Carnegie's exact role is in America's public (and private) higher education has stimulated at least one official explanation from Alan Pifer, the corporation's president: "Its mission is to speak to the nation about the vast enterprise of higher education, not for it."[102]

After noting that private foundations or corporations like Carnegie (with hundreds of millions of dollars in investments) enjoy constitutional rights of free expression "like anyone else," Pifer goes on to describe the unique independence by which Carnegie policy and study groups are characterized:

> It should be evident that Carnegie . . . does not in any respect "represent" higher education, including its associations, institutions, or its estates—that is, trustee, administrators, faculty, students and alumni. . . .[103]

Pifer fails to define further just who or what this large philanthropic foundation *has* been representing through the years, but this chapter has sought to provide some answers to that question. In brief, the interests represented by Carnegie are clearly ruling-class interests, primarily of a corporate-liberal bent. Characteristically liberal aspects have been evident in its advocacy of a controlled expansion of mass higher education, not only to allow for the alleviation of tensions generated by a clearly stratified industrial society, but also to enlarge the profitmaking base upon which monopoly capital itself can operate successfully.

The expansion of mass higher education has been encouraged, insofar as it has created new kinds of workers at many levels for an industrial state controlled by the corporate ruling class of which Carnegie is an interlocked part.[104] At the same time, widespread disruption or rearrangement of the existing class system has been avoided. Carnegie's liberal mission has included the development of new structures to ensure that the corporate ruling class continues to rule in America, and that the middle and working classes stay in their appropriate places in the division of labor, with their same relative share of the social division of wealth.

Concluding Reflections

It is interesting to speculate about the meaning of the organizational changes that were announced by Carnegie at the end of the 1970s.[105] The Carnegie Foundation for the Advancement of Teaching (long a front group and funding conduit for the parent corporation) was reorganized to absorb the activity of the Carnegie Council for Policy Studies in Higher Education, due to terminate with Clark Kerr's retirement at the end of 1979.

Under Kerr, both the council and the commission which preceded it pursued highly visible and activist roles as privately controlled research and development agencies for public policy in higher education. The Carnegie Foundation, on the other hand, has historically functioned more from the background. It appears possible that we will hear fewer public statements about higher education from Carnegie: the reason being, perhaps, that the original need for a publicly visible monitoring and policy promoting agency in the area of higher education no longer exists. At the end of the 1970s it can probably be said that James B. Conant's[106] concerns about the effects of massive expansion on higher education have been resolved. A combination of Carnegie-promoted master plan policies, plus years of economic decay, have taken much of the public appeal out of mass higher education as an answer to private and public social problems—now that significant numbers of graduates are unemployed, or underemployed, in jobs that until recently did not require a college degree.[107]

The flood of expanding demand for higher education has been brought under control for the first time since the end of World War II. Furthermore, this demand has been *restratified*, that is, brought into a state of compatibility with the established class structure. Disruption threatening the basic integrity of that class hierarchy has been headed off by publicly enacted educational policies preventing more "lower class" colleges (like Southern Illinois University) from moving up in the academic hierarchy. Access to the top of the class structure has been preserved for the elite, while the masses have been held in check by a tristratified system allowing them movement up only if they can prove individual merit.[108]

Thus, its work at center stage done, Carnegie can safely move to the background. Higher education has been defused as a mechanism of democratization, and it no longer threatens to confound the established social order of the American corporate system.

Notes

1. C. Wright Mills, *The Power Elite* (New York: Oxford University Press, 1956); G. William Domhoff, *Who Rules America?* (Englewood Cliffs, N.J.: Prentice-Hall, 1967); G. William Domhoff and Hoyt Ballard, *C. Wright Mills and the Power Elite* (Boston: Beacon Press, 1968).
2. E. Digby Baltzell, *Philadelphia Gentlemen: The Making of a National Upper Class* (Glencoe, Ill.: The Free Press, 1958); William Miller, "The Recruitment of the Business Elite" *Quarterly Journal of Economics* 64 (May 1950): 242–253; William Miller, *Men in Business* (Cambridge, Mass.: Harvard University Press, 1952); G. William Domhoff, *The Higher Circles: The Governing Class in America* (New York: Vintage Books–Random House, 1971).
3. G. William Domhoff (ed.), "New Directions in Power Structure Research," Special Issue of *Insurgent Sociologist* 5 (Spring 1975).
4. Domhoff, *Higher Circles*, Part Two: Lawrence H. Shoup, "Shaping the Postwar World: The Council on Foreign Relations and United States War Aims during World War Two," *Insurgent Sociologist* 5 (Spring

1975): 106–116; Thomas R. Dye, "Oligarchic Tendencies in National Policy Making: The Role of the Private Policy-Making Organizations," *Journal of Politics* 40 (May 1978): 309–331.

5. Clarence Karier, "Testing for Order and Control in the Corporate Liberal State," *Educational Theory* 22 (Spring 1972): 154–180.

6. F. Emerson Andrews, *Philanthropic Foundations* (New York: Russell Sage Foundation, 1956); Raymond B. Fosdick, *The Story of the Rockefeller Foundation* (New York: Harper and Bros., 1952); Howard J. Savage, *Fruit of an Impulse: Forty-Five Years of the Carnegie Foundation: 1905–1950* (New York: Harcourt Brace and Company, 1953); David N. Smith, *Who Rules the University? An Essay in Class Analysis* (New York: Monthly Review Press, 1974).

7. Shoup, "Shaping Postwar World"; G. William Domhoff, "Social Clubs, Policy-Planning Groups, and Corporations: A Network Study of Ruling-Class Cohesiveness," *Insurgent Sociologist* 5 (Spring 1975): 173–184; and his *Higher Circles.*

8. Domhoff, "Social Clubs."

9. Domhoff, *Higher Circles*, Part Two: also see the chapter by Mary Anna Culleton Colwell in this book.

10. Ibid.

11. Domhoff, *Who Really Rules? New Haven and Community Power Reexamined* (Santa Monica: Goodyear, 1978), Chapter 4.

12. Ibid., Chapter 5.

13. Savage, *Carnegie Foundation.*

14. Carnegie Corporation of New York, *Annual Report, 1976* (New York: the same, 1977).

15. Even a superficial examination of Carnegie Corporation board members early in the 1970s yielded the following results. Of the seventeen listed trustees, ten were high corporate executives, corporate lawyers, or corporate board members. Four were senior staff at leading academic, cultural, or research centers in the country; the fifteenth was a salaried officer of the Carnegie Corporation itself; the remaining two, one of whom was Margaret Carnegie Miller, were women listing no occupations or occupations of husbands or other male relatives. More recently, new kinds of presumably "safe" board members—women, nonwhites, and a conservative labor leader—have replaced a few white males. Nevertheless, preliminary study indicates that the corporate interlocks and other connections appear to persist (see the Carnegie Corporation, *Annual Report, 1976*). At the present time, a number of students at California State University, Sacramento, are undertaking a study of the corporate connections of all Trustees of the Carnegie Corporation since its founding in 1911. Also see the chapter by Colwell in this book.

16. James O'Connor, *The Fiscal Crisis of the State* (New York: St. Martin's Press, 1973).

17. Karier, "Testing for Order;" see also Russell Marks's chapter in this book.

18. Samuel Bowles and Herbert Gintis, *Schooling in Capitalist America: Educational Reform and the Contradictions of Economic Life* (New York: Basic

Books/Harper, 1977). For an alternative non-Marxist discussion of expansion in American higher education see Martin Trow, "The Second Transformation of American Secondary Education," *International Journal of Comparative Sociology 2 (1961): 144–165.*

19. Carnegie Foundation for the Advancement of Teaching, *State Higher Education in California* (Sacramento: State Printing Office, 1932), p. 15.

20. Ibid.

21. Ibid., p. 66.

22. Savage, *Carnegie Foundation*, p. 209; Neil Smelser, "Growth, Structural Change and Conflict in California Public Higher Education, 1950–1960," in Smelser and Gabriel Almond, *Public Higher Education in California* (Berkeley: University of California Press, 1974); Verne A. Stadtman, *The University of California, 1868–1968* (New York: McGraw-Hill Book Company, 1970).

23. Keith W. Olson, *The G.I. Bill: The Veterans and the Colleges* (Lexington, Ky.: The University Press of Kentucky, 1974), p. 27; David D. Henry, *Challenges Past, Challenges Present: An Analysis of American Higher Education Since 1930* (San Francisco: Jossey-Bass, 1975), Chapter 4.

24. Henry, *Challenges Past*, Chapter 7.

25. James B. Conant, *Shaping Educational Policy* (New York: McGraw-Hill, 1964), p. 52.

26. Ibid.

27. Ibid., p. 51.

28. Ibid., p. 54. Another view, this one more sympathetic to Southern Illinois University and its evolution over the years from Southern Illinois Normal University, founded in 1874 at Carbondale, is to be found in George K. Plochmann, *The Ordeal of Southern Illinois University* (Carbondale: Southern Illinois University Press, 1957). For an updated and also sympathetic view of SIU and its long-term policy of bringing elite educational opportunities to the nonelite masses in the heart of middle America, also see John Gardner, "Southern Illinois University," *Change: The Magazine of Higher Learning* 5 (June 1973): 42–48.

29. Clark Kerr, "Higher Education: Paradise Lost?" *Higher Education* 7 (August 1978): 261–278.

30. William Barlow and Peter Shapiro, *An End to Silence: The San Francisco State Student Movement in the 60s* (New York: Bobbs-Merrill, Inc., 1971), Chapter 1. At a more theoretical level see Randall Collins, "Functional and Conflict Theories of Educational Stratification," *American Sociological Review* 36 (December 1971): 1002–1018; and John W. Meyer, "The Effects of Education as an Institution," *American Journal of Sociology* 83 (July 1977): 55–77.

31. T. W. Schultz, "Investment in Human Capital," *American Economic Review* 51 (March 1961): 1–17; Gary S. Becker, *Human Capital: A Theoretical and Empirical Analysis with Special Reference to Education* (New York: Columbia University Press, 1964). It is interesting to note that the Becker monograph was published with funds from the Carnegie Corporation, suggesting high-level interest in ideas that today appear to be out of

vogue in policymaking circles. For further evidence of the earlier acceptance of such a theory by the U.S. ruling elite, note the use of "human
capital" ideology in the passage quoted from President John F. Kennedy's message to Congress on education in 1963, quoted in Henry,
Challenges Past, 1975, pp. 127–128. This point of view pervaded President Johnson's economic and anti-poverty legislation. By 1967, there is
some evidence that the U.S. corporate ruling class was at least having
second thoughts about further investment in "human capital" (see below:
establishment of the Carnegie Commission on Higher Education).
32. Arthur G. Coons, *Crisis in California Higher Education: Experience under the
Master Plan and Problems of Coordination, 1959–1968* (Los Angeles: The
Ward Ritchie Press, 1968), Chapter 5.
33. Ibid.
34. T. R. McConnell, T. C. Holly, and H. H. Semans, "California Studies Its
Needs and Resources in Higher Education," *Educational Record* 36
(October 1955): pp. 291-303; Ann M. Heiss, Joseph R. Mixer, and James
G. Paltridge, eds., *Participants and Patterns in Higher Education: Research and Reflections; A Festschrift for T. R. McConnell* (Berkeley:
School of Education, University of California, 1973), p. viii.
35. T. R. McConnell, T. C. Holly, and H. H. Semans, *A Restudy of the Needs of
California in Higher Education* (Sacramento: California State Department of Education, 1955).
36. Barlow and Shapiro, *End to Silence*, Chapter 7; Coons, *Crisis in California
Higher Education*, passim; Marc R. Tool, *The California State Colleges
under the Master Plan; A Report of the Academic Senate in the California
State Colleges* (San Diego: Aztec Press, August 1, 1966).
37. Kerr, "Higher Education."
38. McConnell, Holly, and Semans, *Restudy*; Barlow and Shapiro, *End to
Silence*, Chapters 1 and 7.
39. Burton R. Clark, "The Cooling-Out Function in Higher Education," *American Journal of Sociology* 65 (May 1960): 569–576; Barlow and Shapiro,
End to Silence, pp. 182–183.
40. Bowles and Gintis, *Schooling*, pp. 205–223.
41. This was *The Carnegie Series in American Education*, published by McGraw-
Hill Book Company. Nearly two dozen of these volumes were published
in the late 1950s and the early 1960s. Later the same publisher issued the
Carnegie Commission Series, beginning about 1968; see below.
42. From the page facing the title page of T. R. McConnell, *A General Pattern
for American Public Higher Education* (New York: McGraw-Hill Book
Company, 1962).
43. Conant, *Shaping Educational Policy*.
44. McConnell, *General Pattern*.
45. Ibid.
46. Ibid.
47. Burton R. Clark, *Educating the Expert Society* (San Francisco: Chandler,
1962); and his *The Distinctive College: Antioch, Reed, and Swarthmore*
(Chicago: Aldine, 1970), p. 267. Altogether the Center for Higher Educa-

tion researchers at Berkeley developed four "student subcultures" based on their studies at Reed, Swarthmore, Antioch, St. Olaf, and San Francisco State colleges, and from the University of Portland, University of the Pacific, and the University of California at Berkeley. In addition to the academic, collegiate, and vocational subcultures, there was a "nonconformist" subculture. These different subcultures could be found in varying degrees on all campuses and, in some cases, one of the subcultures could be said to characterize a particular campus. According to Clark, the four types of cultures emerged analytically from a combination of two factors: a) the degree to which students are involved with ideas, and b) the extent to which students identify with their college. Collegiate types, for example, were high on identification with a college, but low on involvement with ideas; whereas nonconformists were low on identification, but high on academic involvement. Academic subcultures are high on both factors, while vocational ones are low on both. Some have suggested that it was out of the mix of the nonconformist and academic subcultures that the student movements of the 1960s emerged.

48. Christopher Jencks and David Riesman noted the scramble by elite universities, including leading public universities, for National Merit Scholars in the post-*Sputnik* era; see their *The Academic Revolution* (Garden City: Doubleday and Co., Inc., 1968), pp. 164–165. For an excellent account of the build-up to this in lower schools see Joel Spring, *The Sorting Machine: National Educational Policy Since 1945* (New York: David MacKay Co., Inc., 1976), Chapters 1–3.

49. Barlow and Shapiro, *End to Silence*, pp. 184–185.

50. Ibid.

51. Ibid., Chapter 3.

52. Ibid., Chapters 9 and 10; see also E. Alden Dunham, *Colleges of the Forgotten Americans: A Profile of State Colleges and Regional Universities* (New York: McGraw-Hill Book Company, 1969), pp. 147–150.

53. Barlow and Shapiro, *End to Silence*, Chapter 7.

54. Alan Pifer, "The Nature and Origins of the Carnegie Commission on Higher Education," in *Priorities for Action: Final Report of the Carnegie Commission on Higher Education* (New York: McGraw-Hill Book Company, 1973), Appendix F.

55. Darknell, "The Carnegie Council."

56. Ibid.; and Domhoff, *Who Really Rules?* pp. 134–135.

57. "An Agenda for What? The Carnegie Commission on Higher Education," special section in *Change: The Magazine of Higher Learning* 5 (November 1973): 4–44.

58. "90 Minutes with Clark Kerr," a taped interview of Kerr by George W. Bonham, editor of *Change: The Magazine of Higher Learning*. Available c/o *Change* Cassettes, NBW Tower, New Rochelle, New York, 10801. Note especially Part I: "On the Commission."

59. Ibid.

60. Ibid.

61. Ibid.

62. Ibid.
63. Ibid.
64. Carnegie Commission on Higher Education, *Priorities for Action.*
65. Bowles and Gintis, *Schooling.*
66. Ibid., p. 206.
67. Ibid., pp. 203–213.
68. Ibid., Chapter 8.
69. Norman Birnbaum, "The Politics of the Future," *Change: The Magazine of Higher Learning* 5 (November 1973): 28–37.
70. Ibid., p. 36.
71. Carnegie Foundation for the Advancement of Teaching, press release, New York, January 21, 1974.
72. Ibid.
73. Ibid.
74. Ibid.
75. Dunham, *Colleges of the Forgotten Americans*, Chapter 6.
76. Alden E. Dunham, "Rx for Higher Education: The Doctor of Arts Degree," *Journal of Higher Education* 41 (October 1970): 505–512.
77. Dunham, *Colleges of the Forgotten Americans.*
78. Ibid., p. 157.
79. Ibid., p. 164.
80. Ibid., p. 157.
81. Ibid.
82. Ibid., p. 161.
83. Ibid., p. 158.
84. Ibid., p. 164.
85. Kerr, "Higher Education."
86. Ibid.
87. Dunham, in *Colleges of the Forgoten Americans*, p. 157, appears to agree with this. Generally, most Ph.D.s come from the same thirty to fifty graduate schools.
88. Some science and engineering faculty interviewed recently by the author at a California state college reported citing their own academic qualifications when recommending students to major graduate schools, because of the disdain with which faculty at the latter sometimes view state college applicants.
89. Dunham, *Colleges of the Forgottlen Americans*, p. 160.
90. Paul L. Dressel and Mary Magdala Thompson, *A Degree for College Teachers: The Doctor of Arts; a Technical Report of the Carnegie Council on Policy Studies in Higher Education* (Berkeley: Carnegie Council on Policy Studies in Higher Education, 1977), pp. 4–5.
91. Carnegie Institute of Technology, "A Presentation to the Carnegie Corporation Requesting Support for the Carnegie Education Center" (mimeo), March 21, 1966 (unsigned). This was apparently prepared by teacher-training and other education faculty at C.I.T. the year before the latter became Carnegie-Mellon University. My thanks to colleague Duane Campbell of the School of Education, California State University, Sacra-

mento (who was one of the first Doctor of Arts degree-holders to come out of the program in the late 1960s) for allowing me to examine and use this material.

92. Dressel and Thompson, *Degree for College Teachers*, pp. 15–16.
93. Carnegie Corporation of New York, *Annual Report, 1975* (New York: the same, 1976), pp. 19–20.
94. Carnegie Corporation of New York, *Annual Report, 1970* (New York: the same, 1971), pp. 38–39.
95. Dressel and Thompson, *Degree for College Teachers*, pp. 15–16.
96. Ibid.; see also Carnegie Corporation, *Annual Reports*, 1970–1976.
97. Dressel and Thompson, *Degree for College Teachers*, p. 56. Under Carnegie sponsorship, Dressel and Thompson evaluated the Doctor of Arts program throughout the United States after nearly ten years of operation. Their assessment of the state of "health" and the prospects for the D.A. campaign was highly positive. Funding of this evaluation is noted in the *Annual Report, 1975* of the Corporation. That report also mentions a prior study conducted by Dressel and Thompson in 1972. All of this is cited to indicate the continuing serious and long-term commitment the Carnegie Corporation has provided the Doctor of Arts program in its efforts to establish the use of the degree as a policy in American public state colleges. One cannot imagine an American corporation working harder to promote and establish a market for any commercial product.
98. *The Chronicle of Higher Education*, April 19, 1973, p. 4; May 28, 1974, p. 3; and March 22, 1976, p. 11.
99. Dressel and Thompson, *Degree for College Teachers*, pp. 18–19.
100. Carnegie Corporation of New York, *Annual Report, 1976*, pp. 23–24, 37–38.
101. Ibid., p. 37.
102. Carnegie Commission on Higher Education, *Priorities for Action*, Appendix F.
103. Ibid.
104. See note 15; also Frank Darknell, "The Carnegie Corporation: Directing Higher Education," *Edcentric: A Journal of Educational Change* 36 (October 1975): 14–17, 32; Domhoff, *Higher Circles*, Part 2; and Smith, *Who Rules the University*? Chapter 5.
105. Carnegie Corporation of New York/Carnegie Foundation for the Advancement of Teaching, press release, New York, December 5, 1977.
106. Conant, *Shaping Educational Policy*.
107. James O'Toole, "The Reserve Army of the Underemployed," *Change: The Magazine of Higher Learning* 7 (May 1975): 26–33, 60–63.
108. Kerr, "Higher Education"; Martin Trow, "Aspects of Diversity in American Higher Education," in Herbert Gans, et al., eds., *On the Making of Americans: Essays in Honor of David Riesman* (Philadelphia: University of Pennsylvania Press, 1979); and Martin Trow, "Elite Higher Education: An Endangered Species," *Minerva 14:3 (1976): 335–376.*

Mary Anna Culleton Colwell

The Foundation Connection: Links among Foundations and Recipient Organizations

In a review of the current writing on public policy analysis, political scientist Richard Simeon writes, "We have focused too much on the official decision makers and not enough on the influences which shape the alternatives they consider, the assumptions they make, and the kinds of actions they take."[1] Among the influences which help to set the public agenda of discussion and action are the private policy formation organizations. These organizations have as their principal objective the development of policy options and strategies which are then urged upon the appropriate level of government. Most of the policy-oriented organizations are nonprofit and depend upon several sources for the funding which keeps them in existence. Many of them rely on the philanthropic foundations particularly for new or large projects. This study is part of a research project examining the degree to which philanthropic foundations have the potential to influence public policy in a significant way through the relationships of the foundations to the public policy organizations. One aspect of this relationship between foundations and organizations is the presence of foundation trustees on the boards of directors of the organizations concerned with public policy issues. Although the largest portion of the research project was focused on grants to projects affecting public policy, the literature on the role of institutional directors suggested that overlapping board memberships also were worthy of investigation.[2] As the research progressed, it became obvious there were three kinds of direct links and several forms of indirect links which, together, might form a network of communication and mutual influence. The direct links through trustees or board members are (1) foundation to foundation, (2) foundation to organization, and (3) organization to organization. One individual may be involved in several of these direct links among foundation boards and recipient organization boards. In addition there are several kinds of indirect links which appeared as the data were analyzed. The best way to explain these is by an example. There is no direct overlap between the board of trustees of foundations A, B, and C, but one trustee from each board is a member of the board of Foundation D; a different trustee from each foundation board is on the board of organization F, which also has a trustee from Foundation D on its board. In such a case, the indirect links might provide a channel for relatively easy communication not only between organization F and foundations A, B, C, and D but also among the foundations which are directly and indirectly linked. As such instances multiply, there is a relatively complex web of connections.

The critical connections in this network seem to me to be the links which involve foundation trustees. As John Nason established in his comprehensive study of foundation trustees, in most cases the trustees *are* the foundation.[3] In the relatively small percentage of foundations with professional program staff, the trustees are still responsible for policy and decisions. Nason's study, interviews conducted for this research, and my experience as the executive director of a foundation all suggest that the attitudes, knowledge, values, and goals of the foundation trustees are a critical element in what foundations do, with very few exceptions. Foundation trustees are much less likely to be compliant supporters of staff than are the boards of directors of recipient organizations. Foundation boards of trustees are relatively small, most trustees come to most meetings, and there is strong incentive to develop mutual trust and a close working relationship within the board of trustees. Trustees are fairly consistently on the receiving end of a large flow of information from staff, from applicants, and from prior grantees, as well as their peers and colleagues in their regular occupation or profession. The overlapping board memberships between recipient organizations do not seem to be as significant as those involving foundations because many organizations have very large boards, many of the most prestigious individuals on the boards attend meetings irregularly, if at all, and there is always the potential for different factions to develop over policy disagreements within the board. Nevertheless, multiple overlaps between organizations involving board members, staff, funding sources, and areas of program interest certainly suggest strong connecting links and a channel for communication.

Several authors have identified foundations as part of the elite power structure in the United States which influences public and private policy decisions. The clearest statement of the power structure position related to foundations is found in the writing of G. William Domhoff. In his books and in several articles, he advances a theory of influence and power of the corporate elite which utilizes foundations as one way of influencing the formation of public policy through funding of groups concerned with policy—such as the Council on Foreign Relations and the Committee for Economic Development—and support for the recent proliferation of "think tanks." He also traces foundation influence through the appointment of foundation trustees and staff and foundation created "experts" to high level governmental positions, and to "blue ribbon commissions."[4]

Domhoff describes the way in which the "economically and politically active members of the ruling class, operating as the leaders of the power elite, involve themselves in government at all levels."[5] The four processes are:

1. The special interest process, which has to do with the various means utilized by wealthy individuals, specific corporations, and specific sectors of the economy to satisfy their narrow, short-run needs;
2. The policy-planning process which has to do with the development and implementation of general policies that are important to the interests of the ruling class as a whole;
3. The candidate-selection process, which has to do with the ways in which members of the ruling class insure that they have "access" to the politicians who are elected to office; and
4. The ideology process, which has to do with the formation, dissemination, and enforcement of attitudes and assumptions which permit the continued existence of policies and politicians favorable to the wealth, income, status, and privileges of members of the ruling class.[6]

According to Domhoff, foundations are involved in the second and fourth processes by funding many of the policy-formation groups which bring together members of the elite and their hired experts and "provide a setting in which differences on various issues can be thrashed out and the opinions of various experts can be heard";[7] and the ideology process, through which an attempt is made to convince the public that "this is, for all its defects, the best of all possible worlds."[8] (Also see chapter by Slaughter and Silva.)

In spite of these suggestions by Domhoff and other power structure theorists, there is surprisingly little empirical research on foundations. A few researchers on elite networks have included foundation trustees in the search for connections.[9] A recent study identifying "one large, cohesive group of leaders, representing all major institutions and issue areas, which serves to integrate the network" of American leaders, however, did not include data on the involvement of philanthropic foundations in the key institutional sectors "assumed to exercise power in American society."[10] This very illuminating study is typical of much research on elites in that the "foundation connection" is rarely specified.

My study of foundation linkages began with (1) a sample of foundations with an interest in public policy issues as evidenced by grants and (2) a sample of the organizations funded by these foundations. This is a different approach from that utilized in previous research on foundations.

The trustees for each of the sample foundations and the directors for each of the sample recipient organizations are the individuals who may or may not be involved in overlapping board memberships. By examination of overlapping board memberships, it is possible to establish the potential network of connections among foundations, among organizations, and between foundations and organizations. These overlapping board memberships provide a nexus for communication and interaction which influences grants and may influence the programs and perspectives of the policy formation organizations.

One of the peculiarities of the foundation sector is that there is a wide variation in practice with respect to funding organizations which have a board overlap with a foundation. Such overlaps often are not considered a conflict-of-interest situation. Some foundations, however, have fairly strict conflict of interest guidelines; and the trustee, who sits on the board of an organization applying for a grant, may be excluded from the discussion and/or the vote on an application. Other foundations, probably the majority, expect the trustees who belong to various nonprofit organization boards to be very influential in the decision about how much money to contribute. A prominent example was the controversy on the Rockefeller Brothers Fund board because the "brothers" proposed giving away a large portion of the assets to cultural institutions in which they had a special interest.[11] Interviews conducted during this research revealed, and logic suggests, that many organizations seek trustees of foundations as members of their boards of directors precisely because they improve their access to that foundation, and to the foundation sector as a whole. As the fund raiser of one recipient organization explained, having foundation trustees on the board of directors provides "credibility"; foundation trustees sometimes express the conviction that they can know more about an organization and therefore, make better grant decisions, if they are on the organization's board of directors. One, therefore, would expect some overlaps between foundation boards and the boards of recipient organizations.

The tax laws currently regulating the activity of foundations make it very desirable that organizations receive their funding from several foundations rather than one. If a private foundation contributes more than 33 percent of an organization's budget, it is required to assume what is called in the Tax Reform Act of 1969 "expenditure responsibility."[12] Expenditure responsibility grants entail, as a minimum, greatly increased reporting requirements for most organizations and most foundations and may involve the foundation in legal liability for the actions of the organization. Therefore, there is a strong incentive for foundations to share the funding of organizations. This effort requires communication between trustees of different foundations, especially if the trustees of one foundation have to agree to support certain organizations in return for support by another foundation of the organizations they are primarily interested in. These reciprocal grant arrangements may involve staff as well as trustees in the foundations which have staff, and, in any case, are the results of personal conversations and not formal agreements. This situation generated by the tax law provisions increases the need and desirability of communication among trustees. It does not, however, suggest the necessity or likelihood of overlapping board memberships among foundations. Most of what is written about foundations, on the contrary, describes them as independent and autonomous, if not idiosyncratic, and one would therefore not expect many overlapping board memberships among foundations.

This examination of links among foundations and organizations was based on the assumption that there would be a few connections between foundations and organizations but almost no direct connections among foundations. Before examining the results of the research, it is useful to review some facts about philanthropic foundations and explain the research sample.

The Foundation Sector

There are many thousands of entities listed as foundations by the Internal Revenue Service. The current number is approximately 22,000, although many of these are not grantmaking foundations.[13] Only 10 to 20 percent of this number satisfy the criteria for inclusion in editions 4,5, and 6 of the *Foundation Directory*, as may be seen in Table 1.

For those seeking to understand the place of foundations in American society, fewer than 5,000 and probably only 3,000 comprise the effective foundation sector which accounts for a very high percentage of the total

Table 1 *Criteria for Inclusion of Foundations in Various Editions of the Foundation Directory and Number Included*

Foundation Directory Edition	Minimum Assets	Minimum Grants	Total Included
4 (1971)	$ 500,000	$ 25,000	5,454
5 (1975)	1,000,000	500,000	2,533[a]
6 (1977)	1,000,000	100,000	2,818

Source: F.D., Edition 4, p. vii; Edition 5, p. xi; Edition 6, pp. xi–xii.
[a]This number accounted for 90 percent of all foundation assets and 80 percent of all foundation giving in the year of record.

assets and total giving of all grant-making foundations. A few small family or corporate foundations not included in the *Foundation Directory* may have special impact in a town or county. Recently, the "alternative" foundations established by young liberal heirs to wealth, which are too small to be listed in the *Foundation Directory*, have begun to play a special role.[14] For purposes of social research, however, the appropriate universe is essentially the grant-making foundations included in various editions of the *Directory*. Most social science and popular writing about foundations, in fact, has been limited to a very small percentage of this total— generally the two to four dozen foundations with assets over $100 million (depending on the year) and a few others well known for funding artists, academics, and medical research, such as the Guggenheim foundations, the Russell Sage Foundation, the Milbank Memorial Fund, and so on.

The Research Sample

For the purposes of the larger research project on foundations and public policy, a sample of seventy-seven foundations was drawn from the 400 foundations with assets over $10 million in 1974.[15] The sample includes all the grantmaking private foundations over $100 million in assets (twenty-six foundations), a 20 percent random sample of the foundations between $25 million and $100 million in assets (twenty-five foundations), and a 10 percent sample of the foundations between $10 million and $25 million (twenty-six foundations). The grants for all these foundations were examined for 1972 and 1975 and allocated to the usual categories (Arts and Humanities, Education, Health, Welfare, Religion, International, Science) and a special category of grants constructed for this research. [16] This category included what were considered public affairs, public interest, or policy-oriented programs and projects related to the operation of the political/legal or economic system—the political economy. Selection of public affairs grants followed criteria suggested by Jane H. Mavity and Paul N. Ylvisaker in a report to the Commission on Private Philanthropy and Public Needs (the Filer Commission), "those grants which more permanently and/or fundamentally affect the processes of government, the agenda of public action, and the allocation of public resources."[17] The special category also included grants to what has become known as the "public interest movement" and to organizations which appear to be involved in the processes described by Domhoff. Twenty foundations of the original sample of seventy-seven gave over 5 percent of their total grants or over $200,000 in either 1972 or 1975 in this special category of what are here called public policy grants. (See Table 2 for list of foundations.)

Using the grants in the special category of the subsample of twenty foundations, a sample of recipient organizations was chosen which included all the organizations receiving grants from three or more of the twenty foundations. These thirty-one recipient organizations (see Table 6) cover a very wide range of ideological and political perspectives, as do the programs for which they received grants from the subsample of foundations. The organizations range from the relatively obscure to the well known and vary substantially in size.[18] Those which are relatively obscure include the Alternative Educational Foundation, which publishes the *American Spectator* (formerly the *Alternative*), the monthly voice of young conservatism, and several strongly anti-Communist and pro-free-enterprise organizations (Foreign Policy Research Institute, Freedoms Foundations at Valley Forge, Intercollegiate Studies Institute). Among the better-known policy formation organizations are the Brookings Institution, the Committee for Economic Development, the Council on Foreign Relations, and their more conservative counterparts, the American Enterprise Institute for Public Policy Research and the Hoover Institution on War, Revolution and Peace. Ideologically, the organizations range from those strongly committed to increasing participation of ordinary citizens in public and private policy decisions which affect their lives, such as the Center for Community Change and the Youth Project, to the elitist policy formation organizations listed above. The several legal organizations include the well-known civil rights organizations and some new ones, as well as the antilabor National Right-to-Work Legal Defense Fund.

The trustees of the twenty public policy sample foundations and the members of the board of directors of the thirty-one recipient organizations comprise the group of individuals examined in this effort to look at links among foundations and organizations. The names of these individuals were checked against the Index of Donors, Trustees, and Administrators in Editions 4, 5, and 6 of the *Foundation Directory*. The results of this examination are reported in the next section.

Findings

TRUSTEES OF THE PUBLIC POLICY SAMPLE FOUNDATIONS: FOUNDATION LINKS

Over the period of time covered by the three editions of *Foundation Directory*, 255 individuals served as trustees of the twenty public policy sample foundations; 124 (49 percent) served as trustees of 120 other foundations in addition to the original twenty foundations in the public policy subsample (see Table 2). Only three of the sample foundations did not have direct links through trustees with other foundations. As a minimal conclusion, these data reveal that trustees of the sample foundations have wide access to other foundations as "insiders" and indicate the potential for a network of communication among many foundations. These 120 foundations are geographically dispersed but are largely concentrated in the eastern and midwestern sections of the country, as are the seventeen public policy sample foundations with which they are linked.[19] Given the assumptions discussed above, the large number of foundations directly connected through board overlaps with the public policy sample foundations was unexpected.

Not surprisingly, the size of the foundation board, the number of trustees who served over this period of several years, and the number of trustees who serve on other foundations are highly related, but not perfectly so. For example, the twenty-one individuals associated with the Ford Foundation board included only eight who served on one or more other foundation boards, whereas the nineteen individuals who served on the Rockefeller Brothers Fund board included fifteen who served on other boards. The members of the Rockefeller family, in particular, each appear to serve on several of the boards of the foundations associated with the family. Laurence S. Rockefeller served on the A. P. Sloan board and six other foundations with which the members of the Rockefeller family are associated as donors.

Only two individuals served on more than one of the twenty foundations in the public policy sample during this period: Francis Keppel was listed on the Russell Sage board in *Foundation Directory* 4 and the Carnegie Corporation board in *Foundation Directory* 4, 5, and 6; and Laurence S. Rockefeller was on the Rockefeller Brothers Fund board and the A. P. Sloan board, according to *Foundation Directory* 4, 5, and 6. However, eleven of the public policy sample foundations were indirectly linked in the manner described in the example given above. Trustees from two or more of these eleven foundations served on the boards of twenty other foundations. These overlaps, which can be considered indirect links among some of the public policy foundations, are summarized in Table 3. Part 2 of the table shows the number of other foundations on which each of the eleven mutually had trustees. The strongest indirect links through these twenty other foundations are those of the Rockefeller Foundation, which shares a board member with twelve of the twenty, and the Carnegie Corporation, which overlaps with nine of the twenty. Through these links, as shown in Part 2 of the table, the Rockefeller Foundation is indirectly linked to seven of the eleven public policy foundations which have these mutual links, and the Carnegie Corporation to five of the eleven. As may be seen from Part 1 of Table 3, five of the twenty foundations which provide the indirect links are connected to three or more of the eleven public policy sample foundations. The five foundations are the Carnegie Endowment for International Peace, Carnegie Foundation for the Advancement of Teaching, J. S. Guggenheim Memorial Foundation, Merck Company Foundation, and the Twentieth Century Fund.

TRUSTEES OF THE PUBLIC POLICY SAMPLE FOUNDATIONS: LINKS TO ORGANIZATIONS

Ten of the foundations in the public policy sample are directly linked to eighteen of the thirty-one recipient organizations. Of the 255 individuals who serve or have served recently as trustees of the public policy foundations, forty-eight are now or were members of the boards of these eighteen policy formation organizations. The Rockefeller Foundation has the largest number and percentage of trustees involved in these recipient organizations, as it has the largest number of trustees who were trustees of other foundations (see Table 4). A. P. Sloan and Ford have the next largest number of trustees involved in these recipient organizations. Sloan is second in the number of trustees overlapping with other foundations also. The percentage of Ford Foundation trustees linked with organizations is a little higher than the percentage of A. P. Sloan trustees. As may be seen in Table 2 and Table 4, eight of the ten foundations directly linked to recipient organizations through trustees have half or more of their trustees serving as trustees of other foundations. Of the forty-eight trustees, thirteen are on more than one of these recipient organization boards of directors, as may be seen in Table 5. As described below, there are many links among these organizations in addition to these connections through thirteen trustees of the public policy sample foundations.

The previous two sections presented the results of looking for overlapping board memberships starting with the trustees of the twenty public policy sample foundations. The next two contain the analysis of overlapping board membership starting with the boards of directors of the thirty-one recipient organizations. The names of board members came primarily from 1972 and 1975 annual reports of the organizations, and National Information Bureau reports or IRS returns when published reports were not available. Twelve hundred and thirty individuals served as members of the boards of these organizations during the time span covered by this study. The names of these individuals were compared with the Index of Donors, Trustees, and Administrators in Editions 4, 5, and 6 of the *Foundation Directory.*

MEMBERS OF THE BOARDS OF THE THIRTY-ONE SELECTED RECIPIENT
ORGANIZATIONS: FOUNDATION LINKS

As may be seen in Tables 6 and 7, there is a very substantial overlap
between the group of individuals who are foundation donors and trustees
and the directors of organizations whose programs are related to influencing public policy discussion or public affairs. Table 7 shows that over 50
percent of the board of directors of the Brookings Institution, the Council
on Foreign Relations, and the Hoover Institution are foundation trustees.

The Brookings Institution is "a private nonprofit organization devoted
to research, education, and publication in economics, government, foreign
policy, and the social sciences generally. Its principal purpose is to bring
knowledge to bear on the current and emerging policy problems facing the
American people."[20] The Council on Foreign Relations is "a privately
funded, nonprofit and nonpartisan organization of individual members
devoted to the promotion of a better and wider understanding of international affairs through the free interchange of ideas."[21] The Hoover Institution on War, Revolution and Peace is a "national center for documentation and research on problems of political, social, and economic change
in the twentieth century"[22] which concentrates on public policy analysis
and the analysis of government programs.

Brookings Institution studies are so influential that many observers in
and out of government think it is a governmental agency. In addition,
Brookings has served for many years as a place of employment for high-
level policymakers in Democratic administrations when they are out of
office.[23] The Hoover Institution is growing in importance as a source of
conservative policy studies and serves as a home for Republican politicians
and policy advisors out of office (as does the American Enterprise Institute).[24] For many years the policy positions of the Council on Foreign
Relations have had extraordinary influence over the foreign policy of the
United States. Almost all modern Secretaries of State and their immediate
deputies have belonged to the CFR. There is some disagreement about the
power or influence of the Council on Foreign Relations in the mid-1970s,
but little doubt about its role in the past.[25]

The largest number of foundation related board members are the
ninety-seven trustees who are participants in the Committee for Economic
Development (CED). All the 205 participants in the CED are considered
members of the board of directors and almost all are the chief executive
officers of major U.S. corporations or their immediate subordinates.
"Through a unique business-academic interchange, CED has been a
forum for ideas on vital issues of national policy for thirty-five years" with
a "reputation as a respected, independent business voice."[26] As with
Brookings Institution, the book length studies sponsored by the CED are

frequently regarded as the leading policy statement on the issues discussed. The CED task forces work on a consensus basis and any policy statement from CED clearly reflects the views of the major managers and owners from the corporate sector. These policy communications are, therefore, carefully considered by government policymakers.

Forty percent or more of the board members of three additional organizations (the American Enterprise Institute for Public Policy Research, the Aspen Institute for Humanistic Study, and the Overseas Development Council) are foundation trustees listed in one or more edition of the *Foundation Directory*. The American Enterprise Institute for Public Policy Research (AEI) studies national problems and "fosters innovative research, identifies and presents varying points of view on issues, develops practical options and analyzes public policy proposals. Areas of concentration are economics, law, government and foreign policy."[27]

Although AEI is much younger than Brookings and Hoover, it is more and more regarded as the source of important conservative policy statements and the Republican "government in exile." [28] Government "policymakers often turn directly to Brookings or AEI for counsel. Phone calls are made daily from administration officials and congressional staffs to the eight-story Brookings headquarters on Washington's Embassy row and to AEI's two rented floors in a downtown office building."[29]

The Aspen Institute for Humanistic Studies brings together "leading citizens from the public and private sector in the United States and abroad to consider . . . major issues in contemporary society . . . . All institute programs are concerned with suggesting ways of dealing with current issues, identifying the implications of different alternatives and suggesting possible policies and actions for resolving issues."[30] The purpose of the Overseas Development Council is "to increase American understanding of the economic and social problems confronting the developing countries and of the importance of these countries to the United States in an increasingly interdependent world. The ODC seeks to promote consideration of development issues by the American public, policy makers, businessmen, educators, and the media."[31]

There is little published analysis of the influence of the Aspen Institute and the Overseas Development Council on public policy, as compared with the five organizations listed above. Their potential for influence may be illustrated by the fact that the major statement in 1976 by presidential candidate Jimmy Carter on nuclear proliferation and worldwide control of the spread of nuclear weapons was at a conference of United Nations officials organized by Professor Richard N. Gardner and sponsored by the Institute on Man and Science, Aspen Institute on Humanistic Studies, Overseas Development Council, and Charles F. Kettering Foundation.

This conference was supported financially by the Ford and Rockefeller foundations.[32] Several times a year there are reports in the *New York Times* of recommendations on domestic and foreign policy from the Aspen Institute or the Overseas Development Council.[33] As one foundation official stated in an interview conducted for this research, one of the principal channels for foundation influence on decision-makers is support of a study which is quoted extensively in the *New York Times*.

These seven policy-oriented organizations have an obvious and substantial interrelationship through their boards with the foundation sector in general. The implications of this relationship will be discussed in a later section. Sixteen or seventeen additional recipient organizations have some board member–foundation trustee overlaps (the data about the National Right-to-Work LDF is unclear). Only seven of the thirty-one recipient organizations do not have a verified overlap of board members with foundation boards. As is discussed later, lack of foundation trustee overlap with board members does not necessarily mean lack of a strong relationship to one or more foundations.

Twenty-three recipient organizations have 457 links with 287 different foundations (Table 6). Of these 287 foundations, forty-five also had trustee overlaps with the foundations in the public policy sample. Therefore, 242 additional foundations plus the 120 foundations linked to the public policy sample foundations total over 360 foundations directly linked to the public policy sample foundations or twenty-three of the thirty-one recipient organizations. This total includes seventeen of the twenty public policy sample foundations, the only foundations for which all of the trustees are included in the pool of names examined in this research. Tracing the affiliations of all the trustees of the other 343 foundations would certainly increase the density of interrelationships within this group and would bring in other foundation links. This effort was beyond the scope of this project but even these limited data reveal that 175 of the 343 foundations—over 50 percent—are linked through board members to one of the policy oriented organizations and one or more other foundations and seventy-nine (23 percent) are directly linked to two or more of the organizations and to other foundations. Some of the total of over 360 foundations have multiple links to the recipient organizations and to other foundations. Table 8 lists seventeen foundations in this group which are linked to four or more of the organizations in this sample through trustee-board member overlaps. The Rockefeller Foundation, for example, is linked to fourteen of the twenty-three organizations which have board overlaps with foundations and, as noted in Table 2, thirty-four other foundations. The three Carnegie-related foundations, which have mutual trustees, are related to twelve of the twenty-three organizations and thirty other foundations. The Twentieth Century Fund is directly linked to nine of the other organizations and nine different foundations. As may be seen in Table 8, of the nineteen organizations included, the Mexican-American Legal Defense and Education Fund (MALDEF) has only one link with a foundation which is connected to four or more of these recipient organizations. All of the other eighteen organizations are directly linked to more than one of the seventeen interconnected foundations on this table.

To recapitulate the findings thus far, ten of the twenty public policy sample foundations have trustee overlaps with 120 other foundations; twenty-three of the thirty-one recipient policy-oriented organizations have trustee–board member overlaps with 287 foundations. These, together, equal over 360 different foundations. Almost half of this total is linked both to the recipient organizations and other foundations and almost a quarter to two or more of the organizations and other foundations. Seventeen or 5 percent of this total are linked to four or more of these policy organizations and to many foundations. The remaining kind of link through trustees and board members which completes the network in this particular sample of foundations and organizations is the overlap of board members among the organizations—the interorganizational network, which is discussed in the next section.

MEMBERS OF THE BOARD OF THIRTY-ONE RECIPIENT ORGANIZATIONS:
INTERORGANIZATIONAL LINKS

Table 9 summarizes the data about overlapping board memberships among the recipient organizations in this sample. Twenty-two of the thirty-one recipient organizations in this sample share board members with each other. As may be noted, the Overseas Development Council board members served on fourteen of the other organizations' boards during this period; the Committee for Economic Development had overlaps with twelve of the other twenty-one; the NAACP-LDEF was linked with eleven others; and the Aspen Institute for Humanistic Studies and the Center for National Policy Review, with ten others. Some of these links were through common board members affiliated with foundations and sometimes also with others of these organizations; other links were through board members who did not serve as trustees of any of the foundations included in Editions 4, 5, and 6 of the *Foundation Directory*. Of the total of 138 interorganizational links, eighty-four (60 percent) were through board members who also had foundation affiliations, and fifty-four were through board members not related to foundations.

As may be seen by all of the above, there is a well-connected potential communications network involving trustees and board members of the original public policy sample foundations and the policyoriented organizations which three or more of these sample foundations funded. As mentioned before, lack of trustee-board member overlap does not necessarily indicate a lack of close interaction between the foundations and the organizations. An obvious connection between foundations and organizations is through grants. An examination of the grants (of all the 360 foundations which are linked through individuals to this research sample of foundations and organizations) would indicate connections other than those through trustees and board members. Examination of grants for 360 foundations was well beyond the scope of this project. However, the grants data which were part of the original research project (for the seventy-seven foundations in the stratified sample) do provide one illustrative case—that of the Foreign Policy Research Institute.

As noted above, none of the board members of the Foreign Policy Research Institute (FPRI) is a trustee of foundations listed in the three editions of the *Foundation Directory*. FPRI was established in 1955 with major assistance from the Smith Richardson Foundation, which still contributes to its support twenty-three years later. Smith Richardson and two other of the public policy sample foundations, Lilly Endowment and Pew Memorial Trust, made very large grants to the FPRI in the 1972–1975 period. The William H. Donner Foundation (which is included in the 287 foundations linked with recipient organizations through a trustee-board overlap with the Overseas Development Council) has contributed substantially to the FPRI over the past years and, undoubtedly, many other linked foundations have also.

Similarly, lack of board member overlap does not indicate a lack of relationship among policy-oriented organizations. There is an interesting set of interconnections among the American Enterprise Institute (AEI), the Hoover Institution, National Affairs, Inc. (which publishes the *Public Interest*), the Alternative Educational Foundation (which publishes the *American Spectator*, formerly the *Alternative*), and the Smith Richardson Foundation. For example, Irving Kristol, the editor of the *Public Interest*, is a resident scholar at AEI, and writes feature articles for the *American Spectator*. W. Allen Wallis is an adjunct scholar at AEI and on the board of the Hoover Institution and the Robert A. Taft Institute of Government. W. Glenn Campbell, director of the Hoover Institution, is a program advisor to AEI. Ralph Richardson of the Smith Richardson Foundation is a member of the AEI Advisory Council. William Baroody of AEI and Leslie Lankowsky of Smith Richardson also write articles for the *Alternative*. A complete list of authors for the *Public Interest* would show additional links with the AEI, Hoover Institution, the Alternative Educational Foundation, and the Smith Richardson Foundation.

As the examples above indicate, there are many different ways in which the foundations concerned with public policy issues are linked to the nonprofit policy formation organizations. These examples could be multiplied. In addition, it is obvious there are many other kinds of interconnections utilized in research on elite networks which have not been examined thus far. Therefore, these results minimally indicate the multiple connections among the public policy foundations and this sample of organizations.

OTHER LINKS: THE "HIGHER CIRCLES"

Research on elite networks may include examination of links through family ties, educational institutions, social clubs, membership on corporate boards of directors, and positions in government. Considering the public policy sample of foundations, it is to be assumed the trustees of donor-controlled foundations are connected with each other through family or corporate relationships which precede the foundation connection, that almost all of these trustees belong to the economic elite and many of them to the hereditary or social elite. Almost by definition, these trustees will be linked with other members of elite networks through every form of connection noted above, except governmental positions.[34] The few "independent" foundations which are not controlled by the donor family or corporation might show another pattern. Four of the five independent foundations in the public policy sample (Carnegie Corporation, Ford Foundation, Rockefeller Foundation, Russell Sage Foundation) are all well known for their involvement with public affairs and policy issues.[35] They are all located in New York City, have large boards of prominent people, give nationally and internationally, and contribute to many of the recipient organizations in this research sample. To illustrate the relationship of the foundation-organization network to other elite institutions, some of the other links of the trustees of these four foundations were examined briefly. The data are summarized in Table 10.

The ninety-nine present or former trustees of these foundations include ninety-eight individuals since one person served on both the Carnegie and Russell Sage boards during this period. From 67 to 92 percent of the trustees on these four boards (seventy-nine of ninety-seven individuals) are listed in either *Who's Who* or *Who's Who of American Women*. Listings in these works often do not include all the information collected for this study. Both corporate directorships and social club membership may not be included. In addition, the Standard and Poor's *Index of Corporate Executives and Directors* does not list all those individuals who are on corporate boards as listed in the Standard and Poor's *Register of Corporations*. Therefore the data summarized in Table 10 are incomplete. However these facts clearly support the conclusion that these four foundations are closely related to the "higher circles" in the economic, social, and political elite.

The limited examination of corporate directorships shows that fifty seven of the ninety-eight individuals are directors of major American corporations. Further examination of the entire board of twenty-seven of these corporations which had at least one trustee from these four foundations, showed that eleven of the twenty-seven corporations were linked with two or more of the four foundations. Six corporations had directors who were trustees of Carnegie Corporation and Rockefeller Foundation. Present or former trustees of Carnegie, Rockefeller, and Russell Sage are listed as directors of the New York Stock Exchange and the Teachers Insurance and Annuity Association. In 1978 trustees from Carnegie, Ford, and Rockefeller served as directors of the Cummins Engine Corporation. Present or former directors of Equitable Life Assurance Society include trustees from all four foundations. According to 1977–1978 data, a Ford Foundation trustee is a director of the Chase Manhattan Bank, of which David Rockefeller (of the Rockefeller Brothers Fund) is chairman of the board; the Chase board also includes trustees of the Rockefeller Foundation. A Rockefeller trustee serves as a director of the Ford Motor Company, of which Henry Ford was chairman of the board; he and other directors of Ford Motor Company were previously trustees of the Ford Foundation. This incomplete examination shows ample opportunity for contact among the trustees of these four foundations in the corporate world.

Table 10 also illustrates the potential network of these trustees through upper-class social clubs and through high-level governmental positions in both Democratic and Republican administrations. During an interview conducted for this research an extremely knowledgeable former officer of one of these four foundations stated that there probably were more important decisions about national affairs made at the Century Association, an upper-class club in New York City, than in the White House. To test the relevance of this apparent exaggeration, social club membership, and, separately, membership in the Century Association, were tallied for those trustees who listed this information in *Who's Who*.[36] These incomplete data are summarized in Table 10. They show that over a third of these trustees belong to upper-class clubs[37] and almost a third of the trustees of Carnegie, Rockefeller, and Russell Sage belong to the Century Association. If all the Ford trustees had listed club membership, it is likely a third of them would also belong to Century. The percentages would be higher if only the male trustees on these boards were included in the total. Table 10 also shows that 40 to 47 per cent of the trustees of Carnegie, Ford, and Rockefeller held or hold high level governmental positions. These include cabinet, subcabinet, presidential commission, ambassadorial, and head of major agency positions. Other trustees, not included in these percentages, were members of the Federal Reserve governing bodies at the regional or national level. Over half of the trustees in this group who listed membership in the Century Association also held or hold high-level governmental positions.[38] Certainly the potential exists for discussion and decision-making in a nonpublic environment among this group of trustees and their many associates in the foundations, the corporations, their present and former colleagues in high-level governmental positions in Republican and Democratic administrations, and the policy-oriented recipient organizations. These data clearly support the view that there is a substantial connection between the "independent" foundations and the social and governmental elite as well as the highest-level economic institutions.

Further examination of the same kinds of information for the donor-controlled foundations in the public policy sample would undoubtedly show that some of the other large foundations as well as the smaller or less well known foundations also belong to this well-connected inner group of the foundation-organization network. For example, it is probable that the Field Foundation, the Rockefeller Brothers Fund, and the A. P. Sloan Foundation trustees are also involved in the "higher circles" of the economic and governmental elites. Further research on the extent of this network involving a variety of links is needed. A preliminary observation from the present data is that there may be a "division of labor" in foundation boards. It may be that some trustees are more closely linked to social and economic elites, others are connected to high-level policy-oriented organizations, and both groups have some members who go in and out of policymaking governmental positions. This situation would be analogous to the "division of labor" on corporate boards which has been documented by Soref.[39]

DISCUSSION

What do these networks mean? Most answers to this question are, at best, only partial. In the context of this research, however, they mean at least the following:

1. There is an interconnected foundation "club" not immediately visible to the outside observer among the foundations involved in public policy grants and probably among the majority of the foundations with over $10 million in assets. This means at least mutual access, ease of communication, and a very high probability of shared values and goals with respect to national affairs and the operation of the legal/political and

economic system. Within this foundation network there appears to be an inner group or "higher circle."

2. This foundation network is heavily connected with the major policy organizations, has a substantial voice in the operation of these organizations through board memberships and through grants, and through this relationship influences public policy.

3. These facts, taken together, cast doubt upon the role of nonprofit organizations and foundations in the "third" sector as a balance to the business and government sectors or as a channel of access for citizen/consumers which is more open than business or government.

4. There is need for a great deal more research.

The Interconnected Foundation "Club"

Laumann, Verbrugge, and Pappi in a study in another culture of the impact of a community elite's influence structure demonstrate that "social ties have the largest effect on the community affairs network" [40] and "the community affairs network represents conversations among elite members that have political consequences." There is no better brief description of the activity of trustees of foundations concerned with public policy at their board meetings and other encounters than "conversations among elite members that have political consequences."[41] In fact the ambience of the foundation world is similar to that of a private club where friends, and friends of friends, run into each other casually or gather specifically to discuss ideas and events of importance to the members. Many of the foundation people interviewed for this research acknowledged this characteristic. The "club," of course, includes high-level foundation staff as well as trustees; and much of the collaboration between the largest foundations is arranged by staff.

The foundation world is typical of exclusive private clubs in its secrecy. A wall surrounds the club—not only to control entry by outsiders (non-"foundation people"), but to keep internal proceedings private. Nielsen notes in his study of the big foundations "the reluctance—even the fear—of individuals in the tight little world of philanthropy to talk about the inner workings and problems of foundations."[42] As a case in point, the "Foundation Executives Group," which involves executive directors of major national foundations in quarterly meetings to discuss issues of common concern, is kept as secret as possible. There was substantial alarm when Merrimon Cuninggim mentioned the group in his book *Private Money and Public Service.*[43] Another cause of consternation in foundation circles was Nielsen's study. (Nielsen had been a high-ranking executive in the Ford Foundation and was also president of the African-

American Institute, which was supported by grants from the large foundations.) According to interviews, members of the foundation world made their displeasure known to the trustees of the Twentieth Century Fund, which sponsored Nielsen's research.

Examination of the "inner group" or "higher circle" within this foundation network reinforces the club analogy. As noted, Carnegie, Ford, Rockefeller, and, to a lesser degree, Russell Sage are heavily interconnected with other foundations, with policy organizations and with the corporate world, and almost half of these trustees hold or held high policymaking positions in national government. Nielsen's comment about the big foundations is especially appropriate to this inner group. "These foundations are at or near the center of gravity of the American Establishment. By themselves and also by their positions in an intricate web of powerful men and institutions, they have a significance even larger than their huge resources might suggest."[44] It is extremely likely that other foundations, not all as large as the big foundations Nielsen studied, also belong to this inner group.

Foundations Influence Public Policy through the Major Policy-Oriented Organizations

The multiple overlaps shown here establish that foundations which make grants to projects focused on the operation of the political economy have a substantial voice on the boards of many of the recipient organizations. There is evidence of a well-connected foundation–policy organization network. The seven policy organizations which are most heavily involved in this network—American Enterprise Institute, Aspen Institute, Brookings Institution, Committee for Economic Development, Council on Foreign Relations, Hoover Institution, Overseas Development Council—are clearly influential in American society. AEI, Brookings, and, to a lesser degree, Hoover serve as bases of operation for prominent political leaders out of office.[45] CED includes the leadership of the major corporations in the country and CFR involves all the major actors with influence on foreign policy. It is difficult to read an edition of the Sunday *New York Times* which does not have a background article, column, or feature from one or more of these policy groups. Much of the work of foundation task forces, commissions, and sponsored research is aimed at publication in the *New York Times* and subsequent absorption by decision-makers in the public and private sectors of the society. As noted above, four of these seven organizations were themselves the subject of articles analyzing their influence on public affairs and public policy in newspapers and periodicals in the 1977–1978 period.[46]

The organizations which are interlocked with each other, with foundations, and with major corporations are part of the elite of the organizational world. An interesting example of this is the representation of boards of thirteen of the organizations in this sample (as well as many foundations) on a private supranational policy-formation organization, the Trilateral Commission.[47] The foundation–policy formation organization network "higher circle" appears to be complementary to, and overlaps the networks documented by others in the corporate world.[48] and the political structure.[49]

Although close connections in personal networks are not conclusive evidence of channels of influence,[50] the data in this study tend to confirm the assertion by Domhoff that the agenda of what is discussed, or omitted, in the public arena is heavily influenced by large- and medium-sized foundations and the organizations they support. Foundations are involved in policy-planning and ideology-formation processes. In addition, key individuals from the sample foundations and policy organizations are involved in the candidate-selection process. For example, several articles have described the importance of the Trilateral Commission in the emergence of Jimmy Carter as a national political leader.[51] In short, philanthropic foundations are prime candidates for examination when social scientists consider the "influences which shape the alternatives [official decision-makers] consider, the assumptions they make, and the kinds of actions they take." [52]

Questions about the Role of the "Third" Sector Arising from This Research

The data in this study suggest that the high-level nonprofit policy organizations which are so heavily interlocked with each other, the foundations, the corporate world, and the policy levels of national government reinforce the already disproportionate influence of big business vis-à-vis big government.[53] This concentration of power casts doubt upon the oft-stated assertion that the role of the nonprofit "third" sector is to serve as a balance to the powerful business and government sectors and to provide different viewpoints and many channels through which citizens can influence public policy.[54] Policy differences do exist between the more "liberal" and the more "conservative" public affairs and public interest organizations, but they frequently revolve around the best way to achieve an agreed-upon goal with the least disturbance to the status quo. As Tom Bethell observed in an article about AEI, there are at least three "fundamental tenets of intellectual life in Washington. The first is that opinion, to be acceptable and respectable, must not stray too far to the left or right, but remain close to the middle of the road."[55]

Some of the organizations examined in this research do appear to be channels for access of ordinary citizens to the policymaking process: for example, on the liberal side, the Center for Community Change, Mexican-American Legal Defense and Education Fund, Native American Rights Fund, Puerto Rican Legal Defense and Education Fund, and the Youth Project, and on the conservative side the Americans for Effective Law Enforcement and the National Right-to-Work Legal Defense Fund. These are the organizations which are not especially well connected to the foundation network and probably also not well connected to economic, political, or social elites.

The data in this study suggest that the "third" sector has at least two tiers. One tier is heavily interconnected with the power structure and the second is not. It may be that only the second (and smaller?) tier plays the role of providing different viewpoints and access to citizens which is ascribed to the whole third sector including foundations and nonprofit organizations.

The Need for Additional Research

As the above discussion indicates, there is a need for extensive and detailed research on the role of philanthropic foundations and the organizations they support. There is a need for case studies of specific issues as well as broader, more general, examinations of the connections among foundations and organizations and the types of activities they fund. Recommended research would include an analysis of the activities of a representative sample of smaller but important foundations.

Such research requires better access to current and reliable data than is presently the case, financial support, and a change in the prevailing attitude about third-sector research on the part of foundations. As Lewis Coser, however, observed, foundations serve as gatekeepers of social research.[56] A very experienced foundation person noted in an interview that there has been an unspoken agreement among the foundations which support social research not to turn the spotlight of social analysis on themselves as actors in American society. For example, there is evidence that Floyd Hunter and C. Wright Mills never received substantial foundation support after their major studies of what they considered the power structure in the United States.[57] Nevertheless, as Reynold Levy and Waldemar Nielsen noted in "An Agenda for the Future" for the Filer Commission, "ways need to be found to provide at least modest funding to the work of thoughtful critics of the performance of nonprofit organizations, including foundations." They go on to comment:

The power of the nonprofit sector's establishment has been so great and intimidating upon scholarly and intellectual critics, and its response to criticism in some cases has been so hostile and vengeful, that an attitude of hospitality to research and writing by independent and in some cases dissident voices will not be easy to create. But if it were done, the results on the whole would be stimulating and constructive.[58]

Despite the probable hostility from much of the foundation world, such research is necessary if the exercise of power and the process of decision-making in public policy matters in American society is ever to be clearly understood. This study is a first step in the direction of delineating the networks of influence through which foundations work to shape national policy.

Table 2

Twenty Public Policy Foundations Ranked by Number of Trustees in the Foundation Directory, Editions 4, 5, and 6, with the Number of Affiliations with Other Foundations as Trustees or Donors.

Foundation Name	Number of Trustees in F.D. 4, 5, 6,	Trustees for Only This Foundation	Trustees of Other Foundations	Number of Other Foundations
Rockefeller F.	33	10	23	34
Carnegie Corp.	27	13	14	21
A. P. Sloan F.	26	10	16	27
Ford F.	21	13	8	13
Rockefeller Bro. F.	19	4	15	21
Field F.	18	12	6	7
Russell Sage F.	18	9	9	12
Vincent Astor F.	14	8	6	9
Lilly Endowment	14	8	6	5
A. W. Mellon F.	11	6	5	8
Smith Richardson F.	11	5	5 or 6	5 or 6
Houston Endowment	9	9	0	0
R. K. Mellon F.	7	3	4	6
J. M. Foundation	6	3	3	3
Kerr F.	6	6	0	0
Kirby F.	6	6	0	0
Brown F., Inc.	5	4	1	1
Cowell F.	3	2	1	1
Pew Memorial Trust[a]	1	0	1	2+
J. Howard Pew Freedom Trust[a]	1	0	1	2+
Totals	257[b]	131	126+	120+[c]

Source: Marianna Lewis, ed., *The Foundation Directory, Edition 4(1971), 5(1975), 6(1977)* (New York: The Foundation Center).
[a]The Pew Trusts list only the Glenmede Trust Company as trustees in the F.D.; members of the family serve as decision-makers for these four and several other trusts.
[b]255 individuals.
[c]Excludes the twenty public policy sample foundations. List available from author.

Table 3
Indirect Links among Eleven of the Twenty Public Policy Sample Foundations

Part 1
All Foundations Linked through Trustees with Two or More of the Public Policy Sample Foundations—Numbers Indicate Trustees

Foundations Linked through Trustees with Two or More of the Public Policy Foundations	Public Policy Sample Foundations										
	Vincent Astor F.	Carnegie Corp.	Field F.	Ford F.	Lilly End.	A.W. Mellon F.	R.K. Mellon F.	R. B. F.[a]	R. F.[b]	Russell Sage F.	A.P. Sloan F.
Agricultural Development Council								1	1		
Bodman Foundation	1										1
Carnegie Endowment for International Peace		1							1		2
Carnegie Foundation for the Advancement of Teaching		1				1		1	4		
Carnegie Hero Fund Commission		1					1				
Citizens Research Foundation				1					1		
CBS Foundation		1							1		
Council on Library Resources		1		1							
Cummins Engine Foundation				1					1		
Educational Facilities Laboratories									1		1
First National City Bank Foundation		1							1		
Foundation for Child Development			1						1		
German Marshall Fund					1			1			
J. S. Guggenheim Memorial Foundation		1								1	1
Kettering Foundation		1								2	
Merck Company Foundation		1								1	1
Morgan Stanley Foundation					1						1
New World Foundation								1	1		
Twentieth Century Fund			2						1	1	
United States Steel Foundation								1	1		
Total number of foundations (see Part 2)	1	9	2	3	2	1	1	5	12	4	6

Part 2

Number of Indirect links through Other Foundations for Eleven Public Policy Sample Foundations—Summary of Part 1

Foundations Linked through Trustees with Two or More of the Public Policy Foundations	Public Policy Sample Foundations										
	Vincent Astor F.	Carnegie Corp.	Field F.	Ford F.	Lilly End.	A.W. Mellon F.	R.K. Mellon F.	R.B.F.[a]	R.F.[b]	Russell Sage F.	A.P. Sloan F.
Vincent Astor F.	—										1
Carnegie Corp.		—		1			1	7		1	3
Field F.			—					1	2		
Ford F.				—				1	1	1	
Lilly Endowment	1				—						1
A. W. Mellon F.						—		1			
R. K. Mellon F.	1						—				
R.B.F.					1			—	3		3
R.F.	7	1	1		1			3	—	1	3
Russell Sage F.	1	2	1						1	—	
A. P. Sloan F.	1	3			1			3	3		—

Source: *Foundation Directory*, Editions 4, 5, 6.

[a] Rockefeller Brothers Fund.

[b] Rockefeller Foundation.

Table 4
Direct Links through Trustee/Board Member Overlap—Public Policy Sample Foundations and Recipient Sample Organizations: Foundations Ranked by the Number of Trustees Who Serve on the Boards of Recipient Organizations (10 or 12 of the 20 Public Policy Sample Foundations; 18 or 19 of 31 Organizations)

	AEI	Aspen	Brookings	CCC	CNPR	CED	CFR	Hoover	LCCRUL	NAACP-LDEF	NCUS-China	NRWLDF	NUL	ODC	RPA	SRC	Taft	VEP	WRP-CDF	Number of individual trustees
Rockefeller F.	1	2	1	1			2	4	1	1	2		2	4				1	1	13
A.P. Sloan F.		2	2		1	7							1							8
Ford F.		3				1	1						1	1			1			8
Russell Sage F.															4	1				5
Carnegie Corp.		1	1				1						1		1					4
Rockefeller Brothers Fund			1				1	1						2						4
J.M.F.								2									1			2
Lilly Endowment	1					2														2
Field F.			1																1	1
R.K. Mellon F.			1																	1
Pew Trusts[b]											1?								2	1?
Totals	1[a]	7	7	1	2	12	6	4	1	1	2	1?	5	7	5	1	2	1	2	48 or 49

Source: data from annual reports, IRS reports, National Information Bureau reports, replies to inquiries by mail and Editions 4, 5, and 6, of the *Foundation Directory*.

[a] In addition a trustee of the Smith Richardson Foundation serves on an AEI Advisory Council.

[b] Names of the decision-making members of the Pew family on the Pew Trusts are secret. Mrs. John G. Pew is on the NRW-LDF board and is a member of the family. It is not known if she serves as a trustee.

Table 5
Links between Boards of Recipient Organizations through Trustees of the Public Policy Sample Foundations—Numbers Indicate Trustees (18 of 31 Recipient Organizations with Board Overlaps through 13 Individual Trustees of 10 of the Public Policy Sample Foundations)

	AEI	Aspen	Brookings	CCC	CNPR	CED	CFR	Hoover	LCCRUL	NAACP-LDEF	NCUS-China	NUL	ODC	RPA	SRC	Taft	VEP	WRP-CDF
AEI	—					1												
Aspen		—				1								3				
Brookings			—			1	2				1	1						
CCC				—													1	
CNPR					—							1	1					1
CED	1	1	1			—												
CFR			2				—		1	1	1		1					
Hoover								—								1		
LCCRUL							1		—									
NAACP-LDEF							1			—								
NCUS-China			1				1				—							
NUL			1		1							—	1		1			1
ODC					1		1					1	—					
RPA		3												—				
SRC												1			—			
Taft								1								—		
VEP				1													—	
WRP-CDF					1							1						—

Source: data summarized from Table 4.

Table 6
Number and Percentage of Foundation Trustees Serving on the Board of Directors of 31 Recipient Organizations, 1972 and 1975, with Number of Different Foundations Linked

Organization	Number on Board of Directors	Trustees Listed in F.D. 4,5,6	Percentage	Number of Different Foundations Linked
Alternative Educational Foundation	3	0	0	0
American Civil Liberties Union Foundation (ACLUF)	13	1	8	1
Americans for Effective Law Enforcement (AELE)	9	2	22	3
American Enterprise Institute for Public Policy Research (AEI)	20	8	40	11
Aspen Institute for Humanistic Studies	37	16	43	19
Brookings Institution	20	12	60	29
Center for Community Change (CCC)	27	6	22	7
Center for National Policy Review (CNPR)	14	4	28	6
Committee for Economic Development (CED)	205	97	47	122
Council on Foreign Relations (CFR)	25	14	56	19
Foreign Policy Research Institute (FPRI)	5	0	0	0
Freedom's Foundation at Valley Forge	12	0	0	0
Hoover Institution on War, Revolution and Peace	65	34/5	53	47
Intercollegiate Studies Institute	23	1	4	1
Lawyer's Committee for Civil Rights under Law (LCCRUL)	96	29	30	36
Mexican American Legal Defense and Education Fund (MALDEF)	41	4	10	6

National Affairs, Inc.	3	0	0	0
National Association for the Advancement of Colored People Legal Defense and Education Fund (NAACP-LDEF)	72	13	18	17
National Association for the Advancement of Colored People Special Contributions Fund (NAACP-SCF)	64	2	3	2
National Committee on U.S.-China Relations (NCUS-China)	41	12	29	16
National Right-to-Work Legal Defense Foundation (NRWLDF)a	39	1?	2?	2+?
National Urban League (NUL)	60	13	22	17
Native American Rights Fund	14	0	0	0
Overseas Development Council (ODC)	92	37	40	43
Puerto Rican Legal Defense and Education Fund (PRLDEF)	19	0	0	0
Regional Plan Association (RPA)	49	16	32	21
Southern Regional Council (SRC)	20	2	10	2
Robert A. Taft Institute of Government (Taft)	17	6	35	23
Voter Education Project (VEP)	17	2	11	4
Washington Research Project–Children's Defense Fund (WRP-CDF)b	14	3	21	5

457 Links

Source: data from annual reports, IRS reports, National Information Bureau reports, replies to inquiries by mail and Editions 4, 5, and 6 of the *Foundation Directory*. 287 different foundations: list available from author.
aNames of the decision making members of the Pew family who serve on the Pew foundations are secret. Mrs. John G. Pew is on the NRWLDF board and is a member of the family. It is not known if she serves on the Pew foundations.
bData for WRP-CDF is for recent years and may not reflect 1972 or 1975. Data for these earlier years unavailable.

Table 7
*Recipient Organizations Ranked by Percentage of the Board of Directors (1972 and
1975) Listed as Foundation Trustees in Editions 4, 5, and 6, of the Foundation
Directory.*

Organization	Percentage Listed as Trustees
Brookings Institution	60%
Council on Foreign Relations	56
Hoover Institution on War, Revolution and Peace	53
Committee for Economic Development	47
Aspen Institute for Humanistic Studies	43
Overseas Development Council	41
American Enterprise Institute for Public Policy Research	40
Robert A. Taft Institute of Government	35
Regional Plan Association	32
Lawyer's Committee for Civil Rights Under Law	30
Center for National Policy Review	28
Americans for Effective Law Enforcement	22
Center for Community Change	22
National Urban League	22
Washington Research Project–Children's Defense Fund[a]	21
National Association for the Advancement of Colored People-Legal Defense and Education Fund	18
National Committee on U.S.-China Relations	12
Voter Education Project	1
Mexican American Legal Defense and Education Fund	10
Southern Regional Council	10
American Civil Liberties Union Foundation	8
Intercollegiate Studies Institute	4
National Association for the Advancement of Colored People–Special Contributions Fund	3
National Right-to-Work Legal Defense Foundation	2(?)

Organizations in the Recipient Sample for Which No Member of the Board of
Directors Was Listed as a Foundation Trustee:
Alternative Educational Foundation (publisher of the *Alternative*, now the *American Spectator*)
Foreign Policy Research Institute
Freedom's Foundation at Valley Forge
National Affairs, Inc. (publisher of *The Public Interest*)
Native American Rights Fund
Puerto Rican Legal Defense and Education Fund
Youth Project

Source: data from annual reports, IRS reports, National Information Bureau reports,
   replies to inquiries by mail, and Editions 4, 5, and 6, of the *Foundation Directory*.
[a]Data for Washington Research Project-CDF for recent years may not reflect 1972 or 1975.

Foundations Linked through Trustees to Four or More of the Recipient Organizations with Number of Trustees Serving during the 1969–1975 Period

Foundations	Aspen	Brookings	CCC	CED	CFR	CNPR	Hoover	LCCRUL	MALDEF	NAACP-LDEF	NAACP-SCF	NCUS-China	NUL	ODC	RPA	SRC	Taft	VEP	WRP-CDF	Total of Orgs. Linked to This Foundation
Anderson F.	1	1			1	1						1		1						5
Atlantic Richfield F.	3	1			2							1		2						5
Carnegie Endowment for International Peace	1	1	1	1	1	1		2			1		1	1						9
Carnegie F. for the Advancement of Tchng.	1			1	1	1		1						3				1		7
Carnegie Corporation					1								1		2					4
Chase Manhattan Bank F.				1	1								1	1						4
Field F.	3		1					2						1						4
Ford F.	1		1	1		1								1		1	1	1	1	8
Kettering F.	1		1			1								1						4
Merck Company F.				2				2	1					1						4
New World F.	2		1		1			2	2			1		1						7
Resources for the Future					1							1	1	4	1	1	2			7
Rockefeller Bro. F.	1				1		1							2	1					5
Rockefeller F.	1	2	1	2	4	1	1	1		1		2	2	4	1	1			1	14
Sealantic Fund	1		1	1			1						1	1						4
Twentieth Century Fund		1		1				1		2			1	1			1	1	1	9
World Peace Fund	1			1										2			1		1	4

Source: data from annual reports, IRS reports, National Information Bureau Reports, replies to inquiries by mail, and Editions 4, 5, 6 of the *Foundation Directory*.

Table 9 Direct Links through Board Members of Recipient Organizations: Numbers of Individuals Serving on Both Boards divided between Those Who Are Also Foundation Trustees (F) and Those Who Are Not Foundation Trustees (NF); F/NF (22 of 31 Recipient Organizations: Read down and across to Reach Total of Overlaps in Right-hand Column)

	ACLUF	AEI	Aspen	Brookings	CCC	CED	CFR	CNPR	Hoover	LCCRUL	MALDEF	NAACP-LDEF	NAACP-SCF	NCUS-China	NUL	ODC	PRLDEF	RPA	SRC	Taft	VEP	WRP-CDF	F	NF	Total
ACLUF	—																						1		1
AEI		—				1/3																	1	1	2
Aspen			—	1/	/2	2/3	2/	1/	/3				1/	1/	/1	3/1		1/	/1				8	2	10
Brookings				—		3/										2/							4		4
CCC					—					/1		/1									/1	/1		5	5
CED						—	3/1		1/			/2	3/1	1/3	4/4	4/4		3/2			/1	/1	9	3	12
CFR							—	1/		1/		1/		3/1	3/1	3/1							6		6
CNPR								—		/1		/1	1/1	1/	2/	2/	/1	/1	/1		1/1	/1	5	5	10

Total Organizational Links (one or more individuals)

Hoover	—				2/2			3	1	4
LCCRUL	1/ 3/7	1/	/1					4	4	8
MALDEF	1/	1/						3		3
NAACP-LDEF	—	1/	/1 /1	/1	/2			4	7	11
NAACP-SCF			1/	/1	/1			3	1	4
NCUS-China		—	1/2					7		7
NUL		— 1/2	/1	1/ 1/1				6	2	8
ODC		—	/1	1/ 1/				11	3	14
PRLDEF		—	/1						5	5
RPA		—						2	2	4
SRC		—		2/5 /1				1	5	6
Taft			—					1		1
VEP				—				4	2	6
WRP-CDF				—				2	5	7
TOTAL								84	54	138

Source: data from annual reports, IRS reports, National Information Bureau reports, replies to inquires by mail, and Editions 4, 5, and 6, of the *Foundation Directory.*

Table 10

Additional Information on Trustees of Four Foundations in the Public Policy Sample Which Are Independent of Donor Control

	Carnegie Corporation	Ford Foundation	Rockefeller Foundation	Russell Sage Foundation
Number of Trustees in *Foundation Directory*, 4, 5, 6,	27	21	33	18
Number listed in *Who's Who* or *Who's Who of American Women*	18	17	30	15
Percentage listed in *WW* or *WWAW*	67%	81%	90%	83%
Directors of major corporations, banks, insurance companies	17	10	21	10
Directors of 27 selected corps., banks, insurance companies	11	8	13	5

Members of upper-class clubs[a]	12	8	13	8
Members of the Century Association, New York City	8	4	10	6
High-level government positions[b]	11	10	15	6
Past and present members of the Trilateral Commission[c]	0	2	7	0
Graduate degrees	20	10	25	11
Graduation with honors and/or members of Phi Beta Kappa	6	6	13	7

Sources: *Foundation Directory*, Editions 4, 5, and 6; *Who's Who*, various editions; *Who's Who of American Women*; Standard & Poor's *Register of Corporate Directors and Executives* and *Register of Corporations*, 1978; *Higher Circles*; reports of the Trilateral Commission.

[a] Clubs listed in G. Wm. Domhoff, *The Higher Circles* (New York: Random House, 1970), pp. 21–27.

[b] High-level government positions include cabinet and subcabinet posts, ambassadors, special presidential representatives, members of presidential commissions, commissioners or executive directors of federal regulatory or independent agencies.

[c] The present and former members of the Trilateral Commission include many other foundation people, including a trustee of two other public policy sample foundations, Field and A. P. Sloan.

Note: Except for the data from the *Foundation Directory* and the Trilateral Commission all these figures are minimum numbers since all the sources used are incomplete; some trustees are deceased and no longer listed.

Notes

1. Richard Simeon, "Studying Public Policy," *Canadian Journal of Politics* 9 (December 1976): 554–555.
2. For example, Michael P. Allen, "Structure of Inter-Organizational Elite Cooptation: Interlocking Corporate Directorates," *American Sociological Review* 39 (June 1974): 393–406; Thomas R. Dye and John W. Pickering, "Governmental and Corporate Elites: Convergence and Differentiation," *Journal of Politics* 36 (November 1974): 900–925; Peter J. Freitag, "The Cabinet and Big Business: A Study of Interlocks," *Social Problems* 23 (December 1975): 137–152.
3. John W. Nason, *Trustees and the Future of Foundations* (New York: Council on Foundations, 1977), "Preface," no page number.
4. G. William Domhoff, *Who Rules America?* (Englewood Cliffs, N.J.: Prentice-Hall, 1967); *The Higher Circles* (New York: Random House, 1970); "Some Friendly Answers to Radical Critics," *Insurgent Sociologist* 2 (Spring 1972): 27–39; "State and Ruling Class in Corporate America," *Insurgent Sociologist* 4 (Spring 1974): 3–16.
5. Domhoff, "State and Ruling Class," p. 6.
6. Ibid., pp. 6–7.
7. Ibid., p. 8.
8. Ibid., p. 14.
9. Dye and Pickering "Governmental and Corporate Elites."
10. Gwen Moore, "The Study of a National Elite Network," paper prepared for the 73rd Annual Meeting of the American Sociological Association, San Francisco, September 1978.
11. Richard J. Meislin, "Gardner Quits Rockefeller Fund, Citing 'Special Status' of Brothers," *New York Times,* August 24, 1977, p. 17.
12. Internal Revenue Code Section 4945. Foundations must assume "expenditure responsibility" whenever they give money to an organization which is not a "public charity" in the IRS definition. If a private foundation contributes more than a third of the income of an organization, the "public charity" status of the organization will be jeopardized.
13. Many organizations which seek funds have the word "foundation" in their title and a whole group of organizations which are endowed and have their own income are "operating foundations" and do not make grants—for example, museums, endowed homes for the aged, health research institutes, etc.
14. Chronologically these organizations are Vanguard in San Francisco, Haymarket in Boston, Liberty Hill in Los Angeles, Northstar in New York City. They have been written about extensively. Informative articles are Michael Slattery, "Rich Is Beautiful," *Co-Evolution Quarterly* (Winter Solstice, 1974): 94–103; Patrick Kennedy, "Going Public; Vanguard Foundation," *Foundation News* 18 (May 1977): 43–47.
15. The Foundation Center, a library and information service about philanthropy, supplied the listing of the 400 foundations. I wish to express my

thanks to the Foundation Center for this list and for access to many other sources of data used in this research.

16. A detailed report of the method of categorizing grants and the results of the examination of grants are available from the author.

17. Jane H. Mavity and Paul N. Ylvisaker, "Private Philanthropy and Public Affairs," in Commission on Private Philanthropy and Public Needs, *Research Papers* (Washington, D.C.: U.S. Department of the Treasury, 1977), Vol. II, Part I, p. 801.

18. Data on organizations were obtained from their annual reports, National Information Bureau reports, and public inspection copies of the IRS reports when other information was not available.

19. Ten of the public policy sample foundations are in New York City and one more (Smith Richardson) has its program office there. Three foundations are in Pennsylvania. Two are in Texas. There is one each in New Jersey, Indiana, Oklahoma, and California.

20. Brookings Institution, "Program 1977," p. 1

21. Council on Foreign Relations, *"Annual Report,* 1974–1975, p. iv.

22. Hoover Institution on War, Revolution and Peace, *Annual Report*, 1975, pp. 16–17.

23. See Ira Mathner, "Inside Brookings," *R. F. Illustrated* 3, September 1977, p. 3; and "Two 'Think-Tanks' with Growing Impact," *U.S. News and World Report*, September 25, 1978, pp. 47–48; "New Set of Exiles," *Forbes* 119 (February 1, 1977): 67.

24. Kenneth Lamott, "Right-thinking Think Tank," *New York Times Magazine*, July 23, 1978, p. 16 ff.

25. See Laurence H. Shoup and William H. Minter, *Imperial Brain Trust: The Council on Foreign Relations and United States Foreign Policy* (New York: Monthly Review Press, 1978); Brian Dickerson, "Witch Hunters Still Stalk a Club That Is Ghost of Former Self," *Wall Street Journal* November 1, 1978, p. 1.; Zygmunt Nagorski, "A Member of the CFR Talks Back," *National Review* (December 9, 1977), pp. 1416–1419.

26. Committee for Economic Development, "Report on Activities," 1976, p. 1.

27. American Enterprise Institute for Public Policy Research, "Competition of Ideas," no date, p. 6.

28. "The Conservative's Think Tank," *Business Week*, May 2, 1977, pp. 80–81; Tom Bethell, "The Rewards of Enterprise," *New Republic* 177 (July 9 and 16, 1977), pp. 17–19; "The Other Think Tank: G. O. P. Government in Exile," *Time* 110 (September 19, 1977): 79.

29. "Two 'Think Tanks' with Growing Impact," *U. S. News and World Report* 85 (September 25, 1978): 47–48.

30. Aspen Institute for Humanistic Studies, "Publications Catalog 1976–1977," no date, "Introduction," no page.

31. Overseas Development Council, "World Development: The U.S. Stake" (Annual Report for 1976?), no date, p. 2.

32. *New York Times*, May 14, 1976, I, p. 1.

33. For example, Aspen Institute's recommendation on the future of the Peace Corps, *New York Times*, July 18, 1976, p. 52; Overseas Development

Council recommendations on international and domestic energy policy *New York Times*, June 7, 1976, p. 29; ODC on U.S. role in world food politics, *New York Times*, June 14, 1977, p. 35.

34. According to the data in the larger study, two-thirds to three-quarters of all foundations are governed by boards of trustees on which the donor family and/or the donor corporation representatives are in the majority. These are considered under donor control and, by definition, under the control of the tiny minority who are very wealthy in the United States.

35. The fifth independent foundation, the Cowell Foundation of San Francisco, has a three-person board, gives only locally, and has a very limited interest in public policy. It was included in the sample because of major grants in 1972 and 1975 to the Hoover Institution and the World Affairs Council.

36. Interestingly, some trustees of foundations do not list their foundation affiliation in *Who's Who* and as J. Novak pointed out in his article on the Trilateral Commission (see note 51) David Rockefeller does not list membership in the Trilateral Commission in his entry in *Who's Who.*

37. The list of social clubs is taken from Domhoff, *The Higher Circles*, pp. 21–27.

38. Four out of eight Carnegie trustees who are listed as members of the Century Association have held high-level government positions; the comparable figures for the other foundations are four out of four for Ford, six of ten for Rockefeller, five of six for Russell Sage.

39. M. Soref, "Social Class and a Division of Labor within the Corporate Elite," *Sociological Quarterly* 17 (Summer 1976): 360–368.

40. Edward O. Laumann, Lois M. Verbrugge, and Franz O. Pappi, "Causal Modeling Approach to the Study of a Community Elite's Influence Structure," *American Sociological Review* 39 (April 1974): 170.

41. Ibid., p. 171.

42. Waldemar A. Nielsen, *The Big Foundations* (New York: Columbia University Press, 1972), p. ix.

43. Merrimon Cuninggim, *Private Money and Public Service* (New York: McGraw-Hill, 1972). The Foundation Executives Group is mentioned on pp. 193 and 205.

44. Nielsen, *The Big Foundations*, p. 27.

45. Articles cited in notes 23, 24, 28, 29.

46. Articles cited in notes 23, 24, 25, 28, 29.

47. The membership of the Trilateral Commission as of January 31, 1978, published by the commission lists present or former members of the boards of the following organizations in this research sample:

American Enterprise Institute for Public Policy Research
Aspen Institute for Humanistic Studies
Brookings Institution
Center for National Policy Review
Committee for Economic Development
Council on Foreign Relations

Hoover Institution on War, Revolution and Peace
Lawyer's Committee for Civil Rights under Law
National Association for the Advancement of Colored People
 Legal Defense and Education Fund
National Committee on U.S.-China Relations
National Urban Leage.
Overseas Development Council
Washington Research Project—Children's Defense Fund

The present and former director of the Council on Foreign Relations and
 the present director of Brookings also are members. Many of the present
 members of the Trilateral Commission are also foundation trustees.
48. Allen, "Structure of Inter-Organizational Elite."
49. Dye and Pickering, "Governmental and Corporate Elites;" Freitag, "The
 Cabinet and Big Business."
50. Beth Mintz, Peter Freitag, Carol Hendricks, Michael Schwartz, "Problems of
 Proof in Elite Research," *Social Problems* 23 (February 1976): 314–324.
51. Jimmy Carter was a political unknown when he was invited to join the very
 elite Trilateral Commission. Beginning with the president, vice-president,
 secretary of state, and secretary of defense, twenty or more present or
 former members of the Trilateral Commission are in high-level positions
 in the Carter administration. Two articles which discuss the influence of
 the Trilateral Commission in Carter's election are Robert Manning, "The
 Making of a President: How David Rockefeller Created Jimmy Carter,"
 Penthouse (August 1977): 118–119; Jeremiah Novak, "The Trilateral Connection," *Atlantic* (July 1977): 57–59.
52. Richard Simeon, "Studying Public Policy," pp. 544–545.
53. See Arthur Selwyn Miller, *The Modern Corporate State: Private Government
 and the American Constitution* (Westport, Conn: Greenwood Press, 1976),
 for a persuasive discussion by a constitutional scholar of the ascendancy of
 the big national and multinational corporations and their overwhelming
 influence over national government.
54. Dozens of discussions of the "third sector" contain statements about supporting "pluralism," competing ideas, etc. See, for example, Commission on
 Private Philanthropy and Public Needs, *Giving in America* (Washington,
 D.C.: The Commission, 1975), pp. 12, 42–46; or Robert F. Goheen, "The
 Future of Foundations: The Jeffersonian Potential," in Ciba Foundation
 Symposium, *The Future of Philanthropic Foundations* (Amsterdam, Holland: Associated Scientific Publishers, 1975), pp. 195–203.
55. Bethell, "Rewards of Enterprise," p. 18. The other two points are also
 germane. The second point is that "opinions and studies issued by an
 enterprise like AEI or Brookings acquire (for reasons that are not entirely
 clear) a far greater appearance of legitimacy if the money spent to produce
 them has been "aged" for a decade or two within the intricate machinery
 of a foundation, rather than being funneled directly out of the parent
 corporation. The third point is that if conservative opinions are to be

expressed, they always sound a great deal more persuasive if uttered by academics rather than corporate executives."

56. Lewis Coser, "Foundations as Gatekeepers of Contemporary Intellectual Life," in *Men of Ideas* (New York: The Free Press, 1965), pp. 337–348.

57. Joseph A. Scimecca, *The Sociological Theory of C. Wright Mills* (Port Washington, N.Y.: Kennikat Press, 1977), p. 120. The author states that C. Wright Mills never received a major grant after publishing *The Power Elite* in 1956. See also report of a personal conversation with Floyd Hunter about the lack of research support in Peter J. Seybold, "The Development of American Political Sociology: The Role of the Ford Foundation in the Production of Knowledge" (unpublished Ph.D. dissertation, State University of New York/Stonybrook, 1978), p. 361.

58. Reynold Levy and Waldemar Nielsen, "An Agenda for the Future," in Commission on Private Philanthropy and Public Needs, *Research Papers* (Washington, D.C.: U.S. Department of the Treasury, 1977), Vol. II, Part II, p. 1050.

About the Authors

ROBERT F. ARNOVE, the Editor of this book, is Professor of Education and Chairperson of the Department of Historical, Philosophical, and Comparative Studies of Education, Indiana University, Bloomington. He is the author of *Student Alienation: A Venezuelan Study* (New York: Praeger, 1971); editor of *Educational Television: A Policy Critique and Guide for Developing Countries* (New York: Praeger, 1976); co-editor of *Education and American Culture* (New York: MacMillan Publishing Co., Inc., 1980); and producer of a one-hour documentary film, "Alternative Public School" (1978). He has written extensively on the politics of education in the United States and overseas.

JAMES D. ANDERSON is an Associate Professor of History of Education at the University of Illinois, Urbana-Champaign. He received his Ph.D. from Illinois in 1973. He is the co-editor of *New Perspectives on Black Educational History* (Boston: G.K. Hall, 1978). Professor Anderson has written extensively on philanthropy and black education.

EDWARD H. BERMAN is a Professor of Education at the University of Louisville. His interst in the role of American philanthropy dates from research for his doctoral dissertation on the Phelps-Stokes Fund a decade ago. Since then he has published widely on the educational and political activities of missionaries in Africa and on the attempts by elites in industrialized nations to utilize education to further their hegemony at the expense of certain segments of the populace. He spent the 1978-79 academic year as a Senior Visiting Member at Wolfson College, Cambridge, and is currently completing a study of the idealogical biases which lead the major foundations to subsidize a certain developmental model.

E. RICHARD BROWN is on the faculty of the School of Public Health at the University of California, Los Angeles. He has worked as a health planner and also taught at the University of California, Berkeley, where he received his Ph.D. Dr. Brown is the author of *Rockefeller Medicine Men: Medicine and Capitalism in America*, recently published by the University of California Press.

DENNIS C. BUSS is Associate Professor of Education at Rider College, Lawrenceville, New Jersey. He is coordinator of the program in curriculum and instruction in the Graduate Division, School of Education. He received his Ed.D. degree from Rutgers University, in 1972.

MARY ANNA CULLETON COLWELL holds a PH.D. in Sociology from the University of California, Berkeley. She was the Executive director of the LARAS Fund, a private philanthropic foundation; and she helped research and prepare the *Guide To California Foundations* (1975). Her dissertation is on philanthropic foundations and public policy.

FRANK DARKNELL is Professor of Sociology at California State University, Sacramento, a campus of the California State University and Colleges (CSUC) system. He is interested in how large, privately controlled foundations participate in the development of public policy, especially in the area of higher education. He is currently conducting research on scholarly isolation as it affects science and engineering faculties in state colleges and non-doctoral universities.

DONALD FISHER is Assistant Professor of Education, University of British Columbia, Vancouver. He received his Ph.D. in 1977 from the University of California, Berkeley. His dissertation was on the Rockefeller philanthropies and the social sciences in Britain.

RUSSELL MARKS is an Assistant Professor in History of Education at Indiana University, Bloomington. He received his Ph.D. at the University of Illinois in 1972. He is currently writing a book on the history of the concept of individual differences. He has published on the history of intelligence testing and on moral education in American society.

BARBARA HOWE holds Ph.D. and J.D. degrees and is Assistant Professor of Sociology at the State University of New York (SUNY) at Buffalo. Her interest in foundations stems from her work at Cornell University, where, in 1976, she completed a doctoral thesis on the topic of the emergence of the philanthropic foundation as an American social institution. Since that time, she has done further research on the social history of the Rockefeller Foundation by using the Rockefeller Archive Center (in Tarrytown, New York).

PETER SEYBOLD received his Ph.D. in Sociology from the State University of New York at Stony Brook, in 1978. He is currently an Assistant Professor of Sociology at the University of Wisconsin, Parkside. His research interests include the political economy of knowledge, political sociology, social stratification, and sociological theory.

EDWARD T. SILVA is an Associate Professor of Sociology at the University of Toronto. His work focuses on material and social factors conditioning the circulation of ideas, knowledge, and culture. His empirical and theoretical publications have been on presidential politics, the process of federal constitutional amendment in the United States, and the designation of deviance in society.

SHEILA SLAUGHTER received her Ph.D. in Educational Policy Studies from the University of Wisconsin, Madison in 1975. She is currently an Assistant Professor, teaching Sociology of Education, in the College of Education at Virginia Polytechnic Institute and State University (VPI and SU), Blacksburg, Virginia. Her area of interest is the sociology of knowledge, with special concern for ideology formation in the social sciences. She has published on university academic politics and on publishing in developing countries.

DAVID E. WEISCHADLE is Professor of Education at Montclair State College, New Jersey. He received his Ed.D. from Rutgers University in 1970, in the field of curriculum theory and development. He has published widely on topics pertaining to educational policy formation and the financing of education. He is currently education advisor and contributing reporter with New Jersey Public Television and WNET/13, New York.

Index

Hovey, George Rice, 162
Howard, John B., 228 n
Howe, Barbara, 7, 25, 80 n
Howe, Harold, II, 15, 334, 371, 372, 376
Howe, Irving, 227 n
Home Mission Society: members, 162
House Education and Labor Committee, 341
House UnAmerican Activities Committee, 256
Hunter, Floyd, 433
Huntington, Samuel P., 327 n
Hurn, Christopher J., 23 n
Hyman, Herbert, 282

Ideological: manufacture, 2, 7, 8, 68, 76, 78; dissemination, 59, 79; consensus, 60; variety, 79, 394
Ideology: definition, 55; uses of, 55, 56, 359, 415; formation, 56, 57, 75, 76, 77
Ilchman, Warren F., 327 n, 328 n, 329 n
Imperialism: cultural, 2; American, 127; and "literary colonialism", 322
Indiana Committee on Mental Defectives, 102
"Indirect Rule", 258
Individual differences, 8, 9, 11, 88, 90, 97, 100, 109, 110, 117, 118
Individuals: and freedom, 116
Industrial: society, 55, 253; capitalism, 87, 118, 138; philanthropy, 131, 153, 158, 167; education, 148, 156, 157, 158, 159, 167, 333; schools, 158
Industrial Relations Commission, 48, 69, 77
Influence, 375, 376, 414, 432
Innate ability, 8, 116
Institute for Development Studies, 211
Institute for Economic Research, 70
Institute of Statistics (Oxford), 248
Institutes of Statistics and Experimental Psychology, 246
Instructional television, 348, 349, 350, 358

Intelligence, 8, 18, 93
Integration, 354, 357
Intercollegiate Bureau of Occupations, 61
International Bank for Reconstruction and Development, 223
International Cooperation Administration, 218, 223
International Cooperation Agency, 214
International Education Board, 179, 180, 190
International House of Japan, 317
International Institute of African Languages and Cultures, 249
International Price History Investigation, 245
International Research and Exchange Board, 308
International Training and Research Program, 208
Interracial cooperation: pattern of, 157
Interstate Commerce Commission, 77

Jabavu, D.D.T., 194
Jackson, C.D., 366
Jackson, Frederick H., 383 n
James, William, 96
Jeanes Fund, 179, 182, 188, 189, 195, 196
Jefferson, Thomas, 183, 367, 382 n
Jencks, Christopher, 409 n
Jenks, J.W., 82 n
Jennings, W.I., 262 n
Jim Crowism, 10
John F. Slater Fund, 153
Johnson, E.A. 329 n
Johnson, President Lyndon Baines, 334, 374, 375, 376, 378, 379, 408 n
Johnson, Terence, 125, 143 n
Joncich, Geraldine, 119 n
Jones, Thomas Jesse, 159, 160, 161, 164, 165, 167, 173 n, 175 n, 183, 196, 198 n, 199 n
Josephson, Matthew, 81 n